AFTER HITLER

AFTER HITLER

Recivilizing Germans, 1945–1995   Konrad H. Jarausch

Translated by

Brandon Hunziker

OXFORD
UNIVERSITY PRESS

OXFORD

UNIVERSITY PRESS

Oxford University Press, Inc., publishes works that further
Oxford University's objective of excellence
in research, scholarship, and education.

Oxford   New York
Auckland   Cape Town   Dar es Salaam   Hong Kong   Karachi
Kuala Lumpur   Madrid   Melbourne   Mexico City   Nairobi
New Delhi   Shanghai   Taipei   Toronto

With offices in
Argentina   Austria   Brazil   Chile   Czech Republic   France   Greece
Guatemala   Hungary   Italy   Japan   Poland   Portugal   Singapore
South Korea   Switzerland   Thailand   Turkey   Ukraine   Vietnam

Published in Germany as *Die Umkehr. Deutsche Wandlungen 1945–1995*

Published by Oxford University Press, Inc.
198 Madison Avenue, New York, New York 10016

www.oup.com

First issued as an Oxford University Press paperback, 2008

Oxford is a registered trademark of Oxford University Press

Library of Congress Cataloging-in-Publication Data
Jarausch, Konrad Hugo.
[Umkehr. English]
After Hitler: recivilizing Germans, 1945–1995 / Konrad H. Jarausch;
translated by Brandon Hunziker.
   p. cm.
Includes bibliographical references and index.
ISBN 978-0-19-537400-1 (pbk.)
1. Germany—History—1945–1990. 2. Germany—Social
conditions—20th century. 3. Political culture—Germany.
4. Germany—Economic conditions—1945–1990. I. Title.
DD257.4.J3413 2006
943.087—dc22   2005055486

9 8 7 6 5 4 3 2 1

Printed in the United States of America
on acid-free paper

PREFACE

Americans harbor somewhat ambivalent feelings about Germany. On the one hand, many observers remain skeptical: This is true especially of the individuals whose families suffered during World War II, who hold deep-seated resentments against the country. Seeing Nazi crimes as the embodiment of ultimate evil, many intellectuals remain deeply suspicious of the claim that the country of the perpetrators may have reformed. Even prominent journalists such as Jane Kramer of the *New Yorker* and Mark Fischer of the *Washington Post* are more interested in the dark past than in the changes that followed. On the other hand, other commentators are more charitable: Most soldiers and businessmen who have lived in the Federal Republic fondly remember a friendly and hard-working people that seem to be much like their own. For instance, while fighting in the Vietnam jungle, many GIs dreamed about being stationed "back home in Germany." More recently, President George W. Bush somewhat misleadingly cited the transformation of the Germans after World War II as justification for his democratic crusade abroad.

These contradictory evaluations rest on a disconnect between the prevalence of negative Nazi memories and a lack of appreciation for the positive transformation during the last half century. For instance, in his indictment of "eliminatory anti-Semitism," Daniel J. Goldhagen paints a vivid picture of the complicity of ordinary Germans but suggests without further explanation that somehow the country miraculously transformed after 1945. Compared to the academic attention devoted to exploring Hitler's seizure of power and the effort to educate the public about the crimes of the Holocaust, the difficult process by which the Germans distanced themselves from nationalism and rejoined the international community thereafter remains underexplored. Almost any volume with a swastika on its cover will attract attention, since it promises to satisfy the fascination with ultimate evil. But attempts to explain the subsequent material and moral recovery tend to languish because its success is somehow taken for granted.

Seeking to redress the balance, in this book I intend to tell the neglected story of the struggle to rehabilitate the Germans after Hitler. It is important not only to analyze what went wrong in the past but also to point out how things were put right again after the Nazi catastrophe, since recovering from dictatorship and atoning for massive crimes is an issue facing other nations beyond Germany. Due to the magnitude of the culpability and the extent of the devastation during the war of annihilation, it seemed hardly likely in 1945 that this damage could be undone and the chief culprit actually be reformed. The harsh confrontation of the Cold War that divided not just Germany but Europe and other parts of the world did not make this laborious process any easier. Who should receive the credit for the successful transformation—the victorious powers or the defeated themselves? What measures worked best to reorient an entire political culture—compulsion or incentives? Such questions indicate the need to not just address failure but to explain success.

For analyzing the postwar transformation, the scholarly literature is only somewhat helpful because most works frame the issue in institutional rather than cultural terms. The English-language surveys by Anthony J. Nicholls, Henry Turner, as well as that by Dennis Barck and David Gress, provide much basic information on general developments, but they neglect East Germany and remain state-centered. Political science studies such as the leading textbook by David Conradt offer useful material on the formal government structure, yet they do not pay enough attention to the underlying shift of attitudes. Major German reflections by Axel Schildt, Anselm Doering-Manteuffel, and Heinrich August Winkler point to the important process of Westernization but fail to confront the problematic nature of that concept. Only Mary Fulbrook and Peter Graf Kielmansegg come close to addressing the question of cultural transformation, but even they often lapse into expository narratives.

My own views differ from these authors because I write from a Euro-American perspective that does not quite fit the popular interpretations on either side of the Atlantic. Born during the war, I grew up and was educated in Germany, but I came to the United States over four decades ago to receive my academic training. The division of my institutional responsibilities between the Lurcy Chair for European Civilization at the University of North Carolina at Chapel Hill and the directorship of the Zentrum für Zeithistorische Forschung in Potsdam has deepened this sense of cultural hybridity. Even though I am at home in both the German and American discourses, I sometimes feel like an outsider who is tempted to challenge the basic assumptions of each. Thus, the following reflections emerge from a transatlantic double perspective, which seeks to describe the extent of and explain the reasons for the transformation of my country of birth to skeptics in my adopted home.

In this book I propose the thesis that a collective learning process took place after Hitler, bringing the Germans back from perpetrating unspeakable crimes to a sincere commitment to human rights. Unlike the intellectual preoccupation with German efforts to deal with the Nazi past (explored by Charles Maier and Jeffrey Herf), this investigation focuses primarily on the practical lessons that a disoriented people drew from their past misdeeds. My analysis pays particular attention to the relationship between the outside interventions of the United States and the Soviet Union and the inside insights of the minority of anti-Fascist Germans who were ready to make a new start. In an attempt to integrate both postwar histories, I contrast the Western consequences drawn from the catastrophe with the Eastern efforts to learn from disaster. Since the transformation was a drawn-out process, I concentrate here on three different stages of its development, starting with the postwar period, then focusing on the 1960s, and concluding with the 1990s.

After exploring the alternative of Westernization, I settled on the concept of "civilization" as a standard for evaluating the metamorphosis of the Germans. While postcolonial critics have correctly condemned its misuse as justification for sexist and racist repression, several reasons support this terminological choice. First, prominent contemporaries, from Hannah Arendt to Franklin D. Roosevelt, used the notion of a German deviation from the values of Western civilization as a key argument. Second, in modifying the *Sonderweg* thesis, the Israeli-German historian Dan Diner suggested that the Holocaust constituted a rupture of common ethical norms, a veritable *Zivilisationsbruch*. Third, the surprising resurgence of the concept of "civil society" as a rejection of Communist dictatorship and as a characterization of voluntary social activism links the two dictatorships with each other. Therefore, "civilization" may serve as shorthand for the struggle for human rights.

The methodology used to plumb the relationship between structural transformations and changes in popular consciousness combines an analysis of individual experiences with a study of public discourse. Following the suggestion by the essayist Sebastian Haffner, I proceed from the criterion of the influence that events had on the lives of ordinary people, and thus I investigate the incremental changes in the beliefs and behaviors that shape everyday life. A critical history of the learning process must address both personal reactions to dramatic events and collective debates about key social and political questions. The subsequent observations therefore draw on the individual diaries, autobiographies, and memoirs located in novelist Walter Kempowski's comprehensive collection, as well as on numerous conversations with eyewitnesses. Since personal accounts are generally limited to the early years, the later chapters also have to rely increasingly on print media and other public materials in the Press Archive of the Otto-Suhr-Institute in Berlin.

This source-based reflection seeks to answer the key question concerning the aftermath of the Nazi catastrophe that makes this an exemplary case: How did the Germans succeed in rising out of the physical destruction and moral degradation created by the war of annihilation and Holocaust for which they were to blame? Addressing this problem entails a reconstruction of the distancing from aggression and authoritarianism by eventually embracing a Western conception of human rights. This same issue confronted the former members of the Third Reich in Austria, as well as the Axis allies in Italy and Japan, thereby suggesting comparisons of the differences in their rehabilitations. Moreover, other attempted transitions to democracy in Latin America, the Mediterranean, and Eastern Europe have had to cope with similar problems at a later time. Thus, at the heart of this study lies the issue of the German "return to humanity" that the Social Democratic jurist Gustav Radbruch demanded in 1947, and, by implication, the more general question of recovering from criminal dictatorship.

ACKNOWLEDGMENTS

The completion of such a large undertaking requires the practical help and intellectual stimulation of many colleagues, only a few of whom can be mentioned here. I thank Walter Kempowski for granting me access to his rich collection of autobiographies and Marianne Kerkhoff for helping to select relevant folders of press clippings. In addition, I express my gratitude to Christa Schneider, Inge Schmöker, and Katja Stender for helping with the original German version of the text. Moreover, I am greatly indebted to Brandon Hunziker for preparing a draft translation into English, which I revised based on suggestions by Susan Ferber of Oxford University Press, and to Samara Heifetz for compiling the index. I am also grateful to Michael Geyer, Rüdiger Hohls, Jan-Holger Kirsch, Christoph Kleßmann, and Helga Welsh for selflessly reading the manuscript and offering instructive criticism. Similarly, my thanks go to members of the Zentrum für Zeithistorische Forschung in Potsdam, including Hans-Hermann Hertle, Peter Hübner, Michael Lemke, Thomas Lindenberger, and Martin Sabrow, who turned the last years into a graduate seminar for their director. Finally, I acknowledge that these reflections are an attempt to answer the question raised by my North Carolina graduate students: How could a country that produced Hitler and the Holocaust transform into a new, peaceful, and democratic Germany?

CONTENTS

Contents   xiii

AFTER HITLER

INTRODUCTION

Rupture of Civilization

The full horror of the Nazi dictatorship was only revealed as the end of the war drew near. The "unbelievable spring" of 1945 had finally brought the fighting to Germany—tank treads shredded fields, grenades blew holes into walls, and firebombs torched entire city blocks. Under the energetic attacks of the Allies, the battlefronts, hastily reinforced with poorly trained adolescents and older men of the *Volkssturm*, began to buckle, and the once mighty Wehrmacht crumbled into a mass of civilians who sought above all to evade capture. Not heeding Joseph Goebbels's nihilistic call to resist the enemy at all costs, millions of members abandoned the Nazi Party. While those in the upper echelons got themselves to safety, minor Nazis simply hid their uniforms, hoping that the victors would overlook them. As one journalist wrote, "Everyone is abandoning Adolf and no one had anything to with the regime." At the same time, the greater German Empire began to crumble, with ever larger pieces of territory occupied and the surviving prisoners of war, forced laborers, and concentration camp inmates liberated. Once public administration began to falter, civil order dissolved, water and electricity failed, supplies ran out, and the streets became unsafe.[1]

Looming defeat evoked mixed feelings among the German people. As the journalist Margret Boveri noted at the end of April in Berlin: "Not much is being said about the war. Still, it's obvious that everyone has had quite enough of it." But first one had to survive the final battles and get through the occupation, which held a new set of dangers. To be sure, no longer having to fear being killed came as a great relief. Nevertheless, the arrival of the victors brought new worries of plundering or raping troops, bent on revenge. "Now they have me," another woman described her rape; "I scream, I scream . . . behind me the cellar door thuds closed." Above all for committed Nazis, patriots, and members of the military, the laying down of arms was a defeat. One soldier felt "extremely bitter about how we have been betrayed. So that's what we have fought for during six years, that the Russians are here and we don't know whether our families still live and where they are."[2] But for members of the resistance, forced laborers, and concentration camp prisoners, the arrival of the Allies meant a genuine liberation that offered hope for a better future. In the rest of the population, feelings of deep loss alternated in bewildering succession with the intoxicating joy of survival.[3]

The terrible legacy of the Hitler dictatorship becomes strikingly clear in the impressive photographs taken by the American photographer Margaret Bourke-White as she rode with advancing GIs into the Reich in 1945. Her pictures show the bleak landscapes of scarred ruins, mountains of rubble, blasted bridges, destroyed industrial sites, burned-out houses, and broken machines of war. Not only could suicide victims and individual graves be seen, but also charred bodies hanging from barbed wire and mountains of corpses stacked in front of concentration camp ovens. While the well-fed and imperious faces of Nazi devotees reflect their success in the Third Reich, the more sympathetic countenances of the regime's opponents are marked by deep furrows, and the oversized eyes staring out from the hollow-cheeked faces of the victims seem to plead for mercy. In contrast, the victors look confidently into the camera and, despite all prohibitions, have already begun to fraternize with willing "Fräuleins." Between the bombed-out houses, in the ruined factories, on the packed trains, and across the pot-holed roads, however, life seemed to go on, in spite of everything.[4]

Such shocking images bear stark witness to the destructive consequences of a regime that had overstepped the boundaries of normal warfare with its war of annihilation and mass genocide. While the level of physical destruction was truly breathtaking, the moral disaster was perhaps even greater. Not surprisingly, uncertainty about the future ran rampant. Because the extent of the defeat suffered by the Third Reich far surpassed that of Imperial Germany after the First World War, one question after another confronted the dazed population: Would the hated Germans be allowed to survive at all, or would their liberated neighbors exact a bloody revenge for the crimes that had been committed against them? How would the occupation powers deal with this defeated people —would they divide the country up and demand steep reparations, or would they grant them a minimal sustenance so that they might live on somehow? Would the Allies ever permit their former enemies to reconstitute a more civilized domestic order and return as an active subject to international affairs? The "contempt of the civilized world" that Hitler had engendered thus formed both a prerequisite for and an obstacle to any new beginning for Germany.[5]

The Shock of Inhumanity

The discovery of the ghastly war crimes in early 1945 triggered a deep, world-wide revulsion that darkened the German name for decades to come. Overshadowed by the final battle for Berlin, rumors about the murder of over 5 million Jews in Auschwitz and elsewhere seemed at first too unimaginable to be believed.[6] But gradually, reports of the liberation of "3000 living skeletons and 2700 un-buried bodies" from the underground V-2 rocket factory Dora (Nordhausen) and of the "horror marches" of Allied POWs began to trickle out to media around the world.[7] Still, it was the liberation of the Buchenwald concentration camp near the city of Weimar by American troops in April 1945 that provided unde-niable proof. The deplorable condition of the 21,000 inmates, many of whom stood close to death, as well as the records of the prisoner committee that ac-counted for the murders of 32,705 people, banished any lingering doubts. "What I saw was so horrible," reported the journalist Harold Denny, "that I wouldn't have believed it, if I had not seen it myself." Revolted by such "trained sadism," he vowed: "The world must not forget such things." Denny went on to describe how one liberated Russian, pointing to the murderous Hygienic Institute of the Waffen-SS, commented ironically: "And so, the Germans are civilized!"[8]

To disprove the popular claim of "We knew nothing," the U.S. military forced 1,200 citizens of Weimar "to see for themselves the horror, brutality and human indecency that they perpetrated against their 'neighbors' in the notori-ous Buchenwald concentration camp." According to *New York Times* reporter Gene Currivan, the tour of this "death factory" began first with a look at pieces of human skin that had been processed into tattooed "parchment" for use as a lampshade. "The German people saw all this today and wept. And those who didn't weep were ashamed." Next came the "scientific laboratories" in which human experiments, including deliberate infection with typhoid fever, were conducted, with a death rate of 98 percent. From there the tour proceeded to the barracks, where the "stench, filth, and misery defied description." The no-torious torture chambers and the all too frequently utilized gallows were not left out, either. But worst of all was the crematory, in which corpses lay piled on wagons like wood, waiting to be burned in three modern ovens. Indeed, "They saw sights that brought tears to their eyes, and scores of them, including the nurses, fainted."[9] Even if many patriotic Germans initially did not want believe the reports and images, one thoughtful observer knew that it would be impos-sible for them to deny the crimes for long: "We were, however, appalled by the ghastly reports on the conditions of the liberated concentration camps which reached us."[10]

Confirmed by the discovery of additional camps in Bergen-Belsen (Lower Saxony), Dachau (Bavaria), and Sachsenhausen (outside Berlin), the "indisputable evidence" could only have hardened the Allies' position on Germany's future after Hitler. To overcome the lingering skepticism of "what were called German atrocity stories" from World War I propaganda, the U.S. military commissioned the former prisoner Eugen Kogon to draft an official report on the "extermination factory" at Buchenwald.[11] Numerous U.S. congressmen, leading military officers including General Eisenhower, and journalists also visited the liberated camp to convince themselves of conditions that were "almost indescribably horrible."[12] Shocking images of emaciated prisoners and mass graves served to strengthen the advocates of a punitive policy such as Secretary of Treasury Henry Morgenthau, who along with President Franklin D. Roosevelt, believed that the German people "must have it driven home to them that the whole nation has engaged in a lawless conspiracy against the decencies of modern civilization."[13] The more crimes that were uncovered, the more difficult it would become for moderate, realistic policy makers such as Secretary of War Henry Stimson to argue that a Carthaginian peace would resemble what the Nazis had done to their victims, namely "be a crime against civilization itself." Nevertheless, both sides in this debate agreed it was essential not only to repair the short-term damages wrought by Nazism, but also to break decisively with the long-term, problematic traditions of German political culture that were, at least in part, to blame for them.[14]

For the Germans, the defeat also accelerated the process of distancing themselves from the Third Reich but did not necessarily lead to an acknowledgment of their own responsibility for its crimes. An American opinion poll taken at the beginning of June 1945 revealed an apparently helpless population, which generally held the Nazi leaders responsible for the catastrophe and therefore demanded "the elimination of all traces of the Nazi Party."[15] "The German has become a pariah among other peoples," wrote one bewildered woman from Hamburg. "Germany's honor has been taken by the cruelties which one crazy idea inflicted upon innocent people." She went on to muse: "That such a thing could have been caused by Germans, nobody would have thought possible. . . . That Germany, which proudly counted a Goethe, a Schiller, Humboldt or Kant as its very own possessions, could sink so low."[16] Only in exile did intellectuals like Thomas Mann achieve a more profound analysis of what he called "our disgrace." He understood the "romantic counterrevolution against the . . . rationalism of the Enlightenment" as the chief source of the "hysterical barbarism" of the Nazis and therefore called for a return to the values of Western civilization.[17] To a critical minority of independent observers and anti-Fascists, it was clear that a fundamentally new beginning was necessary in every respect.[18]

As they became known, the contours of the "cold-blooded, scientific mass murder" of the European Jews also cast a shadow over the Potsdam Conference, which was supposed to show the way forward to a "genuinely recivilized Europe." Despite practical problems facing the Allied administration, the ending of German sovereignty on June 5, 1945, already pointed in the direction of strictness.[19] It came as little surprise, therefore, that the initially provisional but then final decisions of the three great powers concerning the future of Germany sought both to punish and rehabilitate. In light of the millions who had died at the hands of the Third Reich, the demand for military security and material indemnification by partitioning off the eastern territories as well as imposing considerable reparations seemed entirely appropriate. An editorial in the *New York Times* described such conditions as "hard and restrictive," as they aimed "to change the direction of the German mind, strip the nation of its war-making potential, change and decentralize its economy." In short, the Potsdam communiqué tried to turn the industrial powerhouse of Europe back into a country of agriculture and peaceful domestic production. Yet for the German people, these conditions of demilitarization, denazification, and decartelization were not altogether "hopeless," as they would give them the chance "to prepare for the eventual reconstruction of their life on a democratic and peaceful basis."[20]

The Allied resolutions put an end to the uncertainty that loomed over the first few months of the occupation and, as General Eisenhower saw it, offered clear terms for step-by-step rehabilitation. "We also were dejected about the communiqué of the Potsdam Conference, which we tried to interpret," wrote the journalist Margret Boveri in her diary. Especially in divided Berlin, people argued "almost always on the basis of the question: East or West"—that is, Bolshevism or Americanism—and whether one "could not perhaps still make, in place of an either-or, a third choice of one's own." The liberal Jewish academic Victor Klemperer, who had barely survived the Nazis' racial persecution, was nevertheless also devastated: "This shrunken, small Germany will become a wretched agrarian state lacking in independence and with no chance of regaining its strength."[21] While the majority of "depressed and disgruntled" Germans did not understand "why the outside world blamed them for the crimes" of Nazism, some members of the decimated elite—for example, the conservative historian Gerhard Ritter—attempted to salvage the better qualities of the nation. Although people still argued over the direction and extent of the required reforms, it became clear to most that militarism and nationalism had driven Germany to misfortune.[22]

However problematic, the Nuremberg trials were a necessary attempt to avenge by judicial means the "violation of the conventions of civilization" wrought by the Nazis' crimes. "All the human and material loss that Europe has suffered since Hitler came to power, including the blood of 5,700,000 Jews that were systematically exterminated, was laid to their criminal machinations." The indictments focused on a rising scale of accusations, derived from the treaties of the League of Nations, from the preparation of Germany for war (charge one) to the waging of aggressive wars (charge two), and to violations of the traditional rules of warfare through the conduct of a war of annihilation (charge three).

The charge of "crimes against humanity," a reaction to the ghastly images from the concentration camps, added a further juristic innovation that applied to the "extermination, enslavement and deportation of civilian populations before and during the war" and to "persecution on the basis of political, racial, or religious grounds." This fourth charge made clear the Allies' attempt to respond not only to Germany's culpability for the outbreak of war and the brutality of its conduct but also to the previously unimaginable quality of the crimes against noncombatants. By avenging these violations through a legal process, the Nuremberg trials sought to reaffirm the principle of human rights for the future.[23]

The German population regarded this spectacle of war-crime trials, which were held in the city of the former Nazi party rallies, with mixed feelings. For some observers, "a boundless lust for power and ignorance came to light, completely free of inhibitions and a maniacal experimentation with people and nations." Still, despite the scrupulous correctness of trial procedures, the Nazis' defenders had little difficulty casting it as "the justice of the victors" because Soviet crimes, such as the mass shootings of Polish officers in 1940 in the Katyn Forest, were also attributed to the Nazis. Nevertheless, the horrific courtroom images of many individuals and organizations that were reported in newspapers, newsreels, and educational films ("Death Mills") did not fall entirely short of their intended effect. As a result, U.S. surveys discovered that roughly half of the German population considered the punishment of the perpetrators to be just. The partial confessions of the participants, moreover, confirmed many of the charges, while the relatively mild sentences for members of the former elite—for example, Minister of Economics Hjalmar Schacht—also demonstrated the possibility of a successful individual defense. All told, the Nuremberg trials bolstered the impression of the leading Nazis' guilt. At the same time, this unprecedented experiment in international justice also contributed to a feeling of exculpation among the population since many Germans could now claim that they had either known nothing of the crimes in the first place or had only followed orders handed down from above.[24]

Under the tutelage of the occupying powers, the process of rehabilitation was likely to be long and arduous, especially since the Allies increasingly disagreed on the goals and methods of the necessary transformation. To be sure, a "strict policy," which, along with the required denazification, deliberately sought to weaken the Germans economically and cripple them politically, was quite popular in Washington and Moscow. But it was equally obvious that such a course would hardly convert a defeated people to democracy. Pragmatic policy makers, like the head of the U.S. military government in Germany, Lucius Clay, advocated instead a "positive program" that included incentives for the difficult physical reconstruction, as well as suggestions for the more problematic reorientation of public life, that lay ahead. At the same time, some observers bemoaned the existence of a "political vacuum" that forced the defeated populace to choose between the competing models of American democracy and Soviet communism. Finally, it was by no means clear whether there would be another central German government or whether the resumption of political life would have to take place according to the ideological views of the occupation power in its respective zone.[25]

From the perspective of the Germans, still filled with self-pity, the conditions for democratization did not seem to be particularly favorable. Only a small minority, above all the regime's opponents and its victims, actually greeted the defeat of the Wehrmacht as a liberation from the dictatorship.[26] Although the majority of the population rejoiced at the end of the war, many also felt resentment against the victors and disappointment at the failure of the Nazis' promises: "They lied to us and betrayed us" was a sentiment felt by many. While American interviewers may have found "a latent and possibly deep-seated feeling of guilt about the brutality of the German Wehrmacht," the almost "compulsive yearning to talk" seemed designed more to blur individual responsibility and attribute blame to the Nazi bigwigs.[27] The search for decent German democrats thus proved largely futile, since the majority still seemed to be held captive to authoritarian patterns of behavior, almost instinctively cozying up to the occupation powers. Upright Christians, untainted by affiliation with the regime, along with Social Democrats, who were "ready to clean house" and would thus risk a new political start, were by contrast scarce commodities.[28]

Given the extent of the Nazi crimes, the renewed attempt at rehabilitation after 1945 demanded a considerably deeper intervention than that required after 1918. To prevent future rearmament, the victorious powers insisted on "unconditional surrender," complete occupation, the end to sovereignty, and legal punishment of war criminals. In light of the massive air bombardments, the carnage on the eastern front, and the flight and expulsion from the eastern territories, many conquered Germans realized that total defeat would bring more drastic consequences than at the end of the First World War. Despite all denials of individual responsibility, the enormous extent and the new quality of the crimes committed during the war of annihilation and genocide could hardly be disputed—especially since thousands of witnesses, be they surviving Jews, former slave laborers, or liberated prisoners of war, still found themselves in Germany. Perhaps more than anything else, this unimaginable shame would render the internal rebuilding of a constitutional state and international readmission into the world community a lengthy process. As Karl Jering, a young intellectual, bluntly put it, "our ostracism is the result of our betrayal of human civilization."[29] It remained to be seen to what extent the victorious occupiers and the uncompromised minority among the occupied would succeed in the necessary cleansing of Germany's political culture.

Interpretations of Nazi Barbarism

Contemporaries and later observers have had great difficulty in explaining the causes of the relapse into Nazi barbarism. American war-time interpretations employed the model of a German deviation from Western civilization, which they considered to be a self-evident standard. Yet it should not be forgotten that the idea of a "Western civilization" had only emerged at U.S. universities after the First World War as an answer to the question, posed by returning soldiers, why farm boys from Iowa needed to die in the trenches of Chateau Thierry. In short, this notion suggested a shared evolution of human rights and democracy among the Western powers, though not the Russian allies, who did not fit the progress of liberty. Ironically German intellectuals during the First World War also emphasized the dichotomy between "heroes and hucksters," as sociologist Werner Sombart put it, or, "culture and civilization," in the words of Thomas Mann.[30] In this way, introductory courses in philosophy and history propagated a universally understood concept of humanity derived from the Enlightenment, suggesting that the Hitler dictatorship ought to be condemned as deviant. The German catalogue of sins could thus seem to extend from the sixteenth to the twentieth centuries, starting with the authoritarian Reformation and territorial fragmentation of the Holy Roman Empire, proceeding to Prussian militarism and Romantic irrationalism, and culminating in the pushy imperialism of the second German Empire.[31]

Interestingly enough, Soviet intellectuals also developed a critique of German barbarism that hinged on the notion of civilization, albeit defined by Marxist standards. The traditional Russian respect for German culture led to a polarized analysis in which the progressive visions of "bourgeois" humanism and the labor movement were placed in stark opposition to the reactionary interests of the Junkers and capitalists. In contrast to the Western emphasis on historical contingency, which located Germany's deviation from its model in various historical turning points such as 1848, the Marxist understanding of fascism was based above all on an economic analysis of class structure, which saw Nazism primarily as the product of the crisis of international monopoly capitalism.[32] While Western "error analysis" favored limited institutional reforms as a corrective, the state-sanctioned "anti-Fascism" of the GDR demanded that a radical social transformation precede any political rehabilitation of the Germans. At the same time, the focus of the Communist Party critique on the traditional elites tended to exonerate the majority of nominal or small-time Nazis.[33]

In the Federal Republic, the American notion of Nazi deviance, now presented as the thesis of Germany's "special path" (*Sonderweg*), gained widespread acceptance by the late 1960s, especially among the younger generation of intellectuals. Positive experiences with Western civil society through exchange programs and personal contacts made them receptive to the critical interpretation of the German past that had been formulated by refugees from Hitler. At the same time, the concept of German deviance offered an answer to the question of structural continuities that had been raised by the Fischer controversy, a heated debate among historians concerning Germany's responsibility for the outbreak of the First World War. Moreover, the methodological shift from political history to a history of society (*Gesellschaftsgeschichte*) facilitated the importation of the methods and theories of the neighboring social sciences. The cumulative effect was an interpretation of the German past that emphasized the long-term weaknesses of the middle class, the belated formation of the nation-state, and, as sociologist Ralf Dahrendorf claimed, its subsequent incapacity for democracy. In this interpretation, the Third Reich no longer appeared as a deviation *from* but, rather, as the logical consequence *of* German traditions.[34] A further strength of the *Sonderweg* perspective was that it helped motivate a new kind of political engagement aimed at breaking with those negative traditions that lingered in the Federal Republic through a rigorous liberalization of society.

During the last two decades, the concept of a German *Sonderweg* has evolved further toward a vision of Westernization, thereby only compounding its problems. In the early 1980s British historians Geoff Eley and David Blackbourn caused something of a stir by strongly objecting to the basic premise of the *Sonderweg* thesis. Since it was not Germany but England that deviated from the general European pattern of modernization, the empirical basis for the critique leveled by scholars like Hans-Ulrich Wehler and Jürgen Kocka was simply insufficient.[35] Out of the ensuing debate emerged a modified version of the *Sonderweg* concept, which now emphasized, in Heinrich August Winkler's formulation, "the long road to the West," stressing the Westernization of the Federal Republic. Nevertheless, it still assigned primary blame for the Nazi catastrophe to the specifically German tradition of a *Reich*, an empire that became conflated with a nation state.[36] This interpretation correctly points to Germany's geographic shift westward, its political and economic bonding to the West, as well as the Americanization of its consumption and popular culture. And yet this view also treats the West as an unreflected standard, failing to scrutinize its historical liabilities such as slavery, imperialism, and exploitation and presents an idealized image that has long since been discredited by feminist and postcolonial critiques.[37]

As an alternative to the *Sonderweg* thesis, the German-Israeli historian Dan Diner coined the concept of a "rupture of civilization at Auschwitz" during the "historians' controversy" of the 1980s. The roots of this neologism can be traced to the profound horror expressed by the émigré Hannah Arendt on hearing reports about the mass murder of the Jews in 1943, which went far beyond all military necessity: "It was truly as if an abyss [had] opened. . . . Everything else could have somehow been repaid, [but] not this. This should never have been allowed to happen." For Diner, therefore, the crime of Auschwitz constituted a "far reaching, fundamental rupture" that touched "the very foundations of certainty about civilization" itself, therefore undermining the most basic premises of human coexistence. "The bureaucratically organized, industrially implemented mass extermination means something like the repudiation of a civilization whose thinking and actions adhere to a logic that required a minimum level of mutual trust." The extermination of a people for the sake of extermination alone not only infringed on universally valid norms of ethical behavior but also, at the same time, repudiated the hopes for secular progress that began with the Enlightenment. At stake was thus more than just the suffering of the Jews: "Auschwitz stands as a universal problem, a problem of humanity."[38]

The rapid colloquial spread of the term "rupture of civilization" indicates that the concept possesses a considerable intuitive appeal. Unlike Western notions of deviance or Marxist class analysis, this neologism explicitly addresses the "moral stigma" of the Holocaust as "an attack on the entire foundations of humanity and civilization."[39] In so doing, the notion of a "rupture of civilization" raises new historical questions about the enigmatic meaning of the term "civilization" that go well beyond the anthropological analyses of Norbert Elias, concerning the control of individual emotions and the state's collective monopoly of power.[40] At the same time, the concept underlines the troubling connection raised by the sociologist Zygmunt Bauman between modernity and genocide: "The Holocaust can only be understood as a failure of civilization (that is, of rationally guided human behavior) to tame morbid instincts or anything else that remains of nature in people."[41] Even if the inflationary use of the term threatens to reduce it to an empty catchphrase, "rupture of civilization" is able to stress more clearly than other concepts (such as "zero hour") that the crimes committed during the war of annihilation and the Holocaust are the necessary point of departure for any history of postwar Germany.[42]

The related concept of civil society, which is enjoying a surprising revival, offers a possibility for specifying the meaning of civilization still further. The idea of a sphere of *societas civilis* outside of one's own house but still below the purview of the state was understood in the political theory of the seventeenth and eighteenth centuries above all as a demarcation from nature and barbarism. Through economic exchange, cultural creativity, and social emancipation, the civilizing of society could be considered a progressive process that would enrich human coexistence. While English thinkers proceeded more from the assumption of the compatibility between civil society and a constitutional state, continental critics such as Immanuel Kant furnished the concept with a potentially antiabsolutist connotation by stressing the self-organizing voluntarism of citizens.[43] Providing an alternative to the discredited notion of "bourgeois society," the concept of *civil society* resurfaced as a keyword of antidictatorial criticism in Eastern Europe, helping dissidents to justify their campaign for restoring human rights during the 1980s. Suggesting a hope for a kind of democratic self-realization beyond both economic necessities and political constraints, the concept also began to reverberate once again in the normative discussions of Western intellectuals.

In order to function effectively as a yardstick of political development, the concept of "civil society," however, requires a historical definition that clarifies its various contending meanings. According to Jürgen Kocka, its most important attribute is social self-organization through the free association of citizens for the pursuit of collective interests in the public sphere. Another significant dimension concerns the norms of civil intercourse among citizens, nonviolent sociability, and a relationship between states that is not marked by militaries and militarism. At the same time, the concept also implies cultural civility along with religious tolerance, civic courage, and a sense of responsibility for the community. A more problematic but still vital aspect is economic self-regulation by means of an unrestricted market, which effectively allows individuals to pursue their own economic interests. Finally, civil society entails civic involvement in both local self-government and national rights of democratic participation.[44] When viewed as a complex web of relationships, civil society emerges not as some codified condition or fixed ideology but as the product of a dynamic process that seeks to foster peaceful exchanges among various elements in society.

Focusing on these core features of civil society might help explain wartime perceptions of the Nazi's breach of the values and practices of Western civilization. To internal critics, the extension of party control over all aspects of society appeared as a perversion of free associations of citizens into compulsory organizations of subjects. Likewise, external observers understood the glorification of violence against dissenters as preparation for military aggression against Germany's neighbors. Nazi victims viewed the consequences of religious, racial, and political intolerance as the cause of their persecution, while German proletarians as well as foreign slave laborers perceived the ideological subordination of the economy as the reason for their own exploitation. Though some Nazi followers were still inclined to balk at the question "Are we the barbarians that newspapers of the entire world call us?," the disastrous results of the war of annihilation and the Holocaust also made it abundantly clear to the rest of the Germans what the consequences of the blind faith they had put into their *Führer* were going to be. Because the Third Reich had barbarized society in nearly every respect, recivilizing the Germans demanded a fundamental reversal of political culture.[45]

In contrast to the *Sonderweg* thesis, the concept of a civilized society therefore offers a more comprehensive standard by which to measure the evolution of different states. Unlike the notion of Westernization, it does not rely on an idealized model of the victorious Western powers, whose own history is marred by considerable racism, imperialism, and exploitation. Instead, the utopia of a civil society is the product of progressive European and American thinkers, including such eminent Germans as Hegel. While civil society embraces the discussion of "bourgeois society," it does not refer primarily to the bourgeoisie as a class or, for that matter, to citizens as members of a state.[46] At the same time, the normative character of the civilizing concept might help avoid the pitfalls of portraying the rehabilitation of the Germans as an uncritical "success story" of modernization and of postulating a teleological progression from a bad past to a better present. The very violation of this standard by both the brown and the red dictatorships makes the deadly ambivalence of modernity itself all too clear, while the manifest imperfections of the democracies illustrate a frustrating incompleteness of realizing their own ideals.

Toward a History of Rehabilitation

The dramatic rupture of civilization by the Nazi dictatorship poses a key question for any postwar history: How could the Germans, after unspeakable crimes, find a way back to the civil society that had already begun to take shape before 1933? Perceptively, the political scientist Peter Graf von Kielmansegg suggests that "it was the catastrophe that rendered the Germans capable of democracy."[47] Conservative observers maintain that the decisive steps in the transformation already occurred in the second half of the 1940s with the currency reform, the promulgation of the Basic Law, and the founding of the Federal Republic. In contrast, liberal intellectuals criticize the incompleteness of the changes, stressing the need for further reforms by the social-liberal coalition, as well as the generational revolt of the 1960s. Similarly, Marxists denounce the Federal Republic as a continuation of fascism, if now in a modern guise, and consider the anti-Fascist, socialist German Democratic Republic (GDR), quite simply, the better Germany.[48] Even after the collapse of communism had decided the competitive struggle between the two states clearly in favor of the Federal Republic of Germany (FRG), the timing, causes, and degree of the Germans' postwar rehabilitation remain open to dispute.

The learning processes, both personal and collective, that aimed to prevent a recurrence of oppression, war, and genocide must therefore be reconstructed historically. In contrast to the unwillingness to learn after the First World War, the even more severe conditions after the Second World War seem to have fostered a drastic change of political outlook among Germans.[49] How did the processes of individual reflection about social learning from the "German misfortune," with its "taste of disgust, sickness, and insanity" that were apparently "incomparable to anything in history," proceed? What were the consequences of the shocking rupture of civilization for specific realms such as attitudes toward the military, understandings of the nation, and the organization of the economy? The mental transformation that did occur in spite of much resistance raises still more difficult questions: Was the superior power of the victors, which encouraged an opportunistic imitation of their rhetoric and forms of behavior, primarily responsible for the changes? Or did the destruction wrought by Nazism, which Germans experienced firsthand, along with the shameful crimes published in the media, so thoroughly discredit racist nationalism that they provoked a search for untainted values?[50]

On several different levels, in this book I approach the long and diffuse process of rethinking that occurred in the defeated society, which both rejected traditions and continued to use them as anchors for salvation. A first focus of analysis is the attempt of individuals to come to terms with their own past, encouraged by hiring practices that demanded the presentation of a convincing account of their activities in the Third Reich. A second subject is the effort made by groups such as student clubs and institutions like churches to explain their more or less enthusiastic collaboration with Hitler's system. A final topic is the public debate about the implications of the Third Reich disaster, because it perhaps more than anything else helped to create the conditions for a renewal of political life at the national level. In all these different arenas, Germans simultaneously tried to make sense of their disparate experiences with Nazism, defeat, and occupation in order to chart political options for the future. To convince a Cold War public of the correctness of their views, they constructed ideological discourses, which tried time and again to deduce lessons from what had happened.[51]

To capture this halting learning process, in this volume I focus on the practical rather than the intellectual ways in which Germans dealt with their problematic past. While many people continued to equivocate about their own complicity in dictatorship and war, the tasks of rebuilding forced them to draw pragmatic conclusions from their experiences during the Third Reich and subsequent defeat. The controversy between leftist critics of the repression of guilt and right-wing apologists of a need for healing silence does not sufficiently consider the practical consequences of either position.[52] Though criticism of a restorative "policy for the past" during the early 1950s correctly calls attention to efforts at evading responsibility, it fails to engage the rebuilding of institutions and the reaffirming of bonds of sociability in order to prevent a relapse into the disastrous Nazi past.[53] The current preoccupation with the halting emergence of a critical memory culture, ready to face the responsibility for the Holocaust, tends to emphasize the moral sensitization toward the victims rather than actual changes in political behavior.[54] Therefore it seems more productive to analyze the often inarticulate efforts of individual resolutions, group discussions, and political decisions to prevent a repetition of the misfortune, to alleviate its disastrous results, and to build a better future.

This exploration of German political culture during the second half of the twentieth century also employs an integrated, problem-oriented approach that contrasts Eastern with Western developments. As long as the histories of the GDR and the Federal Republic are written separately, the postwar division of the country will continue to be perpetuated by scholarship. Since most recent syntheses primarily celebrate the success of Western democracy, they tend to grant the failed communist dictatorship only a subordinate place.[55] Stimulated by historian Christoph Kleßmann's call for a systematic comparison,[56] some efforts to deal with the divided pasts, to be sure, have started to explore the asymmetrical relationship, but they still take the two states as their starting point.[57] A more convincing assessment of the extent of the overall transformation ought instead to proceed sequentially by dealing with a number of key topics and thereby presenting a longitudinal and thematic analysis of the partial similarities, as well as clear differences between East and West. In doing so, the narrative need not strive for schematic balance but should follow the changing locations of key learning processes, while commenting only selectively on the opposite side.[58]

The following reflections on Germany's return to civilization concentrate primarily on three crucial periods in which important changes coalesced. The fundamental decisions that created the conditions for a transformation were made in the period immediately following the war's end. The Potsdam program issued by the victorious powers defined the dual goals of the occupation: While the German people needed to atone for the "dreadful crimes" they had committed, they were at the same time to receive an opportunity to prepare for the "eventual reconstruction of their life on a democratic and peaceful basis." The first means toward accomplishing these goals was the "complete disarmament and demilitarization of Germany" and the admission of defeat; the second condition demanded the dismantling of the "Nazi Party with all of its affiliated organizations," the dissolution of all Nazi institutions, and the prohibition of Nazi propaganda; and the third point called for decentralization of the economy so as to "eliminate the German potential for war" and the "excessive concentration" of economic power.[59] Initially, therefore, I seek to answer the question, How successful was this attempt to eliminate Nazi influences as the spark for subsequent rehabilitation?

Only after the relative stabilization of the Adenauer period, during the "dynamic times" of the 1960s, did the actual breakthrough to a modern civil society occur. While the structural transformation of social conditions had already been set in motion in the late 1940s, the acceleration of the changes during this decade managed to overcome older problematic traditions, since the process was now driven forward by critical Germans themselves. As a result, the trend toward Westernization strengthened, promoted not only by the territorial shift westward and the political alliance with the West, but also by consumerism and popular culture, so much so that one might speak of an Americanization of values and behavior. At the same time, people grew more accustomed to the new political regime, recognizing its achievements in increasing prosperity, internalizing its liberal values, and developing an emotional attachment to representative democracy. While the dictatorial East more and more cut itself off behind the Berlin Wall, the combination of the generational rebellion, election victory of the socialist-liberal coalition, and other changes in societal values gave added impetus to the liberalization of West German society.[60] In this section, I pursue the second issue: Did the 1960s contribute to the loss of time-honored virtues, or did they bring decisive progress to the process of "internal democratization?"

The last, and in many ways still incomplete, step toward the recovery of civilized normalcy is closely connected to the "civic revolution" of 1989–1990. The movement for civil rights in the GDR can be seen as a surprising expression of the reemergence of civil society. But while the democratic awakening may have been able to triumph over the communist dictatorship, the unification of the bankrupt East with the more successful West brought with it new problems for internal unity, forcing the abandonment of many lofty expectations for the future.[61] The unexpected resurrection of a now much smaller nation-state, which was thoroughly embedded in the ongoing process of European integration, necessitated yet another difficult attempt to forge a new identity, inspiring in the process a paradoxical nostalgia for both the old FRG and even the fallen GDR. At the same time, other pressures generated by accelerating globalization of the economy and worldwide migration demanded a new and unfamiliar international openness. Feeling threatened by these rapid changes, a minority soon fell back on the practiced reflexes of racial hatred against foreigners.[62] In the concluding part, I address the final problem: Has the Berlin Republic truly become a "normal state," or is it now the unassuming, but still somewhat unpredictable, hegemonic power of Europe?

In spite of its imperfections, the recivilizing of Germans during the second half of the twentieth century represents an exemplary case, because it suggests the possibility of practical redemption from moral disaster. Critical observers such as U.S. intelligence officer Saul Padover and Jewish survivor Victor Klemperer were initially skeptical about the chances for a fundamental change, since it would require an enormous effort.[63] More optimistic commentators like the Swiss journalist Fritz René Allemann were quick to applaud the renewal of political culture in the mid-1950s, even before the process had been actually completed.[64] The analytical challenge therefore consists of determining the precise extent of the metamorphosis and of deciding what factors spurred this change for the better. Did the Germans really learn from their catastrophe and reject the negative patterns that led them and their neighbors to disaster? Was the subsequent transformation primarily a product of total defeat, a result of transnational processes of modernization, or the outcome of their own decision, based on contrition?[65] The remaining deficits, above all an underlying xenophobia, caution against reading postwar accomplishments as an inevitable success story. Its exemplary interest lies precisely in the dramatic struggles that it took to reach and maintain a tolerant civil society.

PART I

Forced Reorientation

During the Yalta Conference, despite their disagreements concerning the future shape of the peace, the victorious Allies were fundamentally united on how the Germans had to be treated: "It is our inflexible purpose to destroy German militarism and Nazism and to ensure that Germany will never again be able to disturb the peace of the world." Given the Wehrmacht's ruthless conduct of the war, Franklin D. Roosevelt, Winston Churchill, and Joseph Stalin were hardly willing to distinguish between the Nazis who were responsible for the carnage and the wider population that had only lent a helping hand. The mood of their negotiations during the winter of 1945 therefore inclined more toward punishment than rehabilitation. The first occupation directives, as well as order number 1067 of the American Joint Chiefs of Staff, spoke a similarly clear language: "Germany will not be occupied for the purpose of liberation, but as a defeated nation."[1] Because the indubitable attack of 1939 seemed to confirm German war guilt in 1914, the Allies' overriding war aim was the prevention of yet another war of aggression.

The postwar challenge was therefore not just to eradicate the "Nazi tyranny root and branch" but to change German political culture more thoroughly than occurred after the First World War. While the National Socialist institutions and attitudes, which had brought so much suffering to the world, needed to be eliminated, the Allied planners envisaged a more radical break with the traditions that had made Hitler's tyranny and its untold atrocities possible in the first place. The Norwegian author Sigrid Undset, however, deemed a reorientation of "the national mentality" difficult, as the terrible crimes "which were committed as a consequence of German thought" would "never be forgotten."[2] The Potsdam program for occupation, shaped in no small part by impressions produced by the liberated concentration camps, therefore insisted on a far-reaching demilitarization, denazification, and decartelization of the country as a precondition for any later return to the community of civilized peoples through democratization.[3] "The time will come when Germany will once again be able to contribute to civilization," promised one British leaflet for German prisoners of war in the summer of 1945: "But only when you and your countrymen do your part."[4]

The success of this project of a comprehensive "reeducation of the Germans,"[5] however, depended not only on pressure from the occupation powers but also on the willingness of the defeated people to participate in it. "We stand shaken before the ruins of the Third Reich, which collapsed because of the principles upon which it was based," lamented the first edition of the leading newspaper in the Rhineland, the *Neue Rheinische Zeitung*, "and are oppressed by the thought that we as a people bear primary responsibility for the misery that has come over Europe." While the majority of the former Nazi followers were preoccupied with sheer survival, a critical minority emerging from the liberated concentration camps and devastated cities attempted to draw lessons from the catastrophe for which they were ready to accept the blame. "Our goal is to shape a new and better future. That is what we must focus our attention on," insisted Hans Fuchs, the newly appointed president of the North Rhine province. "We must create a new life, not just materially, but also intellectually and spiritually."[6]

Although the need for fundamental change was clear, the extent and method of such a new beginning remained hotly contested. Devastated by their collaboration with the regime and trying to salvage some sense of national continuity in the wake of the collapse, elites sought refuge in those religious beliefs or humanistic traditions that the Third Reich might have left undamaged. In this vein, the philosopher Karl Jaspers pleaded for a "transformation through self-education" that would join a frank exposure of the crimes of the dictatorship with "historical self-reflection" on the basis of Western civilization so as to strengthen the "responsibility of the individual."[7] In contrast, the anti-Fascist authors of the manifesto issued in the Buchenwald concentration camp saw the shameful end of the Third Reich, with the help of the occupation powers, as a chance to achieve more radical changes that had hitherto been blocked. But, like Victor Klemperer, they had to decide between the rival blueprints of the dominant occupation powers: "Which is the right [horse] . . . ? Russia? The U.S.A.? Democracy? Communism?"[8]

Any attempt to explain the transformation of the Germans after 1945, forced from without and wished for from within, has to begin with the key points of the Potsdam agreement. On the one hand, its famous three "Ds"—demilitarization, denazification, and decartelization—comprised the minimal consensus of the increasingly tension-filled Grand Alliance, and thus should be understood as the quintessence of the international critique of the evils wrought by German policy.[9] On the other hand, this hope for a radical rupture with the glorification of the military, the arrogance of the nation, and the concentration of economic power was also shared by many domestic, mostly leftist, opponents of nationalism who had been living in exile or been active in the resistance. The attempt to bring about a fundamental change thus had to be a cooperative project in which the occupation powers and reform-minded Germans worked together to make possible a return to civilized standards.[10] The following chapters consider what measures toward the reeducation of the Germans the Allies undertook, which learning processes occurred in the population, and how successful the changes they engendered were.

CHAPTER 1

Renouncing War

A s defeat became inescapable in 1945, members of the German army spontaneously began to discard their weapons. Some fanatics still heeded the Nazi
call for a "final battle" and fought desperately, especially in the East. But many
retreating soldiers threw away their burdensome rifles, steel helmets, pistols, and
ammunition in what was almost a compulsory ritual: First, they ripped off their
epaulettes and any other signs of their rank and responsibility; then they took
off their uniforms and slipped into civilian clothes; finally, they conveniently
lost their military IDs, dog tags, and anything else that might betray their identity.[1] Driven by the fear of being captured, especially by the Russians, as well as
the urge to make their way home unrecognized, thousands of combatants performed this process of individual demilitarization. By wiping away all traces of
complicity in war and Holocaust, they hoped to save their own lives. Once-
victorious soldiers who had enjoyed being photographed with their military
decorations now transformed themselves, if they had the chance, into seemingly
harmless, defeated civilians.

Despite the partial self-dissolution of the Wehrmacht, the advancing Allies
insisted on the unconditional surrender of the German military. Complete capitulation required above all the systematic demobilization of some 12 million
men of the regular Wehrmacht (Army), the Waffen-SS (Elite Guard), and the
Volkssturm militia. In practice, this meant their capture, transfer to prisoner of
war (POW) camps, and, in some cases, remobilization for reparation labor, and,
above all, a rigorous search for those war criminals who were responsible for
committing atrocities in occupied Europe. At the same time, utter defeat also
implied Allied occupation of the Third Reich's territory in order to secure weapons, ammunition dumps, food depots, troop barracks, and exercise grounds, as

well as to raze all fortifications. To make any circumvention of the regulations impossible, total conquest also meant Allied control over and conversion of the installations of the war economy.[2]

The prevention of another war of aggression required going beyond simply seizing all weapons; it demanded the complete "elimination of the military and military traditions." Predictably, Proclamation No. 2 of the Allied Control Council called for the final dissolution of "all German forces on land, sea, and in the air, the SS, SA [Storm Troops], SD [Security Service], and Gestapo . . . including the general staff and officer corps." Given the poor experiences with disarmament efforts during the Weimar Republic, these conditions aimed at the irrevocable destruction of the military as an institution so as to banish the potential German danger once and for all. At the same time, this announcement decreed a series of sociocultural restrictions that went still further: "All kinds of military training, military propaganda and military activity are forbidden to the German people," including organizations for the maintenance of traditions, veterans' groups, and similar associations.[3] The goal of these measures was nothing less than the complete eradication of militarism as a way of thinking.

Previous research has paid scant attention to this breathtaking experiment of social pacification since the resulting change in the political culture has generally been considered a self-evident achievement of the Bonn Republic. The key term "militarism" remains ambiguous, and the literature on this topic is divided into two approaches: socioeconomic and cultural.[4] Understandably, American histories of the war concentrate more on the dramatic circumstances of the United States' own victory than on the subsequent, more prosaic problems of occupation.[5] While the German literature on military history has meticulously investigated the international negotiations over demilitarization, even the pioneering work of Gerhard Wettig largely ignores the social and cultural dimensions of this process.[6] Likewise, the newer field of peace studies has thoroughly investigated the wide-ranging opposition to West German rearmament, but only recently have scholars turned to the prior psychological distancing from the military that occurred as Germans sought to work through their horrendous wartime experiences.[7]

An analysis of demilitarization therefore demands recalling the extent and explaining the reasons for this largely forgotten change: How did the largest military machine in European history disappear, and how did the military spirit transform itself into a more civil, peaceable outlook? The administrative demobilization decreed by the Allies is well documented by the available sources and thus easily reconstructed. In contrast, the mental demilitarization of the Germans, which went well beyond it, only emerges from the official record in fragments, turning up instead in literary accounts and in oral history interviews.[8] The long-term consequences for the West German attempt to implement a democratic rearmament should also be considered, especially when its civilian form is contrasted with the more obvious efforts to remilitarize attitudes in the

German Democratic Republic (GDR).[9] The first step on the path back to civility after 1945, therefore, was not just taken when soldiers laid down their weapons and shed their uniforms; it occurred, rather, when Germans bid farewell to the mental uniformity of the past.

Allied Disarmament

On May 8, 1945, at 2:41 A.M., the Second World War ended in Europe. After five years, eight months, and six days of the most brutal warfare the world had ever known, an exhausted yet unbowed General Alfred Jodl penned his signature on the instrument of capitulation in Reims, and Fieldmarshal Wilhelm Keitel signed an almost identical document in Berlin. The meeting of Russian and American troops near Torgau on the Elbe, the cowardly suicide of Hitler, and the fall of the Third Reich's capital in Berlin rendered all further resistance futile, even though the Wehrmacht still stood in Scandinavia, as well as in Bohemia and Austria. The attempt by Admiral Hans Georg von Friedeburg to keep fighting in the East in order to have those soldiers also captured by the Western Allies came to nothing, as General Dwight D. Eisenhower insisted that Germans in all theaters of the war lay down their weapons simultaneously. In view of the harsh conditions for capitulation, the defeated Jodl could only appeal to the victors to treat the German people and its troops with magnanimity.[10]

The demand for demilitarization of their enemies was one of the few Allied objectives on which, for the most part, all sides could agree. The idea of permanently disarming the Germans first came up in the principles of the Atlantic Charter, proclaimed by President Franklin D. Roosevelt and Prime Minister Winston Churchill on August 14, 1941. At the Tehran Conference two years later, Joseph Stalin expanded the notion well beyond the military realm into economics as well. The negotiations of the European Advisory Commission, which aimed above all at preventing Germany from obtaining the capacity for future warfare, formed the basis of both the American Draft Planning Directive No. 17 and Joint Chiefs of Staff (JCS) Directive No. 1067. These preparations culminated in the decision of the Yalta Conference:

> We are determined to disarm and disband all German armed forces; break up for all time the German General Staff that has repeatedly contrived the resurgence of German militarism; remove or destroy all German military equipment; eliminate or control all German industry that could be used for military production; bring all war criminals to just and swift punishment.[11]

Going well beyond the demobilization of the Wehrmacht, this program sought to perpetuate the Allied victory by a far-reaching change in Germany's political and economic structures, as well as through its mental dispositions, in order forever to preclude the repetition of aggression.

A primary motive behind the resolution to demilitarize Germany was the widespread fear of Prussian militarism, thought to be embodied by the general staff of the army. An influential 1937 book by German émigré Alfred Vagts had defined the concept as "a vast array of customs, interests, prestige, actions and thought associated with armies and wars and yet transcending true military purposes" and thereby "carrying military mentality and modes of action and decision into the civilian sphere." Trapped by their own atrocity propaganda of World War I, Western intellectuals saw in the Junkers' "lust for war" the real enemy, lurking behind National Socialism, which needed to be eradicated. At the same time, the shock of the Nazis' initial victories made Allied military leaders credit their enemy with "fighting a brilliant patriotic war," which Germany "lost only because of the interference and inefficiency of the party." Eisenhower's headquarters considered the "tightly bound military priesthood" of the Wehrmacht high command the source of German militarism and "the real power in the Reich," which was primarily responsible for planning the war of aggression. Recalling the manifold evasions of the disarmament conditions of the Versailles Treaty, a New York Times reporter wrote, "General Eisenhower and his intelligence officers are resolved that this will not happen a second time."[12]

A further reason behind the insistence on a lasting disarmament was the impression that the Wehrmacht and the SS were guilty of numerous war crimes and had thus gambled away whatever military honor they may have possessed. On the very day of the capitulation, the New York Times carried a report from the Special Soviet State Commission that estimated the number of dead in the extermination camp at Auschwitz to be around 4 million. Statements from 2,819 survivors furnished a shocking picture of the extent of the systematic murder, medical experiments, and forced labor in nearby industrial installations.[13] Similarly, numerous reports from liberated Allied POWs told of the inadequate food supply and frequent cruelties of the guards that violated the Hague Convention's laws on land warfare. Still reeling from his tour of the concentration camps, the American media mogul Joseph Pulitzer demanded that "the entire German general staff, the German industrialists and financiers, and almost all, if not all, of the members of the Gestapo and the SS [some 1.5 million] should be put to death as war criminals."[14] Due to the overwhelming guilt that the Wehrmacht had brought upon itself, the consensus was that it could not be reformed but, rather, needed to be completely dissolved.

The precondition for demobilization was the cessation of all hostilities and the Wehrmacht's laying down of its weapons in all theaters of war. But the implementation of the capitulation could by no means be taken for granted. General Franz Boehme's troops in the Norwegian garrison still felt "unbeaten and in full possession [of their] strength" and only begrudgingly heeded the announcement of the armistice by foreign minister Count Lutz Schwerin von Krosigk. Much against their will did the tenaciously defended enclaves, stretching from the Atlantic coast all the way into the Baltic and Aegean, surrender and withdraw from their positions. Finally, the order to capitulate had to reach over 100 U-boats on the high seas, which were to proceed to designated assembly points from which they would then be escorted into Allied ports.[15] To be sure, isolated exchanges of fire still occurred after the war had officially ended, and German troops continued to harbor a justified fear of revenge from their former enemies, but overall the laying down of arms took place without any major incident.

The capture of the entire German military force following the surrender presented the Allies with enormous logistical problems. Since some 10 million men were still serving in the Wehrmacht at the beginning of May, the defeated masses of soldiers had to be concentrated in large open spaces before actual camps could be set up. In terms of food, protection against the elements, and sanitary facilities, the conditions in these improvised fenced-in areas were often catastrophic, a fact that stemmed more from their captors' being overwhelmed than from any conscious effort to torment the defeated enemies.[16] The repatriation of slave laborers quickly led to an acute shortage of manpower, and one response to the resulting chaos was the rapid release of ordinary soldiers for use in industrial and agricultural production. Further alternatives included the deployment of healthy prisoners for clean-up operations and their transfer to the French or Russians as compensation for war damage. Of the 5,590,996 prisoners originally taken by the Americans, 2,046,757 had been released and 922,566 discharged by the end of July. Some 818,159 had apparently just disappeared. Only about a third of the men, or 1,803,689, remained in custody.[17]

Disarmament also involved the confiscation of military equipment, the demolition of fortifications, the establishment of control over military installations, and the cessation of further arms production: One observer noted that "a poster warned against possession of weapons, promising a penalty of death if they were found." Some 46 million bullets, 24 million small artillery shells, 2.59 million gas masks, 709,000 hand grenades, 82,000 rifles and pistols, 148,000 landmines, 34,000 rockets, 1,842 ships, and 420 airplanes had to be taken out of service by the Americans alone. With the help of prisoners, fortified sites such as bunkers, launching pads for rockets, anti-aircraft positions, and mine fields that were scattered throughout the country needed to be rendered unusable. Hundreds of barracks, troop exercise grounds, airfields, ports, and supply depots of the army, navy, and air force were to be taken over and, in some cases, used further by the Allies for their own forces. The destruction of the various sites of war production, however, proved to be the most difficult task of all, as the "workshops, research institutes, technical documents etc." were not so easily uncovered.[18]

Demobilization similarly entailed a search for war criminals, something that the victorious powers, owing to their belief in a German "conspiracy against the laws of civilization," firmly insisted on. To begin with, to document the crimes and arrest the members of the conspiracy, the Allies endeavored to secure written records such as personnel data and case files from military units and staffs, as well as from paramilitary organizations including the SA, Nazi Motor Corps (NSKK), National Labor Service (RAD), and Todt Organization. Furthermore, in the hope of bringing the perpetrators all the more quickly to trial, the victors systematically screened all prisoners before their release. In doing so, they detained first and foremost generals and field officers, as well as the 250,000 members of the SS, holding them until the decisions of the Nuremberg court were handed down, since both individuals and entire organizations such as the general staff and the High Command of the Wehrmacht and SS had been indicted. The objective of these trials was not merely to atone for the demonstrable crimes of individuals but to demonstrate the criminality of the entire German military establishment.[19]

A logical consequence of this systematic disarmament was the termination of cooperation with the caretaker government of Admiral Karl Dönitz, whose legitimacy rested on a shaky legal foundation. For a few weeks, the Allies were willing to negotiate with Hitler's designated successors, because they needed their signatures on the instrument of capitulation as well as help with the process of demobilization. But especially in the eyes of the British, the former commander of the U-boat fleet was arguably himself a war criminal. His cabinet, composed largely of nobles, civil servants, and businessmen, represented the old elites who had lost their credibility through their collaboration with Hitler. The abolition of German sovereignty on June 5th was thus justified by the "total defeat and unconditional surrender" of the German armed forces, the absence of an effective government, and the need to maintain public order. Consequently, one of the main reasons for establishing a four-power military government by the Allied Control Council was "to carry out the complete disarmament of Germany."[20]

These initial efforts toward demobilization led to an even more ambitious attempt at demilitarization that aimed at a lasting "transformation of the German mentality." "The physical demilitarization of Germany has been successfully accomplished," General Eisenhower noted in greeting the first publication of the occupation paper Neue Zeitung. "But that alone does not guarantee that Germany will not again force the world into war in the future. Militarism must also be eliminated from the German mind. For all civilized peoples of the world, war is in principle something immoral, but the Germans must still be helped to this self-evident truth."[21] On September 25, 1945, the Allied Control Council decreed the dissolution of "all German land, naval, and air forces, the SS, SA, and the Gestapo, with all of their organizations, staffs, and institutions." Going beyond the destruction of the military as an institution, these policies aimed at draining the social and cultural sources of militarism by expressly forbidding the celebration of martial traditions and the pursuit of military training. Along with many neutral commentators, the Allies hoped that these measures would help foster in the Germans "a genuine habit for peacefulness."[22]

A whole host of measures that intruded deeply into the fabric of social life sought to implement the program of demilitarization. Responding to Soviet pressure, at the end of August the Control Council ordered a "ban on uniforms and emblems" that also made the wearing of "medals, decorations, or insignia of rank" subject to punishment. Yet this prohibition proved difficult to implement, as many people lacked even the most basic civilian clothing. Indeed, the saying "dye or die" (*färben oder sterben*) spread quickly in the vernacular. Eight months later this order had to be reiterated, with exceptions for police officers and firemen carefully spelled out.[23] Somewhat surprisingly, it was not until early January 1946 that the Allies forbade the possession of weapons, ammunition, and explosives.[24] This ban was extended in April to the planning, construction, and maintenance of military sites. While the fear of werewolf attacks on the occupation forces motivated the strict restrictions on the possession of arms, the ban on uniforms was supposed to break the defeated population's emotional bond to the military.

Aiming at a similar goal were the successive bans on the maintenance of military traditions, designed above all to prevent the continued glorification of war. On August 20, all "military schools, clubs, or associations of a military sort" were therefore prohibited. Fearing that they might become potential refuges of revanchism, the Allies also dissolved all veterans' associations, even canceling military pensions and other benefits. In mid-December, moreover, the Control Council ordered a "demilitarization of sport," forbidding "all athletic associations of a military character," including, for example, clubs that engaged in flying, parachuting, fencing, or target shooting! Even the American-sponsored newspaper *Neue Zeitung* could not avoid a biting commentary on the absurd classification of gymnastics as a "military sport."[25] Undeterred, the Allies continued to expand their policy and in May 1946 banned "memorials, monuments, posters, placards, statutes . . . which aimed to preserve German military traditions" or otherwise sought to promote militarism.[26] These measures would hopefully banish the glorification of past military achievements from public spaces once and for all.

Also not spared in this cultural demilitarization were schools and libraries, where intellectuals and occupation officers suspected they would find the true roots of militarism. In the British zone, for example, teachers who wished to continue their work had to promise neither "to glorify the military" nor "assist in the preparation for war." In mid-May, the Control Council ordered German publishers, research institutions, and libraries to identify and hand over all books that advocated violence. Specifically affected by this order was "all material that contributed to military training and education or to the maintenance and development of a potential for war." In the Soviet zone, the Deutsche Bücherei in Leipzig went so far as to compile a list of 15,000 books and 150 journals of fascist and Prussian-militaristic literature that were to be withdrawn from circulation. This entire effort somewhat resembled, if under different circumstances, Nazi attempts to purge undesirable writings a decade earlier. Going one step further, Professor Richard Hartman of Marburg University demanded that the German language itself be cleansed: "The demilitarization of concepts is one of the most important tasks in our social reconstruction."[27]

To bring about a lasting pacification of the Germans, in May 1946 the U.S. government proposed a "disarmament treaty for Germany" that would prevent any rearmament for another twenty-five years. Although the British and French governments approved of this proposal, the Soviet Union, which did not want to permit four-power control over East German industry, quickly rejected it. The international community, moreover, was concerned by reports that "considerable amounts of weapons material were once again being produced in the German occupation zones."[28] Nevertheless, after tough negotiations, an agreement on "four-power control over disarmament" was finally reached in October 1946. Among other provisions, it created a joint commission that was charged with guaranteeing the "constant supervision over the liquidation of war and industrial potential according to the Potsdam Agreement." This Military Security Board was to take an inventory of possible war industries so as to destroy purely military plants, monitor factories that could be used to produce war materials, and lift controls on harmless industrial concerns geared toward peaceful production.[29]

Even if some bans proved easier to decree than to implement in practice, the cumulative effects of the Allies' demilitarization measures were considerable. In a detailed report from June 1946 on "demilitarization in the British zone," Lieutenant General Brian Robertson therefore judged that "the progress achieved so far could be viewed as satisfactory." First, "the German Wehrmacht and all of the paramilitary organizations that belonged to it have been entirely dissolved," so that with the exception of the police "no armed, organized body whatsoever" continued to exist. Second, "the removal of all German weapons, military equipment, camps, and depots" had largely been completed, with more than 95 percent of warships, aircraft, and so forth having been destroyed. Third, "the clearing of minefields and the demolition of fortifications and military facilities" was more than three-quarters finished. Nonetheless, Robertson concluded that the "elimination of the German potential for war" could only be accomplished "over a longer period of time," and any attempt to assess the success of the still more important "transformation of the German mentality" would only be possible in the distant future.[30]

Working through Trauma

Years of propaganda proclaiming victory made it initially difficult for many German soldiers to admit their total defeat. In the summer of 1945, Allied reporters repeatedly came across young privates who continued to believe that Hitler was a great man and who insisted that "we have not really lost the war." When presented with the terrible images from the concentration camps, they remained incredulous: "That isn't true. I won't believe it until I've seen the bodies. Photographs can be falsified." Some civilians, especially in those areas that were spared the bombing and ground fighting, claimed still further that "we haven't been beaten in the field," while others "understood their defeat as an accident of chance." Skeptical American observers interpreted the maintenance of military discipline after the surrender as "the arrogance of officers" and construed the rare welcomes for homecoming troops as proof of an unbroken spirit of militarism. Harsh treatment by the victors, therefore, was supposed to make clear to the beaten Germans the full "meaning of their 'conquest.'"[31]

For many former members of the Wehrmacht, it was, nonetheless, the process of defeat that stripped the war of its romantic aura. When battle-hardened soldiers on the Eastern Front recognized that the "situation is hopeless," they concluded: "Now all that's left is the road west, toward the Elbe and the English and Americans," so as not to land in Russian captivity. With the reflexive call of "every man for himself," military discipline quickly dissolved, and units began fleeing in small groups. The brutal attempts by the SS to reinforce discipline through court-martial death sentences proved unable to avert the resulting chaos. The decisive test for survival came during the moment of capitulation by showing "a 'white' flag made from a shirt fixed to the bayonet of a carbine," because it was the reaction of the adversary that decided life or death.[32] The transformation from desperately fighting soldiers to defeated prisoners often claimed still more victims when the victors chose not accept the surrender of their captives. Repeated hundreds of times, such accounts of the military collapse make clear the helpless feeling of being at the mercy of others that shaped the collective memory of the war's end.

For the individual private, the humiliating experience of being captured also revealed the futility of war. The improvised prison camps brought new threats to survival because the unprepared victors could offer neither food nor protection from the elements: "The sanitary conditions were horrendous, and the provisioning nearly broke down after a week." At first, even the Americans treated their captives severely, as feelings of revenge provoked by German atrocities were mixed with hatred inflamed by war propaganda. Especially the Russians and French enlisted prisoners to repair their war damage, so that the German captives would also experience what they had formerly demanded from their own slave laborers. With the help of camp newspapers and various cultural functions, however, those who were detained for longer periods could reflect on the "idol of militarism" or "the new image of man," which meant "freedom and individuality" as well as "human dignity and worth." Others realized that they could obtain their quick release by offering their labor to the Allies, who were desperate to revive agricultural production. But whatever their individual experiences may have been, all German soldiers shared the shock of an undignified captivity.[33]

Nevertheless, most military men were just happy to be alive. "The wonderful feeling of having survived outweighed by far the grief about the awful total defeat which we, of course, also felt," one former officer recalled. "Only a few know whether their families made it through the collapse and many, especially those from the east, now have . . . to fear for their lives," wrote another in his diary in early June. "A powerful revulsion toward the profession has been building up in many, and certainly not the worst of men." Because of the Nazi crimes and the futility of the defense strategy, the military had lost its appeal—an entire generation now just wanted to get home as quickly as possible and return to civilian life. Even though some ex-soldier students, largely for want of clothing, still went around in "dyed uniform pieces," they consciously sought to distance themselves from the "barracks' tone" of the Wehrmacht. "From today's standpoint it might seem absurd, but we went out of our way to treat each other just like civilians." After six years of war, both "civilian" values and "civility" in dealings with others, in contrast to the coarseness of the army, were once again in demand.[34]

For millions returning home from the war, the clearest sign of the defeat was the fraternization of German women with the Allied occupiers, because it demonstrated their lost power. The first opinion poll taken in August 1945 indicated that many recently released soldiers were deeply angry about the relationships that had formed between young women and American GIs. Although they also greeted the repeal of the impractical ban on fraternization, veterans were shocked by the extent of the German women's spontaneous flirtation with the occupiers, complaining: "For six years we risked our lives for them, and now they're running around with the Americans." While older vets admitted that they had once carried on similarly with French and Dutch women, the reversal of roles stung. As one American noticed, the supermen of 1941 had become "the subhumans of 1945, who reluctantly remove the rubble from the destroyed cities or stoically work the land for which they had fought. For this once so proud army, the defeat has an oppressive finality." By experiencing their own impotence, he concluded, "all with the exception of a very few, have accepted the bitter reality of the German defeat."[35]

The collective process of working through wartime experiences centered on the stories that soldiers told among themselves and occasionally also to their wives and children. Through repetition and exchange, they took on a definite shape and became part of the country's social memory, even if politicians, journalists, and historians preferred to ignore them. Oral history interviews, especially among workers, have shown a surprising uniformity of recollections in which the Second World War was almost always apostrophized as a "bad time." To be sure, time and again veterans did mention the war's more positive aspects, such as having "great parties," getting to know distant countries, and experiencing adventures. But, on the whole, there prevailed an astonishingly negative assessment. Talking about cruelty and the constant fear of death, hunger, and humiliating retreat might have been difficult, but these miserable experiences produced a near-unanimous reaction: "War is worse than anything else, the worst that there is." In complete contrast to the heroization of the First World War, the majority of the "burned children" of the second carnage concluded, "that which we have lived through should never be allowed to happen again."[36]

The civilian counterpart to military tales were the accounts, usually passed on by women, of the bombing terror in the cities and the flight and expulsion from the eastern territories. Tales of fear-filled nights in bomb shelters, the roar of bombs, the booming of anti-aircraft guns, the desperate attempts to extinguish fires, and the destruction of all of one's belongings were almost universal. "The memory that war is a terrible thing would remain for the rest of my life" was a common refrain. Reports of the horrors that accompanied the expulsion from Germany's eastern territories, which were, so the victors promised, to be carried out "in an orderly and humane manner," underscored the particularly dismal fate of the refugees. "In June 1945 the Germans in villages and towns were herded together by armed Polish hordes, dragged from their homes, often beaten, and for several days driven west, with no provisions for either food or shelter," reported one of the more reserved descriptions.[37] To be sure, these stories have been used to justify the political efforts of expelled Germans and their children for material compensation and their so-called "right to a homeland." Nevertheless, they underscore the ubiquity of civilian suffering that helped shape a negative memory of the war's consequences.

Literary treatment of the war, which provides a kind of memory archive, emphasizes just as strongly the "suffering of the nation." For all of their differences in stylistic quality, popular representations of the Second World War—for example Hans Hellmut Kirst's 08/15, Theodor Plievier's Stalingrad, and Fritz Wöss's Hunde, wollt ihr ewig leben?—share the same basic tendencies as the more sophisticated texts by Wolfgang Borchert, Heinrich Böll, Siegfried Lenz, Alexander Kluge, and Christa Wolf.[38] Since they focus on the theme of sheer survival amid incomprehensible chaos, these graphic portrayals of the horrors go a long way toward demythologizing the experiences of war. Similarly, portrayals of a complete collapse of order and moral beliefs militate against rash conclusions. In his two volumes on Die große Flucht, Jürgen Thorwald stresses the universal futility of suffering by depicting the Germans more as victims than as perpetrators.[39] Although the privileging of the German experience of terror encourages to some degree a self-stylization of victimhood, it also contributes to a critical memory of the war.

Even as illusory a genre as film could not completely shirk its obligation to represent the destructive effects of the war. Attempts at a vivid representation of death and mutilation during the first postwar years, such as director Bernhard Wicki's *Die Brücke*, were soon replaced by sentimental movies like *Der Arzt von Stalingrad*, which was based on the successful potboiler by Heinz Konsalik. Though the heroization of exceptionally "decent" individuals tried to comfort the audience by providing positive identification figures, it could neither blur the terror of war nor entirely deny the crimes attributed to the Nazi Party and the SS. Even the popular attempt of sentimental movies to reconstruct a healthy, apolitical sense of home in the *Heimatfilm* relied heavily on the contrast of an undamaged world with intimations of tragic wartime fates, which could only be cured through contact with unspoiled nature. Ultimately, the success of Hollywood films forced a reversal of emotional identifications, as American war movies generally portrayed GIs as heroes and Germans as villains, thereby confusing the audiences' sympathies.[40]

In spite of the greater death toll in World War II, commemorations for the dead had a considerably more civil, nonmilitaristic character than after World War I. In reaction to the revanchist death cult of fallen heroes in the Weimar Republic, Allied prohibitions did initially prevent military memorial services. While the war memorials from 1914 to 1918 were expanded by the addition of a few more plaques, new ones were rarely erected, with the exception of numerous monuments for the Red Army in East Germany. The shattering defeat made the sacrifice of life appear all the more futile in retrospect, thus rendering pointless any attempt to use commemorations for inciting revenge. The metamorphosis of the national day of mourning from Nazi "hero commemoration day" to a "day of remembrance for reconciliation, understanding, and peace" indicates that consolation became more important than vengeance. Since war graves were scattered throughout Europe in countries that had a justified reason for hostility, the construction of German heroes' cemeteries was in many cases also physically impossible.[41]

Despite the devastating defeat, positive memories of the war and deeply ingrained militarism did not, of course, disappear altogether. In some private accounts, memories of the initial victories and the courage shown in the final defense against the superior might of the enemy could rekindle lost pride. In semipublic gatherings of former comrades from the front, the discipline of the Prussian military tradition and the toughness of German soldiery might also be celebrated.[42] In their memoirs, generals blamed Hitler's strategic mistakes, the incompetence of the party, and the crimes of the SS for the defeat. And for some, the collective acquittal of the high command at the Nuremberg trials appeared to restore the honor of the Wehrmacht somewhat, even if individual officers were convicted of war crimes.[43] Militaristic thinking did live on in radical right-wing circles, whose members held out hope that the defeat might be reversed sometime in the future.[44] But these attempts to maintain a discredited tradition remained confined to a part of the veterans' milieu and found little resonance among the young. One former soldier noted: "This time the defeat was total; there wasn't the slightest ground for another legend of a stab in the back."[45]

Producing what was effectively a decade-long moratorium on military institutions, the rigorous disarmament and demilitarization policy did enable most Germans to recommence their civilian lives. With the exception of the prisoners still in the Allied camps, only a few 10,000 men in service groups, employed by the victors to search for mines and do other menial tasks, still wore uniforms, without, of course, carrying weapons.[46] Even when some measures—for example, tearing down "dangerous monuments" such as the statue of Emperor William I at the Berlin Palace and removing martial street names like Belle-Alliance-Straße—overshot their mark, the interruption of the military tradition offered a chance to reverse the centuries' old process of social militarization.[47] For haughty officers, the precipitous fall from a privileged position to civilian insignificance was undoubtedly bitter, especially when they had difficulty finding their economic footing. For the political culture, however, the discrediting of the military provided a unique chance to acquire new, more peaceful values and forms of behavior.[48]

The only exception to this policy was the deployment of German police units, which was necessary due to the safety problems resulting from the vacuum of authority. The Allied military police had enough difficulty with trying to maintain discipline among their own soldiers and were thus hardly in a position to deal with the various gangs and black marketeers that were emerging in unsupervised areas. Because the police in the Third Reich had functioned as "an instrument of oppression," it needed to be purged of Nazi thugs and its professionalism restored. The British therefore established courses to train both experienced policemen and fresh recruits. The new blue uniforms were designed to signal a different mindset and "to help the Germans along the road to democracy." Since it put personnel in danger, the policy of strict disarmament could not be maintained, however, and gradually pistols were once again issued to German policemen. In the Soviet occupation zone, the police was shaken up even more radically so as to stabilize the power of the communist Socialist Unity Party of Germany (SED).[49]

Drawn out over several years, the homecoming of the prisoners served as a personified reminder of the otherwise forgotten suffering of the war years. After the first great wave of releases in 1945, the English still held over 300,000 officers and soldiers, the French 700,000, and the Russians perhaps as many as 2 million.

Some were involved in compensatory labor, while others were quarantined for political reasons. The soldiers did not just toil in the camps, however, as some found an opportunity for reeducation in a democratic spirit. With support from the U.S. government and growing pressure from the German public, the pace of releases accelerated in the fall of 1946, largely for political, health, and manpower reasons. At the same time, the contrast between the prisoners who returned home from Western camps and those who survived Soviet captivity was striking, as the latter conveyed "a shocking impression of suffering."[50] "The return of released POWs turned tragic in many cases" because "they were often strangers in a strange world." The reintegration of these broken men proved to be one of the most difficult challenges for postwar German society.[51]

The partly restrictive, partly supportive dealings of the West German authorities with veterans after 1945 successfully prevented the formation of major revanchist pressure groups. The public consternation over the devastating defeat deprived them of social respect, and the cancellation of their pensions forced them to transform themselves into civilians so that they could somehow make a living. The initial ban on organizations also impeded the political representation of their interests. Even after these restrictions were gradually relaxed, veterans were allowed only a limited form of lobbying in matters of material interest, while military propaganda remained strictly off limits. Instead, they stressed their material plight, making the improvement of care (especially for the hundreds of thousands of disabled, as well as the ubiquitous surviving widows) their highest priority. As tax revenues increased, the states tried to offer a minimum level of support, while the federal government, in a series of laws, increased payments to diverse groups that were particularly in need. In addition, many veterans had been sufficiently impressed by the "utter senselessness" of Hitler's war of conquest and annihilation so as to adopt a "very skeptical attitude toward anything having to do with the military."[52]

The West German Basic Law codified the pacifist learning process that began during the first postwar years with a preamble dedicated to world peace. Nonetheless, the constitutional discussions at Herrenchiemsee and in the parliamentary council proved contentious as the renunciation of independent armed forces shifted the defense of the new state to the victorious powers or to an international security system whose reliability remained unpredictable.[53] The Social Democratic Party's (SPD) demand for a complete outlawing of war collided in principle with the Christian Democratic Party's (CDU) advocacy of the possibility of a national defense. The result was an ambiguous compromise, which in article 26, paragraph 1, declared unconstitutional all "acts tending to and undertaken with intent to disturb the peaceful relations between nations, especially to prepare for a war of aggression." Barring special permission from the federal government, the production of weapons of war was likewise forbidden, while a right to conscientious objection to serving in the military was written into the constitution. The first constitution of the GDR also proclaimed the principle of peacefulness, although secret remilitarization by means of the people's police was already under way.[54]

It was the vociferous resistance to a potential rearmament, however, that truly demonstrated the success of demilitarization. When the publicist Eugen Kogon claimed in the fall of 1948 that the English and Americans, in response to the arming of the people's police, "had begun the military training of [West] Germans," the public reaction was quite negative. Ernst Reuter of the SPD had previously demanded "the dismantling of the war ethos," and the first postwar synod of the Protestant Church had pleaded "we do not need war."[55] Yet the conclusion of the North Atlantic Treaty in early 1949 raised the question of West German territory, which NATO would only protect as long as "it remains occupied by Allied troops." In the confused debate about a potential German contribution to Western defense, Chancellor Konrad Adenauer tried to make clear "that Germany [had] lost too much and needed too much of its strength for reconstruction to consider rearming." He did, however, leave the door open by slyly intimating that rearmament would only be possible with full equality and within a "European armed force." Because of negative public opinion, both the cabinet and the Federal Diet came out unequivocally "against armament."[56]

The most important argument for arming West Germany was the fear of East German "rearmament" through the "founding of a Red Army in the Soviet zone." In the fall of 1948, one deserter, military physician Dr. Schreiber, claimed that the People's Police "have been reinforced by German POWs from the Soviet Union . . . equipped with heavy weapons, and quartered in barracks." The deployment of a uniformed "military guard" for the factories likewise worried the Western public. Rumors also circulated of GDR legionnaires serving as "cannon fodder" in the Greek civil war between communists and royalists. In the same vein, the Western press reported the views of General Staimer, since 1946 the commander of the East German People's Police, who envisaged a future civil war: "Our police should be designated to bring about a unified Germany once again." This partially staged agitation had, however, a real core. The SED wanted first to secure its domestic control through a comparative strengthening of the police force and then to prepare itself for political struggles concerning Germany's future after the withdrawal of the Allied forces.[57]

In contrast, Adenauer's strategy for achieving West German rearmament was largely determined by concerns about expected domestic and foreign opposition. After memoranda from former general staff officers such as Adolf Heusinger and Hans Speidel had convinced him that the security of the newly founded state required a capacity for self-defense, the new chancellor maneuvered with extreme caution. Anticipating objections, the initial planning in the office of Theodor Blank, who in 1949 was charged with exploring such possibilities and later became secretary of defense, was largely kept secret, as were the

discussions with the Western powers. Both sides agreed that any German contribution to defense had to be internationalized, be it as part of a European
Defense Community, which failed in the French national assembly, or as member of NATO, the subsequent solution. A final aim of Adenauer's strategy was
to make the offer of West German forces contingent upon their being given full
equality within the Western military structure so as to counter the expected
charge that he had only provided mercenaries.[58] Because the fear of a revival of
the German military was so widespread abroad, it took the Korean War to convince skeptics of its necessity.

The massive "count me out" response to rearmament demonstrates the
extent to which antimilitarism had in the meantime spread among the populace. Surveys suggest that in December 1947, 94 percent of those living in the
American zone agreed with the conclusion that "war does not pay off," while by
early 1948 three-fifths feared another world war. As rumors of preparations intensified, 62 percent of those questioned in the U.S. zone were against rearmament, and at the start of the 1950s over 72 percent, citing their horrific wartime
experiences, wanted nothing to do with it at all. Propagated by the former minister of the interior Gustav Heinemann, and spurred on by the SED, the popular movement against rearmament managed to gather between 4 million and
5 million signatures with the help of churches, unions, and intellectuals. Only
North Korea's attack on the South, which fueled fears of a repetition in a similarly divided Germany, was able to overcome such widespread pacifism, particularly among workers and women, so that by September 1950 some 63 percent of
the population was willing to accept West German forces as part of a European
system of defense.[59]

Yet another consequence of the internal and external skepticism was the comparatively civil form of West German rearmament. To be sure, Adenauer supported
the partial rehabilitation of the German officer corps, already set in motion by the
military tribunal at Nuremberg and ultimately formalized by a letter from General Eisenhower.[60] But in order to be confident of the political reliability and professional competence of former Wehrmacht officers, he also insisted that they be
thoroughly vetted by an independent personnel panel. The recognition of the right
to conscientious objection to military service, which was expanded by subsequent
judicial decisions, also contributed considerably to the social acceptance of rearmament. Still, the new army had a serious problem with tradition, because the
continuity to the Wehrmacht established by the officer corps, no matter how
strictly screened its members were, reinforced their denial of complicity in Nazi
genocide. Only after considerable debate did the Bundeswehr accept the freedom
of conscience displayed by the resisters of July 20, 1944, as an alternative reference
point for the construction of a new tradition. Although fear of a third world war
could not prevent rearmament, the widespread turn away from militarism ultimately gave it a less threatening shape.[61]

Longing for Peace

The newly acquired conviction that no war should ever again emanate from German soil was reinforced by the successive crises of the Cold War. Not only did hundreds of thousands of heavily armed soldiers from the two hostile blocs face off along the iron curtain, but their regional conventional conflict was compounded by the nuclear confrontation of the superpowers, which was justifiably called MAD (mutually assured destruction). As strategic war games and tactical maneuvers transformed the former warmonger Germany into the potential battlefield of a third world war, the renewed destruction of the country, regardless of whether the defense would begin at the Rhine or on the GDR border, appeared inescapable. A cynical *bon mot* formulated the predicament appropriately: "The shorter the range of the missiles, the deader the Germans." In both the West and the East, people found themselves caught in a fundamental contradiction, as they demanded a systematic peace policy while at the same time becoming part of a gigantic arms race.[62]

A consequence of the successor states' integration into the opposing camps was the continuation of the occupation, although in the more benign form of the "stationing" of Allied forces. A considerable part of each state's territory remained under the control of the respective alliance partners: Their military installations, exercise grounds, supply depots, and the like formed extraterritorial islands, while their residential areas, stores, schools, and sport facilities created a kind of parallel society whose only contact with the civilian population was through the German employees who worked there. While most people ignored the street signs in English and Russian, the endless columns of military vehicles which in the summer fanned out to maneuvers, often damaging fields in the process, could hardly be overlooked. The feeling of heightened security that these foreign troops conveyed was also accompanied by a sense of inferiority, since in cases of conflict the locals usually came up short.[63] The presence of Allied soldiers decades after the war restricted German sovereignty and led to a peculiar kind of irresponsibility, as ultimately neither state had final control over the decisions affecting its security.

In a climate marked by the trauma of a world war and fear of nuclear annihilation, it is hardly surprising that the deployment of twelve West German divisions in the mid-1950s proved exceedingly difficult. Only after sharp debates between the CDU and SPD could those compromises be found that shaped the profile of the Federal Republic's newly created armed forces, called the Bundeswehr. By establishing the office of the commissioner of the armed forces, the Federal Diet symbolically asserted civilian control over the military. At the same time, the conception of "internal leadership," propagated by Undersecretary of Defense Count Wolfgang Baudissin, sought to create "civilians in uniform," in order to break with the blind obedience of the past. Moreover, compulsory military service was limited to twelve months, and conscientious objectors could undertake other forms of civilian duty in hospitals and old-age homes. The new uniforms and helmets, which were based on Western models, as well as the more casual tone between officers and enlisted men, signaled a clear departure from Prussian traditions. Already in 1949 a caricature featuring a strange two-headed animal highlighted the contradictory nature of this armed force with the caption: "Bunny rabbits toward the west, watchdogs toward the east."[64]

In contrast, the creation of a national "people's army" triggered a more open push for remilitarization in the GDR. In 1956 the Nationale Volksarmee (NVA) was founded from the ranks of the People's Police as a professional army of volunteers loyal to the Communist Party. But due to the resistance of some segments of the population, it was only after the construction of the Berlin wall that compulsory military service was introduced. Because the GDR, according to the constitution of 1974, was "forever and irrevocably allied with the USSR," the Red Army exercised direct control over its client. Likewise, the leading role of the SED in the NVA was guaranteed by the chairmanship of its general secretary in the National Defense Council and the institution of political officers. Ignoring its own peace campaigns, which were primarily aimed at the West, the Communist Party thoroughly remilitarized its own society by recruiting in schools and among youth groups for the next generation of officers. The traditional field grey of the uniforms, the goose-stepping at parades, and the snappy appearance of the NVA constituted the external expression of a curious revival of Prussian military traditions under the proletarian banner.[65]

Toward the end of the 1950s, the conflict between the longing for peace and security precautions in West Germany came to a head with the question of tactical atomic weapons. While the Federal Republic had explicitly renounced atomic, biological, and chemical weapons in the Paris Treaties, both Adenauer and his energetic Defense Minister Franz Josef Strauß wanted to gain some influence over this *ultima ratio*. Following an Allied air exercise that simulated the millions of German casualties resulting from a nuclear exchange, eighteen physicists, led by the Nobel Prize winner Max Planck, protested against this policy in the sensational Göttingen Manifesto. Leading SPD politicians such as Gustav Heinemann, numerous union members, critical Protestant theologians such as Helmut Gollwitzer, and intellectuals including Heinrich Böll thereupon launched a "campaign against nuclear death," which in 1958 mobilized more than 150,000 people to protest in Hamburg alone. But after Nikita Khruschev's Berlin ultimatum signaled yet another new threat, the movement imploded and the Federal Diet approved the introduction of nuclear delivery systems, as long as control of the warheads remained with the Allies.[66]

The first test case for the potential deployment of the Bundeswehr in the generally unpopular Vietnam War established the FRG's doctrine of military restraint. When in December 1965 American President Lyndon Johnson requested a medical unit and an engineer battalion and Secretary of Defense Robert MacNamara even spoke of combat troops, Chancellor Ludwig Erhard turned them down. The FRG only extended easy credit to the South Vietnamese regime and sent the hospital ship *Helgoland* to the Vietnamese coast. The foreign office argued that for the FRG "freedom for movement in military affairs was limited due to the consequences of the Second World War and the problems created by the division of Germany." Both older Germans, citing the trauma of the world war, and younger ones, strongly criticizing American imperialism, categorically rejected any such engagement. Thus, the interpretation that the Basic Law only permitted the deployment of soldiers in the case of an attack on the Federal Republic itself prevailed.[67] In contrast, the SED leadership, in complete contradiction to their official slogans for peace, had no scruples about sending numerous NVA instructors to aid national liberation movements in Africa.

The West German Social-Liberal cabinet instead concentrated on further reducing international tensions by means of a new "Eastern Policy" (*Ostpolitik*) after 1969. Behind its attempt to achieve "a normalized relationship between the FRG and its eastern neighbors" stood the hope that the consequences of the world war and the strains of the Cold War might yet be overcome. The conclusion of the various "eastern treaties" with the Soviet Union and their client states spun a "web of renunciations of violence," that, by demonstrating the FRG's inherent peacefulness, sought to refute the accusation of revanchism and lessen the lingering fear that many still held of the Germans. Likewise, Bonn's de facto recognition of the GDR was an attempt to diffuse, by way of a contractual agreement, the internal German conflict and, by extension, initiate "change through cooperation." In the end, the Berlin Agreement offered some guarantees against the return of East-West confrontations. The FRG also played a central role in the internationalization and codification of the proceedings of the Conference for Security and Cooperation in Europe (CSCE) as its recognition of the status quo on the continent also required its acceptance of the postwar borders established at Potsdam, as well as the division of Germany.[68] In the long-term, this kind of active peace policy proved to be particularly successful.

The dilemma of maintaining the capability for defense and of pursuing the reduction of tensions reasserted itself even more intensely toward the end of the 1970s. Helmut Schmidt's attempt to prevent the strategic "uncoupling" of Western Europe and the United States while safeguarding the progress made in East-West relations encountered resistance from a public that clearly underestimated the threat posed by the medium-ranged SS-20 missiles recently deployed by the Soviet Union. The chancellor's announcement that Pershing missiles of a comparable range would be stationed on West German soil overshadowed the accompanying declaration of his willingness to continue negotiations, and thus gave birth to a new peace movement. In Easter marches, candlelight vigils, petitions, and prayers for peace, hundreds of thousands came out to protest NATO's dual track decision in a nuclear annihilation panic that the end of the world was near. "We old folks want to act differently now," wrote one former war photographer, "because during the Nazi period we either took part or looked the other way and kept silent."[69] Somewhat ironically, the SPD's refusal to follow its own chancellor led to the 1982 decision by the Free Democratic Party (FDP) to join a conservative government, which then proceeded to implement the deployment anyway.[70]

The emergence of the peace movement was an expression of a social polarization between ecological-pacifist idealists on the one hand and middle-class political realists on the other. The conscientious objectors were part of the new social movements of young, urban professionals, while "service in the army" remained more popular in small-town, traditional milieus. Pacifism was also widespread in the unions, the Protestant Church, and intellectual circles, and advocacy of peace was organized in broad sections of the SPD and the Green Party (the Greens). Support for the armed forces, in contrast, was more likely to be found among industrialists, Catholics, the CDU, and the FDP. With peace slogans and secret financing, the SED tried to bolster criticism of the Bundeswehr, atomic weapons, and medium-range missiles in the West.[71] While the middle-class, conservative camp managed to win the decisive 1983 election, the widespread longing for peace compelled the new Kohl government and its foreign minister Hans-Dietrich Genscher to exercise self-restraint in foreign affairs, a policy that was frowned upon as "Genscherism" in the United States.

Another result of the relaxation of tensions between the two Germanies in the early 1980s was the growing sense of a German "community of responsibility" for the preservation of peace in central Europe. Among the diverse motives, the ideologically distinct, but still common consciousness of guilt for the crimes of Nazism continued to play a considerable role. Still, the FRG was also concerned about its current interest in maintaining intra-German trade, as well as the solvency of the East German economy, by then rapidly slipping into stagnation. Similarly important for its Eastern policy were the "human relief" measures that penetrated the Berlin wall, such as the buying of prisoners' freedom, the easing of mutual visits, and the creation of new city partnerships. Safeguarding this increasingly close network of ties inspired Helmut Schmidt and Helmut Kohl in the West, and to some degree even Erich Honecker in the East, to counteract the superpower confrontation in the renewed Cold War. The spectacular state visits by both sides were a symbolic expression of this new peacefulness between the two Germanies.[72]

In the shadow of détente, a peace movement ironically also developed in the GDR, which seized upon the contradiction between the SED's pacifistic rhetoric and its militaristic practices. A handful of courageous Protestant pastors supported conscientious objectors to military service and preached the "beating of swords into ploughshares," a message that resonated strongly among youth dissatisfied with official militarism. The party found it difficult to respond, because internal critics could cite its own peace propaganda and appeal to international public opinion. Secret police persecution led these dissidents to rediscover the importance of traditional human rights within real existing socialism and to found a group that called itself the "Initiative for Peace and Human Rights."[73] In church services for peace, picket lines, and silent marches, a minority of pacifists endeavored to demonstrate to their reluctant fellow citizens the necessity for peace at all costs. The prominence of dissidents such as Bärbel Bohley, Rainer Eppelmann, and Markus Meckel suggests just how much this movement became a part of the mobilization in the fall of 1989.

This renunciation of war therefore had paradoxical consequences for politics in both German states. Due to the memory of wartime suffering, an elementary longing for peace emerged that transcended the ideological blocks and found expression in the often-repeated slogan "No more war." Nevertheless, the Cold War forced the rearmament of both states within their respective alliances, as neither was able to escape the pressures of their partners. Despite some ugly scandals, however, the West German Bundeswehr turned out considerably more civil than the remilitarized East German NVA. In foreign affairs, moreover, integration into the West and subsequent *Ostpolitik* helped tame West Germany's power by restraining its military and fostering multilateralism. Although something similar occurred in East Germany, it was due more to the state's own weaknesses than to a cultural change of heart. At the same time, the recurrence of peace movements, which were not just staged by the Eastern secret police (Stasi), also demonstrated a learning process of pacification that in some respects overshot its mark, since its irritating claim to moral superiority rested on the protection of other powers.[74]

Forgotten Changes

Over half a century after the end of the Second World War, the process of social demilitarization has largely been forgotten; in restrospect, its success appears self-evident. To understand the extent of this change, one must remember that in 1945 more than half of all German men of fighting age found themselves in some kind of uniform, be it army, air force, or navy; SS or SA; and air-raid wardens or labor service. In addition, there was deep-seated respect for the military, enormous pride in its prior victories, and a widespread belief in war's necessity. In contrast, five decades later more than half of all conscripts refused to perform military service, and Germans instinctively thought like civilians. Not surprisingly, skepticism of military deployments abroad, even when under the multilateral banner of the United Nations or NATO, remains pervasive, as evidenced by surveys taken after the attacks on the World Trade Center.[75] The etymological affinity between "civil," "civilian," and "civilization" suggests that this social distancing from the military and war was a first important step toward the recivilizing of the Germans that has yet to be appreciated sufficiently.

The Allied consensus on the need for demilitarization had a decisive influence on this transformation, aiming as it did at a permanent liberation from "Nazism and Prussian militarism." The wartime debate about the underlying causes of German aggression suggested that achieving this objective required more than just the demobilization of the Wehrmacht and the dismantlement of its machines of war—it demanded nothing less than a "spiritual and intellectual demilitarization." President Roosevelt told the U. S. Congress in September 1943: "When Hitler and the Nazis go out, the Prussian military clique must go with them. The war-breeding gangs of militarists must be rooted out of Germany—and out of Japan—if we are to have any real assurance of future peace." In order to change the militaristic state of mind, a member of the American occupation staff argued in October 1945 that prohibiting military "literature, symbolism, the continuation of traditions and every kind of military schooling and training are all part of the problem of rooting out militarism in Germany."[76] Even if the sweeping bans of everything military sometimes bordered on the ridiculous, their general implementation did succeed in banishing the cult of militarism from public space.

Equally important, however, was how Germans themselves dealt with the trauma of war, because only their break with the glorification of military heroism could keep revanchism from flaring up again. The decisive defeat in battle and its awful consequences at home prevented the Second World War from being glorified in retrospect: "We soldiers from the front have had more than enough. We know what it means to say goodbye and not know if you'll ever come back. . . . I went along with all that when I was 18 years old. I wouldn't like to do it all over again." Cryptic hints about Nazi crimes turn up in numerous stories: "My decisive experiences were, as I said, the terrible conditions of the war. And I can quite understand why Germans . . . are really not very popular in the world. That doesn't come from nowhere." Public admission of the futility of "the totally pointless war" led to a privatization of memory in which the war years were apostrophized as a "lost period of life."[77] Even if the psychological processes of dealing with the aftermath of mass murder and mass death somewhat resist reconstruction, it is likely that the distancing from and subsequent aversion to war were also the result of innumerable ruminations about horrific individual experiences.

The political effect of having been so traumatized was a deeply split public opinion which, while tolerating a limited rearmament, wanted to impose strict limits on the use of military force. While surveys show a principled skepticism against the recourse to arms as a way to solve international conflicts, they also demonstrate a limited willingness for self-defense with conventional weapons in the case of Communist aggression. In the 1970s and 1980s four-fifths of the West German population rejected any deployment of weapons of mass destruction and did not want to see them introduced into the armed forces arsenal, even as a deterrent. Nevertheless, some three-fifths demanded that the Federal Republic be defended against an attack from the East, although merely a slight majority would tolerate a war on German soil. Only a third of those questioned considered duty in the Bundeswehr as a contribution to peace, while a majority of the older generation still supported military service.[78] The attempt to implement a rigorously civilian policy that would avoid all military entanglement was a logical consequence of such public ambivalence.

The rejection of militarism was thus the first important result of the collective learning process that transformed Germany after 1945. The bitter admission of the Wehrmacht's "criminal acts" in the Second World War through "partly active, partly passive participation" in the genocide of the Jews, mass deaths of POWs, deportation of forced laborers, and brutal attempts to crush partisans suggests a fundamental change during the second half of the twentieth century that Thomas Berger has called "a culture of anti-militarism."[79] To be sure, a conservative minority of the older generation continues to protest against this critical verdict by military historians, and young skinheads remain fascinated by military traditions. But the remarkable public success of the traveling exhibit, unapologetically entitled "War of Annihilation: The Crimes of the Wehrmacht," underlines the extent of the metamorphosis of German attitudes. Indeed, one might ask whether this cultural reversal has, perhaps, been exaggerated to the point that regardless of circumstances, peace is now viewed, like war had been before, as an absolute, incontestable, and always valid good. Has the German population today come to possess a new "arrogance of humility" that might have negative consequences of its own?[80]

CHAPTER 2

Questioning the Nation

Due to fear of the victorious powers and disappointment in Hitler's promises, the total defeat initiated a rapid process of distancing from National Socialism and its organizations. For example, "The first thing we did was take an oil portrait of Hitler from its hook, and then we cleaned off the bookshelf." Günter Esdor, a former member of the Hitler Youth, remembered his family's hasty purge in the spring of 1945: "Hitler's book *Mein Kampf* was among the items removed, but even more dangerous were the party insignia, membership lists, and other clear proof of having followed Hitler." Heeding the wise advice of a grandfather who had already lived through several regime changes, the family dumped all objects adorned with the swastika into a fetid manure pit. "I was ashamed, I felt like a blasphemer. But the fear of being shot outweighed everything else." While this process of self-denazification, carried on by the thousands, may have removed the superficial signs of National Socialism, overcoming the nationalism that stood behind it would prove much more difficult. As Esdor conceded, "Of course most Germans . . . mourned the collapse of the Third Reich, that is, as long as they had not been persecuted by the Nazi regime."[1]

From the very beginning, denazification was a central war aim of both the Allies and the regime's anti-Fascist opponents in the resistance or in exile. Destroying the Nazi tyranny, first by banning the Nazi Party and its organizations and then by completely "removing all Nazis from their positions of power," topped the list of the directives for the occupation and the resolutions of the Potsdam conference. Indeed, denazification was viewed as the crucial precondition for bringing peace to a newly liberated Europe.[2] Manifestos of the German resistance likewise called for "an inner purification of Germany from corruption and crimes," insisting that "the violent tyranny of National Socialism must be eradicated root and branch."[3] This demand for the total elimination of Nazi power rested, however, on the somewhat comforting assumption that there existed a fundamental difference between the Nazi Party and the German people, and that by removing a limited number of evildoers, the rest might be brought to their senses. Similarly, the metaphors of Nazi "gangsters" or the "sickness" of Nazism that circulated widely in America suggested the possibility of a rehabilitation of the Germans; they needed only to be liberated from their criminal leadership or from the pathogens that infected their political culture.[4]

Yet not all observers were convinced that the "Nazi government" and the German people could be so clearly separated as to create the basis for building a stable postwar polity. In a private letter that used the polarizing language found in so much war propaganda, Franklin D. Roosevelt therefore described the war as a "crusade to save . . . civilization from a cult of brutal tyranny, which would destroy it and all of the dignity of human life."[5] Behind such words lurked a conception of history that understood Prussian militarism and submission to authority as immutable features of the German national character. Likewise, the Soviet writer Ilja Ehrenburg and U.S. journalist Raymond Daniell regarded the German population's support for the Nazi regime as proof of its utter depravity: "Slowly Europe and the world are growing to realize . . . that the German people themselves, and not just the Kaiser or Hitler, are what we have to contend with, for in any people who can sit idly by and not protest such actions there is some grave moral lack." Believing that more than just a few Nazis were to blame, some Allied politicians such as British diplomat Lord Robert Vansittart and U.S. Secretary of the Treasury Henry Morgenthau wanted to treat "the entire nation as criminals." Above all, they held the Germans' deep-seated nationalism responsible for the crimes of the Third Reich.[6]

Historical scholarship has examined only some dimensions of this complex of personal purification and ideological reorientation while largely ignoring other aspects. Through intensive local research, denazification studies have documented the administrative attempts to eliminate party members, thereby revealing the extent of the exchange of personnel, above all in the Western Zones. But sympathy for the complete rupture demanded by the "anti-Fascist committees" that sprang up with the German surrender has led many authors to interpret denazification as a complete failure, rather than to appreciate the limited, but still significant, discontinuities that it created. They frequently cite its perversion into what West German historian Lutz Niethammer has called a "factory for [absolving] followers," suggesting that the process allowed former Nazis to shed their past all too easily, and often only superficially.[7] Such thinking, in fact, has given rise to the impression of a more rigorous purge of former Nazis in the Soviet Zone, even though in some areas—for example, medicine, technology, and the military—high percentages of Nazis were tolerated there as well.[8] The literature on reeducation policy has not offered a genuine corrective, either, since it is largely limited to the attempts to change the structure of schools, while overlooking the content-oriented and didactic aspects of the reform.[9] Finally, scholarship on the national question after 1945 concentrates almost exclusively on the international and domestic problems of reunification, virtually ignoring the persistence or transformation of cultural identities.[10]

An analysis of the distancing from the nation in the second half of the twentieth century, therefore, must go beyond denazification and probe the broader repudiation of nationalism. To be sure, the purge of the Nazis in the narrower sense of the word remains an essential starting point because it was the elimination of Nazi fanatics from positions of leadership in both the West and the East that provided the foundation for all further changes in political culture. But even more important would be a broader analysis of the retreat from nationalism, the collapse of the nation as a reference point, and the search for other ties of loyalty, because these factors continue to be responsible for the lack or pride in being German, in contrast to other nationalities. Finally, the surprising persistence of a specific kind of German identity, even if its form has changed, should also be addressed, as without its emotional pull the entrance of the East German states in 1990 into the FRG and the reconstitution of a tamed nation-state would not have been possible. The notion of a "postnational nation" goes straight to the conceptual heart of the matter, because its paradoxical character demands an explanation.[11]

Purging the Nazis

In German collective memory, a standard narrative describes the process of denazification, recurring in a stylized version in many autobiographies. As Alexander Dicke, at the time an adolescent in the Ruhr region, recalled decades later:

> Every German had to fill out the Allied government's lengthy questionnaire (with 131 items), which contained some embarrassing questions relating to membership and activities in Nazi organizations. If one wanted a position, he needed a certificate of denazification that included proof of his classification as a nominal follower or beneficiary. Denazification boards attempted to shed light on the darkness of the Nazi past of those under scrutiny. But experiences . . . show that these denazification proceedings met with just as little success as the reeducation programs of the Allies.[12]

This description contains all of the essential elements of the basic storyline of the denazification process: the political objective of screening, the method of filling out a long questionnaire, the judicial proceeding before a denazification board, and a concluding judgment that labeled the attempted purge a failure. The popularity of this narrative and its influence on historiography beg that it be deconstructed: How reliable is this rendition of events, and how conclusive is this judgment of their effects?

What is missing from this description is the contradictory character of denazification, a process whose objectives and methods changed considerably over time. Spurred on by General Lucius Clay's promise that "men with a Nazi viewpoint and who have been active in the Nazi party will be purged, and purged quickly," the initial phase focused on the dissolution of Nazi organizations, the dismissal of Nazis from administrative posts, and the internment of high-level functionaries as well as potential war criminals.[13] For the members of the fallen elite, being committed to an internment camp no doubt came as a terrible shock since they were treated more harshly than ordinary POWs, because they were considered the core of the Third Reich. At first, most could barely grasp the reality of Germany's collapse, and, clinging bitterly to their national pride, claimed to have no knowledge whatsoever of Nazi crimes: "Ultimately, it turned out that they all together rejected any 'blame' for themselves." As reliable documents were lost in the postwar confusion, and even brutal interrogation shed little light on the truth, the hearing of evidence sometimes dragged on, generating new resentment against the supposed "discrepancy between the rhetoric and the actual actions" of the victorious powers.[14]

Although the U.S. military took vigorous action, interrogators did not always possess sufficient language skills or knowledge of local culture to discover all truly guilty parties. While German emigrants in American uniforms, such as the specially trained "Camp Richtie boys," played an important part in the occupation, the vast majority of GIs could barely understand the fine differences between fanatics, opportunists, and nominal adherents—or, for that matter, members of the resistance. Admonitions such as "now *Sie* go back, *nichts* Hitler, *nichts* National Socialism, *nichts* Hitler Youth, *nichts* SS" with which they bombarded POWs upon their release were not, to say the least, very effective. Some die-hard Nazis escaped responsibility altogether by committing suicide, while others went underground. Most, however, tried to conceal their guilt by destroying evidence. In July 1945, the U.S. military governor was able to report proudly that the Nazi Party had been dissolved, 80,000 Nazi leaders had been arrested, and 70,000 Nazi activists were dismissed from positions in the civil service. Still, local differences in the implementation of denazification policies gave rise to a widespread impression of arbitrariness: "In town all officials and public employees who belonged to the Nazi Party are being dismissed. The Americans appear to be much more ruthless in their zeal to de-nazify than the British and the French, and, for that matter, even the Russians."[15]

Following the military guidelines of July 7, 1945, denazification quickly assumed the bureaucratic character for which it would become notorious. Because so many documents had been destroyed by bombing and fighting, the U.S. military government attempted to generate its own information about the extent of involvement with the Nazis with the help of a detailed questionnaire, which ultimately comprised 131 separate questions. Fortunately, a worker in a paper factory had been able to save the Nazi Party's membership files, making it possible to cross-check some of the responses to these questions.[16] In yet another law promulgated on September 26, OMGUS (Office of the Military Governor–United States) forbade the "employment of Nazi Party members" in any occupation above that of ordinary laborer in the hope of catching collaborators still active in business. Above all, the purge concentrated on the 300,000 members of the civil service in the American Zone, of whom approximately half were charged in one way or another. Expulsions based solely on the criteria of party membership and rank did little to distinguish between "nominal Nazis" and dedicated perpetrators, and thus created "a deficit of competent, politically reliable replacement[s]." It is no wonder that this schematic approach seemed "like a scene from the theater of the absurd" to the majority of Germans affected by it.[17]

Not until the promulgation of the "law for the liberation from National Socialism and Militarism" on March 5, 1946, was the task of denazification transferred into the hands of German review boards. While pressure from an American public whose opinions had been shaped by the Nuremberg trials demanded drastic measures, local military authorities faced more pragmatic problems, such as educating children after 80 to 85 percent of the teachers had been dismissed. At the same time, the first German state governments pressed, as the state minister Heinrich Schmitt in Bavaria put it, for an "individual investigation procedure" and for the arrangement of categories of guilt in such a way that investigators would be able to distinguish between the more and less guilty parties. Similarly, the various state governments requested the restoration of at least the perception of legal safeguards through the institution of denazification boards, whose members were to be recruited from anti-Fascists with unblemished records. Hammered out during further negotiations with the military, the new law distinguished between categories such as "I. Chief Nazis; II. Nazis (activists, militarists, beneficiaries); III. Lesser Nazis (probation group); IV. Nominal followers; V. Exonerated." Despite the reversal of the burden of proof, this law created a process that granted the accused the possibility of some defense.[18]

For the large number of people who were incriminated, the denazification procedure was hardly a trifling matter, as without a certificate of exoneration there was no chance of holding onto a normal job. To begin with, all adults over the age of eighteen had to report to their local authorities to register the entire population. At the same time, members had to be selected for the denazification boards from among "people for whom not revenge, but rather equity, is the guiding principle" and who were aware of local circumstances so that they would be able to see through excuses. Moreover, it was possible for citizens to denounce

Nazis and their accomplices, thereby assisting the boards in obtaining much needed information. The recommended sanctions were severe, ranging from up to ten years in a work camp, confiscation of property, and exclusion from public office to the cancellation of pensions and losing one's right to vote. Finally, the military government also supervised the implementation of the review with Argus eyes, reserving for itself the right to intervene directly, as it did when it dissolved the sixth Munich board for its supposed "miscarriage of justice."[19] Since filling out the questionnaire was quite a nuisance, a good many of those who were affected by it considered denazification a real threat to their future.

The impression of leniency that so many remembered, however, derives from the bulk of the judgments rendered by the denazification boards. A typical case was the proceeding against the paper engineer S., who was recommended for group III of the "lesser Nazis." Born in Württemberg in 1903, S. had belonged to sports and singing clubs in his youth. He then worked as a shop supervisor for a few years in Switzerland, before finally becoming a senior engineer in Austria. Not only did he enter the party and the labor front in 1937, the People's Welfare a year later, and finally the National Air Defense League, but from 1944 on he also served as a cell leader in the Nazi Party. In his defense he stated that he "had only participated nominally in Nazism," and he accepted the office of cell leader as an invalid, exempted from military service, under pressure from the higher leadership. Witnesses confirmed these claims, testifying that they were not aware of his party membership and that he "should only be regarded as a nominal follower." Likewise, inquiries revealed "that nothing politically detrimental is known about him." As a result, the board put him into category IV, which was reserved for nominal Nazis, while fining him a hefty 1,000 RM to cover the costs of the proceedings. So well did he appear to have come through the process that in 1969 a local newspaper was able to report on the fortieth anniversary of the business firm that he had subsequently started. Because many party members were opportunists, it does not, in retrospect, seem terribly illogical for the boards to have classified them as such.[20]

In less incriminating circumstances, the review process usually led to an acquittal, thereby allowing the accused to continue his career. Having entered the party in 1937, the SA in 1940, and the NSV as early as 1933, the theater director D., for example, was initially classified as a category IV. But when he came before the board, he claimed that he was "first and foremost an artist and not particularly interested in politics, especially party politics." That, along with the several "strikingly anti-Nazi" statements that he made under oath and his "always tolerant and politically unobjectionable" behavior, earned him a certificate clearing him of all charges. Similarly, an aristocratic school principal who, "because of membership in the Nazi Party," had been forbidden to engage in any pedagogical activities, was classified as "exonerated" on account of her advocacy of the Confessing Church, a wing of the Protestant Church opposed to

Nazi religious policies, and the fact that she had not employed Nazis in her school. Although she found the process humiliating, she was allowed to continue running a renowned private school. These few examples from among thousands demonstrate that in the majority of cases the denazification boards were inclined not to examine critically the whitewashing testimony that was sometimes formulated according to the self-serving principle of "first you testify for me, and then I'll testify for you."[21]

Despite the leniency of many verdicts, the law to purge Nazis from public positions unleashed a storm of outrage. In an open letter, the Council of Evangelical Churches criticized the policy as retroactively "too strict" and, as a result, counterproductive. Likewise, a letter to the editor that appeared in the Swiss daily newpaper *Die Tat* denounced the law as "logical nonsense, judicial perversity and moral perfidy," because it rested on the assumption of collective guilt and sprang "purely from considerations of party politics." In a mimeographed brief, the conservative Catholic Baron von Lünigk polemicized against the "offensive hypocrisy" of the Allies, who had never atoned for their own atrocities, such as the bombing of Dresden: "Who gives to them the moral legitimacy to be the judge of me and my fellow countrymen?" Refusing to recognize the advantages of a judicial process, he claimed: "Even today injustice is being practiced and bondage is being spread, with the very same means and methods of the Nazis."[22] Likewise, the tenor of Ernst von Salomon's successful novel *The Questionnaire* reveals the deep wound this procedure inflicted on Germans' feelings of self-worth, which overshadowed any potential sense of guilt after the war.[23]

Although the military government wanted to continue its rigid policy of purging Nazis, the enormity of the task, along with growing criticism from the German population, eventually forced them to modify its implementation. While U.S. military governor Clay bemoaned the slowness of the process and the "whitewashing" of the accused, the Bavarian minister for denazification pointed out the need to accommodate "nominal party members." To accelerate the processing of the 3.66 million affected (out of a total of 13.41 million in the U.S. Zone), in August 1946 OMGUS announced a general amnesty for youth, exempting all those born after 1919 from further punishment. Drawing on a suggestion made by American trade unions, the Supreme Commander General Joseph T. McNarney amnestied yet another million nominal Nazis with an annual income of less than 3,600 Mk so that the denazification boards could devote themselves to the more difficult cases of the chief culprits.[24] During the summer of 1947, the state governments suggested a further simplification of the process but were unable to convince the military government to adopt it. Only once the Soviet Union ended denazification in its zone in early 1948 did the Americans decide to follow suit.[25]

While the other Western powers generally submitted to American pressure for a thorough denazification, they established their own priorities. For instance, the British proceeded more pragmatically so as not to endanger the "viability of the administration," especially in the Ruhr mining industry, and to allow the populace to participate more actively in the process itself. Nevertheless, they also insisted on implementing the purge "with much vigor" in such key areas as the civil service and education: "It is not the questionnaire, but rather the person who ought to be examined."[26] The English, however, distinguished between the specific judicial guilt of those primarily responsible in groups I and II, whose cases they reviewed themselves, and general political responsibility, the judgment of which they left to the Germans. Given the persistent criticism coming from various quarters such as the Protestant Church, the process was revised in early 1948, then discontinued altogether shortly thereafter.[27] Somewhat surprisingly, the French acted still more magnanimously, perhaps because they primarily sought to achieve security from a renewed attack and thus drew less of a distinction between the various categories of the hated *boches*.[28] They interned and released a smaller percentage of party members, classified almost half as "nominal followers," and let the rest off scot-free.[29] By moving their domicile to another zone, former Nazis therefore could attempt to evade examination.

In contrast, the "eradication of Nazism" in the Soviet Zone was more rigorous, since it aimed above all to secure the power of the Communist minority by restructuring social relationships.[30] During the occupation, Soviet forces as well as Communist Party members arrested and fired all of the Nazis they could find. After the issuing of "purification" laws at the state level and of new guidelines for the "anti-Fascist-democratic" bloc in the fall of 1945, Communists also began distinguishing between Nazi criminals, active Nazis, and nominal party members. As a result, entire professions such as teachers, judges, and police officers were dismissed en masse. Because of regional disparities in implementation, the Soviet Military Administration of Germany (SMAD) in December 1946 insisted on a rigorous application of the Control Council's order No. 12, which required the "removal of all members of the Nazi Party who belonged to it actively, not just nominally," as well as all other enemies of the occupation.[31] The ensuing criticism of the mass dismissals, however, forced the council to revise its decision in order No. 201 of August 1948, which made the rehabilitation of nominal Nazis contingent upon their contributing to reconstruction. To end the uncertainty caused by the expropriation of property formerly held by "the great Junker landholders" and the "monopolistic lords of capital" that resulted from land reform and referenda against "war criminals," the SMAD declared the purge a success and dissolved the commissions in February 1948.[32]

The discrepancy between the contemporary press reports of success and the memory of the purge's failure raises questions about its actual effectiveness. The unreliability of existing statistics, and the mutual accusations of the "elimination of capitalism" in the Soviet Zone and of a "Nazi paradise" in the Western Zones, especially Bavaria, render any answer uncertain at best.[33] Nevertheless, the outlines of the decisions emerging from West German summary figures seem fairly clear: Of the 3,660,648 affected persons, 1,667 fell into the group of chief culprits, 23,060 into that of the majorly "incriminated" (not including British figures), and 150,425 into that of the "less incriminated." Thus altogether, only these 4.8 percent were considered the hard core of the Nazis and punished accordingly. Another 995,874, or 27.2 percent, were classified as nominal members, while 1,213,873, or 33.2 percent, were completely exonerated. Added to these figures were 358,317 amnestied, 782,803 uncharged, and 124,629 people otherwise not classified. According to a similar survey of January 1, 1947, among the 553,170 Nazis in the Eastern Zone, 307,370 had been forcibly dismissed, 83,108 were prohibited from further employment, and the final third working in the railroad, business, or medicine were "temporarily left in place."[34]

What, then, did the vast effort of denazification ultimately achieve? First, as a consequence of the second law of the Allied Control Council of October 15, 1945, stipulating "the termination and dissolution of Nazi organizations," the Nazi Party, its organizations, institutions, and all groups affiliated with it simply disappeared. With the exception of a handful of isolated attempts to carry on underground, the continued existence of Nazism was thus effectively prevented. Second, despite differences in implementation and a number of individual scandals, prominent Nazis were essentially eliminated as a group from public life. During the Cold War, moreover, a critical public sphere on both sides of the iron curtain kept careful watch to ensure that no politician who was too burdened by his Nazi past was allowed to assume a position of major authority.[35] Third, Nazism as an ideology had been so thoroughly discredited by the Nuremberg trials and subsequent court proceedings that Nazi arguments, when they were recognized as such, were no longer tolerated in the public sphere. As a result, the foundation for a fundamental change in the political culture was laid—partly in reaction to modernizing influences emanating from outside of the country, and partly through linkages to progressive traditions within it.

What did not succeed, however, was the complete elimination of all former Nazis from professional life, since that was an unrealistic objective from the start. Despite massive pressure from the international community and the wishes of German anti-Fascists, it proved simply impossible to condemn all 6.5 million Nazi Party members to manual labor in service of reconstruction, since without expert knowledge the administration and economy of the occupied country would have quickly broken down. The experiment also failed to convince all Nazi followers from the old elite to atone for their complicity, as the denazification boards first had to process the questionnaires and lawyers delayed many hearings until finally the purge, largely due to the ensuing Cold War, was ended. The attempt to bring about a reorientation of all opportunistic Nazis, which began in the internment camps and was continued by the licensed media, was also less than successful, as they often only changed their vocabulary while still clinging to their old racist and anti-Communist prejudices. Finally, the process never achieved general acceptance. As public opinion surveys showed, agreement with the policy fell from 57 percent in March 1946 to 17 percent in May 1949. In the end, overly ambitious goals and bureaucratic implementation set the populace against the purge.[36]

The rightist memory of a "failed denazification," nonetheless, appears to be a legend. Since it relies mostly on unspoken criteria, this negative assessment of the purge is similarly misleading when it is presented from a left-wing perspective. If the expectation is that all party members were to be dismissed, then every Nazi who resurfaced after 1945 serves as proof of the failure of denazification. But if the criterion is political influence beyond the immediate collapse, then the long-term success becomes just as clear. Was it not in the Soviet Occupation Zone where denazification was pursued more rigorously and in disregard of the right to self-defense that a second dictatorship emerged? However exasperating it may have seemed to some, the rehabilitation of nominal Nazis was never really a threat, because their internment, release, and screening gave the anti-Fascists and others with an unblemished record a lead in occupying positions in the administration and in forming political parties. Did not the reintegration of Nazi followers under the eyes of the occupation and a critical public actually facilitate the reconstruction and democratization of the Federal Republic, because it prevented the emergence of a subculture of bitter-enders? The actual paradox of the great purge is thus the contradiction between the fact that it undoubtedly petered out in the short term but nonetheless achieved most of its aims in the long run.

Distancing from Nationalism

Behind the debates surrounding denazification lay the still more difficult challenge of breaking with the radical nationalism that was more deeply anchored in German culture than National Socialism. Clear-headed observers understood that a return to the values and practices of Western civilization would require a fundamental change in "national mentality" that would cure it once and for all from its pan-German pretensions. The political journalist Dolf Sternberger thus lamented the "grave perversion" of patriotism through its arrogation by Nazism, countering that "the concept of the Fatherland can be fulfilled only by its *free constitution*."[37] "It was clear to me that an era had reached its end. The world in which I had lived for years and which had given purpose to my life seemed to have perished," Alexander Dicke later recalled. "It was an uneasy feeling, being so disorientated, because no one knew what would come next."[38] The fact that the effort to come to terms with the defeat affected intellectuals as well as ordinary people raises the question of how this reorientation actually occurred, what was repressed, and what, ultimately, was learned.

The precondition for a successful rehabilitation was, of course, the official termination of the Nazi regime though the assumption of sovereignty by the Allies on June 5, 1945. "Admiral Friedeburg poisoned himself on a ship in Flensburg where the members of the government were stripped of their offices," one woman from Hamburg reported succinctly on May 28. "Dönitz [is] removed and taken prisoner." The inglorious end of German statehood did not fail to leave an impression on observant contemporaries. "In the next few days our government is to meet with the inter-allied commission. Its task is to coordinate the measures to be taken by the individual zone commanders, who, incidentally, treat the subjected [Germans] arrogantly and arbitrarily." The rivalry between the superpowers was already beginning to show, for American newspapers gave the impression that "the United States was gradually feeling ashamed at being politically outmaneuvered by the Soviet Union."[39] Among the most important consequences of the Allies' accession to power was Germany's transformation into an object of international politics and the step-by-step division of the country, which, by robbing nationalism of its political stage, ultimately rendered it politically impotent.

More important than symbolic acts such as the final dissolution of Prussia, however, was the demonstration of German powerlessness by the presence of occupation troops in the public space.[40] Even as they were being "overrun," survivors marveled at the "vast and unending stream of vehicles" containing Anglo-American soldiers, who drove in jeeps and trucks, wore clean clothes, and looked well-fed. The directives on curfews, weapons bans, and food controls that people could read from the bilingual signs posted at street corners drove home the fact not only that the Nazi big-shots had disappeared but also that the remaining administrators could act only in the areas granted to them by the occupiers. People also feared the arbitrary quartering of Allied troops, which affected former Nazis as well as ordinary citizens whose homes had survived the fighting. Lastly, profiteering on the black market, prostitution, and similar activities ranked among the uglier manifestations of the occupation. The actor Hans Doerry satirized the feeling of being at the mercy of the victors by recasting the words of the German national anthem:

From the Niers to the Neiße,
From the Eider to the Inn,
It's all one great big pile of shit,
And that is where we now sit.[41]

The Allied program for reorientation in the media, schools, and culture attempted to discredit nationalism through a carrot and stick approach. To put an end to Nazi propaganda, which had been so notorious for its mendacity, the occupying powers first forbade all German newspapers, radio programs, and films. The Allies then attempted to fill the resulting information vacuum, in which rumors strangely flourished, with their own press organs, some of which were produced by returning emigrants. In Soviet-controlled Berlin the *Tägliche Rundschau* began publishing as early as April 1945. "We're dealing with the endless rehashing of party dogmas, with a tasteless glorification of the Soviet system," wrote one critical member of the staff bitterly. In mid-July the *Neue Rheinische Zeitung* was founded as the mouthpiece of the British administration and, by extension, of "public opinion" in the Rhineland as well. It was not until October that the more professionally produced, American-sponsored *Neue Zeitung* appeared, which sought to serve as a model for a reformed press "through objective reporting, unconditional love of truth, and high journalistic standards." Only after a thorough screening were reliable German publishers and journalists licensed to issue their own publications.[42]

A further effort targeted the primary and secondary schools in the hopes that at least the younger generation could be weaned from the drug of nationalism. For that to be successful, it was necessary to purge the teaching staff and install untainted, democratic pedagogues as principals. But detaching youths, who had been disappointed by the defeat and contaminated by the slogans of the Hitler Youth, from the habits of racist and chauvinist thought proved rather difficult. Moreover, "history lessons were not taught, because first a new conception of history needed to be drafted, a task that scholars were charged with." Reading texts on the concentration camps like "The Hell of Buchenwald" and watching films of their liberation like "Death Mills" produced a profound shock. One former pupil recalled: "Although we realized that things would have ended badly for us nonconformists had the Reich lived on, we still didn't want to condemn everything that was preached to us as good and right, without examining it." When teachers wrestled with their own doubts, their lessons came across as more believable. But when, as was often the case in the Soviet Zone, they simply substituted new ideological phrases for old clichés, their efforts frequently "led to defiance and rejection."[43]

In the cultural realm, the occupation powers also attempted to repress harmful influences, while at the same time reinforcing positive traditions and spreading their own views as an alternative. After returning from exile in the United States, the writer Alfred Döblin was deeply impressed with the insatiable appetite for reading among a populace that had been cut off from the rest of the world by the Nazi dictatorship: "People want to know, to hear from the outside, they want novel impulses and to be given new strength." To overcome the disdain felt by the educated for mass civilization, the Americans initially concentrated on importing their own high culture with newly founded "America Houses," which offered access to international modernity. Nevertheless, the first Rita Hayworth film and authentic swing music broadcast by the Armed Forces Network held considerably more appeal for German youth. The East German Cultural Association, in contrast, dedicated itself to the thankless tasks of "eradicating fascist ideology," rediscovering progressive traditions, popularizing Marxist classics in popular editions, and propagating the glorious example of the Soviet Union. But reading previously forbidden works by Jack London, Upton Sinclair, Heinrich Mann, or Lion Feuchtwanger did have a liberating effect. One youth commented: "New worlds opened themselves up. I didn't know that a literature without a nationalistic pathos [even existed], and [so] I was excited."[44]

In addition to Allied initiatives, autonomous learning processes triggered by the defeat similarly helped many Germans drop their nationalist reflexes: "People appeared paralyzed. Would their lives become normal again?" Following the deep shock of the occupation, an ordinary citizen recalled his youthful search: "Questions immediately arose: How could this all have happened? Who was to blame for this catastrophe?" Because the system which years of propaganda had made seem invincible fell apart so quickly, previously suppressed doubts about the war's purpose finally surfaced. "Our sons have all died or been blasted into cripples. Germany lies prostrate. The ruins condemn this system." The terrible reports from the concentration camps appeared incomprehensible, especially to the officers who for years had fought on the Eastern Front. "I suffered something like a nervous breakdown, asking [myself]: 'To what ends have we soldiers been misused; for what [purpose] have the German people stood firm for so unbelievably long?'"[45] Even when individuals admitted their own guilt, such probing questions signaled the beginning of a lengthy process of rethinking basic beliefs.

The unavoidable reexamination of the Nazi experience also led Germans to call into question the nationalism that lay behind it. In retrospect, it was hard for ordinary citizens to understand how a sophisticated people could have followed such a primitive ideology, thereby questioning "the crimes of the Nazis— their unforgivable ideology, their ignorance of basic economic and demographic facts, their brutish biologism, which closed their minds to understanding technical developments, [and] their chiliastic slave mentality, which elected a madman and murderer as its savior." It was precisely because only a minority were convinced Nazis that there had to be broader cultural reasons for the cooperation of the majority with Hitler. The Germans "had become victims of an ideology of fatherland and greatness, authority and obedience, military strength and self-sacrifice, contempt for mankind and racial madness," a contemporary reflected decades later. "They had themselves to blame in part, because they followed false prophets."[46] Even if some fanatics chose to deny the connection, in the end, support for genocidal Nazism, which had endured far too long, could not but discredit more moderate forms of nationalism that were based on older, secondary virtues.

Just how difficult it was for many people to detach themselves from Nazi habits of thought is demonstrated by their emotional reaction to the alleged charge of collective guilt, which came largely from abroad. Indeed, "some incorrigible people, who simply do not want to recognize the crimes," continued to deny all responsibility or attempted to cover up their own role in them. Most nominal followers were more likely to hold the dictatorship of the Nazi "gang of criminals" responsible for the atrocities than to consider their own complicity: "No foreigner can ever appreciate how suppressed we were. No one could rebel publicly, as the specter of the Gestapo lurked above us." Marxist anti-Fascists considered the aristocratic and bourgeois elites as the guilty party, as evidenced by the drastic language of one East German schoolgirl: "The Russians took them into custody in camps as 'capitalist pigs' and 'blood-sucking exploiters.'"[47] Only a few intellectuals such as Martin Niemöller objected to the effort to relativize the Protestant Church's confession of responsibility by referring to the injustices of others: "Nevertheless, this position does not absolve us from confessing our [own] guilt before God and the people." One critical poem even went so far as to justify the Germans' punishment with their own culpability:

> And God said: "No."
> I have to, want to strike you,
> Because you piled guilt upon guilt,
> Your glass is full to overflowing.[48]

Also helping to achieve some distance from nationalism were the reflections of intellectuals on its fatal consequences, as well as their proposals for workable alternatives. By emphasizing the destructive power of radical nationalism, Marburg University rector Julius Ebbinghaus advocated a return to a form of patriotism based on the "rule of law," which would have no need to shy away from "the mirror of the moral world." Similarly, liberal historians such as Walter Goetz attempted to cleanse the love of the fatherland of racism, condemning "the anti-Semitic theory of history" as a "vulgar and intentional falsification of historical facts."[49] In the Eastern Zone, Marxist journalist Alexander Abusch told the story of a "nation that, in the course of its battles against the forces of progress, was driven by its reactionary elites onto a suicidal path." Instead of falling back on "socialist internationalism," democratic Western intellectuals associated with the sociologist Alfred Weber discussed the "development away from the previous nation-state toward an enforceable legal world order" of the United Nations. Other independent minds sought to overcome nationalism by collaborating in the project of unifying Europe, an idea that had already begun to be voiced in resistance circles during the war.[50]

The most radical reaction to the misery of being German was the individual effort to escape the tarnished nation through emigration. One young man remembered: "What we'd like to do most is emigrate, but what German would not want to do that under the present and future circumstances?" In the words of a typical letter of recommendation, this desire to leave "a destroyed and starving homeland" rested above all on the hope of "realizing one's fortune in another country among other people." Most of these plans, however, failed for lack of resources and connections, necessary to start anew in a faraway land.[51] Moreover, other countries usually gave preference to the numerous Nazi victims who had survived the concentration and forced labor camps, and were now called "displaced persons," because they no longer had a home that they wanted to return to. Yet "captured German scientists," Nazis who had gone underground as well as a million ordinary citizens who had been uprooted by flight and expulsion were ready to take their chances abroad.[52] But once they arrived in a new foreign environment, many soon found out how unpleasant it was to stand out even more as German.

As they transformed themselves from the racist "national community" of the Nazis into a collection of victims during occupation, many Germans, nonetheless, managed to preserve a certain sense of identity that transcended defeat: "Due to their common fate, the German people retained a great deal of solidarity even after the war's end." The camaraderie of the front, the fear shared by the women who huddled together in bomb shelters, and the chaos of the Third Reich's collapse shaped new points of reference through collective suffering. Above all, those who had committed no crimes could find "no reason whatsoever" other than their "inborn characteristic of being a German" for being expelled and put to flight. Thus the Czech impulse to punish, exploit, and eject indiscriminately all hated *nemcy* (Germans) derived not only from an understandable passion for revenge but also from a reasoning based on unchangeable national stereotypes. Occupation, captivity, hunger, and cold formed a new kind of collective experience whose inescapable common denominator was membership in the German nation. In wide sections of the populace, feelings of self-pity for their newfound role as victims helped transform the formerly aggressive nationalism into a defensive resentment toward "the awful things that have been done to the German people."[53]

Shared relief measures and support laws to help the struggle for survival also provided a new social foundation for solidarity among Germans during the first postwar years. The "CARE packages" from the United States offered "many treats that had long been missed," and relief actions such as the Allies' school lunch program provided some essential help. At the same time, relatives and acquaintances did provide many with food, shelter, and psychological support during the most perilous moments of the occupation. "At last, the family was together again," recalled one anti-Fascist officer. "Life could begin once more."[54] Churches and unions also helped, although the aid they provided often had a divisive effect on this fragmented society since their efforts might split it still further into groups with different rights, such as the "victims of fascism" or those doing "physical labor," who were favored when it came to food rations. The fact that relief for the suffering, which had been sustained in the name of the nation, could only be obtained at the state level had a decisive impact on Germans' sense of themselves. A comprehensive system of burden sharing, which compensated for the war damage with the help of a special tax on those who emerged unscathed, also helped engender a new kind of social solidarity in Germany. As a result, the erstwhile Aryan master race was forced to transform itself into a welfare community made up of disabled veterans, widows, orphans, refugees, expellees, and the homeless.[55]

At the same time, the humiliation of aggressive nationalism through the territorial losses decreed by the Allies also perpetuated the national question, as the country now once again stood divided. To be sure, the Potsdam Agreement did put an end to the centuries-old tradition of a Reich that encompassed several ethnic groups: "If one counts our eastern lands, the Soviet Union controls half of the former area of the Reich. Europe's borders are whittled down to the territory of Charlemagne." But the consolidation of each occupation zone's borders as administrative and economic units, coupled with the contrast between the Allies' future plans, ironically perpetuated a fixation on the regaining of unified statehood. In the summer of 1946, therefore, the first mass rally of the postwar period in Düsseldorf declared its unanimous support, "regardless of political orientation or world view, for the political and economic unity of Germany." In a related vein, the SED consistently argued from Berlin, the former capital of the Reich, that "the unity of the working class is the unity of Germany."[56] In contrast to earlier quests for hegemony, the competition between the newly formed national parties for a leadership role in "re-"unification could only concentrate on saving the remnants of German territory.

While the Austrians quickly embraced separate statehood, other groups affected by the break-up of the Reich nonetheless adhered to their sense of Germanness in spite of its disadvantages. The continued insistence of the expellees on their "right to a home" as both a demonstration of their origins and a legal basis for a later return could also be explained as arising from a mixture of emotional and material objectives. During the Cold War, older memories of the lost eastern territories lived on in the term "central Germany," which in right-wing circles was the preferred designation for the Soviet Zone. Still, the resistance of 10,000 West Germans to the "border corrections" demanded by Holland, Belgium, and Luxemburg after 1945, through which they might have switched from the camp of the defeated into that of the victors, was striking. Similarly unexpected was the unambiguous wish of the population in the Saarland to be neither annexed by France nor accorded a neutral status between the two countries but, rather, to return to the Federal Republic, which at the time was still under construction.[57] Even when remnants of greater-German nationalism could still be discerned in early postwar rhetoric, such positions were generally the last gasp of those who stubbornly tried to cling to an identity that had grown problematic in the meantime.

The founding of two competing states in 1949 was thus conceived as an interim solution from which a comprehensive German nation-state would redevelop sometime in the future. The reunification mandate in the preamble of the West German Basic Law demanded unmistakably that "the entire German people are called on to achieve in self-determination the unity and freedom of Germany." The claim to legal succession of the German Reich and the comprehensive definition of citizenship on the basis of ethnic descent within the borders of 1937 were expressions of a continuing feeling of nationality that was not satisfied with the Western state then taking shape. Equally clear was the East German constitution's claim to represent the entire nation: "Germany is an indivisible democratic republic that consists of the German states." This perspective persisted, if in a weakened form, when it was restated in the 1968 clause proclaiming that "the GDR is a socialist state of the German nation," before it was dropped entirely in 1974 in exchange for a mere reference to "workers and peasants."[58] The horrifying extent of the second defeat contributed decisively to the transformation of an aggressive nationalism into a defensive, residual sense of nationality.

The absence of an effective revanchist movement is yet another sign of the waning influence of radical nationalism, even if the German question remained unresolved after 1945. The difference between the civil war atmosphere during the early Weimar Republic and the calmer climate that existed after 1945 can be attributed to many factors: Unlike 1918, the second defeat was total in extent, with the lengthy occupation destroying any illusion that its outcome could ever be reversed. Also, the integration of the remnants of the decimated elite into the CDU in the West and the National Democratic Party of Germany in the East achieved greater success than in Weimar, thereby preventing the formation of popular reactionary parties. The interruption of the military's institutional continuity blocked the development of a "state within a state" with territorial ambitions like General Hans von Seekt's Reichswehr in the 1920s. The ban on neo-Nazi groups such as the Socialist Reich Party (SRP) in the West and the organizational repression of the expellees in the East prevented the formation of a broader revanchist movement. Finally, the polarization of the Cold War submerged the national agenda beneath the ideological conflict between the two blocks from which there was no escape. Though a core of incorrigible right-wingers survived, chauvinism lost its broader appeal in the postwar period.[59]

The renunciation of radical nationalism after 1945 was thus the result of a complex mixture of Allied restrictions and reorientation efforts on the one hand and German learning and adaptation processes on the other. The basic decisions for this secular transformation of mentality had already occurred in the early postwar period, when Germany was still reeling from the shock of its total defeat. The loss of the territory annexed by the Third Reich, the cession of the eastern provinces, the abolition of German statehood, and the visible presence of the occupation powers made it clear to even the most obstinate that radical nationalism had led to catastrophe. Apart from individual efforts to avoid responsibility by switching nationalities, it is remarkable, indeed, that a certain sense of ethnic solidarity survived the defeat to form a basis for mutual assistance. Though German identity had been badly damaged by the crimes of the Nazis, it did not disappear entirely but, rather, transformed its character into a "community of fate." As a result of the Second World War, being German became an international stigma that had to be borne stoically and, at best, could be attenuated through good behavior.

A Postnational Nation?

The rejection of radical nationalism left behind a deep emotional uncertainty that conditioned the way Germans dealt with their own identity. Taking the rather low survey results as proof of a "wounded nation," conservative critics such as the pollster Elisabeth Noelle-Neumann lamented the lack of national pride compared with the enthusiasm shown in other European countries. Liberal commentators—for example, the political scientist Karl-Dietrich Bracher —offered a more positive interpretation of this trend and spoke instead of a "postnational democracy among nation-states." Out of the reality of a deeply troubled self-consciousness, they thus made a virtue of postnationality, arguing that, similar to the other "post"-concepts, Germans had survived the malady of nationalism and learned from it.[60] Although the West German public increasingly understood nationalism negatively, East Germans continued to rely on the nation as the primary point of reference when attempting to obtain private or state assistance from the West. The paradox that demands explanation is therefore not simply the widespread turn away from nationalism but the continued existence of some form of national solidarity.

In reaction to the nationalist hysteria of the Third Reich, many otherwise level-headed citizens retreated into a largely prepolitical sense of Germanness in the postwar period. After overcoming their "utter confusion and helplessness," conservative circles began to criticize the mistakes of occupation policy— but they were not in a position to suggest convincing alternatives themselves. For all of the talk about the dangers of a "mass age," authoritarian concepts of government had been discredited by the presidential regime's complicity in the Nazi seizure of power. Moreover, the bloody revenge that Hitler took on the resistance of July 20, 1944, had to a large extent physically destroyed the traditional nationalist, but not dictatorial, elite. In addition, conservatives could not act independently in foreign affairs, since during the Cold War they had to rely on the protection of the Western superpower, which, at the same time, demanded a basic liberalization of domestic politics. The attempt by conservative historians, most notably Gerhard Ritter, to salvage German nationalism by ridding it of its more dangerous elements—for example, its penchant for blind obedience or trust in uniforms— ultimately failed to restore its credibility.[61]

In contrast, patriots on the left foundered both on their internal fragmentation and the contradictory German policy of the Soviet Union. Due to the polarization of the Cold War, the efforts of politicians like Jakob Kaiser, Kurt Schumacher, and Gustav Heinemann to restore political unity between East and West through national neutrality met with little success. The pronounced nationalist rhetoric of the East German People's Congress Movement was also poorly received in the West, since it would have meant nothing less than the dominance of the SED in a united Germany and a full-scale revolution in property rights. Finally, the nonpartisan coalition movement represented by the Committee for an Indivisible Germany was also unable to exert lasting influence on either the political culture or practical policy.[62] The nationalism of the left lost its attraction partly due to the inherent contradiction between its internationalist traditions and national objectives and partly due to the struggle for power between the SPD and the SED. Finally, fluctuations in Soviet policy between punishment through territorial losses or holding hostage a socialist satellite, and a peaceful relationship to a neutral, unified Germany prevented any genuine cooperation as well.[63]

Negative associations and missing perspectives thus led to a veritable flight from Germanness in broad sections of the population and a chameleon-like search for other identities. In the process, West Germans transformed themselves in the direction of the successful democratic model offered by the Americans, whose economic potency and relaxed lifestyle seemed highly attractive in comparison with the other occupation powers. While members of the political elite were reassured by U.S. security guarantees against communism, and managers stood impressed by the possibilities of mass production, intellectuals found the creativity of modernist high culture attractive and youth were fascinated by Hollywood films and rock music.[64] Despite terrible memories of the Red Army's entry into Germany, the victorious Soviet Union and the real accomplishments of socialism could also appear to some East Germans as a guarantor of a more humane future that proved enticing even to skeptical bourgeois scholars like Victor Klemperer.[65] Yet another alternative was the turn toward Europe as a transnational entity that was characterized both by its common consciousness of occidental values and justified by the economic advantages of integration.[66]

The damaged self-confidence of Germans on both sides of the iron curtain began to recover somewhat as they experienced such successes as making progress with reconstruction and winning the 1954 Soccer World Cup. Indeed, in the early postwar period, the guarantee of sheer survival amid chaotic conditions of hunger and cold, occupation and denazification, the dismantling of industry, and reparations gave some cause for satisfaction. After the currency reform in the West, the steadily accelerating growth of the economy created the basis for growing prosperity, while rising international demand for German products offered proof of the country's competitiveness, a fact of which its citizens could be proud. Although it began later and proved much weaker, even in the East an economic upturn allowed for a newfound pride in its own achievement, thereby giving rise to a widespread sentiment of "We are back!" that helped compensate for some of the political humiliations suffered since 1945. Though it was undoubtedly linked to older national stereotypes of diligence and workmanship, this unideological recovery of self-respect offered working Germans a surrogate identity that eventually developed into a downright "Deutschmark nationalism," touting the success of the economy.[67]

In contrast, mounting self-criticism among intellectuals in the course of the 1960s led them to abandon the tradition of positive exceptionalism in exchange for an emphatically negative conception of German identity. Unlike the earlier educated middle class with its affirmative-nationalist orientation, this new stratum of "intellectual workers" possessed a modern lifestyle, international perspective, and critical disposition.[68] In trying to shed light on a sordid past, Western novelists such as Günter Grass and Heinrich Böll, as well as playwrights, including Rolf Hochhut and Peter Weiss, tackled head-on the issue of the crimes of active Nazis, as well the guilt of passive followers. Although their works were exploited as a means of garnering support for the SED regime, Eastern writers such as Christa Wolf and Stefan Heym similarly helped establish some critical distance to the Nazi legacy. In contrast to the increasingly positive self-image of the majority of the populace, the emphasis on German responsibility for the outbreak of the Second World War and the organized mass extermination of the Jews eventually created something like a "Holocaust identity" among intellectuals in the West and an anti-Fascist sense of self among the educated in the East.[69]

The generational revolts of 1968 elevated this literary self-accusation to a paradoxical form of negative nationalism. Although a change in values toward postmaterialism also occurred in other Western societies, in West Germany this development was reinforced by the older generation's extraordinary loss of authority as a long-term consequence of the Third Reich.[70] The charge of responsibility for Nazi crimes played an important part in the indictment of guilt-stricken fathers, as it allowed rebellious sons to reject their traditional nationalist values all the more decisively. In a conscious effort to distance themselves from their own origins, young people championed an emphatic internationalism, a moralizing third-world mentality, and an often naïve sympathy for anti-imperialist liberation struggles.[71] Traces of a persistence of a German exceptionalism turned inside out remained in the radical nature of demands by the new social movements, which emphasized responsibility for peace, the environment, and women's emancipation more emphatically than in neighboring countries. Depending on one's political position, this negation of the nation was either praised as a sign of postnational liberalization or lamented as a form of collective self-hatred.

In the 1970s, the concept of "constitutional patriotism" offered a left-democratic response to the question of what might serve as the basis for political solidarity. This formula, coined by the political scientist Dolf Sternberger and popularized by the social philosopher Jürgen Habermas, represented a decisive departure from an ethnic understanding of the nation and built instead on moral values such as human rights. Indeed, the concept reflected the growing recognition that the Basic Law offered crucial protection for nonconformist individuals and critical groups from the repressive urges of state power.[72] The renunciation of the term "nation" in the 1974 constitution of the GDR pointed in a similar direction, as it made the ideological principle of Marxism the basis of the political system. Because of its explicit connection to democracy, the notion of "constitutional patriotism" appealed strongly to intellectuals, but its pronounced rationalism failed to satisfy the popular need for emotional identification with the community. The result was thus a growing distance between the critical self-image preferred by intellectuals and a more positive, ethnically rooted identification that appealed to the broader population.

In the 1980s, the distancing from the nation accelerated with the development of a binationalism that not just tolerated the existence of two states de facto but sought to justify it morally as well. The call of leftist writers and historians for a full recognition of the GDR and acceptance of East German citizenship relied partly on ethical and partly on political arguments.[73] A somewhat simplistic view of the causes of the crime of "Auschwitz" rooted the Holocaust in the existence of a German nation-state and thus saw its break-up as a historical necessity. An equally facile thesis demanded that Germans make the sacrifice of accepting their division as a precondition for the maintenance of peace in Central Europe so as to atone for their historical guilt in splitting the continent. Due to the failure of reunification rhetoric, more realistic commentators pointed instead to the consolidation of the Federal Republic and the GDR, which had both begun to develop characteristics of separate nations, making dual statehood seem inevitable. Although this diagnosis was correct in recognizing the tendency toward reinforcement of separate statehood, its apodictic nature proved ultimately premature.

Due to such developments, the majority of the West Germans displayed clear signs of a fractured identity a generation after the war's end. Conservative politicians lamented that only about half of the citizens identified with the nation, an abnormally low number compared with other European countries. The generational revolt, moreover, had further weakened the bond between youth and their nation, as did the critical influence of intellectuals in the media and in schools. As a result of the emphasis on historical guilt, the majority of high-school graduates rejected any identification as Germans, while the less-educated classes retained a considerably more positive national self-image, often based on success in international sports competition. Finally, the West German sense of identity was unusually polarized, since only right-wing circles maintained affirmative feelings, while the left distanced itself decidedly from the nation. Fragmentary data do suggest a higher level of national orientation in East Germany, as citizens of the GDR, despite the rhetoric of socialist internationalism, gave the impression of greater Germanness.[74] Though polling results indicate residual feelings of national solidarity, they also show a population that in terms of everyday life was increasingly drifting apart.

In the long run, the social-liberal coalition's "Eastern Policy" (*Ostpolitik*), which partially recognized the GDR, was more successful in maintaining ties between the Germans than the anti-Communist polemics of the CDU that refused to deal with existing reality. As the decades wore on, impassioned Western calls for reunification, ostracism of the SED regime by the Hallstein Doctrine, and symbolic references to the "brothers and sisters in the East" during commemorations of the 1953 rising against the SED all lost their effect.[75] By comparison, the "policy of small steps" helped the Brandt-Scheel government to punch holes in the wall of separation and restore personal, economic, and cultural ties between the two populations. The state visits of West German Chancellor Willy Brandt, his successor Helmut Schmidt, and GDR leader Erich Honecker, along with numerous other contacts between politicians, may not have been able to lift the iron curtain, but they did begin an internal German dialogue that reduced tensions between the two states. During the second Cold War of the 1980s, there arose a conception of a "community of responsibility" between East and West in which the Germans pleaded with their respective superpowers for deescalation. An increasing cross-border trade also contributed to an improvement in East German living standards. While the billions in credit extended by the FRG undoubtedly helped to stabilize the SED gerontocracy, they also created some space for potential dissidence.[76]

Due to the relaxation of détente, the intensity of communication between East and West Germany, which had been reduced by the building of the Berlin wall, returned to a level that far exceeded the exchanges with their other neighbors. Electronic media were particularly helpful, since Western radio and television could be received in most parts of the GDR, once jamming devices were switched off and restrictions on antennas lifted. As a result, every evening East Germans gathered in front of their television sets to emigrate to the West for a few hours, without actually leaving their homes. With the installation of new lines, the number of telephone calls also rose dramatically, while travel between the two states expanded by leaps and bounds in the 1980s. In addition to the privileged "travel cadres" of SED loyalists, some 5 million East Germans, not just pensioners or relatives, visited the West in 1987. Moreover, dozens of partnerships between East and West German cities were established, and in sports as well as culture the number of East-West encounters increased rapidly.[77] Especially for participants in such exchanges among the younger generation, it thus became possible to learn about another part of that abstraction called "Germany" which otherwise lived on only in the memories of the elderly.

The intellectual counterpart to this human networking was the notion of the "cultural nation," a pre-nation-state euphemism signaling a sense of community between all German speakers.[78] The frequent appearance of works by leading East German writers such as Heiner Müller and Ulrich Plenzdorf in the West and the rare publication of critical Western authors like Heinrich Böll and Günter Grass in the East maintained a literary exchange across the border. In the process, past connections to German classicism were just as conspicuous as the parallel preoccupation with the guilt and suffering wrought by Nazism, even if the portrayal of present life experiences by émigrés from the East like Uwe Johnson started to diverge increasingly.[79] In the 1980s scholarly contacts—for example, among social historians—increased as well, and on the political level new attempts were made to establish a dialogue, as occurred in the case of the controversial "discussion paper" on the future of socialism and peace between theorists of the SPD and SED.[80] Although at times somewhat naïve, these attempts were fuelled by a common critique of Nazism, a desire for peace that transcended the Cold War blocs, and a quest for a more just society.

Thus an asymmetrical feeling of solidarity that was no longer inspired by a pronounced nationalism persisted between East and West Germans, however much they had grown apart. While, as polls indicated, explicit patriotism was suspect in the West, hopes for a later reunification endured, and West Germans, though with a slightly patronizing undertone, found their brethren to the East more likeable than their other neighbors.[81] Although similar statistics do not exist for East German citizens, fragmentary evidence suggests that they maintained a higher level of interest in the nation, even if it was motivated by the attraction of Western consumption and popular culture. Especially those East Germans who had relatives in the Federal Republic, obtained their information from the Western media, or had taken trips to the West remained deeply connected to West Germany in spite of all the official skepticism that the regime harbored toward Western contacts. Moreover, the rest of the populace considered the purchasing power of the Deutsche Mark and the higher quality of Western products quite desirable.[82] Although ugly right-wing extremism did occasionally flare up, the extent of irredentist chauvinism remained remarkably low during the period of division.

The long-term consequences of these collective learning processes in the postwar period were thus a fluctuating sense of German identity that might be defined by the contradictory concept of a "postnational nation." On the one hand, the term suggests a clear distancing from previous nationalism, whose destructive effects could not be denied by even the most committed patriots. Aiding this process was undoubtedly an accelerating internationalization brought on by mass consumption, popular culture, and tourism, which broadened the horizons of the leading strata and rendered their mind-set more cosmopolitan. Yet on the other hand, the concept of postnationalism might also imply the recovery of a collective feeling of self-esteem fostered by the economic miracle and the growing identification of the populace with the stability and civility of the Bonn Republic—that is, with all of the things implied by the social democratic campaign slogan of the 1970s, "The German Model." Finally, the contradictory nature of the term recalls the reunification mandate that was reaffirmed by the German Supreme Court: namely, that dual statehood had left the national question unresolved.[83]

The Nation as Burden

Instead of serving as a source for collective pride, as is the case in the United States, the "nation" has remained a rather traumatic point of reference in Germany, even after reunification. The difficulty of generating the same enthusiasm for celebrating unification on October 3rd as a national holiday as for the commemoration of the storming of the Bastille on July 14th in France attests to the deep uncertainty that Germans have in dealing with their own identity.[84] Such unease is not, however, just the product of a widespread sense that the nation-state in general is in crisis at the beginning of the twenty-first century due to the challenges of globalization, international terrorism, and the like.[85] Rather, it is the result of underlying feelings of guilt for the immeasurable suffering of both world wars, the ethnic cleansing of Slavs, and the extermination of Jews, as well as the enslavement of the continent, which have led many self-critical Germans to equate the nation-state with barbarism. Both the aggressive nationalism of young skinheads and the acute lack of self-trust among intellectuals are indications that the issue of national identity has not yet really come to rest in Germany.

In the long-term perspective of the twenty-first century, such a problematization of the nation might be counted as a success of the fundamental process of denationalization that occurred in the postwar period. The racist excesses of Nazism, whose murderous character only became completely clear after its downfall, discredited the nationalism in whose name they claimed to act. No doubt, this transformation was propelled by the denazification imposed by the Allies and carried out with the help of German anti-Fascists. But arguably more important was the collective rethinking that the populace undertook itself in the wake of the utter collapse of the Third Reich. In May 1945 the mayor of Bremen, Theodor Spitta, ascribed the contempt that former followers developed for the Nazi Party to the fact that "the people feel lied to and betrayed" because the "wonder weapons" remained ineffective, the Nazi bigwigs had proven to be cowardly profiteers, and the "wasteful, pointless sacrifice of people and cities" failed to stave off defeat. Because Hitler lacked "any religious and moral grounding and responsibility," his policy achieved the exact opposite of its stated goals: "Hitler strove for a greater Germany of all Germans; the result is the destruction of the German empire and the division of Germany."[86]

By "overcoming nationalism," the older generation attempted to salvage at least a chastened and defensive "sense of nationality," as author Ricarda Huch put it. The solidarity of the "community of destiny," constituted by survivors who understood themselves as victims due to their own suffering, provided the basis for easing the consequences of war through welfare provisions. Because right-wing revanchism, which sought the restoration of the borders of 1937, failed to attract a large following after the second defeat, moderate politicians concentrated on salvaging what was left of German statehood by opposing any further revisions of the border and pushing for the reintegration of the Saarland. In time, the emotional rhetoric of reunification emanating from both the East and West German successor states exhausted itself, since the disunity of the victorious powers condemned it to ineffectiveness as long as the contending camps chose not to give up any asset that might grant the other side an advantage. But perhaps more than anything else, the concept of the nation carried a negative connotation because it tended to be employed, as in the question of reparations, to justify demands for undoing the damage wrought by Nazi crimes.[87]

The intellectual efforts of the younger generation to escape their national identity after 1945 were not, on the whole, any more successful, since the stigma of being German was difficult to cast off. To be sure, German politicians could offer their services to their respective occupation power as "star pupils," not only by toeing their ideological line but also by largely adopting their lifestyle. Moreover, the Europeanization of their self-image, which entailed the transfer of emotional attachments to an emerging Europe, was undoubtedly a constructive contribution to the economic and political integration of the Old Continent. Still, such a negative coding of nationalism—45 percent of respondents were not proud to be Germans—was not understood by other democracies that did not feel the same compulsion to separate themselves from their own past and cast off their identity. The seemingly endless number of symposia that sought to discover a German identity devoid of nationalism often garnered little more than half-hearted smiles from abroad. Ironically, the tense efforts of German intellectuals to gain some "distance from the national legacy" seemed to have become a peculiarly German stance.[88]

From a historical standpoint, this unease raises the central question whether a democratic patriotism can develop that will reconcile allegiance to the nation with a civilized commitment to human rights. The reunification of 1989–1990 could be an important precondition for joining the idea of unity with the concept of freedom, since the return of a shrunken nation-state with recognized borders and without minorities beyond them renders an irredentist radical nationalism superfluous. A further prerequisite might be the intellectual recognition of the need to establish a bond to the political system that would be based on loyalty to the Basic Law, but which also includes a certain feeling of a self-worth that would remain open to other cultures. The program for uniting democracy with patriotism that has been advocated by such different figures as Eastern theologian Richard Schröder, CDU politician Wolfgang Schäuble, and Western historian Heinrich-August Winkler seeks to offer a solution by trying to perpetuate the legacy of the revolutions of 1848 and 1919.[89] At present, therefore, Germans face the challenge of continuing to heed the dangers posed by radical nationalism while also developing a more positive relationship with their own country.

CHAPTER 3

Rejecting the Plan

In early 1945, even the carefully shielded economy was sucked into the maelstrom of the Third Reich's collapse. Behind the rapidly retreating lines, both managers and workers had to decide whether they should heed the order by the private secretary of the Führer, Martin Bormann, and destroy the country's infrastructure or, instead, safeguard the basic conditions necessary for survival after the collapse. As bombing and ground fighting took a heavy toll on water and power plants, energy service began to give out. The disruption of transport rendered food supplies scarce, especially in the cities, with long lines forming and panic buying leading to widespread waste of what little remained. Unprotected depots were plundered by locals and foreign workers alike. As commerce ground to a halt, the mail was no longer delivered, radio stations ceased broadcasting, and newspapers discontinued publishing. Finally, as arms production ended, finding regular work became futile. A local official, Theodor Spitta, noted an acute "shortage of coal and coffins" in Bremen. "The conditions of the economy, currency, and payment are going to be disrupted for a long time, and perhaps even destroyed" altogether.[1] The same suffering that Germans had imposed on the peoples of Europe came crashing down on them with even greater vengeance.

For their part, the allied victors had not yet figured out how to deal with the economic potential of their defeated enemy, which had actually increased during the war. Because the Nazi war economy represented a contradictory mixture of state compulsion and private initiative, analyses of the problem and suggestions for correction were less clear than in the case of militarism or National Socialism. For the leadership of the Soviet Union and Western Marxists, the roots of this unprecedented evil were quite plain, since according to the Komintern definition, fascism represented the highest form of imperialistic monopoly capitalism. In addition to the reparations required for reconstruction, long-term security from further German aggression therefore demanded a fundamental transformation of the social and economic system which in practice would be tantamount to the abolition of capitalism. The only mitigating consideration was that domestic and international alliance policy suggested that these long-term goals should be approached gradually. In its first public appeal in June 1945, the Communist Party of Germany (KPD) thus demanded "the expropriation of all of the assets of the Nazi bigwigs and war criminals," as well as the "liquidation of large landholdings."[2]

For the Americans, by contrast, the problem of the German economy was more complex since they faced a choice between a fundamental reduction or a more limited restructuring. To prevent a third world war, Treasury Secretary Henry Morgenthau, banker Bernard M. Baruch, and Senator Harvey Kilgore proposed a punitive course that aimed at destroying Germany's ability to wage war through a comprehensive deindustrialization: "We must keep Germany—and this applies equally to Japan—from reestablishing herself as a great industrial nation ready to wage war."[3] Arguing against such a harsh policy were more pragmatic voices in business circles and in the military government. These moderates thought that heavily punishing the Germans "is simply not good economics," since transforming a reduced Germany, which had been unable to feed itself even before the war, back into an agricultural economy, would ruin the country completely. If that were to happen, American taxpayers would have to pay the price, as the recovery of Germany's neighbors required the restoration of the largest European economy. Such economic subjugation also contravened the ideals of the Atlantic Charter, not to mention the United States' own interest in free trade. The *New York Times* thus advocated a compromise instead that "would both serve Europe's reconstruction and keep the German menace within bounds."[4]

Despite the ubiquity of hunger and privation in the memoir literature, the issues of outside economic intervention and internal learning processes have figured only marginally in the historiography of the postwar period. On the one hand, this deficit can be attributed to conceptual ambiguity, since the allied decisions refer interchangeably to deindustrialization, decartelization, dismantlement, and reparations, without ever settling on a single term.[5] On the other hand, scholarship has turned its attention to different problems such as the failure to nationalize industry after 1945, which has been interpreted, especially by critical intellectuals, as a "lost opportunity."[6] In contrast, economic historians have concentrated more on the question of continuity, thereby marginalizing the influence of the Marshall Plan or of currency reform on the resumption of economic growth in West Germany.[7] Research on the Soviet Zone has instead identified the more difficult start-up conditions of the planned economy, the effects of the massive expropriation policy, and the coerced changeover of elites as the key issues that contributed to the weakening of the German economy.[8]

The concept of civil society, however, points to a tension-filled connection between the economic order and the political system, since it delineates a space for self-realization through the pursuit of material interests. According to historian Jürgen Kocka, under the influence of industrialization this realm was "[re]defined as a system of necessities, labor, the market, and particular interests, [that] is [both] opposed and subordinated to the state—a sphere of middle-class dominance."[9] The contrast between the construction of a social market economy in the West and the establishment of a socialist-planned economy in the East nonetheless offers a grand social experiment which allows the effectiveness of different ideological systems to be compared in almost textbook fashion: How did the reversion to a market economy, as was demanded by the United States, proceed in comparison with the central planning supported by the Soviet Union? What were the causes, course, and consequences of the "economic miracle" in the Federal Republic and its, albeit somewhat belated, repetition in the GDR? Why did real existing socialism fail as an economic system, and what are the limits of the social market economy for global competition?[10]

Forced Restructuring

In the summer of 1945 the victorious powers confronted the challenge of rendering the threat of Germany's armament production harmless. Given the prior enslavement of Europe and the subsequent Nazi defeat, the problem of converting the German war economy to civilian purposes was especially acute, as the process had to be executed by the Allied Control Council. Its decisions, moreover, were made against the backdrop of negative experiences with Weimar's successful circumvention of the disarmament clauses of the Versailles Treaty, its secret cooperation in weapons development with the Soviet Union, and the open rearmament of the Third Reich, which, in spite of many improvisations, gave the impression of long-term planning and determined action.[11] Added to these concerns were the traumas of inflation and the Great Depression, which made government action, including the nationalization of heavy industry, appear attractive, not just to Communists but to moderate intellectuals as well. Motivated more from such fears than from knowledge of the extent of actual destruction, the Allied planners thus recommended drastic intervention.

The aim of the "economic principles" first suggested in directive JCS 1067 and spelled out more concretely in the Potsdam Agreement was to weaken Germany's economy permanently. Eliminating the German war potential first required that "the production of weapons, munitions, instruments of war as well as all types of aircraft and ocean-going ships [be] forbidden and stopped." Strict supervision was ordered for another category of "metals, chemicals, machines, and other such things" that were indirectly necessary for a war economy. Likewise, provisions were made either to remove nonvital productive capacity as a form of reparations or to destroy it altogether. At the same time, the Allies called for a thorough decartelization so as "to eliminate the existing inordinate concentration of economic power" that could be found in cartels, syndicates, and trusts. Instead, the main emphasis ought "to be placed on the development of the agricultural economy and the peaceful industries of the domestic economy." The 20 billion dollars owed in reparations ought not to consist "of cash payments" but should be accomplished "through the delivery of capital goods, war material, and finished products." The English magazine the *Economist* commented perceptively that "this policy, taken literally, would result in the large-scale de-industrialization of Germany."[12]

In the Soviet zone of occupation, the dismantling of German industry began even before the war had ended, as the Russian leadership considered the breakup of industrial facilities "just another form of warfare against the hated enemy." An understandable reaction to the Nazi "scorched-earth" policy carried out by the retreating Wehrmacht, these Soviet actions also aimed at amassing war booty, so as to demonstrate materially the extent of the victory both in Germany and back home. A summary report from the end of 1946, found in Russian archives after the collapse of the Soviet Union, provides information concerning the dismantling of over 3,000 German companies and offers shocking evidence of the extent of the destruction, which annihilated entire industries. While this process did aim to demilitarize Germany economically, it had as much to do with the reconstruction of the Soviet economy, which visibly profited from the massive transfer despite some misallocation of the captured material. This gigantic pillaging, which reduced the East German industrial plant by one quarter of its former size, only stopped once the Soviets realized that their emerging satellite state, if it were to develop at all, could not be stripped of its entire economic base.[13]

According to the Potsdam Agreement, the Western Allies also undertook a series of drastic measures to reduce any industrial capacity that exceeded "the necessary requirements of the German population and the occupation powers." Thus on July 24, the U.S. military government occupied the factories of the chemical giant IG Farben and placed them in trust in order to break its "monopolistic control of German industry" and to eliminate "its potential for war."[14] In early September, the English arrested forty leading industrialists, including Otto Springorum, with the intention of destroying the coal syndicate in the Ruhr region and holding its leaders personally responsible for their part in war production. In December, they incarcerated another group of eighty-four iron and steel industrialists, who had supported and profited enormously from Hitler's conduct of the war. In addition, the confiscation of large assets sought to demonstrate to the Anglo-American public the seriousness with which the Allies were pursuing the denazification of German warmongers, who were even more difficult to locate in the private sector than in public administration. By requiring numerous permits for companies to restart their production, the Allies showed their resolve to tighten their control over the economic core of the German potential for war.[15]

Although many observers feared that Germany might quickly regain its strength, the economic reality during the first months of peace was anything but rosy. U.S. correspondent Gladwyn Hill witnessed bleak scenes: "The thousand great smokestacks of the Ruhr Valley that once belched defiance against the world now stand lifeless and cold. Grass now grows in the streets" of the city centers, between 50 and 80 percent destroyed, where soldiers and refugees crowded alongside residents. "The water systems generally are working, but some of them only on fire hoses," while sewage did not drain away. "There is no firewood," and only occasionally some coal, despite "the policy of not pampering the Germans." At best, the food supply functioned at a bare minimum that might be sufficient for a disaster area in the United States, and the 800 to 1,500 daily calories allotted to each person were "really only about half enough." Because of the enormous demand for clean-up work and creeping inflation, a labor shortage quickly arose, since "the man who was a bank teller is no use as a miner." Hill's graphic report concluded with the observation: "Under such circumstances, likewise, any menacing industrial revival in the Ruhr is at present inconceivable." The U.S. military governor himself dryly conceded that "less than 10% of industrial concerns" were still up and running.[16]

On the basis of a realistic appraisal of the situation, economic experts pleaded for a more moderate course that would rest on control and structural transformation of the economy rather than on extensive deindustrialization. While various commissions continued to draw up lists of entire branches of industry slated for dismantling, more knowledgeable observers called the "reduction of Germany to [an] agricultural state . . . an economic absurdity," which would have negative consequences for Europe. Only a halfway functioning economy, they argued, would be able to finance the occupation, contribute to the war against Japan, produce reparations, and adequately feed its population.[17] To bring Germany's standard of living up to the level of its neighbors, in early October a pragmatic group of OMGUS economic advisors therefore suggested that exports be resumed and steel production expanded. They stressed the importance of reviving the economy so that it would not become a long-term burden to be shouldered by American taxpayers.[18] The Allied economic plan, passed after lengthy negotiations in early 1946, thus represented a compromise between economic disarmament, demands for reparations, and the maintenance of "significant foundations of livelihood" for the German populace.[19]

The first step toward restructuring the relationships of economic power was the judicial prosecution of economic policy makers and prominent industrialists. Five of the chief defendants at the Nuremberg trials stood accused of organizing slave labor (Fritz Sauckel, Albert Speer), pillaging occupied territories (Walther Funk), making financial war preparations (Hjalmar Schacht), and producing weapons (Gustav Krupp von Bohlen und Halbach). Only Sauckel was hanged. Speer and Funk were given life sentences, while Schacht received a full acquittal, and Krupp was released due to ill health. Beginning in February 1947, the "Flick Trial" against the owner of the "largest private enterprise in the Reich's iron, steel, and armaments industry" for participating in "Aryanization," using forced labor, pillaging defeated competitors, and supporting the SS proved only partly successful as well. While Friedrich Flick, the directors of IG-Farben, and Alfried Krupp all received medium-length prison sentences, most leading businessmen were able to reclaim considerable influence after their terms ended. Therefore many guilty industrialists were only taken out of commission temporarily. But because the West adhered to the idea of private property, no collective transformation of elites occurred. Instead, business leaders were only compelled to return to more humane methods and to accept the loss of their predominance over large segments of the European continent.[20]

In the progressive tradition of "trust busting," Americans also attempted to transform the basic structure of the economy by breaking up large companies. However, the inter-Allied Commission for the Decentralization of the German Economy, initiated in August 1945, found it difficult to define exactly "what represents excessive concentration of power and unfair advantage, that is, what generally should be allowed and what should be prohibited." The English, for example, considered the Soviet suggestion to break up factories with 3,000 or more workers and a yearly volume of 25 million Reichsmark impractical, and their objection prevented the passage of a common law by the Allied Control Council.[21] Despite German protests against the cutting of "organically grown connections," the Allies succeeded in breaking up some of the largest industrial concerns, and, as result, strengthened competition. For example, IG Farben was split up into the Bayer, Höchst, and BSAF companies. Likewise, the highly intertwined coal and steel industries were carved up into twenty-three independent steel producers and dozens of collieries. The financial industry was also not spared, as three of Germany's largest banks were transformed into separate companies, though some of them partially recombined later on. While the leading cigarette producer Reemtsma took it upon itself to split up, the electric giants Siemens and Bosch under more liberal leadership managed to avoid restructuring.[22]

The prohibition of cartels, syndicates, trusts, and other attempts to limit competition was also intended as a bid to force open the corporate encrustation of economic structures. In contrast to Anglo-American free trade, a cartel-friendly practice had prevailed in Germany since 1897 that saw economic agreements as necessary correctives to fluctuations of the market and as advantages for international competition. Because these forms of state-sanctioned cooperation among the different branches of the economy served as the basis for organizing the war economy in both world wars, they were a particularly sharp thorn in the Allies' side. In February 1947 the American law No. 56 thus prohibited "all forms of agreements or joint ventures of people, whose purpose or effect consists of limiting internal or world trade or any other economic activity, of promoting monopolistic control over those areas, or of limiting access to the internal or world market." As a result, price fixing, agreements on market share, production allocations, patent arrangements, and the like were forbidden in order to induce freer competition.[23] But due to marketing difficulties, the Allied holding company "North German Iron and Steel Control" was forced to tolerate the revival of the Ruhr coal syndicate well into the 1950s.

Initiated somewhat later, the dismantling of the industrial concerns in the Anglo-American Zone aimed more at delivering material reparations to the Soviet Union and seventeen other countries than at a structural transformation of the economy. An October 1947 list that resulted from long allied negotiations targeted 682 factories, 302 of which were part of the war industry and had in part already been torn down. While Adenauer grumbled about the "pillaging of German industry," its representatives argued that compensation for the damage Germany had inflicted could only be accomplished through production: "It contradicts economic logic to rob us of the possibility to work by reducing the number of jobs and removing machines and tools."[24] When bulldozers began turning up at those factories that had been slated for demolition, ugly confrontations developed, as demonstrating workers beat up collaborators and resisted so strongly that troops eventually had to intervene. While the French welcomed the tearing down of German war industries, commentators such as the leftist publisher Victor Gollancz and the émigré economist Gustav Stolper criticized the stubborn adherence to dismantlement because it impeded European recovery. Only after many objections from German politicians and tenacious arguments between Allied officials was the dismantling finally ended in December 1949. Although it left behind deep resentment within segments of the German population, the policy only demolished around 5 percent of the total industrial capacity in the West, significantly less than in the East.[25]

In the Soviet occupation zone, economic restructuring proceeded more radically, since, in the eyes of the SED, the middle class had "forfeited its right to property" through its cooperation with the Nazi regime. Along with considerably higher reparations to the Soviet Union, a fundamental upheaval in property relationships and in the structure of the economy took place that sought not only to guarantee peace by dismantling war industries but also to eliminate large landowners and industrialists as a social class. By September 1945, rigorous land reform under the slogan "The Junkers' Land in the Peasants' Hands" began. It stipulated that all landholdings over 250 acres must be distributed to "new peasants" such as former agricultural laborers and expellees from the East.

In the wake of a plebiscite against "war criminals" and "corporate overlords" in June 1946, all owners of large concerns in Saxony were likewise stripped of their possessions, and their factories were nationalized as "the property of the people." At the same time, the foundations of a planned economy were laid as a way of guaranteeing reparation payments, managing shortages, and furthering reconstruction. As a result, a fundamental transfer of elites took place in the Soviet Zone that effectively replaced the propertied middle class with a new socialist leadership stratum.[26] By contrast, the land reform that had also been planned in the West eventually stalled.[27]

Even if some members of the occupation bureaucracies were still working to weaken Germany, this original objective was gradually eclipsed by the growing competition between the different economic systems. The immediate seizure of military researchers and their relocation to the United States and the Soviet Union, where they contributed significantly to the development of weapons technology, was an early sign that the victorious powers did not really trust each other.[28] The polemics leveled by the SED against the half-hearted decartelization and decentralization in the Western Zones as well as American warnings of "democratic appearance and dictatorial reality" in the forced expropriations of the East, pointed clearly to an erosion of the common agenda.[29] Although each side similarly demanded that the defeated enemy be economically disarmed, the divergent strategies of a radical, anticapitalist transformation and a more limited correction within a capitalist framework that reflected the respective ideologies of the superpowers proved to be ultimately incompatible. The Cold War placed a higher priority on confirming the legitimacy of each system and on taking advantage of the potential in each part than on the joint exploitation of Germany.

During the first five years of the postwar period, priorities thus shifted slowly from stripping Germany of its economic power to reviving a transformed economy within the victors' respective sphere of control. To be sure, the Nazi war industry, parts of which initially continued to work for the various occupation powers, was eventually broken up. Even airplanes and ships could no longer be manufactured. But with the 1946 speech of American Secretary of State James F. Byrnes, the fusion of the British and American Zones, and Germany's inclusion in the Marshall Plan, Western policy shifted from reducing the standard of living to embracing gradual recovery. In August 1947 the three Western Allies released a second plan for German industry that, by raising quotas for steel (to 19.7 million tons) and coal production, signaled a change of heart in favor of a revival of the country's economic potential for peaceful purposes.[30] In response, the Soviet Union was forced to end its direct removal of German economic resources and to mask any further exploitation of its zone by creating joint Soviet-German companies (SAGs). Nonetheless, the rebuilding had to proceed within fundamentally changed conditions of the economy, as determined by competing ideologies in both the West and the East.

Return to the Market

In view of the extent of the destruction, any hope of an early reconstruction appeared optimistic and unrealistic in the summer of 1945. Nevertheless, even before the war ended, experts in industry, government, and the universities had attempted to free themselves from Hitler's fantasies of Armageddon and make provisions for the time after the impending defeat. These often secret discussions, however, drew different conclusions from the experiences of the inflation, Great Depression, and war economy: Middle-class anti-Fascists, like the Social Democrat Viktor Agartz, called for the nationalization of large concerns, so as to strip authoritarian industrialists of their power in the process. In contrast, a small minority of neoliberals in the universities centered around Walter Eucken, called *Ordoliberale*, advocated unleashing the energies of the free market, arguing that the only way to spark new economic dynamism was by lifting onerous controls. Lacking a guilty conscience, most leading entrepreneurs were willing to continue working within the framework of their familiar cartels. Only a few outsiders such as Wilhelm Röpke, the Austrian-born economist in Geneva, saw the defeat as a chance for a truly new social and economic beginning that would move beyond collectivism.[31]

To guarantee survival in the interim, the reconstituted local administrations, in cooperation with the occupation powers, continued a kind of command economy. In cities such as Bremen, the collapse had simplified the task by focusing on the provision of basic human needs. "The ruins lying all around [are] sad. Residents had to remove the piles of rubble in the streets." Above all, Deputy Mayor Spitta thought the municipal public works had to be repaired in order to get electricity, water, and gas up and running again. "The houses are nearly all windowless; either they have gaping holes or their window openings are boarded up." To shelter the homeless masses, the ruins needed somehow to be rendered livable again: "Shops are practically nonexistent; there are a few bakeries with long lines of people, otherwise there's nothing [left] to buy." Since stocks were exhausted, new food supplies had to be organized. "For the most part, the offices don't look like they're in business; in the factories mostly cleanup work is being done." New jobs also needed to be created. Many dejected people thus asked themselves: "Does what remains of life have any point at all?"[32]

Individuals found themselves suddenly thrust into a situation in which the "law of the wolves" prevailed and normal rules no longer seemed to apply in the struggle for survival. To leave the ranks of those wandering the country and just to have a place to stay, it was necessary to gain a permit of residency from some local authority. Those buildings that had not been destroyed needed to be made temporarily inhabitable by repairing roofs and installing new windows. Because of Allied troop-quartering and allocation of refugees it was "an existence in the most cramped space with much aggravation. I had to share my bed with my brother," one youth later remembered. "The official from the housing office inspected constantly, always seeking to requisition living space in order to house the many homeless." Because coal extraction had slowed nearly to a halt, "heating fuel was especially sought after," so that many trees were chopped down and coal was even stolen from moving trains. Many an affluent German later remembered: "Never before was I so tortured by cold" as during the first two winters after the war. More than once, the newspapers reported that some malnourished people "had frozen to death in their beds."[33]

Obtaining something to eat was just as difficult, since the food supply had collapsed as a result of the damaged transportation system and administrative chaos. Memoirs are full of descriptions of such hardships: "The supply situation became increasingly catastrophic. There was almost no food left to buy. Rations were reduced time and again. Standing in long lines was [just] a part of everyday life." Because necessity is the mother of invention, many families fell back on earlier "peasant traditions" and attempted to churn butter or make preserves from fruit themselves. "Every square meter of their gardens was put to use. Even tobacco was planted, dried, and cured." In addition, people took foraging trips to the countryside, where they exchanged family silver, carpets, and even oil paintings for potatoes and eggs. Given the shortages, substitute materials also enjoyed a boom. "There was cornbread, yellow and sticky, and the unforgettable hot drink," malt coffee. "Hollow cheeks became the trademark of the Germans. All the bellies had disappeared. The Germans were close to living in a Stone Age." Only the school meals provided by the Quakers and the CARE packets helped to bridge the period of greatest hunger.[34]

With steady work in such short supply, the Germans' efforts aimed above all to safeguard their basic survival needs. While there was an enormous demand for clean-up, repair, and start-up labor, regular employment was paid with valueless money, so that the effort hardly seemed worthwhile. In contrast, temporary work, for which people received payment in kind, flourished. As a result, a considerable amount of economic activity shifted to the black market, where people were able to obtain goods that were otherwise hard to find by paying exorbitant prices or bartering with cigarettes. Since many desirable items, such as cigarettes and coffee, were available primarily in Allied stores like the PX, where soldiers shopped, some of their supplies were passed on to the German population through a "lively trade" in souvenirs such as postage stamps. "For a Leica [camera] you got half a pig," noted one young black marketeer. "Almost everybody stole and pushed their stolen wares in public. Only those who wheeled and dealt could survive in this terrible time."[35] Repeated by the thousands, such experiences of relapsing into a primitive barter economy pointed to both the opportunities and dangers of an unregulated market.

The starting conditions for economic recovery were, nevertheless, not as bad as they may have seemed at the time, because the bulk of industry had survived the bombing far better than private homes. To begin with, the expansion of the war economy had created new productive capacity that, once converted, could be put to use for peaceful, consumer purposes. Moreover, many factories and plants had been repaired, often several times, after the Allied air attacks, so that a remarkable number of machines found in the bombed-out factories still functioned. In addition, the country continued to dispose of the technical skills of engineers, the marketing knowledge of management, and, above all, the manpower of the soldiers returning home from captivity. Despite the enormous suffering that they undoubtedly caused, some of the social problems faced by the defeated country also offered new long-term opportunities for its battered economy. Although at first a terrible burden, the large number of refugees and expellees, for example, added many people willing to work as well as possessing much needed technical skills. Finally, the occupation powers also assisted the recovery by importing their own food supplies so as to guarantee the basic needs of the population.[36]

Such enormous difficulties could only be overcome through common efforts aimed at allowing a rudimentary recovery to get under way. The removal of some 13.5 million cubic meters of rubble from the center of Cologne alone took over a year, to say nothing of the makeshift restoration of canals, bridges over the Rhine, and the central train station. As if the cleanup in the factories had not been hard enough, "the chief problems only emerged when actual production was restarted," because the delivery of raw materials slowed and energy supplies remained unreliable. Time and again, frustrating bottlenecks thwarted a revival of activity. If the mines, for example, managed to extract sufficient coal, there would be "no rolling stock" available to transport it to either factories or homes. Likewise, supplying foodstuffs proved particularly difficult, since domestic production was unable to satisfy the needs of a population whose numbers had rapidly grown with the influx of refugees. Rationing of the shortages, moreover, led to a great deal of injustice, with some groups and areas inevitably getting more than others. Thus despite much hard work, by 1946 industrial production had only reached 50 to 55 percent of its prewar level.[37]

The "hunger winter" of 1946–1947 showed that the economy remained caught in a "deadly cycle," in which an interlocking series of barriers seemed to economists to prevent a genuine recovery. "All plans and measures failed due to the fact that the revival of mining, the extraction of additional coal, and, by extension, the production of more steel, fertilizer, and [other] economic products did not succeed." In part, the Allies had themselves to blame, because arrests of industrialists, continued dismantling, restriction of production, bureaucratic export permits, tightening of the dollar exchange, and other such policies were, to say the least, hardly conducive to stimulating the economy. Under the pressure of denazification and ideologically split by repoliticization, German administrators likewise remained confused about their areas of responsibility and proved unable to do much to foster an economic revival. The freezing of prices for goods on the 1944 level, moreover, did not prevent a further depreciation of currency, which pushed the economy into nonmonetary forms of compensation and channeled what little buying power there was into the black market instead of into strengthening legitimate demand.[38]

Finally, the crisis of the command economy triggered a fundamental change of course away from Allied control and toward the restoration of a free market. The failure of the coal program of early 1947—worked out by English and American advisors inspired by the policies of the Labour Party and the New Deal—motivated U.S. military governor Lucius Clay, who himself had some business ties, to move toward a policy "aimed at establishing as soon as possible a self-sustaining German economy." On July 25, 1947, the convocation of a bi-zonal economic council in Frankfurt offered German politicians "a historic chance" for an active say in the nationwide recovery of their own economy. A further step toward "overcoming the emergency" was taken when the Western Zones were officially included in the Marshall Plan, as the European Recovery Program (ERP) placed Germany's revival within a wider European framework while also offering the prospect of loans to help the economy get off the ground. The final spur came in January 1948 when Johannes Semler was removed as the director of the bi-zonal economic council for criticizing the failed Allied price controls. This firing opened the way for Ludwig Erhard, largely unknown until that time.[39]

In his very first press conference in April 1948, the economics professor from Franconia announced nothing less than "a change of course in economic policy that aims to promote consumer industries. An increase in the production of consumer goods is vital, as people must be offered something [attractive] in return for their labor." Though by no means a dogmatic neoliberal, Erhard had become a free market advocate as a result of experiencing the inefficiency of the Nazi war economy. Even amidst the chaos of the postwar period he placed greater weight on individual "drive and personal initiative"—that is, on "free competition as both an incentive for and measure of achievement" than on governmental compulsion. Still, he continued to recognize the state's key role in creating the conditions for competition, including a free market and unregulated prices. But it was Erhard's extraordinary realization "that our economy must experience a fundamental conversion at the structural level" that enabled him to risk shifting toward "a market economy with free pricing" from "the state command economy with regulatory intervention."[40]

Due to the inflation caused by the Nazi armaments program, the Allies had long discussed the need for a currency reform, only postponing it because of mutual disputes. Although advocates of the market economy, such as Erhard confidant Alfred Müller-Armack collided with supporters of state guidance like Günter Keiser as preparations were made for a drastic devaluation of the currency, the economic advisory council nevertheless proposed a compromise solution. Several of its recommendations, including the reintroduction of price mechanisms and the lifting of controls over production, raw materials, and foreign trade were, in fact, quite liberal. Wages, moreover, were to be negotiated on the basis of contracts, while the abuse of monopolies was to be prevented. The council's more socially oriented proposals sought to maintain the rationing of foodstuffs and rent controls, to keep capital from fleeing abroad, and to steer the economy in such a way as to avoid cyclical upheavals. In a combative speech on June 21, Erhard justified releasing prices of consumer goods as a way of giving the economy an initial push to break its paralysis. Despite the devaluation of the old Reichsmark by 1:10, which wiped out savings and debts, the *Rheinische Post* welcomed the introduction of the new D-Mark with the headline: "Honest Money for Honest Work!"[41]

Although this new currency consisted of "ugly blue bills printed in the USA," the distribution of 40 DM per person marked a crucial turning point in the lives of millions of people who would fondly remember its magical powers for decades to come. When the student Hans Herzog heard Erhard announce that all ration cards and commodity coupons were henceforth abolished, he thought that he must be "dreaming; after all, there was still strict rationing among the victorious European powers. . . . Could he be right? No, not ever, completely impossible, and yet something sensational began overnight." The same experience was repeated millions of times: "The shop windows, which up to now had been completely bare, blossomed. You could buy from butchers to bakers, grocers to linen stores, and soon the still valid coupons were no longer required." Almost instantly, the black market collapsed, because the choice of products grew larger and larger and nobody wanted to part with their new DM bills. "Almost everyone was poor, and many very poor, but from that second on, no one needed to go hungry again. That was an enormous improvement." Judging from the amazed comments of the populace, unleashing the market appeared nothing less than miraculous, which restored optimism and released new energies.[42]

The "shop window wonder" signaled the beginning of an economic revival that got under way with the new value of the money and the step-by-step lifting of controls. For individuals, the loss of their savings meant that "everyone [had] to roll up their sleeves from one day to the next" in order to "earn money at a secure job." Now "that money once again had buying power," it paid off to return to regular employment, to lend an energetic hand to the reconstruction, and to begin planning for the long-term.[43] Once people were earning money with real purchasing power, production of consumer goods also became profitable again. To be sure, the changeover was accompanied by a series of difficulties, as the unregulated prices initially climbed, unemployment increased, and the "previous solidarity . . . suddenly developed a rift." But in exchange, Alexander Dicke noticed that "there were once again many things that we had previously had to do without and which we desperately needed."[44] More than any amount of propaganda ever could, this visible change demonstrated the motivational power of price mechanisms and market competition which reversed the downward cycle of the economy.

The subsequent currency reform in the Soviet Zone had a considerably smaller impact as it favored centralized planning and leveling social distinctions. On the one hand, the Soviet model of Stalinist five-year plans for industrialization pointed in the direction of an economy tightly controlled by the state. On the other, the SED understood itself as the "party of the rebuilding of the German economy" by way of expropriating the property of large landowners and industrialists, who had been branded as "war criminals and war profiteers." To help overcome "the economic chaos" of the postwar period, the Communists embarked on a strategy of "expropriation rather than deconcentration" while at the same time seeking "a better coordination of planning and control." To harmonize the diverging measures of the different Eastern states, in 1947 a German Economic Commission (DWK) was created that mapped out the objectives of an initial plan for the entire zonal economy. Rather than putting its faith in the power of the market, the SED moved toward "a comprehensive planning of the economy so as to utilize all energies sensibly, not to waste anything, and to steer all raw materials and every finished product to where it is most urgently needed and will be used most effectively."[45]

The consequences of this ideological policy decision for a planned economy were rather dire. While it did help the economy to grow faster until 1948 amid more difficult initial conditions, further reconstruction proceeded more slowly and remained at a much lower level than in the West. Following the establishment of the DKW, nationalized businesses could no longer operate independently, but rather had to wait for instructions that were filtered through the main administration for industry and the boards of the people's companies (VEBs). Rather than increasing the production of consumer goods, the first two-year plan followed the Stalinist model and concentrated on expanding the steel and coal industries—that is, the heavy industrial base. The result was an economy of shortages that even the party could not deny ("nobody claimed that these rations were sufficient") forcing it to encourage greater efforts in food production. To channel the mounting displeasure of East German workers, the party paper *Neues Deutschland* published endless essays on the putative famine in the West, the return of Nazi bosses, and the half-hearted nature of the changes in the industrial structure.[46] But for all of the SED's propaganda, it became ever clearer in the 1950s that the social experiment of the planned economy lagged far behind the emerging free market in the FRG.

Because of the frightening example offered by the East and American prevarication, the initially strong movement for nationalizing industry in the Western Zones also came to naught. Citing the collaboration of business owners with the Nazis, union leaders called for the immediate introduction of a "planned economy, socialization [of factories], and co-management" of labor. Likewise, the SPD considered "heavy industry especially suitable for a public takeover." In its Ahlen Program of February 1947 even the CDU advocated "the nationalization of mining" as a step toward a "fundamental restructuring of the economy."[47] In a few states such as Berlin, joint initiatives of the SPD and KPD demanded the adoption of nationalization in the constitution, a proposal that was approved in the elections for the Hessian Diet in December 1946 by a two-thirds majority. The English, who controlled the Ruhr region, were at first willing "to support a socialized economy in Germany," but the neoliberal U.S. military governor Clay delayed its implementation. Owing to the resistance of the business lobby as well as Konrad Adenauer, in March 1947 the Diet in North-Rhine-Westphalia voted against holding a referendum on the "expropriation of the Ruhr furnaces." Though advocates of nationalization did not admit defeat, they achieved little more than the right to nominate representatives to the company board in heavy industry.[48]

Open conflict between the two economic strategies erupted in June 1948 in Berlin, when the city government decided to introduce both new currencies in the divided capital. Soviet Marshall Sokolovskii responded to the Western currency reform by blockading the access roads to the city in order to maintain the economic unity of the Western part with the Eastern occupation Zone. The risky decision by the United States to supply the Western sectors of the capital through an airlift and the images of the "raisin bombers," flying in every minute, represented "only the material form of an intellectual and political struggle in which every Berliner passionately took sides."[49] Even though not all supplies from the East were cut, the living conditions in the two halves of the city functioned as competing alternatives of a market and planned economy, between which people had to decide. On the one hand were "the shop windows of East Berlin, either empty or filled with inferior goods," while on the other people could "now see many household appliances" in West Berlin stores "which had not been available for years." The complete fiasco of the East German currency in free competition with the D-Mark led the SPD to an overwhelming victory in the subsequent city council elections with 64 percent of the votes, while the CDU took another 19.4 percent, a clear vote in favor of the free market.[50]

Although the planned economy seemed a more radical response to economic crimes of the Nazis, it was the more limited correction of the industrial structure by the reintroduction of the market that eventually prevailed. In the end, the vaunted land reform and industrial expropriations in the East served only to maintain the political power of a minority dictatorship. The planned economy proved incomparably less productive and sustainable. Already in the short term, the limited policy of deconcentration and decartelization that was promoted by the U.S. military government and a minority of liberal economists in Germany against the majority of the populace, showed clearly superior results. A year after plunging headfirst into free competition "the miraculous effects of the DM" already appeared to have become self-evident, because a "sharp upward trend" in productivity immediately set in, pushing living standards back up to 85 percent of their prewar level. To be sure, the generous infusion of dollars, Erhard's selective deflationary policy, and social cushioning through the first equalization of burdens law all played an important part in the West's recovery.[51] Still, the populace considered, and not entirely incorrectly, the basic principle of individual initiative, in contrast to collective compulsion, to be responsible for the success.

The Social Market Economy

As a result of its spectacular achievements, the social market economy has so much become a pillar of the political culture of the Federal Republic that even ideological critics such as the SPD or the Greens have made peace with its basic principles. The accession of the new federal states in 1990 has yet again validated the efficacy of this economic system, though it continues to struggle with the consequences of reunification and the effects of globalization. This remarkable consensus, however, conceals the considerable difficulties which it had in establishing its legitimacy among consumers still unnerved by the black market, industrialists accustomed to collusion, and unions hoping for a wide-scale nationalization of industry. At the same time, the successful formula glossed over the tense relationship between the conflicting principles of market liberalism and the welfare state, thus allowing the mixture of components, which over time had changed considerably, to be largely forgotten.[52] How did the social market economy, in contrast to Marxist state planning, develop, and what were the central problems that it had to overcome?

The compromise solution of a competitive, but at the same time socially responsible, economy needed first and foremost to win over a skeptical public. It was not until July 1949 that the new term "social market economy" was laid down with the "Düsseldorf Principles" in the CDU platform: "By this the CDU understands a socially committed constitution of the economy which organizes the performance of free and capable people and yields the maximum economic benefit and social justice."[53] To counter SPD attempts to maintain rationing, Erhard vigorously defended the risk of allowing economic competition: "The demand for democratic freedom will [continue to] ring hollow as long as basic human rights to choose occupation and consumption freely are not recognized as inviolable and inalienable." Even so, the market also needed state regulation: "This freedom does not mean license, and it does not mean irresponsibility, but rather it means steady, obligatory devotion to the common weal." As an experienced marketing expert, Erhard even used advertising methods such as a comic strip, featuring a cute dachshund, to promote the market economy as a superior and ethical economic system.[54]

Aided by his cartel policy, Erhard also had to force free competition on heavy industry, which was accustomed to market collusion. By 1930, some 3,000 cartels had been formed as a way of fixing prices and allocating market share, which subsequently facilitated the Nazi war economy. Rather than lifting the American ban on cartels, Erhard consistently argued "that all market agreements, especially in the area of prices, aim ultimately at some kind of restriction of competition" and, as a result, harmed the consumer. Against the massive resistance of Fritz Berg, the chairman of League of German Industrialists (BDI), Erhard insisted on fostering more competition through a cartel law that he considered the "central principle" of the market economy, and, by extension, economic freedom.[55] Because of stiff parliamentary opposition, the passage of the law dragged on and on, but by allowing a few exceptions, Erhard was able to push the ban on cartels and the institution of a cartel office through the Federal Diet in 1957. Together with the return to world trade, facilitated by floating the D-Mark on international currency markets, the weakened cartel law became a cornerstone of economic liberalization in West Germany.[56]

Was the "social" part of the social market economy ever more than a fig leaf for the introduction of neoliberalism? In response to his critics on the left, Erhard insisted that "in significant areas of our economy, competition has had a beneficial effect, pushing it in the direction of an improvement of our people's living standards." Since this rise in prosperity did not reach everyone, the social policy makers in the CDU, driven by Catholic social doctrine, along with the chancellor, concerned with maintaining power, insisted on tempering the effects of competition through the introduction of tangible social benefits. As a result, the legislation on burden sharing was an important appeasement measure, which, by redistributing some of the wealth of those citizens who emerged unscathed from the war, made life for those parts of the population that had been especially hard-hit somewhat more bearable. Similarly, the state-subsidized housing construction of the 1950s was a necessary step toward addressing basic social needs. Finally, the introduction of a coupling of pension adjustment to wage increases in 1957 was an attempt to help the considerable number of pensioners share in the growing prosperity. While the successes of Erhard's liberalization made the necessary funds available, these social policies also increased purchasing power, thereby furthering the recovery.[57]

For the individual businessman, releasing competition from restrictions meant both enormous opportunities and great risks. On the one hand, the lifting of licensing constraints and allocations on paper, for example, enabled publishers like Heinz Döll once more to budget efficiently, so that the book trade began to rebound. "Furthermore, after the currency reform, business went up and the firm had a lot to do." The improved business climate made the hiring of qualified staff necessary, thus giving the surviving young men new chances for advancement, while also allowing them finally to start families.[58] On the other hand, the intensification of competition heightened economic insecurity, since many firms remained undercapitalized. As the would-be businessman Berhard Recker found out to his chagrin in the Frankish fur industry, hat manufacturing, and wool trade, the introduction of new products and constantly changing consumer tastes made bankruptcies and business failures multiply as well. Nevertheless, many large traditional companies such as the Krupp concern, which had entered bankruptcy in 1953, managed to get back on their feet. Production began to soar, the workforce grew, and optimism returned.[59]

Once initial difficulties had been overcome, the economy experienced an amazing period of growth that was reflected in the rise of all statistical indicators for the 1950s. Between the first quarter of 1948 and the fourth quarter of 1953 industrial production, for example, climbed from 57 percent to 174 percent, that is more than trebling within five years, based on 1950 figures! In the same period, the number of employed, which had initially stagnated at around 13.5 million, grew to around 16 million, so that unemployment, which still stood at 12.2 percent in the first quarter of 1950, declined by roughly half. In the course of the decade the cost of living increased by only about 10 percent, while real wages rose by 51 percent; as a result, actual purchasing power grew by two-fifths. For a population that had only just escaped hunger and cold it was fun to read in the newspapers about ever new statistical records, because the recovery could be felt in their own wallets. Even if much of the growth consisted of making up for the lag in consumption during the Depression, the Second World War, and the aftermath of defeat, during the 1950s the West German economy grew by an astounding 8.2 percent per year, a rate of expansion that would never be achieved again.[60]

The cause of this growth, which soon came to be known as the "Economic Miracle," was a unique constellation of factors that was not created but enhanced by Erhard's economic policy. One crucial reason was the availability of a sufficient workforce that was ready to toil long and hard without complaint. As one worker recalled, "not much time remained for having fun after work." While the annual increase of 7.3 percent in productivity resulted from the introduction of new machines, it also rested to a considerable extent on self-exploitation, as evidenced by the forty-eight-hour workweek.[61] Yet another factor was the rapid accumulation of capital by businesses through tax exemptions (between 1948 and 1953 gross savings grew from 8.8 to 35.4 billion DM), which for the most part was reinvested in the companies. A final cause was the consistent free trade policy, which sought access to the world market and fostered the creation of a single market in the European Community. The ERP credits of the Marshall Plan primarily helped the mining industry and the energy sector as well as contributed to the creation of a positive psychological climate, but they were much less important than the liberalization of the general economic framework.[62]

In contrast, the East German economy got its first real opportunity to overcome its difficult initial conditions only after the reparation deliveries ceased. The nationalization of businesses proceeded apace, so that by 1955 the VEBs were already earning nearly three-fourths of the gross national product, squeezing the private sector ever more. The first five-year plan of 1951 steered almost half of all investment into industry, and about half of that went into heavy industry and mining. Thus, while 13 percent was spent on housing construction, less than 3 percent was left for consumer goods.[63] Fulfilling targets of the plan became the chief steering mechanism of a policy that needed to glorify productive "activists" such as Adolf Hennecke or award bonuses in order to create incentives to work harder. The subsidizing of basic needs such as food, rent, and transportation distorted the allocation of goods, since prices could not cover costs. In contrast, purchasing power was skimmed off in the official shops of the Trade Organization (HO), because there one could buy "a bar of chocolate for 20 marks, for 250 marks one could get a pair of men's shoes, and women's silk stockings cost about 30 marks."[64] Although the reliability of the GDR's official statistics is hard to assess, it is generally agreed that due to its inherent weaknesses and the slower improvement of conditions, the planned economy proved unable to catch up with the market economy.[65]

Not until 1966 did the Western economic miracle lose its glamour by a slight dip in the rate of growth, which cost Ludwig Erhard the chancellorship due to a panicked reaction of the political class. Just a year earlier he had won a resounding election victory and suggested the need for "cooperation of all groups and interests" with the hapless slogan of an "aligned society" (*formierte Gesellschaft*). But as unemployment increased to 0.5 percent, inflation rose to 3.5 percent, and growth flattened out at 2.9 percent, his critics in the CDU and other parties claimed that the stability of the Federal Republic seemed to be in danger.[66] Never one to engage in party-political intrigues, the economics professor in his second government program called for "frugality and austerity," not exactly the message that his countrymen, now accustomed to rapid growth and material prosperity, wanted to hear. While Erhard's popularity allowed him to assert his control over the CDU one last time at its party congress, the Gaullists within the party zealously undermined his authority while the disenchanted coalition partner FDP left the government altogether. As a result, the chancellor, who some thought acted in politics like an "unwitting child," had to resign at the end of November.[67]

While it continued to adhere to the market economy, the grand coalition of CDU and SPD that followed nevertheless moved in the direction of stronger state control in order to overcome the recession of 1967. The new government's leading economic mind was the Hamburg economist Karl Schiller, who in difficult discussions within the SPD had helped inspire the change of course spelled out in the Godesberg Program, with the phrase, "as much competition as possible, as much planning as necessary." Impressed by the dynamism of the market, he nevertheless sought to strengthen the social components of economic policy. In the cabinet, led by chancellor Kurt Georg Kiesinger and foreign minister Willy Brandt, Schiller became minister of economics, alongside conservative finance minister Franz Joseph Strauß, but he succeeded in asserting his "global control" of the economy. His most important innovation was the policy of "concerted action," which was set down in the 1967 Law for Stability and Growth. Specifically, it envisaged discussions about the basic direction of economic policy between the representatives of labor and management as well as the Council of Economic Experts under the aegis of the Federal Bank. Through a series of Keynesian measures, Schiller succeeded in stimulating growth again, so that it reached 4.4 percent by the early years of the 1970s. The strengthening of state intervention, however, represented a backsliding into a problematic tradition.[68]

In the GDR, by contrast, Walter Ulbricht attempted to impart new dynamism to the planned economy by introducing limited market incentives with his "New Economic System of Planning and Guidance" (NÖSPL). Any signs of a "red miracle," however, were among other things interrupted by the mass flight caused by the collectivization of agriculture that could be stopped only by the construction of the Berlin wall. In 1963, the SED introduced "economic incentives," including a more realistic price structure, withholding of earnings for reinvestment, and greater independence of companies in order to stimulate growth. Ulbricht also hoped for a "scientific-technological revolution" and thus guided investments toward electrical engineering, chemical industries, and machine building—that is, to more innovative branches of basic industry. Since indirect control did not function adequately, in 1965 the planning system was also fundamentally overhauled. The result of these measures was a revival of economic expansion, although the annual average of about 3 percent for the 1960s remained altogether disappointing. Erich Honecker's putsch against his patron Ulbricht was thus not simply the product of the party functionaries' fear of liberalization but rather a reaction to the lagging improvement of the standard of living.[69]

In the West, the social-liberal coalition of 1969 appeared to be more successful in merging steady economic growth with a continual expansion of the welfare state. On the one hand, full employment, which was finally achieved in 1961 and led to the recruitment of "guest workers" from abroad, enabled employees to raise wages considerably and, by extension, increase their share of the GDP. On the other hand, the state was able to finance new social initiatives such as the expansion of the primary, secondary, and tertiary educational system (expenditures on education climbed to 15.8 percent of the 1975 budget), thereby increasing its clientele. Because union promoted wage increases of over 10 percent and social redistribution processes transcended productivity gains, they also had negative consequences: As a result of the overheated expansion, the rate of inflation rose considerably, reaching 6.9 percent in 1973 and reactivating old fears. At the same time, between 1970 and 1975 the ratio of social expenditures to GDP, or *Sozialquote*, climbed from 26.7 to 33.7 percent, the greatest increase of the postwar period.[70] The continued shifting of priorities in favor of social policy threw the social market economy increasingly out of balance.

The shock of skyrocketing oil prices in 1973–1974, therefore, triggered a deep crisis that could only be overcome with enormous effort. While the safeguarding of oil imports only cost 15 billion DM annually, a burden that was further reduced by a weak dollar, in 1975 declining exports pushed the economy into its first real postwar recession, which saw the GDP fall by some 2 percent. Branches of industry that concentrated on mid-range technologies had largely missed out on the jump to high technology, so that mining, shipbuilding, camera optics, and consumer electronics encountered increasing problems. In the international realm, chancellor Helmut Schmidt, who styled himself as a "world economist," reacted with a series of partially successful attempts to stabilize the exchange rate. But on the domestic level, he issued frequent stimulus packages which, through their repetition, provided diminishing returns, especially after the second oil shock of 1979 triggered an even deeper recession. As a result of the nasty "stagflation," the total federal debt increased from 45.4 billion DM in 1969 to 309 billion DM in 1982 and base unemployment climbed to 2 million. The number of those receiving some form of welfare assistance, moreover, surpassed 3 million.[71] The much-vaunted German model, it seemed, no longer worked properly.

While Erich Honecker's belated turn to consumer production and expanding social policy helped the GDR to avoid similar recessions, the planned economy nonetheless continued to slide toward its ineluctable final crisis. To be sure, the creation of huge state companies (*Kombinate*) that combined entire branches of the economy, along with the raising of social expenditures—for example, in housing construction—did stimulate new growth during the first half of the 1970s. But in the second half of the decade, the effect of such measures began to wear off. The "unity of economic with social policy," which the SED proclaimed in 1976, was in a way a final attempt to raise productivity in the planned economy by increasing wages and improving consumption. But a good part of the expansion was financed by foreign loans, which became more difficult to repay with the sale of refined derivatives when the Soviet Union reduced oil deliveries and began to raise its prices to world market levels. In the early 1980s, several billions in West German credits as well as rising transfer payments did save the GDR one more time, but in the second half of the decade, mounting foreign debt, a large trade deficit, failed investments, the deterioration of the infrastructure, and other chronic problems effectively drove the state into bankruptcy.[72]

In the Federal Republic, the "turn-around" proclaimed by Chancellor Kohl attempted to bring some relief to the economy, but it remained too weak for a structural reform of the system, especially when compared to the radical neoliberal policies of President Ronald Reagan and Prime Minister Margaret Thatcher. To cope with "the extremely difficult economic situation" the liberal-conservative coalition strove to improve the business climate by reducing expenditures on social services to below 30 percent of the GDP and cutting back total public expenditures to 45 percent. These measures provided some stimulus, but every time the government challenged social entitlements, it encountered vehement protests, not only from the opposition and unions but also from the left wing of the CDU under Norbert Blüm. Although the number of employed grew markedly to over 30 million in the 1980s, the unemployment rate refused to budge and hovered at around the 2 million mark. Despite heavy investment in the single European market, the rate of economic growth barely reached 2 percent, well below that of Great Britain, the United States, and Japan. Due to the shift of emphasis from a free market to social welfare, even before reunification the German economy was starting to lose much of its ability to compete in the international arena.[73]

Limits of the German Model

The development of competing economic systems in the German states after 1945 points to contrasting learning processes derived from the experiences of the dictatorship of the Third Reich. The solution propagated by liberals such as Wilhelm Röpke envisaged the reintroduction of the market as an economic basis of recivilization—a program which, after some vacillation, was adopted by the U.S. military government and implemented in outline by Ludwig Erhard's social market economy.[74] Since the "cooperative capitalism" of the Third Reich had enabled the Nazi dictatorship to enrich itself by pillaging its racial foes and conquered enemies, the economy needed to be changed to the extent that it would no longer pose an external threat or stand in the way of parliamentary democracy internally. A combination of initially tough but then more limited interventions changed the economy's basic structures in the direction of competition, while collective learning processes of entrepreneurs and consumers helped them internalize the opportunities of the market.[75] The strengthening of competition, which was, however, tamed by strong welfare policies, set in motion a dynamic new growth that, despite some scandals, surprised all who took part in it.

In contrast, the East German planned economy, which at first seemed to be more appealing to both leftist intellectuals and the general public, eventually reached a dead end. Rigorous interventions such as land reform and subsequent collectivization of agriculture, coupled with the expropriation of large industrialists' property and repeated attempts to nationalize commerce and trades, amounted to a significantly more rigorous attempt to pull the economic rug out from under reactionary tendencies. Ironically, this drastic change contributed to the establishment of the ideologically opposite minority dictatorship of the SED.[76] Without a doubt, the GDR's starting conditions were more difficult, and its economy registered a modest miracle of its own, so that the widespread pride of the "reconstruction generation" did possess a certain legitimacy. But the nonmonetary control of the economy failed in comparison, not only with the Federal Republic but also with other states, because it could only thrive in relative isolation from the competition of the international economy.[77] The substitution of bureaucratic planning for the market mechanisms created numerous new inequities because the distribution of consumer goods depended on political loyalty or, quite simply, on knowing the right people.

Despite inflated reports in the GDR's statistics, nearly every comparison between the performance of the planned and market economies between 1945 and 1989 comes down in favor of the West. Although long-term trends until the early 1970s exhibit striking similarities, the growth curve of the Federal Republic generally ran at a much higher level. By the time the GDR collapsed, the productivity of the individual worker there only amounted to one-third of his counterpart in the Federal Republic. While the rate of inflation was admittedly higher in the West, available indicators of the German-German exchange rate point to the indisputable loss of purchasing power suffered by the "East Mark" from a level of initial parity to around two-fifths. As a result, the gross nominal income of the average worker was only about one-third that of a Western employee. Moreover, the contrast between the Trabi and the Volkswagen Golf or a rental apartment and a private home makes clear the qualitative differences that caused a fundamental discrepancy in living standards. In spite of all the social inequalities and risks of recession, the colorful consumer capitalism that developed in the West thus proved in the long term incomparably more attractive than the drab socialist consumption in the GDR.[78]

Ironically, the amazing success of the social market economy has also led the West German model to become a barrier to further economic dynamism. On the one hand, the gradual expansion of the welfare state as a result of the competition between the CDU and SPD spurred the continual introduction of new programs such as long-term care insurance. These programs have increased the social expenditures of both employers and employees to the point that the creation of new jobs has come to a halt, the base unemployment rate remains high regardless of economic growth, and a considerable market for illicit work has formed. On the other hand, the practices of the cartel office have been uneven at best and, with the expansion of the single European market, have permitted a higher level of concentration, thereby impeding internal competition. At the same time, the cooperation between unions and employers in "Germany Inc." that has been demanded by the different governments has given rise to a kind of neocorporatism that thwarts painful reforms and, as a result, perpetuates the economy's paralysis. Even without the added burdens of the reunification process, the "German model" was well on its way to refuting itself.[79]

This "Gulliver syndrome" of being fettered by countless state regulations demonstrates that, unlike with militarism and nationalism, the economic lessons of the Nazi experience have only been half learned. No doubt, the memory of the Economic Miracle is one of the most potent founding myths of the Bonn Republic that celebrates hard work, entrepreneurial risk, and consumer sacrifice as the fount of later prosperity. But behind it linger deep-seated fears of two massive inflations, mass unemployment of the Great Depression, and the hunger and cold of the postwar period, which make citizens call for security through an elaborate social safety net. Thus when facing recession, as in 1967, 1975, and 1982, the public time and again asked the state to assume the role of a knight in shining armor rather than trusting in its own strengths and organizing the countermeasures as a civil society. Breaking through the barriers to innovation, therefore, does not require an uncritical adoption of neoliberal "casino capitalism," which is geared toward an unregulated maximization of short-term shareholder value.[80] But only when German party politics, which have become immobilized by clientelism regardless of ideology, once more find the courage to take risks, and make individual initiative worthwhile again, will the social market economy regain its balance and a greater dynamism return.

CONCLUSION TO PART I

Preconditions for Freedom

In the summer of 1945, the Allied occupation powers and a critical minority within the conquered population confronted the dual task of "denazifying and democratizing" the Germans. Removing the visible signs of the Hitler regime was surprisingly easy, as most people distanced themselves quickly from National Socialism by holding a small number of party leaders and fanatical members responsible for its crimes. But "learning the lessons of defeat" in the deeper meaning of the phrase proved considerably more difficult, as it demanded that people call into question hallowed traditions and abandon ingrained habits of thinking. Perceptive observers, such as the émigré writer Stefan Heym, warned of a growing resistance against the experiment of reorienting an entire society: "As Americans, we must above all else develop a long-term educational, political, and economic strategy toward Germany and the Germans and implement it." In order to change the outlook of a post-Fascist society more profoundly, the occupation powers ought to work according to the example "of our own democratic heritage" and put "leadership in the hands of the clean Germans"—that is, Nazi opponents—and support them "until democratic ideals have truly taken root."[1]

Initially, the victorious Allies determined the framework for the renewal of German political culture by intervening—not always wisely but nevertheless drastically enough to compel genuine changes. In the heated debate about the deeper causes of the Third Reich, such as "militarism and pan-Germanism," ideologues, who thought in terms of national stereotypes and considered the Germans to be incorrigible barbarians, argued with pragmatists, who identified specific problems, such as the tendency toward blind obedience, which, once corrected, would allow them to lead the defeated Germans back to civilization. The Potsdam program of demilitarization, denazification, and economic deconcentration was thus a compromise, based on the contradictory desires to weaken, punish, and restructure Germany at the same time. Its overall goal—namely, a fundamental reorientation of politics—was only vaguely formulated. Its practical implementation, moreover, was impeded not only by the different national interests, distinct political styles, and conflicting ideologies that led the occupation zones to develop separately but also by the repeated disputes over the best method (such as change by compulsion or by example), as well as over the alternative of Allied control or German participation.[2]

In the long run, the Germans themselves advanced the reorientation process since they were gradually able to regain control over their own destiny due to the stalemate of the Cold War. To be sure, much bitterness remained over the loss of territory, the expulsions from the East, and the punishment of war criminals, because former soldiers still clung to their military honor, students remained proud of their nation, and business leaders fought the dismantling of industry. But unlike in 1918, the defeat of 1945 could not be denied, since the elites were hardly able to retain a sense of intellectual superiority, let alone brood about revenge. Disgusted with German misdeeds, critical voices, especially in the unions, churches, and intellectual community, thus demanded a radical turning back toward humanity: "The German people are in their entirety responsible for these crimes, and only by recognizing this guilt will it be possible to find the basis for a better system."[3] Derived both from opportunism and the realization of their culture's failings, the gradual embrace of Western ideas of freedom and Eastern notions of equality is the central political development of the postwar period.

By breaking with negative traditions, the three-part program of demilitarization, denazification, and deconcentration sought to lay down a lasting foundation for freedom. Demobilization quickly broke up the military machine, disarmament eliminated the army as an external threat and as a domestic power, and the elimination of militarism as an attitude succeeded so well that subsequent rearmament met with strong resistance from the populace. The purging of the Nazis, in contrast, proved to be more difficult. To be sure, the Nazi leadership was convicted, its organizations dissolved, and its assets confiscated, so that the influence of former Nazis on postwar politics remained slight. Still, many perpetrators slipped through the net, while the division of the country kept nationalism alive as a hope for reunification. The attempt to weaken Germany economically failed even more clearly. Even if war industries were torn down and while widespread dismantling, above all in the Soviet zone, removed industrial production capacity, deconcentration and decartelization had only a limited effect, thus allowing the economy not just to recover but to develop into a new power, at least in the West. Only once these conditions had been created did the occupation powers begin serious efforts toward parliamentary or socialist democratization.[4]

In the West, the elimination of such negative influences allowed a "culture of civility" once again to develop, which would generally determine political opinions well into the 1990s. When Germans shed their uniforms and rejected their ingrained militaristic outlook, they initiated an almost ten-year hiatus without a military, during which men saw themselves once again as civilians and war no longer evoked heroic but, instead, painful memories. The lifting of Nazi control over all aspects of society revived a multifaceted associational culture, which organized society in the prepolitical space both for sociable purposes and the pursuit of collective interests. The reassertion of the rule of law through the passage of the Basic Law with its protections for human rights reconstituted a kind of political life that, in spite of all party-political conflicts, adhered to a basic democratic consensus. Finally, the reintroduction of the free market and the return to a socially more responsible form of economic competition also restored the basic conditions for a recivilization, as they unleashed a new economic dynamism and offered greater freedom for individual self-realization.[5] Conversely, the Marxist project of a more radical reconfiguration of the economy and society in the East tended to smother all initiatives for a civil society and thus led, instead, to a new minority dictatorship of the SED.[6]

Ironically, the contrasting learning processes in both East and West also engendered some excessive corrections, which presented new problems for the further development of the second German democracy. For instance, the rejection of militarism led to a radical ideological pacifism in broad circles of the population that propagated a moralizing foreign policy behind the shield of the occupation powers but lacked understanding for the application of force in the international arena. Similarly, the educated middle class's distancing from fanatical nationalism inspired among their successors, who now styled themselves as intellectuals, a massive self-criticism that was not unjustifiably derided as "negative nationalism." As a result, they embraced other identities such as a European stance—but, in doing so, they revealed an uncertainty of self-understanding that annoyed Germany's neighbors, even if they had promoted it. Lastly, the simplistic Marxist theory of fascism fostered a general critique of capitalism, which misunderstood the economic foundations of freedom because it continued to place its trust in a planned economy. Ironically, the radical learning processes that emerged from the defeat in the East led to an anti-Fascist party dictatorship, while the more cautious changes in the West proved to be a stable basis for building a democracy through the possibility of gradual self-correction.[7]

PART II
Contradictory Modernization

Although important foundations had already been laid after the war, the actual breakthrough of Germany's recivilization did not occur until the middle of the 1960s. During the first postwar years, the consequences of defeat (such as the loss of the eastern lands, the disappearance of the nobility, the mixing of religious denominations, the dissolution of entire social milieus, and the efforts of the expellees to recover their lost status) had already begun to unleash social changes under conservative auspices.[1] Nevertheless, two decades after the constitution of the Federal Republic there occurred yet another upheaval that "from today's perspective appears as an overdue process of political, social, and economic modernization" and, in spite of conservative protests, "is on the whole considered to have succeeded."[2] These West German transformations in the direction of "a cultural modernity" deepened the chasm between the two German states, as the GDR, due to its radical new beginning, rejected any comparable efforts toward reform following the failure of the new economic policy in the 1960s.[3] Unlike the well-researched "long 1950s," the subsequent "decade of accelerated change" raises a series of difficult interpretive questions that have only gradually come into view.[4]

Understanding the 1960s is complicated by the highly charged symbol of "1968," which has generated a peculiar analytical conundrum. The term "sixty-eight" continues to evoke strong emotions because it serves as a marker of ideological identity: Liberals remember it as a "decisive impulse toward democratization," while conservatives deplore it as a "willful dismantlement of the traditional value system."[5] The glaring discrepancy between the participants' retrospective mythologizing of the generational revolt and the relative modesty of the events actually associated with it renders fashioning a narrative of its political history difficult. Moreover, the contradiction between the largely failed attempt to realize its ideological goals and the considerable sociocultural changes that it triggered also eludes conventional attempts to account for them. Finally, the differences in regard to the style and substance between Western anti-Vietnam rallies and East German attempts to protest against the suppression of the Prague Spring prevent a uniform treatment. Gradually, however, historians are coming to the realization that 1968 as a cultural revolution represents a different kind of caesura that requires a cultural approach to be better understood.[6]

To achieve some distance from this charged event, it is necessary to place the generational conflict into the context of the wider social transformation that was occurring in all Western industrial countries during the 1960s. In the case of Germany, these changes might best be considered a kind of catch-up modernization, since the long-range statistical trajectories show the continuity of socioeconomic developments that were interrupted by the two world wars.[7] This process includes, for instance, the rise of a tertiary economy—that is, a flight from agricultural pursuits and the emergence of a service sector, based on training and education. Equally dramatic was the doubling of wages and the reduced cost of mass production that made elite consumer goods accessible to average consumers so that a new prosperity (driven by consumption and a popular culture centered largely on entertainment) could spread quickly. At the same time, in the 1970s, the oil shocks and the introduction of the personal computer signaled the end of high industrialism and with it the transition to postmodernity.[8] These structural changes, which eventually spread to the GDR, militate against the fixation on 1968, as they raise more general questions concerning the transformative processes that stand behind them.

The first problem demanding analysis is the gradual convergence of German patterns of thought and behavior with Western models. The material affluence of the American occupiers had already impressed the defeated Germans because it seemed to offer tangible evidence of the inherent superiority of the Western way of life. Because the Sovietization of East Germany was mostly perceived as a Communist threat, the older generation put their faith in transatlantic protection, although the representatives of German intellectual culture maintained a considerable reserve toward American mass civilization.[9] In contrast, German youths, who were impressed by Hollywood films and rock music, were fascinated by the transformation in lifestyles set in motion by mass consumption and popular culture, because for them this "value change" represented a break with old-fashioned bourgeois virtues and a turn toward a freer sexual morality and a hedonistic way of life. Yet younger Germans also vehemently criticized American foreign policy, especially its support of military dictatorships in the Third World that toed the anti-Communist line.[10] A crucial step was thus the cultural Westernization that overcame anticivilizational reservations and anti-American prejudices, and thereby contributed toward a "fundamental liberalization" of the Federal Republic.[11]

Another important question concerns the connection between these sociocultural developments and the deeper anchoring of participatory democracy in West Germany. The political-historical thesis of "a kind of re-founding of the Second Republic" can be based on evidence such as the end of the Adenauer era, the change in government to a social-liberal coalition, the passage of a new policy toward the east (*Ostpolitik*), and the emergence of citizens' movements, while in the GDR it can only cite the transfer of power from Walter Ulbricht to Erich Honecker.[12] This perspective, however, ignores the problem of the reluctant embrace of democracy by authoritarian elites as well as a skeptical populace, which in the East was blocked by the dictatorship of the SED. To gain a solid footing, the democratic institutions that were implanted by the victors and supported by a minority of the defeated needed a keener appreciation of the value of human rights and a change toward more civil forms of interpersonal behavior. This process of "internal democratization," which only occurred after the passage of the Basic Law and the founding of the Federal Republic, represents the decisive step toward civil society and thus demands a more convincing historical explanation.[13]

A final challenge is to explain the renewed 1960s mobilization of a postwar society, which had only been stabilized with great difficulty. While the majority of the West German populace rejoiced at rising prosperity, critics called for social reforms to go still further. As a result of shocking Nazi scandals and new conflicts, such as the Spiegel Affair, a critical public sphere began to evolve in the West that no longer tolerated the authoritarian style of Chancellor Konrad Adenauer's democracy. At the same time, with the growing influence of the Frankfurt School and an unorthodox Marxism, a "New Left" also emerged that moved beyond the slogans of material redistribution to demand utopian socialist changes. Fearing the extension of emergency powers proposed by the grand coalition, a broad extraparliamentary opposition comprised of diverse elements, ranging from churches to unions, gathered to defend their civil rights. In the East, moreover, isolated intellectuals such as Robert Havemann began to hope for a humanization of socialism in the spirit of Prague.[14] The genesis of a new, nonviolent protest culture that culminated in the new social movements is thus another indicator of the maturing process that brought Germany one step closer to becoming a civil society.[15]

CHAPTER 4

Embracing the West

G ermans greeted the "long-term visit" of the Allied occupiers with a para-doxical mixture of fear and hope. In judging the different powers, elitist resentment toward Western civilization and racist hostility toward the Russians clashed with a fascination for America, admiration for the British, and love of France, as well as interest in the Communist experiment. Even those journalists, who like Margret Boveri attempted to size up the victors realistically, remained ambivalent in their feelings toward them. Written in 1945, Boveri's "America Primer," for example, sought to help Germans appreciate that "the Americans are a new people" who are "not to be measured according to our standards." The characterization of the Western superpower as "a nation of immigrants in the land of freedom," with a conformist "personality type," a penchant for "standardization" of society, a preference for moralizing, a merely superficial politeness, and a marked "desire for newness" offered a mélange of anti-American clichés and perceptive observations.[1] The Germans would need a long process of reorientation to resolve this contradiction between importing reforms while preserving their own identity.

The change in the political culture that was decreed by the victors ran into the twin difficulties of resentment against foreign domination and competition among the new models for orientation. "We will only truly experience our defeat if we let values and [patterns of] behavior be dictated to us by the victors instead of by our own traditions and ask the Americans, what is German," lamented one intellectual in 1946. During the Cold War, however, the consensus of the occupation powers shattered on the conflicting conceptions of the "Occident" or the "free world" on the one hand and of "socialist humanism" on the other,[2] allowing the defeated Germans to play one side against the other.

Likewise, the contradiction between the imposition of changes and their voluntary adoption permitted some passive resistance against those mandates that were thought to be unjust, since lasting reforms presumed a certain amount of cooperation from the Germans. Because it required overcoming deep-seated anti-Western prejudices, the reorientation after 1945 was not a result of a simple, one-way transfer of culture but, rather, of a controversial, long-term process of transnational acculturation.[3]

An analysis of this fundamental transformation, however, has been impeded by the imprecision of terminology, since the most obvious comparison between Americanization and Sovietization has come under criticism for its political overtones.[4] The term "Americanization" is being faulted above all for its naïve and normative usage, which makes it difficult to draw a distinction between external impulses and internal appropriations of American culture.[5] Anselm Döring-Manteuffel has suggested instead the broader notion of "Westernization" so as also to take into account competing influences from England, France, and Italy—signaled by the epithet *Toskana-Fraktion* (Tuscany faction) for the Italophilia of the Left.[6] The term "Sovietization" is similarly handicapped, since it was coined during the Cold War as a Western slogan for criticizing the establishment of Soviet hegemony and the imposition of the Stalinist model on Eastern Europe.[7] Its pejorative counterpart of "Easternization" never became equally popular, as this geographical allusion, invented by journalists during reunification, was considered too defamatory.[8] For examining the prevailing turn toward the West, the more comprehensive approach of "Westernization" therefore appears preferable, even if its content continues to refer primarily to American influences.

Before the concept may be employed, however, the implications of Westernization must be clarified, since its contours can easily become blurred. Above all, it is crucial to recognize that the "West" is itself a complex myth that tends to refer to such disparate meanings as a sociocultural gradient in Europe or American notions of an open frontier that are perpetuated by Western movies, as well as the cigarette advertisements of the Marlboro Man. In the stylization of the West into a general norm for development, its darker sides such as imperialism, racism, slavery, and exploitation tend to be unconsciously suppressed.[9] It is therefore necessary to identify more clearly than has previously been the case the different horizons of meaning associated with the general processes of modernization, the Anglo-American and other European cultural transfers, and the changes that grew out of Germany's own dynamics of development. Despite the validity of postcolonial critiques, the controversial term "Western Civilization" does allude to the existence of a specifically Western idea of civilization, which might analytically fill the somewhat vague concept of Westernization, if it is construed as a shared set of values.[10]

The central question hidden behind this terminological confusion concerns the causes, processes, and consequences of Germany's "long road to the West" after 1945. Should this Westernization be understood primarily as a success of Western policies of reeducation and reorientation along with the failure of the competing Communist model? Or should it instead be considered a kind of "self-colonization" through the selective acceptance of external stimuli, internal parallel development of native traditions, and multiple forms of hybridization of outside offerings and inside learning processes?[11] To do justice to the complexity of Westernization, one might first examine the effect of the thousands of personal encounters after the war that led individuals to turn toward the West. Then it would be important to review the already well researched emergence of political ties to the West from the perspective of the corresponding changes in popular attitudes.[12] Finally, the processes that led to the Westernization of consumption habits and popular culture, which differed according to generational preferences, also need to be compared to determine the repercussions of Americanization in daily life.[13]

Personal Encounters

Individual contacts of the isolated populace with the occupation powers offer a largely ignored key to explaining the decision of many postwar Germans to opt for the West. The crucial first impressions, which were difficult to change, depended on the circumstances in which they occurred: When the arriving victors acted less violently than the dire warnings of Nazi propaganda led them to expect, the defeated could breathe a sight of relief as they began to realize that it just might be possible to get along with the occupiers. The nature of the experience was determined largely by whether individuals who first met the occupation soldiers were harmless elderly citizens, potentially dangerous soldiers, attractive women, or curious youngsters. Even without a functioning media system, various stories of incidents—some traumatic, some pleasant—slowly created a collective image which, although containing some contradictions, did coalesce into an overall judgment. "I was happy as a clam, that the Americans were there," one man remembered, since already "the word Russian sounded . . . rather negative to Berliners." In thousands of similar comparisons "the West" almost always came off better than "the Russians."[14]

The expectations with which the victors and the defeated met each other were conditioned by deep-seated clichés that had been hardened by the enemy images spread by war propaganda. While the French disliked the Wehrmacht's arrogance during the occupation, the British resented the random terror of the Luftwaffe, and the Russians suffered from the devastation of the genocidal war, the Americans had much less reason to hate because the fighting did not reach their shores and they had entered the conflict late. In contrast to German prejudices against the sophisticated yet weak French, bumbling but gallant English, and childlike and vengeful Russians (due to suppressed feelings of guilt), German opinions of the Americans fluctuated more widely. Even confirmed Nazis were unsure whether to admire their friendly affability or to denounce their racial decadence. After the failure of the desperate defensive battles against the Red Army, thousands of fleeing refugees and scattered Wehrmacht soldiers spontaneously started "to move westward," trying to find "the shortest route to the Anglo-American line."[15] How could one otherwise explain that, despite instances of bitter resistance, German troops were more likely to surrender in the West, while even the old men and teenagers of the militia tended to fight until the last bullet in the East, thereby provoking more severe retribution from the Russians than from the Americans?

Comparisons between the victorious powers, which became possible as a result of border adjustments in the occupation zones, almost always favored the Americans. Despite several examples of friendliness shown toward children, Margret Boveri and other eyewitnesses concur in having "seen such shocking things" that the stories of shootings, pillaging, and rapes committed by Russian soldiers could not just have been a legend of the Cold War.[16] In her diary Marianne Kiefer describes similar violations of stealing and the command "Come along, woman!" from Moroccan soldiers, which made the French "odious" to her: "We were such nervous wrecks that we pleaded with the blacks to shoot us."[17] In contrast, Manfred Clausen experienced the regime of the English as distant and imperious, but also correct: "It should be said that on the part of the English soldiers there was not the slightest misconduct toward the German civilian population."[18] And the GIs were widely welcomed as bringing "salvation from this terror" of the other soldiers, since the Americans "were by comparison much more pleasant, didn't act at all like occupiers, and left generous tips."[19] Because of their wealth and poise "the *Amis*" immediately became symbolic of the superiority of the West.

Young women seeking human warmth and amusement had the most intense contacts with the occupation soldiers. Since the Russians were eventually confined to their barracks and the French and the British had to less to offer, the "fun-loving and bored" GIs quickly became the most popular partners. "They had everything, and they were easily able to meet their great demand for 'Frolleins' with cigarettes and chocolate, despite the official 'fraternization ban,'" noted one young German man enviously. It was not just the soldiers' small gifts of coffee and nylon stockings that made such an impression on these young women but also their carefree attitude. "Sometimes they acted like in the wild west" and ignored all traffic laws; one contemporary recalled how "two drunk Americans waved to women with inflated condoms from a jeep." Around the military bases regular amusement areas mushroomed with bars where young women met with the GIs, whether to earn money as prostitutes or to start up a romantic relationship in the hope, usually in vain, of being brought back as a war bride into the land of unlimited opportunities. "The bulk of the German population," a critical observer noted, "had few kind words for these 'Veronikas' and felt that their actions were undignified."[20]

Grown men, in contrast, languishing under the general suspicion of Nazi collaboration, were only useful to the Americans insofar as they could render practical service. The contrast between the "well fed" and "warmly dressed" occupiers and the "pitiful German creatures, all skin and bones," including many who had been disabled in the war, made the dependent relationship physically apparent. Nevertheless, working for the *Amis* was quite popular, since "the job was not paid with money but with a warm meal, which at the time was much more valuable." Anyone who could find some kind of position in a motor pool, kitchen, or officer club could count himself lucky. From this economic gap between occupiers and occupied emerged "a flourishing trade" in food and gas in exchange for Nazi memorabilia and family heirlooms, an informal barter which often grew into a veritable black market. Despite severe penalties, regular raids targeting "any stolen objects" only managed to interrupt their circulation temporarily, not stop it altogether, since the "pushers" became quite adept at hiding their contraband.[21]

Even though some continued to mourn the idols of the Hitler Youth, young people more than any other group became fascinated by the easygoing lifestyle of the American soldiers. Curious youths quickly reactivated their "meager knowledge of English from school," using it "for the first time sensibly and profitably, if also sometimes incorrectly," to coax a piece of gum or bum a ride in a jeep. When troops were billeted in German homes for longer periods of time, real friendships could sometimes form, with boys scrounging up Nazi medals as souvenirs for the GIs in return for "chocolate, coffee, and cigarettes." As one person gratefully remembered, "in the schools the Americans organized school lunches which helped us schoolchildren get through the time of hunger." The private CARE packages, and other parcels from groups like the Quakers, were also a godsend, since they contained desperately needed food and clothing that could, if necessary, be traded for other things. "Our life was gradually, but increasingly colored American," one youngster described, recalling his fascination with U.S. radio broadcasts: "This was the voice of another, unspoiled world," which attempted "to bring the ways of democracy, coated with the comforts of the American lifestyle, to us authoritarian-minded Germans."[22]

To keep inevitable frictions with the populace to a minimum, the Americans more than the other occupiers made an effort to enlist the sympathy of the local civilians. For example, they appointed joint commissions charged with solving such contentious questions as compensation for the repeated damages caused by maneuvers. When they opened new military bases, moreover, they often held an open house, allowing visitors to satisfy their curiosity about what went on behind the compound walls. The establishment of youth clubs where American soldiers played sports with German youths, watched movies, or listened to jazz also helped loosen latent tensions. While the greatest attraction was likely the chocolate and Coca-Cola that were offered to them, these German Youth Activities (GYAs) still brought young Germans together with Americans in a more relaxed, congenial setting. Unlike the strict barracking of the Russians, the possibility of living off base extended the area of contact between GI renters and German landlords. And finally, the joint celebration of festivals such as U.S. Independence Day and Rhenish carnival helped to reduce prejudices, especially against black soldiers.[23]

More effective yet were the official exchange programs that began in 1947–1948, and brought some 12,000 Germans to the United States by 1955. Among their participants were students, including the historian Hans-Ulrich Wehler, who in 1952 received a scholarship from the newly founded Fulbright Program to study American history at Ohio University, as well as professors such as the jurist Walter Hallstein, who was invited as a guest lecturer at Georgetown University. Entire delegations of pedagogues like the group led by Minister for Culture in Baden-Württemberg Theodore Bäuerle also traveled across the Atlantic to learn by inspecting American schools. Likewise, members of social organizations—for example, the trade unionists who attended an AFL-CIO congress where they discussed common problems—also gained firsthand knowledge of the United States. The contrast between their own destroyed and divided country and the peaceful and flourishing United States that spanned an entire continent made as profound an impression as "the very warm reception," thus helping them to forget their former enmity.[24] Even if many American methods could not be directly transferred, the "spirit of true democracy" became so deeply impressed on visitors that some made achieving comparable freedom in Germany into a lifelong challenge.[25]

Among the more important cultural intermediaries were the critical intellectuals and leftist politicians who returned to help build a new and better Germany. The decision to remigrate was not easy, because many, especially the younger refugees, had struck deep roots in their host countries, and some official invitations met with passive resistance from a populace that was preoccupied with its own problems. Nevertheless, the historian Hans Rothfels, the political scientist Ernst Fraenkel, and the social democratic leaders Ernst Reuter and Willy Brandt, to name just a few of the more prominent, brought with them positive experiences from the United States and other Western countries. In contrast, the Communist "Walter Ulbricht" group (named after their ideological leader), despite having itself suffered Stalinist persecution while in Moscow, propagated the superiority of the Soviet system.[26] The left socialist and literary scholar Alfred

Kantorowicz justified his return by citing his "insights and knowledge acquired in exile" that would assist the reconstruction: "The victory of the better, more humane, creative, freedom-loving Germany must still be won. This struggle must be carried out here, in this country." At first, the radical new start in the East seemed to hold more promise for success, but soon the literary critic Hans Mayer, philosopher Ernst Bloch, and other nonconformists switched over to the initially more problematic Federal Republic.[27]

Various experts on Germany also took a central role in conveying foreign ideas to the defeated and German wishes to the outside world. In difficult questions of detail, the occupation powers necessarily relied on "German hands," such as the educator Edward Hartshorne and the jurist Shepard Stone, who had already dealt with Germany before the war. Returning emigrants like journalists Sebastian Haffner and Hans Habe also wrote both English-language reports on the defeated country and German articles that attempted to explain the victors' reform suggestions to a skeptical populace.[28] The various cultural officers who were charged with stirring interest in the creative achievements and political practices of their respective country faced a similar task of transmitting a foreign culture. They had to decide whether they would follow their elitist guidelines and promote, for example, classical music, or whether they would give in to the public's desire for entertainment such as jazz.[29] Due to the need to solve concrete problems of occupation, pragmatic policy makers such as U.S. General Lucius D. Clay and High Commissioner John J. McCloy increasingly saw themselves forced to defer to the desires of the defeated Germans. Especially at the municipal level, occupation authorities had to negotiate practical compromises with mayors, like Wilhelm Kaisen in Bremen, if they wanted to get something done.[30]

As time went on, accidental encounters grew into solid acquaintanceships, transformed into informal networks, and in some cases even coalesced into bilateral organizations. On the level of local bases, individuals might join both German and American clubs—thereby forging overlapping associations. On the national level, the Soviet Union in particular attempted to convey to the educated middle class a more positive image of Russian culture and Communist success ("the victory of socialism in the Soviet Union"). To this end, in 1947 it sponsored the Society for the Study of the Culture of the Soviet Union (later DSF), which would hold meetings, cultural functions, and exhibitions. Founded in 1952, its Western counterpart, the more elitist Atlantic Bridge, was charged with reducing the still widely held reservations toward the Federal Republic in America and cultivating sympathy for the "American way of life" in Germany. At the same time, U.S. service clubs such as the Rotary, Lions, and Kiwanis initiated German branches that, by holding charity events as forums for local businessmen, sought to spread the American service ethos abroad.[31]

The intensification of contacts with the West was also a result of the Germans' own initiatives toward restoring foreign relationships. The oversized economy, for example, had no choice but to try to resume exporting once again, although no longer in the accustomed role of master but, rather, in the much less enviable position of solicitant. During the period of Allied control of firms through military trustees, tentative contacts began to emerge that might gradually develop into a kind of cooperation with the turn toward reconstruction under the influence of the Cold War. The return of European trade promoted by the European Recovery Program of the Marshall Plan allowed previous working relationships to be resumed, which could also be used to reclaim old markets. To be sure, the numerous negotiations occurred under changed political circumstances, and painful memories of German crimes still had to be overcome. Nevertheless, the accompanying trips to the West broadened the horizons of most managers, rewarded truly cooperative behavior, and, as a byproduct, fostered a gradual internationalization of German business style.[32]

Young people in particular were fascinated by the West and sought to escape the narrow confines of Germany by getting to know their neighboring countries. Thus offers from Protestant and Catholic clergy for religious reconciliation meetings, especially in the border regions, proved quite popular among them. In the early 1950s, some of the more daring teachers organized the first field trips abroad, which, to name just one example, took a busload of high school girls from Krefeld to the South of France to expand their language skills, become acquainted with the Provence, and reduce national prejudices through actual human contacts. Likewise, international youth organizations started once again to invite German delegations to their meetings. In 1957 the Boy Scouts asked German representatives to participate in the fiftieth anniversary celebration of their founding in England, where they even got the chance to gaze at the British royal couple.[33] Of course, many youths, no matter how innocent they may have felt, would be reminded of their Germanness by the sometimes negative reactions of their hosts. But through friendly behavior, they could still work to overcome old hostilities and, in so doing, contribute to the emergence of a European sense of community.

The travel wave that began in the 1950s also fostered internationalization, as it led many Germans to associate foreign countries with vacation, diversion, and relaxation. At first in trains or buses, then in their own private cars, and eventually in airplanes, West German citizens flocked to the neighboring lands to the west and south, since the iron curtain blocked off traditional eastern vacation spots. The "second German invasion" of Holland by 200,000 tourists during the Easter holiday of 1954 sparked ironic commentaries that drew on clichés from the Second World War. Industrious shopkeepers, however, certainly did not mind taking the DMs that tourists spent on "tulip bulbs, porcelain windmills, silver spoons, butter, tea, and cognac." Two Danish journalists, disguised as Germans, experienced a "veritable march of triumph, even though we took great pains to break every parking ban." Even when tactless behavior reactivated older resentments, German visitors were for the most part surprisingly welcome: "We had the feeling that we had been missed for ten years."[34] For those tourists who managed to break out of their own cultural umbrella, these trips offered an opportunity to broaden their horizons, be it through cultural studies or by getting to know foreign ways of daily life.

Such diverse contacts opened the door for Western styles of thought and patterns of behavior that seemed increasingly worthy of imitation at both the material and nonmaterial levels. The interest in the East, in contrast, remained more limited, since the areas of contact with the Soviet Union were smaller, encounters were more strictly controlled, and language barriers hindered communication. Once the Red Army had been sequestered in its barracks, the East German populace had little to do with Russian soldiers. Moreover, the various delegations that traveled to the Soviet Union to study for the most part consisted only of convinced members of the SED.[35] In comparison, the West possessed a whole range of attractions: France and Italy offered a pleasing climate and inspiring manifestations of high culture, while England demonstrated forms of a civilized lifestyle and a youth culture characterized by the Beatles and miniskirts. Most of all, the United States displayed impressive examples of military power, political influence, and economic success, not to mention a consumer-oriented popular culture. Since most encounters tended to reduce mutually held prejudices, these experiences of getting to know each other created a psychological foundation for the Germans' gradual turn toward the West in the postwar decades.[36]

Political Bonding

Tying West German politics to the West was not an automatic consequence of positive contacts, however, but the result of a series of controversial choices between the two different blueprints offered by the competing victors. To be sure, Konrad Adenauer, the doyen of the emerging CDU, already avowed his Western leanings in March 1946: "[I am] and remain a German, but also feel like a European and thus lend [my] support to an understanding among and the development of a United States of Europe." At the same time, Kurt Schumacher, the chairman of the SPD in the Western Zone who had himself been disabled in the war, struck a stronger national chord: "Social Democracy is not, however, the party of the Russian or the British, the French or the American workers, but rather of the German worker." Even more radical socialists like Max Fechner pleaded for closer cooperation between the Socialist Unity Party, which was soon to be founded, and the "three-time victor" of history, the Soviet Union.[37] Only after fierce disputes between the representatives of Eastern alignment, the proponents of national neutrality, and the advocates of a turn toward the West was the latter course able to prevail.

The starting point for this political reorientation was the westward shift of German territory through the implementation of the Potsdam decisions in the aftermath the Second World War. However traumatic the flight and expulsion of 12.5 million people had been, the loss of the former eastern territories, caused by the Russians' annexation of part of Prussia and the westward relocation of Poland into the rest of East Prussia, Pomerania, part of Brandenburg, and Silesia actually liberated postwar development from the influence of the East Elbian Junkers who had contributed to the Nazi seizure of power. The subsequent transformation of the central German area into "East Germany" and its separation by the iron curtain forced the West Germans to reorient themselves to the neighboring countries to the west for contact, commerce, and cooperation. By so doing, they were able to develop their own liberal traditions more freely, to deepen cultural and economic relations to France and England, and slowly to begin thinking of themselves as an "integral part of Western Europe." The political scientist Richard Löwenthal therefore considered the Federal Republic that emerged out of these territorial changes as "the most western Germany that has been for centuries," because in it a "civic way of life [could evolve] in a western spirit."[38]

During the first postwar decade, the diffuse concept of a "Christian Occident," which dominated speeches of middle-class politicians, offered an ideological rationale for Westernization. During the Cold War the term's anti-Turkish resonance actually proved advantageous, since it fit *mutatis mutandis* into the anti-Communist crusader mentality of the period. Particularly in the Catholic districts of the south and west it evoked the memory of a Latin-based European culture of the Middle Ages that might perhaps be reconstructed once again through cooperation with France and Italy. Nevertheless, the slogan also left room for some conservative Protestants, as it encompassed the cultural tradition first inspired by the Ancient Greeks. By returning to the fundamental ethical values that had been so heavily damaged by National Socialism, the "Christian Occident" became a bridge between disillusioned neoconservatives and the religiously faithful who were hoping for a re-Christianization of Europe. With its stress on the transnational community of values, this formula seemed to facilitate a spiritual reintegration of German culture into a conservatively understood West. The call for human dignity and a "return to the foundations of the Christian culture of the West" thus assumed a prominent place in the platforms of the CDU.[39]

In the more liberal, Protestant districts of northern Germany, rather, it was the aura of Anglo-American civilization that shaped the concept of a progressive West. The British occupation of the Ruhr valley under the auspices of a Labor government played an important part, but greater material resources made it clear that the United States had become the leading Western power. Due to an inflated sense of high culture, the educated initially remained skeptical of the technical superiority of American civilization, if only because they did not want to lose their self-respect. It was thus a minority of progressive intellectuals, practical businessmen, convinced democrats, and disoriented youths who were attracted by the experimental art, economic dynamism, communal self-government, and hot rhythms of the United States. Only with increased transatlantic travel and the gradual introduction of American Studies into the university curriculum did fragmentary images of the United States begin coalesce into a more coherent picture.[40] The concept of the West as a community of nations with "the same views on the state, the individual, freedom, and property" thus merged quite contradictory notions of the Occident and America.[41]

In spite of countless horror stories, the Soviet model also exerted considerable attraction—not only in East Germany due to the unavoidable presence of the Red Army, but also in some working-class circles in the West. Even members of the battered elite—like the captured officers of the National Committee for a Free Germany, who were impressed by the Russian people's willingness to sacrifice—could draw on memories of the brotherhood in arms that Prussia once shared with the czarist empire. Most of all, the activists of the workers' movement, who considered the merger of the KPD and the SPD long overdue, hoped that Stalin's success with industrialization and collectivization could be replicated so as to build a socialist state in Germany as well. Anti-Fascist intellectuals, such as the Jewish scholar of Romance literature and bourgeois democrat Victor Klemperer, were willing to overlook the excesses and mistakes of Russian occupation, since the Communists promised the most decisive break with the past: "They alone pressed for a truly radical suppression of the Nazis," he noted tersely in his diary.[42] Because of the resonance of the "anti-Fascist unity front" in some spheres of the populace, an eastern bond to the Soviet Union was not entirely out of the question either.

In the "political vacuum" of the postwar period, however, the impression made by the actual policy of the individual occupation powers ultimately determined the allegiance of the Germans. To be sure, the implication of collective guilt at the Nuremberg trials, the bureaucratic character of denazification, the clumsy attempts at reeducation, and the punitive attitude of some U.S. politicians chagrined many people.[43] But speaking at Stuttgart in September 1946, Secretary of State James F. Byrnes pushed open a "gate of hope" by pointing out to "the Germans, as a friend and helper, the way to a new life." The inclusion of West Germany in the European Recovery Program also had a positive effect, since the Marshall Plan placed economic reconstruction in a European context and thereby hastened the recombination of the Western occupation zones into a larger entity, jokingly called "Trizonia"—the future Federal Republic. Finally, the Berlin airlift that was primarily accomplished by American airplanes also sent an encouraging signal of support. The technological feat of supplying over 2 million people in the western part of Berlin with food and other necessities for eleven months offered tangible proof "that the Americans would not leave the Germans in the lurch."[44]

In contrast, many Soviet actions had a chilling effect, and the growing discrepancy between SED propaganda and East German reality undermined the credibility of Communism. Even though the claim of "deliverance by the Red Army" was not entirely without merit, the populace remembered its savagery most of all. "I can't count all of the people who were beaten, shot, or dragged away by the Russians, never to be seen again." While many nominal Nazis were disillusioned with Hitler, they soon grew tired of the exaggerations of the Stalin cult, which transformed the Generalissimo of the Soviet Union into a hero who united "wisdom with boldness, [and] precise scientific calculation with unflagging courage."[45] Some "sections of the populace began to join the German Communist Party (KPD) in the hope of [gaining] certain advantages," but other people withdrew from public life, because "they no longer trusted their own friends and relatives." While many "new peasants" and workers welcomed the expropriation of the large landowners and industrialists, the posting of single candidate lists after the disappointing SED showing in the 1946–1947 elections effectively spelled the end of freedom of opinion. It thus became increasingly clear to East German citizens that they had exchanged one dictatorship for another. As one disappointed old Communist put it: "And that's what we've fought for!"[46]

The West German Basic Law that emerged in this highly charged atmosphere was thus a compromise between reviving Germany's own constitutional traditions and importing new models from the West. The London declaration of the Western Allies did, of course, establish a certain framework for federalism, basic rights, and the realignment of the states that was reinforced by official interventions and informal contacts. But members of the Parliamentary Council were sufficiently familiar with German parliamentary history to be able to preserve its positive aspects while at the same time avoiding the chief mistakes of the Weimar Republic, such as the splintering of the parties and the granting of emergency powers to the president. Moreover, strong personalities such as Ludwig Bergsträsser (SPD), Hermann von Mangoldt (CDU), Anton Pfeiffer (Christian Social Union or CSU), and Rudolf Katz (SPD) were well enough versed in Western varieties of parliamentary government so that, with help from Konrad Adenauer as well as Carlo Schmidt, they could offer positive solutions to difficult problems. Even though it lacked a senate, a powerful president, and plebiscitary elements, the Basic Law made a considerable contribution to Westernization because it combined German traditions of self-government, such as a professional bureaucracy and federalism, with Western concepts of basic rights and constitutional courts.[47]

Discussions on an East German constitution also strove to create the appearance of German control so as to conceal the already ongoing process of Sovietization. The KPD program of June 1945 promised the "creation of democratic rights and freedoms of the people" and the founding manifesto of the SED in early 1946 merely mentioned an "anti-Fascist democratic republic" as a goal.

Drawing on Weimar ideas, the "Draft Constitution for the German Democratic Republic" of November 1946 stressed "the unity of the nation, social progress, and the safeguarding of freedom" as its guiding principles.[48] But outside of Communist circles, the attempt to win the Western workforce for a socialist republic through a nationwide signature campaign for a "referendum for German unity" met with little success. While calls for a "purge of Nazi activists," "democratic land reform," "the expropriation of war and Nazi criminals," as well as economic planning were no doubt popular in the West, they were discredited by the repressive policies of the SED and the Soviet Union in the East. The People's Congress movement therefore remained largely limited to the Soviet Zone, even if the first constitution in the GDR did not adequately reflect the extent to which social change had progressed in the direction of the Soviet model.[49]

Despite some setbacks, Adenauer's policy of cooperation with the Western Allies was on the whole sufficiently successful to convince a skeptical electorate that closer cooperation with the West would bring more tangible benefits. Already the occupation statute of early 1949 helped strengthen German self-rule and treated the rights reserved by the Allies as limited in time. The chancellor could use the leeway, created by the Petersberg Accords, to constitute the Federal Republic as a surrogate state for a Germany that would be reunited in the future and to work toward a rapid "regaining of sovereignty." The "gradual reentry into the community of the free peoples of Europe" made possible an early lifting of occupation controls, membership in European organizations, and the restoration of a certain freedom of action.[50] Even though the maximum demands put forward by nationalists time and again endangered the practice of "trustful cooperation," signs of progress such as the end of a state of war with the United States were undeniable. The "agreement on the German-Allied General Treaty" was thus a success of Adenauer's "steadiness and tenacity." In comparison with the lengthy struggle over revising the Versailles settlement after World War I, formal equality was achieved much more quickly after the Second World War.[51]

In contrast, resistance to the Schuman Plan for the creation of a coal and steel community was considerably stronger as it involved the first concrete step toward a "supranational" union of West European states. Adenauer tirelessly advocated the advantages of the Europeanization of coal and steel production, arguing that it would not only end the unilateral Allied control over the Ruhr valley and constraints on industry but also establish "a peaceful relationship between France and Germany for the long run." Though the German Trade Union Federation (DGB) accepted the European Coal and Steel Community (ECSC), the SPD continued to polemicize against the "weakening of the German economy," the "dictatorship" of ECSC authority, and the creation of a "truncated Europe" without England and Scandinavia that such a union would bring about.[52] The SED rejected this "war plan" still more emphatically by inciting West German coal miners to go on a mass strike. The FRG government, however, remained undeterred and even extended the plan by adding institutions such as a ministerial council, a parliamentary assembly, and a high court as kernels of further integration. In the end, the government prevailed in the debates of the Federal Diet, since it was able to portray the Coal and Steel Community as an end to discrimination and a step toward Europe's "economic and political recovery."[53]

Above all, the lack of feasible alternatives in a reunification policy offered by nationalist and social democratic circles contributed to the consolidation of commitment to the West. Since Bonn rejected "a Communist dictatorship for all of Germany" just as much as East Berlin refused the expansion of democracy to the GDR, demands for "free elections" or a "peace treaty" on a confederative basis cancelled each other out.[54] When the Soviet note of early 1952 seemed to offer a glimmer of hope, the nationally oriented left-wing Protestant Gustav Heinemann claimed that "whoever wants reunification must give up the commitment to the West." But Adenauer was unwilling to reverse his course: "German reunification is possible neither through our own efforts alone nor with Russian support, but only with the assistance of the three western powers." The goal of his policy was "the recovery of German unity in freedom—a status that will never be achieved through a so-called neutralization." Although Schumacher continued to insist on the primacy of reunification, the government and populace considered the risk of unprotected neutrality during the Cold War too great, especially in light of the progress that had already been made toward Western integration.[55]

The surprising East German workers' revolt of June 17, 1953, further discredited nationalist reservations against cooperation with the West, because it provoked Soviet military intervention to keep the tottering SED in power. The spontaneous protests of construction workers on East Berlin's Stalin-Boulevard, of all places, against the raising of their work quotas spread quickly throughout the republic, becoming a general "rebellion against the SED regime." Choruses of demonstrating workers called for "free and secret elections, the repeal of the mandated quota increases, and the removal of members of the government responsible for the deplorable state of affairs."[56] These demands turned a limited labor conflict into a political revolt that signaled nothing less than "the moral bankruptcy of the SED system in the Soviet zone." Since the surprised party members lacked confidence in their police force, the Red Army had to intervene with tanks to restore order. The attempt by the party newspaper *Neues Deutschland* to disqualify the revolt as a "fascist adventure" thus did not have its desired effect. Because the Russian tanks had destroyed "the myth of the workers' party," the Bonn government could feel validated by its policy of "doing everything to unite Germany in peace and freedom."[57]

By the mid-1950s, integration into the West had proceeded so far that the Federal Republic could cope with the rejection of the European Defense Community (EDC) and gain entry into NATO instead. Since a national army "was not compatible with the spirit and purpose of European union," the government had supported the proposal of military cooperation until Gaullists and Communists rejected this solution in the French National Assembly. A disappointed Adenauer nonetheless told the cabinet that "the European policy, pursued till now, must be maintained," and he proposed membership in the North Atlantic Treaty Organization as an alternative to the defunct EDC.[58] Believing that "a wave of protest and resistance would sweep the populace," the opposition put up a strong fight against the ratification of the Paris treaties. In a dramatic rally in the Frankfurt *Paulskirche* on January 29, 1955, the chairman of the SPD, Erich Ollenhauer, supported by intellectuals such as the theologian Helmut Gollwitzer, accused the government of contributing to the "petrification of the division" and the "separation of the Saar." To counteract the rising calls for a referendum, Adenauer emphasized the responsibility of the elected parliament and the benefits of a "restoration of German sovereignty."[59] In the Federal Diet, the government managed to push through the treaties "with a strong majority," since a mere hope for Soviet concessions could not trump the real security offered by Western integration.[60]

Surprisingly enough, the Rome treaties that proposed a European Economic Community were not nearly as contested, even if many of their details were roundly criticized. Jean Monnet's idea of relaunching European integration "through the construction of common institutions, the gradual fusion of national economies, [and] the creation of a common market" encountered much sympathy in Bonn. The benefits of the compromise, which envisioned expanded sales of German industrial products in return for French agricultural subsidies, nuclear cooperation, and colonial preferences, were obvious to all. Because the SPD, chastened by electoral defeats, decided to agree in principle, objections now came from commercial circles and the FDP, which, preferring a free-trade zone that would include Britain, rejected "the high purchase price for Europe." To counter the claim of "many small mistakes" in the treaty, the government pointed to the acceptance of numerous German requests such as the Berlin proviso and the treatment of intra-German commerce as domestic trade. The Belgian foreign minister Henri Spaak was thus able to welcome the signing of the treaties as the "greatest voluntary and organized transformation in the history of Europe."[61]

Only with passage of the Godesberg Program of the SPD, which reversed the course of the largest opposition party, did the commitment to the West became fully accepted in the domestic politics of the FRG. The priority of reunification and negotiations with the Soviet Union, which had been continued from Schumacher's early death, through the chairmanship of Ollenhauer, up to the Plan for Germany of 1959, had not been sufficiently honored by either the Russian government or the West German voters. Toward the end of the 1950s, therefore, a group of younger foreign policy experts such as Fritz Erler, Willy

Brandt, and Helmut Schmidt attempted to lead their party slowly away from its fixation on the East, which had proved to be a dead end. Despite sharp warnings from the SED against such a "capitulation," in November 1959 the SPD's special party congress under the aegis of Herbert Wehner abandoned many "obsolete doctrines" by accepting the market economy as a reality and embracing the "protection of the liberal-democratic order," thereby supporting the armed defense of the country. While the SPD continued to prefer a "European zone of détente," Western integration had become so pervasive by this point that it no longer aroused any controversy as such.[62]

As tensions erupted within the alliance during the early 1960s, a new dispute arose about which "West" the Federal Republic actually ought to emulate. A group of self-proclaimed "Atlanticists" sought close cooperation with the United States and England, an idea that had already been promoted by such different leaders as U.S. President Teddy Roosevelt, British politician Austin Chamberlain, and German Kaiser William II but had never been truly realized. Interest in Anglo-American free-trade concepts could be found primarily in commercial circles and corporate managers who saw in them a way to operate in the international market without restrictions. Members of the military, security experts, and armaments lobbyists also looked to Washington because of the superiority of its conventional weapons tested in the Korean War, the need for its nuclear umbrella against the Russian threat, and the strong political will for defense. Liberal thinkers were able to invoke the congruence of values between the U.S. constitutional tradition and the German "liberal-democratic order." The problem with the Atlantic orientation, however, was the fluctuation of an American foreign policy, heavily influenced by domestic politics, between John Foster Dulles's "roll-back" and President Kennedy's search for détente.[63]

The "Gaullists," who sought a stronger orientation toward Germany's continental neighbor France, took the opposite tack. This partnership harkened back to the cooperation between former Foreign Ministers Aristide Briand and Gustav Stresemann in the 1920s, which had been continued even under Ambassador Otto Abetz during the Vichy regime, albeit in a more problematic vein. Cultural affinities in West Germany, which for centuries had been influenced by France's literature, cultivated lifestyle, and legal system (the Code Napoléon), spoke in favor of a closer relationship to Paris. The "politics of reconciliation," however, had to overcome the tension over the return of the Saarland to the Federal Republic through a referendum in 1956. When a military putsch of 1958 brought Charles de Gaulle to power, the presidential system of the Fifth Republic also finally stabilized the political scene in Paris. In contrast to some of his predecessors, the general was a statesman who thought in historical terms and, largely out of resentment for having been ignored during his wartime exile, strove for greater independence from the United States.[64] But the difficulty of looking to Paris for support derived from its limited military power which, despite the nuclear *force de frappe*, hardly sufficed for genuine protection against the East.

The political alternatives represented by the Atlanticists and Gaullists triggered sharp conflicts during the end of the Adenauer era. Despite successful state visits to Washington and friendships to some Americans, the aging chancellor never quite understood the New World but always felt closer to the old European neighbor and instinctively sympathized with his partner, de Gaulle.[65] On the one hand, the young Turks in the CSU, the Bavarian sister party of the CDU, such as Franz Joseph Strauß and Freiherr zu Guttenberg, believed that cooperation with Paris offered a better chance for further emancipation and the acquisition of nuclear weapons for Germany. On the other hand, the Protestant wing of the CDU in North Germany, led by Foreign Minister Gerhard Schröder and Defense Minister Kai Uwe von Hassel, was more disposed to an Atlantic orientation. For the 1963 Elysée Treaty, which was supposed to seal Franco-German friendship and strengthen practical cooperation, the Atlanticists insisted on a preamble, containing language that would prevent any weakening of transatlantic cooperation.[66] The Gaullists took revenge for this defeat by eventually helping to engineer the fall of Adenauer's successor Ludwig Erhard who, despite his Atlanticist leanings, had been humiliated by President Lyndon Johnson.[67] In the long run, these quarrels only proved that a successful Western policy required both friendship with France and attachment to America.

The ideological justification for Western integration was furnished by a sturdy anti-Communism that united both bourgeois conservatives and social democrats in common defense against the East. To dramatize the threat of totalitarianism, articles in the press claimed that "an unimaginable terror rages over the eighteen million Germans in the Soviet Zone," coordinated by a "seamless network" of secret services, SED organizations, and seemingly harmless social groups. West German government agencies and private organizations such as the "Action Committee against the Fifth Column" warned against the penetration of the Federal Republic by some 200 "Communist front organizations." They alleged that peace groups in particular were "steered and financed by Communists," while the West German Communist Party was dominated by "remote-controlled apparatchiks."[68] Various Western organizations such as the Task Force against Inhumanity, the Federation of Free Jurists, and the Eastern Office of the SPD thus attempted to smuggle their own anti-Communist pamphlets into the GDR. At the same time, the federal government decided "to consider the KPD as unconstitutional" and to apply for its ban on the basis of Article 21 of the Basic Law.[69]

The GDR's chief argument for closer ties to the Soviet Union drew on a heroic notion of anti-Fascist resistance that employed the victory over Hitler as a kind of moral capital. The socioeconomic interpretation of National Socialism as the most advanced form of monopoly capitalism facilitated the claim that fascism lived on in the bourgeois Federal Republic and that American NATO generals were no different than the SS. Crude claims offered by the SED propaganda machine—such as the "inhumane and criminal" dropping of potato beetles from American airplanes, the charge that "Adenauer is the murderer" who was preparing a third world war, and the slandering of the Federal Republic as a "police state"—were designed to hold its own population in check.[70] At the same time, purportedly independent organizations such as the Working Group for German Understanding published appeals against the Western approval of the Schuman Plan, the signing of the General Treaty, the plans of the EDC, and the like. To prevent a lasting integration into the West, the SED leadership tried to appeal to West German nationalism with the help of a broad signature campaign, advocating a peace treaty.[71]

The Cold War confrontation demanded that the Germans make a clear choice, both at home and abroad, for either "the free world" or "the socialist camp." The GDR saw itself as an attempt to realize "a broadened version of democracy" and thus attacked the West for supposedly having "accepted the [legal] succession of the brown monster," the Third Reich. The FRG, in contrast, feared the "aggressive and imperialistic designs of the Soviet bloc" and claimed that it was the "champion of a liberal democratic concept of government that has arisen out of Christianity and has found its values in a rule of law of a democracy." Of these two mutually exclusive conceptions, the Western variant found more resonance in the long term, since it seemed closer to reality and more open to life's opportunities. A tabulation of the Task Force against Inhumanity therefore tried to illustrate the respective "attractiveness of the West and the East" with the following numbers of migrants: Between 1950 and September 1954, 1,584,000 people moved from the East to the West, while only 164,000 went in the opposite direction.[72] The pamphlet argued that the West thus proved to be almost ten times more attractive.

Popular Americanization

Yet another important component of the turn Westward was the Americanization of large parts of popular culture and mass consumption in Germany. In this case, the controversial concept is entirely appropriate, since a concrete, tangible American influence rather than just a general manifestation of modernization was involved. Because many of these new developments first came from the United States, this process was at the time already intensely discussed under the heading of "Americanization."[73] This influence, however, was by no means a sure-fire success or only one part of the general adoption of American styles, substance, and behaviors around the globe. Instead, the deeper imprint on Germany was the result of a unique postwar constellation that encouraged such a fundamental cultural transformation: On the one hand, the policy of the occupation powers sought a "reorientation" that would operate on the basis of its own model and support its own cultural products commercially. On the other hand, disillusioned German youths were extraordinarily open to foreign offerings, thirsting for contacts with the outside world, and therefore they ignored the warnings against Western decadence that were coming from the conservative guardians of tradition.[74]

Initially American cultural officials concentrated on the transmission of high culture so as to overcome inherited notions of German cultural superiority. Its chief instruments were the several dozen "America Houses," which in the larger cities offered a rich selection of U.S. newspapers, journals, and books that would help curious Germans quench their thirst for information. Typical of their political message was the celebration of America by the poet Stephen Vincent Benet: "There is a land of hope, a land of freedom. There is a land in which the most different kinds of people live, descendants of all peoples of this earth living together under the same big sky."[75] Especially appealing were novels by Ernest Hemingway, William Saroyan, and others that furnished a key to understanding this land of contradictions, as well as art exhibits that brought back masterpieces of modernism from their exile in the United States. Attempts to convey the work of classical composers like Aaron Copeland and dramatists such as Thornton Wilder, however, proved more difficult. But when reading Nathaniel Hawthorne, one young English major noted enthusiastically: "Finally, [this is] another America than the one we're used to from the U.S. newspapers, journals, and the occupiers."[76]

In one area in particular these intellectual efforts were surprisingly successful—namely, in establishing the discipline of political science in the universities during the 1950s as a U.S.-oriented "science of democracy." The occupation powers pressed for the resumption of this interrupted tradition in order to provide a kind of "driver's education for politics" that would nourish a more broadly based political education. The founding fathers of the new discipline, including Theodor Eschenburg and Eugen Kogon, were decided democrats who had been trained as jurists, historians, and journalists. Returning emigrants from the United States also played an important part in establishing the new discipline; these included the conservative Arnold Bergsträsser in Freiburg, who strove to develop a scholarly basis for responsible citizenship, and the liberal Ernst Fraenkel at the Free University of Berlin, the author of a brilliant analysis of the dual character of the Nazi dictatorship who wanted to see German democracy follow Western models. With the methodological turn of the second generation toward behavioral science and quantification, the social sciences reclaimed their connection to the international standards established by American researchers and continued to serve as conduits of Western ideals.[77]

The influence of American popular culture such as comic books, which in the 1950s began to replace traditional children's literature, nonetheless reached a wider public in the long run. Fantasy novels, especially those written by Karl May, rather than the realistic portrayals of authors such as Friedrich Gerstäcker, had already contributed to a fascination for Indians among youths who romanticized native Americans as "noble savages."[78] This facilitated the shift in reading interest from combat magazines, which glorified the heroism of the overmatched Wehrmacht, to cowboy stories, based on the movie adventures of Tom Mix and other purported heroes of the wild west, which were especially appealing, because one could identify with their characters without any pangs of conscience. At the same time, translations of the cartoon adventures of Mickey Mouse, Tarzan, and Superman began to appear, all of which proved popular with youngsters, even if their style of word balloons and sound imitations seemed strange at first. Although pedagogues complained that "youth has no serious interests [and] satisfies its educational needs with 'comic strips,'" they had nothing that could even come close to matching the colorful offerings of the Americans.[79]

The influx of American entertainment music had an even more dramatic effect, since it, more than anything else, ignited acrimonious conflicts between the generations. The cult of swing music had already served as a form of youth protest against the Nazi dictatorship, and during the postwar period university students in particular were interested in jazz as an authentic expression of the elemental musicality of suppressed blacks in North America.[80] Rock music, which in the mid-1950s began to be broadcast by Allied stations such as the Armed Forces Network (AFN) and Radio in the American Sector (RIAS), reached a substantially larger audience, since its powerful beat and simple, electronically amplified melodies appealed especially to working-class youth. Alarmed adults saw in the suggestive gyrations of Elvis Presley an unrestrained sexuality, while journalists reported on the "mass hysteria" and teenage brawls unleashed by his and similar artists' music. Indeed, to many critics the entire Christian West seemed suddenly in danger. But there was no escaping when "rowdies" in jeans and petticoats wailed "Hey Barbariba" or other nonsense refrains. How could one protest against the supposedly negative influence of the Western superpower whose protection against the Communist threat was so desperately needed? In the Federal Republic, Cold War liberals eventually did cool down these passions, but in the East the narrow-minded struggle against this "boogie-woogie culture" continued.[81]

Most unsettling were the temptations of the Hollywood films that had flooded the cinemas since the late 1940s, as they seemed to purvey dangerous ideals. The public was fascinated by U.S. movies, especially when they were produced by emigrants such as Billy Wilder, because they were technically superior to domestic films and depicted a dream world, untouched by war, that offered a sugarcoated view of American reality. The U.S. marketing cartel's offensive to carve up the German media market, actually financed by Washington as part of its information policy, contributed to the quashing of German competition.[82]

On one weekend, for instance, West Berlin cinemas showed no fewer than twenty American flicks, including "Cowboy Gangsters, Bandits of Corsica, Tarzan and the She-Devil, Bitter Creek, Fuzzy the Gunslinger, The Creature from the Black Lagoon, Arms Runner, or Satan's Cradle." A Protestant youth newspaper inveighed against such "racy adventure films," arguing that "tolerating them has nothing at all to do with protecting freedom," although German *Heimat* movies that romanticized nature and village life were hardly any better. The CDU demanded that youth be sheltered from the "powerful and often bewildering effects of film and other aspects of the amusement industry," but raising the age limit for cinemas to eighteen years failed to break the attraction of the Hollywood films.[83]

The transmission of new patterns of mass consumption also reinforced the tendency toward Americanization in German society. During the occupation, "chocolate, coffee, and cigarettes" in particular were "highly desirable articles," so that "Luckies" became proverbial and the range of goods in the soldiers' PX stores seemed like paradise to the defeated population. Young women in particular, wanting to look their best for the GIs, yearned for imported cosmetics, nylon stockings, and more fashionable clothes, leading surprised American reporters to speak of a "*Fräulein*-miracle."[84] Along with rock music and cowboy films, novel fashions such as studded jeans and petticoats, as well as greased ducktail and bobbed hairdos, appeared on the scene, which were immediately imitated by the thousand. Since "blue jeans" were initially forbidden in many schools (and for much longer in the GDR), they became a cult object for young men who longed to express their independence from conventions, without, however, realizing that they were also falling victim to a commercial trend.[85] Even businessmen signaled their growing sophistication and cosmopolitanism by drinking scotch or bourbon and donning American business suits, trying to act like the characters in Hollywood films.

The continued improvement of living conditions during the 1960s also led to the acquisition of durable consumer goods that, as in America, were to be paid off over time. Growing prosperity first enabled the modernization of the household through the purchase of vacuum cleaners, electric ovens, and, above all, refrigerators, which were supposed to liberate housewives from the daily burden of grocery shopping. With the acquisition of a radio and a record player, and later a black-and-white television, an entertainment revolution then took place in the living room, that was eventually also complemented by the telephone. Moreover, on the streets the motorization of transportation gathered speed, starting with the moped and motorcycle, proceeding to the motor scooter and minicar (Isetta, Goggomobil), and finally extending to real automobiles such as the VW Beetle. As a result, comforts of daily life that previously had been reserved for the upper strata became accessible to more and more ordinary people, forcing elites to counter this "social leveling" through a distinction in style and quality.[86] Although many appliances were actually designed by German engineers, they spread according to images of affluence derived from the "American way of life."

The skyrocketing demand for consumer goods was also propelled by methods of manufacturing and distribution that underwent a fundamental Americanization. Through American subsidiaries, study in the United States, and advanced training seminars, modern management techniques began to take root, placing greater weight on competition and profit. In addition, the franchise system also gained acceptance, with individual merchants merging into chains wherever possible so as to purchase at lower cost and advertise more effectively. The grocery trade in particular, but also department stores, adopted new forms of self-service so that "king customer" could pick out products himself without having to rely on the help of often unwilling salesgirls. Moreover, advertisements became flashier and more aggressive. Rather than providing information about the advantages of the product in long, tedious texts, their pithy slogans such as "Take a break, drink Coca-Cola" intimated a modern lifestyle. Even German firms therefore began using English labels such as "happy end make-up" as a way of suggesting an aura of worldliness. Since it helped to overcome lifestyle differences with Western neighbors, it is "possible, indeed probable, that the evolution toward a consumer society in the Federal Republic promoted the civilization of Germany."[87]

Ironically, even the antimaterialist protest culture of the student movement borrowed from the model furnished by the American civil rights movement. Although the United States, due to the Vietnam war, represented the chief imperialist enemy, some activists such as Daniel Cohn-Bendit had nonetheless studied there, while others, like Rudi Dutschke, were married to Americans. Their inspiration was Martin Luther King's strategy of nonviolent protest against unjust laws that had proven so effective in exposing racial discrimination in the American South. Students also rapidly adopted protest techniques like the "sit-in" and "teach-in" from campuses like Berkeley and Wisconsin in order to stage an endless seminar, discussing the pros and cons of American military intervention in Southeast Asia. Likewise, the antiauthoritarian forms of the hippie subculture quickly made their way to Berlin, Frankfurt, Hamburg, and other cities, since the protest songs of Joan Baez, the long hair and bell-bottom trousers of the flower children, and the sexual experimentation and drug use in Haight-Ashbury symbolized a new kind of freedom. Stimulated by these and other developments from the outside, the strategy of "direct action" and "limited breach of laws" emerged in the German context as a way of unmasking repression, both real and imagined.[88]

Fragmentary evidence suggests that the transmission of the Soviet model to an East German population under stricter political control appears to have remained rather limited by comparison. Only an educated minority was interested in "the culture of the Soviet Union," which on official occasions was offered as Russian literature, classical music, or ballet. While the broader public grew accustomed to the heroic propaganda films, depicting the construction of socialism, intellectuals were more interested in signs of a realistic debate about the problems of Stalinism during the thaw. To be sure, the successes of the Soviet space program impressed young people with an interest in technology, since Sputnik seemed to prove socialism's ability to succeed in the future. In addition, the *druschba* (friendship) festivals with Soviet delegations, garnished with Cossack dances or balalaika concerts, did sometimes make positive impressions. But the heralded German-Soviet friendship had to overcome traditional prejudices of cultural superiority while at the same time struggling against repressed memories of the brutality of the "liberation from Fascism." The passive resistance against learning Russian, a required subject in school, demonstrated that the majority of the population ultimately refused to adopt the Soviet cultural model.[89]

Despite the official anti-Americanism of the SED, which denounced Washington as the center of capitalist exploitation and international imperialism, a subcutaneous Americanization also emerged in the GDR. In Western Christmas packages and hard currency "Intershops," above all American products including cigarettes, alcohol, and cosmetics transported the aromas of the wider world to the East and set the standards for style and quality with which the country's own goods could not compete. As East Germans emigrated by means of their television sets, they marveled at the outside world through American soap operas like "Dallas" and reruns of old feature films because more realistic comparisons that travel to the United States would have enabled were denied. The appeal of rock music, broadcast by Western stations such as Radio Luxemburg (RTL) to about one-third of East German youth, was so powerful that Walter Ulbricht had to authorize a counterprogram of his own, the youth station called DT64.[90] When East German bands played Western hits, they often overstepped the bounds of what was permitted, creating a perennial problem with young "rowdies." While the Communist Party portrayed the United States as an oppressor and aggressor, citing internal critics like Angela Davis, attempts to ban its culture actually led East German citizens to fantasize about America as an incarnation of a better life.[91]

Another drastic indication of Americanization was the sharp increase in the use of Americanisms in the decades after the Second World War. So many words and phrases were either borrowed directly from English or transposed into German—particularly in the media, but also in slang—that Federal President Gustav Heinemann demanded: "The deluge of Americanisms must finally be pushed back." On the one hand, the adoption of some military terminology such as "Jeep" or technical jargon like "personal computer" was probably unavoidable.[92] On the other hand, this trend was increasingly driven by advertising that primarily targeted young people with catchwords that sounded "modern, dynamic, young, stylish, vital, [or] sexy." Ultimately, however, efforts of diverse groups such as the German Language Association (VDS) to protect the German language "against being displaced by English" could do little to hinder the spread of some 4,600 Americanisms (another list even goes up to 20,000). Many of the fashionable imports are even incorrect, since in the United States nobody knows what a "handy," the German term for a mobile phone, is supposed to be! The frequent borrowing of American words has contributed to the emergence of a hybrid "New English German," also sometimes called "Germlish" or "Denglisch," that shows better than anything else the extent of America's cultural influence at the everyday level.[93]

Ironically, the spread of anti-Americanism might be considered a further indicator of Americanization, since only a strong sense of being threatened could give rise to such virulent protests. To begin with, the defeated German elite possessed a long tradition of cultural pessimism that abhorred America as decadent, plebeian, corrupted by Jewish influences, and ruled by the rabble. Moreover, Marxist circles also denounced the United States, as one GDR pamphlet with the title "Ami Go Home!" showed, as a capitalist exploiter, an imperialistic oppressor, and, after 1968, as the author of "consumer terror" or proponent of "globalization." Among the motives of this hostility were anger at the harshness of the occupation and resentment at having lost so much power, as well as jealousy of American prosperity and disappointment in the gap between U.S. ideals and actions: "After everything that I've learned to this point . . . I'll say it straight out that the Americans are the biggest hypocrites." This hostility had less to do with the undeniable problems of U.S. society than with German struggles that cited the American example to justify their own reservation against parliamentary government, objection to military deployment, or opposition to anti-Communism. The United States has come to serve as a convenient screen upon which a wide range of entirely different critiques of the West could be projected.[94]

The Americanization that occurred in the postwar decades was therefore a lengthy process that affected various areas of society and culture in contradictory ways. The conscious attempt to promote lasting change on the U.S. model, such as the "new orientation" toward a Western democracy, was, as evidenced by the frequent complaints of occupation officers, only a partial success. More effective were German adaptations of popular culture and mass consumption that occurred not just through direct importations but through parallel development of similar trends. During the Cold War, those on the right of the political spectrum required U.S. protection against the Communist threat but generally rejected the transmission of American culture, at least until the relationship eased somewhat under Chancellor Erhard. In contrast, the West German left, which embraced the more relaxed lifestyle represented by clothing, music, and films, protested against Washington's nuclear weaponry and policies in the Third World. Between these extremes, however, the majority developed unambiguously positive feelings for America, its democratic system, its dynamic economy, and its entertainment culture.[95] Only in the GDR did there remain a peculiar ambivalence, in which official hostility collided with private interest.

Contradictions of "De-Germanization"

Since the Second World War—in part by foreign compulsion, and in part by their own volition—the Germans have shed many of the threatening aspects of their former appearance. Young people in particular can hardly be distinguished anymore from their West European neighbors in terms of their casual dress, cultural habits, food preferences, and body language. On supermarket shelves many groceries come from abroad, and in upscale specialty stores there are more international products than ever before. German hosts have an increasingly hard time finding restaurants that offer "typical German" fare for their foreign guests. When driving across the country, one is more likely to hear English-language music on the radio, even if it is played by native bands, than German tunes. Likewise, the films shown on commercial television and in movie theaters are for the most part imported from Hollywood. Moreover, four-fifths of the expressions used on the Internet stem from the United States—the list goes on and on. Indeed, the changes in lifestyle have been so extensive that the cultural anthropologist Hermann Bausinger has asked ironically: "How German are the Germans?"—one would be tempted to add "still."[96]

The gradual formation of a "civil character" through "informalization" signals the end of the special path between East and West that Germans once so proudly claimed. Since the Communist alternative, because of the threatening policies of the Soviet Union, did not seem especially attractive, the Western model of capitalist democracy was able to overcome considerable reservations and prevail in the long run. Although not always consciously desired, the resulting Westernization consisted of overlapping processes of positive individual encounters, attachment to the Western alliance for military protection, and youthful fascination with American popular culture, all of which mutually conditioned and reinforced each other. Integration into the "West" or the "free world" demanded fewer drastic changes than cooperation with the egalitarian East would have entailed, because Germany's own civic traditions needed only to be liberated from their nationalist excesses and not abolished altogether through a social revolution. The result of these changes in values and behavior, carried out over several decades, was a reorientation of the political culture, which is sometimes celebrated as the return of a chastened apostate to a common Western civilization.[97]

Interpreting the Westernization of the Federal Republic as an exemplary success story, however, elides the considerable struggles and problems that were associated with this transformation. As the traditional anti-Americanism of Leo Matthias indicates, some conservative circles originally harbored strong reservations against this form of modernization that ironically resurfaced during the 1960s in the leftist polemics of Rolf Winter against American imperialism.[98] At the same time, the "star-pupil syndrome" shown in the defeated nation's unconditional embrace of the parameters set by the respective occupation powers also bore witness to a widespread opportunism that made many Germans into accomplices in the division of their own country. Was not the escape from feelings of guilt through a renunciation of previous identity as much proof of repression of memory as it was part of a constructive process of coping with a problematic past?[99] Even if alarmist warnings against the culturally destructive consequences of turning toward the west turned out to be exaggerated, not all of the models that were uncritically adopted had a truly positive effect. Their impact depended entirely on the particular version of the "West" that Germany had now arrived in.[100]

The widespread criticism of the dark underside of the "free world" indicates that even for many of its supporters "the West" was by no means an unproblematic standard in the postwar period. Did not leading Western countries such as Great Britain and France have an imperialist past whose evil effects persisted despite decolonization and was not this imperialism, in fact, indirectly continued by the United States? Was the West not tarnished by a hideous racism that had justified slavery and apartheid, and, even after they had been abolished, continued to foster violence against immigrants? Did capitalist greed unregulated by law not lead to the exploitation of the workforce, while unbridled competition produced time and again new economic crises that wrecked the previous advances? Was mass consumerism itself not a form of compulsory acquisition of endless novelties, whose possession satisfied the consumer less and less, and was popular culture not a kind of drug, which made people dependent on shallow entertainment in the long run?[101] In order not just to exchange their own pathologies for the problems of their mentors, German intellectuals had to embark on a critical encounter with the West that would allow them to adopt its positive sides without taking on its historic liabilities.

The cumulative process of a "normative Westernization" could only succeed if its advocates oriented themselves on an ideal notion of the West that encompassed the central values of the American and French Revolutions. The philosophical point of departure of these liberating ideas was the postulate of releasing the individual from authoritarian tutelage and affording him greater opportunities for self-realization. Central to this ideal was therefore a guarantee of the human rights of "freedom, equality, and fraternity," that was to prevent a relapse into right- or left-wing dictatorships. These lofty notions also contained the principle of a civil society based on civic responsibility that preceded the state and allowed bringing people together in groups to pursue collective goals. Finally, the public sphere that emerged from such initiatives offered the chance for self-criticism that was lacking in dictatorships and, despite all ideological prejudices and political missteps, could put the democracies back on the right path.[102] The gradual adoption of this civilizational canon of values is a historical achievement of the postwar period that ironically has imposed a new responsibility on the Germans to serve as agents of Westernization in the current transformation of East Central Europe.

CHAPTER 5

Arriving at Democracy

As the country struggled to rebuild, "the great majority of the German people" succumbed "to [political] apathy." Observers from the U.S. military government explained the widespread retreat into private life by claiming that the Germans, suffering "from the consequences of the long Nazi dictatorship and the impact of the recent total defeat," were "much too preoccupied with questions of survival such as food and shelter" to think of anything else. As a result of such traumatic experiences, "only a minority regarded" a fresh start as an "opportunity," while the majority thought of it as an "onerous obligation."[1] Although the idea of democracy, which the Allies promoted with different accents, seemed to have been tarnished by the Weimar debacle, some intellectuals —such as the left-leaning Catholic, Walter Dirks—called for a fundamental renewal of Europe through a "productive utopia," based on freedom and socialism: "It requires the passionate efforts of those who are committed to keeping the constructive anxiety of the best members of society alive" in order to seize "the precious opportunity for a 'transformation.'"[2]

Democratizing the defeated Reich was also an essential war aim of the Allies who mentioned it in the Potsdam Agreement as a general, but distant task for the future. But preparing for the eventual "restructuring of Germany's political life on a democratic basis" remained a problematic compromise formula because it sought to reconcile the open approach of the American spirit of freedom with the controlled concept of a Soviet "people's democracy." In principle, both versions agreed that democratization entailed the restoration of basic rights such as the freedom of speech, the reconstitution of local and regional self-government, and the refounding of "all democratic political parties." But in practice the priority of assuring military security and the contrasting interpretations of this agenda soon led to endless conflicts. Even some advisors in the U.S. military government tried primarily to reestablish representative institutions, while others pursued a more far-reaching project of cultural reorientation. Behind General Eisenhower's promise that "we want to help you to rebuild your lives on a democratic basis,"[3] lay a fundamental paradox: How could an authoritarian occupation regime impart the spirit of freedom to a skeptical, defeated people?

There was good reason, nonetheless, to answer the question whether democracy was possible in Germany more positively than, for example, in Japan, whose defeat was no less thorough. To begin, such an effort was able to draw on the liberal traditions of the 1848 revolution, which had deep roots in the southwestern regions of Baden and Württemberg. Moreover, it could build on the "creeping parliamentarization" of the semiconstitutional Second Empire, as well as resume the constitutional development of the Weimar Republic while avoiding its flaws.[4] Finally, it might also use the moral capital of the anti-Nazi resistance and respond to the demand of liberal émigrés for a "sociological, moral, economic, and politically democratic renewal."[5] In the fall of 1945, Rudolf Agricola, the editor in chief of the *Neue Neckar Zeitung*, thus called on Germans "to create the conditions for this [rebirth] themselves." By explaining that "the essence and responsibility of democracy" was based on natural law, leading politicians such as Konrad Adenauer and Kurt Schumacher strove to embed a "democratic development with a European spirit" in the core values of Western civilization.[6] Democracy, therefore, was not just to be implanted by force from the outside but needed to be founded anew from within and learned through active participation.

The voluminous literature on postwar history pays relatively little attention to the problem of democratization as such. As in the portrayal of the House of History in Bonn, the process is often subsumed under the general perspective of a success story, with the failed dictatorship of the GDR serving as a dark foil.[7] The surveys that appeared for the twenty-fifth and fiftieth anniversaries of the Federal Republic's founding evince a growing sense of satisfaction with the "political miracle" that is, of course, not entirely unjustified.[8] Conservative commentators tend to exude a Whiggish optimism and locate the breakthrough of democracy early on with the passage of the Basic Law and Konrad Adenauer's lengthy chancellorship. Leftist critics of "restoration," by contrast, point to a later process of liberalization in the symbolic year of 1968 and voice a "perpetual concern" about the remaining deficits of German democracy.[9] How one ought to treat the democratic rhetoric of the German "Democratic" Republic remains an open question as well—was it only a thinly veiled attempt to conceal the dictatorship of the SED, or did an alternative conception actually lie behind it?[10] It appears that formal categorizations and normative approaches have largely prevented this line of questioning from being properly historicized.

One way to approach this transformation of political culture might be an analysis of the gradual recovery of democracy's legitimacy during the postwar period. Such a cultural perspective would move beyond the dominant institutional focus of the literature and look more closely at the processes through which West Germans gradually came to accept the provisional arrangement of the Federal Republic. In her pioneering analysis of the stability and collapse of the GDR, the political scientist Sigrid Meuschel distinguishes between a merely "conditional loyalty" toward and a more "fundamental legitimacy" of the political system. Her distinction raises the question why attitudes toward the FRG were able to evolve from passive acceptance to active support, while public opinion failed to warm up to the SED dictatorship. This approach addresses economic, social, and cultural dimensions beyond the realm of politics that also play an important part in the emotional attachment to a system.[11] The following reflections will thus begin with the formal establishment of democracy, then proceed to analyze the internal acceptance of self-government, and finally discuss how the parliamentary system met the test of subsequent crises.

Formal Democratization

The second German democracy did not emerge on its own volition but, rather, by fiat of the competing victorious powers. Initially the Soviet Union took the lead by permitting "anti-Fascist parties" to organize and combining the Communists (KPD), Social Democrats (SPD), Christian Democrats (CDU), and Liberals (LDPD) into a united front in order to work for "a transformation of German politics."[12] Already in its first declaration of June 1945, the KPD called for the "creation of the democratic rights and freedoms of the people" that would lead to a new government, which, freely elected by the entire nation, would form the basis of a "new democratic republic."[13] This goal, which also appealed to non-Communists, went beyond simply reintroducing the failed structures and practices of Weimar democracy since it presumed the unity of the left. "Without a unified working class [there can be] no democracy," argued one leading voice in the KPD.[14] The problem with this Communist initiative, however, was that the Soviet understanding of the concept of democracy differed from Western notions of freedom by requiring, above all, an end to economic exploitation and nationalist oppression: "The dictatorship of the working class is the democracy of those who work."[15]

Since they considered the Germans too "immature for political life," the Americans began somewhat later with their own attempt "to lead Germany back into civilized society and the European economy." To provide a roadmap, General Lucius Clay commissioned Michigan political scientist James K. Pollock to come up with a comprehensive plan "to prepare the German people for democratic self-government." His wide-ranging effort to reorient an entire political culture was to concentrate primarily on the transformation of the schools, the press, the churches, and public life.[16] However, the expected conversion was impeded by the apparent contradiction of the military government's actions with its own ideals. As one U.S. employee fumed: "They don't give a damn about democratic rules when they've got someone in their pocket." Because of the disappointment brought on by unrealistic expectations, enormous patience was required of the Allies if the "misunderstanding of democracy" as simply a parliamentary form of government was to be overcome and the meaning of a democratic "way of life" was to be explained. Convinced German democrats like Dolf Sternberger thus had to resolve the contradictions of the "tyranny of freedom" for their skeptical countrymen.[17]

The Allied project of reorienting the Germans toward democracy already began in the POW camps, albeit with contrasting ideological priorities. Amid the terrible conditions of the Russian gulag, the promise of more food led volunteers to participate in anti-Fascist courses where some young soldiers, such as the future Dresden party chief Hans Modrow, found their way to communism through genuine remorse.[18] The better material situation for officers of the Africa Corps in camps within the United States facilitated the development of a more lively discussion. Although ardent nationalists refused to give up hope for victory until the end, critical minds such as Gustav H. Blanke began holding lectures for their fellow soldiers on the Weimar Republic and "American democracy." In early 1945, Blanke and 150 other carefully chosen candidates were sent to Fort Kearney in Nebraska, where they discussed how to lead the German people back to an improved version of Weimar democracy. In these courses speakers included, for instance, the well-known historian Howard Mumford Jones who lectured on American history, the émigré Henry Ehrmann who portrayed "German history in a new light," and the political scientist T. V. Smith who introduced the theory of democracy. As a result, a number of dedicated advocates of democratization emerged from these courses.[19]

To win over the younger generation for democracy, reorientation policies also paid special attention to the schools. Paul Wandel, the director of the Central Administration of People's Education in the Soviet Zone, outlined an ambitious agenda: "It is essential to fashion new learning objectives, new curricula, new teaching methods, new teachers, new relationships between the people, the teachers, and the school." With support from the SED, that meant establishing comprehensive schools, hiring uncompromised teachers, and introducing different curricula. But this forced reorganization met with considerable resistance from pupils who were subjected to it: "Democracy = rule of the people = total tyranny of the new bigwigs."[20] Similarly far-reaching plans for structural reform in the Western zones failed after meeting stiff resistance from traditional pedagogues who clung to religious education, as well as from the association of high-school teachers who fought to maintain the elitism of the secondary schools. Moreover, the individual German states jealously guarded their independence in matters of education and culture and thus rejected reforms aimed at standardizing education. But with help from America Houses and exchange programs, reformers were able to liberalize teaching styles, produce new textbooks, and introduce student self-government, all of which subtly contributed to the democratization of schooling in Germany.[21]

Since large-scale efforts at reeducation often engendered more resentment than success, the occupation powers, at least in the West, began to adopt more indirect forms of reorientation. The press proved to be an especially important field, though "newspapers only appeared irregularly due to the paper shortage, were only [slightly better] than skeleton editions, and as a rule could only be obtained 'under the table.'" In the Soviet zone, Communist censorship rendered the media boring and, worse still, unbelievable.[22] In the West, by contrast, the Allies implemented a strict licensing procedure that only permitted anti-Fascists without Nazi ties to establish publishing houses in order to create a new media that would give the younger generation a greater appreciation for facts than opinions. Young journalists, such as Rudolf Augstein, fortunate enough to receive one of the coveted licenses, were able to found new publications such as *Der Spiegel* and to embark on a lifelong career. Nevertheless, the shortage of experienced personnel eventually allowed networks of publicists that had already been active in the Third Reich to return. For all of the criticism it received, this reorientation policy did establish a new, democratic public sphere, thus compelling even conservative commentators such as Hans Zehrer, Giselher Wirsing, and Karl Korn to accommodate themselves to the media's changed tone.[23]

The authorization of self-government at the local level proved more effective than other efforts at reorientation since it enabled the defeated population to participate in finding solutions to their own problems. Although they had assumed sovereignty, the occupation powers could not carry out basic administrative tasks themselves due to lack of personnel and inadequate language skills. As a result, they were forced to bring in German experts to help, provided that these had not been too compromised by collaborating with the Nazis. Not surprisingly, conflicts repeatedly erupted between local officials and their Allied overseers, especially in areas such as the absorption of refugees from the Eastern lands, leading General Clay to burst out in anger: "The Germans don't have a democracy yet, therefore they ought not to deceive themselves into thinking that they can claim its benefits."[24] In spite of the inevitable friction that shifting responsibility to local experts entailed, strong working relationships developed when Germans and Americans tackled issues of survival together. "But we did allay the chaos," announced Arthur Werner, the mayor of Berlin, so "everyday life in our city has returned to an orderly course." By the end of the year, this "testing ground for the practice of democracy" could thus point to its first real successes.[25]

At the same time, regional and national political parties began to reemerge, which, while built upon traditional camps, modified them in important aspects as well. The first grouping was the Communist Party (KPD), which by June 1945 was already promoting itself as a decidedly anti-Fascist party, thereby giving it a head start in political agitation. The reconstituted Social Democratic Party (SPD) could also claim not to have voted for the 1933 Enabling Law, and with Kurt Schumacher they possessed a passionate democrat for whom the preservation of German unity was a top priority. By contrast, the Christian Democratic Party (CDU), led by the Rhenish regional politician Konrad Adenauer, was a truly new creation—an interdenominational party of the middle class that led Catholics out of their isolation in the Center Party and weaned Protestants from nationalism. Similarly, the Free Democratic Party (FDP), chaired by Reinhold Maier, was an attempt to combine the fragmented liberal camp into one comprehensive party. This consolidation succeeded because Allied prohibitions of neo-Fascist organizations forced rightists to join the other middle-class parties. Since the CDU and the SPD triumphed in the first local elections, the Communists, looking for a way to become more competitive, accelerated the forced merger of the SPD into the SED in the spring of 1946.[26]

A further step toward democratization was the reconstitution of states as larger administrative units within the occupation zones. Some of these *Länder* (for example, Bavaria and Saxony) were based on their historical predecessors, while others (such as North-Rhine Westphalia and Thuringia) were largely new creations. These states offered "an opportunity for German officials to gain experience in self-government, since they ... [assumed] responsibility for food, supplying heating fuel, and all of the other necessities of life."[27] The governments were appointed by the Allies from among Weimar politicians, members of the resistance, and technical experts on the basis of a "white list," and consisted of representatives from all democratic parties, a fact that forced them to make frequent compromises. Nevertheless, the occupation powers intervened whenever they deemed policies to be too conservative, as occurred in Bavaria with the Schäffer cabinet, which was replaced with the more liberal Hoegner government. By the summer and fall of 1946, the new states began to gain legitimacy by drafting constitutional documents and holding elections to their legislatures, bringing success to the SPD and CDU in the West, and the SED in the East. While their minister presidents were the first elected spokesmen for German interests, they remained too weak to push through a collective national government at their last joint conference in Munich.[28]

The Basic Law that emerged from the Parliamentary Council formulated these learning processes into a constitution, taking into account the errors of the Nazi past and the experiences of the postwar period. To be sure, the Frankfurt documents put forward by the Allies in July 1948 were an important catalyst toward "working out a democratic constitution," while the informal influence of

Western advisors reinforced the tendency toward federalism and a guarantee of basic rights. But the text itself was an independent German achievement that was worked out in various committees such as the "Ellwangen Circle" of the CDU, the Herrenchiemsee Constitutional Convention, and finally the debates of the Parliamentary Council.[29] On the one hand, the Basic Law attempted to create an ethical foundation for the provisional structure of the Federal Republic by invoking the moral precepts of natural law and the sanctity of human life. On the other hand, it sought to stabilize parliamentary government through procedural safeguards such as weakening the office of the presidency, requiring a constructive vote of no confidence and instituting a "5 percent barrier" in elections to prevent splinter parties from entering parliament. Since the Basic Law was not drawn up by the largely disinterested populace but by a minority of committed democrats, its basic orientation proved surprisingly successful.[30]

The Soviet Zone's response to the failure of the unity campaign waged by the people's congresses was to found its own "German Democratic Republic." In its first manifesto, the SED downplayed its communism and presented itself somewhat misleadingly as the "party for the construction of an anti-Fascist, democratic, parliamentary republic." Nonetheless, it also promised to go beyond the bourgeois rights of "formal democracy" and break the power of the warmongers, capitalists, and bureaucrats so as to "truly" embody the will of the people.[31] Although the SED emerged from the state elections in the fall of 1946 as the strongest party, it failed to get a majority in the larger cities due to the appeal of the middle-class parties, and it came in a distant third in the Berlin city elections. This partial failure forced the party to formalize an alliance policy that removed the uncertainty of balloting by a prior agreement on candidate lists, thereby degrading the vote into an acclamation ritual.[32] To prevent the founding of a Western state, the SED then started a massive campaign for a people's congress in which an assembly elected through self-nomination would draft a unified German constitution. Since only a small minority of Westerners participated, the passage of the document ultimately led to the constitution of the GDR, based largely on the Weimar model.[33]

In actual practice, however, the two constitutions developed in quite opposite directions. In the Federal Republic, Adenauer's "chancellor democracy" helped cement democracy in the long run, perhaps because of its "semiauthoritarian" character. By weakening the presidency and establishing his authority to issue guidelines to other ministers, the Basic Law had strengthened the position of the chancellor. Moreover, with deliberate use of his seniority, no-nonsense manner, tenacity in the pursuit of objectives, and deftness during difficult negotiations, Adenauer carried out his duties in such a way that the reigns of power converged in his hands. By strengthening the office of chancellor and by retaining the chairmanship of the CDU, he was able to consolidate his authority in decisive moments, outmaneuver rivals, and impose his views on the cabinet and parliament. Likewise, in foreign affairs his great experience and natural gravitas exuded an aura of serious leadership, proving to the skeptics that even a democratic government was capable of acting decisively.[34] Thus, to his critics Adenauer appeared to be a kind of "surrogate kaiser," but, unlike the mercurial Wilhelm II, he was soon accepted as a respected statesman on the international stage.

In the GDR, by contrast, Walter Ulbricht's more radical "people's democracy" quickly evolved into an outright Communist dictatorship. The increasing discrepancy between the SED's democratic rhetoric and repressive policies gradually discredited the pretense of creating a "better Germany." Since the attempt to construct an anti-bourgeois "alternative society" resonated among the populace even less than the limited renewal in the West, it had to be imposed with more draconian methods according to Ulbricht's cynical motto: "It has to look democratic, but we've got to have everything in our hands." To make the party into an effective instrument of transformation, the SED was rigorously purged of right-leaning Social Democrats and left utopian members of Marxist splinter groups. By eliminating all open opposition, the party was, in effect, internally Stalinized.[35] At the same time, independent politicians like Jakob Kaiser of the CDU were pushed aside, and the bloc parties were reduced to acclamatory accomplices of the SED. In the long run, the violation of civil rights by the secret police, the censorship of the media, and the degradation of elections to "rubber stamping" robbed the claims of "democratic politics" of their credibility.[36]

Representing both an external military threat and a potential for domestic subversion, the Cold War had a paradoxical effect on democratization as it both accelerated and hindered the process. On the one hand, Western anti-Communism allowed nationalist members of the old elite to reconcile themselves to the provisional arrangement of the Bonn Republic as the lesser evil, because some Nazi involvement would be overlooked in the fight against the Bolshevist menace. Widespread fears of an attack by the Red Army legitimated the prohibition of the KPD in the name of "defending democracy" and facilitated efforts to bring together all middle-class forces by absorbing the Union of Expellees and Disenfranchised (BHE), the German Party (DP), and the Bavarian Party into the CDU/CSU, except for the openly neo-Nazi *Sozialistische Reichspartei* (SRP).[37] On the other hand, the East-West conflict made it easier for GDR anti-Fascists to overlook violations of the party's internal democracy or human rights in public, since coercive measures, while not exactly pleasant, might be justified as necessary by the new start. In the process, however, the hopes of a group of radical democratic and socialist intellectuals, such as Walter Dirks and Hans Mayer, to unite the best principles of both ideologies, fell by the wayside.[38]

The second German democracy was initially only tolerated by the majority but not exactly loved, to say the least. Many members of the former elite were openly bitter about Germany's precipitous fall from power: "Without a doubt, a true democracy cannot be achieved in the impoverished state in which the German people are still living today." Disappointed in the Nazi betrayal of their promises, ordinary citizens were often confused about which party they might trust. During discussions with other disillusioned youths searching for a new worldview, one disappointed SS-cadet officer encountered "pathetic remains of an undigested ideology of the past, more or less half-baked . . . phrases of Marxist theory or utopian fantasies about world improvement." Due to their "negative experiences," most people did not want anything to do with politics and persisted in maintaining "a 'without me' attitude." Merely a few responsible souls joined the emerging parties, "for something new could only be built through active participation." Young people, however, were somewhat more open: "After the experiences of the past I only wanted to be a democrat." The nineteen-year old Helmut Kohl was "downright excited" about the Basic Law, since, like many members of his generation, he felt that "this will be our republic."[39]

Was the Federal Republic, therefore, an attempt at "restoration" and thus a lost opportunity for a fresh start? Already during the founding phase, Eugen Kogon massively criticized the "incomplete renewal," a disappointment that was echoed by intellectuals in the 1960s and has informed much of the historical literature ever since. Even though much "restoration of what had been" was obvious, the question remains as to what had actually been restored—the Second Empire, the Weimar Republic, or the Third Reich? Without doubt, there was a "return of [elements of the] past" through specific efforts to reclaim supposedly uncorrupted traditions in the churches and universities and through attempts to reconstitute social cohesion under middle-class auspices. But on the whole, the thesis of a "conservative modernization" seems more accurate, since many real innovations such as the Federal Constitutional Court were introduced and technology became a new model for society to follow. "That, of all things, democracy [should] have benefited in Germany from this mentality," combining bourgeois restoration with technical modernization strikes one as an irony of history.[40]

The formal democratization that has been roughly sketched here thus laid the foundation for a gradual process of growing into democracy. Unlike in the strife-torn Weimar Republic, the second time around the Germans did not really have a choice, since the new form of government was effectively imposed on them by the Western powers. This crucial push from the outside gave the minority of native democrats the chance to establish a parliamentary framework to which an apolitical majority would gradually become accustomed. The provisional nature of the Bonn Republic, moreover, facilitated a pragmatic relationship with the new institutions, which were able to prove themselves by solving practical problems and provided a means to resist the more onerous demands of the Allies. Finally, the contrast with the dictatorship of the SED in the East helped illustrate the advantages of the democracy that was taking shape in the

West. Because the frictionless functioning of the constitutional organs suggested that the Germans were rapidly gaining practice in democracy, the parting American high commissioner James B. Conant looked confidently into the future in 1954: "The German people seem to have broken with their undemocratic past."[41]

Internalizing Democratic Values

Despite the successful establishment of democratic institutions, the cultural process of adopting the spirit of democracy remained difficult, as authoritarian thought patterns and habits of behavior tended to persist. Even after the founding of the Bonn Republic, domestic observers detected "greatest distrust [toward] and internal rejection" of the newly implanted form of government, coupled with a quest for genuine participation that one might call "perhaps somewhat romantically, a German, organic or functional democracy." This contradictory mixture of outright skepticism and inflated expectations produced both dissatisfaction and apathy: "It should be said clearly that all efforts toward a truly lively democracy still lack the broad resonance that is needed."[42] Leading American social scientists such as Gabriel Almond and Sidney Verba also found the discrepancy between the outward practice of parliamentary rituals—for example, voting—and inner reservations against democratic ideals problematic.[43] These observations raise a number of important questions: How did various social groups find their way to democracy? What factors encouraged their acceptance? And by what means did an appreciation of its values develop?

The conscious integration of members of the prior elite into the emerging democratic system through granting opportunities for wielding influence was a first step toward overcoming their aversion to "mass rule." Despite internment and denazification, indisputable expertise in administrative and economic questions permitted many tainted bureaucrats to continue their careers, serving not only the Allies but the democratic leaders as well. The reestablishment of social networks, moreover, allowed the former political class to cope with the loss of its locational advantage in Berlin and win influence in the new capital in Bonn. The controversial reinstatement of dismissed public servants according to article 131 of the Basic Law facilitated the return of discredited experts to their former offices—albeit mostly in mid-level positions in the bureaucracy, the Foreign Office, and the Bundeswehr. As a result, they succeeded in maintaining key advantages for themselves, such as the three-tiered educational system, preference for jurists in official appointments, and a career civil service despite the reformist efforts of the U.S. occupiers. The CDU and CSU not only offered opportunities for advancement to young talents such as Kurt Georg Kiesinger and Franz Joseph Strauß, but the authoritarian style of Adenauer's chancellor democracy also convinced older people that it could guarantee respect and order.[44]

In addition, the attention paid to the wishes of the churches persuaded the religiously bound middle class that democracy could become a more "Christian form of government" than the traditional authoritarian state. For a long time, members of the Protestant Churches of Germany (EKD) hesitated to distance themselves from their former nationalism and the Nazi-aligned "German Christians." Traditional Protestants were loath to admit that "because of us infinite suffering has been brought upon many peoples and countries," as the more self-critical members of the Confessing Church like Martin Niemöller admitted. Only through the ceaseless efforts by laymen such as Gustav Heinemann to convince their religious brethren did it become possible to create a feeling of democratic responsibility: "The state is no longer our master, but should be our servant. We are all responsible for its character and its decisions."[45] Similarly, the Catholic Church preferred to pass with merciful silence over the Center Party's vote in favor of the Enabling Law in 1933 and the Concordat with the Third Reich which helped legitimize Nazi rule. Among Catholics it was likely renewed concern with basic Christian values of human dignity that opened the door to their reconciliation with democracy through the founding of an interconfessional party.[46] Because of their strong moral position, the two denominations were able to exercise enormous influence on decisions relating to educational issues and family policy.

Finally, the struggle for a social democratization of the emerging Federal Republic, although not always successful, also helped the working class to integrate itself more fully.[47] While electoral success in proletarian districts and industrialized states allowed the SPD to achieve local and regional power, at the federal level it remained stuck in the less enviable role of the opposition. Adenauer was sufficiently prudent to offer unions some concessions in particular issues, such as in granting limited co-determination for labor in managing heavy industry. However, the more far-reaching and popular hope for a comprehensive nationalization of the means of production proved illusory. Moreover, the personality clash between Schumacher and the chancellor impeded continuous cooperation in formulating legislation, so that the SPD had no choice but to carve out an effective role as a parliamentary opposition. Finally, the emotional extraparliamentary movement against rearmament failed due to a Supreme Court judgment and repeated defeats at the polls; therefore, the decisions of the federal government effectively gained plebiscitary legitimacy.[48] Thus for the SPD, the advocacy of democracy on principle turned into a difficult test of conscience in practice.

Because only fringe groups continued to be excluded from participation in democratic processes, extremism found fewer opportunities to develop than had been the case in the 1920s. To be sure, former Nazis initially lost their civil rights and all explicit neo-Nazi activities were forbidden. Therefore the *Sozialistische Reichspartei*, as the successor organization of the Nazi Party, was declared unconstitutional. But the subsequent softening of denazification led to the exoneration of the majority of nominal members and even some former perpetrators, while article 131 of the Basic Law reinstated many dismissed public servants. Hence, most fellow travelers were allowed to participate in public affairs, if they had recanted sufficiently.[49] In contrast, the Communists were at first favored by many occupation officers, despite the complaints of middle-class advisors, because they ranked among the most committed anti-Fascists. But eventually their zeal for radical measures proved to be their undoing, since the ideological East-West confrontation discredited them as an appendage of Moscow. The subsequent ban of the Communist Party had only a limited effect, because it was counteracted in part through material and propagandistic support from the East.[50]

Since the GDR systematically antagonized large groups of the population, its legitimacy remained more precarious throughout its four-decade lifespan. While neo-Nazis were also banned, the East, barring a few exceptions, eliminated the members of the old elite through expropriations and purges, despite the establishment of a refuge in the National Democratic Party of Germany (NDPD). In addition, initial offers of cooperation with religious socialists quickly gave way to discrimination against the churches, which refused to bow to the totalistic claims of Marxism, so that the Eastern CDU atrophied into the role of a "fellow traveler" within the communist system. After 1950, moreover, the expellees—euphemistically called "resettlers" by the state—were no longer allowed to organize or articulate themselves. Through the forced unification of Socialists and Communists, the entire workers' movement was brought under the control of the SED and nominally became the ruling party. At the same time, the influence of union members steadily eroded after they were absorbed in the comprehensive Federation of Free German Unions (FDGB). In spite of its putative privileges, the working class therefore no longer possessed any means to assert itself. Other social organizations like the Women's League were similarly instrumentalized and, as a result, largely lost their character as representatives of collective interests.[51]

In the end, it was probably its practical performance that allowed the Federal Republic to win the numerous skeptics over to democracy. In a nutshell, Bonn could point to better "results" than either Weimar or East Berlin. Due to the visible improvement in its living situation, the undecided majority that placed little faith in the Germans' ability to govern themselves gradually became convinced that a democratic polity could master practical problems of everyday life. Initially, this involved ensuring sheer survival by providing food, shelter, and work—and in these areas even critics of the occupation acknowledged the assistance from the Western Allies. Subsequently, it meant the rebuilding of factories, transportation networks, and residential areas through the Germans' own "hard work," all of which was organized by an efficient administration and supported by the Marshall Plan. Lastly, the economic upturn played a decisive role in creating popular loyalty, since due to the lifting of emergency controls the recovery could be claimed as a success of the social market economy.[52] Because the West overcame these problems more quickly than the Soviet Zone, the good will that emerged as a result ultimately benefited the democratic system.

In the area of foreign policy, the Federal Republic was also able to point to the guarantee of security from a new world war. As a result of the wartime trauma, about half of the West German population lived in fear of a new conflict between East and West, an anxiety that was further heightened by the Korean War. Despite inevitable frictions, the presence of Western soldiers therefore came to be seen as welcome protection, demonstrated vividly by the Berlin airlift, which contributed to a positive perception of NATO as well. For this and other reasons, the majority of the populace also supported the attempts to integrate with their West European neighbors, even if it would entail a certain loss of sovereignty, as was the case with the European Coal and Steel Community. While most West Germans continued to hope that the division of the country could be overcome, their anti-Communism prevented them from going over to the Soviet camp, and only a minority of about one-third of the population called for a neutral course between the blocs.[53] For a people tested by suffering, the maintenance of peace in Europe at a time when armed conflicts were breaking out across Asia was no mean achievement, therefore helping to legitimize democracy.

In domestic politics, West German citizens were most impressed by the remarkable stability of the Adenauer cabinets, especially when compared to the governmental crises that afflicted the Weimar Republic and the Fourth Republic in France. Of course, two-thirds of the populace first needed to shed their political passivity and be convinced of the blessings provided by the largely ignored Basic Law. Surveys show that this reversal of attitudes was propelled not just by the success of Erhard's economic policies but also by the social concessions granted by Adenauer. Not surprisingly, a solid majority considered the currency reform necessary, while worrying about unemployment that only vanished with the upturn driven by the Korean War. Since socialist ideas initially had much support, most people welcomed the right of unions to participate in managerial decisions. An overwhelming majority, moreover, supported the basic ideas behind proposals for a system of burden sharing between various segments in the population that aimed to alleviate the losses suffered by some special groups such as disabled veterans or refugees in the war. As economic prosperity and social support measures reached ever greater segments of the population by the beginning of the 1950s, satisfaction with the democratic system grew appreciably.[54]

The GDR could certainly also boast of some successes, but they came later and remained at a much lower level. Poor start-up conditions such as the massive reparations demanded by the Soviet Union made it difficult for the SED to get its version of the planned economy moving, so that after 1948 a productivity gap began to open between East and West that could not be closed again. With large projects such as construction of the East Berlin boulevard Stalinallee and new industrial sites like Eisenhüttenstadt, urban reconstruction also made progress in the DDR, but the once picturesque city centers decayed for want of attention and building materials. While the hunger and cold that accompanied the first postwar years were also overcome in the East by the end of the 1950s, the state's preference for large-scale investments thwarted the development of a differentiated offering of consumer goods. As long as the border remained open, the discrepancies between the modest socialist state in the East and the dynamic, if less egalitarian, society in the West became increasingly visible, evident in the contrast between the colorful and well-stocked shop windows in the FRG and the drab and sparse displays in the GDR. As one Berliner mused: "How beautiful it was to live in West Berlin, to have Western money in our wallet. What luck we had."[55]

Another sign of West German democratization was the emergence of a critical public sphere that was willing to defend the "free constitutional state, based on the rule of law," which had emerged in 1949. With their strict licensing policy, the Allies wanted to break the habits of the Nazi-led press and irresponsible, opinionated journalism and to deliver more factual information to the public. Due to the lack of skilled newcomers, old media networks did eventually reconstitute themselves. Nevertheless, in the course of the generational change, younger journalists such as Rudolf Augstein and Marion Döhnhoff, who were more open to the West, developed a new professional ethos that favored "contemporary criticism" over approval of government policies. As a result, by the early 1950s the opinions presented by such important weeklies as *Die Zeit* and *Der Spiegel* began to grow more liberal, enabling them to become a better counterweight to the announcements of the Federal Press Office, which was controlled by the CDU. The establishment of new broadcast formats such as the muckraking television magazine "Panorama," as well as the founding of radical magazines like *konkret*, created a platform for exposing scandals and leveling criticism at the government.[56]

This cultural liberalization was reinforced by the emergence of a number of socially critical writers who strove less for philosophical introspection than for accurate portrayal of the shortcomings of postwar society. While initially authors of the "inner emigration" had dominated the literary scene with symbolic reflections on German fate, new kinds of intellectuals began to gather in the discussion circles like the famous Group 47, who spoke out publicly so as to resume the engagement of Weimar leftists. The ironic short stories by Heinrich Böll, the picaresque novels of Günter Grass, and the shocking plays by Peter Weiss challenged the traditional canon of humanistic cultivation in both style and content.[57] On the one hand, dramatists like Rolf Hochhut addressed the persistence of Nazi behavior in the Federal Republic, breaking through the wall of repressive silence that many Germans had erected between their prosperous present and problematic past.[58] On the other hand, authors such as Martin Walser furnished satirized portraits of the increasingly "affluent society" that unmercifully exposed its weaknesses. On the cultural pages of newspapers and in various journals, there thus emerged a new, subversive intellectual culture that was oriented toward human rights.

As a result of such impulses, a critical discourse on democracy developed in the early 1960s that advocated a broader social self-determination. In his reflections on *The Structural Transformation of the Public Sphere*, the young Frankfurt theoretician Jürgen Habermas formulated a justification of public discussion as a crucial precondition for civic freedom. Instead of understanding democracy merely as a series of political game rules, he portayed self-government as a social process of arriving at common understanding through debate in a civic sphere characterized by "critical publicity."[59] Similarly, in his seminal work on *Society and Democracy in Germany*, the Constance sociologist Ralf Dahrendorf located the causes of his country's "structural incapacity for democracy" in its modernization deficit, which he attributed to conflict aversion, the monopoly of elites, and withdrawal into private life. Only a fundamental liberalization of the Federal Republic would be able to truly realize the "socially founded constitution of freedom."[60] Due to the persuasiveness of such analyses, democracy became a catchword of the 1960s, expressing a general desire for more cultural openness and public participation.[61]

This new appreciation for democracy that went beyond politics enlarged the concept into a demand for a continuous transformation of society and culture. For instance, the sociologist Willy Strzelewicz did not consider the concept as "a completed condition with regard to, for example, the constitution"; instead, he understood it as "a process that is far from finished and consists not only of political, but also social, economic, and cultural relationships in society." Such an expansive notion of democracy that aimed at a liberalization of basic convictions and behavior implied a comprehensive reform of the "economy, family, and school." In other words, West Germany needed to break with its remaining authoritarian structures in the pre-political realm.[62] Going far beyond the democratic right to vote, such intellectual demands for more participation appealed especially to young people who had grown up in the Bonn Republic and chafed against its remnants of authoritarianism. One crucial element of the generational rebellion of 1968 was therefore the leftist call for the "mobilization and practice of an emancipatory and democratic counterpower, codetermination, and self-determination in all subsystems of society."[63]

Worried about the collapse of all established authority, conservative circles, in contrast, demanded that democracy be clearly restricted to the formal system of government. Bruno Heck, the general secretary of the CDU, insisted that democracy was a form of organization for the polity, but not for society: "The politicization of society, which also means democratization of society, leads to a loss of freedom."[64] The philosopher Wilhelm Hennis formulated his objections to the demands of the 68ers even more sharply, arguing that due to its misguided egalitarianism "the complementary democratization of all social areas" was nothing less than an unconstitutional "relinquishment of the foundations of Western political culture." Citing the experience of totalitarianism, he urgently warned against any blurring of the difference between the political and the nonpolitical aspects of life: "This demand" for radical democratization "is therefore not an ideology," or "just a false social consciousness, but a revolt against nature."[65] This staunch repudiation of the expansive claims of the advocates of radical reform set in motion a principled debate on the narrow and broad meanings of democracy.

Due to these developments, Western opinion polls taken in the postwar period reflect a gradual turn away from authoritarian patterns of thought and a tentative embrace of democratic values. On the one hand, memories of Nazism—more than half initially agreed with the conclusion that National Socialism was a good idea that was carried out poorly—and older authoritarian reflexes that manifested themselves primarily in patriarchal claims to superiority continued to influence thinking and behavior. But on the other hand, there were clear indications that political attitudes were shifting, because in surveys the rejection of the extremes of National Socialism and Communism tripled from 22 to 66 percent between the summer of 1945 and the fall of 1946.[66] While a minority continued to call for strong leadership, most put their faith in the people, not the experts, and preferred self-government. The great majority remained reluctant to engage in politics, but from 1948 on about half of the respondents in Berlin and somewhat fewer in the U.S. Zone began to advocate democracy as the preferred form of government. Even though social safeguards continued to have an important role, indications that Germans began to appreciate the importance of freedom of opinion and human rights grew stronger by the late 1940s.[67]

In contrast, the GDR remained far less attractive in the eyes of its own population. By the end of 1950, the general mood among three-fourths of those questioned when exchanging currency in West Berlin was either poor or very poor. People complained above all about the lack of freedom, material shortages, and feelings of powerlessness, therefore generally approving Adenauer's demand for "free elections." While four-fifths of East German youths already belonged to the Free German Youth (FDJ) by 1951, they continued to be highly interested in the West. Indeed, skepticism toward the Soviet Union and the SED remained strong, even among those who participated in official events, such as the national congress of the FDJ at Pentecost. Despite SED prohibitions, the majority listened to Radio in the American Sector (RIAS) for both serious news and lively entertainment. Of course, those groups who were adversely affected by compulsory measures (such as the farmers who faced the pressure of collectivization and most refugees) held negative views of SED leader Walter Ulbricht. But while some criticized the West's lack of response to the 1953 uprising, most supported Adenauer's "policy of strength" toward their own government.[68] A host of problems thus impeded the formation of an emotional bond to communism.

As a result of the negative impressions of the SED system and the positive perception of the Bonn government, the apolitical majority of the population slowly reconciled itself to democracy. The SPD's initial edge in voter identification lasted only until January 1953, when it began to be overtaken by the CDU. Likewise, the share of the total vote held by right-wing and left-wing splinter parties fell from one-fifth to one-tenth and thus no longer presented much of a threat. The general approval of the federal government, which until the end of 1951 had hardly exceeded its disapproval rating, climbed markedly in the course of 1953 before stabilizing at an astounding 70 percent. The election results show a similar trend: the outcome was quite close in 1949, then the CDU won a clear victory in 1953, only to gain an unprecedented absolute majority in 1957. The growing popularity of Adenauer's cabinet also extended to democracy as a form of government, which some 44 percent of voters considered stronger by the end of 1953 than in the years before.[69] The personal authority of the first federal chancellor and the approval of his policies thus undoubtedly helped to anchor the West German system in the hearts and minds of its citizens.

According to autobiographical accounts, generational change played a decisive role in overcoming deep-seated reservations against popular sovereignty.[70] Among the elderly who had been socialized in the Second Empire, it was above all the uncontested authority of Adenauer's chancellor democracy that made the Bonn state at least partly acceptable. For middle-aged citizens who had been unnerved by the political and economic chaos of the Weimar Republic, it was not so much the "adjustment to each changed political situation" as the prosperity of the social market economy and the stability of the middle-class coalition government which cast a favorable glow on the FRG. For the members of the Hitler Youth generation who had been deeply disappointed by the collapse of the Third Reich, it was the chance to realize a peaceful and secure future that slowly reduced skepticism toward political engagement: "For only through active cooperation can something new be built, because we have to take responsibility for the past as a result of our own faults." But among the different age groups, those young people who had grown up in the Federal Republic were most likely to consider democracy self-evident and to call most loudly for genuine "democratic thinking and action" in the 1960s.[71]

The acceptance of democracy, which remains underexplored in the existing historical literature, was thus a lengthy learning process that only really gained steam after the formal establishment of parliamentary institutions. Ironically, the difficult structural conditions created by the downfall of the Third Reich, the occupation, and the Cold War proved more favorable to the implantation of a parliamentary system than did the collapse of the Second Empire. In a conscious attempt to learn from the mistakes of the past, the federal government disarmed its potential critics among the old elite with a strategy of integration that, by including them in decision-making processes, helped to avoid engendering antidemocratic resentment. Through its indisputable accomplishments, especially in reconstruction, the economic miracle, and western integration, the Bonn state eventually succeeded in convincing apolitical skeptics that the Western system was superior to its socialist East German counterpart. Finally, the emergence of a critical public sphere promoted the internalization of democratic values and behavior among intellectuals, since it endowed them with the role of guardians of political conscience and the mission to reform society through an expanded notion of democracy.[72]

Testing Parliamentary Government

It was precisely the spectacular success of democracy, however, that nourished doubts among some thoughtful observers as to whether its acceptance rested merely on fickle opportunism or on solid principle. "I never got rid of the feeling," the liberal politician Hildegard Hamm-Brücher put it, "that we were really just a fair-weather democracy that had not yet passed any true test." These intellectual misgivings suggest that the approval of the Federal Republic remained conditional and might just as easily have been countermanded in more difficult times. Indeed, this is exactly the difference that Sigrid Meuschel has tried to conceptualize with her contrast between a temporary loyalty to and the fundamental legitimacy of a political system.[73] Beyond the functioning of parliamentary institutions and material rewards from democracy, this distinction implied the necessity of an affective bond between citizens and their political system, based on feelings rather than reason. What trials did the second German democracy need to overcome to achieve such an emotional anchoring in the hearts of the majority of its people?

The first piece of evidence regarding democratic reliability came with the transfer of power within the ruling party from Konrad Adenauer to Ludwig Erhard in the fall of 1963. His entanglement in the *Spiegel* scandal of 1963 cost the power-hungry chancellor the support of his own parliamentary delegation, since he stood by his compromised defense minister Franz Joseph Strauß too long, thereby raising doubts about his attachment to legality. When plans for a grand coalition with the SPD collapsed on the question of revising the proportional voting system, the FDP forced Adenauer, in the coalition agreement of December 1962, to give "the binding promise" that he would "relinquish his office by October 1963." Although he believed that his popular economic minister lacked the forcefulness to be an effective head of government, the departing chancellor could not prevent Ludwig Erhard's nomination as his successor. The conservative *Frankfurter Allgemeine Zeitung* was delighted with this outcome: "The strongest proof of democracy that anyone could present during these days was the refusal to return to the parliamentarianism of the Weimar Republic" by guaranteeing the "stability of parliamentary democracy." The first change at the top of the government thus occurred "in a way that corresponded to the best conventions of democracy."[74]

A more controversial confirmation of "the normal functioning of a constitutional state," was Erhard's replacement by Kurt Georg Kiesinger, since it resulted from the creation of the grand coalition in the fall of 1966. Although Erhard had guided the party to electoral victory, his "leadership style" came under increasing fire since he lacked Adenauer's personal authority. When the first postwar recession robbed him of the aura of economic infallibility and Francophile Gaullists spun intrigues against his pro-American foreign policy, Erhard increasingly seemed "hapless and forlorn."[75] But all alternatives to him appeared equally problematic. While cooperation of the CDU with the FDP had run its course, the Liberals and Social Democrats lacked the courage to enter a coalition with a bare majority in the Bundestag. Justified as the result of an "emergency," the "magic solution" therefore turned out to be a grand coalition, which allowed the CDU to maintain power while at the same time proving the SPD capable of governing. A cabinet composed of the two largest parties, however, risked weakening parliamentary opposition and strengthening right-wing radicalism—a point that demonstrating students did not fail to make. Long-term cooperation also appeared worrisome to intellectuals, who saw in it a "cartel of fear."[76]

The "overdue experience of transferring governmental responsibility to the other large party" in opposition occurred only with the formation of the Social-Liberal cabinet in October 1969. Despite the close outcome of the election, SPD leader Willy Brandt seized the initiative and persuaded Walter Scheel of the FDP to take the risk of entering into an alliance for modernization. That agreement largely ended the need for cumbersome compromises and revived "democratic enthusiasm." The generational replacement of leading personalities and the substantive change of course signaled the end of the postwar period and the beginning of an era of "renewal" through changes in society.[77] In his inaugural speech, interrupted several times by heckling, Brandt formulated his government's motto with the programmatic phrase: "We want to risk more democracy." The promise of a political opening for greater participation, as well as reforms in the areas of education, social policy, and the like, began an effort to expand the scope of democratization in line with the proposals made in intellectual discussions. By reconstituting a strong opposition, this first changeover of power and policy direction revitalized parliamentary democracy.[78]

Even the spy scandal that forced Willy Brandt to resign and transfer power to Helmut Schmidt did little to change this positive impression. After the election victory of 1972, the "trials of everyday" governance had proven difficult for the Social-Liberal coalition to master. The oil shock unleashed by the OPEC cartel's price increase had destroyed the fiscal means for further domestic reforms, while the great breakthroughs of the "Eastern policy" (*Ostpolitik*) of reconciliation with the neighbors were over. Brandt himself was beset by a strange lethargy and despondency that spoiled his "zest for governing," so that he decided to step down because of an annoying but hardly lethal scandal, sparked by the revelation that Günter Guillaume, one of his trusted aides, was an East German spy.[79] His successor Helmut Schmidt proved "more energetic and determined" and, because of the threat of inflation, worked toward "reclaiming the economic and financial trust of the broad middle strata." As chancellor of "continuity and concentration," he strove for "greater efficiency in state administration" and thus attempted to consolidate previous reforms through a policy of austerity. For liberal observers, this successful change in government offered further evidence of "the stability of parliamentary democracy in the face of crisis."[80]

In stark contrast to the public discussion of the chancellor question in the West, the smooth "changing of the guard in East Berlin" from Walter Ulbricht to Erich Honecker only confirmed the dictatorial character of the GDR. As the seventy-eight-year-old general secretary had already been in power for a quarter of a century, in May 1971 he justified his "phased withdrawal" by citing his advanced age: "Unfortunately there's no remedy for the years." His successor Honecker, who as a former prisoner of the Nazis, head of the FDJ, and chairman of the Defense Council, came from the inner circle of the SED, then promised: "The present course will be maintained." Since Ulbricht had assumed the duties of his predecessors Wilhelm Pieck and Otto Grotewohl gradually, this was the only real leadership change in the four decades of the GDR before its final crisis in the fall of 1989! This transfer of power derived neither from open debate within the SED, nor was it based on free elections. Instead, it resulted from Soviet pressure and the intrigues of the successor, both of whom were unhappy with Ulbricht's slight internal liberalization and timid initiation of contacts with the West.[81] Although concealing the actual reasons for the switch maintained a façade of unanimity, it failed to bolster the legitimacy of the Communist system.

A more difficult test of democracy was the question of how the Federal Republic would cope with the threat of political extremism, which once again became acute toward the end of the 1960s. Due to concerns over a return of National Socialism, many commentators feared rightist nationalism, which in the form of the National Democratic Party of Germany (NPD) had managed to overcome the 5 percent hurdle and enter several state assemblies, such as the one in Hesse. Despite the NPD's rhetorical acceptance of the Bonn state, in 1967 the Federal Office for the Protection of the Constitution accused this effort to gather various rightist groups of having "a basic outlook hostile to democracy," since its ultimate aim was to change the system of government. The unanimous reaction of all democratic politicians, leftist intellectuals, and critical youths against the attempted revival of "fascism" succeeded nonetheless in blocking the NPD from the federal parliament in the elections of 1969.[82] Because of this failure, political infighting quickly took hold of the party, leading it to split into rival factions and withdraw from the state diets. In spite of some predictions of doom, the Federal Republic therefore proved itself capable of standing up to populist assault from the Right.

In contrast, the conflict with leftist radicalism turned out to be more problematic, since its spokesmen "demanded [more] democracy from below." The Left's concept of democracy aimed at an "economic realization of basic rights," as well as "institutional support for a critical public sphere"—in other words, at dismantling authoritarian structures and reforming social relationships of power.[83] However, defenders of the parliamentary system warned against a "dictatorship through the back door" and called the "democratizing of institutions with a functional or executive character absurd," since it would break with the principle of competence.[84] This debate became explosive when leftist critics started to demand a neo-Marxist revolution, which would overthrow parliamentary democracy: "Society must be changed radically and the entire system needs to be abolished." Government circles reacted to the emergence of 316 radical groups with some 95,000 members with panicked resolve: "Democracy must be defended." On January 28, 1972, the Social-Liberal coalition passed an extremist resolution that called for checking the constitutional reliability of all applicants for public office. Alarmed, critical writers warned "against another destruction of the seeds of the liberal democratic order under the pretext of defending it."[85]

The advent of leftist terrorism with the Red Army Faction (RAF) intensified the struggle to define the limits of democracy, since the RAF sought to impose their minority version of the people's will with violence. Although Federal President Gustav Heinemann warned that "democracy needs radical criticism," the unnerved deputies voted for tough antiterror laws that entailed a certain "loss of liberality," triggering a prolonged conflict with the terrorists.[86] It took the spectacular murders of the federal prosecutor Siegfried Buback and the head of the employers' association Hanns-Martin Schleyer, the armed liberation of the hijacked passenger airplane in Mogadishu, and the mysterious suicides of the RAF leaders Andreas Baader and Ulrike Meinhof to restore a sense of proportion, because "terror has changed the republic." In the desire for "security above all else" conservatives saw a chance to stop the trend away from traditional values that had weakened state authority.[87] The moderate left denied the accusation of co-responsibility and rejected a "backward-looking stabilization," while some thoughtful activists of the protest scene began to distance themselves from fantasies of violence.[88] The shock of the "German Autumn" of 1977 therefore forced people to reflect on the values of the constitution as the crucial basis for democracy.

A constructive development, in contrast, was the rise of citizen movements, claiming "a right to participation" through direct action, which could not easily be ignored. Progressives welcomed local initiatives aimed at improving the environment under the slogan "Citizens, defend yourself!" as "a sign of political maturity," while conservatives warned against such "limitations of authority and parliamentary committees' ability to act."[89] Even massive police power, heavy water canons, and exorbitant fines could not break the spontaneous resistance to the establishment of nuclear power plants in Wyhl and Brokdorf, since the officials discredited themselves "through a series of blunders."[90] To be sure, "civil disobedience" frequently spilled over into "severe riots," but eventually pleas "for a different way of dealing with state power" and substantive discussions with activists succeeded in working out a "nonviolent course for the demonstrations."[91] The evolution of the environmental organizations of the Federal Association of Citizens' Initiatives (BBU) into their own Green Party (GAL) channeled the diffuse protest potential back into the parliamentary process while at the same time changing the protest's political style. Likewise, the success of this upstart helped push the established political parties toward the realization that citizens needed "to participate more vigorously in political decisions."[92]

The peace movement of the 1980s turned out to be a more difficult test, since in it the will of a large minority of the populace collided with the majority of members of parliament. The Western decision to match the Soviet SS-20 deployment with its own intermediate-range missiles made "fear of atomic arms run rampant." Since the Schmidt-Genscher government had initiated the dual-track NATO resolution, it remained deaf to the eschatological angst of the Krefeld appeal, which was signed by almost a million citizens.[93] Supported by elements in the unions, churches, and German Communist Party (DKP), the protests posed the key question: "Can the peace movement compel the chancellor to change his course?" Converging on Bonn, some 250,000 citizens marched "for disarmament and détente in Europe," in the words of SPD moralist Erhard Eppler, "out of exasperation about a conception of security that in the end only threatens suicide." Conservatives, however, criticized the demonstration as a "procession of dropouts from history," while leftists prophesied "the bankruptcy of the established party system." Because the CDU staunchly supported the deployment of new missiles, the government did not have to alter its policy of rearming and negotiating at the same time. Nevertheless, the Social-Liberal coalition eventually collapsed due to the "longing for opposition" in the left wing of the SPD.[94]

While the change from Helmut Schmidt to Helmut Kohl resolved the chancellor crisis, its questionable procedure fostered a creeping dissatisfaction with politics. The "internal split of the SPD" between moderate government support-ers and leftist radicals provoked the rupture, because a strong minority refused to follow the chancellor's lead in questions of NATO rearmament, use of nuclear energy, and financial retrenchment. Due to the decreasing reliability of its part-ner, the leader of the FDP, Hans-Dietrich Genscher, began to flirt "with the thought of desertion." Instead, he advocated a coalition with the CDU, although its chairman, Helmut Kohl, tended to "bore" the public as the liberal journalist Theo Sommer smugly put it.[95] Though Schmidt claimed "I'm not thinking of withdrawing," the Social-Liberal coalition collapsed in September 1982 with the resignation of the Liberal ministers and the SPD's rejection of the social budget cuts, demanded by the neo-liberals in the FDP.[96] Even though Kohl signaled his wish for continuity, the FDP's change of sides left behind a bitter aftertaste, since such a parliamentary maneuver was no longer accepted by the public and the Basic Law had to be bent to dissolve the Bundestag so that new elections could take place in the following year.[97]

The "intellectual about-face" pronounced by the Kohl-Genscher cabinet propagated the reconstitution of state authority through a return to a formal understanding of democracy. The change of course was most noticeable in cul-tural and social style, since it meant "going back to the unspoiled world of the fifties, the bourgeois *Biedermeier*." An important part of the new government's agenda was the attempt to "risk more state and less democracy"—that is, to limit the "proliferating rights of minorities." Accompanying this agenda was also a mistrust of "popular sovereignty" and of plebiscitary practices, as well as a clear preference for delegating decisions to parliament.[98] Middle-class commentators therefore welcomed the "distancing from utopianism" of the Kohl era as an overdue normalization, which would give Germans a "new confidence" in the future. Nevertheless, leftist critics pointed out that the Federal Republic was in danger of withering to a "spectator democracy" and that a deep "chasm" had opened in the political culture between the majority of well-satisfied citizens and a minority of critics in an alternative subculture.[99]

While Kohl's neocorporatist practices did bring a reduction in public strife, they ran the risk of discrediting democracy through numerous scandals. The po-litical integration of various social forces through the distribution of favors fos-tered a collective immobility, as well as a self-service mentality. Liberals like Ralph Dahrendorf thus lamented "a 'certain decay' of the German political class," while Theo Sommer welcomed the Greens' campaign against the "decline of political mores."[100] The occasion for such Cassandra calls was the Flick scandal, precipi-tated by the notebook of the company's agent Eberhard von Brauchitsch, which carefully recorded financial contributions to Kohl, Strauß, and other leading poli-ticians. Similarly, the Barschel scandal, concerning the manipulation of elections by the CDU in Schleswig-Holstein, triggered widespread acrimony. While the author Günter Grass railed against "a republic of scandals," the Hessian minister president Walter Wallman warned about "holding democracy itself responsible for the 'political misconduct' of the politicians." Ironically, it was neoconservative policies that led directly into a new "crisis of confidence and credibility."[101]

Passing the tests of such difficult challenges slowly created the conviction that the Federal Republic was "not just a fair-weather democracy." In contrast to the paralysis of the SED dictatorship, the often controversial, but ultimately accepted changes of government offered clear proof of the ability of parliamentary institutions to function under duress.[102] The challenges posed by the NPD or RAF terrorism did not lead to a relapse into fascism but to an intense discussion of "basic values" which increased appreciation for the "liberal-democratic order" while at the same time setting boundaries for the use of political power.[103] Moreover, the charges of political disinterest and discouragement triggered such constructive reactions as the recognition of citizens' initiatives, the expansion of opportunities for participation at the local level, and the intensification of criticism of politicians' scandals.[104] To be sure, the Federal Republic was by no means as perfect as conservative apologists made it out to be. Still, leftist caricatures of a "supposedly growing illiberalism" were equally exaggerated. It is thus not surprising that by the end of the 1980s nearly four-fifths of all West German citizens were either "very satisfied or fairly satisfied" with the democratic system.[105]

Learned Democracy

With every passing decade, the number of anniversary commentaries testifying to the amazing success of the Federal Republic multiplied. While in the beginning evaluations merely argued "Bonn is not Weimar," over the years approval of the republic grew considerably: "There she stands, well fed, neat, and tidy, thirty years old and uncannily healthy, just as the comedian says—the Federal Republic of Germany." Because criticism was able to correct many faults, the balance sheet of this "broadly accepted German polity" became quite positive: the Bonn state boasted firm guarantees of freedom, a high degree of legal security, much effective legislation, a government well aware of problems, a smoothly functioning federalism, a dense social safety net, and a broad associational base— the list of civilizational achievements was long and impressive.[106] This outcome was by no means inevitable but was the product of a long-term learning process that drew important lessons from the failure of Germany's first attempt at democracy. The Second Republic also showed itself to be surprisingly capable of reform by adapting time and again to new challenges within the framework established by the Basic Law. Why, then, was the Bonn democracy more successful than its Weimar predecessor?

First and foremost, the Federal Republic was a result of Nazi defeat and a product of Allied occupation that determined the structural conditions for future development more drastically than had the defeat and revolution of 1918. In a negative sense, the attempt to break rightist traditions through demilitarization, denazification, and decartelization had helped to clear enough space for a new beginning, even when their implementation did not always go far enough. At the same time, the cautionary example of the SED dictatorship in the Soviet Zone discredited left-wing utopias and enabled a moderate parliamentarianism to appear as the only sensible option in the propaganda battles of the Cold War. In a more positive respect, the Western superpower, the United States, served as an attractive model of democratic institutions and economic success that was broadcast into West German living rooms through radio, films, and television. In this process, Jewish remigrants such as Theodor Adorno and American German experts like Shepard Stone played important parts as mediators between the two cultures, thereby helping to transmit democratic values into a German context.[107] Cultural Westernization and Americanization of lifestyles therefore reinforced the process of political democratization.

Yet the Germans' own contribution to the anchoring of democracy was almost certainly more decisive, because without their active cooperation the parliamentary system could not have taken root in the long run. Though this aspect is often slighted, the minority of committed democrats could draw on self-government traditions of their own which had been expressed in the revolutions of 1848 and 1918, even if these were unable to win a lasting majority before 1945.[108] While the Basic Law consciously attempted to link itself to such constitutional precedents, it was also characterized by a strong determination to avoid the mistakes of the Weimar Republic. The Parliamentary Council was thus called on to overcome the widespread reservations against democracy by establishing an institutional framework that would on the one hand guarantee authority, order, and stability and on the other safeguard legal security and freedom of opinion. Although in retrospect some provisions—for example, the financial burden-sharing among the states and the strong role of the Bundesrat in passing legislation—have proven problematic, the overall framework of this constitution proved to be remarkably resistant to crises, as well as highly adaptable through amendments.[109]

Several decades were needed, nonetheless, before the majority of citizens grew into their new democratic home, settled into it, and could no longer do without it. This gradual acceptance was facilitated by a series of positive experiences: At the beginning, the parliamentary system allowed citizens an emotional time-out during which they could reorganize their private lives by demanding only a formal fulfillment of their duties. As they then began to register their own demands, the Bonn state proved itself to be surprisingly responsive. Among other things, it organized a remarkable economic recovery, provided for social security through indexed pensions, helped prevent a much-feared new war, and earned international recognition. Triggered by repeated scandals, a critical public sphere developed under judicial interpretations of the constitution, which came to function as an early warning system for urgent problems. The transfer of power between chancellors and coalitions not only offered those who were interested in politics good entertainment but also proved to skeptics the ability of democratic institutions to function under pressure.[110] In contrast to the GDR, the greater extent to which citizens of the Federal Republic could participate in solving their own problems created a more robust legitimacy for the parliamentary system.

The subsequent controversy over issues such as the extension of participation and the limits of freedom demonstrated that democracy had become the new standard for political debate. Since conflicts only revolved around the interpretation of its principles, democracy itself was no longer in question except among a small number of extremists. The leftist critique of the "crass discrepancy between the formal democratic principles of the system and the de facto exclusion of the majority of the populace" motivated demands for revolutionary change through more participation, expressed in citizens' initiatives. Conservative politicians objected instead to the Stasi infiltration of the Left and denounced acts of civil disobedience as "clearly punishable offenses," warning: "These constitutional rights of parliament should not be unhinged by minority coercion that has not been legitimated democratically." Here opposing models of democracy confronted each other—a critical notion of a grass-roots democracy according to the model of revolutionary councils (Soviets) clashed with a conception of parliamentarianism limited by the articles of the constitution.[111] This conflict of principles centering on the democratization of democracy reflected fundamental differences in civil values and behaviors that helped shape the course of the Federal Republic and would continue to change it further in the future.

CHAPTER 6

Protesting Authority

After the steps toward democratization during the first two postwar decades, the "outbreak of great dissatisfaction with the state and society" in the middle of the 1960s came as quite a surprise.[1] While sociological studies still lamented the apathy of the student body, unrest began to grow at several universities. For example, on June 22, 1966, over 3,000 students at the Free University (FU) in Berlin gathered in front of the academic senate for Germany's first "sit-in" to protest the dismissal of the leftist assistant Ekkehard Krippendorf from the Otto Suhr Institute. This confrontation had grown out of a conflict concerning the authority of the rector who, among other things, forbade the writer Erich Kuby from speaking at FU, because he had the temerity to question the merits of anti-Communism. The suddenly rebellious students also demanded a general reform of the university that would give professors, assistants, and themselves one-third—that is, equal—representation in university governance. At the same time, they called for a political mandate, empowering the organized student body to take positions on social questions. The demonstrators thus sought nothing less than "the dismantling of oligarchic tyranny and the realization of democratic freedom in all areas of society."[2]

The generational revolt of the 1960s left behind a severe trauma among many authority figures, which condemned the surprising attacks as "relapse into romanticism" and "cultural rupture." The older generation of democrats that had lived through the collapse of the Weimar Republic and the crimes of the Nazi dictatorship saw in the Federal Republic a well-ordered constitutional state, and they believed that the parliamentary form of government represented enormous progress, in spite of its noticeable weaknesses. The spontaneous crossing of established boundaries by the youth protests appeared to them as nothing less than a new wave of irrationalism that would recklessly jeopardize the civil normality that they had worked so hard to regain.[3] Added to that fear were suspicions, not entirely unjustified, about the GDR's Ministry for State Security's (Stasi) role in financing radical journals, such as *konkret*, and about the SED's control over leftist groups from afar.[4] Critics of the "cultural premises of intellectual radicalism," such as the philosopher Hermann Lübbe, also warned that this "neo-totalitarian element" might have terrorist consequences.[5] The conservative interpretation has therefore deplored the student revolt as a dangerous protest that imperiled the very values of Western civilization.

By contrast, more sympathetic observers considered the movement of the "68ers" as the "first fairly successful German revolution," that, in the words of critical theorist Jürgen Habermas, effected a "fundamental liberalization" of West German society.[6] Numerous autobiographical texts indicate that the postwar generation, less burdened by memories of the catastrophes of the Third Reich, was more likely to chafe against the oppressive narrowness of the Adenauer period. Not surprisingly, dissatisfied youths proved more open to criticisms of restoration coming from leftist authors and intellectuals than to the self-praise dished out by Bonn politicians. In retrospect, former participants thus remember the revolt as an intense but somewhat confused search for ideological perspectives and anti-authoritarian lifestyles, based on an unsystematic mélange of the ideas of the young Marx, the Frankfurt School of critical theory, and psychoanalytic critics like Herbert Marcuse. These recollections represent the movement as an individual attempt to break out of familial constraints and a collective effort to throw off social conventions, which had a politically liberating effect.[7] On the whole, the left has judged the changes unleashed by the generational revolt more positively, seeing them as an expansion of civil society through "a kind of re-founding of the second republic after the fact."[8]

For contemporary historians, the symbolic date 1968 is thus at once fascinating and problematic, as it is difficult to capture its import within the conventional framework of a political narrative.[9] The first hurdle is the emotional polarization of personal memories, which makes it difficult to achieve the necessary analytical distance.[10] A second problem is the only modest importance of the events that accompanied the revolt, from the shooting of student demonstrator Benno Ohnesorg to the street "Battle on Tegeler Weg," as they are incommensurate with the storm that they unleashed in the media.[11] Yet another difficulty is the underexplored relationship between the international generational revolts (which engulfed the universities) and political developments (such as the demise of the grand coalition and the beginning of the social-liberal reform era) that occurred on the national level.[12] A final obstacle to effective analysis is the lack of clear criteria for judging the effects of long-term sociocultural changes on the more short-term alterations in values and behaviors.[13] How, then, is the paradox of the utter failure of the revolution's political project to be reconciled with the unexpected success of the simultaneous transformation in cultural attitudes?

To analyze how the mobilization of the late 1960s contributed to the civilizing of Germany, it is necessary to concentrate less on ideology and events than on the hopes and experiences of both its proponents and its detractors. To begin, it might help to review the forgotten West German protest tradition, which, at least according to leftist critics, can be understood as a defeated but still far-reaching antithesis to the successful attempts at bourgeois restoration of the 1950s. Following this, it would be important to discuss the origins of the generational unrest in the following decade, probe its ideological search and protest methods, and recapitulate briefly the main events of the turbulent year 1967–1968. To arrive at a balanced judgment about the long-term impact of the effort to expand chances for participation, it ought then to be useful to ponder its contradictory consequences by comparing some of its negative outcomes like terrorism with some of its more positive legacies like the New Social Movements. Finally, some comparisons with East German developments ought to suggest several dimensions that partially connect the caesurae of 1968 and 1989.[14]

Opposing Restoration

The roots of the social mobilization of the 1960s reach back into the preceding decade, because the generational revolt built on the experiences of earlier protest movements. The conservative portrayal of the 1950s as a quiet and generally apolitical era in the Federal Republic is somewhat misleading; in fact, there were important mass movements by people dissatisfied with the restorative compromises of the Adenauer period. For example, the Allied dismantling of factories, the suffering of Nazi victims, the problems of the expellees, and the needs of former soldiers all gave rise to spontaneous protests, as well as organized demonstrations, that only appear on the margins of accounts that focus on the progress of parliamentary democracy.[15] This vocal criticism in the West created intense political debates, even when it failed to reach its stated goals, while in the East the SED controlled public life through wide-ranging propaganda campaigns that allowed no dissent. The forgotten history of Western protest bequeathed an arsenal of political objections, active individuals, and incipient networks whose potential for criticism accelerated the mobilization efforts of the next decade.

The target of successive waves of protest was the recovery of "a modest normality of life," allowing the *Bürgertum* a kind of "Indian Summer," in which it could restore West German institutions in its own image. The social leveling promoted by National Socialism had eliminated the last remnants of aristocratic predominance, while the working class, whose large unions were just reemerging, remained too weak to assume political leadership. The necessity of reconstituting order and security had given the old-fashioned bourgeois virtues of diligence, thrift, and cleanliness a new lease on life. The reestablishment of a patriarchal family structure, the refounding of voluntary associations, the reopening of social institutions, the reintroduction of a professional civil service, and the revival of a sense of civic pride were, as the prefix "re" indicates, all attempts to go back to the self-governing traditions of the late Second Empire. But because of the enormous damage to both the material foundation and the nonmaterial values of German society, there was something forced about the reconstruction of civic structures that often made it seem lacking in genuine liberality.[16]

The first group of critics consisted of those leftist intellectuals in the East and West who strove for a radical renewal of political culture. They gathered in loose discussion circles, cooperated in the publishing of journals such as the *Frankfurter Hefte* and *Der Ruf*, and maintained intellectual exchanges with each other across the iron curtain. Such diverse thinkers as Eugen Kogon, Hans Werner Richter, Hans Mayer, and Ernst Bloch agreed in their sharp condemnation of the elites who had collaborated with National Socialism, and they demanded a fundamental democratization of public life. At the same time, they called for social reforms that, drawing on both Christian and Marxist conceptions, proposed a socialization of economic enterprises and envisioned a more equitable distribution of land so as to reduce social inequality.[17] Even if the polarization of the Cold War and the founding of competing states soon overshadowed these ideas, the programmatic statements and literary representations of these early postwar critics offered a trenchant critique of both Stalinist repression in the East and restoration trends in the West.

A larger source of protest consisted of the workers who struggled for greater rights and better pay by striking—for example, 75,000 Hessian metalworkers walked out in 1951. When the Labor Relations Act granted union representatives only a right to object but left them in the minority in company boards, 1,660,550 workers took to the streets in May 1952 in order to obtain a "genuine right to co-determination" in all realms of the economy. But despite a three-day newspaper strike, Adenauer was willing to grant only limited concessions to workers' involvement.[18] Still more dramatic was the East German revolt of June 17, 1953, which began with spontaneous protests against the raising of work quotas but led to the voicing of political demands by workers and citizens in some 270 locations. To defend its precarious hold on power, the SED called on the Red Army for help, and the subsequent repression cost the lives of about fifty-five people.[19] In the aftermath of this defeat, Eastern workers were in effect powerless to change their conditions, while West German unionists concentrated their collective bargaining on gaining the forty-hour week, higher wages, and other benefits. In spite of the ban of the KPD, there remained a latent potential for protest in the Federal Republic, especially on the far left margins of the working class.

Even more widespread were the protests against rearmament, since in addition to unionized workers they included clergymen, intellectuals, and Communists. The GDR supported the "peace movement" in the West in order to block the establishment of the Bundeswehr, without, however, tolerating similar objections in its own realm. In the Federal Republic, the first wave of opposition between 1950 and 1952 was led by prominent pastors such as Martin Niemöller and politicians like Gustav Heinemann, and concentrated on preventing the basic decision to rearm. After the failure of the European Defense Community, a second phase of the "St. Paul's Church movement" of 1955 attempted to prevent the Bundestag's approval of NATO membership, with more than a million demonstrators speaking out against the Paris treaties. A third stage of protest actions was the "Campaign against Atomic Death," seeking to prevent the nuclear arming of the Bundeswehr. Set in motion by the "Göttingen Declaration," some 1,644,000 people voiced their fears of nuclear annihilation through a concerted petition drive between 1957 and 1958.[20] Although the campaign collapsed shortly after the Constitutional Court prohibited petitioning for referenda, this extraparliamentary mass movement illustrated the power of an outraged public.

Another important, if much smaller, circle was composed of journalists, who proved their solidarity following the government's violation of free speech in the *Spiegel* affair. This occurred when Rudolf Augstein's personal vendetta against the dynamic but unpredictable CSU defense minister Franz Josef Strauß culminated in the publication of an article entitled "Partially Ready for Defense" in October 1962, exposing the inadequacies of the Bundeswehr. Angry about the disclosure of secret information concerning the NATO maneuver "Fallex 62," which simulated the horrific consequences of a nuclear war in Central Europe, Strauß immediately ordered the offices of the leading news magazine, *Der Spiegel,* to be searched and his nemesis Augstein, as well as the author of the article, Conrad Ahlers, arrested for high treason. When the opposition declared a "crisis of the constitutional state" and even conservative papers such as the *Frankfurter Allgemeine Zeitung* showed their outrage, the focus of the scandal shifted from the issue of a supposed betrayal of secrets to an attack on the freedom of the press. The public protests resulted in a coalition crisis between the CDU/CSU and the FDP that ultimately forced Strauß to resign, while also damaging the reputation of Adenauer, who covered for his defense minister too long.[21] In the media, this affair strengthened the tendency toward critical reporting.

The most influential attempt to provide a theoretical foundation for the widespread discontent came from the "New Left," which attacked both West German affluence and East German party dictatorship. The concept of "a new socialist movement of the left" was an allusion to the English journal *New Left Review,* put out by the historian Edward P. Thompson and the cultural critic Raymond Williams, which propagated an unorthodox Gramscian Marxism. In Germany, the Frankfurt School, under the leadership of the sociologist Theodor Adorno, and the Socialist League, a group of left Social Democrats and independent socialists around Marburg political scientist Wolfgang Abendroth, stood behind similar endeavors.[22] To provide a more up-to-date critique, the New Left focused on developing a fresh interpretation of the problem of alienation posited in Marx's early writings, which reacted to the subtle, but no less invidious, forms of exploitation in a consumer society. Because the proletariat seemed mostly content with its share of prosperity, hopes for a revolutionary class to confront this exploitation shifted to the new intelligentsia of dissatisfied students and white-collar employees. With the help of a critical media, they might form "a countervailing power," expose the lingering fascistic tendencies of capitalism with original strategies, and, as a result, mobilize the still disadvantaged workers.[23]

The student vanguard of critical Marxism was the Socialist German Student League (SDS), an intellectual debating club that made the transition to direct action in the mid-1960s. Having participated in labor conflicts and the campaign against rearmament, most of its members, largely out of youthful radicalism, refused to go along with the SPD's ideological about-face in the Godesberg Program, which recognized the social market economy and Western integration. Forced to fend for itself after being disowned by the parent party in October 1961, the SDS offered a fertile ground for a renaissance of unorthodox Marxism that refused to surrender its hopes for a fundamental change in the existing order. Its activists debated a wide range of socialist classics, ranging from V. I. Lenin to Rosa Luxemburg, as well as the work of newer social critics, including C. Wright Mills, Herbert Marcuse, Wilhelm Reich, and Georg Lukács, a heterogeneous ensemble from which they tried to fashion a contemporary revolutionary theory. At the same time, they attacked the "brown past" of many professors and began to rail against poor educational conditions by drafting a "university memorandum."[24]

The media paid even more attention to the self-conscious provocations of a small, anti-authoritarian subculture in the artistic bohemia of a few large cities. Influenced above all by French existentialists and situationists, avant-garde groups began forming, first in Schwabing, then later in Frankfurt and Berlin, under the name Subversive Action, searching for ways to dramatize their loathing for the "oppressive claustrophobia of the Adenauer period." This kind of individualistic rebellion attracted nonconformist youths—especially those who sought to escape authoritarian discipline so they could experiment with freer lifestyles and, not least of all, act out their sexual impulses. Dieter Kunzelmann, one of the leading free spirits, wrote disarmingly about the founding of the first commune: "We are trying here to set up a communist and situationist nucleus within capitalist society." The guardians of morality were above all angered by the playful forms of protest that wished to provoke the established conventions of middle-class society—for example, the appeal: "In all seriousness we demand a bit of fun."[25] Although the revolutionary ideas of these anti-authoritarians remained vague, they nonetheless managed to develop new forms of protest with their original "happenings" that exposed authoritarian patterns through exaggeration.

These diverse protest traditions coalesced in the extraparliamentary opposition, when critical intellectuals, left trade unionists, and radical clergy campaigned with rebellious students against the passage of an Emergency Law in parliament. The "Emergency Committee for Democracy" organized a mass movement against a constitutional amendment that would enlarge the power of the executive in national emergencies, because it feared that the FRG might be undermined by emergency decrees just like the Weimar Republic had been. At the Frankfurt Congress of 1966, the philosopher Ernst Bloch swore before 5,000 listeners that basic rights were being eroded: "We come together to nip this development in the bud."[26] Since the SPD, as part of the grand coalition, was also responsible for the draft, the protesters formed an Extraparliamentary Opposition (APO) by organizing strikes, holding demonstrations, and, finally, marching 60,000 people on Bonn in order to stop the legislation. In the end, the hysterical fears of fascism proved to be exaggerated, since in its final form the bill sharply curtailed the authority of the executive branch. By failing to prevent the law, this campaign contributed to the alienation of young protestors from parliament and the system it represented.[27]

In spite of the evident success of the Federal Republic, a considerable potential for protest had nonetheless accumulated by the mid-1960s. The preferred topics of self-criticism involved social inequalities in the distribution of wealth, the inner emptiness of consumer society, the dangers of the nuclear arms race, and threats to human rights. Within representative democracy, networks of critical intellectuals, mass organizations of employees, nuclei of student agitation, and forms of cooperation between critical voices had emerged that together might sustain a social mobilization.[28] In contrast, the GDR remained as quiet as a cemetery in the years that immediately followed the construction of the Berlin wall. After August 13, 1961, the SED succeeded in suppressing the last remnants of anti-Communist criticism in the unions and churches and in eliminating all internal Marxist alternatives of a Trotskyite or other color by rigorously deploying party control commissions.[29] While in the East autonomous social organization had generally been rendered impossible, in the West civil society allowed tensions to vent themselves dramatically, as long as these did not become a threat to the basic social, economic, and political order.

A Cultural Revolution

The plethora of competing attempts to explain the "68 movement" shows a certain helplessness of intellectual commentators and academic observers in trying to make sense of the generational revolt. Moreover, the inevitable exaggeration in the media during rituals of remembrance has produced more retrospective nostalgia than analytical understanding, even among the original participants.[30] The political polarization of interpretations, which range from horrified condemnation of the rebels' youthful terrorism via ambivalent verdicts of their "successful failure" to praise for their liberating impact, has not exactly facilitated scholarly understanding, either.[31] Sociological theories, positing the rebellion of a "new class" of white-collar workers and social-psychological theses of an all too "permissive upbringing" (red diaper theory), compete with political science approaches to "new social movements" and pedagogic analyses of "youthful alienation" in educational institutions.[32] But scholars have only slowly come to realize that this phenomenon needs also to be placed into a historical context in order to achieve a more nuanced, multidimensional explanation with the help of detailed descriptions.

The autobiographical allusions to abnormally strong generational tensions between adults and young people at the beginning of the 1960s offer a first clue to analysis. In the case of Dieter Kunzelmann in Bamberg, it was the endless "guidelines, unfathomable rules, and reproaches of the schools," as well as the boredom of a safe apprenticeship at a bank, that led to the rejection of the "predictable middle-class way of life" and gave rise to "a downright revulsion against any form of order, security, and uniformity." For Inga Buhmann it was more "the problems with my father," as well as "our rejection of school and the teachers," not to mention the "mendacity and meanness of most people" and the refusal of adults "to speak of happiness and sex." With Rudi Dutschke, who lived in the East German Luckenwalde, it was the attempt to resolve "the social question and the question of faith," as well as to understand the causes for the outbreak of the Second World War. For Friedrich-Martin Balzer in Islerlohn, by contrast, it was the strong inner need to resist the "resigned rationality" that accompanied becoming an adult as well as to find his own, independent way in life.[33]

During the 1960s the normal problems of adolescence in many cases became so pronounced that they ended with a symbolic break of some sort. On his mother's fiftieth birthday, the nineteen-year-old Kunzelmann ran away from home, hitchhiked to Paris, and began the sobering life of a tramp, sleeping under bridges at the Seine. Although remorsefully returning home a few months later, he still managed to persuade his parents to fund him in a nonconformist life in Schwabing. While Buhmann initially began a regular course of studies, she turned to poetry, drifted into the Bohemian life, fell into the "nuthouse," and became a prostitute in Paris before she finally pulled herself together through political engagement with the SDS. Dutschke confronted a surprised FDJ assembly with critical views that forced him to decamp to West Berlin: "When I hear the word 'shooting,' a chill runs down my spine. Nobody wants war. The travel ban to the West is a violation of personal freedom. All Germans should be brought together at one table." Balzer shocked his graduation audience with an idealistic valedictorian speech as well: "We want to be inconvenient to the powerful of the world. We want to stand up bravely for justice. We want to be critical and to doubt all that is offered to us as tried, true, and sacrosanct."[34]

For liberal adults, the youth rebellion seemed a "highly curious occurrence" that evoked mostly amazement but little understanding. In the weekly *Die Zeit*, Marion Dönhoff contrasted it with the Czechs' heroic fight for freedom, noting that "a part of the youth generation that has inherited [democracy] at birth dreams of a Soviet system, condemns pluralism, and hates liberals more than fascists." When this "childhood sickness" would not pass, Theodor Eschenburg, the rector of the University of Tübingen, could not help but offer a negative appraisal, despite his sympathy for the "need for freedom and emancipation" among the young: "But more significant to me seemed to be the impulse to bad behavior—since the struggle against convention was perhaps the most important aspect of this revolution." Behind this instinctive rejection lurked the disappointment of an older generation that saw its civilizational accomplishment of reclaiming the rule of law and self-government from the ashes of the Third Reich insufficiently appreciated: "It was characteristic of the [younger] generation that it had grown up in the era of the economic miracle and could know nothing from its own experience about the terrible times that Germany had gone through before."[35]

This discrepancy of perceptions points to a process through which individual conflicts deepened so much that they exploded into a collective revolt that took hold of almost an entire generation. When the inevitable "separation of youth from the adult world" occurs publicly and collectively, "because the individual biographical conflict [blends] with socio-economic contradictions," a generational rebellion can take shape in which the confrontation becomes generalized and emotionalized. In this process, the creation of solidarity—that is, the establishment of a self-proclaimed generational community, which is recognized by others—has a central role.[36] In comparison with the numerically strong but mostly working-class "rowdies" (*Halbstarke*) of the 1950s, university and high school students, as well as apprentices to trades, created a broader sense of generational solidarity, expressing itself both in life style and in political actions.[37] To be sure, only a minority were truly active, but their confrontations energized the majority of the age cohort and overcame, at least in part, the boundaries that separated classes, genders, and indeed entire nations.[38]

One of the first areas of generational friction involved inadequate learning conditions at the universities, which had been restored in their traditional form. Prompted by Georg Picht's complaints about the "crisis of education," the United Student Councils launched a campaign in the summer of 1965 to dramatize the overcrowding that plagued institutions of higher learning.[39] With the memorable slogan of "Under academic gowns [grows] the mildew of thousands of years," Hamburg students protested two years later against the "dictatorship of the chairs"—that is, the authoritarian control of powerful professors. When the Free University attempted to reimpose discipline in Berlin, students objected to the "curtailment of their 'democratic rights'" by heeding Peter Schneider's ironic call to "stop arguing and sit down on the floor in the hall." Since liberal professors did not prove radical enough for their tastes, activists founded a "critical university" of their own that would offer a "permanent critique of the universities," as well as promote "practical university reform." At the same time, they occupied their academic departments so as to force a politicization of their respective curricula.[40] Thus, out of the problems of everyday student life developed a fundamental critique of the university as a social institution.

A second point of contention was the German government's support for the American intervention in the Vietnamese civil war against the Communist Vietcong. The presence of students from the Third World encouraged a romanticized sympathy with anti-imperialistic liberation struggles against local dictatorships, such as Moise Tschombe's rule in the Congo, that were propped up by Washington. At the same time, the Vietnam War was the first conflict that was carried live on television. West German audiences received a steady stream of shocking images of American and South Vietnamese brutality, since similar shots from the North Vietnamese could not be so easily obtained. A growing peace movement could thus denounce the "tortures and killing of prisoners" in Saigon, as well as the American use of "napalm bombs [and] poisonous chemicals." Students demonstrated against such "murder," while pamphlets demanded that the "*Amis* get out of Vietnam!" At the Frankfurt Vietnam Congress of the SDS in 1966, Herbert Marcuse declared that "there is no need, neither strategic, technical, nor national, that could justify what is happening in Vietnam: the slaughter of the civilian population."[41] Ironically, the protests against the Vietnam War criticized the Western superpower for disregarding its own ethic of civilization.

A third, somewhat vaguer cause for protest among young people was their resentment of the "bourgeois conformity that characterized affluent society." Above all, sensitive adolescents criticized traditional middle-class virtues as leading directly to careerist conformity and idolized the disobedience of the artistic avant-garde with the motto: "Stay Loyal, Stay German, Stay Dumb." For many young people, the fetishization of consumption by their elders, whose artificial needs were spurred on by advertising, was an outrage from which they tried to escape. Thus Dieter Kunzelmann interpreted the Brussels department-store fire of 1967 as a Vietnamization of Europe by asking rhetorically, "When will the chain stores in Berlin [begin to] burn?"[42] The prudery and double standards of bourgeois sexual morality also aroused much resentment. "We have to liberate sexuality and at the same time rediscover the relevance of a sensual pornographic literature." Radical leaflets also scorned the possession of property as a petit bourgeois abomination: "If you want to leave your wallet at home, STEAL WITHOUT CASH!"[43] The logical consequence of such frustrations with adult society was to drop out, to band together, and to develop an alternative lifestyle.

A final reason for generational alienation in Germany was the silence of the fathers about their own involvement in the Nazi regime. Even if the rebels, like Niklas Frank and Bernward Vesper, only rarely hailed from prominent families who were linked with the National Socialists, many asked the disturbing question: "Daddy, what did you do during the war?" If a son could counter the reprimand "you misfit!" with the accusation "you member of the Hitler Youth!" parental authority and discipline went out the window. More generally, the scandalous discovery of numerous "brown" judges, politicians, and professors raised the issue of the incompleteness of denazification and the continuity of compromised institutions. A popularized Marxist analysis of fascism took the existence of capitalism in the Federal Republic as proof of the quasi-Fascist character of Western Democracy. Another flyer urged melodramatically: "Let's end the fact that Nazi racists, Jew-murderers, Slav-killers, and Socialist-executioners, that the entire Nazi shit of yesterday, continues to pour its stench over our generation!" In a kind of after the fact anti-Fascism, the rebels therefore demanded a "permanent ANTI-NAZI campaign. Let's prepare a REVOLT against the Nazi generation."[44]

As a result of such different irritations, a considerable part of the younger generation started to believe the slogan "trust no one over thirty!" Already in the 1950s, conflicts between rebellious youths and adults had flared up around questions of lifestyle such as wearing jeans and listening to rock music. Even in the GDR, repeated confrontations about such issues emerged among the generally more docile children of the republic who were born after 1949. But in the 1960s when such generational conflicts became politicized, they turned these normal tensions into a fundamental critique of Western society. An anonymous poem from 1968 illustrates the close connection between lifestyle revolts and political rebellion: "That you like beat music,/ want to dance and most of all to fuck,/ that's what I love." Since some adults, behaving like superiors or Nazi block wardens, might "have something against that," the author warned: "Watch out and bloody do something about it." His call for anti-authoritarian protest, for throwing eggs and blocking traffic, ended in a principled threat: "If the state wants to spoil your/ dancing and your fucking,/ then smash the state!"[45]

These generational tensions inspired an attempt to create a counterideology that eclectically assembled its social criticism out of various traditions of the Left. Youthful theorization, however, was impeded by the fact that many critical ideas had been obliterated by the Nazi dictatorship and thus first had to be painstakingly reconstructed by contacts with survivors and forgotten treatises. Moreover, the SED regime, which had not truly been de-Stalinized, stood as a barrier to Marxism, since it not only persecuted its own dissidents but also gave socialism a bad name due to its bigoted provincialism. While some of the movement's leading minds, such as Rudi Dutschke and Hans-Jürgen Krahl, read voraciously in order to extract from sociological texts a critical understanding of the present, they hardly came close to achieving theoretical formulations that possessed any real interpretive strength. While their views became more and more radical as the intensity of the conflict grew, they nonetheless remained too focused on the situation at hand to convey any lasting insights.[46] The 1968ers are thus perhaps best understood as a movement in search of theoretical answers that possessed a contextual and instrumental relationship to ideology

Despite previous disappointments, Marxism remained the reference point of all ideological work, since the long struggle of the labor movement had made it synonymous with social emancipation from oppression. Out of a feeling of personal alienation, many rebels became interested in the writings of the young Karl Marx, which dealt explicitly with this topic. GDR refugees, such as Rudi Dutschke and Bernd Rabehl, had been forced to study the works of Lenin in school, of course. But because of the Stalinization of the Soviet Union, they now preferred the insights of unorthodox Communists such as Leo Trotsky, Rosa Luxemburg, and Nikolai Bucharin. Even more relevant seemed to be the ideas of neo-Marxists such as Georg Lukács, Ernst Bloch, and Herbert Marcuse, since they analyzed "late capitalist society" in order to accelerate its coming dissolution. As the movement grew more radical, the slogans of Mao Tse-tung, Che Guevera, and Frantz Fanon also gained influence as the revolution ostensibly shifted its focus to the anti-imperialistic periphery.[47] Although the SDS draped its calls for revolutionary change in popular Marxist language, its attempts to work out a theory of revolution for an affluent society ultimately failed due to its fixation on the unwilling workers.

Another theoretical impulse derived from the social-psychological concepts of anti-authoritarianism that called for a change in interpersonal relations. First formulated by Franfurt School theorist Theodor Adorno during his exile in the United States, this criticism sought to identify traits of an "authoritarian personality" whose fixation on bourgeois virtues made it susceptible to the temptations of fascism. His colleague Max Horkheimer expanded this concept into a critique of the integral, "authoritarian state," which had abandoned the tactics of open repression associated with dictatorship and moved toward the more subtle suppression of democracy. Also important was the rediscovery of Wilhelm Reich, who, with an amalgam of Marx and Freud, criticized bourgeois prudery and thus seemed to legitimize the youthful desire for freer sexuality. But the key text of the 68 movement was Herbert Marcuse's book *The One-Dimensional Man*, which denounced the evolution of capitalism from a welfare state to a technological warfare state and argued that its "repressive tolerance" could only be broken through "extra-legal" resistance.[48] Taken together, these assorted writings furnished a vocabulary of protest that seemed to lend intellectual justification to the youth revolt.

An often ignored, but nevertheless crucial, aspect of the theoretical debate was, finally, the problem of mass democracy within a capitalist society. The entrance of the SPD into the Grand Coalition shocked intellectuals because it left the Bonn government "without an opposition," thus rendering it incapable of reform. The Berlin sociologist Johannes Agnoli therefore drew much attention with his Marxist critique of parliamentarianism when he argued that the pretense of pluralism only masked the true nature of power relations in the FRG.[49] As an alternative, progressive historians rediscovered the council form of direct democracy that had briefly appeared during the revolution of 1918–1919. Unlike the current parliamentary system, it would allow for direct citizen participation in a revolutionary situation and provide for a more spontaneous expression of their political will.[50] But the refusal of the masses to follow a revolutionary minority posed the crucial question of how to achieve further democratization—through direct action, the formation of revolutionary cadres, or, as moderates preferred, a "long march through the institutions?" Although the demand for more "direct democracy" informed most appeals to one degree or another, it was not always clear what that was supposed to mean.[51]

The impact of this ideological cocktail, drawn from unorthodox Marxism, anti-authoritarian psychology, and notions of participatory democracy, was rather ambivalent. To be sure, the basic orientation did foster some genuinely positive developments: Marxist rhetoric fostered a social critique and greater solidarity with the Third World; anti-authoritarian thinking, moreover, encouraged personal nonconformism, sexual liberation, and communitarian lifestyles; and participatory impulses justified criticism of existing institutions as well as direct forms of mobilization. But the negative effects of these impulses were just as serious: The continual repetition of Marxist phrases created a simplified understanding of social conflict, while at the same time nourishing false hopes of new revolutions. The anti-authoritarian gestures, repudiating middle-class virtues, destroyed interpersonal civility and deepened individual life crises. Finally, the illusions of grass-roots democracy paralyzed entire universities through demands for co-determination, while also lowering the quality of instruction. Despite all attempts to create a "revolutionary-scientific analysis," the lack of a mature theoretical base ultimately hastened the movement's demise.[52]

By contrast, more innovative were the movement's mobilization strategies and protest techniques that attempted to unmask power through symbolic initiatives. These nonviolent forms of criticism derived mostly from the American civil rights movement that, much like youthful consumer styles, quickly migrated from Berkeley to Berlin. German demonstrators thus liberally borrowed English terms such as "sit-ins," "teach-ins," and "happenings" to supplement their own evolving vocabulary of protest. The playful character of the protests continually surprised the forces of law and order, since they were only prepared for the orderly demonstrations of the workers' movement and the political parties, not for the spontaneous, chaotic, and colorful productions put on by students. The conspicuous helplessness of the police inspired the protestors to come up with ever new ideas, so that frustrated officials always seemed to lag one step behind in their reactions.[53] Yet in practice, nonviolent protest methods required the functioning of a public sphere, guaranteed by the rule of law, and thus relied directly on the same civic culture that they theoretically rejected. Indeed, the absence of such conditions prevented a comparable movement, despite some lifestyle tensions, from developing in the GDR.

The banners, placards, and slogans of the revolt displayed a surprising wit and irony. No doubt some boring sayings such as "Learn from the people to serve the people" recalled the stale rallies of the SED. But slogans such as "Professors are paper tigers" and "By day they are cops, at night they are flops" were eminently more effective in making fun of the authorities. Appropriating the methods of the police, while at the same time inverting their meanings, was another successful tactic. As a show of solidarity with Iranian revolutionaries, for instance, protestors printed a poster that read "MURDER: Shah Mohammed Reza Pahlawi is wanted for murder and torture." Another placard indicted the "commander of the West Berlin Police, SS-Werner," for the "murder of Ohnesorg."[54] By carrying red flags and images of Mao, Che, and Ho like monstrances, activists imitated Catholic processions so as to ridicule the anti-Communism that prevailed in the West. Perhaps most original of all were symbolic actions such as escorting a single demonstrator with hundreds of so-called marshals. During the solemn state funeral for the Social Democrat Paul Löbe, Kunzelmann, clad in a white nightshirt, sprang from a coffin carried along in the procession and began distributing leaflets.[55]

The nonviolent forms of protest sought to circumvent official prohibitions by using unconventional methods and to unnerve the custodians of order by "breaking the established rules of unreasonable power." The tactic of the sit-in, so successful in the U.S. civil rights struggle, effectively blocked the movement of nonparticipants, although it entailed little more than placing bodies on benches, on steps, and in hallways. Moreover, once people began sleeping on the floors, the sit-in could turn into an occupation of an institute that could last for days or even weeks. More popular yet at the universities was the teach-in as a way to agitate against the Vietnam War, because this method attempted to convey a subversive viewpoint on a contested issue in an emotionalized form. Finally, activists engaged in a series of novel street protests such as "strolling demonstrations" of groups that could form and dissolve over and over again to get around a ban on demonstrations in the literal sense.[56] The conspicuous peacefulness of the participants made it difficult to prevent the protests or to remove the demonstrators, because in doing so the police forces would appear to bystanders as the aggressors.

Due to the inequality of respective resources, the "confrontation with state authority" consciously intended to provoke repression so as to unmask the oppressive nature of its power. "With provocations we can create a public space for ourselves," Rudi Dutschke argued, "in which we can spread our ideas, our wishes, and our needs. Without provocation we will not be noticed at all." Transgressions of university rules were meant to lead to expulsions and disciplinary proceedings in order to unleash still more protests, because they would increase the feeling among students that their wishes were not taken seriously by the administration. This mechanism functioned similarly on the street. When armed police forcefully arrested young demonstrators for a minor violation of order, the fascistic character of the state would become apparent to all observers. Likewise, by demonstrating the absurdity of such trifling offenses during court proceedings, defendants tried to expose the authoritarian character of the judicial system.[57] In time, the strategy of provoking repression led to the formation of a choreographed ritual between the initiatives of the protestors and the reactions of the police, in which each side seemed to play a preordained part.

The media reporting that directed the attention of the majority public to the actions of the minority protesters contributed decisively to the spread of the movement. Above all, the alarmist and disparaging headlines carried by newspapers of the Springer Verlag, especially the sensationalized tabloid *BILD*, aroused the populace against the protests: "If you produce terror, you have to bear its harsh consequences." Although leftist newspapers offered more nuanced coverage, the SDS called for the creation of "an informative alternative public sphere" that would be able to convey its own critical version of events through leaflets and samizdat literature.[58] More important yet were the images that spread their message on TV and the front pages without needing any words: Photographs of uniformed policemen, faces flushed with anger, clubbing down peaceful, well-dressed students suggested an excessive use of state violence. In contrast, pictures of long-haired, drug-using communards, stone-throwing hooligans, and wounded West German policemen reinforced the fears of upright citizens.[59] The sensationalized news coverage and controversial commentary brought this new kind of symbolic politics into the lives of nonparticipants and shaped the opinion of bystanders.

Despite adult skepticism, the new forms of protest enabled the movement to spread, intensify, and radicalize remarkably quickly between 1966 and 1968. While the demonstrations began in large cities such as Berlin, Frankfurt, Munich, and Hamburg, they soon reached smaller university towns, including Göttingen, Marburg, Heidelberg, and Tübingen, and finally spread to new locations like Bochum and Bielefeld, whose institutions were still in the process of emerging. Stimulated by dramatic events like the killing of Benno Ohnesorg, the number of participants also grew, allowing the movement to extend into other social circles like apprentices, as well as new age cohorts like high-school pupils. This dramatic growth turned the heads of leaders like Rudi Dutschke who had initially aimed at creating a "revolutionary opposition" and as a result began to believe in the feasibility of a "revolutionary seizure of power."[60] Nevertheless, the rebels could not realize this hope because the Bonn government, unlike its besieged counterpart in Paris, was never really endangered, and society, unlike in Chicago, was not as deeply split. Most important, the system itself, unlike in Prague, was never fundamentally called into question by anything close to a majority of the population.

Propelled by provocative campus protests, an intellectually diffuse movement emerged by the late 1960s, in which thousands of students came together in common action. The civil rights movement against racial discrimination in the United States, whose ideas and methods were conveyed through direct contacts, served as its primary model. But the German student revolt was also stimulated by the attempts of the anarchist Dutch Provos to liberate themselves from bourgeois constraints through the "revolutionizing [of] everyday life." At the same time, complaints about the "misery of the university," proven by the "misery of those who have to study there," combined with older pacifist traditions calling for the "Amis" to "get out of Vietnam!"[61] Through the Marxist theorizing of the SDS, a limited academic critique of "poor working conditions with miserable lectures, mindless seminars, and absurd examination requirements" gradually grew into an assault on the "liberal democratic order" in general. Thus an initial demand for more "self-organization" of students and greater voice in social discussions developed into a call for a fundamental change of the political system.[62]

Though the SDS strategy of "active disobedience" carried the message into wider circles, the actual breakthrough to a mass movement occurred only with the tragic death of a student in the summer of 1967. Sophisticated leaflets criticized democracy as an empty shell, and happenings such as the pudding attack on U.S. Vice President Hubert Humphrey made the apparatus of state power look ridiculous.[63] But only when the frazzled officer Karl-Heinz Kurras shot the student Benno Ohnesorg during the anti-Shah demonstration in front of the West Berlin opera house, did a more general mobilization take place. "June 2nd was decisive for me and many others," Inga Buhmann described her shock. "Until then I had always hesitated about whether I should really become involved. All at once, it became clear and irrevocable." When Mayor Heinrich Albertz tried to cover up the responsibility of the police, thousands of students attended spontaneous funeral services, adult intellectuals proclaimed their sympathy, and rebellious high-school pupils showed their solidarity with the movement. The SDS concluded that "the post-Fascist system in the FRG has become a pre-Fascist one" and called for closer cooperation between all of its opponents so as "to attack the capitalist oligarchy's positions of power in the economy, public sphere, and in the state apparatus itself."[64]

During the winter of 1967–1968, "direct actions" led to a rapid radicalization, making the movement increasingly embrace "revolutionary counterviolence" against the state. The impatient rebels began to go beyond their cautious mentors, provoking a disappointed Jürgen Habermas to reproach them with "fascism of the left." During demonstrations against hated symbols like America Houses, protestors took to hurling cobblestones at windows, since "only an act of destruction is an act of liberation."[65] Public attention climaxed with the Berlin Vietnam Congress in February 1968 where delegates from around the world called for "the creation of a second revolutionary front against imperialism in its metropolitan centers" through the "fight for revolutionary solutions in businesses, offices, universities, and schools."[66] But on April 11, the smear campaign, waged by the tabloid *BILD* against the student rebels, claimed another victim when the neo-Nazi Josef Bachmann shot their charismatic leader Rudi Dutschke several times in the head: "We all felt deeply hurt and our indignation knew no bounds." This second bloody deed in the span of one year broke all inhibitions: "There was no doubt as to who the truly guilty party was for this assassination." In Berlin, Hamburg, and Munich, outraged demonstrators stormed the buildings of Springer Verlag and set fire to delivery trucks.[67]

Despite "nonstop assemblies and demonstrations," the protest movement did not succeed in seriously challenging the power structure of the Federal Republic during the months that followed. The transformation of a "prerevolutionary situation" into an actual revolution failed for a number of reasons: Although labor conflicts in factories led to several wildcat strikes, union organizers in the DGB refused to join the cause, since they wanted to jeopardize neither their material benefits nor their political influence.[68] At the same time, the APO campaign against the emergency laws in May 1968 absorbed all energies when it sponsored a march on Bonn so as to prevent their passage with pressure from thousands of demonstrators. The disappointment was thus all the greater when the Federal Parliament paid no attention to the massive protests and approved the bill nonetheless.[69] Finally, the various factions in the SDS found it increasingly difficult to agree on which strategy they should follow—a principled opposition within the system or an armed struggle in the metropolitan centers in the style of urban guerrillas.[70] The mobilization of the academic milieu thus met its limits in the reluctance of labor unions to join and the resistance from political parties against its demands.

The failure of the attempt to seize power triggered a rapid ideological and organizational fragmentation that imploded the movement as quickly as it had grown. The passage of the emergency laws deprived the APO of its common cause, since it illustrated the ineffectiveness of extraparliamentary opposition, as well as the exaggeration of its underlying fears. When "the glorious Red Army" brutally crushed the attempt at "socialism with a human face" in Prague in August of 1968, radical circles were "greatly disillusioned" since the USSR had ignored all protests of its Western sympathizers.[71] Moreover, the so-called Battle on Tegeler Weg, occasioned by the honor court trial of the leftist lawyer Horst

Mahler, proved to be a pyrrhic victory for the rebels, fighting in the midst of tear gas, who injured over a hundred policemen with stones. Afterward, law officers were outfitted with protective helmets and shields, thereby reversing the balance of power on the streets. The core of the movement, the SDS, which had been rendered leaderless by Dutschke's slow convalescence abroad, quietly dissolved in 1969, because it never came up with a unified response to the confusing situation brought on by declining support.[72]

The cardinal problem, on which unified action of the Left foundered, was the question of violence that became urgent in the winter of 1968–1969. The example of the Parisian May and the street battles in Chicago tempted hard-core radicals to organize an effective "counterviolence" against the police, as well as to confront the "structural violence" of the system with at least "violence against things," although this strategy seemed more anarchist than Marxist.[73] In the search for ideological clarification of the current class relationships, competing ideological groups formed that were oriented in part on Maoism, in part on Trotskyism, and in part on Stalinism. However, their attempt to gain a wider basis in the oppressed proletariat by organizing in factories rarely met with success. The reestablishment of a West German Communist Party, the DKP, which was controlled and financed by the SED, offered yet another alternative. But joining it would entail subordination to "the real existing socialism" of the GDR, which most Western radicals rejected.[74] In wall posters, assemblies at institutes, and individual actions, these rival "K-groups" (Communist splinter groups) fought each other bitterly and, by assuming sectarian characteristics, rendered themselves increasingly irrelevant.

A More Liberal Society?

Although the student movement rapidly disintegrated, the youth revolt had profound consequences for political participation, social behavior, and cultural styles. Already during the 1970s perceptive social scientists like Ronald Inglehart began to notice a profound "value change" in the younger generation across all Western societies that repudiated the traditional bourgeois norms of hard work, cleanliness, and thrift. Instead, surveys discovered that young people preferred "postmaterial" ideals, such as social equality, sexual freedom, and international peace, and they became more hedonistic in their attitudes as well as tolerant of a plurality of personal lifestyles. Conservative commentators like Gerd Langguth considered this erosion of respect for traditional authority dangerous since it threatened to upset the established order: "In this respect one has to judge the influence of the 68–movement especially critically." More progressive observers like the Freiburg historian Ulrich Herbert argue instead that the long process of sociopolitical "liberalization" in Germany culminated with this shift in values and the new social movements of the 1970s.[75] These contradictory evaluations raise the question: What were the actual effects of the generational revolt?

The critics of the 1968 upheaval can point to a considerable amount of evidence that supports their negative evaluation. To begin, the effect of the revolt on the place where it all started, the universities and schools, proved to be highly problematic. For instance, occupying institutes in order to "transform the study of German literature into a productive force of enlightenment" sought to force research and teaching into a Marxist ideological mold. But coming up with new curricula and developing radical theories beyond the Frankfurt School demanded much intellectual effort that could only rarely be mustered, even if new leftist organs such as the Berlin *tageszeitung* (*taz*) added a fresh voice to the media.[76] Ironically, the co-determination of student and staff in educational decisions tied up institutional governance in endless meetings, a general repudiation of discipline undermined educational standards in the schools, and the ideologicalization of intellectual approaches led to a decline in scholarly creativity. But the turn from action toward analysis also inspired some rebels to undertake a new, and ultimately more successful, project of a "long march through the institutions."[77]

Another questionable aspect was the exaggeration of an anti-authoritarian stance that claimed to liberate the individual and thereby renew society from the ground up. Often the rejection of bourgeois values just turned into sloth, dirtiness, and generally uncouth behavior. Typically, Kunzelmann's spectacular communes I and II fell apart due to the egotism of their founder, quarrels stemming from sexual licentiousness, and overexposure in the media. Moreover, when money was short, some nonconformists began to occupy empty tenements and other buildings, which soon developed into unpoliced "liberated zones" where all kinds of experiments such as freer sexuality were permitted. Not only did their ratty appearance offend most adults, but also such places began to attract petty criminals and to spawn occasional violence. When the use of drugs was added to the mix, which, as Bernward Vesper depicted in his cult novel *Die Reise*, went from the relatively harmless smoking of joints to heavy acid trips, the consequences often became deadly. At the same time, some entrepreneurs discovered the youth market, commercializing rock music, t-shirts, and other accoutrements, and, as a result, exploited the alternative lifestyle for their own gain.[78]

Even more problematic were the orthodox Marxists in the K-groups, since they got stuck in a fundamentalist opposition to "the system." Due to the expansion of the welfare state, their expectation that social contradictions in the industrialized countries would intensify proved to be illusory, while the admired anti-imperialist liberation movements turned out to be left-wing developmental dictatorships, which oppressed their opponents as mercilessly as their reactionary counterparts. While doctrinaire rivalries in interpreting the Marxist classics prevented common action, they could never entirely disprove the suspicion that they were being financed by the SED. Finally, the Communist Party's "complete break with reality" led to a sect-like isolation from the majority of students. Although Maoists and Trotskyites continued to dominate elections in the social science departments, they were increasingly pushed to the margins and never gained a wider following, not even by going to work in the factories. As Peter Schneider portrayed in his novella *Lenz*, Marxist involvement thus became a rite of passage for intellectuals that afterward was to be forgotten as quickly as possible.[79]

The most dangerous product of student radicalism was the drift of some activists into terrorism, dressed up with Marxist phrases. The Berlin "hash rebels" and Frankfurt "Spontis" started to assemble Molotov cocktails—affectionately called "Mollis"—used, for example, to set fire to the offices of the Springer Verlag as they engaged in a furtive game with the police under the cover of darkness. While arrests in the wake of denunciations and house searches were able to take individual activists temporarily out of commission, such police "repression" actually increased youth subculture's fascination with dramatic actions. The decisive step toward violence against people was the spectacular liberation of the petty hoodlum Andreas Baader, organized by the gifted journalist Ulrike Meinhof.[80] When they used weapons to spring the prisoner from a courtroom, the radicals were forced to go underground. This break with legality led to further criminalization by leading the group to rob banks to obtain money for still more terrorist attacks. A small minority of "Leninists with guns" thus made the decision to use violence explicitly. This Red Army Faction (RAF) proved capable of shaking the Bonn Republic but never came close to bringing it to its knees.[81]

Ultimately, the terrorist glorification of violence discredited itself through its inhumane disregard for human life. To be sure, the RAF, the June 2nd Movement, and other successor groups managed to organize a series of spectacular attacks that were initially excused by intellectual circles as a kind of extralegal defense against neo-Fascist tendencies. But the massive response of "armed democracy"—such as sealing off the government district in Bonn with concrete barriers, extending personal protection to leading managers or politicians, and rigorously searching for perpetrators by the police—made further successes increasingly difficult for the terrorists. The high point of the confrontation came in the "German Autumn" of 1977. The murder of the president of the League of Employers Schleyer, the liberation of a highjacked passenger plane in Mogadishu, and the controversial suicides of Baader and Meinhof, ultimately had a sobering effect. With the "Mescalero Declaration" the radical scene disavowed further violence, while sympathizing intellectuals distanced themselves from assassination attempts, so that the terrorists lost their support structure and were isolated.[82] Due to the failure of the strategy of violence, the rest of the Spontis, including Joschka Fischer, slowly found their way back to the constitutional state.

Countering this long list of strictures, defenders of the liberalizing impact of the generational revolt could also point to some important positive consequences.

To begin, the Social-Liberal coalition succeeded in reintegrating the moderate democratizers into the political system because Brandt's programmatic pledge to "to risk more democracy" addressed their reform wishes and his attempt at reconciliation with the Eastern neighbors (*Ostpolitik*) ended the Cold War confrontation, thus seeming worthy of support. Moreover, the expansion of education through founding new high schools and universities opened up creative possibilities for an entire cohort of young academics who could thereby contribute to the transformation of the curricula. In Bremen, critical pedagogues were able to found a "democratic-progressive teachers' league," institute "new school subjects, openness in grading, democratic school institutions," and rejuvenate the faculty as well as administration. In addition, they stimulated "initiatives for comprehensive schools" and were able to compel the founding of a more liberal university. "Suddenly, there was more air to breathe."[83] For these moderate activists, the Brandt-Scheel government's receptiveness for innovating and expanding social policy seemed to offer evidence of the Federal Republic's ability to reform.

The cultural anti-authoritarians also advanced some constructive changes in lifestyles with their aura of anarchical "fun." Youthful appearances transformed to a remarkable degree: While students who participated in the sit-ins of the mid-1960s were serious, well-groomed, and smartly dressed, five years later they behaved casually and provocatively, had long hair, and wore tattered jeans.[84] Moreover, the commune's practice of unrelated young people living together soon spread for financial reasons, so that *Wohngemeinschaften*, or "living communities," proliferated, especially in the large cities. In matters of sex, young people enjoyed their newfound freedom most, shedding the restrictive conventions of bourgeois respectability. Especially in larger urban areas, "anti-authoritarian islands" formed that established a "scene" of alternative bars, shops, and social initiatives in some neighborhoods—an unregulated space for experiments, which almost magically attracted the next generation of high school pupils and apprentices.[85] Since it accommodated the youthful need for freer development, this liberalization of lifestyles slowly brought about a broader change in values, while local initiatives laid the basis for the development of new social movements.

Another positive change was the initiation of a new women's movement that aimed at greater equality between the genders. It all began during an SDS meeting in which Helke Sander, tired of making coffee, threw tomatoes at the patriachical activists in a symbolic effort to cast off women's passive role as an object of male desire.[86] The public got involved through the dispute over abortion, when Alice Schwarzer and dozens of other prominent women admitted in a newspaper advertisement that they had aborted their fetuses. The Social-Liberal coalition liberalized the law in 1974, but it was struck down by the German supreme court. Women advocates did not give up, however, and they got the Bundestag to work out a compromise, allowing abortions in the first trimester under special medical and social conditions. Feminist activists pushed not only for greater legal equality but also for more educational opportunities and chances in the job market. Moreover, they founded self-help networks with equality officers (*Frauenbeauftragte*), women's houses, and informal kindergartens, creating a wide-ranging support system.[87] In spite of some separatist exaggerations, the new feminism gradually did gain a greater political voice and achieved more personal freedom for women in the Federal Republic.

A further positive consequence of the generational rebellion was the development of a strong ecology movement. Germans were particularly sensitive to environmental problems because they had a long tradition of protecting nature, called *Naturschutz*.[88] The warnings of authors like Rachel Carson and the memorandum of seventeen scientists on "the limits of growth," sponsored by the Club of Rome, resonated strongly in the Federal Republic where the effects of ecological deterioration were felt quite directly in this densely settled country. Intellectuals like the ethical socialist Erhard Eppler therefore pleaded for giving the quality of life priority over further economic growth. At the same time, citizens, upset by the insensitivity of technocratic planning, began to gather in spontaneous protests to resist the destruction of their neighborhoods as was being done by razing old buildings in the name of "urban renewal" and constructing highways for "traffic improvement."[89] The preservation of local neighborhoods against the decisions of government bureaucrats and business interests led to a series of symbolic confrontations in which citizens opposed prestige projects that would infringe on the quality of their daily lives.

The failure of elected authorities to respond to such civic needs triggered the development of a series of grass-roots movements that spread beyond the local level and created wider national and transnational networks. Public officials proved especially inept in handling the issue of nuclear power, which triggered eschatological fears that any large malfunction of commercial plants would produce a devastation similar to the A-bombs over Hiroshima and Nagasaki. These quickly growing citizen initiatives were a strange coalition between local farmers, city residents, committed students, leftwing intellectuals, and other idealists who adopted the nonviolent protest methods, learned from the civil rights movement, even if a radical fringe was all too willing to meet repression with violence of its own. Believing in technological progress, the established parties like the SPD lacked any strategy for dealing with this civic unrest. As a result of not receiving a hearing, a minority of radical activists began to occupy nuclear construction sites in places like Wyhl and Brokdorf and create "free communities," thereby violating property laws in the self-appointed service of a higher cause.[90]

The spectacular growth of the peace movement followed a similar trajectory from local initiatives to national, even transnational, coalition building. When the NATO dual track decision of 1979 threatened another round in the arms race, domestic concerns over nuclear accidents combined with lingering memories of the world wars into an all-consuming fear of a nuclear Armageddon, which would make the whole globe go up in flames. Since the issue had a "special importance" for a country "located at the border between two alliances," many trade unions, churches, and youth groups passed resolutions in favor of peace. More than 4 million people eventually signed the Krefeld appeal that denounced the proliferation of atomic weapons and called for a halt to armaments, without equally engaging their cause—the Soviet deployment of intermediate SS-20 missiles. The movement culminated in October 1981, when about 300,000 frightened citizens marched on Bonn to demonstrate "for disarmament and détente in Europe."[91] Though these protests split the SPD and led to the resignation of Chancellor Schmidt, his successor Helmut Kohl refused to yield in "this crucial question," and the Bundestag voted to deploy the Pershing II missiles to redress the strategic imbalance on the western side.[92]

In spite of such heated confrontations, the Federal Republic eventually managed to channel these new social movements back into regular politics through the foundation of a new political party. After scoring some local successes, in January 1980 the diverse initiatives coalesced into the Green Party, which propounded an ecological, social, participatory, and pacifist program. Though riven by ideological disputes between value conservatives and leftist radicals, as well as by ideological idealists and political pragmatists, the new party attracted a well-educated and youthful following due to a pervasive climate of nuclear fear that combined ecological concerns with a profound longing for peace.[93] Moreover, scientific evidence of the dying of forests due to acid rain demonstrated that industrial capitalism needed a fundamental course correction, if decent living conditions for plants, animals, and human beings were to be maintained. By the mid-1980s, the Green Party managed to gather enough votes to make former youthful rebel Joschka Fischer into the first Hessian minister for ecology, clad in jeans and tennis shoes. The subsequent nuclear disaster of Chernobyl thus seemed like a confirmation that traditional politicians had "failed."[94]

The changes initiated by the generational revolt were so profound that their Christian-conservative opponents were unable to reverse most of them when the CDU returned to power in 1982. A majority of adults and a minority of career-oriented young people in religious groups and student fraternities had never approved the criticism of the Federal Republic or the relaxation of lifestyles. For the "League for the Freedom of Scholarship" and the Association of Christian Democratic Students (RCDS), leftist attacks on the system had constituted a "moral terror of ideologically fanaticized groups" that had to be fought as a menace to culture. Finally, the formation of Helmut Kohl's government in 1982 gave conservative opponents of radicalism the chance to proclaim their own "spiritual-moral turn" against the legacy of 1968.[95] But this change of course could only register a few small successes, such as the restoration of professorial authority at the universities, because its actual measures never lived up to its lofty expectations. To the disappointment of cultural conservatives, the democratization of the institutions and the transformation of lifestyles were already too far advanced to be rolled back by a simple change in government.

Consequences of Failure

Decades after the dramatic events of 1968, this symbolic date continues to serve as a marker of personal identity, dividing commentators into opposing cultural camps. Stimulated by the rhetoric of successive anniversaries, former protagonists, now the "grandpas (*Opas*) of the APO," have a tendency to mythologize their acts of resistance, while their critics equally exaggerate the negative effects of the rebellion. Those "shaped by the protests" like to point to their contribution to the democratization of institutions, relaxation of lifestyles, intensification of attempts to deal with the Nazi past, completion of the social welfare state, and emergence of new social movements. But those "hurt by the protests" stress their conspicuous negative consequences; it is hard to deny an ideological stultification through dogmatic Marxism, paralysis of the universities through committee work, loss of qualification by reducing academic standards, and glorification of violence through terrorism.[96] This cycle of glorification and condemnation can only be broken by conscious attempts at historicization that inquire comparatively into the causes, course, and consequences of the movement for the consolidation of civil society.[97]

The intellectual challenge therefore consists of transcending the contending memories in order to provide an analytical explanation of this generational revolt that is able to account for its many contradictions. In retrospect, the internationality of the movement, which can be attributed to the integrative effects of the media, as well as to personal experience (Daniel Cohn-Bendit in France, Gretchen Klotz-Dutschke in America), remains impressive. Likewise, the intensity of the ideological searching of the New Left, whose mixture of unorthodox Marxism, anti-authoritarianism, and passion for direct democracy distinguished it clearly from the older communism and socialism of the labor movement, does not cease to astonish. Finally, the generational context, which despite a few adult reference figures led the activists of an entire generation of youths into radical antagonism toward their parents, is all too obvious.[98] But in the German context, the partial repression of memories of collaboration with the Nazi dictatorship and the division of the country into ideologically competing successor states must also be mentioned as complicating circumstances. What, then, caused the revolts, how did they unfold, and, in the end, what were their implications?

The simultaneity of the revolts in Berkeley and Berlin, Paris and Prague, suggests that their causes are to be found in a transnational constellation of factors that transcended local contexts. The rebellion was a product of a postwar generation that no longer had to worry about securing the basic needs of life but could take a certain level of affluence for granted. As a result, critical youths were able to perceive the difference between the political promises and actual realities of modern civilization more keenly and did not have to content themselves with the compromises of their parents. They thus experienced the ideological polarization of the Cold War as increasingly restrictive and wanted to break free of the conflicts between the superpowers that were shifting to the Third World. This postwar cohort therefore reacted rather ambivalently to the development of consumer society and popular culture, rejecting its ostensible materialism and yet adopting commercial rock music and jeans as symbols of protest.[99] Because the traditional demands of the workers' movement had largely been satisfied through wage increases and other concessions, only restless college and high school students and some trade apprentices remained, along with established intellectuals, to undertake spontaneous mass protests.

The course of the revolts, however, showed both the potential and the limits of any attempt at revolution in modern mass society that was so completely centered on generational conflict. The escalation of nonviolent protests of a minority of activists to a movement that encompassed a good part of the entire age cohort by provoking repression surprised even its leaders: "We lived as if we were high," one participant recalled, "and we believed that we could change the whole world." Intensified clashes with the police led to a radicalization of the demands that went far beyond the reforming of universities and ending the Vietnam War, by calling for greater freedom and equality for the entire society. But in the decisive test of power, it became clear that the unions, despite a few isolated strikes, would refuse to join in the rebellion because they did not want to jeopardize their hard-won gains by making common cause with the revolutionary romanticism of students. As a result, the parliamentary governments in the West succeeded in shaking off the protests by passing partial reforms, while in Czechoslovakia the Red Army had to intervene to restore "order." In the aftermath, there remained only the memory of May 1968 as an extraordinary moment of mobilization, a fleeting chance to effect greater change.[100]

Nonetheless, political failure made possible a dismantling of authoritarian structures, a spread of emancipated lifestyles, and a growth in political participation, all of which profoundly changed West German culture. The experience of self-organization and nonviolent methods of protest laid the foundation for the development of a "colorful and fantasy-filled protest and demonstration culture." The conflict-laden, partial reform of institutions that extended even to the police changed both their internal climate and their behavior toward citizens. The individual transformation of mentality liberalized social values toward greater tolerance for unconventional lifestyles and unleashed a veritable "sexual revolution."[101] The general absence of such changes in the GDR, which added to the difficulty of integration after reunification, illustrates the importance of this gentle "cultural revolution" for the civilizing of the FRG. "The year [1968] was like a firestorm that set ablaze everything that was conventional, from Czechoslovakia to America, leaving behind a landscape in which much had changed in the consciousness" of people. Despite some frightening terrorist aberrations, the sociocultural impact of the generational revolt ultimately made a vital contribution to the establishment of a more tolerant civil society.[102]

CONCLUSION TO PART II

Paradoxes of Modernity

The sweeping sociocultural transformations of the 1960s established competing versions of modernity on both sides of the iron curtain. Neither the defensive attempt at a "partial modernization" of Imperial Germany nor the contradictory project of "reactionary modernism" in the Third Reich had succeeded in combining technological progress and social tradition in such a way as to reconcile their antithetic tendencies.[1] After the postwar crisis, another effort at modernization therefore took the notion of modernity as an unquestioned model, since it alone promised a chance both to catch up with international progress and to liberate oneself from the burden of an unpleasant past. In the urban landscape this hectic endeavor remains apparent everywhere in the contrast between the simple makeshift buildings of the early 1950s that tried to offer a roof over one's head and the gleaming glass and concrete structures of the 1960s that attempted to suggest a cosmopolitan sense of modernity. This frantic attempt to modernize, however, brought with it all the problems of advanced industrial society.[2]

The Cold War ironically demanded that the Germans choose between two alternative models of modernization—socialism and capitalism. In this contest the Soviet Union was able to draw on the revolutionary aura of the Marxist utopia, the successes of Stalinist industrialization and collectivization, and the victory of the Red Army over the Wehrmacht. The Western powers, by contrast, had to rely on the evolutionary attractions of political freedom, material affluence, and civil society, which, though less imposing, were more effective in the long run.[3] The greater intensity of personal encounters that resulted from casual contacts with soldiers, the efforts of numerous intermediaries, and elaborate exchange programs increased the appeal of the West. In addition, the political bond to the NATO alliance and the economic integration with neighboring countries resulted primarily from freely made decisions rather than from dictatorial demands. Finally, American consumer society and popular culture promised greater fulfillment for individual desires than the socialist subsidy of basic needs. Hence the public on both sides of the iron curtain was generally inclined to choose the West over the East.[4]

When compared to the dictatorship of the SED, West German parliamentarianism also proved to be the more attractive political system. While it may seem ironic that the anti-Fascist beginning in the East vociferously invoked democracy, it rested on a Leninist understanding of the general will (*volonté générale*), whereby the party was the vanguard of the working class that ruled in the name of the people. The East German sociologist Detlef Pollack thus considers "the absence of democracy and the resulting deficit of legitimacy" as the chief cause of the GDR's general backwardness.[5] The West German parliaments, by contrast, allowed for more open debate concerning fundamental questions, a different distribution of power in the state diets, and the possibility of a change of course through free elections. The integration of diverse interest groups, achievements such as the economic miracle, and the chance to criticize the system thus slowly convinced the populace of democracy's capabilities. It also helped that the Bonn system was able to pass diverse practical tests such as the transfer of power, the rise of radicalism, and the advent of new social movements.[6] Unlike in the East, where citizens were limited to an acclamatory role as spectators, West Germans enjoyed more influence on policy decisions at both the national and local levels. As a result, the democratic system there showed itself to be more capable of further development.

West German pluralism permitted the conflicts that accompanied these social changes to be resolved more constructively than did its Eastern counterpart of a welfare dictatorship. The systematic dismantling of civil society and the middle class during the building of socialism had crippled voluntary organizations by placing them under the control of the SED, thereby effectively robbing them of the possibility for autonomous interest representation. Differences of opinion could only be debated within the party, or they were silenced through repressive measures.[7] In contrast, the recovery of civil society in the Federal Republic allowed for the reconstitution of autonomous institutions and associations that were able to articulate the varied wishes of their members. The human rights set down in the Basic Law, moreover, furnished a public platform for numerous protest initiatives to spread their ideas, attract followers, and influence politics. Within the public sphere of the West, the cultural revolutionary departures of the 1960s were able to develop more effectively, challenge the governing authorities, and, even though they failed to seize power, initiate an anti-authoritarian transformation of values that, in the following decades, fundamentally changed the republic.[8]

East German propaganda never tired of pointing out that the Federal Republic came to face the same social problems that afflicted other advanced industrial societies. In order to make its welfare dictatorship more palatable, the SED continually warned its citizens of the danger of unemployment, and this became a sad reality with the recessions of the 1970s. Yet another popular criticism that confirmed the forced egalitarianism of the GDR was the inequality of the "two-thirds" society in the West, in which the lowest third, comprised mostly of the working poor, remained excluded from the blessings of affluence. East German journalists also enjoyed denouncing the higher crime rate in the West with their drastic portrayals of the consequences of drug abuse in order to cast their own police state in a more positive light.[9] In addition, West German critics complained about the mounting destruction of the environment through unbridled motorization, industrialization, and urbanization.[10] Growing criticism of modernization's negative consequences, however, was itself an indication of its powerful effect on the lived experience of Germans in the postwar period.

Unlike the culturally pessimistic mandarins of the Weimar Republic, West German intellectuals nonetheless welcomed this leap into modernity as an overdue success of the civilizing process. Since it was revered as the legacy of the Enlightenment, the notion of progress long remained uncontested, as the changes that it set in motion were viewed as beneficial, not destructive. Western commentators argued that the processes of Westernization, democratization, and mobilization finally ended German deviance and transformed the country into a normal member of Western civilization—except for its troubled past. As a result, such elements of civil society as associational culture and urban self-government, which had begun to develop previously, were now able to prevail in all social and political areas.[11] In contrast, it remained debatable to what extent the command economy, social support, and cultural tutelage in the GDR could also be considered "modern." Since it dismisses the objections leveled against it by postmodern and green critics, the tenacious adherence of key thinkers such as Jürgen Habermas to the "project of modernity" illustrates just how deeply the modernization of the 1960s has changed German identity.[12]

PART III
Challenges of Civil Society

The third great wave of change descended on Germany with unexpected fury at the end of the 1980s and the beginning of the 1990s. Just as everything seemed to be deadlocked, as the Federal Republic and the GDR had come to terms with the division, Communism suddenly collapsed in Eastern Europe, and East German citizens rebelled, demanding reunification with the West. On unification day, October 3, 1990, domestic commentators had good reason to celebrate the opening of the border, symbolized by the Berlin wall, and hail the chance to share in the blessings of the social market economy, as well as the extension of freedom and the rule of law, to the Eastern part of the country, previously denied these benefits. Even skeptical observers from abroad could welcome the recovery of full sovereignty for Germany, the reconstitution of a chastened nation-state, and the international recognition of established borders.[1] The conclusion of the Cold War permitted the resolution of problems left over from the Second World War so that the postwar era could finally come to an end. However, those new citizens of the Federal Republic who were most affected by the reunification process were plunged into an unforeseen crisis, as many were overwhelmed by the change of systems.[2]

Celebrating unification as a success story, as campaigning politicians were wont to do, has nonetheless impeded an understanding of the manifold changes that the process involved. Conservative commentators were especially happy to interpret the "unexpected unity" as an affirmation of the Federal Republic, since the majority of the East German populace had unambiguously chosen the West German model.[3] At the same time, even leftist circles considered the failure of "real existing socialism" proof of the impossibility of the Communist experiment, although a certain phantom pain over the lost dreams of a socialist utopia tended to linger.[4] Yet these opposing accounts often ignored the fact that the collapse of communism encompassed the entire Soviet empire, that everywhere the opposition struggled to reconstitute human rights, and that the reintegration of the Eastern European countries was a challenge for all of Europe.[5] The concentration on the special features of the German case, such as reconstituting instead of splitting the nation-state, transferring the Western system to the East, and offering massive economic aid has at times threatened to overshadow this wider European context of the post-Communist transition.

Thus a few problems ought to be singled out from the discussions of the causes, courses, and consequences of the upheaval in 1989–1990 that are especially relevant to the consolidation of civil society in a comparative perspective. Its "protective function" for the freedom of citizens against the illegitimate encroachments of the state might mark a first focus.[6] Totalitarianism theory, which emerged from the horrible experiences of the refugees fleeing National Socialism, highlights the repressive features of Communist dictatorship, which applied particularly to the initial Stalinist phase, by stressing the systematic destruction of social self-organization.[7] Its concentration on repression, however, offers little guidance for analyzing the reemergence of individual dissidence and of independent social groups from below. Indeed, such initiatives are more easily comprehended through the approaches of "everyday history" which emphasize the "limits of dictatorship" in the "self-will" (*Eigen-Sinn*) of the governed population.[8] Despite the impressive features of the "democratic awakening" during the fall of 1989, the ensuing transformation of the system in most affected countries seemed to suffer from a continuing weakness in the newly emerging structures of civil society.[9]

A second problem area, which results from the "community function" of civil society points to the implications of reconstituting the nation-state. Should the unexpected reemergence of a common state for all Germans prove to be an occasion for a "renationalization"—that is, a revival of buried national traditions which some right-wing critics such as Karl Heinz Bohrer felt was long overdue? Or did the German nation-state, as some postnational intellectuals such as novelist Günter Grass claimed, pose a threat to domestic freedom and peace in Europe through its very existence? Was a middle course of democratic patriotism possible for the "difficult fatherland," as the theologian Richard Schröder called it, which would unite freedom with love of one's country?[10] The international version of this identity debate revolved around the implications of Germany's greater responsibility in Europe, such as requests to participate in military deployments and the primacy of orientation toward the United States or integration into the European Union. How could the revival of ethnic nationalism, observable in East-Central Europe, be reconciled with domestic pluralism and European integration without provoking new internal repression or hostility?[11]

A final area of conflict relates to the "socialization function" of civil society, especially in the practice of civic virtues such as tolerance and cosmopolitanism. One important measuring stick for the liberality of a democracy is how it deals with "others," whether they are fellow countrymen who return from abroad or refugees from different cultures who would be more difficult to integrate. As a result of the post-Communist migration movements, ethnic claims to citizenship for migrants of "German ancestry" collided with moralistic imperatives to provide a refuge to asylum seekers, which were shaped in part by memories of flight from National Socialism.[12] What relative priority should be granted to the familiar refugees from the GDR and somewhat related resettlers from Eastern Europe, and to strange emigrants from the civil wars in the Balkans and truly foreign economic asylum seekers from the Third World? The ambivalent reaction of the enlarged Federal Republic, which has found it difficult to achieve a more open attitude toward naturalization and immigration due to economic difficulties of its own and older social prejudices, shows the clear limits of current tolerance.[13]

The problems issuing from communism's collapse thus raise the question: Have the changes after German unification contributed to the consolidation of a "reflexive civil society?"[14] Some indicators support an optimistic assessment. Not only has the attraction of the second, Communist, dictatorship been broken, but the question of the nation-state has been amicably resolved, although how cosmopolitan the country ought to be has not yet been decided definitively. Other noticeable advances involve the intermediary role of social self-organization and the communication function of a pluralistic public sphere. Yet lingering difficulties indicate the need for some skepticism as well. The intensity of Holocaust memories shows that older traumata continue to be influential due to the imposition of changes in the postwar period, the controversial legacy of the 1960s, and the incomplete tasks of the reunification crisis. Moreover, entirely new problems have developed out of the globalization process that point to the economic and political limits of the "German model." Since it ought to be considered a normative "concept of expectation," the civil society that has evolved over the last five decades is therefore not an irreversible achievement but, rather, an ever-changing challenge for the future.[15]

CHAPTER 7

Abandoning Socialism

A t the celebrations of the GDR's fortieth anniversary in 1989, two "contrast-ing demonstrations" suggested portents of its rapidly approaching demise. Calls of "Gorbi, Gorbi" welcomed the Soviet guest of honor during the central commemoration on October 6, and Gorbachev's report on the Soviet reforms reaped enormous applause. In contrast, his host Erich Honecker, in a "fragile, thin voice," praised the successes of the GDR and solemnly promised that so-cialism would master its current challenges. Indeed, a festive torchlight proces-sion of over 100,000 members of the FDJ suggested that the future of "our country" was secure.[1] But the mood was completely different the following evening, when some 6,000 to 7,000 people in East Berlin publicly protested against the SED, something that the GDR had not witnessed for decades. By chanting "New Forum" and "Freedom of the Press" and demanding other basic rights, the demonstrators rehearsed what would become a democratic uprising in their own state. While the surprised police force was initially restrained, later on that evening the Stasi and other security forces stepped in with brutal vio-lence, beat the protestors, and arrested hundreds.[2] What led to this challenge to the East German state?

The GDR's primary liability was its dependence on the other world power of the Cold War, the Soviet Union. Because of the enormous price it had paid in blood to overcome the Wehrmacht in the "Great Fatherland War," the Red Army believed it had earned the annexation of most of East Prussia and control over the central region of Germany as its victory trophies. During their occupation, the Russians initially assigned a higher priority to repairing war damages and guar-anteeing protection against a third attack than to establishing a new client state.[3] With its "truly unlimited . . . capabilities," the Soviet system introduced in East

Germany was therefore supposed to serve as a promising alternative to the corrupt, capitalist West. However, it was not the revolutionary council communism of 1917–1918 but the late Stalinism of 1945–1953, with its cult of "the greatest genius of our time," that shaped the founding phase of the GDR and thereby gave its structures a particularly repressive form.[4] Therefore, the SED itself had no choice but to denounce the latent resentment against "the Russians" as slanderous propaganda in order to defend "the progressive policies of the Soviet occupation power."[5]

Another burden was the compulsory nature of the SED regime, because its attempt to draw on progressive traditions was only supported by a minority. To be sure, the founders Wilhelm Pieck and Otto Grotewohl understood the GDR as the completion of the Revolution of 1848 and the realization of the hopes of the workers' movement that had finally overcome its crippling division. But the Communist core had already assumed an anti-democratic disposition during the Weimar Republic, veterans of the resistance had become practiced in conspiracy, and Soviet émigrés had been largely Stalinized.[6] Moreover, accusations of "social fascism" against the SPD were not truly forgotten, and the purges of the Central Party Control Commission hit both the returning emigrants from the West and the left-wing dissenters and Trotskyites especially hard.[7] At first, the anti-Fascist alliance policy was able to persuade progressive intellectuals, such as the Dresden scholar of romance literature Victor Klemperer and the Leipzig professor of German Hans Mayer, to cooperate in the construction of what was promised to be a better Germany.[8] In the long run, however, the outlook of the SED leadership proved to be deeply anti-bourgeois and illiberal due to its limited intellectual horizon.

In retrospect, the failure of the GDR, as portrayed in the journalistic, social scientific, and historical literature, seems almost overdetermined. Moreover, the remarkable boom in research, which access to previously inaccessible sources unleashed, has generated a broad spectrum of ideologically incompatible discourses.[9] While the renaissance of totalitarianism theory, advocated by conservative scholars, has illuminated the mechanisms of repression employed by the SED state, as well as the attempts at resistance, it has contributed little to the understanding of the developmental dynamics of the collapse.[10] The concept of a "failed experiment," by contrast, illustrates the aspirations of the actors in building socialism but is largely silent on the regime's negative aspects, as well as the causes of its downfall.[11] By contrast, a third variant of a differentiated comparison between the Nazi dictatorship and other Soviet satellites, preferred by liberal scholars, seems to be less burdened by ideology since it conceives of the GDR as a system of inherent contradictions and thus attempts to relate repression and everyday life to each other in a paradoxical way.[12]

Rather than trying to draw a complete portrait of the GDR's evolution, the following reflections sketch the role of civil society within its collapse. Since the

Communist governments in East-Central Europe systematically eliminated the independence of all social forces, dissidents like Tadeusz Mazowiecki and Vaclav Havel rediscovered this concept as justification for the creation of a sphere of autonomous, critical activity outside of politics. In this quest, civil society acted both as the normative goal and as the agent of change, because they hoped that a repressed society would be able to reclaim its ability to act independently through the creation of prepolitical networks and an alternative public sphere.[13] Although the concept did not come to the GDR until relatively late, the cyclical course of civil society from initial repression, through partial reemergence, until its explosive return and difficult consolidation, offers unusual insights on East German development. The analysis must therefore begin from an action perspective that unites political conditions, economic requirements, and organizational possibilities.[14]

Dismantling Civic Culture

Unlike Western individualism, the collectivism of the Marxist-Leninist social utopia left little space for independent civic activity. The polarized thinking engendered by the dogma of class conflict saw in the bourgeois "monopolistic lords of capital" and the aristocratic "Junkers" the chief enemies whose power needed to be broken before an "anti-Fascist democratic" renewal could be risked: "Its goal is a socialist society that abolishes all exploitation of people by people, eliminates class contradictions between poverty and wealth, finally secures peace, and ushers in a fully developed democracy." The political preconditions for the realization of this program were on the one hand the "unity of the working class" that would be achieved with the founding of the SED and on the other the "cooperation of all constructive, democratic popular forces," joined together in the Unity Front of the other parties and organizations.[15] This vision aimed to create social harmony by overcoming class conflict, as well as to bring about cooperation among progressive elements with the leading SED—that is, an alternative model to bourgeois society that would level social differences rather than observe human rights.[16]

The first step toward imposing social uniformity was the securing of Communist dominance, initially through informal favoritism, but soon through formal privileges as well. The conquest of Berlin by the Red Army made possible the installation of an administration that was composed of elements affiliated with the KPD, thereby giving it an organizational head start over its middle-class rivals. As a result, denazification was employed not only against former members of the Nazi Party but also against all undesirable competitors who might challenge the Soviet regime. At the same time, the founding of the Socialist Unity Party led to a considerable increase in Communist influence that was based on widespread hopes of nationalization of the economy. Through preferential allotment of paper for leaflets and access to radio for broadcasts, the SED won about half of the votes in the state elections during the fall of 1946, and thereby it somewhat legitimated itself through plebiscitary acclamation. But after its crushing defeat in the subsequent free elections in Berlin, the SED abandoned all democratic pretenses, predetermined the distribution of seats in the "national block" before the vote, and fell back on the expansion of the police as well as other security forces.[17]

In keeping with Marxist logic, the next step was the revolution of economic structures through a series of emergency measures, aimed at a permanent transformation of property relationships. On July 23, 1945, the nationalization of banks and other parts of the financial sector initiated this process, since the Soviets wanted to establish control over the currency. In addition, on September 1, "the implementation of land reform" began on a large scale. This measure aimed not just at "giving land to many agricultural workers, refugees, and land-poor peasants" but also at stripping "large land owners," denounced as the bastion of reaction, "of their economic and, by extension, political power." Moreover, the largest industrial concerns were expropriated as a punishment for the collaboration of "war criminals" with National Socialism, and in subsequent years other businesses in the mining, steel, and energy sectors were nationalized "for the general public good." The gradual introduction of a planned economy sought to coordinate the newly emerging "nationally owned enterprises," which were sworn to contribute to the construction of a "democratic economy" that would soon demonstrate the superiority of socialism by improving the living standard of workers and peasants.[18]

Yet another element was the transformation of various associations into Communist-dominated mass organizations, a process similar to the "coordination" undertaken by the Nazis in 1933. Most important was the founding of a "united labor union," called the Federation of Free German Labor Unions (FDGB). This new organization was designed to overcome the fragmentation of the working class and to lead it toward cooperating in the "improvement of the economic basis"—in the new role of supporting, not opposing, nationally owned companies.[19] The creation of an "independent youth organization," the Free German Youth (FDJ), pursued a similar goal of bringing together different youth groups so that they would become "a powerful instrument in the rebuilding of democracy."[20] Likewise, the founding of a comprehensive "Cultural League" was supposed to protect "the indivisible unity of German intellectual life" through the stimulation of reflection among intellectuals about German guilt.[21] At first, new creations such as the Democratic League of Women (DFD) talked as if they were still "free of partisanship," but in time it became clear that they were also controlled by the SED. In short, within a few years society had largely lost its capacity for self-organization.[22]

The only force that, at least in part, was able to elude the SED's claim to total power was the Protestant Church, since there were too few Catholics to have any political impact. At first, the widespread current of "Christian socialism" formed a certain bridge to the new political authority. But soon the East-West confrontation, the power struggle between the SED and the CDU, and the conflict between the FDJ and Christian youth groups created sharp tensions. Thus in August 1945, Pieck and Grotewohl saw themselves forced to affirm the religious tolerance of the SED and to stress the opportunities for cooperation between "Christianity and Marxism." Nevertheless, the conservative Protestant bishop Otto Dibelius criticized the changes in the Eastern Zone as founded on "compulsion and dishonesty." Indeed, he even compared the behavior of the People's Police with the Gestapo, and he complained bitterly about the state's infringement on worship. In contrast, a country pastor loyal to the regime defended the "policy of peace" in the Soviet occupation zone, while the SED intellectual Wilhelm Girnus branded the Christian obligation to take public positions as political meddling.[23] The conflict between church and state could thus be temporarily abated, but never completely resolved.

With the founding of the GDR as a separate state, concern for West German reactions disappeared, and pressure on the remaining elements of civil society intensified. For instance, the SED began calling for the "eradication of [SPD-]opportunism" from its own ranks so as bring the "new type of party" totally in line with Marxism-Leninism.[24] As the Communists repressed the last independent stirrings of the Western-supported CDU, new, more submissive groups, such as the post-Fascist National Democratic Party of Germany (NDPD), were founded, and the bloc parties were completely subordinated to the SED. More and more, mass organizations such as the FDJ, then under the leadership of Erich Honecker, openly adopted the Communist goal of "securing and consolidating the anti-Fascist dictatorship."[25] In an attempt to defame the emerging Federal Republic, the SED criticized the West German elections as a "product of a reactionary electoral system," whose results amounted to a "national disgrace." At the same time, it initiated a massive people's congress petition drive so as to justify the founding of its own separate state as the "establishment of a unified, independent, and democratic Germany" with 7.9 million signatures.[26]

During the "construction of socialism" from 1952 onward, the SED proclaimed an "intensification of the class struggle" in order to socialize further areas of the economy. By launching a "campaign against economic criminals," the party succeeded in arresting and expropriating business owners, accusing them of sabotage, which included doing business with firms in the West.[27] Indirect methods, such as reducing the allocation of raw materials, refusing credit for investment, discriminating in delivery contracts, inventing tax liabilities, and compelling the acceptance of state partnership, proved even more effective. Due to such a "system of snares," between 1948 and 1952 the proportion of industrial production in private firms declined from 60 percent to 19 percent, and only the more complicated consumer goods industries and crafts were able to preserve their independence a little longer. Toward the end of the 1950s, 95.2 percent of transportation and communication, 89.1 percent of industrial production, and 75.3 percent of retailing, but only 53 percent of agriculture and 22.1 percent of the crafts, had been nationalized.[28] This rigorous expropriation gradually destroyed the economic basis of civil society.

The multifaceted resistance against such coercive measures, which culminated in the popular uprising of June 1953, failed largely because of its lack of organization and the superior power of the state. Courageous individual protests undertaken by bourgeois politicians, former Social Democrats, and students fell short because of their isolation for which even the Eastern office of the SPD, the "Task Force against Inhumanity," and the reporting of West Berlin radio stations could not compensate.[29] Only when anger over inadequate supplies, increases in work quotas, and discrimination against the middle class seized hold of broad sections of the population did the demonstrations of the Berlin construction workers on June 16 spread "like wildfire from street to street," with the crowds chanting: "More pay, free elections, freedom for political prisoners!" Surprised by the rapid expansion of the protests to 300 other locations, SED functionaries could only regain control by calling in Russian tanks. Though the party leadership defamed the rising as a "Fascist putsch," independent investigations showed "that the rebellion was really an uprising of the repressed masses, particularly the industrial working class," and was neither planned nor guided by external forces.[30]

With its "new course," which had been proclaimed just a few days before the rebellion, the shaken SED attempted to salvage the basic direction of its repressive policy through partial concessions. "Bold, tangible steps" such as the reopening of the zonal border, the increase of resources for the private economy, the allocation of more consumer goods, the release of thousands of prisoners, and the readmission of expelled high schoolers were designed to placate a restless population. In addition, the SED called on members of the FDGB to "redouble all their efforts," since that would supposedly "raise their material and cultural standard of living [and] reinforce trust in the state and in the policies of the party of the working class." At the same time, however, 10,283 of the demonstrators were arrested, 1,359 were handed over to the courts, and dozens were executed on the basis of specious evidence; altogether, some 55 people lost their lives. Moreover, the forces of the Ministry for State Security, the Barracked People's Police as the core of East German rearmament, and the industrial militias were expanded, better armed, and more intensely indoctrinated.[31]

The SED also had an ambivalent relationship to intellectuals, since it needed them for the construction of socialism but mistrusted their independence. At first, the party relied on the persuasive power of Marxist ideology, moral appeals to older academics to take part in rebuilding, and, among younger research-ers, the desire for advancement. In a typical appeal, the economic historian Jürgen Kucynzki warned of bourgeois illusions and pointed out the superiority of the "socialist concept of the freedom of scholarship," which was not beholden to objectivity but was dedicated to progress.[32] To stop the westward flight of scientists, engineers, and doctors, the SED offered a "differentiated system of privileges for the members of the 'intelligentsia'" that tried to maintain their loyalty through special salaries, individual contracts, and official recognition. Within the party apparatus, by contrast, it was more the chance for a career, the opportunity to exercise authority, and the possibility for influencing policy that not only appealed to fanatical functionaries but also attracted a flock of fellow travelers. Grotewohl, nonetheless, demanded still more dedicated partisanship from the newly created socialist elite: "Abandon your negating neutrality!"[33]

In collectivizing agriculture, by contrast, the SED openly employed coer-cion, since its various incentives only attracted a minority of peasants into the production cooperatives. At the beginning of the 1950s, the party attempted to persuade "new farmers" to give up their marginal holdings by establishing "ma-chine lending stations" that were to be outfitted with Soviet tractors. As one proponent put it, the goal was to bring about "a complete political, technical, and cultural transformation in our villages."[34] The ideal productive unit sought by the Agricultural Productive Co-Operative (LPG) was a "machine village," in which the merger of land parcels would permit mechanized production and the mass husbandry of animals would enable more efficient breeding. In practice, the system reduced independent farmers to wage laborers and initially led to a drop in production because, when nobody felt responsible for them, many fields grew thick with weeds and animals got sick.[35] To break the resistance of peas-ants who clung tenaciously to the soil, the SED waged another campaign of agi-tation and intimidation by the People's Police at the end of the 1950s that forced expropriations by raising taxes. These modern "enclosures" compelled diehard resistors to take flight and reluctant farmers to enter the LPGs, so that by the end of 1960 compulsory collectivization had effectively been completed and "mass socialist production" could begin.[36]

The resumption of the struggle against the Protestant Church also showed that the SED was bent on destroying all remnants of space for independent civic activity which might still exist. Conflicts flared, for example, over the rivalry between the FDJ and Protestant youth such as the Junge Gemeinde, since the state youth organization would not tolerate any group beyond itself. By intro-ducing an "atheistic youth consecration" as a substitute for confirmation and by banning religious instruction from the schools, the SED attempted to keep new recruits away from the church through a "systematic guerrilla war."[37] More-over, the party initiated a "campaign for leaving the church," when Grotewohl declared that the "socialist world view" could never be truly reconciled with religion which was nothing more than "a legacy from the capitalist past." Behind this conflict stood the paradox of the existence of a state church in an atheistic state, which raised the troubling question: "How should a Christian behave toward an ideological state, without compromising himself or becoming an enemy of the state?" While conservative church circles associated with Berlin Bishop Otto Dibelius clung to unity with the West, leftist theologians such as Bishop Moritz Mitzenheim proved more willing to come to terms with the GDR and create a "church in socialism."[38]

As a result of these and other measures, the compulsory process of dismantling civic culture was largely complete by the end of the 1950s. In regard to politics, the GDR had become a state "dominated through and through" by the SED in which democratic civil rights were eroded and the block parties, despite subtle differences in style, no longer represented genuine alternatives.[39] From a social perspective, East German society had been effectively "deactivated," as expropriations and expulsions had leveled class differences to the point that bourgeois remnants could only be found among a few Protestant pastors, academics, and artisans, who until 1972 retained a precarious independence. But these middle-class traces had little formative influence on the rest of society.[40] In the realm of associations, the Communist-led mass organizations had established a virtual monopoly, so that even innocuous athletic clubs and gardening groups fell under SED control. In short, outside of the embattled churches, no space remained for independent cooperation among autonomous citizens. Since the press was considered a "collective organizer of the socialist transformation," a free public sphere that was capable of criticizing the destruction of civil society had also ceased to exist.[41]

Reactivating Society

The actual surprise was not that the majority of the population conformed to the SED regime but that, nonetheless, critical minorities gradually developed in the GDR. From a governance perspective, this phenomenon is generally discussed as a transition to post-Stalinism or late totalitarianism in which forms of repression evolved from direct coercion to indirect sanctions.[42] The literature of the opposition similarly shows a slow progression from passive reluctance to open resistance, but its fixation on typologies of protest keeps it from offering a convincing explanation of the causes of this change.[43] In contrast, by focusing on the limits of dictatorship, one can begin to discern some clues to the unintended consequences of repression. For instance, the concept of "self will" of the populace, developed by historians of everyday life, emphasizes the independent potential of popular desires, which the SED was never able to break completely.[44] The crucial precondition that enabled the renewed articulation of deviating opinions, however, was the reconstitution of social spaces—a process labeled "redifferentiation" by sociologists—which allowed groups to develop autonomous political alternatives in partial public spheres, thereby reviving civil society.[45]

Even the SED's own governing methods offered people some leverage for pursuing their own interests, as long as they claimed to support instead of challenge the system. The ideological illusion of voluntary cooperation in the building of socialism permitted the largely suppressed population a range of strategies of microresistance because the party, no matter how dominant, required its assent in symbolic acts of acclamation. Since "publicly none of the social organizations could be used as a basis for the development of political opposition," the widespread "inner reserve" could only "express itself as passive, but still collective defiance." This kind of refusal to go along cropped up, for example, when "a worker defies the increase of quotas or a farmer, squeezed into the collective farm, grudgingly performs only the most necessary work. It is resistance when an electrician installs a hidden TV antenna for 'Western reception' for his customers . . . ; when a teacher encourages his students to think critically rather than indoctrinating them ideologically."[46] Numerous examples of recalcitrance in the workplace, youthful rebelliousness, and intellectual criticism of the party demonstrate a considerable amount of self-will that implied a refusal to comply with SED demands.

The most frequent compromise between maintaining personal integrity and showing public conformity was the so-called retreat into private life. For "at home, in the living room, among friends," one could express criticism of SED policies, as long as no state informant (IM) reported these sentiments to the Stasi: "More and more people, once they reach[ed] a certain point, renounce[d] further careers in their profession so as to avoid the social obligations that accompany them."[47] If someone chose not to enter the party and was willing to sacrifice the modest rewards of real existing socialism, such as a small car or an official trip abroad, he could attempt instead to live an independent life of sorts. One expression of this "retreat into the private sphere" was the *dacha* culture that found expression in the allotment garden, the camp site on a Mecklenburg lake, or the weekend cottage in the country, instead of political engagement. But this strategy called for the cultivation of a conscious double life that meant conformity in public and defiance in the private sphere. Such a split consciousness was especially difficult for children to maintain, and in the long run it helped to stabilize the system as it diverted the pressure of dissatisfaction with the regime inward.

A more subtle and, as a result, often successful tactic was the appropriation of socialist institutions for purposes of one's own independent interests. Membership in the FDJ did not just have to mean conformity but could also be used for the sake of recreation, allowing, for example, a group of friends to collectively refuse "to enlist in military service." In intensive discussions within SED university groups destined for indoctrination, forbidden literature might also be read, which could sometimes lead to "subversive views," especially if the author's name was the critical scientist Robert Havemann. Even the proven institution of the brigade, designed to implement socialism at the workplace, might at times risk making demands on management and push them through forcefully, as attested by numerous spontaneous work stoppages. In addition, neighborhood collectives which were charged with enforcing socialist guidelines could occasionally rouse themselves to bring petitions for the preservation of historic buildings or cultural memorials such as a Berlin swimming pool built in art nouveau style.[48] Rather than confront the party head-on, this tactic of reinterpretation allowed the repressed populace to use the regime's organizations for its own contrary purposes.

Petitions that addressed specific problems might also serve as a lightning rod for irritation, provided they requested help in socialist terms. For instance, in the summer of 1961 fifty-six locomotive builders in Hennigsdorf complained about the "completely insufficient supply [of foodstuffs] that was offered as reward for our years of intensive work in building the people's economy." They demanded the "immediate end" to the shortages that were "brought about by the hasty collectivization of agriculture," as well as the dismissal of those who were responsible. As long as pleas involved "constructive criticism," the SED sent its district administrators to justify its policies and promise corrective measures. In contrast, the party responded less tolerantly when an anonymous worker in Leipzig denounced Ulbricht's "conscious lies," such as "catching up and surpassing of the West German standard of living," and inveighed against "daily injustice, daily arbitrariness, daily violence, daily ridicule." Accusations like "you've got blood on your hands" or demands like "Tear down the disgraceful Berlin wall!" inevitably led to a search for the guilty party and further repressive measures.[49] The GDR was, therefore, only in a very limited sense a "negotiation society."[50]

More controversial yet was the attempt of many GDR citizens to carve out spaces of their own by expanding the limits of taste and criticism. As in the Third Reich, dance music provoked generational conflict, since the puritanical SED denounced "this decadent amusement," disparaging it as the "cultural rubbish of a decaying social order." Though rock'n roll was also initially criticized in the West, it was frowned on even longer in the East due to the "shallowness of [its] texts and music." In the 1960s, the Communist Party did yield somewhat to Beatlemania by establishing the youth radio station DT-64. But it required that 60 percent of the music played derived from Amiga Productions, the GDR's own recording label.[51] As a "socialist alternative" the "music grandpas in the GDR" favored a "singing movement," which was "positively disposed" toward Marxist achievements. International festivals of "red chansons" that celebrated the worldwide "anti-imperialistic struggle" were also among the regime's favorites. Beyond the hot rhythms of rock, songs that referred to the refusal of military service and to flight from the republic provoked the SED guardians of virtue to forbid concerts by the "Renft Combo," while allowing the apolitical "Puhdys" to dash from one success to another.[52]

In fact, most of the rare public conflicts that occured in the GDR began as riots at rock concerts. In October 1977, some 8,000 to 10,000 young people on Berlin's Alexanderplatz became so enraged when a performance of the rock group "Express" was stopped that a street battle broke out with the People's Police. When the mayhem was over, two policemen had been killed and 200 concert goers were wounded, in addition to one other accidental death. As a result, 700 youths were temporarily detained. While the official newspaper *Neues Deutschland* blamed "rowdies," the Western media emphasized the political chants, such as "Germany" and "Russia Out."[53] Ten years later the scene repeated itself when on Pentecost David Bowie and other bands performed for three days in West Berlin, blasting their music to several thousand fans who had gathered on the other side of the wall. As the cops tried to push them away, "stones, cans, and bottles" began flying, and the crowd vented its disaffection with loud calls of "freedom," the "wall must go," and "Gorbachev." Since similar confrontations took place in Leipzig and elsewhere, it was the massive police repression of their desire for a freer lifestyle that politicized part of East German youth against the regime.[54]

Novels and plays, which managed to elude censorship during periods of relaxation, played a comparable role for intellectuals. Proceeding from a class definition of fascism, the SED sought to create "a socialist culture for the entire nation," prompting artists to find a "connection to our life" by going into the factories. This conception of "socialist realism" was called "the Bitterfeld Way" after the industrial town where it was proclaimed in 1958. Controversies erupted over issues such as the use of modernist styles that censors rejected as "rudiments of late bourgeois thought," as well as the ideological loyalty of attempts to portray the "contradictions of our socialist development" by authors such as Peter Hacks.[55] When writers used the freedom of discussion too openly and criticized the imperfections of real existing socialism, as Wolf Biermann did in his songs, the eleventh plenum of the SED intervened, charging them with displaying an "anti-socialist attitude." As a result, artists who lacked "the higher quality of Marxist understanding" were forbidden to make public appearances, had their publications blocked, and were dismissed from official positions. The policy begun by Ulbricht, which reduced culture to a "struggle against imperialism," inevitably discredited all appeals to humanism.[56]

Erich Honecker's personal preference for "clean art in a clean state" was no more successful in channeling the artists' propensity toward critical creativity into service to the state. As the 1970s began, some "indications of de-ideologization" appeared in Ulrich Plenzdorf's novel *The New Sufferings of Young W.*, the beat film "Paul and Paula," and the TV show "A Colorful Kettle," which satirized conflict situations of socialist society, thereby thrilling its audience.[57] But in the second half of the 1970s, a more severe, restrictive course returned, because party hardliners suspected that "the principle of socialist realism" was being challenged in formal and ideological ways. Above all, the unexpected protest of leading GDR writers such as Christa Wolf and Heiner Müller against Wolf Biermann's expatriation served the party as a welcome pretext to repeal its informal "edict of tolerance" and muzzle those literary figures still partly loyal to the state by demanding from them "firm positions of socialism." Honecker's boast that "mind and power" were united in the GDR proved wholly incapable of solving this perennial conflict.[58]

Clashes over cultural policy carried "particular weight" in East Germany, since novels, plays, and films served as surrogates for free expression in a closed society. People in the GDR read differently from their counterparts in the West, as "books were scrutinized by many readers . . . particularly for those 'hidden spots,' where rightly or wrongly criticism was suspected." The SED thus established a thorough system of cultural guidance that entailed the review and approval of manuscripts, whose content and form were examined and corrected time and again by functionaries before publication. As an incentive for cooperating with suggestions for change, the party granted material and nonmaterial privileges to writers, such as travel to the West and access to international literature. Negative sanctions, by contrast, ranged from prison terms that could last many years, a fate that befell Erich Loest, to expatriation into the West, a luckier outcome that happened to Reiner Kunze. For loyal critics within the system like Stefan Heym and Christa Wolf, readings created a small public sphere, a kind of "sanctuary for the intrepid" in which intellectuals could exchange critical opinions. As a result, a limited, but somewhat independent, cultural scene slowly emerged in the GDR.[59]

Due to the repression of anti-Communist impulses, critical voices that pointed out the discrepancy between the utopian promise and the meager reality of the GDR could only develop on the basis of socialism. The first major critic was the natural scientist Robert Havemann, who as a Communist was arrested by the Nazis and as a Stalinist helped carry out the postwar purge at Humboldt University. Despite his privileged position, Havermann became so disillusioned by SED practices by the 1960s that he openly criticized their dogmatism in a lecture series entitled "Scientific Aspects of Philosophical Problems."[60] The brutality of his subsequent disciplining—which included dismissal, removal from the academy, and exclusion from the party—made Havemann realize the importance of human rights, and he went on to articulate them in the Western media so as to circumvent the silencing in his own country. His demand for "an opposition and a critical press" led to a "psychological terror" campaign via house arrest that lasted many years. Ironically, these repressive measures elevated Havemann to a symbol of democratic socialism that demonstrated the possibility of resistance against the system from within and thus attracted a group of similarly persecuted dissidents.[61]

Another irritant for the regime was Wolf Biermann, whose biting songs were particularly popular among East German youth. When he was seventeen, Biermann had left Hamburg for the GDR so that he could take part in the building of a better Germany as a "critical Communist." But much like his friend Havemann, he chafed at the "monopolistic bureaucracy" of the SED and jokingly propagated a "red democracy," which brought him the charge of wanting "to negate and tear down everything." Biermann got around the resulting ban on public appearances through tape recordings, semiprivate performances, and church concerts, so that he slowly became a cult figure for rebellious intellectuals. Under the pretext of his supposed "crass violation of civic obligations," the SED prevented his return to the GDR after a concert in Cologne in the fall of 1976.[62] Surprisingly, some 100 intellectuals—including Jurek Becker, Stephan Hermlin, Heiner Müller, and Christa Wolf—protested with Stefan Heym against his expatriation and advised "tolerating [his songs] calmly and thoughtfully." Though the SED succeeded in compelling many signatories to retract, the "Biermann case" was a cultural defeat, because his banishment demonstrated the party's lack of tolerance for constructive criticism.[63]

The next well-known dissident to emerge was the philosopher Rudolf Bahro, who considered himself a leftist Communist. A member of the SED for more than two decades, Bahro sympathized with the Prague Spring and, since he was employed as a work planner at the state-run rubber corporation, was particularly interested in ecological issues in the industrial economy. In 1977, he published a sensational indictment of real existing socialism under the somewhat ironic title *The Alternative*.[64] This book charged the SED with "industrial despotism," perpetuating the "late class society" in the guise of state socialism, and demanded the founding of a new "League of Communists." When he voiced his criticism of the "disastrous excess of the bureaucratic principle" during interviews broadcast on Western television and charged the party with dictatorship, he was arrested and sentenced to eight years in prison for "espionage activity." To prevent deviations from the party line, the loyalist newspaper *Bauernzeitung* denounced dissidents like Bahro as "asssorted cranks and vain fellows in socialist countries," who slander their own society: "They are something foreign, an artificial product from abroad."[65]

Due to multiplying cases of dissidence, the term "civil rights movement in the GDR" began to appear in the late 1970s. This designation alluded to Honecker's signing of the Helsinki Declaration, which the SED used to stabilize the borders, but some citizens seized on the opportunity to demand human rights, even if the entire text was never published in the East. For example, thirty-three signatories associated with Jörn Riedsel in Riesa cited the UN Charter, while another hundred led by the internist Karl Nitschke referred to the final act of the Conference for Security and Cooperation in Europe (CSCE) in order to justify their petitions for travel to the Federal Republic.[66] Artists such as Jürgen Fuchs and the songwriters Gerulf Pannach and Christian Kunert were more interested in having access to a public to ply their trade: "We don't need any muzzle/, freedom is the razzle-dazzle/ for which we're standing in line." Another group of young people in Jena, centered around Michael Sallmann and Thomas Auerbach, tried to build their "socialist opposition" on the basis of freedom of thought. In all cases, the SED reacted with prison sentences and eventual deportation of its detractors to the West, a strategy that hindered the formation of an internal opposition but at the same time invited imitation from others.[67]

Not until the formation of a peace movement in the shadow of the Protestant Church did a broader basis for opposition in the GDR emerge. Despite the establishment of a separate Union of Evangelical Churches (BEK) in the East and the decline in congregation membership from around 80 to 30 percent of the population, the church's fundamental conflict with the SED persisted. One spectacular victim was Pastor Oskar Brüsewitz, who in the summer of 1976 publicly burned himself alive to dramatize his criticism of the regime: "The churches accuse Communism of repressing the young." Although the party dismissed his suicide as "abnormal and insane," it functioned as a signal. Additional conflicts arose, especially around the issue of compulsory military service, because not all young men wanted to obey the draft. Those refusing to go into the NVA, such as the East Berlin youth Nico Hübner, who even came from a loyal party family, suddenly found themselves isolated and exposed to massive repression, especially if they did not find support among their peers. Nonetheless, Hübner vowed: "I won't bow before a system that can only maintain its power through the manipulation of consciousness, through spying on nonconformists, through blackmail and slander."[68]

During the 1980s, conscientious objectors, opponents of the arms race, and critical theologians began to form peace groups within the Protestant Church. Ironically, all they did was to take the official protestations of peace that were being made by the state and the church at their word. For example, they criticized the militarization of East German education and demanded the recognition of a substitute for military service beyond the provision for a few hundred construction soldiers per year, introduced in 1964. Above all, the badge "Swords into Plowshares," which illustrated the biblical injunction for a change of heart, was a thorn in the side of the authorities since it drew attention to the contradiction between their peace propaganda and their actual militarism. To break this resistance, the SED proceeded brutally, imposing prison sentences and forcefully deporting ringleaders, such as Roland Jahn in Jena, to the West.[69] The remaining pacifists, nonetheless, persisted in organizing peace workshops, holding silent vigils, and spreading the Berlin appeal "Make Peace without Weapons." While the official church attempted to cooperate with the government, diverse peace circles ignored police sanctions and formed the core of an active opposition.

Another issue raised by critics of the system was environmental pollution, which had assumed dangerous proportions in many industrial locations due to the use of sulfurous lignite fuel. The visible dying of forests in the Erzgebirge and the choking air pollution in the "chemical triangle" of Halle-Leipzig-Bitterfeld drew attention to an ecological crisis in the GDR, prompting concerned citizens to collect statistical data and join together to take action. When young environmentalists carrying signs reading "Return to Life" sought to meet in Buna for a bicycle demonstration, they were doused with foam by Halle's fire department and fined 500 DM, because they had supposedly "endangered public order." The SED demonized all independent criticism, even when its only purpose was to remedy undeniable problems. Activists would even encounter "suspicion from above" when they just "wanted to clear out a streambed or clean up a playground." In the mid-1980s, an unofficial "environmental library" and a new network called "Noah's Ark" were founded in East Berlin. With its radiation stretching across central Europe, the "catastrophe of Chernobyl" confirmed such worries and led to a written protest of 300 citizens against the use of atomic energy.[70]

Mounting reprisals against the peace and ecology movement eventually forced a discussion of "the close connection between peace and human rights." In January of 1986, Berlin civil rights activists and radical socialists founded an "Initiative for Peace and Human Rights" (IMF) because they noticed that "working for peace depends on achieving basic democratic rights and freedoms." Although controversial, this was an important step toward the emergence of a political opposition outside the confines of the Protestant Church, as the group's demands merged several individual issues into a global critique of the GDR. Its founders, Peter Grimm, Ralf Hirsch, Wolfgang Templin, and Rainer Eppelmann, called for "unlimited freedom to travel for all citizens," which would have meant tearing down the wall. In addition, they demanded an end to the limitations on "elementary human rights" imposed by the criminal code and the dispensation of justice. They also asked for "the nomination of independent candidates for local elections and for the People's Parliament," as well as the repeal of all restrictions on "the right of assembly, demonstration, and association." This program to democratize socialism aimed essentially at reconstituting a functioning civil society.[71]

Instead of waiting for repression to end, the opposition groups strove for the immediate creation of an alternative public sphere. For this purpose Western journalists who were allowed to work in the East after the Helsinki Declaration provided important help, as their reports on the use of force documented the violation of human rights, and their accounts of dissident appeals informed not only the Federal Republic but the GDR as well.[72] More restricted to the movement itself was the development of an East German underground press, or *samizdat*, consisting of mimeographed publications that were not subject to official approval since they claimed to be "for internal church use" only. Topical pamphlets and congregational newssheets gradually turned into more ambitious journals such as the *Borderline Case* of the IFM and the *Environmental Pages* of the Ecology Library, replete with satirical illustrations which not only transmitted information from the outside world but also spread organizational news and articulated an increasingly intense critique of the GDR.[73] Despite immediate sanctions, the protest groups also attempted to draw the attention of a broader public with nonviolent methods such as banners, silent marches, and sit-down strikes.[74]

As a result of this process of social redifferentiation, an opposition slowly formed within the Communist dictatorship that self-consciously professed its "hostility to the politics practiced" by the SED. It recruited its members in part from among anti-authoritarian youth, in part from an artistic-literary "alternative culture," in part from socialist dissidents, and in part from Protestant friends of peace. By the end of the 1980s, this oppositional scene consisted of over 200 groups with several thousand members who added to their list of grievances discrimination against women and exploitation of the Third World. Unlike the Stasi's notion of a "diversion" by the class enemy from abroad, this was an internal creation which, while influenced by opposition movements in neighboring countries as well as Gorbachev's perestroika, tried to develop an ideological outlook of its own. Though the groups had a fluid, decentralized structure and were only very loosely networked through friendships and meetings as "church from below," they nevertheless increasingly came together for joint actions. Their most spectacular initiative was the observation of the local elections in May 1989 that documented the manipulation of the SED in its own brochure, called "Election Case."[75]

The SED observed the reconstitution of elements of a civil society with growing "confusion among its ideological masterminds." One the one hand, the splintered opposition was so small that a few manifestations, such as the Olof-Palme peace march, could be tolerated without risk. On the other hand, the totalitarian claims of dictatorship demanded that the state organs continue to proceed "rigorously against the independent groups." But measures such as searching the Environmental Library and expatriating "provocateurs" like Freya Klier and Stephan Krawczyk following the Liebknecht demonstration in January 1988 only tarnished the GDR's image abroad.[76] Therefore, it seemed better to combat the growth of a "typical revolutionary class" by expanding the Stasi, whose "unofficial informants" had infiltrated all oppositional groups. But vigilance became more difficult when even party intellectuals such as Jürgen Kucynzski began citing the reforms of Michael Gorbachev as example. The formation of a group scene posed little danger to the well-organized SED as long as the populace, increasingly disappointed by the economy and yearning for freedom to travel, did not throw its weight behind the opposition demand for "a transfer of power to an enlightened civil society."[77]

A Civic Revolution

After four decades of mostly silent acquiescence, East German citizens suddenly began to speak up in the fall of 1989. Following the opposition lead, they began to vent their frustrations about the shabbiness of the GDR, shed their fears of the omnipresent Stasi, and express their disappointment with real existing socialism. In numerous assemblies and demonstrations, holding placards, the hitherto silent majority spontaneously overcame its resignation and publicly voiced its critical opinions. Leading dissidents like Bärbel Bohley, who had long demanded a "legal space of resistance and debate"—that is, "recognition as citizens of this country" by upholding constitutional rights—now found unexpected support from the masses. Standing behind this dramatic process of "self-liberation" was nothing less than the reconstitution of civil society which partially reactivated older institutions and at the same time created new forms of collective action.[78] How did the democratic awakening transpire, what were the limits to the self-organization of society, and what weaknesses did the SED dictatorship leave behind?

The first act of social self-determination was the achievement of the right to public demonstration. Time and again restive citizens had emphasized their demand "we want to get out!" by public protest, for which they were regularly punished. But more menacing to the SED was the criticism that demonstrators leveled against its "election fraud" and the bloody repression in Tiananmen Square, as well as their insistence on the "freedom to assemble" inside the GDR. Due to nonviolent methods such as "silent vigils," pamphlets saying "China is not far," banners that read "For an open country with free people," and chants proclaiming "We're staying here," the brutal intervention of the security forces only helped generate more solidarity with the arrested protestors among the bystanders, so that the number of participants swelled from a few hundred in August to several hundred thousand by November.[79] Though the epicenter of the demonstrations was the St. Nicholas Church in Leipzig, because a dissident scene had formed there, the protests soon spread throughout the entire republic. The crucial breakthrough came on October 9, when the local SED leadership, lacking instructions from Berlin, chose to renounce violence against the protestors, thereby clearing the way for a social dialogue.[80]

The next step was the transformation of informal groups into firm organizations that could act effectively in public. On September 9, for instance, the "New Forum" in its call for "Awakening 89" bemoaned the "lack of social communication" and offered itself as a "political platform for the entire GDR" so as to initiate a "democratic dialogue," concerning the necessary reforms. Its founders were some thirty intellectuals from various peace, human rights, and ecology groups, including Bärbel Bohley, Katia Havemann, Rolf Henrich, Jens Reich, and Reinhard Schult. When they attempted to register the New Forum officially, based on article 29 of the constitution, their petition was immediately rejected by the Ministry of the Interior, which labeled the group a "platform hostile to the state." But with demonstrators loudly chanting, "allow the New Forum," and supporters gathering thousands of signatures in its favor, this diffuse coalition of dissidents and ordinary citizens could no longer be stopped.[81] Shortly thereafter, another group, called "Democracy Now" emerged, which advocated in a more sophisticated platform a "democratic transformation in the GDR" by recognizing civil rights, reforming the economy, and fostering environmental consciousness.[82]

At the same time, the media miraculously liberalized and almost overnight created an independent East German public sphere. Because citizens, bored by predictable ideological indoctrination, preferred Western television shows, artists demanded a "new media policy" that would set in motion "a comprehensive public conversation." Though the SED tried to keep indirect control over information by offering a "dialogue between the people and the government," it proved unable to keep the dam from bursting.[83] Having long grown tired of being spoon-fed by the party, journalists began issuing detailed reports on taboo topics, not least of all the growing demonstrations. In addition, they conveyed various viewpoints and even offered critical commentary of their own. A flood of readers' letters poured across the editorial pages, giving vent to previously suppressed complaints. With the increasing accuracy of its coverage, the official television news program "Current Camera" saw its ratings shoot up from about 10 percent to nearly half of the households. Conversely, the anti-Western "Black Channel," produced by the propagandist Karl Eduard von Schnitzler, was shut down. Indeed, one refugee commented sarcastically: "Really, what they're showing these days borders almost on freedom of the press."[84]

An even more important development was the founding of new political parties that challenged "the SED's claim to leadership head on." First announced on July 24th, the Social Democratic Party took the lead and was officially formed on October 7 in the vicarage of Schwante. This social and ethical movement for democracy arose from peace and human rights' groups affiliated with the Protestant Church, as their founding by clergymen such as Markus Meckel, Steffen Reiche, and Martin Gutzeit suggests. In sharp contrast to the bureaucratic socialism of the SED, the revived SDP saw itself as the party of "ecologically oriented social democracy," which consciously drew on the traditions of the SPD.[85] Although it also stemmed from the same Protestant milieu, the "Democratic Awakening" (DA) Party, formally established in mid-September, was somewhat more conservative in its basic orientation, yet it also aimed at becoming a comprehensive organization. While pastors such as Edelbert Richter, Rainer Eppelmann, and Friedrich Schorlemmer wanted to unite the entire opposition politically, the DA, through its contacts with the West German CDU and its endorsement of the popular desire for reunification, gradually moved into a more bourgeois direction.[86]

As unexpected byproduct of the ferment, East German parliamentarianism revived by insisting on actually practicing those rights provided for in the constitution. At first Manfred Gerlach, the leader of the Liberal-Democratic Party (LDPD), admitted to "errors and illusions," making the case for moderate reforms within the socialist system in a series of unusually candid interviews. Then a critical group of young Christians in the CDU, in their letter from Eisenach, demanded such unheard of rights as the freedom to travel, open debate, and democratization of their own party. After overthrowing the old leadership, their less tainted successors like Lothar de Maizière made the other parties revoke their cooperation with the SED so that the "national bloc" collapsed.[87] This desertion forced the government to put forward a coherent program in the People's Parliament as its leadership switched from Honecker to the designated successor Egon Krenz and finally to the more open-minded Hans Modrow. For the first time in its history, the SED had to justify itself in the face of public criticism. Heeding the demands of citizens who expected free discussions and effective solutions to their problems, the East German parliament thus began to stir even before the new elections.[88]

The democratic awakening culminated in the establishment of the Round Table, which institutionalized the reform discussion outside the untrustworthy channels of the state. After the opening of the Berlin wall, loyal critics of the system such as Christa Wolf worried about the hemorrhage of the GDR and thus pushed for energetic changes. Roundtable meetings were an expression of the sociopolitical stalemate: the SED and its mass organizations all the way down to company militias still controlled all formal instruments of power, but the opposition, split into rival organizations and new parties, possessed credibility and, by extension, popular support. Through the mediation of the churches, the central Round Table offered a neutral site at which reform initiatives, such as the New Forum and the SDP, could meet with the government, mass organizations, and bloc parties to discuss the future of the country. This project rested on a basic consensus that inspired both sides to compromise: "It is the democratic-socialist idea of a GDR capable of being reformed."[89] The round tables that began sprouting up throughout the country were thus attempts at institutionalizing civil society, because they allowed their representatives to influence the process of reform.

Though the civic movement excelled in mobilizing the masses, suspicion of power put it at a disadvantage in the struggle over the future of the GDR. By storming the Stasi headquarters in the Normannenstrasse, civil rights advocates were able to prevent the consolidation of the SED, renamed as Party of Democratic Socialism (PDS); but during the subsequent election campaign the dissidents, as political amateurs, were clearly overwhelmed.[90] Western parties proceded more professionally, printed larger numbers of posters, offered practiced speakers, and researched rapidly changing attitudes through polling. Struggling with "extremely unequal start-up conditions," the Eastern opposition such as the New Forum relied on witty, mimeographed fliers and put up media-shy candidates who sought to "find themselves" rather than appeal to the public. A fusion of the new parties with their stronger "sisters" in the West was thus inevitable. At first, the unified Social Democrats enjoyed an edge, but then the "Alliance for Germany," forged from the CDU block party and the DA, as well as some liberals, caught up.[91] Due to the open border to the FRG, the motley collection of civil society groups in the Alliance 90 was unable to compete successfully as long as it refused to transform itself into a party as well.

The surprising electoral victory of the Alliance for Germany, with 48 percent of the vote in March 1990, accelerated the channeling of civic protest into traditional parliamentary forms. The "democratic election campaign" proved decisive in changing the attitude of the East Germans because only Helmut Kohl's personal intervention made the newly created electoral alliance known and popular. In terms of substance, the outcome was above all "a vote for unity," and, more precisely, for the "fast track" of joining the BRD as promised by the CDU rather than the slower and socially better cushioned stance of the SPD. At the same time, the result was to a certain extent "a negative decision . . . against all that had until now determined politics here," that is, against real existing socialism, even if some of its values such as the right to work remained anchored in popular attitudes. Ultimately, the vote was about improving the material conditions of life through a rapid economic and currency union, which Western intellectuals mocked as a "banana reflex." Ironically, members of the surviving PDS and the small group of citizens' rights advocates emerged on the same side as the defenders of a Third Way that envisioned the continuation of a reformed socialism in an independent GDR.[92]

After their defeat in the election, the citizens' rights advocates attempted to perpetuate their legacy by issuing a draft constitution from the Round Table. Although the carefully constructed text had lost its practical function with the formation of the unification coalition in East Berlin, its authors hoped to trigger a "constitutional debate for all of Germany." The draft was quite innovative, because it did not conceive of the constitution as an "authoritative statute of the sovereign" but rather as a "reciprocal promise of citizens" who "through it constitute themselves into a 'civil society.'" New were also the explicit allowances made for civic movements, party financing through a tax credit, elements of direct participation, and social mandates such as the right to work, environmental protection, and abortion. Not surprisingly, conservative jurists criticized such a left-liberal document, which might have served as a model for reforming the Western constitution as well, as a "third way to a second collapse." Instead they portrayed the Basic Law, since it had "proven superb," as a superior constitutional basis for all of Germany: "It contains in its principles those ideas for which the revolution in the GDR has fought."[93]

The bankruptcy of the East German state rendered further attempts to map out an independent future irrelevant since it forced a quick "economic and currency union" with the Federal Republic. Chancellor Kohl seized on this suggestion, made by the New Forum in early February, because he wanted to stop the mass migration to the West and limit subsidies to the Modrow government. While the SPD warned of social upheaval, demanding a "social union," the majority of the populace hoped that the purchasing power of the D-Mark would finally allow them to fulfill their consumerist desires. The safeguarding of East German income and savings called for an equal exchange rate of 1:1, while the "stability of the D-Mark," lower Eastern productivity, and the lack of international competitiveness required a higher rate. Western economists also puzzled over what the potential consequences of "the transformation of the GDR economy into a social market economy" would be for business. While critics rejected the shock therapy of introducing the D-Mark as a "capitulation after a lost war," Minister-President Lothar de Mazière instead emphasized the chances of the social market economy by demanding a "pioneering spirit and new courage."[94]

The unification treaty cast the accession of the new states into a legal form that incorporated the fledgling East German initiatives into an established West German civil society. Already the drafting process made the discrepancies of power clear, because well-prepared Western bills usually prevailed over hazy Eastern wishes. As a result, the negotiations could only cushion the process of assimilation to an existing system rather than create something entirely new. The advantage of a contractual regulation of the transition was that it created "legal certainty" for the affected population by establishing clear conditions for the merger, such as the recognition of East German educational degrees. The SPD's exit from the coalition government during the summer forced a series of substantive compromises such as the clarification of property issues, regional economic support, admission into the social security system, and a continued right to abortion which responded to the East German desires to maintain a "uniformity of living conditions" and, as a result, eased the psychological adaptation to unity. While critics denounced the agreement as a "liquidation treaty" for the GDR, its authors from both the East and the West celebrated it as "a success for democracy."[95]

Although East German citizens had every reason "to proceed into unity confidently and with their heads held high," their sanguine expectations were only partially fulfilled.[96] From the perspective of civil society, the unification process yielded ambivalent results because the civic movement splintered programmatically and organizationally to such a degree that it quickly lost its independence and was forced into cooperation with various West German partners. Among activists like Angela Merkel, a pragmatic majority succeeded in entering political parties or in using the new chances for launching professional careers. But a more idealistic minority in groups such as the New Forum was disappointed by the end of the "beautiful revolution," and they withdrew once again from public life. In the bitter words of Bärbel Bohley, "We fought for justice, but what we got, was the rule of law." Instead, managing the transformation of the new states became a playground for the former members of the block parties and post-Communists in the PDS, as well as dubious "development helpers" from the West. Not surprisingly, the initial optimism of a population struggling with the difficult consequences of the transition soon gave way, thus setting off new worries about the future.[97]

While a greater variety of organizations emerged, this diversification only rarely allowed for the articulation of Eastern interests due to the structural preponderance of the West. On the one hand, local groups such as sport clubs could finally shed their dependence on a factory, as well as their socialist names such as "Locomotive," resuming older traditions of relying on a voluntary spirit. On the other hand, large Western organizations such as parties, unions, and charities spread eastward in order to create a power base throughout Germany on which they could pursue their goals. Even if East German functionaries hoped that joining Western associations would help win them greater influence on the federal level, most often they found themselves in a minority position from which they hardly ever managed to escape in order to register their desires, let alone achieve them. The remnants of independent East German associations were only to be found in the shrunken post-Communist groups and the organizations of regime victims, as well as memory initiatives, which formed a polarized, nostalgic subculture. Because of this weakness of institutionalization, most quantitative indicators point to a considerable deficit of participation in the East.[98]

Furthermore, the collapse of the East German economy did not render the revival of civic engagement in public affairs any easier. The exchange rate, which was set too high at 1:1.5, brutally exposed the inferior productivity of the labor-intensive planned economy, which was simply not equal to the dual challenge of market competition and postindustrial transition. The excessive profit orientation of privatization through the Trusteeship Agency (*Treuhandanstalt*) forced the rapid dismantling of ailing conglomerates and their takeover through stronger Western partners, so that only a few remnants of the GDR economy survived the upheaval. While the enormous financial transfers from the West eventually managed to renovate the material infrastructure and cushion the social consequences of the transformation, there was insufficient investment in new productive operations, so that unemployment quickly assumed shocking proportions at around one-fifth of the workforce. Despite all of the measures to create jobs and retrain workers, especially women, the migration to the West resumed. Because a new middle class could only gradually consolidate, little investment capital was available, and property disputes paralyzed new initiatives, the economic preconditions for civic initiatives remained modest at best.[99]

The impressive awakening of an East German public sphere therefore ended in a contradiction between colorful newness and indirect dependency. To be sure, the informational content of the print media, except for the notorious magazine *Super-Illu*, was considerably higher than in the GDR, so that citizens could follow political events with greater ease. More international exchange also improved the entertainment offerings in film and television, while freer access to the products of the global music culture promoted Westernization. But tough competition quickly led to the failure of new East German initiatives, promting the takeover of most newspapers by publishers in the West and the occupation of the boardrooms of the reformed television and radio stations by Western media executives. Although a regionally distinctive media market did manage to form, a number of East German intellectuals from Daniela Dahn to Hans-Jürgen Misselwitz lamented "the cultural colonization," expressing their resentment at the difficulties of gaining a hearing for their different views. Yet it was precisely the self-assertion of a few journals such as *Wochenpost* and *Berliner Debatte Initial* that facilitated their long-term incorporation into a new media culture for all of Germany.[100]

Since Eastern initiatives tended to be overwhelmed by Western institutions, the subjective viewpoints of the new citizens revealed a certain weakness of civil society. The varying reactions to unification, which ranged from the joy of being liberated via uncertainty about a strange system all the way to socialist phantom pain, were increasingly overshadowed by new experiences with the "unification crisis." Although retirees were generally satisfied with their pensions, women and young people worried about the future. In surveys, more than one half described themselves as "winners of unification," while one third considered themselves to be losers in the upheaval. The bad memories of real existing socialism and the enormous demands of the radical change led to a widespread withdrawal into private life, a shying away from all forms of social engagement. Numerous surveys showed that East and West distinguished themselves in the respective priority that they attributed to social security and individual freedom. Even if most viewed unification positively, the lack of respect for Eastern achievements nourished a widespread skepticism toward democracy, which could only be overcome by positive experiences with their own engagement in the united Germany.[101]

The Loss of Utopia

The break with socialism was, in the end, inevitable because, among other problems, the SED regime had systematically destroyed the foundations of civil society in East Germany. Even if skepticism is warranted when politicians praise "citizens' engagement" in "honorary offices," volunteer work, and "self-help," one must admit that the "social capital" produced by the free association of responsible individuals is an undeniable strength of the democratic form of government since it promotes the formation of political will through public discussion.[102] Despite its appeal to humanist traditions, the utopia of Marxism instead relied primarily on the collectivism of the proletariat to achieve future justice: in its Leninist form on disciplined cadres of a vanguard party, and in the Stalinist version on bureaucratic and police repression. While in the West the conflicts of civil society offered citizens practice in democracy, the elimination of the middle class, control of the public sphere, and ideological compulsion of the East demanded daily conformity to the dictatorship. It was only the oppositional "experience of civic courage and resistance" that managed to break through this passive bondage and make possible the spectacular self-liberation of civil society in the autumn of 1989.[103]

Due to the suppression of public criticism, the erosion of the socialist model was a gradual process that began to intensify from the mid-1960s onward. To be sure, the KPD was able to overcome the initial difficulties of Soviet occupation, economic pillaging, and lack of popularity by fusion with the SPD, emphasis on its resistance record, and claims of success in reconstruction. In the long run, however, anti-Fascism lost its credibility precisely because it became ritualized, while censorship measures aimed at youth rock music, as well as literary experimentation, generated resentment against the petit bourgeois philistinism of the SED. But it was above all the military repression of the workers' revolt of 1953 and the squashing of subsequent attempts at democracy in Hungary, Poland, and Czechoslovakia that robbed the ideology of its aura of justice, because the use of force unmasked Communism as a minority dictatorship. Finally, the undeniable defeat in the material competition with the consumer society of the Federal Republic made the majority of the population skeptical toward the promises of socialism. As a result, more and more citizens of the GDR, feeling "foreign in their own country," distanced themselves from the SED system.[104]

Civil society played a key part in the collapse of socialism because it prescribed normative goals while at the same time suggesting practical methods for change. To begin, the emergence of dissident groups laid the groundwork for undermining the SED dictatorship from within by demanding civil rights, formulating public criticism, and creating networks of collective action. Then the unexpected appearance of an opposition accelerated the recovery of the right to demonstrate, the reconstitution of a pluralist public sphere, and the articulation of alternative concepts that together broke down the SED's monopoly on politics. Moreover, the unexpected mobilization of citizens forced the SED to change leaders, debate necessary reforms, and agree to a division of power at the roundtable discussions, which through the holding of free elections channeled the transformation of the system in a nonviolent direction. Unfortunately, during the subsequent consolidation, the emerging East German initiatives were eclipsed by the institutions of an established West German civil society, because of its economic superiority and well-tested Basic Law. As a result, social mobilization in the new states once again declined drastically.[105]

Due to their differing expectations, observers disagree about the character of postsocialist civic culture in East Germany. To be sure, clichés of vulgar "Ossis" (Easterners) without cosmopolitan finesse, which a disappointed wife of a Western doctor enunciated, can easily be ridiculed as postcolonial exaggerations.[106] Nevertheless, some serious social scientists also contend that in central values, such as participation in politics, "the East must move more strongly toward the West than the West to the East." From the perspective of the middle class, "the transformation of East German elites and the East German economy, culture, and society appears as a process of embourgeoisement," even if socialist value orientations still linger, particularly in the working class.[107] Although Western critics tend to bemoan the emergence of a specific form of East German identity as an aftereffect of socialist socialization, it could also have the reverse function of becoming a "vehicle for an aggregation of interests," which might alleviate the transition into a foreign world of competition. Signs of Eastern self-will and self-organization might thus be viewed more positively as indicators of necessary self-assertion in the conflicts of a united German society.[108]

The fading memories of socialism in the GDR therefore possess a thoroughly contradictory nature. Former adherents of the SED regime and some leftist intellectuals still suffer from a sense of utopian loss, which, while stressing emancipatory desires, ignores the actual practices of real existing socialism. In contrast, former Stasi victims recall only the massive repression of the "lawless state" in the hope of receiving better compensation for their suffering in the second German dictatorship. Between these extremes, most East Germans cultivate, in part out of disappointment in the "unification crisis," a certain nostalgia, which often fixates on material products as a way of evoking a lost life.[109] The writer Günter de Bruyn therefore warns that the dramatic moment of the democratic awakening should not be allowed to sink into oblivion, "because it would be disastrous if, instead of [honestly confronting] our past we would merely perceive an illusion of it." Though it was embedded in a wider East European movement, the collapse of Communism was one of the few genuine successes of democracy in Germany. While favorable international conditions undoubtedly helped, this act of self-liberation ought to retain an exemplary meaning for the emerging common civil society.[110]

CHAPTER 8

Searching for Normalcy

The tapping of the "wall peckers" in the winter of 1989–1990 signaled the removal of the physical barrier in Berlin and with it the end of the German division. Armed with screwdrivers, chisels, and pickaxes, hundreds of people braved the cold in order to hammer away at the concrete and thereby remove the hated border between East and West with their own hands. While resourceful vendors rented tools to tourists who wanted to take home a piece of the wall as a souvenir, East German border police attempted in vain to impede the destruction of the "anti-Fascist protection wall." Soon the first holes appeared, which opened up some surprising views, even if the remaining steel struts continued to keep people from slipping through to the other side. Ultimately, it took dozens of bulldozers and construction cranes to tear down the about 100-mile-long barrier with its 190 watchtowers so thoroughly that a decade and a half later hardly a trace of it remains.[1] The rigorous removal of this hated symbol of division, Cold War, and oppression was motivated by an understandable urge to return to normalcy, even if most people were unable able to say what might really be "normal" after all of the ruptures of the preceding fifty years.

After conquering the defeated Reich, even the Allies had difficulty defining what they would consider as "Germany" in the years to come. The previous territorial fragmentation and the aggressiveness of the Bismarckian nation-state seemed to recommend that they first satisfy their own security needs by dividing the country into several German-speaking states. The Potsdam Conference therefore reached a general consensus concerning the "de-annexation" of Hitler's conquests—restoring Austrian independence, returning the Sudetenland to Czechoslovakia and Alsace-Lorraine to France, turning most of East Prussia over to Russia, and provisionally ceding the rest, Pomerania and Silesia, to Poland.

Economically, however, what remained of Germany was still to be treated as a single unit as a means of securing reparations.[2] But despite the presence of all major powers in the destroyed capital of Berlin, the establishment of four separate occupation zones reinforced centrifugal tendencies since each of the victors implemented the collective resolutions in their territories according to their own priorities. Finally, as the Cold War emerged, cooperation in the Allied Control Council collapsed altogether, so that the division into two ideologically hostile successor states slowly became the new normality.

The palpable yearning for "normalization" thus possessed quite different meanings in the postwar period. After the mass murder undertaken in the Third Reich, the concept mainly referred to the search for a regular life free from economic crisis, war, and occupation. During the *Ostpolitik* of the 1970s, the notion instead signaled the creation of normal relationships between the Federal Republic and the GDR, the attempt "to progress from a regulated next-to-each-other to co-existence" or, in other words, an acceptance of the division.[3] With the collapse of Communism, the idea changed once again to signify a chance to overcome the German division and resume being a normal nation-state in Europe: "After its long odyssey the country has returned to itself." Neoconservative ideologues went even one step further and promoted an explicit "renationalization" that not only sought to dispose of the past but also aimed to change the present through a more self-confident role on the world stage. To defend the hard-won progress in the recivilizing of Germany during the previous four decades, leftist critics such as Jürgen Habermas branded such attempts at normalization as "the second fundamental lie [*Lebenslüge*] of the Federal Republic."[4]

Historical scholarship on unification has thus far offered only a cursory treatment of the changes in the notions of normalcy that were triggered by the return of the nation-state. While the various document collections and analytical studies have carefully reconstructed the course of domestic political conflicts, as well as the process of decision making in foreign affairs, they have for the most part ignored its cultural dimensions.[5] The longer-range syntheses written by moderate scholars have tended to be satisfied with narrating the complementary successes of Konrad Adenauer's strategy of Western integration and Willy Brandt's Eastern policy, which ultimately led to the reconstitution of a postclassical nation-state, firmly embedded in a European framework.[6] In contrast, Mitchell Ash, a historian of science, has criticized the discourse on normalization as a justification for Western attempts at modernization, system transfer, and reorientation of the East and suggested instead "a more neutral vocabulary of reconstruction and renewal." Since intellectuals frequently deride "the normal" as "proto-totalitarian," a more differentiated analysis of the implications of the desire to become once again "a normal people" is now in order.[7]

Behind these debates about the elusive concept of normalcy lurks the difficult question concerning the relationship between the nation-state and civil society. Because of the horror of Auschwitz, many intellectuals such as Günter Grass consider the two inherently incompatible and are content with the continued existence of a German "cultural nation."[8] But other commentators like the theologian Richard Schröder strive to reconcile a nation-state structure with a democratic civil society in the hope of moving Germany closer to the European mainstream.[9] The deadlock between these normative positions can only be broken by a historical reflection that analyzes blueprints for political and social order as malleable concepts instead of thinking in categories of a fixed national character. Problematized in this way, the perspective of normality poses new questions about the causes, course, and consequences of the unification process: Did the normalization of the 1980s imply an acceptance of the division, or were the foundations of unity already being laid before 1989–1990? What notions of internal and external normality collided during the struggle for unification? Did the accession of the East German states represent a return to a normal nation-state, or did it endanger the civilizing successes of the Federal Republic?

Accepting Division

With each passing decade since the founding of competing states, Germans grew increasingly accustomed to the abnormal normality of their country's division. The failure to destabilize by attempts at spreading socialism to the West or rolling back communism in the East led to a stalemate that was elegantly redefined by the Brandt-Scheel formulation of "two states in one nation" but in practice produced an endless series of contradictions.[10] To guarantee its survival, the SED regime insisted on a rigorous internal demarcation (*Abgrenzung*) against Western influences and a speedy international recognition of its sovereignty. At the same time, the Social-Liberal government in Bonn stressed the maintenance of ties across the divide and envisioned a strategy of "change through getting closer" to the GDR. Their common interest in continuing the relaxation of tensions during the second Cold War between the superpowers in the 1980s facilitated laborious efforts to negotiate compromises between East and West that were aimed at bringing "humanitarian relief" to citizens, especially in the GDR.[11] But would concessions to the SED only deepen the division in the long run, or would they help overcome it?

While the FRG government clung tenaciously to the long-term goal of political unification, its German policy nevertheless pursued short-term steps toward a "normalization of relationships between both German states." The "Letter on German Unity," attached to the German-Soviet Treaty of 1970, confirmed the goal of "peace in Europe . . . in which the German people once again achieve their unity in free self-determination." The 1973 decision of the Federal Constitutional Court also reaffirmed the unification mandate of the Basic Law, even though this legal position appeared increasingly anachronistic to some skeptics. Likewise, each year speeches given on June 17 recalled the popular uprising of the "brothers and sisters in the East," although the holiday was increasingly considered as an early summer occasion for family excursions.[12] Finally, the cabinet presented its assessment of the status of German-German relations in an annual "Report on the State of the Nation," which usually produced controversial discussions in the Parliament. Nevertheless, in practice, negotiations with East Berlin concentrated on concluding mutual agreements over such things as easing travel between the two states and providing economic aid, which, at least initially, strengthened the hand of the SED.[13]

To overcome this dilemma, intellectuals increasingly spoke out in favor of abandoning the goal of national reunification by the early 1980s. To critics such as Günter Grass, the division seemed to be a just punishment for the crimes of the Nazis, a moral verdict that could no longer be revoked. Other commentators, like the journalist Peter Bender, argued that "freedom comes before unity" and advocated a Europeanization of the German question so as to achieve more room to maneuver. Based on the impression "that the majority of citizens have effectively come to terms with the division of Germany," Günter Gaus, the head of Bonn's permanent representation in East Berlin, pleaded for "detaching the concept of the nation from the state." If one wanted to serve a "policy of peace in Germany," one needed to recognize "that for the foreseeable future . . . there [will be] no reunification." But moderate observers like Hermann Rudolph challenged this assessment by maintaining that "despite everything there is no reason to abandon" the belief "that the Germans are and want to stay one nation."[14] With surveys indicating that the hope for unity was fading fast, a growing number of commentators began arguing in favor of accepting the existence of two German states.

The GDR leadership, not surprisingly, welcomed this development, as it facilitated its policy of asserting its separate statehood. After the trauma of June 17, 1953, the regime's decisions continued to be driven by its "fear of the people," whose loyalty after the "collapse of socialist ideology" was conditional at best. In reaction to the potential subversiveness of Bonn's Eastern policy, the SED contrived a complicated system of internal prohibitions that was designed to keep party members and other authority figures from Western contacts and to limit travel privileges to nonsocialist countries to a small number of carefully chosen loyalists. The spread of the "Polish virus," as the party called the independent trade union movement in the neighbor to the East, put further pressure on the regime, which responded by suspending the previously permitted cross-border traffic. At the same time, the SED pursued an expansion of international recognition through cultural exchanges and athletic successes. To cement dual statehood further, Honecker in a programmatic speech in Gera demanded the transformation of the permanent representations into regular embassies, the acceptance of GDR citizenship, the regulation of the border along the Elbe River, and a stricter compliance with the transit agreement.[15]

In the early 1980s it was primarily the poor condition of the economy that forced the SED to make concessions to the Federal Republic. Honecker's attempt to create his own consumer communism by proclaiming the "unity of economic and social policy" far exceeded the economic resources of the GDR. At the same time, cutbacks and price increases in oil and other raw material imports from the Soviet Union undermined the export of refined products by the chemical industry, the chief means for earning hard currency from the West. The SED reacted by raising the minimum amount of currency that visitors from non-socialist countries were required to exchange, as well as the *Autobahn* transit fees and the ransoms for freeing imprisoned dissidents—measures that further irritated the Western partner. Intra-German trade demanded especially large sums of credit, since the East bought more from the West than it sold to the West. Though the *Neues Deutschland* foregrounded disarmament policy, chancellor Helmut Schmidt's 1981 state visit in Hubertusstock had more to do with improving economic relations because many East Germans considered that the main issue was to "maintain our standard of living." The "network of treaties and understandings between our two states" was supposed to bring "a little bit of normality."[16]

While the border remained a lethal place for anyone trying to flee, the easing of travel restrictions gradually rendered it less fearsome by making it more penetrable. In 1979 some 3.1 million people traveled from West Berlin into the eastern part of the city, while another 3.6 million entered the GDR from West Germany. Similarly, in 1982 some 1.55 million pensioners and 46,000 other GDR citizens were able to travel to the West for familial reasons. The transit traffic to and from West Berlin also climbed to 19.5 million, as highway and train connections steadily improved. Although both sides acted "as if it were the most normal thing in the world," these encounters often created embarrassing situations, since the "Good Samaritan attitude" of Western guests unwittingly reinforced the inferiority complex of their Eastern hosts. Likewise, the stories brought back by pensioners painted too positive a picture of the Federal Republic as the "land of milk and honey," with unlimited possibilities for consumption and travel.[17] But for all the misunderstandings that inevitably resulted from decades of division, such contacts nonetheless maintained a certain feeling of togetherness within the divided population, especially when constrasted to the complete lack of connection between North and South Korea.

The transition to the more conservative cabinet of Helmut Kohl and Hans-Dietrich Genscher in the fall of 1982 made little difference for the functioning of the German-German relationship. Pressured by the CSU, Western rhetoric hardened by stressing the legal reunification mandate, inveighing against the order to shoot those trying to escape, and demanding greater reciprocity for concessions. In practice, however, the new government strove to abide by the agreements inherited from its predecessor so as not to endanger the "human gains" for the citizens of the GDR. The difference from the SPD was thus more philosophical than practical. While the previous government proved more willing to abandon "reunification in the sense of reconstituting that which existed before," Kohl's report on the state of the nation claimed: "We are not resigned to accepting that fellow German countrymen are denied the right to self-determination."[18] In spite of massive support for the West German peace movement, the SED also decided to adhere to a "pragmatic position" due to its deteriorating economic situation. One of the most dramatic expressions of the continuity in German policy was the granting of a credit of 1 billion DM, even without an explicit "return," negotiated by none other than Franz Josef Strauß.[19]

Despite the intensification of the German-German relationship, the tendency toward self-recognition of the Federal Republic, which had developed from a stopgap measure to a permanent solution, strengthened during the 1980s. As a result of growing apart, at sporting events, in television news, and in travel guides, journalists spoke of "Germany," even though they were referring only to the West. For many travelers, the GDR seemed to be a nearby foreign country —still somehow related, to be sure, but basically strange because of its Communist character. While 78 percent of all West German adults considered reunification desirable in 1979, only 59 percent of the county's youths clung to this goal. Moreover, 64 percent of those surveyed believed that real chances for a return to German unity were slim. Because people were quickly losing interest in disputes over national history, the Federal Republic built a museum to celebrate its own success, the House of History in Bonn. Thus the plea of conservative fraternity students for the "unity of the nation" sounded increasingly anachronistic, while academic efforts "to keep alive the German question" yielded a "discouraging picture."[20]

In the GDR a separate sense of identity also slowly emerged, but this feeling did not necessarily correspond to the SED slogan of a "socialist nation." Officially, the constitution of 1974 had bid farewell to the nation when it based the political system entirely on class solidarity: "The GDR is a socialist state of the workers and peasants." But however much official propaganda rejected reunification and insisted on the recognition of separate citizenship, the question of nationality remained unsettled, for the majority of the population continued somehow to feel "German." The SED's turn to "heritage and tradition" during the 1980s was thus an attempt to place the state on a broader basis that was rooted in regional history and recognized cultural figures beyond the heroes of the workers' movement.[21] Instead of a socialist nationalism, a certain "we feeling" slowly began to coalesce that consisted of a contradictory mixture of common memories of suffering and pride in the GDR's own material and athletic success. Nevertheless, the isolated East Germans remained for the most part more intensely fixated on their Germanness than their more cosmopolitan cousins in the West.[22]

Due to the lack of progress with unification, the long-standing consensus of the major parties in the Federal Republic began to crumble in the mid-1980s. The Greens, for instance, gave priority to the "question of peace" over unity and even began to fancy notions of neutrality. Likewise, leading thinkers in the SPD, such as Egon Bahr and Jürgen Schmunde, suggested closing the Salzgitter office (set up to register human rights violations in the GDR) and recognizing a separate East German citizenship. Distancing itself from national revisionism, a SPD position paper clearly stated that "the unity of the nation does not mean reunification."[23] The CDU, by contrast, maintained, in the words of the chancellor's advisor Horst Teltschik, that "the German question must remain open," while the CSU increased its criticism of SED human rights violations and demanded an easing of emigration to the West. Similarly, the Sovietologist Wolfgang Leonhard pointed to the possibility for "great changes" in the Eastern block through dissidents, and the jurist Rupert Scholz argued: "The way to unity through the nation-state is not forbidden."[24] Despite direct conversations between the SED and SPD concerning a "partnership for security," most Social Democrats started to doubt the reunification mandate.[25]

The basic paradox of normalizing intra-German relations manifested itself in Erich Honecker's long-awaited state visit to Bonn in 1987. While the SED interpreted the trip, finally permitted by the Soviet leadership, as "the sealing of the German division," Chancellor Kohl saw the meeting as proof of "the unbroken resolve to preserve" unity. The honors demanded by protocol, such as the East German anthem and hammer-and-compass flags, undoubtedly signaled some recognition of GDR sovereignty, but President Richard von Weizsäcker's welcome of Honecker as a "German among Germans" indicated the continued closeness of both states.[26] The joint communiqué therefore proclaimed the "further development of good neighborly relationships" through easing travel regulations and intensifying youth exchanges, city partnerships, and scholarly contacts, which underlined, despite different social systems, a common will to "guarantee peace." Due to its contradictory interpretations, it was by necessity "a visit that left many things open," since it only strengthened the mutual connections, without, however, being able to bridge the still very real antagonisms. Thus afterward Bonn and East Berlin remained "divided together."[27]

In the neighboring countries, however, the German rapprochement evoked barely concealed nervousness, as it seemed to challenge the stability of the postwar order. While Honecker could rightly claim that "capitalism and socialism relate to one another like fire and water," Kohl was also not entirely wrong when he spoke of a "breakthrough in German policy." Although a certain easing of tension in the "European house" was even welcomed by the new Soviet leader

Michael Gorbachev—as long as the wall between the two German rooms did not collapse—all of its satellite regimes lived in fear of German unification. Similarly, West European politicians had voiced support for unity countless times, but they did so fully believing that they would never have to keep such a promise.[28] However, some surprising agreement on the intra-German détente anticipated future developments. Thus American President Ronald Reagan bluntly declared: "We want the Berlin Wall to fall so that the reunification of all four sectors of the city . . . will become a reality." Moreover, East European dissidents like Vaclav Havel also supported unification as a precondition for the rejoining of a peaceful Europe.[29]

Despite some successes, a mere "management of the consequences of division" remained somewhat unsatisfying, as it left the question of the long-term future undecided. To be sure, one could strike deals in the waiting room to unity, even if intra-German commerce had begun to shrink due to the weakness of GDR exports. Likewise, one could consider the 10 million annual trips between the two states as "a small miracle for the Germans," since they vastly increased the number of human encounters.[30] Yet "a new patriotism" remained "in search of [novel] forms of unity," while the left argued along with Green Party leader Joschka Fischer that one needed to "understand division not as a curse" and, instead, work toward cultivating unofficial forms of cooperation. A joint paper by the SPD and SED on peace policy thus tried to contribute to this goal, as it promoted détente through ideological competition between democratic and dictatorial socialism. While critics such as SPD notable Egon Bahr labeled the "CDU commitment to reunification hypocrisy," other observers like Hans-Otto Bräutigam claimed that "the cohesion of the Germans [has] become stronger."[31]

In the end, no single party possessed a perfect recipe for overcoming the division since none wanted to jeopardize the hard-won normalization of relations with the GDR. While the CDU pursued the "ending" of the "unnatural" separation, it found no practical method for doing so, leading its liberal wing to conclude that "reunification cannot now be achieved." The CSU clung to a strict anti-Communism, which only produced sterile confrontations, despite all of its rhetorical fury. The FDP, under Genscher's leadership, pushed for further attempts at disarmament in connection with the Helsinki process but in doing so did not really want to change the postwar order.[32] By contrast, the SPD had developed a practical concept of "transformation through closeness" but increasingly lost sight of the final goal of reunification, since it invested so much in cooperation with the SED. The leadership of the GDR also remained caught in the dilemma of "striving for a good relationship" and simultaneously "maintaining old feelings of hatred." Only the Greens established closer relations to the emerging East German opposition, but they merely wanted to reform socialism and not work toward reunification.[33]

Choosing Unification

During the summer of 1989 the democratic awakening in Eastern Europe posed a fundamental challenge to the normality of the continent's division and, as a result, to the separation of the German states. The efforts of Mikhail Gorbachev and George H. Bush toward détente had softened the two fronts to the point that, for the first time in decades, nuclear disarmament and even the lifting of the iron curtain began to be conceivable. Soviet toleration of the independent trade union, Solidarity, in Poland and the commemoration movement for the 1956 uprising in Hungary made it clear that the Brezhnev doctrine had been effectively revoked, a drastic change that promised greater freedom for internal reforms among the satellite states. Finally, Bonn's Eastern policy had engendered sufficient trust in the Soviet bloc to reduce traditional fears of German revanchism. These developments, which Kohl and Gorbachev discussed during the latter's visit in Bonn, also infused new life into the question of reunification, which had "long lain dormant in the shadow of 'political realities.'" How would the Germans, how would their neighbors, react to these new opportunities?[34]

The first response was an intense controversy that revealed the extent to which everyone had become accustomed to the division. In June, a federal government spokesman predicted "Honecker's remaining in office beyond 1990," while the SED head hoped that "the development of good-neighborly relations" would continue. The Young Socialists also advocated "transnational cooperation" rather than the pursuit of the illusion of unity, while left intellectuals such as Gerhard Zwerenz criticized the concept of "reunification" as "an empty nationalist phrase, which does not even appear in the Basic Law."[35] By contrast, a growing number of commentators, including dramatist Rolf Hochhuth, believed that "the German clock has struck unity" and in light of the reforms in the Soviet Union predicted, like CDU politician Ottfried Hennig, that "the wall will fall." Foreign observers, such as the French historian Joseph Rovan and the former Italian ambassador Luigi Ferraris, also began to ponder "the possibility of the reunification of the continent which had been split since 1945." Although the Federal Republic was not pursuing a "policy of destabilization," these differences in opinion made it clear that "people were once again discussing the German question."[36]

The end of stability signaled by the mass exodus from the GDR threw the Bonn government into a quandary over the future of its Germany policy. The East Germans' elemental urge to emigrate plunged the "policy of small steps" into a crisis, because the normal exchange of economic help for humanitarian concessions could no longer master the new dimension of the problem. Should operative policy, even in this situation, "simply stay its course" and continue the tested cooperation with the SED, or was the wave of emigration a sign of such a "widespread dissatisfaction" as to necessitate a policy change, pushing for the democratic self-determination of the GDR population?[37] While leftist politicians like Gerhard Schröder continued to reject reunification as an "unsuitable term," conservatives, such as the journalist Karl Friedrich Fromme, now demanded an active policy aimed at unification. After much discussion, Chancellor Kohl and opposition leader Hans-Jochen Vogel finally agreed "to offer [the GDR] broadly conceived cooperation, were it to introduce political and economic reforms." Having underestimated the opposition in the GDR, West German politicians initially responded by intensifying their well-tested Eastern policy.[38]

Ultimately "the precipitous development in East Berlin" forced a fundamental rethinking of options, which shattered the normality of the division. The rapid growth of the Leipzig demonstrations and their spread to other cities demanded greater adherence to human rights, while Honecker's fall signaled a generational transfer of power within the ossified SED leadership. The decisive event, however, was the partly planned and partly accidental opening of the Berlin wall on November 9 because it made possible a spontaneous unification from below in the divided Berlin: "The Germans are celebrating their reunion," the media proclaimed. Bonn's policy supported this democratic awakening with further calls for reform, contacts with the newly emerging opposition groups, and demands for "free elections in the GDR" as a condition for an "entirely new dimension of economic assistance."[39] To be sure, the SED continued to insist that reunification "was not on the agenda," and opponents called for concerted action "against unification." But in international commentaries "the sleeping lioness of unity" raised her head, and the West German populace began to consider the return of political unity not only desirable but also suddenly possible.[40]

Only in late November did Helmut Kohl risk the crucial step of declaring unification the goal "of operative daily policy" in his "Ten Point Plan." Even if misunderstood hints by Soviet diplomat Nikolai Portugalow triggered the idea, it was Horst Teltschik who suggested that the chancellor might reclaim the leadership of public opinion with a daring initiative. The text itself was worked out in the close confines of the chancellery without input from Foreign Minister Genscher or consultation of Western allies so as not to dilute it.[41] On its face, the plan contained little more than an evolution of previous policy, since in addition to immediate aid it began with the continuation of "cooperation with the GDR." Going somewhat further, it made the expansion of assistance contingent on the condition that "a change of the political and economic system of the GDR [should] be bindingly resolved and irreversibly set in motion." More explosive yet was the reference to Hans Modrow's suggestion of a treaty community that would be expanded by "confederative structures between two states in Germany" with the clear goal of creating a "federal state order." Despite concluding allusions to European integration and the CSCE, this reference was the real provocation that set in motion the process of reunification.[42]

Not surprisingly, the reaction to Kohl's unexpected initiative was rather divided. Conservative circles were overjoyed, since they believed that "we have earned our unity." Even the SPD brought itself to agree, largely because the elder statesman Willy Brandt insisted that "what belongs together is growing together," though the Saarland populist Oskar Lafontaine remained skeptical. In contrast, the Greens saw "no reason to deviate from our position." West German intellectuals inveighed "against the sweaty arrogance from Oggersheim," and Berlin leftists demonstrated in "unity against the Kohl plantation."[43] Likewise, Germany's allies and neighbors were hardly enthused by the chancellor's coup, since they felt slighted by not being consulted and had major substantive reservations. U.S. President George Bush proved the most amenable to the plan, but on the condition that Germany remain in NATO. French President François Mitterrand, however, had ambivalent feelings toward a potential increase in German power, while British Prime Minister Margaret Thatcher flatly rejected unification. Most distraught of all was Mikhail Gorbachev, who did not consider his policy of détente as permission for unity and thus gave Genscher a firm dressing down, replete with allusions to Hitler's attack on the Soviet Union some fifty years before.[44]

Once again, the East German populace forced hesitant politicians to take further action with its open endorsement of unity. In the second half of November, the chants ringing forth from the Monday demonstrations in Leipzig began to change from "we are *the* people" to "we are *one* people," and even to "Germany, united Fatherland." While socialist intellectuals continued to hope for an independent "third way" that would reform the GDR, more and more opposition groups began to demand outright unification.[45] Recruited from conservative church circles, the Democratic Awakening Party was the first to call for the reconstitution of national unity, the SDP advocated "a democratic and unaligned Germany in a European house," and the citizens' rights group Democracy Now presented a step-by-step plan for a "mutual convergence" through political and social reforms enacted by both states. When a huge crowd of Dresden citizens triumphantly received Kohl just before Christmas with shouts of "Helmut, Helmut" and black-red-gold flags, the silent majority made the continuation of division untenable. The chancellor realized, "this regime is finished. Unity is coming!" With the wind clearly at its back, the federal government in Bonn decided to discontinue support for East German statehood and instead to push for unification.[46]

The growing pressure for "unity from below" unleashed an intense domestic and international debate over the legitimacy of a German nation-state. Many foreign commentators, such as the editorial staff of the *New York Times*, feared that "this development is unavoidable," although "hardly anyone is for it." But most domestic observers saw the "merger of both states in Germany as the only way out of the economic, social, political, and moral crisis of the GDR."[47] In fact, both reactions were emotional, because the return of a German nation-state touched on a dual taboo: On the one hand, the entire postwar order in Europe was based on the division of Germany; on the other hand, the identity of German intellectuals rested on a "postnational" self-understanding conditioned by the Holocaust.[48] As a result, in the winter of 1989–1990, the state chancelleries and various commentators searched frantically for past models that would yield somewhat to the aspirations for national unity without allowing the problematic pre-1945 nationalist state to return. In the process, positive and negative notions of normality played a key role, as their competing slogans determined the respective recommendations.

Fearing a "Fourth Reich," opponents of unification insisted on the continuation of the division since they considered multiple statehood the normal condition of the German past. The quasi-historical "arguments against reunification" were quite diverse: A German nation-state was immoral, because it had been discredited by Auschwitz; anti-Semitic, since racism still lingered; "reactionary and aggressive," because it rested on the borders of 1937; "utterly impossible," for it required the annexation of the GDR; and, finally, "illusionary," because East German living standards could not be raised quickly to Western levels.[49] This negative and oversimplified memory shaped above all the feelings of the political and racial victims of National Socialism in Israel, the United States, the Soviet Union, and Poland, whose suffering had been inextricably tied to the name "Germany." But ironically, German intellectuals such as Günter Grass, in a kind of anti-Fascism after the fact, also wished to avoid a relapse into the horrors of the Third Reich and thus remained fixated on old fears.[50] In the long run, however, their refusal could not be maintained because it ignored the fundamental changes that had taken place during the generation and a half since 1945.

Searching for a "Third Way," reformist socialists, by contrast, favored the idea of a "treaty community" because it allowed the possibility of a "socialist alternative to the FRG." This solution, worked out by the chancellor's office in the form of a detailed draft treaty, rested on continued GDR independence that would be developed through closer ties in all areas of the economy and culture into a kind of dual state. The main supporters of this East German attempt to "develop a solidarity society" of their own came not only from the former SED, now reborn as the Party of Democratic Socialism (PDS), but also from elements within the citizens' movement of the Round Table, as well as Western radicals who refused to give up the project of democratizing socialism without a fight.[51] Initially, Gorbachev also sought the renewal of the GDR through internal reforms, while some Western intellectuals and trade unionists preferred continuing the project of a "better Germany" to creating a united one. In the long run, however, the obvious failure of real existing socialism and the East German people's longing for unity pulled the rug out from under the project of establishing just a loose treaty community between a self-reforming East and an affluent West that would have to finance it.[52]

The compromise of a "confederation" offered a more gradual progression toward unification since it accommodated the desire for unity without immediately ending the independence of the GDR. In many ways, it hearkened back to the "German Confederation" of the nineteenth century because it tried to make the incompatible compatible by aiming for greater community while simultaneously maintaining separate sovereignty. The SED had actually made this suggestion in the 1950s so as to avoid "free elections" and codify the "achievements of socialism" through legal equality during a potential merger. Plans for a confederation were propagated primarily by the PDS, the leftist currents in the SPD, and the Greens who had grudgingly accepted unity but did not want to see a complete fusion.[53] Several neighboring states also saw in such a solution the lesser, but still tolerable, evil. However, Modrow's loss of credibility that stemmed from the discovery of SED corruption, his further support of the Stasi, and the state bankruptcy rendered even a partial salvaging of dual statehood obsolete. After sharp debates, even the Soviet government realized the inevitable "necessity" of unification, making its concession public in early February during successive press conferences with Modrow and Kohl in Moscow.[54]

Advocates of unity, by contrast, called for an "accession" to the Federal Republic according to the Basic Law, based on the precedent of the return of the Saarland in 1956. An orderly transition could be accomplished, either through a joint constitutional convention spelled out in article 146 or through a quick entry of the new states according to article 23, thereby avoiding a "long adventure" of transition. Arguments for this "given process" referred to the achievements of democratization, the reputation of the Basic Law as "the most peaceful and liberal political order," and the integration into Europe and the Western alliance system. As a nation within the recognized borders, a truncated German state would no longer represent an anomaly in the international community. Proponents of accession were primarily the governing parties, as well as the SPD, the Protestant churches that had helped maintain cohesion, and a growing majority of the East German population.[55] Equally important was the steady support of the American government and of dissidents from East Central Europe, because their encouragement reduced foreign resistance. The core problem of this alternative, however, was the clarification of controversial positions such as the recognition of the Eastern border with Poland, as well as the continuation of NATO membership.[56]

By contrast, the final variant of creating a "European peace order" stressed the interdependence of German unity and European integration. Above all, Foreign Minister Genscher pointed out that the new Germany ought to be embedded into Europe so as to gain the approval of its neighbors through "full respect for existing treaties," the "inviolability of borders," and the "establishment of structures for cooperative security." But Chancellor Kohl also steadfastly supported Germany's "European responsibility with no ifs or buts," since he considered national unity and European integration "not [as] competing, but rather as complementary mandates of the Basic law." The SPD, the Greens, and the skeptics of unity among the East German citizens' rights advocates supported this position as well.[57] Of course, Europeanization was also popular among the neighboring states because it permitted a still-hesitant Mitterrand to accept the inevitable under certain conditions and opened the door for East Central Europe's return to the West. Nonetheless, it remained highly controversial whether that alternative meant the abolition of the nation-state and neutralization within the CSCE or Germany's incorporation into the European Union.[58]

Ultimately, the dispute over the "path to Germany" was not decided by an academic jury but by the population of the GDR in the first free elections of March 1990. The unexpected victory of the "Alliance for Germany," which received over 48 percent of the vote, as well as the disappointing results for the SPD, which came in at just under 22 percent, and the Liberals who received about 5 percent, resulted in a three-quarter majority in favor of unity. While the East German government of Lothar de Mazière, which comprised this coalition, wanted to "set its own priorities," it proved to be a more willing partner in the negotiations with Bonn than its predecessor, which had been dominated by the PDS.[59] The influence of this clear "affirmation of unity" on the form and pace of the process was undeniable: On the one hand, the result was a signal to hesitant intellectuals, who remained skeptical of unity because of a misunderstood lesson of history, as well as those West Germans who feared that it might bring "material disadvantages."[60] On the other hand, the clear mandate strengthened the hand of those powers such as the United States who advocated "quick unification" and insisted on membership in NATO. Thereafter the task would be "to shape this unity in appropriate steps."[61]

For the international community the chief challenge was realizing the German right to self-determination without, however, destabilizing Europe in the process. Among the affected countries, the implementation of this desire unleashed many anxieties since they feared that "Pandora's box is once again open." As a result of numerous closed-door conversations, American, Russian, and German statesmen agreed on "two-plus-four negotiations" to accommodate the wishes of both German states while at the same time respecting the residual rights of the victors of the Second World War.[62] Despite the protests of the smaller neighbors who felt ignored, this formula proved advantageous because both German states were for the most part able to agree, in spite of the differences between the neutralism of Markus Meckel and the multilateralism of Hans-Dietrich Genscher. At the same time, strong American support for unity overcame the resentment of Margaret Thatcher, derived largely from the loss of her special status in the White House, and the wavering attitude of François Mitterrand. The key role, however, fell to Mikhail Gorbachev, since unification meant that the Soviet Union had to give up its East German satellite.[63]

The result of the dramatic negotiations was neither a neutral confederation nor a European peace order but an expanded Federal Republic that remained firmly anchored in the West.[64] First, the Two-Plus-Four Treaty of September 12, 1990, established that "the unified Germany will encompass the territories of the FRG, GDR, and all of Berlin." This statement in effect recognized the Oder-Neisse line as the eastern border with Poland, even if agreement was difficult for those who had been expelled in 1945.[65] Second, it reaffirmed Bonn's peace policy such as the "renunciation of the production, possession, and power to determine the use of ABC weapons." This also meant a drastic reduction in the size of the Bundeswehr to 370,000 soldiers following the integration of the Eastern NVA, thereby preventing any possibility of new aggression. Third, the Soviet Union promised to withdraw its troops from East Germany by 1994, as long as Bonn would bear the costs and only conventional forces would be stationed there. The fourth, and for Moscow the most difficult concession, was that Germany would retain the right to choose its alliances and thus maintain its membership in NATO as a whole. Fifth, the victorious powers dissolved "their rights and responsibilities," returning to unified Germany "full sovereignty over its internal and external affairs." The conclusion of the treaty was "a historical hour for Europe and a fortunate hour for the Germans."[66]

At the same time, the domestic aspects of unification had to be organized, which in effect amounted to the transfer of the Western system to the new states. Although many felt "steamrolled" by its pace, the economy cried out for "rapid unification" to prevent the bankrupt GDR from "bleeding dry" through the "exodus of hundreds of thousands." By proposing an "economic and currency union," which recalled the Zollverein of the nineteenth century, Chancellor Kohl wanted to give East Germans a "perspective for the future, that is, courage and confidence to stay." In order to overcome the "intensifying crisis," the Federal Republic offered "its strongest economic asset, the D-Mark."[67] Rather than "growing together as slowly as possible," this offer called for an abrupt, fundamental change of systems by "creating the legal preconditions for the introduction of the market economy." Since in setting the exchange rate the interests of the East and West Germans collided with one another, a compromise of 1:1.5 was finally worked out. The financial conversion, which required sums reaching into the billions, would be facilitated through a fund for German unity on the capital market. Ignoring the warnings of leftist Cassandras, the signing of the State Treaty was a "decisive step toward unity," because the East Germans "had faith in an economic rebound."[68]

The unification treaty was thus a necessary attempt to find a legal form for the GDR's integration into the Federal Republic because most East Germans insisted on adopting the Western model.[69] Though some wished to modify the Basic Law by inserting a "right to work," both governments preferred accession on the basis of article 23 because of the "uncertainties" of a lengthy constitutional discussion according to article 146.[70] Lothar de Maizière's intention to bring about unity "as quickly as possible and as orderly as necessary" failed due to the collapse of GDR finances, which rendered an "emergency annexation unavoidable." After a long "skirmish," the East German Parliament therefore set the date for unification as October 3, 1990.[71] The content of the voluminous treaty tried to regulate the chaos of the transition as much as possible. The easiest step was the political incorporation, which was accomplished through the reestablishment of the five Eastern states that had existed until 1952. More difficult was the recognition of Eastern diplomas and acceptance into the Western benefits system without having paid anything into it. The most controversial aspects proved to be determination of property rights, the legality of abortion, and access to the files of the Stasi, which had kept detailed records on millions of citizens. To cope with all these difficulties, Federal President Richard von Weizsäcker exhorted: "Accept each other."[72]

The unification celebration on October 3, 1990, symbolized the transition "from normalization to normality"—from management of division to restoration of unity. A Swiss reporter described the festive scene: "Amid the exultation of tens of thousands . . . a huge black, red, and gold flag has been hoisted . . . in front of the Reichstag in Berlin at midnight as a sign that the entrance of the GDR into the FRG has been completed." On the rostrum Chancellor Kohl and Premier de Maizière, as well as other dignitaries, listened to the ringing of the freedom bell from the Schönberg town hall and sang the national anthem, intoned by a choir. "A brief moment of emotion" passed, with the "indefinable feeling of having witnessed a historic occasion." Champagne corks popped, fireworks lit up the evening sky, and "a cheerful festive mood" permeated the air. The celebration was deliberately unostentatious, so as not to produce any "patriotic ardor" that might evoke bad memories. By demonstrating the continued existence of its civility, the unified Federal Republic wanted to soothe the fears of both domestic and foreign skeptics who persisted in the opinion "never again Germany!"[73]

Uncertainties of Normality

The elemental joy over the unexpected unity soon gave way to uncertainty about the consequences of returning to normality. To the question posed by the SPD politician Klaus von Dohnanyi in the summer of 1991, is "Germany—a normal country?" many intellectuals emphatically responded: "After Auschwitz there can never be political normality for Germany." For commentators such as Kurt Sontheimer who were sensitive to tradition, the return to the nation-state was "a miracle of history," which, as the neoconservative Rainer Zitelmann hoped, would put an end to the agonizing discussion of the past and inspire a more self-confident stance in international affairs.[74] In contrast, critical thinkers such as Jürgen Habermas, for whom the East German "Deutsch-Mark nationalism" was an abomination, were concerned with maintaining the civilizing advances of the postwar period that a revulsion against the Nazi crimes had inspired and with pushing forward the evolution toward a postnational global community. With amazement, foreign observers thus registered in the Germans a certain "fear of becoming normal once again."[75]

Highest priority belonged to the attempt to expunge all traces of the division as quickly and as thoroughly as possible. This included, above all, removing the notorious fortifications such as watchtowers, minefields, firing zones, and guard dogs that stretched along the 800–mile border between the two states like a deep wound. With assistance from the "Fund for German Unity," blocked streets were reopened, demolished bridges rebuilt, rail lines restored, telephone lines reactivated, high-tension wires reconnected, and new gas and oil lines laid. Long-separated families were reunited, and interrupted friendships, particularly in towns near the border, could be refreshed and new encounters made, which helped to rekindle human relationships. From more distant regions, bus trips were organized into unknown parts of the country, in which the younger generation could satisfy its curiosity and establish new contacts. Amid all of the euphoria, however, the very first meetings revealed just how far the Germans had grown apart in attitudes and life experiences during the previous four decades. It came as little surprise, therefore, that the people carried "the wall in their heads" much longer than it took to remove its physical remains.[76]

Another aspect of the transition was the rapid Westernization of the outward appearance of East German cities, streets, and people. While most things stayed the same in the West after October 3, the changes in the East during the first years of unity were breathtaking. Flashy new cars began to dominate the streets; gas stations, stores, and shopping centers sprang up everywhere; houses were repainted; and sparkling advertisements banished the dreary gray that had only occasionally been punctuated by red propaganda banners. With hard Western currency in hand, customers at first bought only Western products instead of their own well-known but boring goods, so that cherries from Werder outside Berlin lay rotting while fruit was flown in from the American west coast! From postage stamps to insurance forms and tax bills, a strange new regulatory world from the West assailed the new citizens, who had trouble learning to cope with its unfamiliar demands. Occasionally Western development helpers offered support, if not always for selfless reasons. Ultimately, there was little alternative to this pervasive "dominance of the West," especially if East Germans quickly wanted to become full citizens of the new state.[77]

Less welcome as a byproduct of the transformation was the breakup of many GDR institutions, partly out of necessity and partly because of misunderstanding. Due to the closing of many companies, an industrial wasteland emerged that covered broad stretches of land with rusting factories and orphaned collective farms. Following the withdrawal of the Russian troops, empty barracks and abandoned exercise grounds, often contaminated with old munitions, added yet another blemish to the post-Communist landscape. As a result of the dissolution of the Stasi, many of its former "objects" also fell into decline, if they no longer promised to yield any private gain. Finally, many daycare centers, culture houses, and other social institutions, which could no longer be financed, sank into disrepair. The "blooming landscapes" promised by Helmut Kohl during the election campaign, fertilized by consumption subsidized from the West, thus contrasted starkly with the ugly ruins of the defunct SED dictatorship. As a result, disappointment over the "tearing down" and anger over the "selling out" of the East took hold of many former GDR citizens. For those who lost their job, it didn't much matter if the air quality had improved and the water become cleaner in cities of the "chemical triangle."[78]

The understandable "unification shock" soon turned into anxiety over a far-reaching "crisis of unification" since there seemed no end to the bad news. Had the excessive market orientation of the Trusteeship's privatization policies not ruined many renowned industrial firms such as the camera company Pentacon? Were the inflated wage demands of the united trade unions not pushing up the level of unemployment to the point where it was twice as high in the East than in the West? Was the exodus of labor, above all of young people, not continuing unabated, despite all of the retraining initiatives taken by the government?[79] The belated policy reactions to the collapse of the structures of the planned economy mounted a truly remarkable effort, which saw the transfer of 1,250 billion Euros for the renovation of the infrastructure and the financing of social costs through a solidarity surcharge added to the income tax. Unfortunately, only a fraction of the money went into actually new, productive investments. Many East Germans therefore felt as if they were "foreigners in their own home, strangers in the new era," while impatient, know-it "better Westies [Wessis]" railed against the ingratitude of "whining Easties [Ossis]."[80]

The real difficulties and the political mistakes created a veritable "psycho-drama of political unity" that became a favorite topic of editorials and cultural comments in German newspapers. Opinion polls discovered a growing alienation between Easterners and Westerners, reinforced by the asymmetry of their income and access to the media. The systematic delegitimizing of the GDR through the parliamentary Commission of Inquiry and the media's exposure of scandalous Stasi collaboration triggered a "deep depression in the East and apathy in the West," which threatened to lead to "distance, disappointment, and hatred."[81] The arrogance of some Western advisors, the loss of the familiar East German products, and the incessant feeling of being overwhelmed by rapid changes helped nourish a feeling among many East Germans that they were "second-class citizens." As the distance from the shabbiness and repressiveness of real existing socialism grew, there thus emerged, stoked by the election propaganda of the PDS, "something like a cultural identity" of the East, based on a "misty-eyed memory of the GDR," that expressed itself as nostalgia (*N-Ostalgie*).[82] Hence the numerous initiatives for creating a new "togetherness" had a hard time bridging these emotional chasms.[83]

As a "central component" of the "new European order," unification also represented a caesura in international affairs since it raised the issue of "the future German role in European and international politics." Once the new states were integrated, the increase in population, enlargement of economic potential, and expansion of territory seemed to make a growth of German power inevitable. Although such a development might be tempered by expectations of assuming more responsibility, it also awakened understandable historical fears among German neighbors. Domestically, moreover, intellectuals harbored anxieties about a return to ascendancy. Two opposing perspectives thus faced off in the public sphere: Along with Oskar Lafontaine, the left considered the "nation-state obsolete" and hoped that "one day in the not too distant future" unified Germany would be absorbed into "a greater Europe." Conservative commentators such as Arnulf Baring, by contrast, demanded a fundamental rethinking of Germany's international role that would allow it to define its own interests and resume its old mediating function between East and West, modified by postwar civilizing ingredients.[84]

During the first Gulf War against Iraq, the expanded Federal Republic did not exactly pass the test of its greater responsibilities with flying colors. Under the banner of "no blood for oil," a mass movement arose that considered the liberation of Kuwait, in Peter Glotz' words, an "unjustified war." While in the West the tradition of civil abstention from conflicts lived on, in the East it was rather the lingering influence of SED-fostered anti-Americanism that fueled passions against the war. Only after Hans Magnus Enzensberger characterized Saddam Hussein as "Hitler's ghost" and Wolf Biermann stressed the menace posed to Israel by SCUD missiles did a more sober appraisal set in.[85] Under massive American pressure, the Kohl-Genscher government changed course and sent, in addition to billions of dollars in aid, support troops to Turkey and the Mediterranean, as well as military equipment to Israel. Washington, however, was not the only capital that was disappointed by the Germans' attempt "to remain political dwarfs." Slowly the realization "that we also must assume our portion of political responsibility for the increasingly difficult course of world events" began to dawn on the political class in Bonn.[86]

Brought on by the dissolution of Yugoslavia, the next important trial hardly went any better, since a more active German foreign policy also awakened old prejudices. To be sure, it was Slobodan Milosevic who had aggravated the conflict between nationalities in the multiethnic south Slavic state as a way of salvaging "at least the dream of a greater Serbia" from the wreckage of Titoism.

The Western powers and Russia, however, as the godfathers of the founding of Yugoslavia in 1919, wanted to maintain the federal state for as long as possible. At the same time, the Balkans were emotionally traumatized by the memory of the Austro-German occupation during the First World War and the Nazi crimes of the Second World War, especially since the Croatian Ustashi had been loyal allies of Hitler. Genscher's rapid recognition of Slovenian and Croatian independence in the name of their right to self-determination not only unleashed a military counterstrike by the Serbians but also aroused indignation over a "big and arrogant" Germany in Western capitals. It appeared as if any attempt to assume a regional leadership role was also bound to trigger "old-new resentments."[87]

Obtaining domestic approval of military peacekeeping missions was an equally controversial process since it called for a rethinking of Germany's international posture. Several barriers such as the constitutional limitation of the military to the defense of the country, the Bundeswehr's outdated focus on a conflict with the Warsaw Pact, and the "culture of restraint" promoted by the peace movement had to be overcome. The first foreign deployment under the aegis of the UN in Somalia therefore remained largely limited to providing logistical support. Gradually, the "nightly television images of the Balkan horrors" forced Germans to realize that nonintervention could also be a moral failure and the lesson of the Holocaust might point to the need to combat injustice more actively. In 1994 a decision of the Federal Constitutional Court finally opened the way for participation in peacekeeping operations within a UN or NATO framework. During the Kosovo War, airmen from the Luftwaffe went into battle for the first time since 1945, while ground troops were made available for a possible land invasion. Despite historical fears still harbored by some neighbors, this reluctant assumption of military responsibility was welcomed internationally as a necessary step toward normalization.[88]

By contrast, engagement for European integration was less controversial since German and European unity appeared to be "inextricably intertwined." The political class, regardless of party affiliation, promoted the continuation of Europe's unification process, not least of all because it provided a kind of insurance policy against possible nationalist relapses in the future. Due to his personal convictions, Chancellor Kohl was willing to sacrifice the D-Mark, the symbol of Germany's economic revival, to the creation of the Euro by agreeing to the Maastricht Treaty, as long as the new currency was stable and the European Central Bank was located in Frankfurt am Main. Toward NATO expansion into Eastern Europe, however, the Federal Republic maintained a more reserved posture and instead let the Americans take the lead. Nevertheless, it did nothing to prevent the admission of its former enemies into the alliance, since that would increase Germany's security in the East. In spite of popular fears of low-wage competition in the labor market, the federal government took a more active role in promoting expansion of the EU into East Central Europe, because it promised advantages for industry and would restore Germany's traditional central position.[89]

Though the initial steps were marked by continuity with the old Federal Republic, the foreign policy of the united Germany did slowly assume contours of its own. To be sure, the basic coordinate system that included a commitment to NATO and European integration, as well as simultaneous friendship with the United States and France, remained firmly in place. But perceptive observers such as the Polish historian Adam Krzeminski discovered a few slight shifts in emphasis—for example, "the desire for an active policy in the East and Southeast of Europe." Such a course also entailed a closer relationship to Russia, which expressed itself in considerable investment and attempts at mediation when tensions cropped up between Moscow and Washington. In addition, there were some indications of a bolder assertion of Germany's own interests within a multilateral context, such as, for example, the demand for limiting agricultural subsidies in the EU and for keeping the East German states in the regional support program of Brussels. Despite warnings from abroad, these new initiatives did not signal a return to the affectations of Wilhelmine world politics but represented attempts to deploy the increased weight of a European "middle power" cautiously.[90]

Dealing with the ideological repercussions of the "return to normality" proved still more difficult, since most intellectuals were completely unprepared for it. Citing a widespread "aversion to facing up to the tasks and responsibilities which the reestablishment of the nation-state has brought with it," Wolf Lepenies lamented "the lack of consequences of this astounding event." The leftist majority, which had long since bid farewell to the nation, complained along with Habermas about "the discrediting of our best and most vulnerable intellectual traditions" and portrayed the failure of state socialism as the "destruction of reason." The rightist minority, by contrast, agreed with the cultural critic Heinz Bohrer that unity offered a chance to highlight the "lack of an unconsciously effective, self-evident feeling of nationality" that had provincialized the "half-nation West." The challenge of finding an identity soon produced an ideological power struggle, revolving around discursive hegemony within the reconstituted nation. The East German theologian Richard Schröder therefore commented sarcastically: "Every party has considered unification . . . as a chance to push through some agenda that has not yet succeeded in the Federal Republic—on our backs."[91]

A first bone of contention was the future orientation of German democracy: Should the advances of the old Federal Republic be continued, or should a new hybrid with more East German characteristics be created? Proud of the overthrow of the SED dictatorship, Lothar de Maizière had promised that the unified country would become "more Eastern, Protestant, and socialist." Western commentators such as Kurt Sontheimer, however, did not consider a "farewell from the Federal Republic" to be necessary, because "nothing fundamentally new [is] emerging." In his obituary for the GDR, the sociologist Niklas Luhmann ironically noted that the left was finally discovering that the Bonn state, which it previously criticized, was a civil society, characterizing this attitude as a paradox of "going along while being opposed."[92] By contrast, conservative cultural commentators wanted to leave this "republic of political weaklings and intellectual windbags" behind by appealing to the nationalist feelings of the new states. East German intellectuals found it difficult to define which positive elements, apart from the walk-in polyclinics, they wanted to salvage from the wreckage of socialism, but they still claimed that unity was "the dowry of the GDR."[93]

Yet another ideological battlefield was the attempt to deal with the past, a task that became doubly difficult through the collapse of Germany's second dictatorship. The heretical hope expressed by Martin Walser in his 1998 Peace Prize speech at the Frankfurt book fair—that "the Germans are now a normal people, an ordinary society"—was bound to founder on the objections of the rival victim groups.[94] On the one hand, East Germans, scarred by the repression of the SED as well as conservative cold warriors in the West, demanded a retrospective delegitimation of the GDR as a "state based on injustice," which would confirm a forceful anti-Communism. On the other hand, in both parts of the country survivors of the Nazi crimes and intellectuals on the left who remained conscious of German guilt insisted on an unflinching engagement with the Holocaust in order to justify a retrospective anti-Fascism. Although the frontlines were inverted, both debates were closely linked, as each concerned the respective priorities within a broader anti-totalitarianism as the legitimating ideology of the expanded Federal Republic. Only slowly did it begin to dawn on some that both issues suffered from instrumentalization and instead required a more differentiated analysis.[95]

The most explosive controversy, however, revolved around the implications of reconstituting the nation-state, since an "intellectual right" demanded a decided "renationalization." With his sibylline essay "Goat Song Crescendo," the poet Botho Strauß launched a philippic against the shallowness of the 1968 intelligentsia and called for a "far-reaching change of mentality born amid dangers." Willy Brandt's conservative widow Brigitte Seebacher broadened this critique of "German self-hate" into a rejection of the widespread denial of the fatherland: "Normality means to be as others are, other democrats who each in their own way have had to find normalcy." As a precondition for a more independent national policy, the publicist Rainer Zitelmann went on to challenge Western integration so as "to debunk the almost mythical glorification of the West." Rejecting the German "metaphysics of guilt," the Göttingen high school teacher Karlheinz Weißmann similarly called for a return to the traditions of the nation-state. These currents culminated in the attempt to use the effort to create a new normality of unity as a means of returning to a "self-confident nation."[96]

"Constitutional patriots" on the left who were suspicious of the whole concept of the nation reacted with a touch of hysteria to such neonationalist attacks on their discursive authority. For instance, Günter Grass deplored the "rampant growing together" that occurred during the "ugly process of unification" and prophesied bleak consequences of an "unchecked greed for profit" for neighbors in East Central Europe. Defending the civilizational gains of the old Federal Republic, the social democratic thinker Peter Glotz also warned of "German dangers" such as the rise of a new "national intelligentsia," which would relapse into outdated nationalist patterns under the banner of "normalization." Similarly, the prominent Bielefeld historian Hans-Ulrich Wehler castigated the "new dreams of the intellectuals" as a "mystical nationalism." Even more explicitly, Jürgen Habermas criticized those intellectuals "who long for a new 'normality of the nation-state'" and denounced their dreams as a "third revival" of neoconservative ideas dating from the Weimar Republic.[97] This reflexive rejection, while rhetorically impressive, hardly addressed the new challenges posed by reunification.

Between these fronts, more moderate intellectuals strove to develop a democratic patriotism that built on the learning processes of the postwar period but accepted the task of constructing a new identity. Christian Meier, a well-known historian of antiquity, pleaded for "the necessity of constructing a (new) nation," while the contemporary historian Heinrich August Winkler called for a "new construction of a German nation" with a decidedly European orientation and Western values. In addition, the East German theologian Richard Schröder justified "why we must consider ourselves as a nation or a people" with the burdens of history and the tasks of the unification process: "Nations without a state and divided nations make problems for themselves and others. Fortunately, we are now rid of this." Finally, the CDU politician Wolfgang Schäuble called for an emotional attachment through "love of the homeland, patriotism, [and] national feeling," so that "the national community [can exist] as a communal protection for peace and freedom."[98] It was precisely in order to prevent relapses into a dangerous nationalism that these commentators advocated the acceptance of a postclassic, Westernized nation-state firmly embedded within Europe.

Despite all unsolved problems, retrospective appraisals of the unification process after the first five years struck a decidedly positive note. Minister-President of Saxony Kurt Biedenkopf stated, if a bit prematurely, that "German unity has succeeded." While "many desires of the GDR dissidents" remained unfulfilled and serious mistakes such as the principle of "restitution before compensation" had hampered the attempt to bring East and West closer together, the extent of rebuilding was still "an impressive common achievement of all Germans."[99] "The international [aspect] has succeeded," summed up Alfred Grosser, a French authority on Germany, adding the wish: "Try to be optimists!" Mental integration turned out to be the most difficult task of all, since some observers like Christoph Dieckmann claimed that "East and West are once again drifting apart," because Eastern voices did not find enough of a hearing in the unified Germany. Such disappointment may have been partly due to unrealistic expectations created by a "false myth of a community" that suggested total consensus. Hence the conservative columnist Hans-Joachim Veen argued, if acceptance of the "foundations of the Federal Republic's legitimacy" was the basic criterion, then internal unity existed already.[100]

Civil Society and Nation

In view of the multiple upheavals, normality was an understandable "object of desire" for many Germans in the twentieth century. Initially, this vague concept meant a middle-class life that could be planned without undue worries of political instability, military violence, economic crises, or cultural uncertainties. However, the ideological basis and substantive form of a normal existence were endlessly debated, since each party, church, or interest group sought to realize its own, usually incompatible, notion of what that entailed. As a result, during the 1980s "normalization" could imply either the recognition of the division, an interpretation favored by those on the left, or the disavowal of the Nazi past, as rightists advocated during the historians' debate over German responsibility for the Holocaust. After unification, a similar controversy pitted pessimists, who warned of an "unnoticeable transformation of the Germans" in the direction of a "false normalization," against optimists, who saw "the republic on the way to normality." Behind such disputes lurked the trauma of the nation, which hampered "the acceptance of the Federal Republic as a democratic and stable system of government."[101]

The German reception of the fashionable concept "civil society" has rarely posed the question of its compatibility with the nation-state explicitly. That is hardly surprising, since Zivilgesellschaft is primarily considered as a signifier of the "third sector" that is located somewhere between politics and the economy. In other words, the concept denotes a sphere of autonomous civic action in society, which pertains to the entire range of problems, from the local to the global level.[102] But closer study of "real civil societies" leads inevitably to the question of the political conditions that either favor or hamper their development. In addition, a historical look at the German case shows that certain regimes such as Wilhelmian semi-constitutionalism, presidential cabinets, and National Socialist or Communist dictatorships have not exactly helped transnational cooperation or promoted independent activity by their citizens. Precisely because authoritarian traditions and reactionary nationalism have repeatedly repressed civil society, Germany's special path suggests rather a reverse conclusion: namely, that without constitutional guarantees and political unity, a civil society can only develop with great difficulty.[103]

Is the expanded Federal Republic finally "on the way to civil society," or do relapses into repression and aggression threaten, as suggested by the metaphor of a "two component poison"? While overly optimistic assessments of reunification as "a German success story" may be premature, leftist pessimism, which posits a kind of compulsory repetition of catastrophe, appears less convincing still.[104] Even if during the first decade following unification the postwar learning processes, which changed political culture for the better, have been pruned of some exaggerations, their basic civilizing thrust has not been fundamentally challenged. For instance, the limited acceptance of multilateral peacekeeping deployments has done little to reverse the demilitarization of mentalities; the rise of a democratic patriotism has failed to undo the rejection of radical nationalism; and the return of neoliberalism has failed to break the sense of social solidarity that supports a clientelist welfare state. The rediscovery of East Central Europe has not shaken the foundations of Westernization, either, because even the new citizens stand by democracy, and protest movements, as shown in the leadup to and aftermath of the Gulf and Iraq wars, continue to flourish.[105]

Such positive findings do not mean that all problems that have resulted from unification have already been solved. The collapse of the East German planned economy has led to such widespread deindustrialization, unemployment, and emigration that even an enormous transfer of money and expertise from the West has only managed to stimulate economic growth in a few especially favorable areas. Misunderstandings between countrymen who had quite different formative experiences and expectations were bound to happen, because both sides knew too little about each other's lives. Added to an already difficult situation were new frustrations brought on by Western tutelage perceived as colonization, as well as resentment toward Eastern ingratitude seen as obstinacy. Only slowly have "common experiences on thin ice" been able to overcome these contradictions so that conflicts in the "scenes from a difficult marriage" could be considered enriching rather than upsetting.[106] Ironically, it was precisely the intense preoccupation with the unification crisis that has prevented the new, more powerful Germany from becoming as overbearing as skeptics had predicted.

The real challenge is thus not to deny unification, for which it is already too late, but rather to civilize the new nation-state in a European and global context. The accession of the East German states to the old Federal Republic was not necessarily the wrong step toward achieving this goal, even if it did prevent the fusion of East and West on a more equal basis. Domestically, it transferred a model that had proven itself over the previous four decades to the new states; internationally, it embedded the strengthened Germany into the Western alliance, as well as into the process of European integration. No doubt, a more intelligent investment policy, the adoption of proven solutions such as the polyclinics, and greater respect for the vast difference in biographies would have helped.[107] A bit more courage in the discussion of the reform of the Basic Law would also not have hurt. Nevertheless, there remains sufficient reason to hope that embedding unification in the broader process of overcoming the division of Europe might prevent the recurrence of nationalism, thereby helping the entire continent to grow together again. In the end, everything depends on the character that the new nation-state will assume in the future.

CHAPTER 9

Fearing Foreignness

The flames that engulfed several homes for asylum seekers signalled a growing hostility toward foreigners in the enlarged Federal Republic. In the early 1990s, mobs of young people shouting "Foreigners Out!" and cheered on by adult spectators, stormed hostels in the East German cities of Hoyerswerda and Rostock with the goal of forcing the deportation of refugees. Shortly thereafter, radical right-wing skinheads set fire to the homes of Turkish families in the West German cities of Mölln and Solingen, burning several people to death.[1] Surprised by daily reports of horrific "violence against foreigners," politicians stood by helplessly as a mounting wave of xenophobia, which some of them had helped foment through their populist criticism of "asylum abuses," washed over the newly united Germany. In reaction, alarmed citizens in churches, unions, and cultural associations called for a "common front against hatred of foreigners" and thus mobilized hundreds of thousands in candlelight demonstrations for tolerance. This conflict between xenophobic racism and multicultural cosmopolitanism posed the fundamental question: "How civil is the unified Germany?"[2]

Somewhat unintentionally, Allied decisions to punish the crimes of the Nazis had in fact created the basis for an ethnically homogenous, but much smaller German state. Although Hitler had begun the process of ethnic cleansing by unleashing a war of annihilation that culminated in the genocide of the Jews and the Slavs, the measures undertaken at the Potsdam Conference to prevent the recurrence of such crimes completed the destruction of the centuries-old multiethnic settlements in East Central Europe. The undoing of the Nazi conquests in such places as the Sudetenland returned disputed areas to Germany's neighbors, while the westward shift of Poland with the cession of parts of East Prussia, Pomerania, and Silesia detached still more territories that had been ethnically mixed before the war. The supposedly "orderly and humane" transfer of population that began with the spontaneous flight of Germans fearing revenge quickly turned into a state-sanctioned expulsion of some 12.5 million people. At the same time, several million "displaced persons" from Eastern Europe were either returned to their home countries or transported across the ocean.[3] With the exception of a small Danish minority, the population that remained between the Rhine and the Oder Rivers thus became more uniformly German than it had ever been.

In its dealings with foreigners, the Federal Republic inherited a highly ambivalent tradition. On the one hand, the 1913 definition of citizenship according to *jus sanguinis* had been built on the principle of cultural origin in the hope of keeping ties to the German diaspora in Eastern Europe and overseas after a century of emigration. In contrast to the French and American practice of *jus soli*, however, this ethnic preference discriminated against foreigners who had established roots in the country and, as was the case with East European Jews, sought to obtain German citizenship. As a result, the foreign workers who were recruited to advance economic growth saw themselves treated as temporary help instead of as permanent immigrants.[4] On the other hand, among the fathers of the Basic Law the experience of Nazi exile had engendered a principled openness toward all those seeking protection. Memories of their own flight inspired them to make the extraordinarily liberal promise that the "politically persecuted enjoy the right of asylum."[5] During the Cold War, the dual goals of admitting ethnic Germans relocating to the FRG and accepting political asylum seekers could still be reconciled since in the case of the GDR refugees they were largely identical.

Due to its fragmentation, the scholarly literature is only somewhat helpful in trying to explain the connection between immigration and xenophobia. Most of the impressive research on migration concentrates on German emigration rather than on Germany's subsequent transformation into an immigration country, a highly charged topic during the last few years.[6] In contrast, the literature on right-wing radicalism focuses primarily on marginal parties and youth subcultures such as the skinheads and thus explains the phenomenon largely as a form of domestic protest or the result of generational tensions.[7] Legal histories tracing the development of citizenship are more interested in the changes of rules pertaining to admission and naturalization, while sociological studies on the problems of assimilation often slight the historical background.[8] Since the troubling rise of xenophobia so shortly after unification can hardly be a coincidence, a more integrative and cultural approach is required to elucidate some of the psychological connections between immigration and xenophobia.

Indeed, acceptance of foreignness is a key indicator of the maturity and vitality of a civil society. Therefore critical commentators saw the outbreaks of violence as an assault against the liberal constitutional state that Germany had worked so hard to build over the preceding four decades: "The sickening, pogrom-like incidents in Saxony's Hoyerswerda and their Western [as well as] Eastern imitators mark a *casus belli* for civil society."[9] Such massive xenophobia violated some of the central tenets of civil society, such as its orientation toward "conflict, compromise, and understanding"; its "recognition of plurality, difference, and tension"; and its mandate to "act nonviolently, peacefully." Yet one might object to such an idealization of civil society by arguing that "uncivil tendencies," such as right-wing radicalism and xenophobia, were also a part of modern society and revealed a negative side of intolerant, but still voluntary, association.[10] Any reflection on the extent of German transformation since 1945 must therefore conclude with the question: "What kind of society did the new republic become?"

Instrumental Opening

In the topsy-turvy world of Nazi defeat, ethnic separation and consolidation seemed to have a clear priority. One journalist noted a seemingly random movement: "Everywhere one sees family caravans with hand carts—refugees from Berlin's surrounding area who are trying to get home." Cut off by new international and zonal borders, children who had been sent off to the countryside wanted to return to their parents, evacuated adults rushed back to the destroyed cities, and captured soldiers hoped for quick release and a way home. At the same time, surviving slave laborers demanded rapid repatriation to their homelands, while stateless Nazi victims waited in camps alongside erstwhile collaborators to emigrate to America, Canada, or Australia. But the dissolution of the Nazi racial hierarchy also brought new foreigners to Germany in the form of occupation troops, who now came not as inferiors but as the new masters, living in a superior universe of their own in the West or in completely segregated compounds in the East.[11] Solidarity was extended only to the closest friends, and beyond that perhaps to "ethnic comrades," but rarely to foreigners, whose spontaneous acts of revenge Germans had ample reason to fear.[12]

The greatest challenge involved the absorption of expellees from the East who streamed in individually, in joint treks, and in endless columns. "At the border the Czechs take the shirt right off the Germans' back and hit them with a dog whip," one man reported angrily. His stoic wife, however, replied: "We can't complain. We asked for it." By 1949, 7,945 million Germans had arrived in West Germany from the former Eastern territories, Czechoslovakia, the Soviet Union, Hungary, Romania, and Yugoslavia; 4,070 million came to the Soviet Occupation Zone and Berlin; and another 470,000 landed in Austria.[13] Finding accommodation for the homeless in the shattered cities required mandatory quartering, feeding the masses necessitated the issuing of ration cards, and providing work for the idle compelled the organization of public clean-up or reconstruction.

Despite widespread resentment against this influx, most refugees succeeded in gaining admission into postwar society by insisting that they were fellow Germans in need of assistance from their better-off countrymen. While the GDR declared integration completed in the early 1950s, in the West expellees were able to organize freely and, as a result, achieve some material compensation for their losses, as well as obtain a law that allowed the further immigration of ethnic Germans.[14]

Just as unexpected was the arrival of numerous East Germans who could invoke their German citizenship, since Bonn refused to recognize the GDR as a separate state. When authorities took his ration card away, the student Hans Herzog realized: "I had to leave [my] girlfriend as well as friends and flee immediately. 'Illegally,' that is, without official travel documents, I had to get across the zonal border into the West." By the time the Berlin wall was erected in 1961, as many as 3.8 million people had left East Germany for economic and political reasons. In contrast, only about half a million people migrated in the opposite direction.[15] Although they initially wanted to slow this stream, West German politicians eventually grasped the political value of refugees since they not only delegitimized the SED but also offered a source of cheap labor for the economic miracle. Hence both large parties supported the acceptance of Easterners and provided generous assistance such as compensation for lost property, recognition of pension entitlements, housing aid, and budget allowances that facilitated their integration. Even if Westerners resented the newcomers in the beginning, they were soon so impressed by their competence and diligence that most welcomed their brethren from the East.[16]

Despite the extent of this influx, German society continued to view itself as an ethnically homogenous unit, rooted in the soil, and not as an immigration country. The primary reason for this perception lay in the continuation of the traditional pattern of emigration abroad. Between 1954 and 1973 some 1.6 million Germans emigrated, some of whom were simply continuing their journey from the East and others were seeking to better their life overseas. Another reason included the limited influx of non-German asylum seekers, who as victims of Communism could count on receiving particular sympathy in the FRG. Because wartime destruction rendered Germany an unattractive destination and the iron curtain protected the country during Cold War crises like the Hungarian uprising of 1956 and the Prague spring of 1968, only about 7,100 asylum seekers registered annually between 1954 and 1978.[17] Finally, various refugees from the East, despite their different dialects, could invoke their German heritage and cite ethnic discrimination as a result of the war. Because their integration was usually successful in the long run, these ethnic migrants were not really perceived as foreigners.[18]

The building of the wall abruptly ended ethnic immigration from the East, and forced the Federal Republic to seek workers elsewhere, primarily from the

Mediterranean region. Due to shortages in some branches of the economy, the Federal Republic had already concluded agreements with Italy (1955) and Greece (1960), but now added Turkey (1961), Portugal (1964), and Yugoslavia (1968) to the list. To fill the open positions, especially in areas requiring physical effort, companies recruited "guest workers" who, in the tradition of seasonal labor, were supposed to come to the FRG temporarily and to return home after completing their tasks. Already in 1964 Armando Rodriguez from Portugal was celebrated as the one-millionth guest worker, for which he was given a moped. The number of foreign workers continued to rise until 1973, when it reached 2.6 million, nearly 12 percent of the dependent workforce. Some 605,000 labor migrants came from Turkey, 535,000 from Yugoslavia, and 450,000 from Italy. Unlike the slave laborers under the Nazis, they came voluntarily, and while they had to perform backbreaking toil and live in crowded dormitories, they received better pay than they would have gotten at home.[19]

When their temporary stay gradually turned into permanent residency, many guest workers became unexpected immigrants. Although their home countries at first pressed for a quick return of their citizens, more and more labor migrants decided, at least for the medium term, to continue working and living in Germany. Many companies pressured the federal government to extend time limits on work visas because they wanted to lose neither their skilled nor their unskilled workers.[20] Although a considerable portion of the migrants returned home within a few years and the recession of 1967 brought about a negative balance in migration, the decision of the rest to stay contradicted the theory that guest laborers would serve as a buffer to economic cycles. The growing number of foreigners, which by 1973 had climbed to 3.97 million, rendered parts of the aliens' law obsolete and finally led some observers to the grudging acknowledgement: "The Federal Republic is an 'immigration country.'" Although Bavaria insisted that "Spaniards should not become Germans," the Social-Liberal government arrived at a contradictory conclusion: "Integration yes, immigration no."[21]

While the oil shock of 1973 accelerated attempts to contain immigration, such restrictions ultimately encouraged more family members to immigrate. Claiming that the limit of "the ability to absorb [new migrants] has been reached," the government first raised fees for employer permits. Then Bonn announced an official "recruitment stop" and intensified the practice of deportation in the hope of forcing guest workers to return to their country of origin. However, the recession of 1974–1975 proved to be a more effective deterrent, since it created the first "unemployed guests," dimming job prospects. Hence the annual influx declined from a peak of about 1 million in 1970 to around 300,000 in 1975, and the level of homeward remigration also increased, reducing the total number of foreigners in the Federal Republic once again to below 4 million.[22] With the improvement of the economic cycle, however, the number of foreigners grew to 4.5 million in 1980 in spite of further attempts to limit it. Workers living in the FRG for the long term now brought their wives and children, aided by a special provision that allowed the reuniting of families, and thus struck even deeper roots into German society. The paradoxical attempt to develop an integrationist nonimmigration policy had thus led itself ad absurdum.[23]

As a result of the unrealistic policy of inviting "temporary guests," minorities collected in urban centers with all of the problems usually associated with the formation of ghettos. In 1981, for example, there were 232 foreigners for every 1,000 Germans in Frankfurt, 183 for every 1,000 in Stuttgart, and 173 for every 1,000 in Munich. Insufficient language knowledge led to their concentration in certain city quarters, while poor and overcrowded dwellings created endless frictions. Moreover, the foreign children's lack of success at school impeded their integration. While sympathetic observers concluded that "life in the ghetto is imposed on them," other critics stressed the "social explosiveness" of conflicts with German residents, as well as the foreigners' penchant for criminality.[24] Many Berliners felt foreign in "Little Istanbul," since they neither spoke Turkish nor understood Anatolian customs. Likewise, on the "'Front Street' of Hüttenheim," at the edge of the Ruhr region, confrontations flared up repeatedly between foreigners and local youths. Although they faced their share of prejudice, Italians and Yugoslavs were for the most part accepted as individuals by the populace. In contrast, the Turks, clinging to their Muslim lifestyle, were often considered "incapable of integration."[25]

In response to the irrational fear of "being overrun by foreigners," an ugly xenophobia emerged, especially among the lower classes, which rekindled dormant racist prejudices. Sensationalist reports of a "fratricidal struggle" between Serbs and Croats, the "smuggling of humans" by crime rings, violent acts committed by "foreign extremists," and frequent "crimes by foreigners"—all created a xenophobic mood among regulars at bars and pubs.[26] The radical right-wing NPD therefore inveighed against the "monstrous assault on our national traditions" by organizing a "citizens' initiative to stop foreigners" and clamoring for a law that would roll back immigration. In less inflammatory language, but with an unmistakable intent, the CSU also inveighed against the "aberration of 'Germanization'" through the naturalization of foreigners. Drawing similarly on nationalist resentment, even some conservative university professors demanded rigorous measures against the "overruning of the German people by foreigners" in their Heidelberg manifesto of 1982. As a result of such agitation, four-fifths of the Federal Republic's citizens thought "that too many foreigners live among us today" and demanded greater restrictions on immigration.[27]

Acknowledging the paradox that "we called for labor, but people came," liberal circles, in contrast, insisted on greater tolerance, above all because of the "trying situation" of foreign children. Due to their poor knowledge of German, minority youths were often "shunted aside at school" so that two-thirds dropped out before receiving their diplomas. Concerned observers pointed out that blocked job access resulting from poor educational performance was a "social time bomb" that would generate resentment against the majority society among the more than 1 million youths who had "immigrated, but [felt] excluded."[28] When an SPD commission in 1980 warned "of a new racist arrogance," the Federal government felt forced to lay out a "program of integration for young foreigners" so as to improve their "equality of chances."[29] Since the "new social question" of foreign "fellow citizens" posed enormous problems, the government named the former North Rhine–Westphalian Minister-President Heinz Kühn an "ombudsman for foreigners' affairs" to represent their interests. Critics understood the issue of foreigners as proof of civility: "Only everyday life can show whether we live up to the ideals of freedom, equality, and brotherhood toward our guest workers as well."[30]

In the early 1980s the sluggish economy, the continued arrival of family members, and the growing number of asylum seekers triggered a new wave of xenophobia. Although the size of the foreign workforce stagnated, women and children increasingly joined their husbands, while some 108,000 asylum seekers knocked on the door. Under pressure from conservative politicians and trade unionists who feared for their jobs, the Social-Liberal government passed measures that sought to curtail "the abuse of the right to asylum" and place "limits on family members."[31] After 1982 the conservative Kohl government proved even more receptive to the anxious slogan "the boat is full," offering foreigners return bonuses of 10,500 DM per person. While 140,000 guest workers took advantage of the possibility to draw on their retirement pensions early, leading the population of resident aliens to decline slightly, the return of economic growth in the mid-1980s robbed the measure of its limited effectiveness. Further attempts by the CSU Interior Minister Friedrich Zimmerman to facilitate deportation by tightening legislation pertaining to foreigners collapsed due to energetic protests by the FDP and the opposition.[32]

In contrast, an informal coalition of humanitarian groups continued to fight for the acceptance of a "multicultural togetherness." For instance, the bishops of both churches proclaimed a "day for foreign fellow citizens" that sought greater understanding for their problems. Self-critical union representatives overcame their fears and advocated more mutual respect between German and foreign workers. Left Social Democrats demanded more rights for newcomers because "the Federal Republic is an immigration country." Even industrial leaders acknowledged the economic advantages of employing migrants due to the shortage of qualified workers: "Foreigners are needed."[33] Intellectuals, by contrast, stressed the imperative to accept cultural difference: "Why should Turks not be Turks?" Human rights activists likewise demanded: "It is essential to create a society in which all people, regardless of whether they are of German or non-German origin, are able to live as equal citizens before the law." The journalist Günter Wallraff finally dramatized the daily discrimination faced by Turks in a bestselling expose, describing his experiences as a presumed contract worker named "Ali" in a steel factory.[34]

Surprisingly, foreign voices were hardly heard in this discussion, since they lacked recognized representatives and avenues for publication. "The Turks have it hardest of all," it was said, because they comprised the largest group (1.6 million) with the greatest cultural distance. In the workplace, laborers described the situation as still relatively positive: "I can make myself understood in German; I work hard; therefore everyone likes me and I love everyone." But conflicts were likely to arise in crowded apartment buildings because of different culinary habits and unfamiliar religious practices. Above all, "Turkish women felt like outcasts," because most were illiterate, could not speak German, and continued wearing traditional headscarves.[35] Tensions were even more intense in the schools, as foreign pupils who did not know the language were unable "to say what [they] felt." Since teachers did not understand Turkish, endless disciplinary problems arose and academic performance remained disappointing. In dealing with the bureaucracy, moreover, foreigners often encountered arrogance, reacting to their arbitrary treatment as "second-class people" with "fear and disgust." Only a few attempted to organize themselves, while some youths "learned karate" for protection .[36]

Toward the end of the 1980s, however, a paradoxical modus vivendi began to evolve that made the Federal Republic a "nonimmigration country with immigrants." On the one hand, more and more second-generation newcomers achieved success in education and at work. Indeed, hybridization progressed so that the first indications of a mixed German-Turkish culture could be discerned. Although many recent arrivals continued to cling to their former lifestyle, many Germans, especially youths, grew accustomed to their foreign neighbors. Eating at "the Italian" or shopping for vegetables from "the Turk" was increasingly taken for granted.[37] Pollsters also registered "more friendly" experiences in personal contacts with foreigners, which suggested a growing ease on both sides in their dealings with each other. The "ordinary hatred against foreigners" that continued to plague the country came more from a youthful minority that tended toward "violent action, incited by words and alcohol." Due to the lack of a social consensus, however, the emerging "multicultural society" remained fragile and was threatened each time the number of asylum seekers started to rise.[38]

In the end, the so-called foreigner problem remained largely unresolved in the old Federal Republic, because German society proved unable to achieve a consensus on the issue of immigration. With such an emotionally charged topic, it became difficult to obtain even simple data on the consequences of employing foreigners, so that negative myths of "welfare cheating" grew like weeds. Closer investigation, however, revealed that migrants served as a crucial reserve for the labor market "and above all performed jobs that were rarely taken by Germans."[39] Hence right-wing parties found it easy to exploit underlying fears of competition and ethnic prejudices—for example, the populist Franz Josef Strauß could claim, contrary to all evidence, "We are not an immigration country." Moral appeals by the Left for tolerance toward other lifestyles, which stemmed from "concerns for cosmopolitanism," likewise failed to take into account the realities of immigration because they often ignored the importance of the newcomers learning to respect the rights and obligations of the host society.[40] This societal stalemate also hindered the federal government's efforts to get a handle on the situation, as they aimed more at pleasing confused voters than at solving problems.

The situation of foreigners in the GDR was still more difficult, because the closing of the border thoroughly cut it off from international contacts. While the SED nurtured a Slavic minority of Sorbs in a separate organization called *Domowina*, it dealt with the remnants of the Jewish community in a more intolerant fashion.[41] According to the motto of "socialist internationalism," the GDR similarly practiced an anti-imperialist asylum policy that accepted civil war refugees from Greece, Chile, and diverse African countries as privileged friends. But the experience of contract laborers from neighboring socialist countries and especially from Vietnam was anything but pleasant, as they had to live in barracks, earned far less than their German coworkers, and were systematically prevented from establishing contacts with the local populace. Due to the regime's restrictive travel policies, moreover, fewer East Germans had the opportunity to get to know foreign countries and, by extension, acquire a greater understanding of other cultures. Though their numbers—some 191,000 in all—remained relatively small, "the foreigners" evoked, perhaps for that very reason, even more deeply rooted prejudices in the East.[42]

Unexpected Refugee Crisis

The sins of omission created by this illusionary policy exacted a high price when ethnic and foreign immigration increased explosively at the end of the 1980s. As long as the iron curtain kept the numbers of ethnic resettlers and GDR refugees below 25,000 annually, the programs for integrating them into West German society continued to function fairly effectively. As long as the number of incoming and outgoing labor migrants was more or less balanced, and applications for asylum did not exceed 100,000 annually, the total number of foreigners in the FRG remained relatively constant at about 4.5 million.[43] Conservative politicians could thus continue to welcome the return of ethnic Germans as being in the "national interest," while spokespersons for the Greens were able to demand a multicultural "open republic" for refugees from around the world. But when the numbers of refugees from the GDR, ethnic repatriates, asylum seekers, and family members joining their relatives shot up with the collapse of

Communism and the outbreak of civil war in the Balkans, a new wave of immigration commenced that overwhelmed all existing barriers and unleashed an acute crisis.[44]

The onslaught began with the mass exodus from the GDR, whose elemental pressure finally ruptured the iron curtain. Although the SED had allowed some 40,000 citizens to leave in 1984, applications for permission to move to the West for economic or political reasons increased dramatically after 1987. Partly through discrimination, and partly through persuasion, the GDR attempted to convince these applicants to stay. But such measures only strengthened the desire to leave.[45] The opening of the Hungarian border in the summer of 1989 permitted the first mass flight, while the occupation of FRG embassies by desperate refugees led to subsequent departures. As thousands crowded the grounds, a humanitarian crisis emerged that forced the SED to relent and allow the emigrants to board sealed trains for West Germany. The growing panic triggered by this mass flight compelled the SED to draft a new travel ordinance whose premature announcement led to the fall of the Berlin wall. Between July 1989 and June 1990 this exodus brought 518,000 officially registered GDR citizens into the FRG.[46] While West Germans initially welcomed "the countrymen from over there [with] balloons," the enormous costs of their integration gave rise to a dangerous mixture of "resentment and existential fear."[47]

The stampede continued with a dramatic increase in the number of ethnic Germans seeking to resettle in the FRG due to the lifting of administrative restrictions in the Eastern bloc. With the collapse of Communism, the last barriers to migration disappeared in those countries of East Central Europe that still harbored some German minorities. As one elderly woman from Russia put it, "We can only thank Gorbachev's policies for our departure." While Willy Brandt's Eastern policy had already made possible an annual influx of some 50,000 resettlers, primarily from Poland and Romania, in the second half of the 1970s, this stream swelled to 203,000 by 1988. During the crisis year of 1989, that number, which now also included ethnic Germans from Russia, nearly doubled to 397,000. The long-held desire to live in safety with other Germans swept all other considerations aside: "We would have also come on foot," one recent arrival recalled. The claim of these ethnic resettlers to a speedy naturalization, however, involved considerable costs, since often the children could hardly speak German and migrants from rural areas had to be retrained before they could find suitable work in industry.[48]

The generous assistance provided to refugees from the GDR and resettlers from Eastern Europe created widespread resentment, especially among those West Germans who were struggling with difficulties of their own. Support payments to cover short-term expenses, home loans, and unemployment assistance awakened a good deal of social jealousy: "The silent majority of Germans is largely in agreement: These people take our jobs, our homes, our pensions, our

money." Well-intentioned government appeals for "greater acceptance of resettlers" hardly helped alleviate the "fear of new competitors" that gripped two-
thirds of the populace.[49] Leftist politicians, such as SPD leader Oskar Lafontaine,
stoked popular passions by calling for a reduction of immigration as well as a
cut in social assistance. Though the Kohl government welcomed ethnic returnees, it was compelled to make resettlement less attractive through administrative measures such as a wider geographical distribution of resettlers and cutbacks
in integration assistance. In order to somehow master the immigration pressure, the Bundestag passed a new "resettler admission law" in 1990 that required
applying for entry in the country of origin. As a result, the number was cut nearly
in half, to 221,000, in the following year.[50]

The immigration wave crested when the number of applications from asylum seekers, wishing to escape political persecution and begin a better life,
climbed rapidly as well. The repression of the Tamils in Sri Lanka; the persecution of Kurds in Turkey, Iraq, and Iran; and the ethnic cleansing in the former
Yugoslavia each unleashed new streams of refugees. Since the introduction of
new visa requirements could no longer contain the pressure, the number of
applicants climbed more than twentyfold between 1983 and 1992, from 20,000
to more than 438,000 annually! Even after cutting the acceptance quota from
four-fifths to less than one-third, the overwhelmed authorities were unable to
cope with this new influx. Right-wing politicians such as Alfred Dregger fulmi-
nated against these supposedly "bogus asylum seekers" and the "abuse of asylum" by "economic refugees." As a result, applicants were forbidden to work
before a decision about permission to stay was handed down. The camps swelled
because bureaucratic processing required more and more time. Rejected applicants could appeal decisions, and many continued to be tolerated even after their
final rejection, so that only about one-fifth of all such people were deported in
the end.[51]

Since the number of family members joining workers already in Germany
also continued to grow, the different migration flows combined to form a veritable flood that triggered a widespread panic. Newspapers fueled xenophobic
fears with headlines that "Germany admitted the most foreigners in 1989." Indeed, the number of newcomers reached an astounding 1.6 million in 1992, so
that in spite of numerous departures a positive migration balance of some
822,000 remained.[52] For those communities chiefly affected, this proved a mid-
level catastrophe. Though there was some federal assistance, most of the costs
for ethnic resettlers and foreign asylum seekers had to be borne by local welfare
agencies. Because larger urban areas such as Berlin, city-states such as Hamburg
and Bremen, and heavily industrialized states such as North Rhine–Westphalia
registered the highest influx, they insisted on a wider regional dispersion into
rural areas. As a result, foreigners who looked different and spoke little or no
German were transferred to small towns that had no experience at all in dealing

with strangers. Even those foreigners who had lived in Germany for a long time noticed a deterioration of the climate: "You can feel much more strongly that you are unwanted."[53]

The government reacted to these alarmist reports with a contradictory amendment of the Aliens Act, which was pushed through by Wolfgang Schäuble in 1990. On one hand, the bill tried to contain the influx by "tightening the right to asylum"; on the other hand, it proposed integrating foreigners through the transformation of the conditional "resident permit" into a more secure "right to residency." While the CSU demanded that new limits be placed on residency permissions and on family members seeking to join their relatives, the churches, unions, and welfare organizations called for an improvement in legal security for foreign residents and a liberalization of immigration regulations. For the first time, foreigners—above all, the Turks, for whom unification had spurred a "surge of consciousness"—protested in nationwide demonstrations against the deterioration of the conditions of their residency.[54] The new Aliens Act of April 1990 was thus a paradoxical compromise. While bringing some limited progress in consolidating residency rights and easing naturalization procedures, it sought primarily "to restrict the influx of foreigners, because there are limits to the ability to integrate them."[55]

At the same time, an alienated minority of the population grew increasingly hostile to foreigners, expressing its resentment with ugly nationalist slogans. A survey conducted by the Leipzig Institute for Youth Research in the summer of 1991 discovered an "abyss of hatred toward foreigners" in East Germany, since it registered a "decidedly authoritarian-nationalist attitude" among 15 to 20 percent of those questioned. Among apprentices, for example, 46 percent agreed with the demand "Foreigners Out!," 54 percent rejected the Turks, and 60 percent believed "there are too many foreigners." Just as alarming was the result of a similar poll of Berliners, in which at least one-third in the West and East worried about "the danger of being overrun by foreigners." While East German disorientation due to unification certainly played a considerable role in this resentment, the "passive toleration" of nationalist excesses was just as widespread in the West. A further representative poll of September 1992 revealed an "increasingly broad consensus" of anti-foreign viewpoints. Every fourth citizen supported the slogan "Foreigners Out!" and over half agreed with the motto "Germany for the Germans."[56]

This rampant xenophobia soon led to outbreaks of violence, which escalated in a deadly dynamic from verbal disparagement to physical assaults. Still relatively harmless was the nightly scrawling of malicious slogans such as "German Power" and the drawing of swastikas on the outsides of houses. More repulsive were the repeated vulgarities and "verbal insults," directed in the streets against visibly distinctive strangers such as Africans or Vietnamese, since they spread fear that limited freedom of movement especially at night. Worse still were the racist assaults on individual foreigners, such as the intoxicating hunt of so-called nigger bashing, which frequently turned from "a regular drubbing" into uncontrolled brutality that left victims permanently disabled. Most dangerous of all were, however, the oranized attacks on the apartments of foreigners and asylum hostels, during which skinhead assailants not only smashed windows with stones but also set fire to the buildings with homemade Molotov cocktails. If the police showed up at all or if the foreigners collectively defended themselves, outright street battles broke out in which "sympathetic spectators" sometimes prevented the restoration of order.[57]

Youthful perpetrators who released their anger with violent acts could hardly articulate why they wanted to persecute foreigners. Their dull "hatred for Jews, foreigners, homosexuals" and for everything strange or different expressed itself in slogans such as "shoot the foreigners, shoot the Turks" and in threats such as "we're going to cut you dirty foreigners down to size." On the one hand, their readiness for "gay bashing" or throwing "Mollis" stemmed from sloganeering and drinking, the adrenalin rush of illicit adventure, the comradship feeling of male bonding, and the sense of power over those weaker than themselves. On the other hand, their propensity for violence was encouraged by a xenophobic worldview of German superiority, propagated by adult right-wing extremists, and repeated in the brutal songs of neo-Nazi rock bands:

They're always eating garlic
and they stink like pigs.
They come here to Germany
and live with dirty tricks.
They fuck the whole place up
and only make a mess.
So you've just got to kill them
there's no point in doing less.

Since those accused of hate crimes shed little light on their motivations during trials, social commentators found themselves puzzling over why Hannah Arendt's "banality of evil" still seemed to infect Germany.[58]

For their part, foreign victims felt increasingly "misunderstood, discriminated, and excluded." Harassment by officials, isolation at the workplace, and discrimination when looking for a place to live were already bad enough, although one could always steel oneself against "everyday xenophobia" by being patient. But the dramatic increase in violence created a new "sense of being threatened," of being exposed without any legal protection, especially since the police usually only intervened when it was already too late. The insults and assaults that strangers suffered on a daily basis signaled "a creeping poisoning of society," which placed a heavy burden on the relationship between indigenous and foreign residents. "We live in constant fear," one African woman from

Magdeburg confessed in the fall of 1992. "When darkness falls, I am glad when I'm in my apartment. Almost all of us ask ourselves whether we can go on living here. When I consider the hatred toward foreigners, I see little future for us." Neither self-defense by groups of youth nor well-intentioned fraternization through sports did much to help counter this hatred.[59]

Intellectuals also had great difficulty in attempting to explain xenophobia, since they were quite distant from the world out of which these excesses arose. Journalists, for example, described Hoyerswerda as an anonymous and soulless "socialist town" whose residents were taking their "last revenge on the GDR" through racist violence. "Betrayed by the older system, and sold down the river by the new one," youths who lacked any hope for the future seemed to have no alternative but to express blind rage toward a world that they did not understand.[60] But when the "terror against foreigners" spread westward to Mölln and Solingen, commentators had to admit that the problem affected the entire country, not just the new states. Thereafter they needed to find broader explanations that would include the growth of the West German skinhead subculture as well. Were there not signs of "violence tourism" by youths who went looking for action beyond their hometowns? And were not young neo-Nazis spurred on by the slogans of adult extremists in the NPD who came from the middle classes? Somewhat helpless, psychoanalysts concluded that the sudden outbreak of hatred and violence "was triggered by the recent far-reaching political changes" that made foreigners into scapegoats.[61]

Surprised by the spread of violence, the political parties also proved incapable of bringing their ideological "concepts into harmony with the reality." While the CDU wanted to admit ethnic resettlers "without restriction" and immediately deport foreign asylum seekers, the SPD called for exactly the opposite policy. Since Chancellor Kohl was reluctant to take a stand, Minister of Interior Schäuble had to profess "contrition for the violent acts" and Family Minister Angela Merkel had to try "slowing down the violence against foreigners" through an intensification of support for East German youth.[62] When the federal ombudsman for foreigners Liselotte Funcke resigned out of frustration over the lack of government support, her colleagues at the state level demanded a clear "acknowledgment [that Germany was] a country of immigration" so as to pull the rug out from under xenophobia. Her successor, Cornelia Schmaltz-Jacobsen, therefore claimed that "Germany [is] already a multicultural society" and advocated a legislative initiative aimed at allowing dual citizenship. Federal President Weizsäcker saw the violence not as a "sign of the rebirth of racist or nationalist ideologies" but, instead, spoke of a "crisis of human understanding."[63]

Due to such waffling, liberal personalities took it upon themselves to explain the practical and moral reasons for tolerance. Bundestag President Rita Süssmuth (CDU) condemned the violence as a "violation of the most elementary human rights," while former Chancellor Willy Brandt argued: "Whoever opens himself up, gains in humanity." The president of the Association for Industry and Commerce, Hans Peter Stihl, also warned that xenophobia was having a negative effect on business abroad, while the Chamber of Commerce stressed that "manual labor in Berlin is unimaginable without foreigners."[64] Similarly, the German Trade Union Federation and the churches proclaimed "Ten Theses against Rightist Prejudice," which culminated in the provocative claim: "To be German means to be multicultural." On the basis of these impressive appeals, an "alliance against xenophobia" formed from the ranks of the churches, unions, employers' associations, athletic leagues, and youth groups that sought to coordinate a campaign for tolerance under the motto "without foreigners we are alone." East German SPD politician Wolfgang Thierse made clear what was at stake: "Our democracy is threatened by both: radical right-wing violence and approval of it."[65]

Since expressions of shame over the "stigma of xenophobia" failed to stem the violence, disgusted citizens began asking themselves: "What [can we] do against the hatred?" One answer was mobilizing the public's conscience through appeals such as "Against Violence and Xenophobia," which deplored "the outbreak of German racism and the widespread acceptance of the attacks on foreigners" in no uncertain terms: "We imagine a more civilized, humane society differently." Another plea, called "Foreigners need friends" was issued by twenty-eight organizations who pleaded for "human dignity and cosmopolitanism."[66] Even more effective were "demonstrations against the hatred toward foreigners," which began hesitatingly in 1991 but in the following year assumed the character of "mass protests." Organized by groups such as Pro Asylum, these rallies found an impressive form in candlelight vigils of hundreds of thousands of people who gathered peacefully in Hamburg, Munich, and other large cities in order to signal: "Foreigners are my friends." The progressive commentator Micha Brumlik concluded that "the candlelight vigils have attested to a civilizational minimum—people are simply not permitted to beat each other to death because they seem different."[67]

Finally, the mass protests against the rise in violence compelled leading politicians in the center and right parties to distance themselves unmistakably from xenophobia. Although the police only slowly began collecting exact statistics, the increase in the number of crimes against foreigners (from 2,426 in 1991 to 6,636 in 1992) could hardly have been clearer, especially since they included the deaths of seventeen people.[68] At a rally in Berlin, FRG President Richard von Weizsäcker therefore offered a stern warning against the tendency to look away: "It is high time to fight back. We are all called on to act." In the parliamentary debate that followed the assault in Mölln, the chairman of the SPD caucus, Hans-Ulrich Klose, launched a sharp attack against the government "because the way in which asylum has been handled has contributed to the poisoning of the political climate." Chancellor Kohl, in contrast, cited the May riots of the Berlin anarchists to demand that both "terror from the right and left" be fought simultaneously. While the debate did result in a "unanimous condemnation of xenophobia and violence" and in a clear statement of the collective will to apply the existing law more resolutely, it failed to alleviate the underlying migration pressure.[69]

One solution was to restrict the right to asylum so as to prevent its abuse by economic refugees while not blocking entry to those who were indeed being politically persecuted. But to separate the applicants, the guarantee of asylum needed to be altered in the Basic Law, which required a two-thirds majority in the parliament. Minister of the Interior Rudolf Seiters wanted "to develop a process that would exclude those who do not need our protection from a lengthy asylum procedure because they come from a safe third state or a country of origin free of persecution." While a quota provision would be maintained for civil war refugees, those arriving via other European Union countries or post-Communist states would be automatically deported. Applications from peaceful countries of origin, moreover, would be rejected across the board, so that the rest could be examined more carefully. Especially the SPD stood "under enormous pressure" in this discussion, since it had to decide either to keep the door open in remembrance of its own emigration during the Nazi era or shut it according to the wish of many of its members to decrease competition for jobs. The Greens, the PDS, and the churches, by contrast, rejected any limitation of the right to asylum as a matter of principle.[70]

After much agonizing, the Bundestag worked out an asylum compromise that signaled a fundamental change of course since it reduced the influx but did not close the door altogether. Contentious issues included the maintenance of legal safeguards through the guarantee of an individual procedure without thereby permanently blocking the courts. The judgment of whether a country of origin was really free of persecution was equally open to debate, because the legitimacy of the application was largely dependent on the assessment of the internal situation of distant places by German immigration authorities. In addition, deportation into secure third-party states transferred control to the outer borders of the EU and the East European neighbors, which would not be possible without their assent.[71] Despite loud protests from the left wing of the party, the majority of the SPD voted with the CDU and FDP to approve this "asylum reform": not to "seal off" the border but to restrict the "previous abuse of the right to asylum." While the Left decried this "unholy alliance," the "majority of citizens agreed with the deep cut into article 16" which tightened the asylum clause of the Basic Law. The Right, by contrast, celebrated the law as a long overdue "end to the self-blockade."[72]

This "dubious compromise" may have reduced the fears of being overrun by foreigners through restricting asylum, but it did not really provide a solution to problems of immigration and multicultural coexistence. In a brilliant analysis of the problem, the sociologist Claus Leggewie therefore called on Germans "to adapt themselves to the new quality of the refugee problem," which could no longer be solved by simply sealing off the border. The poverty migration from Africa, the post-Communist exodus from Eastern Europe, and the wave of civil war refugees from the former Yugoslavia demanded more flexible responses. Moreover, Germany needed to guarantee "adequate protection, especially for ethnic, cultural, and religious minorities," while at the same time reducing xenophobia. Instead of merely reacting to migration pressure and xenophobic violence, Leggewie proposed a more conscious "governmental process of guiding" migration in order to create a clear legal and institutional foundation for immigration.[73] In spite of such sage advice, the question remained whether German society, deeply split between cosmopolitanism and a fear of foreignness, would prove equal to this task.

The Immigration Struggle

The shocking answer came in the form of "a new xenophobic crime" just a few days after the asylum compromise. On Pentecost Sunday of 1993, a firebomb attack on an apartment house in Solingen killed two young Turkish women and three girls. In response, hundreds of young people took to the streets to demonstrate, chanting "Nazis Out!" and laying waste to parts of the downtown in the process. Shaken adults reacted with "disbelief, rage, and sadness" to the new anti-foreign excess. Though Chancellor Kohl apologized to the Turkish government for this "perfidious crime," Solingen citizens booed politicians who hurried to the scene: "Do something finally! Respectable men like you are the arsonists."[74] After this cowardly murder, many embittered Turks feared for their lives. Said one: "Now I know that I can't have any real friends here." Politicians on the Left and spokespersons for foreigners demanded "a radical change in the policy toward foreigners and asylum," through tougher measures against right-wing radicalism and guarantees of civil rights for immigrants. In a moving commemoration of the victims, Federal President von Weizsäcker reminded the country: "Hospitality has always been considered a symbol for the civilization to which we claim to belong."[75]

The Solingen hate-crime triggered a noticeable shift in public opinion because it finally prompted the silent majority to distance itself from xenophobia. In a policy statement, Helmut Kohl deplored the "incomprehensible extent of moral brutalization," while economic leaders worried about its harm to "a positive image of Germany" abroad. Studies conducted by the Federal Criminal Investigation Agency and the Ministry for Family Affairs, moreover, proved that the attacks came "from the middle of society" and evidently could be traced back to "feelings and notions of a general threat to and discrimination of Germans in contrast to 'foreigners.'"[76] Appeals for tolerance slowly yielded results, when Rita Süssmuth reminded the country that "foreigners are not the cause of violence," and Frankfurt Ombudsman for Foreigners Daniel Cohn-Bendit argued that "they are not guests who can be invited and then later sent home." Public opinion watchers thus detected a "drastic change in attitudes" that led to a "more positive relationship toward foreigners than in 1982." While negative viewpoints became rarer, approval of giving foreigners the right to vote as well as to hold dual citizenship grew considerably.[77]

The number of xenophobic attacks only slowly declined in the mid-1990s, since it proved easier to "reject violence and extremism" rhetorically than to put this resolve into practice. Thus the police sometimes sympathized with the hostility that many of their fellow citizens felt toward foreigners—for example, they stood idly by during the disturbances in Eberswalde. Similarly, well-intentioned appeals for "humane interaction with immigrants" and rational arguments about the economic advantages and demographic necessity of immigration did not reach those youths who were most ready to use violence.[78] In addition, legal prosecution proved disappointing, since those accused of committing violent crimes often appeared "almost harmless" at their trials. As a result, a certain "leniency with the perpetrators" tended to prevail among the judges who decided their fate. Only when the violence claimed yet more victims, as happened in Mölln, did the courts impose harsher penalties in the hopes of deterring imitators. In fact, "attacks on foreigners" reached their horrible peak in 1993 with some 6,721 reported offenses, before declining by about one-third thereafter.[79]

The implementation of the asylum restrictions, however, markedly reduced the influx of refugees through across-the-board rejections, quicker decisions, and harsher treatment. Since the main route from the former Eastern bloc led through the Czech Republic, Austria, and Poland (89 percent in 1993), the border police was able to deport asylum seekers on the basis of special agreements with those countries.[80] Doubling the number of bureaucratic "decision makers" also led to a drastic reduction in processing time, making it possible to work through the over 400,000 applications that had piled up over the previous two years. Because political persecution, and not economic need, was now the only criterion considered for granting asylum status, the new provisions had their intended effect: "Only very infrequently did someone have a chance." When the airport decision-making offices were confronted with translation difficulties and denials of the country of origin, they now felt freer to reject an applicant in case of doubt. As a result, in the overcrowded deportation camps, an atmosphere of chaos and depression prevailed: "Humanity often falls by the wayside."[81] Although Amnesty International sharply criticized German restrictions, the CDU and FDP judged the "new right to asylum as a success" because the tightening worked as a deterrent.[82]

The Kohl government therefore pursued a dual policy of "limiting immigration and [promoting] integration," with a clear preference for restriction. While the FDP, representatives of foreigners, and the opposition pushed for easing naturalization for the younger generation, the CDU/CSU continued to pander to fears of "foreign inundation" and demanded "a tougher stance against foreigners."[83] In early 1994, the chancellor used the blockade of a superhighway by Kurdish extremists as an occasion to condemn "the violent actions as an intolerable abuse of the German right to hospitality." After more such incidents occurred, the parliament passed a law which stated that "the conviction of a foreigner for serious breach of the public peace" would entail "a prison term of at least three years and mandatory deportation." The legal situation further deteriorated with the introduction of a visa requirement for foreigners under the age of sixteen in order to slow the influx of children.[84] Small improvements for wives, such as an independent right to residency, carried less weight in comparison. Since the coalition was unable to reach agreement on a "guarantee of naturalization for the children of foreigners," its alien policy continued to stagnate.[85]

Although the tide of immigration receded noticeably as the restrictions took hold, the number of foreign residents continued to grow through the mid-1990s. To be sure, the introduction of a language test in 1993 made it more difficult for resettlers to apply for admission, while tougher countermeasures against smuggling rings reduced the number of asylum seekers entering the country illegally. Though immigration reached an absolute peak in 1992 with a surplus of 822,000 new arrivals, by 1998 the migration balance once again turned negative with a deficit of 54,000 departures, largely because of the deterioration of the economy.[86] Even if horror stories such as "over 13 million people have moved to Germany this decade" were vastly exaggerated, the number of legal foreigners finally stabilized at 7.3 million in 1996, or about 9 percent of the total population. Almost half of them had lived in Germany for more than ten years and thus could no longer be considered temporary labor migrants. Although a quarter stemmed from other European Union states, the over 2 million Turks, about 30 percent of the foreigners, formed a separate subculture.[87] As a result, the challenge to German society's capacity for integration continued to grow as the 1990s wore on.

Among those foreigners already in Germany, especially the Turks, the challenge of "living in two worlds" led both to separation and integration. On the one hand, many newcomers sought refuge in a Turkish-speaking subculture, with its own newspapers and cable television programs, to retain their familiar customs. Increasingly frustrated by discrimination, a sizable minority turned toward a form of Islamic fundamentalism that propagated an antimodern world view of masculine superiority and ethnic difference: "Turkishness is our body, our soul is Islam." The ghettoization of living conditions reinforced this trend toward the emergence of a "parallel Muslim society."[88] On the other hand, many more open and venturesome immigrants succeeded with integration, especially in the second and third generations. The educational level among foreigners rose since about one-third reached some sort of advanced training, some 45,000 small businesses succeeded in achieving economic independence, and also increasing numbers of older immigrants remained in the country for their retirement.[89] To avoid an identity conflict between cultural background and place or residence, educated young Turks often cultivated a dual identity so as not to "bind themselves to any country."[90]

Only for Jewish immigration did the Liberal-Conservative coalition make an exception to its restrictive policy in a kind of belated compensation for the Holocaust. With the collapse of the Soviet Union in 1991–1992, an increasing number of Jews who wanted to live in a European country closer to Russia chose Germany over both the United States and Israel as their new home. The federal government reacted generously to this desire by simplifying the application process as long as they were able to prove their Jewish origin. To the astonishment of the Jewish Agency, over 80,000 Russian Jews emigrated to Germany during the 1990s. In fact, in 1992 alone, some 19,000 Jews arrived there, more than went to Israel. Overhelmed at first, the 30,000 Jews still residing in the country of the former persecutors tried to attend to the needs of their coreligionists in order to increase their chances for a successful integration. Nonetheless, conflicts between the older local residents and the Russian newcomers over religious and social issues were inevitable. Despite some right-wing resentment, this unforeseen immigration led to the reemergence of a lively Jewish community in Germany, as is depicted in the ironic stories of Wladimir Kaminer.[91]

In the fall of 1998 the formation of a new government composed of the SPD and the Greens finally offered a chance "to break the decades-old 'reform blockage'" and initiate a modern immigration policy. While the CDU continued to call for restricting the influx of foreigners, the victorious parties of the left could now seize the opportunity to implement new concepts of openness and integration. Churches, unions, academics, and immigrant groups supported this initiative to "acknowledge the realities of immigration" and pass a more humane alien law that would be aimed at "integration, not exclusion."[92] Citing the 4 million unemployed and the overtaxing of community resources, the new Minister of the Interior Otto Schily, however, surprised the public by declaring: "More immigration is not bearable." The Greens and spokesmen for foreigners were greatly disappointed when Chancellor Schröder also spoke out in favor of a more cautious approach to the issue. As a result, the advocates of reform decided to concentrate initially on easing naturalization under certain conditions, if need be even by accepting "dual citizenship."[93]

The very mention of a right to naturalization incensed the union parties that feared it would cheapen citizenship by making it available so to speak "for free." In order to compensate for his last-minute defeat in the federal election, CSU chairman Edmund Stoiber suggested a petition drive against such a "dual passport." Roland Koch, the CDU's candidate for minister-president of Hesse, took up the hint in the hope of finding a "hot-button issue" for his campaign.[94] A storm of indignation broke out against this crass instrumentalization of xenophobia. Not just the government but also the churches, the Central Jewish Council, intellectuals, and representatives of foreigners spoke out in favor of ending their status of "second-class citizens" through a legalized form of integration.[95] Despite such warnings, the collection of signatures was surprisingly successful: "Those who want to be Germans must decide for one passport," grumbled one disgruntled citizen, while an old woman, whose opinions were shaped by diffuse anxieties, added: "This here is my country." Apparently the petition drive touched a nerve, because two-thirds rejected a dual passport, allowing Koch to eke out a win with this demagogic campaign.[96]

After the Hessian debacle, the SPD retreated from dual citizenship and instead sought a way to ease naturalization that could form the basis of a legislative compromise. Since the party depended on the assent of the FDP, its coalition partner in the Palatinate, for a majority in the Bundesrat, it adopted the Liberals' proposal that suggested allowing dual citizenship only for immigrant children. After the age of twenty-three, young foreigners would have to choose one or the other nationality. Irritated by this partial retreat, the Greens continued to insist on a "more rapid naturalization," while the CDU, emboldened by the success of its populist strategy, rejected any compromise whatsoever.[97] Nevertheless, intense negotiations with the FDP and the Greens finally yielded an acceptable compromise: Youths would need to chose one nationality after they turned twenty-three; the adult application time for citizenship would be reduced to eight years; and naturalization would be made contingent on "adequate knowledge of the language," an "adherence to the Basic Law," a clean police record, and the ability to support oneself. While conservatives denounced this "poor compromise," Minister of the Interior Schily praised the succesful reform as "a symbol for a modern and cosmopolitan Germany."[98]

Although intense controversy overshadowed the reception of the naturalization law, such criticism was unable to impede its positive impact. Commentators were strangely reserved, dubbing this "a second-best solution" that was "insufficient, but nevertheless good." Yet the reform represented a long overdue break with the ethnic tradition of *jus sanguinis* that had been established in 1913 and thus marked the transition to the territorial principle of the *jus soli* that was common in other Western states. This change finally overcame the ethnocentrism of the German concept of citizenship and cleared the way for "the reality of life" that promised immigrants a more secure possibility for integration.[99] Despite the restrictions placed on the dual passport, irritating bureaucratic hurdles to be overcome, and vague provisions that could be construed in contradictory ways, about half of the foreigners living in Germany now had a chance to become full citizens. Although a narrow-minded implementation deterred some applicants, the number of naturalizations increased rapidly. While only 61,700 foreigners became citizens in 1994, five years later their number had climbed to 143,000. It was undeniable: "The German passport is coming into vogue."[100]

Due to the societal stalemate, the immigration issue remained politically charged. In early 2000, Chancellor Schröder surprisingly proposed a limited recruitment of skilled foreign workers in information technology to fill the deficit in this important sector, estimated at some 75,000 specialists. Called "Green Card" after the American model, this five-year work visa for up to 20,000 applicants intended to overcome the labor shortage in a key technology that stemmed from insufficient engineering training. At the same time, such a measure would demonstrate the economic benefits of highly qualified immigration. Successful applicants for this visa needed to possess a college degree and the promise of a job with an annual salary of at least €50,000.[101] Although this proposal was quite limited, Jürgen Rüttgers, the CDU's candidate for minister-president in North Rhine–Westphalia, pandered to the fear of foreigners by running a populist campaign with the motto "Children, not Indians." Fortunately, the xenophobic slogan helped lead to his defeat. Despite some reservations, the "Green Card" therefore went into effect in the summer of 2000, and during the first two years some 15,000 IT experts availed themselves of it.[102]

In his courageous "Berlin Address" of May 2000, Federal President Johannes Rau sought to break the immigration deadlock by calling on the country "to overcome insecurity and fear." On the one hand, immigration was "in our enlightened interest" for demographic, economic, and cultural reasons. On the other hand, greater efforts toward fostering integration were also necessary. To facilitate a parliamentary compromise, Minister of the Interior Schily created a commission of experts that was chaired by Rita Süssmuth of the CDU and included immigration advocates in the churches, unions, and the Greens; neutral representatives from academe, the economy, and the communities; and opponents in the conservative parties.[103] The "nonpartisan social consensus" that the commission hammered out after intense deliberation envisioned a new way of steering immigration according to the needs of the labor market by setting an annual quota (of around 50,000 persons) while at the same time intensifying efforts toward integrating those migrants who were already living in Germany. This recommendation satisfied the Left's desire for greater openness and mollified the Right's fears of being overrun by foreigners.[104]

As an alternative to a multicultural "mishmash," the CDU nonetheless insisted on the recognition of a "German lead culture" so as to speed the integration of foreigners. The CSU demanded unequivocally that "anyone who wishes to live here permanently must be willing to assimilate into the German language and value system." Insufficient language skills did, in fact, pose one of the greatest barriers on the labor market for immigrants, especially Turkish youths. Another problem was the tendency among some Muslims to embrace a fundamentalist version of Islam that rejected Western ideas of human rights and sought to maintain male dominance over women, such as through mail-order brides from Anatolia.[105] The controversy intensified when on October 19, 2000, the chairman of the CDU parliamentary delegation Friedrich Merz tossed the term "*Leitkultur* (lead culture) of Germany" into the debate. In contrast, the government continued to insist on the goal of a "multicultural society" and was at most willing to add the concept of "constitutional patriotism." Behind this ideological debate lurked the key question: "How much difference can Germany really stand?" At least, all parties agreed on the need to improve German-language acquisition by immigrants.[106]

The immigration law of June 2004 was therefore a compromise, designed both to allow controlled immigration and to promote integration. The initial draft proposed an acceleration of asylum processing, a reduction of the maximum age for children joining their parents, a partial opening for labor migration, and an intensification of integration. In the summer of 2002 it foundered on the resistance of the CDU/CSU in the Bundesrat, since the Constitutional Court declared the split vote of the SPD-CDU coalition in Brandenburg invalid.[107] Nevertheless, two years later Schily succeeded in getting the opposing CDU/CSU and the Greens to agree on a "law to limit and control immigration and regulate the residency and integration of citizens from the [European] Union and foreigners." The complicated title indicated a contradictory mix of "protection and opportunities": The bill limited immigration to highly qualified workers, college graduates, and wealthy applicants; it increased security by facilitating the deportation of terrorist suspects; it supported the integration of newcomers by making language training obligatory; and it introduced humanitarian exceptions for nonpolitical persecution to be decided by a hardship commission. While the government welcomed the reform as "a historic turning point," advocates of further opening such as Pro Asyl were disappointed that more could not be achieved.[108]

Touchstone of Civility

When xenophobia climaxed in the early 1990s, FRG President Weizsäcker had warned that the manner in which Germany dealt with foreigners would be a "yardstick for our entire democratic order." Theoretically at least, one could no doubt argue that "civil society integrates *and* discriminates against foreigners in equal measure," since the voluntary union of like-minded people also implies a corresponding demarcation from nonmembers. Still, it was equally clear that the "civility" of the Federal Republic would be judged according to how well it adhered to universal standards of human rights, which applied not only to its own members but also to outsiders trying to get into the country. Moreover, foreigners already living in German society depended above all "on civilized forms of conflict resolution" to prevent xenophobic violence. Although right-wing populism, xenophobia, and outbreaks of violence were even more frequent in some neighboring countries, Germany was held to a higher standard because of its terrifying Nazi past.[109] How well, then, did the Federal Republic pass this test in the past, and how would it face this challenge in the future?

While politicians debated whether Germany was "a cosmopolitan country," its record of admitting foreigners in the second half of the twentieth century was nothing less than remarkable. When one includes the influx of expellees, refugees from the GDR, and later resettlers, "it appears that about one-third of the resident population of the Federal Republic in 1989 had immigrated since 1945." Even if one only considers "foreigners" in a cultural sense, the Federal Office of Statistics counted some 30 million immigrants and 21 million emigrants between 1959 and 1999, which amounted to an immigration surplus of 9 million. The influx of guest workers and their families, along with contingents of civil war refugees, waves of asylum seekers, and labor migrants within the European Union, had increased the resident population of the Federal Republic by 9 percent by 2000. Compared with similar migrations elsewhere, the specific German problem stemmed from a mix of ethnic returnees and foreign immigrants. Establishing an effective system of controlling migration, which would be guided by Germany's own interests, proved impossible as long as large sections of the public continued to answer the question "Are we an immigration country?" negatively.[110]

German reactions to the consequences of "immigration without an immigration policy" were thus marked by considerable uncertainty and ambivalence. The Right's welcoming of ethnic remigration ignored the foreignness of the newcomers in the hope that lingering cultural affinity would make rapid integration possible. Its aversion to foreigners, based in large measure on stereotypical notions of criminality and welfare fraud, presumed that they were incapable of acculturation. Violent attacks on strangers that emerged from a "family culture of intolerance and hate" stemmed from a distorted notion of the "other" that sought to compensate for a sense of inferiority through the use of force.[111] The Left's "excessive enthusiasm for a multicultural society" also hindered integration, because it tended to glorify the alterity of foreigners without demanding respect for the basic rules of democracy. Uncritical tolerance of fundamentalism fostered ethnic ghettoization that only fed hostility toward integration, especially in larger immigrant communities such as among the Turks. The well-intentioned institution of the Ombudsman for Foreigners proved unable to mediate between the cultures of the guests and the hosts as long as the will to linguistic and legal integration was lacking.[112]

The development of a rational system to regulate the influx required a clear admission that "we need immigration" due to its undeniable benefits. Demographers such as Rainer Münz urgently warned of the "graying" of the German population, which due to its low birthrate of 1.4 children per couple, well below the 2.1 needed to maintain the current level, would shrink markedly without further immigration in the future. Despite the high unemployment rate, business leaders, citing Germany's dependence on exports, also pointed out the necessity of "immigration of foreign specialists" in order to make up for the deficit of trained workers in the most innovative industries. Writers and intellectuals, in contrast, ususally stressed the cultural enrichment of immigration through different habits and lifestyles.[113] Skeptics cautioned nonetheless that immigration should not be taken as a panacea, since it also created enormous problems of adapting newcomers to different workplaces, social systems, and cultures. Hence it was crucial that this process not be left to the chance of ethnic disputes, economic crises, or civil wars. Instead, it had to be deliberately guided according to the needs of the labor market and the ability to absorb and integrate different migrants. Only in that way could immigration be made more humane for both sides.[114]

As "a modern civilization," the Federal Republic needs both greater tolerance for cultural differences and a more consistent policy of integration. If it is not to result in a one-sided assimilation, this dual goal calls for a common "effort by Germans and non-Germans." On the one hand, in welcoming migrants the indigenous will have to open themselves more than previously to different religious practices and social habits. On the other hand, the newcomers will have to leave the cocoon of their "ethnic subculture" and internalize the rules of their host society, if they ever hope to lay down lasting roots in it.[115] The Turkish writer Zafer Senocak concludes that "beyond labor market planning, a concept of immigration for the future poses challenges to educational and cultural policy," which had been ignored for too long. While "a special program to combat racism and xenophobia" must, of course, aim to reduce nativist prejudices, more support for language acquisition is needed to facilitate the understanding of German culture by foreigners. By highlighting the advantages of hybridity, bicultural politicians such as Cem Özdemir, intellectuals including Feridun Zaimoglu, and movie directors like Fatih Akin can do much to ensure the success of this process of cultural mediation.[116]

CONCLUSION TO PART III

Implications of Upheaval

One and one-half decades after 1989–1990, the meaning of this caesura remains controversial, both in public opinion and in scholarly debate. Disagreements about its significance stem not only from the short temporal distance, the asymmetrical consequences for East and West, and the habitual self-doubt of intellectuals but also from the complexity of the events themselves. To begin, it is unclear what to call the upheaval. Was the overthrow of the superannuated GDR leadership only a "turn-about" (*Wende*) of SED policy? Was it, rather, a collapse of Communist rule from above, or was it a real revolution from below?[1] Moreover, the causes of the transformation are similarly in dispute: Did the impetus come from the inside, from the long-term structural problems and the short term exodus crisis of the GDR? Or was it, rather, a product of international developments such as the détente between the superpowers as well as the dissident movements among the East European neighbors?[2] Finally the implications of unification for the development of German civil society also remain in doubt: Does the return of the nation-state pose a threat to the civilizing advances of the postwar period or does it signal the end of a long deviation from Western development?[3]

Concerning the democratic awakening in the East, the answer seems to be largely positive, because the revival of civil society played a central role in its preparation, course, and consequences. Borrowing the concept from East European dissidents, the GDR opposition that emerged from small groups, informal networks, and cautious public actions understood itself as a grass roots challenge to the SED dictatorship. Even if the mass exodus was a largely unorganized event, the growing demonstrations during the fall of 1989 were dominated by competing groups of a civic movement that offers a classic example of societal self-organization against a repressive government.[4] This impressive mobilization of dissatisfied citizens culminated in the forced sharing of power at the central Round Table that sought a way to reform the GDR. However, the first free election of March 18, 1990, began channeling the protest into parliamentary forms, which ended the experimentation of grass roots revolutionary action through the transfer of the West German system to the East. Though it dissipated the revolutionary euphoria, the advent of an established civil society also provided channels for articulating Eastern views, if only they were used enough.[5]

Regarding the unification process, the picture is somewhat contradictory, since accession to the Federal Republic realized some hopes but also brought new disappointments. While the Basic Law provided legal security and political freedom, the many unfamiliar Western practices, ranging from sales contracts to insurance policies, produced initial consternation. Moreover, the collapse of the Eastern economy, accelerated by the harsh privatization policy of the Trusteeship Agency, created widespread unemployment for which the repair of the infrastructure and the massive social transfer payments seemed an inadequate compensation. No doubt the increase in security through NATO and EU membership was preferable to the nuclear arms race, but with it came demands for the assumption of new international responsibilities and military deployment that ran counter to pacifist habits. Finally, the unexpected return of the nation-state produced considerable uncertainty over the nature of future identity, since Germans had to cope with the burden of two dictatorships and find a new role in a Europe that was trying to grow together at the same time.[6] Adjusting to these paradoxes confused many Western intellectuals, but it was even more difficult for citizens from the East.

The impression regarding German treatment of foreigners was even more negative as outbreaks of xenophobic violence contradicted self-satisfied claims of multicultural civility. No doubt taking in millions of fleeing East German ethnic remigrants from East Europe, as well asylum seekers and civil war refugees from the Third World, was an impressive accomplishment. But the widespread hatred of foreigners revealed an ugly impulse of discrimination among the lower classes whose fears were inflamed by populist propaganda of right-wing parties, bourgeois politicians, and neo-Nazi youths. Nonetheless, even in this area, some positive indications of greater civility could be observed as well: Candlelight vigils for tolerance, alliances against xenophobia, and groups like Pro Asyl expressed widespread sentiment in favor of cosmopolitanism. Growing self-organization of the Turkish subculture also showed the possibilities for articulating the wishes of a discriminated minority. The passage of an immigration law after endless wrangling was therefore a contradictory compromise between a stubborn defense of domestic interests and a growing receptiveness to the world. The commission's chair, Rita Süssmuth, correctly commented: "We are opening the door a crack."[7]

In many ways, as Timothy Garton Ash perceptively observed, the upheaval of 1989–1990 has reopened some of the fundamental questions that have been debated ever since the revolution of 1848.[8] The collapse of Communism has posed the problem of reconciling civil rights with adequate social security, which Westerners tend to resolve more in favor of liberty, whereas Easterners rather prefer equality, according to survey results. In contrast to the breakup of other countries, the end of division has created the challenge of once more constituting a democratic national state for an estranged people, without thereby sliding back into the horrors of an excessive nationalism. The unexpected transformation of the Federal Republic into an immigration country has confronted society with the task of treating strangers in a civilized fashion, without thereby instituting a "xenophobic normalcy" of discriminating difference.[9] After the failure of the Weimar Republic, the enlarged Federal Republic has received a surprising "second chance" to find solutions for such long-range problems, which might be accepted by the majority of the populace, as well as by the neighboring countries.[10]

In mastering the difficulties shared by other advanced industrial societies, the Germans can, however, rely on a series of positive experiences reinforced through the upheaval of 1989–1990. Even if it is not complete in some East German circles and among certain Western intellectuals, the disenchantment with the socialist utopia has produced a break with collectivism, which ought to increase the appreciation of individual human rights.[11] At the same time, the postnational identity of the old Federal Republic, which was a product of division, has created preconditions for the establishment of a "postclassic" nation-state that might help prevent dangerous relapses into an aggressive nationalism.[12] Finally, concern about a rapidly aging society due to the low birthrate has led to a more realistic attitude toward the problem of immigration, which could construe encounters with foreigners not as social danger but as cultural enrichment.[13] The abiding challenge that results from the unexpected unification is therefore the taming of the recovered national state according to the positive aspects of Western civilization.

CONCLUSION

Contours of the Berlin Republic

The debate about the future capital and seat of government revealed a fundamental conflict about the identity of united Germany. For critics, Berlin symbolized the "Prusso-German mystique," the crimes of the Third Reich, and the tendency toward centralization—in short, the danger of a relapse into arrogance. Instead, they saw Bonn as symbol of a democratic new beginning and as "our federalism and tie to the West"—that is, the civilizing progress of the postwar period. Opponents of the provisional capital on the Rhine decried its provincialism and inbreeding, invoked promises of relocation repeated in the unification treaty, and stressed the urbanity of the metropolis and its symbolic contribution to unification. Since public opinion was also deeply split, it took an emotional debate in the Bundestag on June 21, 1991, to decide the issue in favor of Berlin with the slim majority of seventeen votes. The winning compromise envisaged a "fair division of labor" between the transfer of "core areas of governmental function" to the traditional capital and the continuation of other administrative offices in Bonn.[1] Though controversial, this result marked both a return to the past and a fresh start.

The slogan that embodied all fears and hopes surrounding the move of the government was the term "Berlin Republic." Even if intellectuals had debated this concept as shorthand for the enlargement of the Federal Republic since the early 1990s, it was mainly the publicist Johannes Gross who sparked a new controversy in 1996 with his impassioned plea for "the establishment of a Berlin Republic." Because he considered the governmental practice of Bonn as none "too serious" and thus not really "to be taken seriously," he hoped that "Berlin as federal capital will produce a fundamentally different political style." The transfer of the government would bring more flair, cosmopolitanism, and

267

intellectual dialogue into politics.[2] Sharp attacks of skeptics (who feared a cultural "Easternization," a new nationalism, or a forgetting of the Nazi past) turned the slogan into a political "battleground," which subsequently served as a projection screen for competing identities and contrasting analyses. The excitement over this issue made the discourse on the "Berlin Republic" itself into a phenomenon of the postunification decade.[3]

Behind the journalistic debate lay differing judgments about the extent of the postwar transformation and the consequences of the changes after unification. For Kurt Sontheimer, the accession of the new states, the only minor modifications of the Basic Law, and the stability of the parliamentary institutions suggested that "the Federal Republic which will be governed from Berlin shall essentially not be a different republic" from its predecessor in Bonn. Nonetheless, the enlargement of the population, the shifting of the frontiers to the East, and the rapid transformation of society would pose a set of novel problems, which could not remain without consequences for political culture. Assessing the impact of these factors was compounded by another significant departure, however: the end of the sixteen years of CDU hegemony through the election victory of the Social Democrats and the Greens in 1998 that brought the generation of the "68ers" to power and strengthened the trend to symbolic media politics. Even if it is still somewhat too early to judge whether the expectations of or reservations about Berlin will be fulfilled, some contours of the new constellation are gradually becoming visible enough to be discussed.[4]

The key area of disagreement involved predicting which historical heritage would inform the new "identity of the Berlin Republic." Many foreign commentators, leftist politicians, and pessimistic intellectuals feared that unification would revive the dangerous pattern of the first half of the twentieth century and that a strengthened Germany would therefore resume its hegemonic, aggressive, and exploitative behavior. In contrast, a minority of observers from abroad, more conservative parties, and somewhat more optimistic columnists hoped that the learning processes of the second half of the century would prevail and the enlarged Federal Republic would act in a multilateral, peaceful, and cooperative fashion. Whereas critics of unification tended to argue in immutable negative national stereotypes, defenders of unity emphasized the positive possibilities of collective learning from the past. Conducted in exemplary fashion among the advisers of British Prime Minister Margaret Thatcher at Chequers castle, this acrimonious debate revolved around the issue which legacies and lessons would shape Germany's future.[5]

Since all too often destructive conclusions are drawn from history, it is important to clarify why Germans responded to the second, even more devastating, defeat in one century more constructively than to the first.[6] Due to disappointment in the loss of the First World War and the ensuing revolution, antidemocratic nationalists had concluded that another, more radical attempt needed to be made in order to regain dominance over Europe. Why then did a more crushing defeat in World War II and the attending collapse of the Nazi dictatorship lead most Germans instead to eschew war, to abjure radical nationalism, and to reject special paths of modernization in the future?[7] But even positive learning processes can have negative consequences in different circumstances, if they are pushed too far. How have the lessons of the National Socialist past affected the German response to the new challenges of globalization? Finally, in recent decades, postcolonial criticism has begun to question the goal of transformation—whether it is called Westernization, liberalization, or civilization. To what extent were the successive changes really a positive gain? Answering such questions requires not just a reexamination of the record but some reflection on the criteria used to pass judgment.

Civil Learning Processes

The popularity of the various terms springing from the Latin word *civis* might perhaps serve as an indicator of the transformation of German political culture after 1945. Dictionaries have increasingly begun to include compound concepts, based on the adjective "civil," which among other things means "civilian" in contrast to "military," according to the Brockhaus encyclopedia. The turn-of-the-century conflict, articulated by Thomas Mann, between an inward German "culture" and an outward Western "civilization" was attenuated in the postwar period, because during the Cold War the concept of "Western civilization" came to denote those shared values that seemed to be threatened by Communism. Moreover, Norbert Elias's anthropological interpretation of civilizing as "an advancing process of controlling instincts and emotions, decreasing the inclination to violence, and refining customs and forms of behavior" grew in importance, so that the notion of "civilization" could gradually turn into a positive social goal. Finally the Anglo-American notion of "civil society" became popular among intellectuals as a "counterconcept to the state" and as an intermediary sphere of societal self-organization. Only in corresponding GDR dictionaries are these concepts completely absent.[8]

To characterize the learning process that derived from the shock of the Nazi crimes, one might thus speak of a "recivilizing" effort so as to describe the core of what is meant by the "long path to the West." The cultural critic Jürgen Habermas has suggested that "the Federal Republic only became politically civilized to the extent that our barriers against realizing the previously unthinkable rupture of civilization have disappeared." This perspective starts from the paradoxical failure of a cultivated nation to prevent the inhuman policy of genocide: "It is a difficult truth to comprehend that in as culturally highly civilized a society as the German one a liberal political culture could only emerge *after* Auschwitz."

It took the realization of the implications of the Holocaust to force a keener appreciation of the fundamental importance of human rights and democracy, "namely the simple expectation not to exclude anyone from the political community and to respect equally the integrity of everyone in his otherness."[9] Building on such reasoning, in this book I propose the thesis that internalizing these lessons manifested itself less in the troubled effort to come to terms with the past than in the active penitence of the new beginning.

Intellectual engagement with the Nazi crimes was at best partial and half-hearted because many Germans found it difficult to confront their own ghosts. Initially, allied disclosures of the National Socialist atrocities during the Nuremberg Trial and subsequent court cases created shock and outrage among the defeated, who refused to believe them. But soon the imperative of unflinching confrontation with war and genocide, imposed from the outside, triggered a defensive reaction against the presumption of collective guilt, which legitimized a policy that spread the mantle of silence over the past.[10] Only a courageous minority of democratic politicians like Theodor Heuss and Kurt Schumacher, as well as critical intellectuals like Eugen Kogon and Karl Jaspers, tirelessly advocated an open admission of guilt. Since each side accused the other of perpetuating the Nazi legacy, the ideological competition between East and West during the Cold War led to a double simplification: In the GDR fascism was equated with capitalism, while in the FRG the brown and red dictatorships were subsumed under the notion of totalitarianism.[11] A good deal of the rebuilding and some of the reorientation therefore took place with only an incomplete understanding of the Third Reich.

The eventual emergence of a more self-critical approach to the past owed as much to the general transformation of West German society as to the intellectual efforts to deal with the issue of responsibility. It took until 1958 for a central documentation office for prosecuting National Socialist crimes to be established in Ludwigsburg and until 1963 for a trial about Auschwitz to be initiated by German authorities in Frankfurt. It required the rise of social criticism in literature, the broadcasting of unvarnished documentary TV series, and new curricular guidelines for schools to promote a more critical consciousness of the past, subsequently amplified by the generational rebellion.[12] It needed the pressure of international public opinion, the dramatization of the fates of individuals in the U.S.-made TV soap opera, and the importation of the "Holocaust" concept to break through German self-stylizations as victims and prompt a recognition of their role as perpetrators in the murder of the Jews and Slavs. While it helped to legitimize the political changes, the public memorialization of the moral lessons of the Nazi crimes, which combined paradoxical elements of moral insensitivity and self-flagellation, could not have taken place without the practical learning that preceded it.[13]

This pragmatic heeding of lessons that transformed German political culture largely took place in three distinctive phases: in the years after 1945, around 1968, and during 1989–1990. The changes began with the "programs of civilizing or recivilizing Germany under the protectorate of the victorious powers," which were initially supported by only a minority of the defeated. Already during the war Americans in particular had discussed a fundamental transformation, which would go beyond the overthrow of the National Socialists and seek to prevent future wars through the elimination of their deeper causes. Hoping that the totality of the defeat would prevent the emergence of revanchism, German exile leaders and resistance groups also demanded: "If we do not want to sink into the abyss of nihilism, we must once again recognize the ethical values of the Western world and reestablish their authority."[14] The Potsdam program of demilitarization, denazification, and decartelization was supposed to lay the foundation for a second, more successful, attempt at democratization. The long-range result of this imposed reorientation was a turn toward pacifism, post-nationalism, and economic competition, which transformed the old Federal Republic into a civil state.

The development of a Western form of civil society nonetheless took another generation, since it required a more fundamental transformation of social structures and cultural orientations. Even if the thesis of a "refounding of the Federal Republic" somewhat exaggerates the importance of the Social-Liberal coalition, the controversy about the constructive or destructive effect of the concurrent cultural revolution nonetheless signals that the changes associated with it were crucial for further advancing the recivilizing process in Germany.[15] But the controversial year of 1968 should be understood as a symbol for a series of catch-up modernization processes, which Westernized West German society through the rise of mass consumption and popular culture. Such changes facilitated the cultural acceptance of the "imposed democracy" that only gradually gained emotional appeal through practice in its procedures and proof of actual achievements.[16] Finally, the conflicts caused by the younger generation's attempt to widen political participation were also a difficult test of democratic civility. The products of this second phase were Westernization, inner democratization, and protest mobilization, all of which increased the sociocultural distance to the GDR.

But the transformation could only be called complete when the collapse of Communism extended these changes to East Germany, even if not all new citizens were enthusiastic about the transfer of structures from the "civilized West." Undoubtedly, the formation of elements of a civil society within the SED dictatorship propelled the democratic awakening of the fall of 1989, but the accession of the new states and the ensuing unification crisis hampered voluntary initiatives of East German citizens.[17] Moreover, the normalization debate in the wake of unification demonstrated that the relationship between a German national state and a concept of civilization based on human rights remained insecure. This problem manifested itself especially in the ugly outbreaks of xenophobic violence as a result of fears of being overrun by immigration, which showed clear limits of tolerance.[18] Nevertheless, by also reaching the East, this third wave of changes contributed to a greater appreciation of human rights, national solidarity, and cultural difference. While the liberalizing thrust of these processes has generally been accepted, some of their specific consequences continue to be controversial.

On the one hand, noticeable deficits have remained in every dimension of civilizing advancement, which limited the success of the learning processes. For instance, in spite of all attempts at enlightenment, a fascination with war and an unbroken nationalism have persisted among youthful skinheads and right-wing adults.[19] Also, the market and competition, sponsored by Ludwig Erhard's neoliberalism, have not prevailed permanently, since during the recessions Rhenish capitalism developed neocorporative traits that have inhibited further growth.[20] Even if the cultural critiques of the shallowness of imports from American popular culture have declined considerably, signs of disinterest in politics, distrust of political parties, and hostility to public protest have reappeared time and again.[21] The radical fringe of the leftist milieu has also refused to distance itself from violence even after the defeat of the Red Army Faction, and a phantom pain has lingered in spite of the discrediting of real existing socialism.[22] Finally, the right-wing effort at aggressive renationalization has also fed xenophobic violence.[23] Thus the problems that were constructively resolved by the majority have continued to fester with various minorities and led to new conflicts.

On the other hand, excessive learning has created some distortions of the opposite kind, which also proved to be impediments for the united Germany. Thus an ideological pacifism bred by semisovereignty has complicated the assumption of international responsibility through multilateral military deployment; similarly an ethical postnationalism has prevented an emotional bonding to the nation-state in the form of a democratic patriotism.[24] Moreover, a radical market liberalism has spread among entrepreneurs close to the FDP and justified waves of shareholder-driven dismissals. Even if slavish imitation of Western lifestyles discredited itself by its exaggerations, illusions of grass-roots participation have infatuated particularly the Greens, while the vulgar Marxism of the student movement has misled an entire generation of intellectuals into a simplistic, materialist outlook.[25] Similarly problematic have been an anti-Fascism after the fact, a clinging to a German exceptionalism, and a naïve multiculturalism, which closed its eyes before fundamentalist violations of human rights.[26] Though well intentioned, exaggerated lessons of history in areas like genetics research have therefore tended to create as many problems as insensitive obduracy.

In the beginning, the victorious allies promoted the learning processes from the outside through a mixture of interventions and incentives, which left the defeated little choice but to comply. The suspension of sovereignty and the military occupation created political preconditions for the implementation of the Potsdam program that were well nigh inescapable. Though the Cold War deepened the division among the occupation zones, the ideological confrontation simultaneously prompted a reversal in German policy toward rehabilitation, thereby accelerating the subsequent rebuilding. NATO's military protection and the solution of the problem of controlling the Ruhr through European integration strengthened the incipient ties to the West, while the Warsaw Pact and COMECON failed to achieve a comparable attraction for an orientation to the East. The stunning success of the economic revival, sparked by the Marshall Plan, facilitated the consolidation of the new democratic order and the stabilization of social peace through an expansion of the social safety net. With the return of semisovereignty in the mid-1950s, direct external interference decreased and outside influence assumed the indirect, but still effective form of watchful commentary by international public opinion.[27]

Thereafter, the Germans themselves continued to propel the rethinking internally by realizing the terrible consequences of the Nazi dictatorship and appreciating the improving circumstances of the Federal Republic. As a prod to the learning process, the totality of the defeat played an important role since it consigned potential desires for revenge to the realm of illusion. At the same time, the insight that the Germans had "excluded themselves from civilized humanity through a unique crime" reinforced the readiness for convincing contrition so as to be accepted once again into the international community.[28] Due to the shock of the disclosure of Nazi crimes, the prevention of potential relapses into barbarism became a central goal of the creation of the Basic Law and of the new political institutions. Gradually, international recognition and domestic stability helped buttress the nascent democracy and the attractiveness of the Western lifestyle facilitated the acceptance of a normative understanding of the meaning of "civilization." In spite of a widespread repression of guilt and self-stylization as victims, a critical attitude nonetheless gained ascendancy in the long run, which made a fundamental reorientation of political culture possible.

Ultimately the civilizing process had a stronger impact on the Federal Republic than on the GDR because only in the former was society free enough to correct some of its own shortcomings. In the Soviet Zone, the Communist and Socialist leaders who had survived in the resistance or returned from exile undoubtedly propagated a more radical anti-Fascism as the founding ethos of a "better Germany," which attracted intellectuals like Berthold Brecht and Stefan Heym. But since only a minority of the people supported the "socialist experiment," the SED was inevitably trapped into establishing a new dictatorship.[29] In the Western Zones, the remaining Weimar democrats and the former Nazis who had come to their senses through the defeat proceeded less radically while trying to build a democracy from below, allowing denazification all too often to turn into a whitewashing effort. Nevertheless, the Federal Republic proved to be more capable of learning in the long run, since it developed a critical public sphere, which could force reforms by exposing scandalous Nazi remnants or initiating debates about issues such as environmental protection. Finally, international pressure was more effective in the West, because the Federal Republic wanted to belong to Western civilization.[30]

From the perspective of the Potsdam reorientation program, postwar development looks like an impressive but incomplete success. German pacification has been surprisingly complete, and racist nationalism has given way to a sincere commitment to European integration. The prospering social market economy won the ideological competition with the planned economy and served as a model for neighboring states. Since democracy eventually took root in the West, its attraction contributed to the overthrow of the SED dictatorship in the East. The lively civil society that has emerged decreased bureaucratic regimentation through a critical public and established greater citizen participation. But advances in understanding, such as the recognition of the July 1944 resistance, were achieved only through sharp conflicts because authoritarian patterns lingered and traditionalists proved reluctant to accept liberalization.[31] Moreover, some excesses of learning have complicated the emergence of a pragmatic common sense and erected new taboos concerning German suffering during bombing, rape, and expulsion.[32] Not an inevitable triumph but a long struggle over the internalization of civilizing standards therefore forms the historical foundation for the Berlin Republic.

Global Challenges

While Germans were still wrestling with the consequences of World War II, the shift to postindustrial society initiated another transformation toward the era of globalization. The worldwide transition to high technology created new growth centers in electronics beyond the classic industries of steel, chemicals, and cars; the outsourcing of much production to the Asian tiger states led to a rapid deindustrialization in the old manufacturing areas, and as a result the structure of employment in advanced countries shifted from industrial labor to the service sector. At the same time, the oil shocks of 1973 and 1979 demonstrated the limits of unchecked economic growth and the ecological dangers of continually rising energy consumption. In his restrospective on the "short twentieth century," the British historian Eric Hobsbawm treated the beginning of the 1970s as a caesura that separated the golden postwar era from a new period of profound insecurity. The German political scientist Hans-Peter Schwarz emphasized the later rupture of 1989–1990 instead, but he also designated the following years as "most recent contemporary history."[33] How have the civilizing learning processes prepared the Berlin Republic for these new challenges?

A cursory look at some central dimensions of the German metamorphosis produces somewhat mixed answers. In foreign and security policy, the adherence to multilateral alliances, preference for negotiations, use of economic incentives, and commitment to European integration have undoubtedly served the country well. But the renunciation of force, itself a product of the Soviet-American condominium of the Cold War, proved to be inadequate for the increased importance of the Federal Republic after unification. With difficult soul-searching, the German government therefore had to convince itself first to participate in peace missions and then to take part in actual military combat as a result of the shocking TV images of the Yugoslav civil war. Similarly, the much praised "culture of restraint" could not be maintained in the long run since the population demanded a more forceful pursuit of German interests and the Allies a more active leadership role in Europe.[34] When during the reelection campaign of 2002 the Schröder-Fischer cabinet actually tried to pursue a more independent foreign policy by rejecting German participation in the preemptive war against Iraq, a great outcry ensued, since conservative critics predicted the end of the transatlantic community.

The ambivalence of the emotional and symbolic reaction to the restoration of the nation-state also suggests that the national question remains somewhat unsettled. The old Federal Republic had good reason to be proud of overcoming traditional nationalism and to celebrate the emergence of a sense of "constitutional patriotism," which allowed liberal commentators to speak of a "postnational" state.[35] But based on the euphoria of unification, populist intellectuals such as Rainer Zitelmann attempted to propagate a "renationalization" in order to restore the nation as orienting value and as emotional bond. Tired of the confessions of guilt and rituals of contrition that were demanded by critics abroad and commentators at home, rightist thinkers called for a revival of pride in their freshly unified country. A confused Left responded to this onslaught by seeking at all costs to avoid the historically contaminated category "nation" and fleeing into advocacy of multiculturalism or European integration. Moderate observers, such as the Berlin theologian Richard Schröder, have therefore had great difficulties in proposing "a democratic patriotism" as a reasonable compromise by arguing that it was the solution preferred by other Western countries.[36]

The current economic malaise indicates, moreover, that problems also stem from incomplete rather than excessive learning from the past. Although the market and competition, along with the extension of the welfare state, had been chiefly responsible for the economic miracle in Germany, government intervention had already returned during the first recession of the mid-1960 so that a form of "coordinated capitalism" emerged as a result of close cooperation between entrepreneurs, trade unions, and the state. Even if this "German model" of mutual consultations succeeded in guaranteeing exceptional labor peace for decades, it proved too rigid and expensive during the transition to globalization due to its excessive regulation, steep social costs, and high taxes. Taking neoliberal deregulation in the United States as an example, employers and economists thus systematically campaigned for the dissolution of cartels, privatization of public companies (the postal service and state railroads), and rationalization through massive lay offs in order to create more freedom for competition.[37] A stricter adherence to the original market-oriented maxims of Ludwig Erhard might have rendered such calls for reform superfluous.

In contrast, the Westernization of the Germans seems a real gain, unlikely to be reversed in spite of some anti-American resentment. Both the mass flight in the summer of 1989 and the March election of 1990 revealed how much the East Germans wanted to move collectively to the "West," which they associated with prosperity and freedom. Critical warnings of an "Easternization" of the enlarged Federal Republic have proven unfounded, because the completion of internal unification did not suffer from Eastern dominance but, rather, from the weakness of voices from the new states.[38] The question of whether Germany wanted to fall back into its historical role of vacillating between East and West has arisen rather from a different context—namely, the integration of Europe. Since the East Central European dissidents were instrumental in preparing the ground for the overthrow of the SED dictatorship, the FRG, for reasons of gratitude, market potential, and military security, emphatically advocated extension of the European Union, as well as expansion to the East by NATO. Even if the burden of the past makes the normalization of relations with Poland and the Czech Republic difficult, the Germans themselves have now ironically become transmitters of Westernization to their Eastern neighbors.[39]

Judgments on prospects for democracy remain more divided, since parliamentary practice often appears to fall short of the ideal of "civilized conflict management, nonviolent power struggle, and peaceful leadership change." Critics deplore the development of a "spectator democracy" in a media society, without direct participation or responsibility of citizens. As remedy they propose stronger grass-roots involvement—that is, more possibilities for initiatives, referenda, and plebiscites, which have been adopted in progressive cities and in some of the states but not yet on a federal level.[40] Moreover, in the former Eastern Germany widespread disappointment with the "unification crisis" has made it difficult for democratic values to take root. Formally, institutions function well enough, but they appear to lack an emotional grounding independent of their performance. Similar difficulties encountered by the post-Communist transformation in other East European countries pose the question of whether German postwar learning processes are transferable to other settings. Finally, the debate about the "democracy deficit" and the failure of the constitutional referenda also suggest that the EU needs to make more of an effort to increase civic participation and popular appeal.[41]

The legacy of the protest culture of 1968 also remains contested, because the war against international terrorism puts liberality to a hard test. As numerous peaceful rallies have shown, the right to demonstrate has become firmly established as a result of the activities of citizen initiatives, because courts only intervened when protesters did considerable material damage or used violence.[42] But the toleration of foreign extremists, as long as these did not directly endanger internal security, unfortunately also created a "kind of sanctuary" in Germany, which a Hamburg cell of Al Qaeda used to prepare the attack of September 11, 2001, on the World Trade Center in New York City. To prevent its recurrence, the federal government tightened up the legal rules with several new security laws that forbade subversive associations from hiding behind religious claims, checked airport personnel more thoroughly, and extended the electronic surveillance powers of the Federal Criminal Office (BKA). However, these initiatives immediately aroused liberal critics, who saw "the foundations of the rule of law" in danger and "all citizens under general suspicion."[43] Even if these restrictions are regrettable, the memory of Nazi abuses limited the reduction of civil rights to less than those in the concurrent Patriot Acts in the United States.

The debate about the welfare state also reveals a continuing discrepancy between ideological discrediting of socialism and clinging to government support. The German compromise between free competition and social security proved quite successful, as long as prices remained steady, strikes were rare, and benefits could be extended even to long-term care insurance. But the double pressure of globalization, which brought irreducible unemployment due to high wage costs and anemic growth, and of unification, which overtaxed the social insurance systems through inclusion of people who had never contributed, has created an acute crisis for the transfer system. In contrast to neighboring states like Holland and Sweden, the necessary welfare reforms became extraordinarily difficult, since the political parties had to reduce the privileges of their own clientele, who protested loudly against cuts. Though neoliberal economists demonstrated the necessity of reductions to increase "competitiveness," the halting implementation of proposals by reform commissions, chaired by experts like Bert Rürup and Peter Hartz, shows that the collective security reflex all too often prevails over the willingness to assume individual risks.[44]

The frustrating discussions about the direction of normalization similarly illustrate the problems of finding a stable identity for the enlarged Federal Republic. Instead of having just to bear the customary burden of the Nazi past, the collapse of Communism confronted the public with the legacy of a second, ideologically opposed dictatorship, thereby doubling the vexation.[45] No longer complaining about the division of the country, commentators now deplored the lack of progress in "internal unity," grousing alternately about a "nostalgia" that glorified the GDR in retrospect and a "westalgia" that wanted to preserve the customs of the Bonn Republic.[46] Even if the economic mistakes made by the rapid privatization of the Trusteeship Agency were eventually corrected through enormous transfer payments, a self-sustaining growth in the East is not yet in sight. Moreover, the extension of the Western system to the new states has for a decade delayed the necessary reform discussion in important areas, such as restructuring the schools and universities.[47] Similarly, the German role in the European Union remains contradictory, since the refounding of their own national state and the continuation of progress in integration tend to hinder one another.[48]

Finally, the long struggle over the shape of an immigration law suggests that the practice of cosmopolitanism remains politically contested. The growing birth deficit of the Federal Republic has left even conservatives little choice but to accept immigrants if pensions are to be safeguarded, since a shrinking population cannot produce enough contributions. Leftist circles have similarly been forced to realize that the social integration of migrants demands more respect for the values of the constitution and a basic knowledge of language and culture of the host country. Among trade unions, employer organizations, churches, and parties, a broad consensus has therefore emerged in favor of regulating immigration so as to recruit necessary specialists without increasing mass unemployment. But the general population remains fearful of too many foreigners and envious of their social benefits. In order not to antagonize these potential voters, populists in the CDU/CSU prevented a possible agreement by insisting on stiff protections.[49] Only the practical implementation of the new regulations will show if the recent immigration compromise has found a workable solution.

For mastering the new challenges of globalization, the learning from the Nazi past is therefore a necessary precondition but not always a sufficient guide. No doubt, the Westernization of values, democratization of political decisions, and mobilization of citizen initiatives provide a laudable foundation for the policy of the Berlin Republic at the beginning of the twenty-first century. But the excess of demilitarization has already had to be corrected to allow participation in peace-keeping missions, and denationalization has been rendered somewhat pointless through reunification. In contrast, the decartelization of the economy, the distancing from Communism, the creation of internal unity, and the opening toward multicultural tolerance have not yet gone far enough, as shown by the continuing obstacles to competitiveness, the insistence on preserving social benefits, the tensions between East and West Germans, and the prejudices against foreigners.[50] The liberalization of German political culture that has emerged out of the collective learning from the mistakes of the past is an impressive achievement in itself, but it alone cannot offer guidance for all the new problems. Reaching the level of other Western democracies now confronts the Federal Republic with all the problems of advanced societies.

These reflections raise the following question: Does a continuing concentration on avoiding a repetition of the catastrophes of the twentieth century not somehow block the perception of the novel challenges of the twenty-first century? For Klaus Naumann, trends like the "aging of institutions, the weakening of [informal] arrangements, and the erosion of parliamentary structures" even suggest a certain "pattern of wearing out" of the Federal Republic. "The respectable generational experience of the war, postwar, and founding of democracy . . . threatens to turn into an immobilism, which is oblivious to the tasks of the Berlin Republic, because they are neutralized by an insistence on normative and institutional continuity." In other words, might the learning achievements of the past not in some way be responsible for the protracted crisis of the "German model"? Especially in face of the weakening of international competitiveness through rising government deficits and excessive development of the welfare state, but also regarding other issues, such a warning seems not completely unjustified.[51] Without thereby relativizing the double burden of the dictatorial past, the time appears to have come to probe more insistently into a different genealogy of the globalization problems of the present.[52]

The Task of Civilization

Marked by the ravages of the past, the shining face of the new old capital Berlin is itself a mirror of the civilizing transformation. The move of the Bundestag into the renovated Reichstag with its Soviet graffiti and Norman Foster's glass dome has transformed the ugly Wilhelmian building into a living center of democracy that attracts thousands of visitors. The construction of a modern chancellor's office and other administrative buildings in the "federal ribbon" has turned a deserted area in the shadow of the Berlin wall into a representative government quarter, which presents itself as open and close to its citizens. In contrast, the contemporary skyscrapers at Potsdamer Platz represent an urbane media culture and consumer society, which radiates dynamic internationalism and connects the West Berlin cultural forum with the Eastern downtown. The erection of an impressive Holocaust memorial close to Brandenburg Gate and the planned reconstruction of Hohenzollern Palace at the other end of Linden Boulevard suggest an embrace of the painful as well as proud legacies of the past. From these contrasts between visible war damages or traces of dictatorship and new postmodern edifices, the capital and thereby also the Berlin Republic are gaining a new, tension-filled identity.[53]

In international comparison, the extent of German professions of contrition over the Holocaust seems almost exemplary. In Japan, criticism of imperialist expansion, admission of responsibility for the war, and remorse over the atrocities committed during its course appear to be less widespread in spite of the insights of some courageous intellectuals.[54] In Italy the switch of sides in the summer of 1943 made the acceptance into the front of the victorious powers possible, while the spread of the *resistenza*-myth hampered a serious debate about popular involvement in Fascism.[55] In Austria the Allied offer to treat the country as the first victim of aggression was so tempting that the soul-searching over complicity with Nazi crimes only reached wider circles through the Waldheim scandal of the 1980s.[56] Even among the liberated victors, such as France, "the Vichy syndrome" for a long time made it difficult to speak publicly about the topic of German collaboration or about the excesses of *épuration* during the immediate postwar period.[57] International pressure and intellectual criticism prevented a comparable mythologization in the Federal Republic and ultimately compelled the elites to recognize the necessity of a fundamental transformation.

Hence the claim that German democratization is transferable, promoted by the Bush administration as justification for the invasion of Iraq, ought to be treated with some skepticism. Appealing to the public memory of postwar success, the president and his top advisors have argued that "we lifted up the defeated nations of Japan and Germany and stood by them while they built representative governments."[58] But even a cursory reflection suggests that the 1945 constellation was as unique as the preceding Nazi crimes. On the one hand, the Wehrmacht was completely defeated for a second time within a generation, while Hitler's dictatorship was utterly discredited by the suffering of soldiers, the nightmare of bombing, and the flight of civilians from the East. Because the atrocities, committed in the German name, were so horrible that they could not be denied, there was no alternative but a new beginning that would radically break with the Nazi past.[59] On the other hand, a sizable minority of Weimar democrats, resistance survivors, and returning émigrés was committed to humanistic values and ready to make a fresh start that drew on minority traditions of democracy. Without their passionate struggle for a better Germany, the allied reorientation project could not have succeeded.

In the meantime, postcolonial criticism promoted by Third World intellectuals has called into question the very concept of "civilization" by claiming that it has served to perpetuate the hegemony of white males. Manifold negative experiences with European and American imperialism have badly tarnished the model of "Western civilization" by exposing the ubiquitous practices of racism, economic exploitation, and discrimination against women that are conducted in its name.[60] Nonetheless, a postmodern relativizing, which rejects the possibility of a universal standard out of respect for other cultures, is equally misleading because it justifies violence and repression as cultural difference. The problem does not lie in the notion of human rights but in their imperfect realization among non-whites, lower classes, and women![61] Without a measuring rod of humane behavior, as formulated in the "general declaration of human rights" by the UN after the Second World War, it is impossible to live together on the globe in peace and justice. By highlighting the terrible consequences of a departure from this norm, the German example demonstrates that it is the great strength of the ideal of civilization, on which democracy builds, that it is capable of self-correction even in case of terrible abuse.[62]

If defined as respect for human rights, the notion of civilization should not be considered as permanent achievement but as an open-ended task for the future. In contrast to the militarism, nationalism, and statism of 1945, Germans have heeded Kurt Schumacher's call for "a great turnabout," transforming their political culture according to the values of the Basic Law.[63] Especially nongovernmental organizations of civil society, which work together in the "Forum on Human Rights" seek to follow these norms as ethical standard in practice. Nonetheless, there is no reason for complacency, since even within parliamentary democracy new dangers to basic rights can threaten through growing disinterest in politics, financial corruption, abuse of the media, and excessive surveillance. Moreover, the insights gained from the Holocaust offer only a limited guidance for the new challenges of globalization, since they illuminate the horrors of ethnic cleansing but not the problems of deindustrialization. Hence, the difficulties of historical learning processes sketched above imply that the civilizing of politics ought to be understood as a goal for which one must continually strive.[64]

NOTES

ABBREVIATIONS

AfS	*Archiv für Sozialgeschichte*
AHR	*American Historical Review*
APuZ	*Aus Politik und Zeitgeschichte*
BDI	*Berliner Debatte Initial*
BfdiP	*Blätter für deutsche und internationale Politik*
BK	*Bayern-Kurier*
BZ	*Berliner Zeitung*
CEH	*Central European History*
DA	*Deutschland-Archiv*
DAS	*Deutsches Allgemeines Sonntagsblatt*
DUD	Deutschland Union Dienst, Bonn
DZ	*Deutsche Zeitung*
DzD	*Dokumente zur Deutschlandpolitik*
FAZ	*Frankfurter Allgemeine Zeitung*
FJNSB	*Forschungsjournal Neue Soziale Bewegungen*
FR	*Frankfurter Rundschau*
GG	*Geschichte und Gesellschaft*
GK	Globus Kartendienst, Hamburg
GSR	*German Studies Review*
HAZ	*Hannoversche Allgemeine Zeitung*
HB	*Handelsblatt*
HSK	H-Soz-u-Kult
HZ	*Historische Zeitschrift*
JMH	*Journal of Modern History*
KA	Kempowski Archiv, Nartum
ND	*Neues Deutschland*
NRZ	*Neue Rhein Zeitung*
NYT	*New York Times*

NZ	Neue Zeitung
NZZ	Neue Zürcher Zeitung
PNN	Potsdamer Neueste Nachrichten
RhM	Rheinischer Merkur
RP	Rheinische Post
SBZArch	SBZ-Archiv
SZ	Süddeutsche Zeitung
taz	tageszeitung
TR	Tägliche Rundschau
TSp	Der Tagesspiegel
VfZ	Vierteljahrshefte für Zeitgeschichte
VSWG	Vierteljahrschrift für Sozial- und Wirtschaftsgeschichte
WaS	Welt am Sonntag
WdA	Welt der Arbeit
WZB	Wissenschaftszentrum für Sozialforschung, Berlin

INTRODUCTION

1. Alexander von Plato and Almut Leh, *"Ein unglaublicher Frühling": Erfahrene Geschichte im Nachkriegsdeutschland 1945–1948* (Bonn, 1997). See also Anonyma, *Eine Frau in Berlin: Tagebuchaufzeichnungen vom 20. April bis 22. Juni 1945* (Frankfurt, 2003), 186.

2. Margret Boveri, *Tage des Überlebens: Berlin 1945* (Frankfurt, 1996), 91 ff. See also Anonyma, *Eine Frau in Berlin*, 62 ff. Cf. Burkhard Asmuss, Kay Kufeke, and Philipp Springer, eds., *1945: Der Krieg und seine Folgen* (Bönen, 2005).

3. Arnd Bauerkämper et al., eds., *Der 8. Mai 1945 als historische Zäsur: Strukturen, Erfahrungen, Deutungen* (Potsdam, 1995). See also Jörg Hillmann and John Zimmermann, eds., *Kriegsende in Deutschland* (Munich, 2002).

4. Margaret Bourke-White, *Deutschland April 1945* (Munich, 1979). The text depicts the situations out of which the images came.

5. These fundamental questions are also posed in the brilliant synthesis by Graf Kielmansegg, *Nach der Katastrophe: Eine Geschichte des geteilten Deutschland* (Berlin, 2000), 10, 81. Quotation from SHAEF-Directive from 3/30/1945, in Klaus-Dietmar Henke, *Die amerikanische Besetzung Deutschlands* (Munich, 1995), 187.

6. The first reference is in the article "5,000,000 Reported Slain at Oswiecim," *NYT*, 4/11/1945. Earlier reports on the liberation of Majdanek were also hardly believed in the West.

7. "Germans Forced to Bury Victims" and "More Tell of Horror March," *NYT*, 4/15/1945. Norbert Frei, "'Wir waren blind, ungläubig und langsam.' Buchenwald, Dachau und die amerikanischen Medien im Frühjahr 1945," *VfZ* 35 (1987), 385 ff.

8. Harold Denny, "Despair Blankets Buchenwald Camp," *NYT*, 4/20/1945, and Bourke-White, *Deutschland April 1945*, 90–96. See also Frank Stern, *Im Anfang war Auschwitz: Antisemitismus und Philosemitismus im deutschen Nachkrieg* (Gerlingen, 1991), 59–64.

9. Gene Currivan, "Nazi Death Factory Shocks Germans on a Forced Tour," *NYT*, 4/18/1945. See also "Richmond Sargeant Writes Dr. Curt Bondy of Mass Burial of Internees in Germany," *Richmond Times Dispatch*, 6/3/1945.

10. Alexander Dicke, "Mit 'Vorwärts, vorwärts' war es nicht getan . . . Erinnerungen von 1931 bis 1950," MS, 1991, KA 3228, 127. See also Karl Jering, *Überleben und Neubeginn: Aufzeichnungen eines Deutschen aus den Jahren 1945/46* (Munich, 1979), 18; Heinz Döll, "Skizzen und Daten 1919/1949," MS, n.d., KA 5940/3, 255, and Wolfgang Prüfer, "Berlin—Rädnitz und dreimal zurück, 1939–1949," printed as manuscript, 1995, KA 4379, 185, 214–215.

11. "Todeslager Sachsenhausen," *TR*, 5/26/1945; "Buchenwald," Editorial, *NYT*, 4/19/1945. "Atrocity Report Issued by Army," *NYT*, 4/29/1945. See also David A. Hackett, ed., *The Buchenwald-Report* (Boulder, 1995), 16 ff., and Henke, *Die amerikanische Besetzung*, 862 ff.

12. "Congressmen and Army Chiefs Get a Firsthand View of Nazi Horror Camps," *NYT*, 4/21/1945, and "American War Chiefs See Concentration Camp Atrocities in Germany," *NYT*, 4/24/1945.

13. "Soviet War Writer Rebuked by Chief," *NYT*, 4/15/1945, and Franklin Delano Roosevelt to Secretary of War, 8/26/1944, in Cordell Hull, *The Memoirs of Cordell Hull* (New York, 1948) 2:1603. Cf. Michaela Hönicke, "'Prevent World War III': An Historiographical Appraisal of Morgenthau's Programme for Germany," in Robert A. Garson and Stuart S. Kidd, eds., *The Roosevelt Years: New Perspectives on American History, 1933–1945* (Edinburgh, 1999), 155–172, and Henke, *Die amerikanische Besetzung*, 67 ff.

14. Henke, *Die amerikanische Besetzung*, 108–109. See also Michaela Hönicke, "'Know Your Enemy': American Interpretations of National Socialism, 1933–1945" (Ph.D. diss., University of North Carolina at Chapel Hill, 1998), and Hönicke, "Wartime Images of the Enemy and German-American Encounters at 'Zero Hour,'" *Borderlines* 2 (1995), 166–194.

15. "Anti-Nazi Feeling Rises, Says Army," *NYT*, 6/8/1945. See also Jering, *Überleben und Neubeginn*, 18 ff.

16. Agathe Matthiesen, "Tagebuch," KA 5958/1, 8.

17. Thomas Mann, "Die deutschen KZ," *TR*, 9/5/1945. See also Mann, *Deutschland und die Deutschen 1945* (Hamburg, 1992), 32, 36.

18. Lutz Niethammer et al., eds., *Arbeiterinitiative 1945: Antifaschistische Ausschüsse und Reorganisation der Arbeiterbewegung in Deutschland* (Wuppertal 1976). See also Jering, *Überleben und Neubeginn*, 21 ff.

19. "Four Allies Take Control of Reich, Impose '37 Borders, Stern Terms," *NYT*, 6/5/1945. G. Hill, "Running Germany Harder Than Expected," *NYT*, 6/10/1945. See also Bundesminister des Innern, ed., *Dokumente zur Deutschlandpolitik*, 2. series, vol. 1: *Die Konferenz von Potsdam*, 3 parts (Neuwied, 1992), 3:2101 ff.

20. "Germany Stripped of Industry by Big Three: Five Powers to Plan Peace," *NYT*, 8/3/1945; Editorial, "The Potsdam Decisions," *NYT*, 8/3/1945; and Raymond Daniell, "Big Three Dealt Boldly with Great Problems," *NYT*, 8/5/1945. See also "Geschicht-liche Entscheidung," *TR*, 8/5/1945.

21. "Germans Warned, Fate Is Their Own," *NYT*, 8/7/1945. Boveri, *Tage des Überlebens*, 299–230. See also Victor Klemperer, *So sitze ich denn zwischen allen Stühlen*, 2 vols., edited by Walter Nowojski (Berlin, 1999), 1:64–65.

22. Gerhard Ritter, *Geschichte als Bildungsmacht: Ein Beitrag zur historisch-politischen*

Neubesinnung (Stuttgart, 1946), as well as Klaus Schwabe and Rolf Reichardt, eds., *Gerhard Ritter: Ein politischer Historiker in seinen Briefen* (Boppard, 1984).

23. "Big Four Indict 24 Top Nazis for Plotting against Peace: Atrocities in War Charged," *NYT*, 10/19/1945; Editorial and excerpts from the indictment, "The Nazi Regime Indicted," *NYT*, 10/19/1945. Telford Taylor, *Die Nürnberger Prozesse: Hintergründe, Analysen und Erkenntnisse aus heutiger Sicht* (Munich, 1994), 36–61.

24. Jering, *Überleben und Neubeginn*, 166. Robert M. W. Kempner, *Ankläger einer Epoche: Lebenserinnerungen* (Frankfurt, 1983), and Prüfer, "Berlin," 216, 268–269. See also Peter Reichel, *Vergangenheitsbewältigung in Deutschland: Die Auseinandersetzung mit der NS-Diktatur von 1945 bis heute* (Munich, 2001), 42 ff.

25. G. Hill, "Running Germany Harder Than Expected," *NYT*, 6/10/1945; Drew Middleton, "Extremists Lead German Politics," *NYT*, 8/8/1945, and Middleton, "Germans Unready for Political Life," *NYT*, 8/19/1945.

26. Christoph Kleßmann, *Befreiung durch Zerstörung: Das Jahr 1945 in der deutschen Geschichte* (Hannover, 1995), and Konrad H. Jarausch, "1945 and the Continuities of German History: Reflections on Memory, Historiography and Politics," in Geoffrey J. Giles, ed., *Stunde Null: The End and the Beginning Fifty Years Ago* (Washington, D.C., 1997), 9–24.

27. Saul K. Padover, *Experiment in Germany: The Story of an American Intelligence Officer* (New York, 1946), 18, 34, 36, 42, 60. See also the criticism of Henke in *Die amerikanische Besetzung*, 284 ff.

28. Kathleen McLaughlin, "Reich Democracy Tested in Munich," *NYT*, 8/3/1945.

29. Jering, *Überleben und Neubeginn*, 158. See also Stern, *Im Anfang war Auschwitz*, 65 ff.

30. Harry Elmer Barnes, *The History of Western Civilization* (New York, 1935), and Columbia College (subsequently Columbia University), ed., *Chapters in Western Civilization* (New York, 1948). See also Werner Sombart, *Händler und Helden: Patriotische Besinnungen* (Munich, 1915), and Thomas Mann, *Betrachtungen eines Unpolitischen* (Berlin, 1918).

31. See the quotations from contemporary texts in the preceding note. See also Alan J. P. Taylor, *The Course of German History: A Survey of the Development of German History since 1815* (London, 1945). This book was written to give information to British occupation troops, but because of its anti-German tendency it was never distributed among them.

32. Despite the pioneering study by Norman M. Naimark, *The Russians in Germany: A History of the Soviet Zone of Occupation* (Cambridge, 1995), there exists relatively little research on Soviet German policy. Since the concept of civilization is largely informed by Western viewpoints, the following reflections proceed more from this perspective, without, however, completely neglecting the Russian point of view.

33. "Die Toten mahnen die Lebenden," *TR*, 9/11/1945. See also Fritz Klein, *Drinnen und draußen: Ein Historiker in der DDR* (Frankfurt, 2000), 101 ff., and Georg G. Iggers et al., eds., *Die DDR: Geschichtswissenschaft als Forschungsproblem* (Munich, 1998).

34. Bernd Faulenbach, *Ideologie des deutschen Weges: Die deutsche Geschichte in der Historiographie zwischen Kaiserreich und Nationalsozialismus* (Munich, 1980), as well as Helga Grebing, *Der "deutsche Sonderweg" in Europa 1806–1945* (Stuttgart, 1986).

35. Hans-Ulrich Wehler, *Das Deutsche Kaiserreich 1871–1918* (Göttingen, 1973) and Jürgen Kocka, *Sozialgeschichte* (Göttingen, 1977) versus David Blackbourn and Geoff Eley, *The Peculiarities of German History: Bourgeois Society and Politics in Nineteenth-Century Germany* (New York, 1984).

36. Heinrich August Winkler, *Der lange Weg nach Westen*, 2 vols. (Munich, 2000).

37. See also the debates surrounding "political correctness" in the United States. For an introduction, see Marilyn Friedman, ed., *Political Correctness: For and Against* (Lanham/MD 1995), as well Cyril Levitt et al., eds., *Mistaken Identities: The Second Wave of Controversy over "Political Correctness"* (New York, 1999).

38. Dan Diner, "Vorwort des Herausgebers," in Diner, ed., *Zivilisationsbruch: Denken nach Auschwitz* (Frankfurt, 1988), 7–13. See also Diner, "Zivilisationsbruch, Gegen-rationalität, 'Gestaute Zeit': Drei interpretationsleitende Begriffe zum Thema Ho-locaust," in Hans Erler et al., eds., *"Meinetwegen ist die Welt erschaffen": Das intellektuelle Vermächtnis des deutschsprachigen Judentums* (Frankfurt, 1997).

39. Ian Kershaw, "Trauma der Deutschen," *Der Spiegel* 55 (2001), no. 19, 62 ff. An Internet search on January 30, 2006, registered over 22,000 hits for the term, ranging from newspaper articles to academic treatises.

40. Norbert Elias, *Über den Prozeß der Zivilisation: Soziogenetische und psychogenetische Untersuchungen*, 2 vols. (Frankfurt, 1976).

41. Zygmunt Bauman, *Dialektik der Ordnung: Die Moderne und der Holocaust* (Hamburg, 1992), 26 ff.

42. Dan Diner, "Den Zivilisationsbruch erinnern: Über Entstehung und Geltung eines Begriffs," in Heidemarie Uhl, ed., *Zivilisationsbruch und Gedächtniskultur: Das 20. Jahrhundert in der Erinnerung des beginnenden 21. Jahrhunderts* (Innsbruck, 2003), 17–34. See also Michael Geyer, "War, Genocide, and Annihilation: A Reflection on the Holocaust," in Konrad H. Jarausch and Michael Geyer, *Shattered Past: Recon-structing German Histories* (Princeton, 2003).

43. For an introduction to the enormous literature on this topic, see John Keane, *Democ-racy and Civil Society: On the Predicaments of European Socialism, the Prospects for Democracy, and the Problem of Controlling Social and Political Power* (London, 1988), 31–68.

44. Jürgen Kocka, "Zivilgesellschaft als historisches Problem und Versprechen," in Manfred Hildermeier et al., eds., *Europäische Zivilgesellschaft in Ost und West: Begriff, Geschichte, Chancen* (Frankfurt, 2000), 13–39. See also the project descrip-tion at www.wz-berlin.de.

45. Wilm Hosenfeld, *"Ich versuche jeden zu retten": Das Leben eines deutschen Offiziers in Briefen und Tagebüchern* (Munich, 2004), 302. See Frank Trentmann, ed., *Para-doxes of Civil Society: New Perspectives on Modern German and British History* (New York, 2000), 3–46.

46. Jürgen Kocka, "Das europäische Muster und der deutsche Fall," in Kocka, ed., *Bürgertum im 19. Jahrhundert: Deutschland im europäischen Vergleich*, 3 vols. (Göttingen, 1995), 1:9–84. See also Gerhard Schröder, "Die zivile Bürgergesellschaft," *Die Neue Gesellschaft: Frankfurter Hefte* 47 (2000), 200–207.

47. Kielmansegg, *Nach der Katastrophe*, 10.

48. Hans-Peter Schwarz, *Die Ära Adenauer*, 2 vols. (Stuttgart, 1981/1983), versus Axel

Schildt et al., eds., *Dynamische Zeiten: Die 60er Jahre in den beiden deutschen Gesell-schaften* (Hamburg, 2000). See also Rolf Badstübner et al., *Die antifaschistisch-demokratische Umwälzung: Der Kampf gegen die Spaltung Deutschlands und die Entstehung der DDR von 1945 bis 1949* (Berlin, 1989).

49. Jering, *Überleben und Neubeginn,* 27. See also Peter Graf Kielmansegg, "Lernen aus der Geschichte—Lernen in der Geschichte: Deutsche Erfahrungen im 20. Jahr-hundert," in Peter R. Weilemann et al., eds., *Macht und Zeitkritik: Festschrift für Hans-Peter Schwarz zum 65. Geburtstag* (Paderborn, 1999), 3–16.

50. Anonyma, *Eine Frau in Berlin,* 278; Karl Heinrich Knappstein, "Die versäumte Revolution," *Die Wandlung* 2 (1947), 677. See also Walter L. Dorn, *Inspektionsreisen in der US-Zone: Notizen, Denkschriften und Erinnerungen aus dem Nachlaß,* edited by Lutz Niethammer (Stuttgart, 1973).

51. Konrad H. Jarausch, "Towards a Social History of Experience: Some Reflections on Theory and Interdisciplinarity," *CEH* 22 (1989), 427–443. See also Martin Sabrow, *Das Diktat des Konsenses: Geschichtswissenschaft in der DDR 1949–1969* (Munich, 2001).

52. Ralph Giordano, *Die zweite Schuld oder Von der Last Deutscher zu sein* (Cologne, 2000), versus Hermann Lübbe, "Der Nationalsozialismus im politischen Bewußtsein der Gegenwart," in Martin Broszat et al., eds., *Deutschlands Weg in die Diktatur* (Berlin, 1983), 329–49.

53. Norbert Frei, *Adenauer's Germany and the Nazi Past: The Politics of Amnesty and Integration* (New York, 2002), xii. See, however, Frei, "Deutsche Lernprozesse: NS-Vergangenheit und Generationenfolge seit 1945," in Heidemarie Uhl, ed., *Zivilisa-tionsbruch und Gedächtniskultur: Das 20. Jahrhundert in der Erinnerung des beginnenden 21. Jahrhunderts* (Innsbruck, 2003), 87–102.

54. Aleida Assmann and Ute Frevert, *Geschichtsvergessenheit–Geschichtsversessenheit: Vom Umgang mit deutschen Vergangenheiten nach 1945* (Stuttgart, 1999). Reichel, *Vergangenheitsbewältigung,* 199 ff. at least goes into the judicial consequences.

55. Manfred Görtemaker, *Geschichte der Bundesrepublik Deutschland: Von der Grün-dung bis zur Gegenwart* (Munich, 1999), and Ulrich Mählert, *Kleine Geschichte der DDR* (Munich, 1998).

56. Winkler, *Der lange Weg,* vol. 2, versus Christoph Kleßmann, *Die doppelte Staats-gründung: Deutsche Geschichte 1945–1955,* 5th ed. (Göttingen, 1991), and Kleßmann, *Zwei Staaten, eine Nation: Deutsche Geschichte 1955–1970,* 2nd ed. (Bonn, 1997).

57. Peter Bender, *Episode oder Epoche? Zur Geschichte des geteilten Deutschland* (Munich, 1996). See also Arnd Bauerkämper et al., eds., *Doppelte Zeitgeschichte: Deutsch-deutsche Beziehungen 1945–1990* (Bonn, 1998), and Christoph Kleßmann et al., eds., *Deutsche Vergangenheiten—eine gemeinsame Herausforderung: Der schwierige Umgang mit der doppelten Nachkriegsgeschichte* (Berlin, 1999).

58. "Protokoll einer Podiumsdiskussion des Geschichtsforums," *Potsdamer Bulletin für Zeithistorische Studien* no. 15 (1999), and Konrad H. Jarausch, "'Die Teile als Ganzes erkennen': Zur Integration der beiden deutschen Nachkriegsgeschichten," *Zeithistorische Forschungen* 1 (2004), 10–30.

59. *DzD: Die Konferenz von Potsdam,* 3:2101 ff. See also the discussion about the JCS-directive 1067, in Henke, *Die amerikanische Besetzung,* 112 ff., and Udo Wengst,

"Kontinuität und Wandel in Deutschland während der Besatzungszeit," paper given at ZZF, 5/3/2001.

60. Schildt et al., *Dynamische Zeiten*; introduction to Philipp Gassert and Alan Steinweis, eds., "Coming to Terms with the Past in West Germany: The 1960s" (forthcoming 2006); and Ulrich Herbert, "Liberalisierung und Radikalisierung: Die BRD auf dem Weg nach Westen," Centre-Marc-Bloch-Lecture on 5/21/2001. In contrast to the misleading comments of Andreas Rödder, "Die Umkehrer," *FAZ*, 10/19/2004, the reorientation of German political culture was wider and went deeper than the postmaterialist value shift in the wake of 1968.

61. Konrad H. Jarausch, *The Rush to German Unity* (New York, 1994), and Charles S. Maier, *Dissolution: The Crisis of Communism and the End of East Germany* (Princeton, 1997).

62. Konrad H. Jarausch, ed., *After Unity: Reconfiguring German Identities* (Providence, 1997), and Klaus J. Bade, *Europa in Bewegung: Migration vom späten 18. Jahrhundert bis zur Gegenwart* (Munich, 2002).

63. Padover, *Experiment in Germany*, 399–400, and Klemperer, *So sitze ich denn zwischen allen Stühlen*, 2:6 ff.

64. Fritz René Allemann, *Bonn ist nicht Weimar* (Cologne, 1956).

65. Kielmansegg, *Nach der Katastrophe*, 661 ff. See also Andrei S. Markovits and Simon Reich, *Das deutsche Dilemma: Die Berliner Republik zwischen Macht und Machtverzicht* (Berlin, 1998).

PART I

1. Gerhard L. Weinberg, *A World at Arms: A Global History of World War II* (Cambridge, 1994).

2. "Programmatische Richtlinien der Association of Free Germans vom Oktober 1942," in Clemens Vollnhals, ed., *Entnazifizierung: Politische Säuberung und Rehabilitierung in den vier Besatzungszonen 1945–1949* (Munich, 1991), 74–75, and Sigrid Undset, "Die Umerziehung der Deutschen," *NZ*, 10/25/1945.

3. U.S. Department of State, ed., *Foreign Relations of the United States, 1945* (Washington, DC, 1960), II: 1502–1505. See also Manfred Müller, *Die USA in Potsdam 1945: Die Deutschlandpolitik der USA auf der Potsdamer Konferenz der Großen Drei* (Berlin 1996), and Hans-Jürgen Küsters, *Der Integrationsfriede: Viermächteverhandlungen über die Friedensregelung mit Deutschland 1945–1990* (Munich, 2000).

4. Alliierte Militärbehörde, ed., "Merkblatt für zur Landarbeit entlassene deutsche Kriegsgefangene," reprinted in Heinz Döll, "Skizzen und Daten 1919/1949," MS, n.d., KA 5940/3.

5. The American concept of reeducation ("Americans Facing Shifts in Germany: Emphasis Now Being Placed in Re-education but Economic Crisis Makes This Hard," *NYT*, 6/24/1946) went well beyond just schools to encompass all of German culture.

6. "Der Anfang" and "Der 'Neuen Rheinischen' zum Geleit," *NRZ*, 7/15/1945. See also K. Hofmann, "Der Weg zum Wiederaufleben Deutschlands," *TR*, 5/25/1945, and Dicke, "Mit 'Vorwärts, vorwärts' war es nicht getan," KA 3228.

7. Karl Jaspers, "Antwort an Sigrid Undset," *NZ*, 11/4/1945. See also the foreword by

Werner Krauss, Alfred Weber, und Dolf Sternberger for their journal, *Die Wandlung* 1 (1945), 3–6.

8. Text of the Buchenwald manifesto, in Clemens Vollnhals, ed., *Entnazifizierung: Politische Säuberung und Rehabilitierung in den vier Besatzungszonen 1945–1949* (Munich, 1991), 81 ff. See Klemperer, *So sitze ich denn zwischen allen Stühlen*, 1:57 ff.

9. Hönicke, "'Know Your Enemy.'" In Potsdam, democratization was still a distant objective, for which the three "Ds" were to create the proper conditions. See chapter 5 in this volume.

10. Peter Graf Kielmansegg, "Konzeptionelle Überlegungen zur Geschichte des geteilten Deutschlands," *Potsdamer Bulletin für Zeithistorische Studien* no. 23–24 (2001), 7–15, and Konrad H. Jarausch, "Geschichte der Deutschen 'diesseits der Katastrophe': Anmerkungen zu einem großen Werk.," *Potsdamer Bulletin für Zeithistorische Studien* no. 23–24 (2001), 16–18.

CHAPTER 1

1. Dicke, "Mit 'Vorwärts, vorwärts,' war es nicht getan," KA 3228; Erwin Schmidt, "Vom Eisernen Vorhang zum Golden Gate," KA 4595, and Jering, *Überleben und Neubeginn*, 16 ff. See Michael Geyer, "Der Untergang," *TSp*, 2/29/2004.

2. Armin Nolzen, conference report, "Das Kriegsende 1945 in Deutschland," Potsdam 11/17–19/2000, H-Soz-u-Kult (http://hsozkult.geschichte.hu-berlin.de/), 1/23/2001.

3. "Kapitulationsforderungen an Deutschland," *NRZ*, 9/29/1945. Also Earl F. Ziemke, *The U.S. Army in the Occupation of Germany 1944–1946* (Washington, 1975), 291 ff.

4. Volker Berghahn, *Militarism: The History of an International Debate, 1861–1979* (New York, 1982); Ulrich Albrecht, "Der preussisch-deutsche Militarismus als Prototyp: Aspekte der internationalen wissenschaftlichen Diskussion," in Wolfram Wette, ed., *Militarismus in Deutschland 1871 bis 1945: Zeitgenössische Analysen und Kritik* (Münster, 1999), 41–46; and Ute Frevert, *A Nation in Barracks: Modern Germany, Military Conscription and Civil Society* (Oxford, 2004).

5. John Gimbel, *The American Occupation of Germany: Politics and the Military* (Stanford, 1968). See Edward N. Peterson, *The American Occupation of Germany: Retreat to Victory* (Detroit, 1978).

6. Gerhard Wettig, *Entmilitarisierung und Wiederbewaffnung in Deutschland 1943–1955* (Munich, 1967), and Militärgeschichtliches Forschungsamt, ed., *Anfänge westdeutscher Sicherheitspolitik 1945–1956*, 4 vols. (Munich, 1990).

7. Hans-Erich Volkmann, "Die innenpolitische Dimension Adenauerscher Sicherheitspolitik in der EVG-Phase," in Militärgeschichtliches Forschungsamt, ed., *Anfänge westdeutscher Sicherheitspolitik 1945–1956*, 4 vols. (Munich, 1990), 2:235–604. See also the praiseworthy exception of Klaus Naumann, ed., *Nachkrieg in Deutschland* (Hamburg, 2001), 9–26, as well as Thomas U. Berger, *Cultures of Antimilitarism: National Security in Germany and Japan* (Baltimore, 1998).

8. For example, Robert G. Moeller, *War Stories: The Search for a Usable Past in the Federal Republic of Germany* (Berkeley, 2001), and Richard Bessel and Dirk Schumann, eds., *Life after Death: Approaches to a Cultural and Social History of Europe during the 1940s and 1950s* (Cambridge, U.K.: 2003).

9. For an introduction, see David Clay Large, *Germans to the Front: West German Rearmament in the Adenauer Era* (Chapel Hill, 1996).

10. See "The War in Europe Is Ended; Surrender Is Unconditional" and "Germany's Act of Military Surrender," as well as the description in "Germans Played for Time in Reims," *NYT*, 5/9/1945.

11. "Appendix 'A' Draft Directive to the US UK USSR Commander-in-Chief: Elimination and Prohibition of Military Training in Germany," 9/19/1944, National Archives, RG 260, OMGUS Records, Control Council, Box 11, cited in Kathryn Nawyn, "Striking at the Roots of German Militarism" (M.A. Thesis, University of North Carolina at Chapel Hill, 2001). See also Wettig, *Entmilitarisierung und Wiederbewaffnung*, 28–74.

12. Drew Middleton, "Reich's Staff Seen as Uncurbed Peril," *NYT*, 5/10/1945, and Middleton, "Germans Start to Disband Army," *NYT*, 5/12/1945. For the emergence of the concept, see the influential study by the emigrant Alfred Vagts, *A History of Militarism: Romance and Realities of a Profession* (New York, 1937), 15, and "Zur Geschichte des deutschen Militarismus," *TR*, 11/10/1945.

13. "Surrender of Criminals Required" and "Oswiecim Killings Placed at 4,000,000," *NYT*, 5/8/1945. See "Wehrmacht unterstützte Massenermordungen," *TR*, 1/4/1946.

14. "US Soldiers Bitter at Brutality, Enemy Plainly Well Treated," *NYT*, 5/14/1945, and "Urges Executions of 1,500,00 Nazis," *NYT*, 5/23/1945.

15. "Boehme Says Troops Were Unbeaten," *NYT*, 5/8/1945; "Germans Yielding to Russian Army" and "Contacts Made with U-Boats Expected to Yield in US Ports," *NYT*, 5/12/1945. See also "Latvia Fighting Goes On,"*NYT*, 5/9/1945, and Lutz Graf Schwerin von Krosigk, *Memoiren* (Stuttgart, 1977), 247–248.

16. For an attempt at whitewashing, see "Für Deutschland wurden sie gefangen," *TR*, 8/13/1945. See also Arnold Krammer, *Nazi Prisoners of War in America* (New York, 1979).

17. OMGUS, "Report of the Military Governor" No. 1, August 1945, addendum to "Demobilization." See also "Nazi Prisoners Work in France," *NYT*, 5/18/1945, and "British to Free 1.500.00 Germans," *NYT*, 5/31/1945.

18. Dicke, "Mit 'Vorwärts, vorwärts' war es nicht getan"; 120; OMGUS, "Report of the Military Governor," no. 1, August 1945, Materials on "Disarmament," "Demobilization of German Air Force," and "Naval Disarmament and Demobilization." See "Germans Start to Disband Army," *NYT*, 5/12/1945, and "Befehl Nr. 3," *TR*, 6/18/1945.

19. "War Crime Trials Near, Wright Says," *NYT*, 6/1/1945; "German Staff to Be Kept in Exile," *NYT*, 6/22/1945; "US Counts Link Germans in a Conspiracy against the Laws of Civilization," *NYT*, 10/19/1945.

20. "Allies to Reject Doenitz Regime," *NYT*, 5/18/1945, and "Allies Take Control of Reich, Impose '37 Borders, Stern Terms," *NYT*, 6/6/1945. See also "Unterzeichnung der Deklaration über die Niederlage Deutschlands," *TR*, 6/5/1945, and OMGUS, "Report of the Military Governor," no. 1, August 1945, introduction.

21. Leopold Schwarzschild, "Occupy Germany for Fifty Years," *NYT*, 7/8/1945; "General Eisenhower an die NZ," *NZ*, 10/18/1945. For the sociocultural demilitarization, see also the forthcoming dissertation by Kathryn Nawyn (Chapel Hill, 2006).

22. "Big Four Issue Code to Bar German Rise," *NYT*, 9/26/1945, and Schwarzschild, "Occupy Germany for Fifty Years." See Wettig, *Entmilitarisierung und Wiederbewaffnung*, 102 ff.

23. "Befehl Nr. 12," *TR*, 7/26/1945; "Verbot von Uniformen und Abzeichen," *NRZ*, 9/15/1945; "Keine militärische Kleidung mehr," *NRZ*, 6/4/1946. See also Dicke, "Mit 'Vorwärts, vorwärts' war es nicht getan," 148, 150.

24. For a detailed narrative of the preparation of the individual prohibitions, see Nawyn, "Striking at the Roots," and Wettig, *Entmilitarisierung und Wiederbewaffnung*, 104 ff.

25. "Berlin Council Ends Militaristic Schools," *NYT*, 8/21/1945; "Entmilitarisierung des Sports," *NZ* , 12/21/1945; "Militaristischer Sport," *NZ*, 9/16/1946. See James Diehl, *The Thanks of the Fatherland: German Veterans after the Second World War* (Chapel Hill, 1993), 6 ff.

26. Wettig, *Entmilitarisierung und Wiederbewaffnung*, 104 ff.

27. "Grundsätze der Schulerziehung," *NRZ*, 8/15/1945; Richard Hartmann, "Entmilitarisierte Begriffe," *NZ*, 11/30/1945; "Welche Literatur ist verboten?" *NZ*, 5/31/1945; and "Allies to Wipe out All Pro-Nazi Books," *NYT*, 5/14/1946. See Wettig, *Entmilitarisierung und Wiederbewaffnung*, 105 ff.

28. "Ein Abrüstungsvertrag für Deutschland," *RP*, 5/1/1946, and "Prüfung der deutschen Rüstung beschlossen," *RP*, 5/15/1945. See also "Erklärung Achesons zur deutschen Abrüstung," *NZ*, 8/30/1946.

29. "Vier-Mächte Kontrolle der Abrüstung," *NZ*, 10/4/1945; "Entmilitarisierung wird geprüft," *NZ*, 1/6/1947; and "Sicherheitsamt für Westdeutschland," *NZ*, 1/20/1949. See also Wettig, *Entmilitarisierung und Wiederbewaffnung*, 153 ff. Because the economic dimension of demilitarization is closely connected to decartelization, they are treated together in chapter 3.

30. "Entmilitarisierung in der britischen Zone," *NZ*, 6/17/1946. For a similar judgment of Lucius Clay in 1948, see Jean Edward Smith, ed., *The Papers of General Lucius D. Clay: Germany 1945–1949* (Bloomington, 1974), 2:966.

31. "U-Boat Commander Says His Men Should Be Treated Like 'Brothers,'" *NYT*, 5/18/1945; "Surly Germans Still View Allies Victory as 'Fluke,'" *NYT*, 5/26/1945; "Germans Hail Own Army," *NYT*, 5/28/1945; and "'Conquest' Meaning Dawns on Germans," *NYT*, 5/15/1945.

32. Egon Schönmeier, "Der gestorbene Idealismus: Erinnerungen eines ehemaligen Ordensjunkers," KA 6235, 47–50. See also Ernst von Salomon, *Der Fragebogen* (Hamburg, 1951), 409 ff.

33. Schönmeier, "Der gestorbene Idealismus," 54 ff.; Friedrich Hermann Jung, "Mein Jahrhundert," MS, 1996, KA 6352/1, 89 ff.; Jürgen Reinhold, *Erinnerungen* (Essen, 2000), 215 ff.; Kurt Wrubel, "So war's! Erinnerungen," MS, 1996, KA 5573, 80 ff.; Manfred Clausen, "Lebenserinnerungen," KA 6451, 21–22.

34. Hans Herzog, "Eine bewegte Zeit," KA 6368, 64, 108, and Jering, *Überleben und Neubeginn*, 26 ff. Cf. Svenja Goltermann, "The Imagination of Disaster," in Paul Betts et al., eds., *Death in Modern Germany* (New York, 2006).

35. "Fraternizing Irks Reich's Ex-Soldier," *NYT*, 8/23/1945; Anonyma, *Eine Frau in Berlin*, 51. See Elizabeth D. Heineman, *What Difference Does a Husband Make?*

Women and Marital Status in Nazi and Postwar Germany (Berkeley, 1999), and Maria Höhn, GIs and Fräuleins: The German-American Encounter in 1950s West Germany (Chapel Hill, 2002).

36. Quotes from Hans Joachim Schröder, Die gestohlenen Jahre: Erzählgeschichten und Geschichtserzählung im Interview: Der Zweite Weltkrieg aus der Sicht ehemaliger Mannschaftssoldaten (Tübingen 1992), 284 ff. See also Robert G. Moeller, "War Stories: The Search for a Usable Past in the Federal Republic of Germany," AHR 101 (1996), 1008–1048, and Andreas Austilat, "Das Schweigen der Männer," TSp, 3/28/2004.

37. Helmut Kohl, Erinnerungen 1930–1982 (Munich, 2004), 45; "Als letzter Deutscher in Schlesien," RP, 1/3/1948, and "Im Herzen deutsch geblieben: Wiedersehen mit Ostpreußen," RP, 8/4/1948. See Moeller, War Stories, 51 ff., and Jörg Friedrich, Der Brand: Deutschland im Bombenkrieg 1940–1945 (Berlin, 2002).

38. Harro Müller, "Stalingrad und kein Ende: Zur Präsentation des Zweiten Weltkriegs in drei historischen Romanen," in Wolfgang Küttler et al., eds., Geschichtsdiskurs (Frankfurt, 1993–1999), 5:297–313.

39. Jürgen Thorwald, Die große Flucht: Es begann an der Weichsel: Das Ende an der Elbe (Stuttgart, 1991). See also Peter Fritzsche, "Volkstümliche Erinnerung und deutsche Identität nach dem Zweiten Weltkrieg," in Konrad H. Jarausch and Martin Sabrow, eds., Verletztes Gedächtnis: Erinnerungskultur und Zeitgeschichte im Konflikt (Frankfurt, 2002), 75–97.

40. Heide Fehrenbach, Cinema in Democratizing Germany: Reconstructing National Identity after Hitler (Chapel Hill, 1995), and Moeller, War Stories, 123 ff. See also Reinhold Wagnleitner, Coca-Colonization and the Cold War: The Cultural Mission of the United States in Austria after the Second World War (Chapel Hill, 1994), 222 ff.

41. "Wo ruhen unsere Kriegsgefallenen?" RP, 10/11/1949. See George L. Mosse, Fallen Soldiers: Reshaping the Memory of the World Wars (New York, 1990), and Jörg Echternkamp, "Von Opfern, Helden und Verbrechern: Anmerkungen zur Bedeutung des Zweiten Weltkriegs in den Erinnerungskulturen der Deutschen 1945–1955," in Jörg Hillmann and John Zimmerman, eds., Kriegsende in Deutschland (Munich, 2002), 301–316.

42. Otto Schulz to the U.S. news control office in Regensburg, 8/22/1947, KA 4707. See Thomas Kühne, "Zwischen Vernichtungskrieg und Freizeitgesellschaft: Die Veteranenkultur der Bundesrepublik 1945–1995," in Klaus Naumann, ed., Nachkrieg in Deutschland (Hamburg, 2001), 90–113.

43. "Soldaten vor Gericht," NZ, 12/7/1945; "Das OKW auf der Anklagebank," NZ, 1/7/1946; "Soldatische Ehrbegriffe," NZ, 4/8/1946; "Das Fazit von Nürnberg," NZ, 10/21/1946. See also "Das Urteil des hohen Gerichts," RP, 10/2/1946.

44. The persistence of militaristic thinking has received little scholarly attention. For a start, see Donald Abenheim, Bundeswehr und Tradition: Die Suche nach dem gültigen Erbe des deutschen Soldaten (Munich, 1989).

45. Jering, Überleben und Neubeginn, 26, 38.

46. "Zufriedenstellende Fortschritte in der Entwaffnung," RP, 6/15/1946, and Schmidt, "Vom Eisernen Vorhang," 31 ff.

47. "Gefährliche Denkmäler und Straßennamen," RP, 2/21/1948; Wolfgang Prüfer, "Berlin—Rädnitz und dreimal zurück, 1939–1949," printed as manuscript (1995),

KA 4379, 238. The other option was the French foreign legion, which during the early postwar period recruited many German soldiers who did not want to return to civilian life.

48. For example, Schönmeier, "Der gestorbene Idealismus."

49. "Die Reorganisation der deutschen Polizei," *RP*, 10/30/1945, and "Polizei: Diener des Volkes," *RP*, 4/20/1946. See "US-Zonenpolizei: Eine neue Sicherheittruppe," *NZ* 7/1/1946, and Thomas Lindenberger, *Volkspolizei: Herrschaftspraxis und öffentliche Ordnung im SED-Staat 1952–1968* (Colonge, 2003).

50. "Monatlich 15.000 Heimkehrer," *RP*, 9/14/1946; "Das Gefangenenlager als Akademie," *RP*, 11/13/1946; "Die USA fordern Freilassung deutscher Kriegsgefangener in Westeuropa," *RP*, 12/7/1946; "Heimkehrer aus Afrika and aus Rußland," *RP*, 10/22/1947; "Wie leben sie hinter Stacheldraht?" *RP*, 1/14/1948; "Wo blieben die zwei Millionen?" *RP*, 1/15/1949; "Gebt die Kriegsgefangenen frei," *RP*, 12/23/1949.

51. Dicke, "Mit 'Vorwärts, vorwärts' war es nicht getan," 140, and Frank Biess, "The Protracted War: Returning POWs and the Making of East and West German Citizens 1945–1955" (Ph.D. diss., Brown University at Providence, 2000).

52. "Das Problem der Kriegsinvaliden," *NZ*, 11/5/1946; "Kriegsbeschädigten muss geholfen werden," *RP*, 8/10/1949; Herzog, "Eine bewegte Zeit." See Diehl, *Thanks of the Fatherland*, 227 ff., and Birgit Schwelling, "Krieger in Nachkriegszeiten: Veteranenverbände als geschichtspolitische Akteure der frühen Bundesrepublik," in Claudia Fröhlich and Horst-Alfred Heinrich, eds., *Geschichtspolitik: Wer sind ihre Akteure, wer ihre Rezipienten?* (Stuttgart, 2004), 68–80.

53. Heinz Medelind, "Bonn unterscheidet sich von Weimar," *NZ*, 10/28/1948; Theodor Steltzer, "Laßt uns einen neuen Anfang finden!" *NZ*, 12/24/1948; "Das Recht auf Sicherheit," *NZ*, 2/22/1949, and "Besetzte Gebiete durch Pakt geschützt," *NZ*, 3/15/1949.

54. "Dienst am Frieden Deutschlands und der Welt," *RP*, 9/8/1949. Carl-Christoph Schweitzer et al., eds., *Politics and Government in the Federal Republic of Germany. Basic Documents* (Leamington Spa, 1984), 31 ff., and Wettig, *Entmilitarisierung*, 221 ff., 238 ff.

55. "Deutsche Miliz ohne deutsches Wissen?" *RP*, 11/27/1949; "Remilitarisierung: Eine Theorie," *NZ*, 12/14/1948; and "Wir brauchen keinen Krieg," *NZ*, 1/12/1949. See Norbert Wiggershaus, "Die Überlegungen für einen westdeutschen Verteidigungsbeitrag von 1948 bis 1950," in Militärgeschichtliches Forschungsamt, ed., *Entmilitarisierung und Aufrüstung in Mitteleuropa 1945–1956* (Herford, 1983), 93–115.

56. "Widerstand gegen jeden Angriff," *RP*, 3/19/1949; "Nicht unter deutschem Befehl," *RP*, 11/29/1949; "Keine deutsche Wehrmacht," *RP*, 12/5/1949; "Diskussion unzweckmäßig," *RP*, 12/7/1949; "Bundestag gegen Aufrüstung," *RP*, 12/17/1949.

57. "Bedenkliche deutsche 'Wiederaufrüstung,'" *RP*, 11/4/1949; "Militärischer 'Werkschutz' in der Ostzone," *RP*, 3/16/1949; "Deutsches Kanonenfutter in Griechenland," *RP*, 5/18/1949; "Volkspolizei soll Deutschland erobern," *RP*, 6/7/1949. See Helmut Bohn, *Die Aufrüstung der sowjetischen Besatzungszone Deutschlands* (Bonn, 1960).

58. Konrad Adenauer, *Erinnerungen* (Stuttgart 1965–1966), 1:341 ff, 442 ff, 513 ff, 2:163 ff, 270 ff, 328 ff. See Large, *Germans to the Front*, 31 ff.

59. Survey data from Anna J. Merritt and Richard L. Merritt, *Public Opinion in Occupied Germany: The OMGUS Surveys, 1945–1949* (Urbana, 1970), as well as Merritt and Merritt, *Public Opinion in Semisovereign Germany: The HICOG Surveys, 1949–1955* (Urbana, 1980). See Hans-Erich Volkmann, "Die innenpolitische Dimension Adenauerscher Sicherheitspolitik in der EVG-Phase," in Militärgeschichtliches Forschungsamt, ed., *Anfänge westdeutscher Sicherheitspolitik 1945–1956*, 4 vols. (Munich, 1990), 2:235–601.

60. "OKW-Urteil wird verkündet," *NZ*, 10/28/1948. Cf. Norbert Frei, *Adenauer's Germany and the Nazi Past: The Politics of Amnesty and Integration* (New York, 2002), 164.

61. Georg Meyer, "Zur inneren Entwicklung der Bundeswehr bis 1960/61," in Militärgeschichtliches Forschungsamt, ed., *Anfänge westdeutscher Sicherheitspolitik 1945–1956*, 4 vols. (Munich, 1990), 3:851–1162. See Douglas Peifer, *Three German Navies: Dissolution, Transition and New Beginnings, 1945–1960* (Gainesville, 2002).

62. Michael Geyer, "The Place of the Second World War in German Memory and History," *New German Critique*, no. 71 (1997), 5–40.

63. Little research has been done on this dimension.

64. "Der ideale Deutsche," *RP*, 11/24/1949. See Large, *Germans to the Front*, 265 ff. Cf. Detlef Bald, *Die Bundeswehr: Eine kritische Geschichte 1955–2005* (Munich, 2005).

65. Helga Haftendorn and Lothar Wilker, "Die Sicherheitspolitik der beiden deutschen Staaten," in Werner Weidenfeld and Hartmut Zimmermann, eds., *Deutschland-Handbuch: Eine doppelte Bilanz 1949–1989* (Bonn, 1989), 605–620.

66. Helga Haftendorn, *Sicherheit und Entspannung: Zur Außenpolitik der Bundesrepublik Deutschland 1955–1982*, 2nd ed. (Baden-Baden, 1986), as well as Dennis L. Bark and David R. Gress, *A History of West Germany* (Oxford, 1989), 1:366 ff., 386 ff., 399 ff.

67. "Einsatz im Machtspiel," *Der Spiegel* 55 (2001), no. 46, 34 ff. Chancellor Helmut Kohl even allowed the Federal Security Council to declare that the deployment of the Bundeswehr outside of NATO territory was unconstitutional.

68. Willy Brandt, *Erinnerungen* (Frankfurt, 1989), 239 ff. Werner Link, "Die Außenpolitik und internationale Einordnung der Bundesrepublik Deutschland," in Werner Weidenfeld and Hartmut Zimmermann, eds., *Deutschland-Handbuch: Eine doppelte Bilanz 1949–1989* (Bonn, 1989), 578 ff.

69. Helmut Hoffmann, ed., *Nachbelichtet* (Dresden, 1997), 135 ff.

70. Helmut Schmidt, *Menschen und Mächte* (Berlin, 1987). See Helga Haftendorn, *Sicherheit und Stabilität: Außenbeziehungen der Bundesrepublik zwischen Ölkrise und NATO-Doppelbeschluß* (Munich, 1986), and Jeffrey Herf, *War by Other Means: Soviet Power, West German Resistance and the Battle of the Euromissiles* (New York, 1991).

71. Detlef Bald, *Militär und Gesellschaft 1945–1990: Die Bundeswehr der Bonner Republik* (Baden-Baden, 1994), 89 ff., 113 ff. For a sensationalized account of the SED's penetration, see Hubertus Knabe, *Die unterwanderte Republik: Stasi im Westen* (Berlin, 1999).

72. Konrad H. Jarausch, "Nation ohne Staat: Von der Zweistaatlichkeit zur Vereinigung," *Praxis Geschichte* 13 (2000), no. 3, 6–12.

73. Erhart Neubert, *Geschichte der Opposition in der DDR 1949–1989* (Berlin, 1997), 597–600.

74. Christian Hacke, *Weltmacht wider Willen: Die Außenpolitik der Bundesrepublik Deutschland* (Frankfurt, 1993).

75. "Abmarsch in die Realität," *Der Spiegel* 55 (2001), no. 46, 22 ff. See also the cover page with a montage of a birch cross with a helmet as a pictorial reminder of those fallen in the spring of 1945.

76. U.S. Department of State, *Occupation of Germany: Policy and Progress, 1945–46* (Washington 1947), 2, and Harper to the deputy military governor, 10/16/1945, OMGUS, Records of Executive Office, Box 96, National Archives.

77. Letter to the editor of the *FR* on 9/21/1950; Schröder, *Die gestohlenen Jahre*, 911–920; Jering, *Überleben und Neubeginn*, 62; and Otto Nickel, "Der totale—der total zwecklose Krieg," *Die Wandlung* 2 (1947), 116–123. See also Richard Bessel and Dirk Schumann, eds., *Life after Death: Approaches to a Cultural and Social History of Europe during the 1940s and 1950s* (Cambridge, 2003), as well as the review by Michael Geyer on H-German (http://www.h-net.org/~german/), 10/21/2004.

78. Joyce M. Mushaben, *From Post-War to Post-Wall Generations: Changing Attitudes toward the National Question and NATO in the Federal Republic of Germany* (Boulder, 1998), 171 ff.

79. Berger, *Cultures of Antimilitarism*, x.

80. Hamburger Institut für Sozialforschung, ed., *Verbrechen der Wehrmacht: Dimensionen des Vernichtungskrieges 1941–1944*, exhibition catalogue (Hamburg, 2002), 3 ff. See Henryk M. Broder, "Die Arroganz der Demut," *Der Spiegel* 55 (2001), no. 47, 42 ff., and Klaus Naumann, *Der Krieg als Text: Das Jahr 1945 im kulturellen Gedächtnis der Presse* (Hamburg, 1998).

CHAPTER 2

1. Günter Esdor, "'Haben Sie das gehört: Es ist Krieg!!!' Die Geschichte meiner ersten 23 Lebensjahre in einer bewegten Zeit von 1933 bis 1955," MS, Bremen 1998, KA 6479. See also Stadtarchiv Karlsruhe, "Das Tagebuch der Marianne Kiefer," KA 6515/3.

2. Ruth-Kristin Rößler, ed., *Die Entnazifizierungspolitik der KPD/SED 1945–1948: Dokumente und Materialien* (Goldbach, 1994); "Mission and Objectives of the US Occupation," U.S. Army pamphlet from 1947, reprinted in von Plato and Leh, *"Ein unglaublicher Frühling,"* 98.

3. Planned radio address of Carl Goerdeler from 7/20/1944, and "Programmatische Richtlinien der Association of Free Germans aus dem Jahre 1943," in Vollnhals, ed., *Entnazifizierung*, 67 ff., 74 ff.

4. Hönicke, "'Know Your Enemy,'" 159 ff.

5. Hönicke, "'Know Your Enemy.' American Wartime Images of Germany 1942–1943," in Ragnhild Fiebig von Hase and Ursula Lehmkuhl, eds., *Enemy Images in American History* (Providence, 1997), 245 ff.

6. "Genosse Ehrenburg vereinfacht," *TR*, 5/15/1945; Raymond Daniell, "To Wipe out the Mark of the Beast," *NYT Magazine*, 5/13/1945. See also Michaela Hönicke, "'Prevent World War III': An Historiographical Appraisal of Morgenthau's Programme

for Germany," in Robert A. Garson and Stuart S. Kidd, eds., *The Roosevelt Years: New Perspectives on American History, 1933–1945* (Edinburgh, 1999), 155 ff.

7. Lutz Niethammer, *Die Mitläuferfabrik: Die Entnazifizierung am Beispiel Bayerns*, 2nd ed. (Berlin, 1982), 653–666, and Armin Schuster, *Die Entnazifizierung in Hessen 1945–1954: Vergangenheitspolitik in der Nachkriegszeit* (Wiesbaden, 1999). See also Michael Hayse, *Recasting German Elites: Higher Civil Servants, Business Leaders and Physicians in Hesse between Nazism and Democracy, 1945–1955* (New York, 2003).

8. Helga Welsh, *Revolutionärer Wandel auf Befehl? Entnazifizierungs- und Personalpolitik in Thüringen und Sachsen (1945–1948)* (Munich, 1989), as well as Olaf Kappelt, *Die Entnazifizierung in der SBZ sowie die Rolle und der Einfluß ehemaliger Nationalsozialisten in der DDR als ein soziologisches Phänomen* (Hamburg, 1997).

9. Karl-Heinz Füssl, *Die Umerziehung der Deutschen: Jugend und Schule unter den Siegermächten des Zweiten Weltkriegs 1945–1955*, 2nd ed. (Paderborn, 1995), and Caspar von Schrenck-Notzing, *Die Politik der amerikanischen Umerziehung* (Frankfurt, 1994). See also Brian Puaca, "Reform before the Reform" (Ph.D. diss., Chapel Hill, 2005).

10. Michael Lemke, *Einheit oder Sozialismus? Die Deutschlandpolitik der SED 1949–1961* (Cologne, 2001), and Peter Brandt, *Schwieriges Vaterland: Deutsche Einheit, nationales Selbstverständnis, soziale Emanzipation. Texte von 1980 bis heute*, 2nd ed. (Berlin, 2001).

11. Konrad H. Jarausch, "Die Postnationale Nation: Zum Identitätswandel der Deutschen, 1945–1995," *Historicum* 14 (Spring 1995), 30–35. See also Dieter Langewiesche, *Nation, Nationalismus, Nationalstaat in Deutschland und Europa* (Munich, 2000), 228.

12. Dicke, "Mit 'Vorwärts, vorwärts' war es nicht getan," KA 3228, 146–147.

13. "Hard Policy Fixed for Ruling Reich," *NYT*, 5/17/1945. See also the wording of JCS directive no. 1067 in Vollnhals, *Entnazifizierung*, 98 ff.

14. For a description, see von Salomon, *Der Fragebogen*, 535–633. See also Niethammer, *Mitläuferfabrik*, 663.

15. Figures under "Denazification during the First Month," in OMGUS, "Report of the Military Governor," no. 1, August 1945. See also Jering, *Überleben und Neubeginn*, 29, 36, and Christian Bauer and Rebekka Göpfert, *Die Richtie Boys: Deutsche Emigranten beim US-Geheimdienst* (Munich, 2005).

16. "Namen unter Abfallpapier: Wie die NS-Parteikartei gefunden wurde," *NZ*, 10/28/1945. For the Schäffer-Patton scandal as a crisis of denazification, see Niethammer, *Mitläuferfabrik*, 159 ff.

17. OMGUS, "Report of the Military Governor," September 1945, and Heinz Döll, "Skizzen und Daten 1919/1949," MS, n.d., KA 5940/3, 275.

18. "Frontbericht der Säuberung," *NZ*, 8/11/1945; "Deutsche Pläne zur Säuberung," *NZ*, 12/20/1945; "'Entlastete': Ein neuer Begriff," *NZ*, 1/17/1946; and "Das Gesetz zur politischen Säuberung," *NZ*, 3/8/1946. Cf. "Entnazifizierung," *TR*, 3/10/1946, and Vollnhals, *Entnazifizierung*, 16 ff.

19. Heinrich Schmitt, "Die Reinigung," *NZ*, 3/3/1946; "Die Durchführung des Säuberungsgesetzes," *NZ*, 4/11/1946; "Probleme um das Säuberungsgesetz," *NZ*, 5/19/1946; "Ernste Worte zum Säuberungsgesetz," *NZ*, 6/13/1946.

20. Denazification Board Decision of 10/1/1946; "Military Government of Germany: Fragebogen" of 3/18/1946; "40jähriges Betriebsjubiläum," *Heimatnachrichten aus Neustadt*, 8/11/1969, KA 3760; and Nedebock to Hüttenbach, 5/30/1948, KA 6457/1. See also Michael H. Kater, *The Nazi Party: A Social Profile of Members and Leaders* (Cambridge, MA, 1983), 72 ff.

21. British Control Office, "Einreihungsbescheid" of 6/6/1947; Military Government of Germany, Fragebogen, n.d.; and Letter on the Advisory Council for Theater from 4/8/1947. For depositions under oath, see Clearing Certificate of 9/1/1947, KA 6349. See also Juliane Freifrau von Bredow, *Leben in einer Zeitwende* (privately published, n. d.), 53 ff.; draft of a testimonial letter for Dr. Ing. A. H. vom 6/28/1946, KA 1099; and Jering, *Überleben und Neubeginn*, 200 ff.

22. "Säuberungsgesetz unverändert," *NZ*, 5/26/1946; "Reserviert für Nazis," *NZ*, 9/2/1946; and "Krise der politischen Säuberung," *NZ*, 11/7/1946. See also "Gedanken zum Entnazifizierungsgesetz," copy from *Die Tat*, early September 1946, KA 662; Hermann Freiherr von Lünigk to the Deutschen Entnazifizierungsvorstand Rhein-Berg Kreis, 10/1/1946, and sermon of Dr. H. Thielecke on Good Friday, 1947.

23. von Salomon, *Der Fragebogen*, 8 ff.

24. "Krise der politischen Säuberung," *NZ*, 11/7/1946; "Kontrolle der Säuberung verschärft," *NZ*, 12/2/1946; and "Eine Millionen amnestiert," *NZ*, 12/29/1946. See also Vollnhals, *Entnazifizierung*, 20 ff.

25. "Für Revision des Säuberungsgesetzes," *NZ*, 8/3/1947; "Keine Einigkeit über Säuberung," *NZ*, 9/25/1947; "Bizonaler Postdirektor verteidigt Pgs," *NZ*, 10/20/1947; "Neue Entlassungen von Internierten," *NZ*, 2/12/1948; and "Säuberung vor dem Abschluß," *NZ*, 5/6/1948.

26. "Nazi-Säuberung in den Verwaltungsstellen," *NRZ*, 10/3/1945; "Stand und Ergebnisse der Nazisäuberung," *NRZ*, 11/24/1945; "Säuberung der Wirtschaft und Verwaltung," *NRZ*, 3/20/1946; "Ein Jahr Entnazifizierung," *NRZ*, 4/15/1947.

27. "Reform der Entnazifizierung," *RP*, 12/6/1947; "Politische Säuberung verhindert," *RP*, 2/11/1948; "Neues Entnazifizierungsgesetz," *RP*, 4/30/1948; and Vollnhals, *Entnazifizierung*, 24 ff.

28. *Les boches* was a derogatory term applied to the Germans. It is the abbreviated form of *Alboche*, meaning *Allemand*, and was likely first used widely during the Franco-Prussian War of 1870–1871.

29. Edgar Wolfrum, *Französische Besatzungspolitik und deutsche Sozialdemokratie: Politische Neuansätze in der "vergessenen Zone" bis zur Bildung des Südweststaates 1945–1952* (Düsseldorf, 1991).

30. For a more thorough discussion of denazification in the Soviet Zone than can be offered here, see Timothy R. Vogt, *Denazification in Soviet-Occupied Germany: Brandenburg, 1945–1948* (Cambridge, MA, 2001).

31. Documents in Vollnhals, *Entnazifizierung*, 168 ff., and Rößler, *Die Entnazifizierungspolitik*, 64 ff. See also Welsh, *Revolutionärer Wandel*, 18 ff., 167 ff., and Damian van Melis, *Entnazifizierung in Mecklenburg-Vorpommern: Herrschaft und Verwaltung 1945–1948* (Munich, 1999), 321 ff.

32. "Achtung, getarnte Nazis," *ND*, 5/10/1946; "Eingliederung in den demokratischen Neuaufbau," *ND*, 9/6/1946; Wilhelm Pieck, "Der Sinn der Entnazifizierung," *ND*,

2/21/1947; and "Gerechte Entnazifizierung," *ND*, 8/27/1947. See also "Entnazifizierung in der Ostzone," *NZ*, 8/21/1947.

33. "Säuberung, nicht Entkapitalisierung," *NZ*, 2/21/1947, versus "Nazi-Eldorado in Bayern," *ND*, 8/20/1946. For the difficulty compiling statistics, see Vollnhals, *Entnazifizierung*, 224 ff., 332 ff.

34. Vollnhals, *Entnazifizierung*, 333, and Rolf Badstübner, *Vom "Reich" zum doppelten Deutschland: Gesellschaft und Politik im Umbruch* (Berlin, 1999), 254.

35. "Schlußstrich unter die NSDAP," *NRZ*, 10/17/1945; "Weiteres Nazikomplott zerschlagen," *NRZ*, 3/29/1947; "Liste Prominenter in Verwaltung und Industrie des Westens," *ND*, 12/3/1946. Vollnhals, *Entnazifizierung*, 55 ff. Cf. Annette Weinke, *Die Verfolgung von NS-Tätern im geteilten Deutschland: Vergangenheitsbewältigung 1949–1969* (Paderborn, 2002).

36. Vollnhals, *Entnazifizierung*, 55 ff. See also Steven P. Remy, *The Heidelberg Myth: The Nazification and Denazification of a German University* (Cambridge, MA, 2000).

37. Sigrid Undset, "Die Umerziehung der Deutschen," *NZ*, 10/25/1945, and Dolf Sternberger, "Der Begriff des Vaterlands," *Die Wandlung* 2 (1947), 494–511. See also "Der lange Weg," *NRZ*, 12/29/1945.

38. Dicke, "Mit 'Vorwärts, vorwärts' war es nicht getan," KA 3228, 124.

39. Matthiesen, "Tagebuch," KA 5958/1, 14; Jering *Überleben und Neubeginn*, 31. See also Boveri, *Tage des Überlebens* 195 ff.

40. "Die Auflösung Preußens," *ND*, 2/15/1947. These measures were based on a one-sided view of history that held Prussia responsible for both world wars.

41. Dicke, "Mit 'Vorwärts, vorwärts' war es nicht getan," 120; Agathe Matthiesen, "Tagebuch," KA 5958/1, 10 ff.; "Deutschlandlied 1949" from Hans Doerry, KA 6349.

42. "Die Zeitung der Roten Armee in Berlin," *TR*, 5/13/1945; Heinrich Graf von Einsiedel, *Tagebuch der Versuchung* (Frankfurt, 1985); "Der Anfang," *NRZ*, 7/15/1945; and Dwight D. Eisenhower, "Zum Geleit," *NZ*, 10/18/1945. See also Boveri, *Tage des Überlebens*, 223 ff.

43. Prüfer, "Berlin," KA 4379, 208, 214; Ruth Reimann-Möller, *Die Berichterstatterin von Burg: Schule–mein Leben* (Norderstedt, 2000), 2 ff., 216 ff.; and Hans Herzog, "Eine bewegte Zeit," KA 6368, 80. Cf. Kimberly Redding, *Growing up in Hitler's Shadow: Remembering Youth in Postwar Berlin* (Westport, 2004).

44. Arnold Döblin, "Die beiden deutschen Literaturen," *NZ*, 2/5/1946; "Gründung des Kulturbundes zur demokratischen Erneuerung Deutschlands," *Sonntag*, 7/3/1960; Prüfer, "Berlin," 230 ff.; and Dicke, "Mit 'Vorwärts, vorwärts' war es nicht getan," 149. See also Konrad H. Jarausch and Hannes Siegrist, eds., *Amerikanisierung und Sowjetisierung in Deutschland 1945–1970* (Frankfurt, 1997).

45. Dicke, "Mit 'Vorwärts, vorwärts' war es nicht getan," 121; Matthiesen, "Tagebuch," 8; Döll, "Skizzen und Daten," 255.

46. Jering, *Überleben und Neubeginn*, 28 f.; Dicke, "Mit 'Vorwärts, vorwärts' war es nicht getan," 145.

47. Dicke, "Mit 'Vorwärts, vorwärts' war es nicht getan," 126 ff.; Matthiesen, "Tagebuch," 10–11; and Reimann-Möller, *Die Berichterstatterin*, 221 ff. See also Bernhard Recker, "Die Geschichte der Familie Zita und Bernhard Recker," KA 6406, 13: "In the eyes of the victors, all Germans shared the guilt."

48. "Wortlaut der umstrittenen Rede," *NZ*, 2/21/1946, and the quote from a poem by someone called Hildebrandt with the title, "Hammerschlag!" in Matthiesen, "Tagebuch," 14–15.

49. Julius Ebbinghaus, "Patrioten und Nationalisten," *NZ*, 4/22/1946; Veit Valentin, "Antisemistismus und Nationalsozialismus," *NZ*, 1/17/1947; and Walter Goetz, "Nationalsozialistische Geschichtsfälschungen," *NZ*, 2/14/1947.

50. Paul Merker, "Der Irrweg einer Nation," *ND*, 9/7/1946; "Aussprache über die Friedensfrage," *NZ*, 2/14/1947; and Wilfried Loth, *Der Weg nach Europa: Geschichte der europäischen Integration 1939–1957*, 3rd ed. (Göttingen, 1996).

51. Jering, *Überleben und Neubeginn*, 37; Letter of recommendation from Heinrich Döll, August 1946, in Döll, "Skizzen und Daten," 275 ff. See also Erwin Schmidt, "Vom Eisernen Vorhang zum Golden Gate," KA 4595.

52. Johannes Dieter Steinert, "Drehscheibe Westdeutschland: Wanderungspolitik im Nachkriegsjahrzehnt," in Klaus J. Bade, ed., *Deutsche im Ausland—Fremde in Deutschland: Migration in Geschichte und Gegenwart* (Munich, 1992), 386–392; Fritz-Bauer-Institut, ed., *Überlebt und unterwegs: Jüdische Displaced Persons im Nachkriegsdeutschland* (Frankfurt, 1997); and Burghard Ciesla, "Das 'Project Paperclip': Deutsche Wissenschaftler und Techniker in den USA (1946 bis 1952)," in Jürgen Kocka, ed., *Historische DDR-Forschung: Aufsätze und Studien* (Berlin, 1993), 287–301.

53. Reinhold, *Erinnerungen*, 222; report by Dr. August Wolfgang Koberg on his expulsion from Czechoslovakia, n.d.; and Otto Schulz to Trix-Günter Stövhase, 8/25/1947, KA 4707. See also Elizabeth Heineman, "The Hour of the Woman: Memories of Germany's 'Crisis Years' and West German National Identity," *AHR* 101 (1996), 354–395.

54. Dicke, "Mit 'Vorwärts, vorwärts' war es nicht getan," 155 ff., and Herbert Puin, "Eine Familiengeschichte," KA 6175, 56 ff. See also Herzog, "Eine bewegte Zeit," 91 ff.

55. Michael L. Hughes, *Shouldering the Burden of Defeat: West Germany and the Reconstruction of Social Justice* (Chapel Hill, 1999). See also Hans Günter Hockerts, ed., *Drei Wege deutscher Sozialstaatlichkeit: NS-Diktatur, Bundesrepublik und DDR im Vergleich* (Munich, 1998).

56. Jering, *Überleben und Neubeginn*, 32 ff.; Boveri, *Tage des Überlebens*, 279 ff.; "Düsseldorfs Bekenntnis zur Reichseinheit," *NRZ*, 7/3/1946; "Es gibt nur einen Staat: Deutschland," *NRZ*, 7/10/1946; "Die Einheit der Arbeiterklasse ist die Einheit Deutschlands," *ND*, 4/23/1946; "Für die Wirtschaftseinheit Deutschlands," *ND*, 5/12/1946.

57. "Die deutschen Länder untrennbar verbunden," *RP*, 6/7/1947; "Protest gegen Gebietsabtretung," *RP*, 11/15/1947; "Nationalismus," *RP*, 4/30/1948; "Grenzberichtigungen?" *RP*, 12/2/1948. See also Kohl, *Erinnerungen*, 94 ff.

58. Schweitzer, *Politics and Government*, 373 ff.

59. For a more critical view see Hajo Funke, *Brandstifter: Deutschland zwischen Demokratie und völkischem Nationalismus* (Göttingen, 1993).

60. Elisabeth Noelle-Neumann and Renate Köcher, *Die verletzte Nation: Über den Versuch der Deutschen ihren Charakter zu ändern* (Stuttgart, 1987), versus Karl Dietrich

Bracher, *Wendezeiten der Geschichte: Historisch-politische Essays 1987–1992* (Stuttgart, 1992), 272–296, and Konrad H. Jarausch, "Die Postnationale Nation: Zum Identitätswandel der Deutschen 1945–1990," *Historicum* 14 (Spring, 1995), 30–35.

61. For example, see Kurt Georg Kiesinger, *Dunkle und helle Jahre: Erinnerungen 1904–1958* (Stuttgart, 1989), 331. See also Rainer Zitelmann et al., eds., *Westbindung: Chancen und Risiken für Deutschland* (Frankfurt, 1993).

62. Rainer Zitelmann, *Demokraten für Deutschland: Adenauers Gegner–Streiter für Deutschland,* (Frankfurt, 1993), and Leo Kreuz, *Das Kuratorium Unteilbares Deutschland: Aufbau, Programmatik, Wirkung* (Opladen, 1980).

63. See the controversy about Wilfried Loth, *Stalins ungeliebtes Kind: Warum Moskau die DDR nicht wollte* (Berlin, 1994). See also Lemke, *Einheit oder Sozialismus?*

64. Jarausch and Siegrist, *Amerikanisierung und Sowjetisierung.* See also Volker Berghahn, *Unternehmer und Politik in der Bundesrepublik* (Frankfurt, 1985), and Uta G. Poiger, *Jazz, Rock and Rebels: Cold War Politics and American Culture in a Divided Germany* (Berkeley, 2000).

65. Klemperer, *So sitze ich denn zwischen allen Stühlen,* and Michael Lemke, ed., *Sowjetisierung und Eigenständigkeit in der SBZ/DDR (1945–1953)* (Cologne, 1999).

66. Loth, *Der Weg nach Europa,* passim, and Wolfgang Schmale, *Geschichte Europas* (Vienna, 2000).

67. Jürgen Habermas, *Die nachholende Revolution: Kleine politische Schriften VII* (Frankfurt, 1990), 205–224. See also Harold James, *A German Identity: 1770–1990* (New York, 1990). Cf. Tina Pfeiffer and Norbert Seitz, "Was symbolisiert das Wunder von Bern?" *APuZ* B 54 (2004), 3–6.

68. Konrad H. Jarausch, "Die Krise des deutschen Bildungsbürgertums im ersten Drittel des 20. Jahrhunderts," in Werner Conze et al., eds., *Bildungsbürgertum im 19. Jahrhundert* (Stuttgart, 1989–1992), 4:180–205. See also Paul Noack, *Deutschland, deine Intellektuellen: Die Kunst, sich ins Abseits zu stellen* (Stuttgart, 1991), 16 ff.

69. Dirk van Laak, "Der Platz des Holocaust im deutschen Geschichtsbild," in Konrad H. Jarausch and Martin Sabrow, eds., *Die historische Meistererzählung: Deutungslinien der deutschen Nationalgeschichte nach 1945* (Göttingen, 2002), 163–193. See also Bernhard Giesen, *Kollektive Identität* (Frankfurt, 1999).

70. Ronald Inglehart, *The Silent Revolution: Changing Values and Political Styles among Western Publics* (Princeton, NJ, 1995).

71. Konrad H. Jarausch, "1968 and 1989: Caesuras, Comparisons, and Connections," in Carole Fink et al., eds., *1968: The World Transformed* (Cambridge, 1998), 461–477, and Wolfgang Kraushaar, *1968: Das Jahr, das alles verändert hat* (Munich, 1998).

72. Diverse texts in Dolf Sternberger, *Verfassungspatriotismus* (Frankfurt, 1990), 11–38, and Jürgen Habermas, *Eine Art Schadensabwicklung: Kleine politische Schriften VI* (Frankfurt, 1987), 161–178.

73. Hans Mommsen, "Aus Eins mach Zwei: Die Bi-Nationalisierung Rest-Deutschlands," *Die Zeit,* 2/6/1981. See also Winkler, *Der lange Weg,* 2:435 ff. A criticism of Winkler's position is offered by Jens Hacker in *Deutsche Irrtümer: Schönfärber und Helfershelfer der SED-Diktatur im Westen,* 3rd ed. (Berlin, 1992).

74. Noelle-Neumann and Köcher, *Die verletzte Nation,* passim; Heinz Niemann, *Meinungsforschung in der DDR: Die geheimen Berichte des Instituts für Meinungs-*

forschung an das Politbüro der SED (Cologne, 1993), 30 ff.; and Peter Förster, "Die deutsche Frage im Bewusstsein der Bevölkerung in beiden Teilen Deutschlands: Das Zusammengehörigkeitsgefühl der Deutschen. Einstellungen junger Menschen in der DDR," in Deutscher Bundestag, ed., *Materialien der Enquete-Kommission "Aufarbeitung von Geschichte und Folgen der SED-Diktatur in Deutschland,"* vol. 5: *Deutschlandpolitik, innerdeutsche Beziehungen und internationale Rahmenbedingungen,* part 2 (Frankfurt, 1995), 1212–1380.

75. Edgar Wolfrum, "Nationalstaat und Nationalfeiertag: Gedächtnis und Geschichtspolitik in Deutschland (und Österreich) 1871–1990," *Historicum* 14 (Spring, 1995), 26–29, and Wolfrum, *Geschichtspolitik in der Bundesrepublik Deutschland: Der Weg zur bundesrepublikanischen Erinnerung 1948–1990* (Darmstadt, 1999).

76. Timothy Garton Ash, *In Europe's Name: Germany and the Divided Continent* (New York, 1993); Heinrich Potthoff, ed., *Die "Koalition der Vernunft": Deutschlandpolitik in den 8oer Jahren* (Munich, 1995); and Konrad H. Jarausch, "Nation ohne Staat: Von der Zweistaatlichkeit zur Vereinigung," *Praxis Geschichte* 13 (2000), no. 3, 6–11.

77. Heiner Best, "Nationale Verbundenheit und Entfremdung im zweistaatlichen Deutschland," *Kölner Zeitschrift für Soziologie und Sozialpsychologie* 42 (1990), 1 ff.

78. Erhard Hexelschneider and Erhard John, *Kultur als einigendes Band? Eine Auseinandersetzung mit der These von der "einheitlichen deutschen Kulturnation"* (Berlin, 1984).

79. Mark Lehmstedt and Siegfried Lokatis, eds., *Das Loch in der Mauer: Der innerdeutsche Literaturaustausch* (Wiesbaden, 1997).

80. Jan Herman Brinks, *Die DDR-Geschichtswissenschaft auf dem Weg zur deutschen Einheit: Luther, Friedrich II, und Bismarck als Paradigmen politischen Wandels* (Frankfurt, 1992); Dieter Dowe, ed., *Die Ost- und Deutschlandpolitik der SPD in der Opposition 1982–1989: Papiere eines Kongresses der Friedrich-Ebert-Stiftung am 14. und 15. September 1993 in Bonn* (Bonn, 1993).

81. Gerhard Herdegen, "Perspektiven und Begrenzungen. Eine Bestandsaufnahme der öffentlichen Meinung zur deutschen Frage," *DA* 20 (1987), 1259–1272, and 21, 1987, 391–401.

82. Stefan Wolle, *Die heile Welt der Diktatur: Alltag und Herrschaft in der DDR 1971–1989* (Berlin, 1998), 63 ff.

83. See also Gebhard Schweigler, *Nationalbewußtsein in der BRD und der DDR*, 2nd ed. (Düsseldorf, 1974), versus Tilman Mayer, *Prinzip Nation: Dimensionen der nationalen Frage, dargestellt am Beispiel Deutschlands*, 2nd ed. (Opladen, 1987).

84. Klaus Harpprecht, "D-Formation der Geschichte," *SZ*, 9/29/2000, and Klaus Hettling, "Ein Picknick für die Freiheit," *FAZ*, 6/16/2001.

85. Eric J. Hobsbawm, "Eine gespaltene Welt geht ins 21. Jahrhundert," *FR*, 12/4/1999, versus Carsten Dippel, "Renaissance des Nationalstaates?" *PNN*, 8/2/1999.

86. Fritz René Allemann, *Bonn ist nicht Weimar*, edited by Xenia von Bahder (Frankfurt, 2000), 115–116, and Theodor Spitta, *Neuanfang auf Trümmern: Die Tagebücher des Bremer Bürgermeisters Theodor Spitta 1945–1947*, edited by Ursula Büttner and Angelika Voß-Louis (Munich, 1992), 100 ff.

87. Ricarda Huch, "Loslösung vom Nationalgefühl?" *TR*, 4/13/1946, and Heinrich August Winkler, "Nationalismus, Nationalstaat und nationale Frage in Deutschland seit

1945," in Winkler and Hartmut Kaelble, eds., *Nationalismus—Nationalitäten—Supranationalität* (Stuttgart, 1993), 12–33. See also Heiner Timmermann, ed., *Nationalismus in Europa nach 1945* (Berlin, 2001), 41 ff., 361 ff.

88. European Commission, ed., "The First Year of the New European Union," *Report on Standard Eurobarometer* 42 (1995), 66 ff. See also Klaus Wagenbach, "Distanz zum nationalen Erbe?" *Freitag*, 10/3/1997.

89. Richard Schröder, *Deutschland, schwierig Vaterland: Für eine neue politische Kultur* (Freiburg, 1993), and "Man muss nicht stolz sein, aber man darf," *TSp*, 3/21/2001. See also Heinrich-August Winkler, "Abschied von der Abweichung," *Die Zeit*, 12/14/2000.

CHAPTER 3

1. Spitta, *Neuanfang auf Trümmern*, 72 ff. See also Walter Rohland, *Bewegte Zeiten: Erinnerungen eines Eisenhüttenmannes* (Stuttgart, 1976), 107 ff.

2. "Aufruf der Kommunistischen Partei Deutschlands," *TR*, 6/14/1945. See also Fritz Schenk, *Das rote Wirtschaftswunder: Die zentrale Planwirtschaft als Machtmittel der SED-Politik* (Stuttgart-Degerloch, 1969).

3. "Baruch Urges Plan for Foe in Defeat," *NYT*, 6/1/1945; Drew Middleton, "US to Push Curb on Reich Industry," *NYT*, 7/1/1945; C. P. Trussell, "Reich War Power Declared Strong," *NYT*, 7/10/1945.

4. Howard S. Ellis, letter to the editor, *NYT*, 6/9/1945; Hanson W. Baldwin, "Occupation and Peace," *NYT*, 7/11/1945; and "European Reconstruction," *NYT*, 7/12/1945. See also Wilfried Mausbach, *Zwischen Morgenthau und Marshall: Das wirtschaftspolitische Deutschlandkonzept der USA, 1944–1947* (Düsseldorf, 1996).

5. Gimbel, *The American Occupation of Germany*.

6. Eberhard Schmidt, *Die verhinderte Neuordnung, 1945–1952: Zur Auseinandersetzung um die Demokratisierung der Wirtschaft in den westlichen Besatzungszonen und in der Bundesrepublik Deutschland* (Frankfurt, 1970).

7. Werner Abelshauser, *Wirtschaftsgeschichte der Bundesrepublik Deutschland 1945–1980* (Frankfurt, 1983), and Abelshauser, *Kulturkampf: Der deutsche Weg in die Neue Wirtschaft und die amerikanische Herausforderung* (Berlin, 2003).

8. Andre Steiner, *Von Plan zu Plan: Eine Wirtschaftsgeschichte der DDR* (Munich, 2004), and Peter Hübner, ed., *Eliten im Sozialismus: Beiträge zur Sozialgeschichte der DDR* (Cologne, 1999).

9. Jürgen Kocka, "Was heißt 'Zivilgesellschaft'?" *TSp*, 3/25/2002, and Helmut Fehr, "Die Macht der Symbole: Osteuropäische Einwirkungen auf den revolutionären Umbruch in der DDR," in Konrad H. Jarausch and Martin Sabrow, eds., *Weg in den Untergang: Der innere Zerfall der DDR* (Göttingen, 1999), 213–238.

10. For preliminary responses, see Berghahn, *Unternehmer und Politik*, and Anthony J. Nicholls, *Freedom with Responsibility: The Social Market Economy in Germany 1918–1963* (Oxford, 1994).

11. Joseph Borkin and Charles A. Welsh, *Germany's Master Plan* (New York, 1943); "Disarmed Germany Urged by Crowley: Bombed and Defeated County Has Power to Rebuild War Machine, Says FEA Chief," *NYT*, 6/27/1945, and "Reich War Power Declared Strong," *NYT*, 10/7/1945.

12. Meeting minutes of the Potsdam Conference on 8/2/1945. "Die deutsche Regelung," *Economist*, 8/11/1945. See also "Germany Stripped of Industry By Big Three: Economy Mapped," *NYT*, 8/3/1945.

13. "Die Wiederaufnahme der Industrie," *TR*, 8/5/1945; Rainer Karlsch and Jochen Laufer, eds., *Sowjetische Demontagen in Deutschland 1944–1949: Hintergründe, Ziele und Wirkungen* (Berlin, 2002), 19–78.

14. Report of the U.S. Military Governor, "Control of IG Farben," September 1945. See also "Hitlers Geldgeber und Brandstifter des Krieges," *TR*, 7/21/1945, and Rohland, *Bewegte Zeiten*, 115 ff.

15. Drew Middleton, "US to Push Curb on Reich Industry," *NYT*, 7/1/1945; Middleton, "US Seizes Farben Plants To Bar Reich Arms Output," *NYT*, 7/6/1945; "Forty Industrialists in Ruhr Arrested," *NYT*, 9/7/1945; "British Seize Ruhr Industrialists as Allies Investigate Six Trusts," *NYT*, 2/12/1945; and "Ruhr Trusteeship Urged as War Curb," *NYT*, 12/21/1945. See also Günter Henle, *Weggenosse des Jahrhunderts: Günter Henle als Diplomat, Industrieller, Politiker und Freund der Musik* (Stuttgart, 1968), 75 ff.

16. Gladwyn Hill, "Allies' Delay Bars Recovery in Ruhr," *NYT*, 8/6/1945, and Military Government of Germany, "Monthly Report of Military Governor US Zone 20, August 1945," section on "German Industry and Utilities." See also the descriptions in Spitta, *Neuanfang auf Trümmern*, 94 ff.

17. Drew Middleton, "German Industry's Fate Studied," *NYT*, 7/15/1945; Middleton, "More German Factories Will Run in US Zone Than First Implied," *NYT*, 7/21/1945; "Reduction of Germany to Agrarian State Branded Economic Absurdity by Experts," *NYT*, 8/29/1945; "Engineers Offer Plan for Germany," *NYT*, 9/27/1945. For further warnings, see Harley H. Kilgore, "Germany Is Not Yet Defeated," *NYT Magazine*, 8/12/1945.

18. Raymond Daniell, "US Experts Urge Reich Export Rise: Russia Suspicious," *NYT*, 10/8/1945; Anthony H. Leviero, "Smash IG Farben Empire, Eisenhower Advises Allies," *NYT*, 10/21/1945; Raymond Daniell, "US Agents Clash on Reich Cartels," *NYT*, 11/18/1945.

19. "12 Punkte für Deutschland," *NZ*, 12/14/1945; "Stahlproduktion und Zukunft," *NZ*, 1/28/1946; "Neuplanung der deutschen Industrie," *NZ*, 4/1/1946. See also "Plan für Reparationen und den Nachkriegsstand der deutschen Wirtschaft entsprechend den Beschlüssen der Berliner Konferenz," *TR*, 3/28/1946.

20. "Der Nürnberger Prozeß," *NZ*, 11/15/1945; "Erster Tag des Flick-Prozesses," *NZ*, 4/20/1947; "24 IG Direktoren vor Gericht," *NZ*, 5/5/1947; "Der dritte Industrieprozeß," *NZ*, 8/18/1947; "IG-Farben Urteil verkündet," *NZ*, 7/31/1948. See Rohland, *Bewegte Zeiten*, 134 ff., and Berghahn, *Unternehmer und Politik*, 40 ff.

21. See the detailed report of OMGUS on the "Activities of the Directorate of Economics, Allied Control Authority 1945–1949" of August 1949, Part 1, and Werner Plumpe, "Desintegration und Reintegration: Anpassungszwänge und Handlungsstrategien der Schwerindustrie des Ruhrgebietes in der Nachkriegszeit," in Eckart Schremmer, ed., *Wirtschaftliche und soziale Integration in historischer Sicht: Arbeitstagung der Gesellschaft für Sozial- und Wirtschaftsgeschichte in Marburg 1995* (Stuttgart, 1996), 290–303.

22. "Die Mitschuld der deutschen Bankwelt," *NZ*, 11/7/1946; "Erster Schritt zur Konzernentflechtung," *NZ*, 7/27/1947; Dr. Bauer, "Entflechtung der Stahlindustrie," *NZ*, 7/18/1947; "Auswirkungen der Entflechtung," *NZ*, 10/30/1948; "IG Farben Entflechtung steht bevor," *NZ*, 12/16/1948. See also Rohland, *Bewegte Zeiten*, 154 ff., and Günther Schulz, "Die Entflechtungsmaßnahmen und ihre wirtschaftliche Bedeutung," in Hans Pohl, ed., *Kartelle und Kartellgesetzgebung in Praxis und Rechtsprechung vom 19. Jahrhundert bis zur Gegenwart* (Stuttgart, 1985), 210–228.

23. "Einzelheiten des Antitrustgesetzes," *NZ*, 2/21/1947, and "Neues 12–Punktememorandum der USA zur Entkartellierung veröffentlicht," *NZ*, 7/1/1949. See also H. G. Schröter, "Kartellierung und Dekartellierung 1890–1990," *VSWG* 81 (1994), 457–493, and Robert Franklin Maddox, *The War within World War II: The United States and International Cartels* (Westport, 2001).

24. "Die Demontagen und ihr Echo," *NZ*, 10/20/1947, and "Demontage-Echo wird ruhiger," *NZ*, 10/24/1945. Berghahn, *Unternehmer und Politik*, 69 ff., and Nicholls, *Freedom with Responsibility*, 122 ff., underestimate the political impact of the protests against dismantling.

25. "USA gegen Demontage Einstellung," *NZ*, 2/12/1948; "Demontagestopp für 18 deutsche Werke," *RP*, 11/25/1949; and "Kein Zutritt für Demonteure," *RP*, 11/26/1949. See also Gustav Stolper, *Die deutsche Wirklichkeit: Ein Beitrag zum künftigen Frieden Europas* (Hamburg, 1949), 159 ff. Rather one-sided is Hanns D. Ahrens, *Demontage: Nachkriegspolitik der Alliierten* (Munich, 1982).

26. "Die Rolle des Grundbesitzes in Deutschland," *TR*, 9/14/1945; "Die deutschen Industriemagnaten müssen bestraft werden," *TR*, 10/20/1945; "Der Volksentscheid ist Sache jedes friedliebenden Menschen," *ND*, 6/14/1946; "Der Sieg des Volksentscheids," *ND*, 7/2/1946; "Wirtschaft des Friedens!" *ND*, 8/8/1946. See also Badstübner, *Vom "Reich" zum doppelten Deutschland*, 153 ff.

27. "Bodenreform-Zwischenbilanz in den Westzonen," *NZ*, 7/15/1946, and "Die umstrittene Bodenreform," *NZ*, 3/14/1947.

28. Burghard Ciesla, "Das 'Project Paperclip.' Deutsche Naturwissenschaftler und Techniker in den USA (1946 bis 1952)," in Jürgen Kocka, ed., *Historische DDR-Forschung: Aufsätze und Studien* (Berlin, 1993), 287–301.

29. "Die Hungersnot im Westen," *ND*, 11/22/1946, and "Das Entkartellisierungsgesetz," *ND*, 2/12/1947; "Entflechtung?" *ND*, 2/25/1947, versus "Die Parteien vor ernsten Entscheidungen," *NZ*, 6/24/1946.

30. "Zwei-Zonen-Pakt unterzeichnet," *NZ*, 12/6/1946; "Der neue Industrieplan," *NZ*, 9/1/1947; "12–Punkteplan für den Ruhrbergbau," *NZ*, 9/12/1947.

31. Karl Albrecht, *Das Menschliche hinter dem Wunder: 25 Jahre Mitwirkung am deutschen Wirtschaftsaufbau* (Düsseldorf, 1970), 16–17, and Rohland, *Bewegte Zeiten*, 143 ff. See also Wilhelm Röpke, *Die deutsche Frage*, 3rd ed. (Erlenbach-Zürich, 1948), 251 ff.

32. Spitta, *Neuanfang auf Trümmern*, 120 ff. See also Jering, *Überleben und Neubeginn*, 33 ff.

33. Dicke, "Mit 'Vorwärts, vorwärts' war es nicht getan," KA 3228, 122–144, 161. See the equally impressive descriptions in the diary of Agathe Matthiesen, KA 5958/1, 15 ff; and Döll, "Skizzen und Daten ," KA 5940/3, 265 ff; Kurt Wrubel, "So war's!

Erinnerungen," MS, 1996, KA 5573, 87 ff.; and Hans Herzog, "Eine bewegte Zeit,"MS, 1998, KA 6368, 87 ff.

34. Dicke, "Mit 'Vorwärts, vorwärts' war es nicht getan," 131–156.
35. See note 33 for sources. See also Schmidt, "Vom Eisernen Vorhang zum Golden Gate," KA 4595, 28 ff.
36. This perspective of hindsight is emphasized above all by economic historians. For example, see Werner Abelshauser, *Wirtschaft in Westdeutschland 1945–1948: Rekonstruktion und Wachstumsbedingungen in der amerikanischen und britischen Zone* (Stuttgart, 1975), 167 ff.
37. "Wiederaufbau einer Großstadt," *RP*, 3/23/1946; "Wirtschaftsfragen der Eisenverarbeitung," *RP*, 10/17/1945; "Kohle genug—aber keine Waggons," *RP*, 11/21/1945; "Gedanken und Anregungen zur Ernährungslage," *RP*, 4/3/1946; and "Deutsche Industrieproduktion 50–55 Prozent von 1938," *RP*, 3/30/1946. See also Paul Kleinewefers, *Jahrgang 1905: Ein Bericht* (Stuttgart, 1977).
38. "Der Anfang des deutschen Wiederaufstiegs," *NZ*, 1/30/1947; "Weitere Demontage der Untergang Deutschlands," *RP*, 12/11/1946; and "Kohle als Schlüssel zum Erfolg oder Mißerfolg," *RP*, 1/25/1947.
39. "Feierlicher Auftakt in Frankfurt," *NZ*, 6/27/1947; "Positive amerikanische Politik in Deutschland," *NZ*, 7/18/1947; and "Dr. Semler seines Amtes enthoben," *RP*, 1/28/1948. See Theodor Eschenburg, *Letzten Endes meine ich doch: Erinnerungen 1933–1999* (Berlin, 2000), 74 ff; Henle, *Weggenosse des Jahrhunderts*, 85 ff.; and Volker Hentschel, *Ludwig Erhard: Ein Politikerleben* (Munich, 1996).
40. Ludwig Erhard, *Gedanken aus fünf Jahrzehnten: Reden und Schriften*, edited by Karl Hohmann (Düsseldorf, 1988), 55 ff., 69 ff., 95 ff. See, for example, Albrecht, *Das Menschliche hinter dem Wunder*, 34 ff., and Nicholls, *Freedom with Responsibility*, 151 ff.
41. "Für ehrliche Arbeit wieder ehrliches Geld!" *RP*, 6/19/1948, and "Erste positive Wirkungen der Geldreform," *NZ*, 6/20/1948. See also Erhard, *Gedanken aus fünf Jahrzehnten*, 120 ff.; Albrecht, *Das Menschliche hinter dem Wunder*, 78 ff.; and Nicholls, *Freedom with Responsibility*, 178 ff.
42. Dicke, "Mit 'Vorwärts, vorwärts' war es nicht getan," 163 ff. and Herzog, "Eine bewegte Zeit," 111–112. See also Wrubel, "So war's!" 90, "Bankkonten werden 1:10 abgewertet" and "Eine Woche neues Geld," *NZ*, 6/27/1948, and "Die Stadt mit den zwei Währungen," *RP*, 6/26/1948.
43. Döll, "Skizzen und Daten," 277; Wrubel, "So war's!" 90–91; Reinhold, *Erinnerungen*, Teil VI; Herzog, "Eine bewegte Zeit," 111 ff.
44. Dicke, "Mit 'Vorwärts, vorwärts' war es nicht getan," 164–165; "Wie man mit der D-Mark lebt," *NZ*, 8/4/1958; Eschenburg, *Letzten Endes meine ich doch*, 125 ff.; and Nicholls, *Freedom with Responsibility*, 216 ff.
45. "Sieben Monate Wirtschaftsaufbau," *TR*, 1/4/1946; "Manifest an das deutsche Volk," *ND*, 4/23/1946; "Wirtschafts-Chaos abgewendet," *ND*, 7/2/1946; "Enteignung statt Entflechtung," *ND*, 3/23/1947; Walter Ulbricht, "Der Weg zum wirtschaftlichen Aufstieg," *ND*, 5/23/1947; and A. Ackermann, "Kann es für unser Volk wieder besser werden?" *ND*, 7/12/1947. See André Steiner, "Zwischen Länderpartikularismus und

Zentralismus: Zur Wirtschaftslenkung in der SBZ bis zur Bildung der Deutschen Wirtschaftskommission im Juni 1947," *APuZ* B 49–50 (1993), 32–39.

46. R. Reutter, "Erhöhung des Lebensstandards," *ND*, 2/12/1947. See also "Die Hungersnot im Westen," *ND*, 11/22/1946; "Liste prominenter Nazis in Verwaltung und Industrie des Westens," *ND*, 12/3/1946; and "Ostzone vorbildlich gegen Trusts," *ND*, 2/2/1947.

47. "Entschließung des 1. Hessischen Gewerkschaftskongress am 8/25/1946," 425–426; speech by Viktor Agartz at the first party congress of the SPD May 1946, 411–421; and "Ahlener Wirtschaftsprogramm der CDU für Nordrhein-Westfalen 2/3/1947," 428–430, all in in Klaus-Jörg Ruhl, ed., *Neubeginn und Restauration: Dokumente zur Vorgeschichte der Bundesrepublik Deutschland 1945–1949*, 3rd ed. (Munich, 1989). See also "CDU fordert Gemeinwirtschaft," *RP*, 2/3/1947.

48. "Die Berliner fordern Übereignung der Kriegsverbrecherbetriebe," *ND*, 9/19/1946; "Mehrheit in Großhessen," *ND*, 12/3/1946; and "Mißachtung des Volkswillens," *ND*, 3/2/1947. See also General Robertson to the zonal advisory council, 8/14–15/1946, 1:661 ff., and "Clay at the meeting of the state council of the US zone, 9/8–9/1947," 3:402 ff., both in in Bundesarchiv und Institut für Zeitgeschichte, ed., *Akten zur Vorgeschichte der Bundesrepublik Deutschland 1945–1949*, 5 vols. (Munich, 1976–1983). See Wolfgang Rudzio, "Die ausgebliebene Sozialisierung an Rhein und Ruhr: Zur Sozialisierungspolitik von Labour-Regierung und SPD 1945–1948," *AfS* 18 (1978), 1–39.

49. "Die Stadt mit den zwei Währungen," *RP*, 6/26/1948; "Nur noch Luftbrücke nach Berlin offen," *NZ*, 7/1/1948; and "Berliner behalten die Ruhe," *NZ*, 7/3/1948. See also Prüfer, "Berlin," KA 4379, 310 ff.

50. "Berlin wählte trotz Terror die Freiheit," *NZ*, 12/7/1948; "Überraschendes Echo der Berliner Wahl," *RP*, 12/8/1948; and Burghard Ciesla et al., eds., *Sterben für Berlin? Die Berliner Krisen 1948 und 1958* (Berlin, 2000).

51. Horst Heffle, "Leben in Deutschland: Ein Jahr nach dem Währungstausch," *NZ*, 6/18/1949, and "Dollarmilliarden aus Onkel Sams Tasche," *NZ*, 7/7/1949. See Nicholls, *Freedom with Responsibility*, 167 ff.

52. Alfred Müller-Armack, *Wirtschaftslenkung und Marktwirtschaft* (Munich, 1990), 6 ff. "The complete elimination of the market economy must be considered the deepest cause of our present problems."

53. "Vertrauen für Dr. Erhard," *RP*, 8/18/1948; "Geburtstag der D-Mark," *RP*, 6/20/1949; and "Soziale Marktwirtschaft," *RP*, 7/18/1949.

54. "Zur Kritik an der neuen Ordnung," 8/6/1948, and "Marktwirtschaft im Streit der Meinungen," 8/28/1948, both in Erhard, *Gedanken aus fünf Jahrzehnten*, 127 ff., 134 ff.

55. Erhard, *Gedanken aus fünf Jahrzehnten*, 217 ff., 346 ff., 393 ff., 450 ff. Gerold Ambrosius, "Die Entwicklung des Wettbewerbs als wirtschaftspolitisch relevante Norm und Ordnungsprinzip in Deutschland seit dem Ende des 19. Jahrhunderts," *Jahrbuch für Sozialwissenschaft* 32 (1981), 154–201.

56. Horst Satzky, "Grundsätze, Entstehung und Novellierungen des Gesetzes gegen Wettbewerbsbeschränkungen," in Pohl, *Kartelle und Kartellgesetzgebung*, 229–243; and Berghahn, *Unternehmer und Politik*, 152 ff.

57. Erhard, *Gedanken aus fünf Jahrzehnten*, 249 ff., 252 ff., 478 ff. See also Werner Plumpe, "'Wir sind wieder wer!': Konzept und Praxis der Sozialen Marktwirtschaft in der Rekonstruktionphase der westdeutschen Wirtschaft nach dem Zweiten Weltkrieg," in Marie-Luise Recker, ed., *Bilanz: 50 Jahre Bundesrepublik Deutschland* (St. Ingbert. 2001), 242 ff., and Nicholls, *Freedom with Responsibility*, 322 ff.

58. Döll, "Skizzen und Daten," 265 ff., and Bernhard Recker, "Die Geschichte der Familie Zita und Bernhard Recker," KA 6406, 34 ff.

59. Herbert Puin, "Eine Familiengeschichte," KA 6175, 61 ff., and Reinhold, *Erinnerungen*, 291 ff.

60. Numbers cited in Plumpe, "Wir sind wieder wer!" 240 ff. Cf. Christoph Buchheim, lecture comparing East and West German economic growth, Akademie für politische Bildung, Tutzing, April 23, 2005.

61. Wrubel, "So war's!" 90 ff.; Dicke, "Mit 'Vorwärts, vorwärts' war es nicht getan," 169–170.

62. Albrecht, *Das Menschliche hinter dem Wunder*, 109 ff., and Plumpe, "Wir sind wieder wer!" 270 ff. Cf. Abelshauser, *Wirtschaftsgeschichte der Bundesrepublik*, 32 ff.; Nicholls, *Freedom with Responsibility*, 390–397.

63. "Anteil der Eigentumsformen am Aufkommen des gesellschaftlichen Gesamtprodukts," *Statistisches Jahrbuch der DDR* (1973), 39; "Daten zum ersten Fünfjahrplan," in Hellmuth Kalus, *Wirtschaftszahlen aus der SBZ: Eine Zusammenstellung statistischer Daten zur wirtschaftlichen Entwicklung in der Sowjetischen Besatzungszone und in Ost-Berlin*, 2nd ed. (Bonn, 1960), 120.

64. Prüfer, "Berlin," 316 ff. Cf. Jeffrey Kopstein, *The Politics of Economic Decline in East Germany, 1945–1989* (Chapel Hill, 1997).

65. Albrecht Ritschl, "Aufstieg und Niedergang der Wirtschaft der DDR: Ein Zahlenbild 1945–1989," *Jahrbuch für Wirtschaftsgeschichte* 2 (1995), 11–46.

66. Friedrich-Wilhelm Henning, *Das industrialisierte Deutschland 1914 bis 1992*, 8th ed. (Paderborn, 1993), 194 ff.

67. Erhard, *Gedanken aus fünf Jahrzehnten*, 915 ff., 940 ff., 978 ff., 1021 ff. See Eschenburg, *Letzten Endes meine ich doch*, 172 ff.; Nicholls, *Freedom with Responsiblility*, 364 ff.

68. Karl Schiller, *Der Ökonom und die Gesellschaft: Das freiheitliche und soziale Element in der modernen Wirtschaftspolitik* (Stuttgart, 1964). See Manfred Kern, *Konzertierte Aktion als Versuch einer Verhaltensabstimmung zwischen Regierung und Interessenverbänden* (Cologne, 1973), and Abelshauser, *Wirtschaftsgeschichte der Bundesrepublik*, 111 ff.

69. André Steiner, *Die DDR-Wirtschaftsreform der sechziger Jahre: Konflikt zwischen Effizienz- und Machtkalkül* (Berlin, 1999), and Monika Kaiser, *Machtwechsel von Ulbricht zu Honecker: Funktionsmechanismen der SED-Diktatur in Konfliktsituationen 1962 bis 1972* (Berlin, 1997).

70. Henning, *Das industrialisierte Deutschland*, 238 ff.; Abelshauser, *Wirtschaftsgeschichte der Bundesrepublik*, 87 ff.

71. Schmidt, *Menschen und Mächte*. Cf. Jens Hohensee, *Der erste Ölpreisschock 1973/74: Die politischen und gesellschaftlichen Auswirkungen der arabischen Erdölpolitik auf die BRD und Westeuropa* (Stuttgart, 1996), and Harm G. Schröter, "Ölkrise und Reaktionen in der chemischen Industrie beider deutscher Staaten," in Johannes

Bähr and Diemar Petzina, eds., *Innovationsverhalten und Entwicklungsstrukturen* (Berlin, 1996), 109 ff.

72. André Steiner, "Zwischen Konsumversprechen und Innovationszwang: Zum wirtschaftlichen Niedergang der DDR," in Konrad H. Jarausch and Martin Sabrow, eds., *Weg in den Untergang: Der innere Zerfall der DDR* (Göttingen, 1999), 153–192.

73. Henning, *Das industrialisierte Deutschland*, 268 ff. Cf. Helmut Kohl, *Erinnerungen 1982–1990* (Munich, 2005), 50–54.

74. Röpke, *Die deutsche Frage*, passim; Erhard, *Gedanken aus fünf Jahrzehnten*, 55 ff.

75. Berghahn, *Unternehmer und Politik*, 9 ff. Cf. Götz Aly, *Hitlers Volksstaat: Raub, Rassenkrieg und Nationaler Sozialismus* (Frankfurt, 2005).

76. For a self-representation, see Institut für Wirtschaftsgeschichte der Akademie der Wissenschaft der DDR, ed., *Handbuch für Wirtschaftsgeschichte*, 2 vols. (Berlin, 1981), 2:862 ff.

77. Charles S. Maier, *Dissolution: The Crisis of Communism and the End of East Germany* (Princeton, 1997).

78. Oskar Schwarzer, "Der Lebensstandard in der SBZ/DDR 1945–1989," *Jahrbuch für Wirtschaftsgeschichte* 2 (1995), 119–146. See also Ina Merkel, *Utopie und Bedürfnis: Die Geschichte der Konsumkultur in der DDR* (Cologne, 1999).

79. Kielmansegg, *Nach der Katastrophe*, 456 ff., versus Werner Polster and Klaus Voy, "Von der politischen Regulierung zur Selbstregulierung der Märkte: Die Entwicklung von Wirtschafts- und Ordnungspolitik in der Bundesrepublik," in Klaus Voy et al., eds., *Marktwirtschaft und politische Regulierung* (Marburg, 1991), 169–226.

80. Gabriele Metzler, "Von Wundern und Krisen: Wirtschaft und Gesellschaft der Bundesrepublik seit 1949," in Eckart Conze and Gabriele Metzler, eds., *50 Jahre Bundesrepublik Deutschland: Daten und Diskussionen* (Stuttgart, 1999), 167 ff. See Konrad H. Jarausch and Michael Geyer, *Shattered Past: Reconstructing German Histories* (Princeton, 2003), 269–314.

CONCLUSION TO PART I

1. Sidney Shalett, "General Defends Rule of Germany," *NYT*, 2/15/1946; Stefan Heym, "But the Hitler Legend Isn't Dead," *NYT Magazine*, 1/20/1946; Edwin L. Sibert, "The German Mind: Our Greatest Problem," *NYT Magazine*, 2/17/1946.

2. "Grundlagen für den Wiederaufbau," *TR*, 8/13/1945; Tania Long, "US Teaching Plan in Germany Fails," *NYT*, 2/23/1946; and Raymond Daniell, "McNarney Report and Aides Differ," *NYT*, 3/1/1946.

3. Drew Middleton, "Pan-Germanism, Militarism Goals of Ex-Soldier Students at Erlangen," *NYT*, 2/18/1946, and Middleton, "Germans Return to Nationalism," *NYT*, 2/25/1946, versus Paul Herzog, "Cholm–Schädelstätte," *Die Wandlung* 1 (1946), 143–147, as well as Marie Louise Kaschnitz, "Von der Schuld," *Die Wandlung* 1 (1946), 431–448. See Wolfgang Schivelbusch, *Die Kultur der Niederlage: Der amerikanische Süden 1865, Frankreich 1871, Deutschland 1918* (Berlin, 2001), 9–49.

4. Drew Middleton, "Germans Unready for Political Life," *NYT*, 8/19/1945; Raymond Daniell, "Germans to Regain County, City Rule," *NYT*, 10/9/1945; Drew Middleton,

"Rebirth of Nazism Called Possibility,"*NYT*, 1/14/1946; C. L. Sulzberger, "US Psychology Fails in Germany," *NYT*, 3/26/1946.

5. Dana Adams Schmidt, "Land of Questions without Answers," *NYT Magazine*, 5/26/1946. See also Manuel Borutta and Nina Verheyen, "Akteure der Zivil- gesellschaft: Individuelle Ressourcen, soziale Basis, Vergesellschaftung," Berlin 4/18–20/2002, H-Soz-u-Kult, 7/18/2002.

6. "Das Wollen der antifaschistischen Einheitsfront," *TR*, 8/14/1945, and "Antifaschis- tische Parteien und Deutschlands Zukunft," *TR*, 8/15/1945.

7. The topic of the formal democratization is not included here, as it has already been treated elsewhere. For an introduction, see Winkler, *Der lange Weg*, vol. 2.

PART II

1. Axel Schildt and Arnold Sywottek, eds., *Modernisierung im Wiederaufbau: Die westdeutsche Gesellschaft der 50er Jahre* (Bonn, 1998).

2. Claus Leggewie, "1968 ist Geschichte,"*APuZ* B 22–23 (2001), 3–6. For an introduc- tion, see Detlef Siegfried, "Forschungsbericht 1968," H-Soz-u-Kult, 12/12/2002.

3. Schildt et al., *Dynamische Zeiten*, 13 ff. See Stefan Wolle, "Die versäumte Revolte: Die DDR und das Jahr 1968,"*APuZ* B 22–23 (2001), 37 ff.

4. Schildt et al., *Dynamische Zeiten*, 16 ff. See also the perspective of Hanna Schissler, ed., *The Miracle Years: A Cultural History of West Germany, 1945–1968* (Princeton, 2001), and Matthias Frese et al., eds., *Demokratisierung und gesellschaftlicher Aufbruch: Die sechziger Jahre als Wendezeit der Bundesrepublik* (Paderborn, 2003).

5. Elisabeth Peifer, "1968 in German Political Culture, 1967–1993: From Experience to Myth," (Ph.D. diss., University of North Carolina at Chapel Hill, 1997), and Fink et al., *1968*.

6. Ingrid Gilcher-Holtey, *Die 68er Bewegung: Deutschland, Westeuropa, USA* (Munich, 2001). See also Edgar Wolfrum, "'1968' in der gegenwärtigen deutschen Geschichts- politik," *APuZ* B 22–23 (2001), 28 ff.

7. Thomas Welskopp, "Identität ex negativo: Der 'deutsche Sonderweg' als Metaer- zählung in der bundesdeutschen Geschichtswissenschaft der siebziger und achtziger Jahre," in Konrad H. Jarausch and Martin Sabrow, eds., *Die historische Meistererzählung: Deutungslinien der deutschen Nationalgeschichte nach 1945* (Göttingen, 2002), 109.

8. Axel Schildt, "Materieller Wohlstand, pragmatische Politik, kulturelle Umbrüche: Die 60er Jahre in der Bundesrepublik," in Axel Schildt et al., eds., *Dynamische Zeiten: Die 60er Jahre in den beiden deutschen Gesellschaften* (Hamburg, 2000), 21– 53. See also Michael Geyer, "In Pursuit of Happiness: Consumption, Mass Cul- ture and Consumerism," in Konrad H. Jarausch and Michael Geyer, *Shattered Past: Reconstructing German Histories* (Princeton, 2003), 269 ff.

9. Jarausch and Siegrist, *Amerikanisierung und Sowjetisierung*.

10. Ronald Inglehart, *The Silent Revolution: Changing Values and Political Styles among Western Publics* (Princeton, 1977), and Andreas Rödder, *Die Bundesrepublik Deutschland 1969–1990* (Munich, 2004).

11. Anselm Doering-Manteuffel, *Wie westlich sind die Deutschen? Amerikanisierung und Westernisierung im 20. Jahrhundert* (Göttingen 1999). See also Ulrich Herbert, ed.,

Wandlungsprozesse in Westdeutschland: Belastung, Integration, Liberalisierung 1945–1980 (Göttingen, 2002), 7 ff.

12. Leggewie, "1968 ist Geschichte," 3, and Görtemaker, *Geschichte der Bundesrepublik,* 475 ff.

13. Arnd Bauerkämper, Konrad H. Jarausch, and Markus Payk, eds., *Demokratiewunder: Transatlantische Mittler und die kulturelle Öffnung Westdeutschlands 1945–1965* (Göttingen, 2005).

14. Axel Schildt, "Vor der Revolte: Die sechziger Jahre," *APuZ* B 22–23 (2001), 7–13.

15. Jarausch und Siegrist, *Amerikanisierung und Sowjetisierung.*

CHAPTER 4

1. Margret Boveri, *Amerika-Fibel für erwachsene Deutsche: Ein Versuch Unverstandenes zu erklären* (Freiburg, 1946). See Michaela Hönicke Moore, "Heimat und Fremde. Das Verhältnis zu Amerika im journalistischen Werk von Margret Boveri und Dolf Sternberger," in Arndt Bauerkämper et al., eds., *Demokratiewunder: Transatlantische Mittler und die kulturelle Öffnung Westdeutschlands 1945–1970* (Göttingen, 2005), 218–252.

2. Jering, *Überleben und Neubeginn,* 161. See Axel Schildt, *Zwischen Abendland und Amerika: Studien zur westdeutschen Ideenlandschaft der 50er Jahre* (Munich, 1999).

3. Jering, *Überleben und Neubeginn,* 161. Jessica C. E. Gienow-Hecht, "Shame on US? Academics, Cultural Transfer, and the Cold War: A Critical Review," *Diplomatic History* 24 (2000), 465–494, and Gienow-Hecht, *Transmission Impossible: American Journalism as Cultural Diplomacy in Postwar Germany, 1945–1955* (Baton Rouge, 1999).

4. Jarausch and Siegrist, *Amerikanisierung und Sowjetisierung.* For a defense of the former concept, see Richard Kuisel, "Commentary: Americanization for Historians," *Diplomatic History* 24 (2000), 509–515.

5. Axel Schildt, "Sind die Westdeutschen amerikanisiert worden? Zur zeitgeschichtlichen Erforschung kulturellen Transfers und seiner gesellschaftlichen Folgen nach dem Zweiten Weltkrieg," *APuZ* B 50 (2000), 3–10, and Bernd Greiner, "'Test the West': Über die 'Amerikanisierung' der Bundesrepublik Deutschland," in Heinz Bude und Bernd Greiner, eds., *Westbindungen: Amerika in der Bundesrepublik* (Hamburg, 1999), 16–54.

6. Doering-Manteuffel, *Wie westlich sind die Deutschen?* See Axel Schildt, *Ankunft im Westen: Ein Essay zur Erfolgsgeschichte der Bundesrepublik* (Frankfurt, 1999).

7. Ernst Birke and Rudolf Neumann, eds., *Die Sowjetisierung Ost-Mitteleuropas: Untersuchungen zu ihrem Ablauf in den einzelnen Ländern* (Frankfurt, 1959), and Hans Lemberg, ed., *Sowjetisches Modell und nationale Prägung, Kontinuität und Wandel in Ostmitteleuropa nach dem Zweiten Weltkrieg* (Marburg, 1991).

8. Lemke, *Sowjetisierung und Eigenständigkeit.*

9. Blackbourn and Eley, *The Peculiarities of German History,* as well as Gienow-Hecht, "Shame on US," 489 ff. See also Ruth Nattermann, "Die Imagination des Westens," report on a German-Italian conference on H-Soz-u-Kult (HSK), 10/29/2004.

10. Matthias Middell, "Europäische Geschichte oder *global history—master narratives* oder Fragmentierung? Fragen an die Leittexte der Zukunft," in Konrad H. Jarausch

and Martin Sabrow, eds., *Die historische Meistererzählung: Deutungslinien der deutschen Nationalgeschichte nach 1945* (Göttingen, 2002), 214 ff.

11. Winkler, *Der lange Weg*, and Wagnleitner, *Coca-Colonization*, xii ff.

12. Ronald J. Granieri, *The Ambivalent Alliance: Konrad Adenauer, the CDU/CSU, and the West 1949–1966* (New York, 2003).

13. Kaspar Maase, *BRAVO Amerika: Erkundungen zur Jugendkultur der Bundesrepublik in den fünfziger Jahren* (Hamburg, 1992). Cf. Agnes C. Muller, ed., *German Pop Culture: How 'American' Is It?* (Ann Arbor, 2004).

14. Prüfer, "Berlin," KA 4379, 195 ff.

15. Egon Schönmeier, "Der gestorbene Idealismus: Erinnerungen eines ehemaligen Ordensjunkers," KA 6235, and Philipp Gassert, *Amerika im Dritten Reich: Ideologie: Propaganda und Volksmeinung 1933–1945* (Stuttgart, 1997).

16. Boveri, *Tage des Überlebens*, 99 ff. See Naimark, *The Russians in Germany*.

17. "Das Tagebuch der Marianne Kiefer," Stadtarchiv Karlsruhe, KA 6515/3, 2.

18. Manfred Clausen, "Lebenserinnerung," KA 6451, 22.

19. "Das Tagebuch der Marianne Kiefer," 3; Hans Herzog, "Eine bewegte Zeit," KA 6368, 133. See Henke, *Die amerikanische Besetzung*, 187.

20. "Dicke Luft in Kaiserslautern," *SZ*, 7/2/1952; Esdor, "'Haben Sie das gehört," KA 6479, 208, 228 ff. Prüfer, "Berlin," 242 ff. See also Höhn, *GIs and Fräuleins*.

21. Esdor, "Haben Sie das gehört," 196–197, 208–209, 228 ff.

22. Esdor, "Haben Sie das gehört," 195–196, 221, 227, 239. See Petra Goedde, *GIs and Germans: Culture, Gender, and Foreign Relations, 1945–1949* (New Haven, 2003).

23. "Das Ludwigsburger Experiment," *RhM*, 9/30/1951; Hermann-Josef Rupieper, *Die Wurzeln der westdeutschen Nachkriegsdemokratie: Der amerikanische Beitrag 1945–1952* (Opladen, 1993), 156 ff.; and Höhn, *GIs and Fräuleins*, 60 ff. See Ilko-Sascha Kowalczuk and Stefan Wolle, *Roter Stern über Deutschland: Sowjetische Truppen in der DDR* (Berlin, 2001).

24. Theodor Bäuerle, "Deutsche Erzieher in den USA," *NZ*, 12/7/1948; "Deutsche Studenten erleben internationale Verständigung" and "Deutsche Gewerkschaftler und ihre amerikanischen Kollegen," *NZ*, 5/12/1949; and Walter Hallstein, "Ein aufgeschlagenes Buch von Jahrmillionen Erdgeschichte," *NZ*, 7/4/1949. See Oliver M. A. Schmidt, "A Civil Empire by Co-optation: German-American Exchange Programs as Cultural Diplomacy, 1945–1961" (Ph.D. diss., Harvard University, Boston 1999).

25. Annette Puckhaber, "German Student Exchange Programs in the United States 1946–1952," *GHI Bulletin* 30 (2002), 123–141. See Richard H. Pells, *Not Like Us: How Europeans Have Loved, Hated and Transformed American Culture since World War II* (New York, 1997), and Rupieper, *Die Wurzeln der Nachkriegsdemokratie*, 390 ff.

26. Alfons Söllner, "Normative Verwestlichung: Der Einfluß der Remigranten auf die politische Kultur der frühen Bundesrepublik," in Heinz Bude und Bernd Greiner, eds., *Westbindungen: Amerika in der Bundesrepublik* (Hamburg, 1999), 72–92. See also David Pike, *Deutsche Schriftsteller im sowjetischen Exil 1933–1945* (Frankfurt, 1981).

27. Alfred Kantorowicz, "Mein Platz ist in Deutschland," *NZ*, 2/14/1947, and Hans Mayer, *Der Turm von Babel: Erinnerungen an eine Deutsche Demokratische Republik*

(Frankfurt, 1991), 16 ff. See also Mario Keßler, *Exil und Nach-Exil: Vertriebene Intellektuelle im 20. Jahrhundert* (Hamburg, 2002), 33 ff.

28. Volker Berghahn, *America and the Intellectual Cold Wars in Europe: Shepard Stone between Philanthropy, Academy, and Diplomacy* (Princeton, 2001), and Uwe Soukup, *Ich bin nun mal Deutscher: Sebastian Haffner: Eine Biographie* (Berlin, 2001), 156 ff.

29. Manfred Heinemann, ed., *Umerziehung und Wiederaufbau: Die Bildungspolitik der Besatzungsmächte in Deutschland und Österreich* (Stuttgart, 1981), and David Pike, *The Politics of Culture in Soviet Occupied Germany, 1945–1949* (Stanford, 1992).

30. Smith, *The Papers of General Clay*, and Thomas A. Schwartz, *Die Atlantik-Brücke: John McCloy und das Nachkriegsdeutschland* (Frankfurt, 1992).

31. Höhn, *GIs and Fräuleins*, 52 ff.; Jan C. Behrends, "Gesellschaft für Deutsch-Sowjetische Freundschaft," in Wolfgang Benz, ed., *Deutschland unter alliierter Besatzung 1945–1949/55* (Berlin, 1999), 266 f.; and Ludger Kühnhardt, *Atlantik Brücke: Fünfzig Jahre deutsch-amerikanische Freundschaft* (Berlin, 2002).

32. Henle, *Weggenosse des Jahrhunderts*. See Christian Kleinschmidt, *Der produktive Blick: Wahrnehmung amerikanischer und japanischer Management- und Produktionsmethoden durch deutsche Unternehmer 1950–1985* (Berlin, 2002).

33. The schoolgirls' field trips to the Riviera were organized by my own mother, and I myself participated in the scout jamboree in England.

34. "Auf die zweite germanische Invasion," *Der Spiegel* 8 (1954), no. 18, 10, and "Unsere deutschen Helden," *Der Spiegel* 8, no. 30, 16 ff. See Rudy Koshar, *German Travel Cultures* (Oxford, 2000).

35. Evemarie Badstübner-Peters, "Ostdeutsche Sowjetunionerfahrungen: Ansichten über Eigenes und Fremdes in der Alltagsgeschichte der DDR," in Konrad H. Jarausch and Hannes Siegrist, eds., *Amerikanisierung und Sowjetisierung in Deutschland 1945–1970* (Frankfurt, 1997), 291–311.

36. Axel Schildt, *Moderne Zeiten: Freizeit, Massenmedien und 'Zeitgeist' in der Bundesrepublik der 50er Jahre* (Hamburg, 1995), 398 ff. See Greiner, "Test the West," 21.

37. "Wesen und Verantwortung der Demokratie," as well as "Dr. Schumacher sprach in Düsseldorf," *RP*, 3/27/1946. See "Es lebe der 28. Jahrestag der großen sowjetischen Oktoberrevolution" and Max Fechner, "Offener Brief an Dr. Schumacher," *TR*, 11/7/1945 and 3/23/1946.

38. Adenauer, *Erinnerungen*, 1:40–41; Richard Löwenthal, *Gesellschaftswandel und Kulturkrise: Zukunftsprobleme der westlichen Demokratien* (Frankfurt, 1979), 274. See Kurt Sontheimer, *So war Deutschland nie: Anmerkungen zur politischen Kultur der Bundesrepublik* (Munich, 1999), 34 ff.

39. Kohl, *Erinnerungen*, 56. See Schildt, *Zwischen Abendland und Amerika*, 24–38, and Vanessa Conze, "Das Europa der Deutschen: Ideen von Europa in Deutschland zwischen Reichstradition und Westorientierung (1920–1970)" (Ph.D. diss., University of Tübingen, 2001).

40. Carl Misch, "Wie die Amerikaner zu Deutschland stehen," *NZ*, 12/23/1946.

41. Adenauer *Erinnerungen*, 1:96–97; Schildt, *Zwischen Abendland und Amerika*, 167–195.

42. Klemperer, *So sitze ich denn zwischen allen Stühlen*, 1:57–58, 146–147, and "Das Wollen der antifaschistischen Einheitsfront," *TR*, 8/14/1945.

43. "Deutschland: Ein politisches Vakuum," *RP*, 7/16/1947, and von Salomon, *Der Fragebogen*.

44. "Tor der Hoffnung," *NZ*, 9/13/1946; "Europa berät Marshall Plan," *NZ*, 6/20/1947; "Berliner behalten die Ruhe," *NZ*, 3/7/1948. See Franz Josef Strauß, *Die Erinnerungen* (Berlin, 1989), 65, 80 ff.

45. "Hitler: Der Mörder der deutschen Arbeiterschaft," *TR*, 6/1/1945; "Generalissimus der Sowjetunion," *TR*, 6/29/1945; and "Grundlagen für den Wiederaufbau," *TR*, 8/13/1945. See Prüfer, "Berlin," 221–222; Anonyma, *Eine Frau in Berlin*, 164 ff.; and Naimark, *Die Russen in Deutschland*, 91 ff.

46. Schmidt, "Vom Eisernen Vorhang zum Golden Gate," KA 4595, 13 f., and Herzog, "Eine bewegte Zeit," KA 6368, 89.

47. "Das Memorandum der Gouverneure," *Die Welt*, 3/5/1949, and Edmund Spevack, "Amerikanische Einflüsse auf das Grundgesetz: Die Mitglieder des Parlamentarischen Rates und ihre Beziehungen zu den USA," in Heinz Bude und Bernd Greiner, eds., *Westbindungen: Amerika in der Bundesrepublik* (Hamburg, 1999), 55–71.

48. "Aufruf der Kommunistischen Partei Deutschlands," *TR*, 6/14/1945; "Manifest an das Deutsche Volk," *ND*, 4/23/1946; "Deutsche Einheit als nationale Aufgabe: Warum Verfassungsentwurf?" *ND*, 11/16/1946.

49. "Volksentscheid für die Einheit Deutschlands," *ND*, 3/2/1946; Otto Grotewohl, "Das ganze Deutschland muss es sein," *ND*, 6/8/1947; "Der Volkskongress tagt," *ND*, 12/7/1947.

50. "Die Bestimmungen des Besatzungsstatuts," *Telegraf*, 4/12/1949; "Kommuniqué der Außenminister: Schnelle Aufnahme in die Europa-Gemeinschaft," *Der Tag*, 5/8/1950; "Ende und Anfang," *DUD*, 3/6/1951.

51. "Deutschland und der Westen," *Englische Rundschau*, 9/14/1951; "Kernfrage Souveränität," *DUD*, 9/22/1951; "Schlusspunkt hinter Washingtoner Konferenz," *DUD*, 11/22/1951; "Versailles ist tot!" *DUD*, 11/23/1951; and "Adenauer erreicht Gleichberechtigung," *Der Tag*, 11/23/1951.

52. Paul Sehte, "Die europäische Lösung," *Die Zeit*, 3/29/1951; Bundesregierung, "Mitteilung an die Presse," 5/9/1950; and SPD-Vorstand, "Was weißt Du vom Schumanplan?" (Hannover, 1951).

53. "Bergarbeiter organisieren Kampf gegen Schuman-Plan," *TR*, 1/20/1952; Walter Hallstein "Wandlung und Entwicklung des Schuman-Planes," *Die Zeit*, 3/29/1951; "Alles oder nichts?" *DUD*, 6/28/1951; "Die Annahme des Schuman-Plans," *Das Parlament*, 1/16/1952; and "Die Erklärung der Bundesregierung," *NZZ*, 1/11/1952.

54. "Die verzögerte Antwort," *Deutsche Politik*, 12/28/1950; "Klare Fragen an Moskau," *DUD*, 2/26/1952; "Was will Rußland?" *DUD*, 3/7/1952. See Adenauer, *Erinnerungen*, 2:63 ff.

55. "Es gibt kein Gegenargument mehr," *National-Zeitung*, 3/14/1952; "Die Antwort der Westalliierten," *DUD*, 3/26/1952; "Einheit nur mit Hilfe des Westens," *Der Tag*, 4/4/1952; "Jetzt muß das deutsche Volk seinen Willen bekunden!" *TR*, 5/22/1952; and "Zuallererst die Wiedervereinigung," *FAZ*, 8/7/1952. See Rolf Steininger, *Eine vertane Chance: Die Stalin-Note vom 10. März 1952 und die Wiedervereinigung: Eine Studie auf der Grundlage unveröffentlichter britischer und amerikanischer Akten* (Berlin, 1985).

56. "Demonstrationen in Ostberlin," *DUD*, 6/17/1953; "Ostberlin im Aufruhr gegen SED-Regime," *NZ*, 6/17/1953; "Niederlage," *FAZ*, 6/17/1953; and "Der Volksaufstand in der deutschen Sowjetzone," *NZZ*, 6/18/1953.

57. "Schüsse in Ostberlin," *DUD*, 6/18/1953; "Der Zusammenbruch des faschistischen Abenteuers," *ND*, 6/19/1953; Herbert Wehner, "Die Unterdrückten siegen," *Berliner Stimmen*, 6/20/1953; and "Panzer zerstören 'Arbeiterpartei'-Mythos," *NZ*, 6/22/1953. See Christoph Kleßmann and Bernd Stöver, eds., *1953: Krisenjahr des Kalten Krieges in Europa* (Cologne, 1999).

58. "Volle Übereinstimmung mit Bonn," *DUD*, 2/6/1953; "Rundfunkansprache des Bundeskanzlers im Wortlaut," *Deutsche Kommentare*, 9/11/1954; "L'admission de l'Allemagne à l'OTAN est la solution la plus rapide et la plus simple," *Le Monde*, 9/12/1954; and Adenauer, *Erinnerungen*, 2:270 ff.

59. "Deutschlands Schicksal steht auf dem Spiel," *Vorwärts*, 1/21/1955; "Die westdeutsche Opposition gegen die Pariser Abkommen," *NZZ*, 1/31/1955; "Integrität des Grundgesetzes," *DUD*, 2/3/1955; "Verantwortungsbewusstes Ja," *DUD*, 2/7/1955; and Wilhelm Pieck, "Pariser Verträge ablehnen," *TR*, 2/24/1955.

60. "Das Ja des Bundestages," *DUD*, 2/27/1955; "Die Schlussdebatte im Bundestag," *FAZ*, 2/27/1955; "Bewegte Ratifikationsdebatte in Bonn," *NZZ*, 2/27/1955; and Hans Baumgarten "Mit dem Westen zum Osten," *FAZ*, 2/28/1955. See Adenauer, *Erinnerungen*, 2:384 ff., and Strauß, *Die Erinnerungen*, 261 ff.

61. "Neue europäische Phase," *DUD*, 6/7/1955; "Hoher Kaufpreis für Europa," *DZ*, n.d.; "Sechs europäische Länder als einheitliches Zollgebiet," *Das Parlament*, 3/2/1957; "Die Debatte über den Gemeinsamen Markt in Bonn," *NZZ*, 3/22/1957; and Wilfried Loth et al., eds., *Walter Hallstein: Der vergessene Europäer?* (Bonn, 1995).

62. "Ollenhauer vor dem Parteitag: Absage an überholte Doktrin," *Die Welt*, 11/14/1959; "Programmrevision der deutschen Sozialdemokratie," *NZZ*, 11/14/1959; Harri Crepuck, "Schwarz und kein Rot," *ND*, 11/16/1959; and "Leben in Freiheit ohne Ausbeutung," *Die Welt*, 11/19/1959. See also Detlef Lehnert, *Sozialdemokratie zwischen Protestbewegung und Regierungspartei 1848 bis 1983* (Frankfurt, 1983), 184 ff., and Hartmut Kaelble, "Deutschland, Frankreich, Nordamerika: Transfers, Imaginationen, Beziehungen," report on a conference on HSK, 10/28/2004.

63. Granieri, *The Ambivalent Alliance*, passim, and Bernd Stöver, *Die Befreiung vom Kommunismus: Amerikanische Liberation Policy im Kalten Krieg 1947–1991* (Cologne, 2002).

64. Maurice Couve de Murville, "Deutschland und Frankreich seit 1945," *Deutsche Rundschau* (June 1958). See also the forthcoming dissertation by Elana Passman on German-French rapprochement.

65. "Adenauer bei de Gaulle," *NZZ*, 9/15/1958, and "Paris spricht von vollem Erfolg in Kreuznach," *FAZ*, 11/27/1958. See Rudolf Morsey and Hans-Peter Schwarz, eds., *Adenauer: Teegespräche 1961–1963* (Berlin, 1992).

66. Frank Roy Willis, *France, Germany and the New Europe, 1945–1967*, 2nd ed. (London, 1968).

67. Strauß, *Die Erinnerungen*, 415 ff., and Granieri, *Ambivalent Alliance*, passim.

68. Aktionskomitee gegen die fünfte Kolonne, *Stalins Agenten als 'Friedenskämpfer'* (n.p. 1950); "Warnliste Nr. 3" and "Kommunistisch gesteuert und finanziert," *RP*,

6/28/1952; "Zweierlei Reaktion," *DUD*, 3/23/1953; and Carola Stern, "Ferngesteuerte Apparatschiks," *SBZArch* 4 (1953), 251–252.

69. Untersuchungsausschuss Freiheitlicher Juristen, *Kommunistische Infiltration und ihre Abwehr*, 6/4/1956; "Menschliche Offensive gegen die Sowjetisierung," *WdA*, 4/7/1955; "Vor einem Hungersommer," Eastern edition, *WdA*, May 1953; and "Alarmzeichen für Schwerhörige," *DUD*, 12/27/1955.

70. Dieter Vorsteher, "The Image of America as the Enemy in the former GDR," *Deutsches Historisches Museum Magazin* 3 (1993), no. 3; pamphlet: "Der Ami-Käfer fliegt in den kalten Krieg!" of 1950; Robert Havemann, "Der Mörder ist Adenauer!" *TR*, 5/14/1952; and "Polizeistaat Westdeutschland," *TR*, 7/21/1954.

71. "Wochenbericht des Arbeitskreises für deutsche Verständigung," *TR*, 1/7/1952; "Die ganze Welt horcht auf!" *TR*, 3/22/1952; and "Deutsche Verständigung für gerechten Friedensvertrag," *TR*, 7/14/1952.

72. "Der Unrechtsstaat," *ND*, 5/27/1956; Franz Thedieck, "Kommunistische Infiltration: Maßnahmen zu ihrer Bekämpfung," *Bulletin des Presse- und Informationsamtes der Bundesregierung*, (August, 1956); and Kampfgruppe gegen die Unmenschlichkeit, "Anziehungskraft des Westens und Ostens" (March, 1955).

73. Kaspar Maase, "'Amerikanisierung der Gesellschaft': Nationalisierende Deutung von Globalisierungsprozessen?" in Konrad H. Jarausch and Hannes Siegrist, eds., *Amerikanisierung und Sowjetisierung in Deutschland 1945–1970* (Frankfurt, 1997), 219–241. See also Alf Lüdtke, Inge Marssolek, and Adelheid von Saldern, eds., *Amerikanisierung: Traum und Alptraum im Deutschland des 20. Jahrhunderts* (Stuttgart, 1996); and Alexander Stephan, ed., *Americanization and Anti-Americanism: The German Encounter with American Culture after 1945* (New York. 2005).

74. F. Panter, "Die Kriegsgeneration ist nicht verloren," *Neuer Vorwärts*, 12/24/1953. Cf. Maase, *BRAVO Amerika*, 73 ff., and Richard Kuisel, *Seducing the French: The Dilemma of Americanization* (Berkeley, 1993).

75. "Amerika," *NZ*, 11/21/1946, and "Den Frieden noch gewinnen! Der amerikanische Militärgouverneuer zum zweiten Jahrestag des alliierten Sieges," *NZ*, 5/8/1947.

76. Jering, *Überleben und Neubeginn*, 162. Wagnleitner, *Coca-Colonization*, 128 ff., 166 ff.; and Schildt, *Zwischen Abendland und Amerika*, 167 ff.

77. Eschenburg, *Letzten Endes meine ich doch*, 189 ff., and Sontheimer, *So war Deutschland nie*, 67–86. See Matthias Stoffregen, *Kämpfen für ein demokratisches Deutschland: Emigranten zwischen Politik und Politikwissenschaft* (Opladen, 2002).

78. As introduction see Willi Paul Adams and Knut Krakau, eds., *Deutschland und Amerika: Perzeption und historische Realität* (Berlin, 1985).

79. "Das Problem der jungen Generation," *DUD*, 7/26/1956, and the Mäckie figures of the radio and tv magazine *Hör-Zu*. See also Sabrina P. Ramet and Gordana P. Crnkovic, "*Kazaam! Splat! Ploof!*" *The American Impact on European Popular Culture since 1945* (Lanham, MD, 2003).

80. Detlef K. Peukert, *Die Edelweißpiraten: Protestbewegungen jugendlicher Arbeiter im "Dritten Reich": Eine Dokumentation*, 3rd ed. (Cologne, 1988), and Michael H. Kater, *Different Drummers: Jazz in the Culture of Nazi Germany* (New York, 1992).

81. "Das Problem der jungen Generation," *DUD*, 7/26/1956; "Eine Jugend, die sich

langweilt," *DZ*, 9/15/1956; and "Deutsche Jugend in Ost und West," *Das ganze Deutschland*, 7/17/1954. See also Poiger, *Jazz, Rock and Rebels*.

82. Prüfer, "Berlin," 230. See Fehrenbach, *Cinema in Democratizing Germany*, and Wagnleitner, *Coca-Colonization*, 222 ff.

83. Ludwig Kroll, "Erweiterter Jugendschutz beim Film," *DUD*, 11/2/1956, and Elisabeth Pitz, "Sinnvoller Jugendschutz," *DUD*, 12/17/1956, versus "DGB-Jugend fordert mehr demokratische Aktivität," *DGB Nachrichten*, 5/9/1959.

84. Esdor, "Haben Sie das gehört," 196–197, 241. See Höhn, *GIs and Fräuleins*, 109 ff.

85. Uta G. Poiger, "Rock 'n' Roll, Kalter Krieg und deutsche Identität," in Konrad H. Jarausch and Hannes Siegrist, eds., *Amerikanisierung und Sowjetisierung in Deutschland 1945–1970* (Frankfurt, 1997), 275–289. See Michael Geyer, "In Pursuit of Happiness: Consumption, Mass Culture and Consumerism," in Konrad H. Jarausch and Michael Geyer, *Shattered Past: Reconstructing German Histories* (Princeton, 2003), 269 ff.

86. Michael Wildt, "Amerika auf Raten: Konsum und Teilzahlungskredit im Westdeutschland der fünfziger Jahre," in Heinz Bude und Bernd Greiner, eds., *Westbindungen: Amerika in der Bundesrepublik* (Hamburg, 1999). 202–230. See Schildt et al., *Dynamische Zeiten*.

87. Michael Wildt, *Am Beginn der "Konsumgesellschaft": Mangelerfahrung, Lebenshaltung, Wohlstandshoffnung in Westdeutschland in den fünfziger Jahren* (Hamburg, 1994), and Erica Carter, *How German Is She? Postwar West German Reconstruction and the Consuming Women* (Ann Arbor, 1997).

88. Wolfgang Kraushaar, "Transatlantische Protestkultur: Der zivile Ungehorsam als amerikanisches Exempel und bundesdeutsche Adaptation," in Heinz Bude und Bernd Greiner, eds., *Westbindungen: Amerika in der Bundesrepublik* (Hamburg, 1999), 257–284, and Uwe Timm, *Heißer Sommer: Roman* (Munich, 1974).

89. "Kultur des Sowjetlandes," *TR*, 5/27/1945. See Simone Barck, "Die fremden Freunde: Historische Wahrnehmungsweisen deutsch-sowjetischer Kulturbeziehungen in der SBZ in den Jahren 1948 und 1949," in Konrad H. Jarausch and Hannes Siegrist, eds., *Amerikanisierung und Sowjetisierung in Deutschland 1945–1970* (Frankfurt, 1997), 335–359.

90. Stephan Merl, "Sowjetisierung in der Welt des Konsums," in Konrad H. Jarausch and Hannes Siegrist, eds., *Amerikanisierung und Sowjetisierung in Deutschland 1945–1970* (Frankfurt, 1997), 167–194, as well as Heiner Stahl, "Hausherren von Morgen: Die Jugend- und Medienpolitik der SED und ihre Umsetzung bei Jugendstudio DT64 im Zeitraum von 1964 bis 1971," MA thesis (Potsdam, 2002).

91. For the ambivalent impressions of an East German spy, see Ingrid Deich, *Zwischen Dallas und New York: Wie ich die USA erlebte—Notizen eines Aufenthalts* (Leipzig, 1986).

92. Barbara Engels, *Gebrauchsanstieg der lexikalischen und semantischen Amerikanismen in zwei Jahrgängen der Welt 1954 und 1964* (Frankfurt, 1976). See also die *Bibliographie zu Anglizismen* of the Institut für deutsche Sprache (Mannheim, 2002).

93. Verein Deutsche Sprache, *Die VDS-Anglizismenliste* (http://www.vds-ev.de/denglisch/anglizismen/anglizismenliste.php, 2005), and Gerlinde Ulm Sanford, "Amerikanismen

in der deutschen Sprache der Gegenwart," *TRANS: Internetzeitschrift für Kulturwissen-schaften* 3 (1998), n.p. See Dieter E. Zimmer, *Deutsch und anders: Die Sprache im Modernisierungsfieber* (Reinbek, 1997).

94. DDR Informationsamt, *Ami go home!* (Berlin, 1950); Otto Schulz to Trix-Günter Stövhase, August 25, 1947, KA 4707. See Konrad H. Jarausch, "Mißverständnis Amerika: Antiamerikanismus als Projektion?" in Arndt Bauerkämper, Konrad H. Jarausch, and Markus Payk, eds., *Demokratiewunder: Transatlantische Mittler und die kulturelle Öffnung Westdeutschlands 1945–1970* (Göttingen, 2005).

95. Sebastian Knauer, *Lieben wir die USA? Was die Deutschen über die Amerikaner denken* (Hamburg, 1987), 15–31, 51 ff., 81 ff., 128 ff., 148 ff.

96. Hermann Bausinger, *Typisch deutsch: Wie deutsch sind die Deutschen?* (Munich, 2000).

97. Maase, *BRAVO Amerika*, 14–15; "'Die Sonderwege sind zu Ende,'" *Der Spiegel* 54 (2000), no. 40, 85 ff.

98. Leo L. Matthias, *Die Entdeckung Amerikas Anno 1953 oder das geordnete Chaos* (Hamburg 1953), and Rolf Winter, *Ami go home: Plädoyer für den Abschied von einem gewalttätigen Land* (Frankfurt, 1989).

99. Frei, *Adenauer's Germany and the Nazi Past*.

100. Axel Schildt, "Überlegungen zur Historisierung der Bundesrepublik," in Jarausch and Sabrow, eds., *Verletztes Gedächtnis*, 253–272.

101. Philipp Gassert, "Die Bundesrepublik, Europa und der Westen," in Jörg Baberowski et al., *Geschichte ist immer Gegenwart: Vier Thesen zur Zeitgeschichte* (Munich, 2001), 67–89.

102. Alfons Söllner, "Ernst Fraenkel und die Verwestlichung der politischen Kultur in der Bundesrepublik Deutschland," *Leviathan* 39 (2002), 151–154. Cf. also the other essays in Bauerkämper et al., *Demokratiewunder*, passim.

CHAPTER 5

1. OMGUS, "Report of the Military Governor" No. 1, August 1945, "Political Situa-tion," 1–2; Allemann, *Bonn ist nicht Weimar*, 101 ff.

2. Walter Dirks, *Die zweite Republik* (Frankfurt, 1947), 10, 23 ff., 112 ff.

3. *Das Potsdamer Abkommen* (Offenbach, 2001); "Germans Warned Fate Is Their Own" and "Statements by Eisenhower and Montgomery," *NYT*, 8/7/1945. See Felicitas Hentschke, *Demokratisierung als Ziel der amerikanischen Besatzungspolitik in Deutschland und Japan, 1943–1947* (Münster, 2001), 10 ff.

4. Recently, Wolther von Kieseritzky and Klaus-Peter Sick, eds., *Demokratie in Deutsch-land: Chancen und Gefährdungen im 19. und 20. Jahrhundert: Historische Essays* (Munich, 1999), and Margaret L. Anderson, *Practicing Democracy: Elections and Political Culture in Imperial Germany* (Princeton, 2000).

5. Josef Wirth et al., eds., *Das demokratische Deutschland: Grundsätze und Richtlinien für den deutschen Wiederaufbau im demokratischen, republikanischen, föderalis-tischen und genossenschaftlichen Sinne* (Bern, 1945); Hans Mommsen, "Von Weimar nach Bonn: Zum Demokratieverständnis der Deutschen," in Axel Schildt and Arnold Sywottek, eds., *Modernisierung im Wiederaufbau: Die westdeutsche Gesell-schaft der 50er Jahre* (Bonn, 1998), 745–758. See Winfried Becker and Rudolf Morsey,

eds., *Christliche Demokratie in Europa: Grundlagen und Entwicklungen seit dem 19. Jahrhundert* (Cologne, 1988), 189 ff.

6. Rudolf Agricola, "Ist Demokratie in Deutschland möglich?" *NZ*, 11/11/1945; "Wesen und Verantwortung der Demokratie," *RP*, 3/17/1946; and Kurt Schumacher, "Deutschland und die Demokratie," *NZ*, 3/27/1946.

7. *Haus der Geschichte der Bundesrepublik Deutschland*, www.hdg.de. See also Diethelm Prowe, "Demokratisierung nach 1945: Neubeginn, Amerikanisierung, konservative Integration," *Potsdamer Bulletin für Zeithistorische Studien*, no. 16 (1999), 5–13.

8. Richard Löwenthal and Hans-Peter Schwarz, eds., *Die zweite Republik: 25 Jahre Bundesrepublik Deutschland—eine Bilanz* (Stuttgart, 1974), 9 ff. See also Peter H. Merkl, ed., *The Federal Republic of Germany at Fifty: The End of a Century of Turmoil* (Houndmills, 1999).

9. Hans-Peter Schwarz, *Der Ort der Bundesrepublik in der deutschen Geschichte* (Opladen, 1996), versus Rainer A. Roth and Walter Seifert, eds., *Die zweite deutsche Demokratie: Ursprünge, Probleme, Perspektiven* (Cologne, 1990), 23 ff., and Ulrich Herbert, "Liberalisierung als Lernprozeß: Die Bundesrepublik in der deutschen Geschichte—eine Skizze," in Herbert, ed., *Wandlungsprozesse in Westdeutschland: Belastung, Integration, Liberalisierung 1945–1980* (Göttingen, 2002), 7 ff.

10. Klaus Schroeder, *Der SED-Staat: Partei, Staat und Gesellschaft 1949–1990* (Munich, 1998) versus Mählert, *Kleine Geschichte der DDR*.

11. Sigrid Meuschel, *Legitimation und Parteiherrschaft: Zum Paradox von Stabilität und Revolution in der DDR, 1945–1989* (Frankfurt, 1992), 23. See Gert-Joachim Glaeßner and Michal Reiman, eds., *Systemwechsel und Demokratisierung: Russland und Mittel-Osteuropa nach dem Zerfall der Sowjetunion* (Opladen, 1997).

12. "Die Demokratie im Werden," *TR*, 6/16/1945, and "Das Wollen der antifaschistischen Einheitsfront," *TR*, 8/14/1945.

13. "Aufruf der Kommunistischen Partei Deutschlands," *TR*, 6/14/1945, and declaration of Wilhelm Pieck, *TR*, 11/1/1945.

14. Theodor Schulze, "Ohne geeinigte Arbeiterschaft keine Demokratie," *TR*, 11/1/1946, and Max Kreuziger, "Ehrliche Demokratie—ehrliche Einheit," *TR*, 1/25/1946.

15. Kornejew, "Über die Demokratie," *TR*, 2/7/1946 and 2/10/1946, and Walden, "Die künftige deutsche Demokratie," *TR*, 3/10/1946.

16. Drew Middleton, "Germans Unready for Political Life," *NYT*, 8/19/1945; Jering, *Überleben und Neubeginn*, 44, 183; Lucius D. Clay, *Decision in Germany* (Westport, 1950), 84 ff; James K. Pollock, *Besatzung und Staatsaufbau nach 1945: Occupation Diary and Private Correspondence, 1945–1948*, edited by Ingrid Krüger Bulcke (Munich, 1994), 50 ff, 60 ff, 80 ff.

17. Dolf Sternberger, "Herrschaft der Freiheit," *Die Wandlung* 1 (1946), 556–571; Sternberger, "Über die Wahl, das Wählen und das Wahlverfahren," *Die Wandlung* 1 (1946), 923–942; Hans Habe, "Mißverstandene Demokratie," *NZ*, 3/6/1946; and Jering, *Überleben und Neubeginn*, 127.

18. Hans Modrow, *Ich wollte ein neues Deutschland* (Berlin, 1998).

19. Gustav H. Blanke, *Vom Nazismus zur Demokratisierung Deutschlands: Erinnerungen*

und Erfahrungen 1933 bis 1955 (Hamburg, 1999), 121–197. See also Friedrich Hermann Jung, "Mein Jahrhundert," MS, 1996, KA 6352/1, 98.

20. Paul Wandel, "Die Demokratisierung der deutschen Schule: Eine nationale Forderung," *TR*, 10/24/1945. See Ruth Reimann-Möller, "Die Berichterstatterin von Burg: Zwischen den Schatten von Königin Luise und Hermann Matern" (Norderstedt, 2000), KA 6122, 211 ff., 229 ff.

21. Tania Long, "US Teaching Plan in Germany Fails," *NYT*, 2/24/1946; "Bekenntnisschule als Probefall," *RP*, 4/20/1946; and "Der christliche Volkslehrer," *RP*, 11/20/1946. See Brian Puaca, "Learning Democracy: Education Reform in Postwar Germany, 1945–1065" (Ph.D. diss., Chapel Hill, 2005).

22. Alexander Dicke, "Mit 'Vorwärts, vorwärts' war es nicht getan," KA 3228, 161, and Einsiedel, *Tagebuch der Versuchung*, 231 ff.

23. Christina von Hodenberg, *Konsens und Krise: Eine Geschichte der westdeutschen Medienöffentlichkeit 1945–1973* (Göttingen, 2006), 101ff. See also Markus Payk, "Der Amerika Komplex," in Arndt Bauerkämper, Konrad H. Jarausch, and Markus Payk, eds., *Demokratiewunder: Transatlantische Mittler und die kulturelle Öffnung Westdeutschlands 1945–1970* (Göttingen, 2005).

24. Raymond Daniell, "Germans to Regain County, City Rule," *NYT*, 10/9/1945; Jering, *Überleben und Neubeginn*, 86l and Spitta, *Neuanfang auf Trümmern*.

25. Arthur Werner, "Unsere Stadt im ersten halben Jahr der antifaschistischen Ära," *TR*, 11/18/1945; "Militärgouverneur erläutert neues Verwaltungssystem," *RP*, 12/4/1945; and "Probefeld für demokratische Praxis," *FAZ*, 1/1/1953. In the Soviet Zone, anti-Fascist committees took over the distribution of food and living spaces. See Rebecca Boehling, "U.S. Military Occupation, Grass Roots Democracy, and Local German Government," in Jeffrey M. Diefendorf et al., eds., *American Policy and the Reconstruction of West Germany, 1945–1955* (Cambridge, 1993), 281–306.

26. "Eisenhower Bars Nazis from Polls," *NYT*, 10/13/1945; Daniel E. Rogers, *Politics after Hitler: The Western Allies and the German Party System* (Houndmills, 1995); and Andreas Malycha, ed., *Auf dem Weg zur SED: Die Sozialdemokratie und die Bildung einer Einheitspartei in den Ländern der SBZ* (Bonn, 1995).

27. "Wege zum demokratischen Staat," *NZ*, 12/14/1945, and "Die Selbstverwaltung auf einer neuen Stufe," *TR*, 7/5/1945.

28. Kathleen McLaughlin, "Schaeffer Is Ousted by Patton: Pro-Nazi Leaders Seized in Raid," *NYT*, 9/30/1945, and Henric L. Wuermeling, *Die weiße Liste: Umbruch der politischen Kultur in Deutschland 1945* (Frankfurt, 1981).

29. "Forderungen für föderalistische Staatsform werden formuliert," *NZ*, 4/23/1948; "Arbeit auf Herrnchiemsee beendet," *NZ*, 8/22/1948; and "Väter der Verfassung," *NZ*, 9/25/1948. See Edmund Spevack, *Allied Control and German Freedom: American Political and Ideological Influences on the Framing of the West German Basic Law* (Münster, 2001).

30. "Deutschlands Weg zum neuen Staat," *NZ*, 5/7/1949, and "Bonner Werk auf fester Basis," *NZ*, 5/10/1949. Heinrich Oberreuter, "Die Demokratiebegründung im westlichen Deutschland als Verpflichtung für die Zukunft," in Rainer A. Roth and Walter Seifert, eds., *Die zweite deutsche Demokratie: Ursprünge, Probleme, Perspektiven* (Cologne, 1990), 231–254.

31. SED, "Manifest an das deutsche Volk," *ND*, 4/23/1946, and Fred Oelßner, "Was ist Demokratie?" *ND*, 7/11/1946.

32. "Die SED die weitaus stärkste Partei," *ND*, 9/2/1946, and "Absolute Mehrheit der sozialistischen Einheitspartei," *ND*, 9/9/1946. In Saxony a majority was only achieved by declaring 212,000 votes invalid.

33. "Entwurf der Verfassung," *ND*, 11/15/1946, and Otto Grothewohl, "Warum Verfassungsentwurf," *ND*, 11/16/1946.

34. Karl Dietrich Bracher, "Die Kanzlerdemokratie," in Richard Löwenthal and Hans-Peter Schwarz, eds., *Die zweite Republik: 25 Jahre Bundesrepublik Deutschland—eine Bilanz* (Stuttgart, 1974), 179–202. See also Hans-Peter Schwarz, *Adenauer*, 2 vols. (Stuttgart, 1986, 1969), and Gordon A. Craig, *From Bismarck to Adenauer: Aspects of German Statecraft* (Baltimore, 1958).

35. Wolfgang Leonhard, *Die Revolution entläßt ihre Kinder*, 21st ed. (Cologne, 2003), and Thomas Klein, *"Für die Einheit und Reinheit der Partei": Die innerparteilichen Kontrollorgane der SED in der Ära Ulbricht* (Cologne, 2002).

36. Kurt Rabl, "Die Durchführung der Demokratisierungsbestimmungen des Potsdamer Protokolls in der SBZ Deutschlands und später in der DDR," *Zeitschrift für Politik* 17 (1970), 246 ff. See also the disillusionment of Klemperer, *So sitze ich denn zwischen allen Stühlen.*

37. Barbara Mettler, *Demokratisierung und Kalter Krieg: Zur amerikanischen Informations- und Rundfunkpolitik in Westdeutschland 1945–1949* (Berlin, 1975). See Berghahn, *America and the Intellectual Cold Wars.*

38. See Sean Forner, "Catastrophe and Democratic Renewal: German Left Intellectuals between East and West, 1945–1960" (Ph.D. diss., University of Chicago, 2005).

39. Otto Schulz to the American news control office, 8/22/1947, KA 4707; Egon Schönmeier, "Der gestorbene Idealismus: Erinnerungen eines ehemaligen Ordensjunkers," KA 6235, 53; Juliane Freiin von Bredow, *Leben in einer Zeitenwende*, n.d., 67 ff; Reinhold, *Erinnerungen*, 227–228; and Kohl, *Erinnerungen*, 70–71.

40. Eugen Kogon, *Die unvollendete Erneuerung. Deutschland im Kräftefeld 1945–1963: Politische und gesellschaftspolitische Aufsätze aus zwei Jahrzehnten*, edited by Hubert Habicht (Frankfurt, 1964), and Allemann, *Bonn ist nicht Weimar*, 106 ff. See also Arnold Sywottek, "Wege in die 50er Jahre," in Axel Schildt and Arnold Sywottek, eds., *Modernisierung im Wiederaufbau: Die westdeutsche Gesellschaft der 50er Jahre* (Bonn, 1998), 13–39.

41. James B. Conant, "The Foundations of a Democratic Future for Germany," *Department of State Bulletin*, 5/17/1954.

42. See the press release on "Die deutsche Demokratie zwischen innerer Lähmung und äußerer Hemmung," *Informationsdienst Presse und Rundfunk* (Bonn), 4/25/1950.

43. Gabriel A. Almond and Sidney Verba, *The Civic Culture: Political Attitudes and Democracy in Five Nations* (Princeton, 1963).

44. Kiesinger, *Dunkle und helle Jahre*, and Strauß, *Die Erinnerungen*. See Wilfried Loth, "Verschweigen und Überwinden: Versuch einer Bilanz," in Loth and Bernd-A. Rusinek, eds., *Verwandlungspolitik: NS-Eliten in der westdeutschen Nachkriegsgesellschaft* (Frankfurt, 1998), 353–360, and Frei, *Adenauer's Germany and the Nazi Past*, 42 ff.

45. Martin Niemöller, "Der Wortlaut der umstrittenen Rede," *NZ*, 2/21/1946; Gösta von Uexküll, "Drei Tage Demokratie zwischen Klostermauern," *Die Welt*, 6/30/1969; and Gustav W. Heinemann, *Einspruch: Ermutigung für entschiedene Demokraten*, edited by Diether Koch (Bonn, 1999), 58 ff., 65 ff.

46. See the forthcoming dissertation by Benjamin Pearson on the democratization of Protestantism, as well as the research by Klaus Große Kracht on lay Catholicism in the postwar period.

47. Jering, *Überleben und Neubeginn*, 172–173.

48. Richard Löwenthal, "Bonn und Weimar: Zwei deutsche Demokratien," in Heinrich August Winkler, ed., *Politische Weichenstellungen im Nachkriegsdeutschland 1945–1953* (Göttingen, 1979), 9–25. Because the integration of the SPD is assumed, its tension-filled relationship to the early Federal Republic has yet to be analyzed as a problem.

49. Otto Büsch and Peter Furth, *Rechtsradikalismus im Nachkriegsdeutschland: Studien über die "Sozialistische Reichspartei" (SRP)*, 2nd ed. (Cologne, 1967).

50. Spitta, *Neuanfang auf Trümmern*, 128.

51. Schroeder, *Der SED-Staat*.

52. Heinz Liepmann, "Politik? Um Himmels willen . . . ," *Die Welt*, 7/2/1960, and Henle, *Weggenosse des Jahrhunderts*, 137 ff. See Merritt and Merritt, *Public Opinion in Occupied Germany*, 103 ff., 167–168, 191–192, 210 ff., 294 ff., and Merritt and Merritt, *Public Opinion in Semisovereign Germany*, 65, 78, 85.

53. Of the numerous surveys, see in particular, Meritt and Merritt, *Public Opinion in Occupied Germany*, 87, 134, 139, 163, 172, 205, 218, 221, 241, and following. See also Merritt and Merritt, *Public Opinion in Semisovereign Germany*, 68, 79 ff., 103, 113, 144, 153, 167, 203, 213, 255.

54. Merritt and Merritt, *Public Opinion in Occupied Germany*, 286 ff., 294, 307, 314 ff.; Merritt and Merritt, *Public Opinion in Semisovereign Germany*, 57, 71, 75, 116, 123–124, 147, 150, 154, and following.

55. Prüfer, "Berlin," KA 4379, 317. See the research project by Michael Lemke on both parts of Berlin as "display windows" of their respective political systems.

56. Sebastian Haffner, "Rückfall in Schrecken und Willkür," *Der Spiegel* 16 (1962), no. 46, 53. See Hodenberg, *Konsens und Krise*, 293 ff.

57. Hermann Glaser, *Deutsche Kultur: Ein historischer Überblick von 1945 bis zur Gegenwart*, 2nd ed. (Bonn, 2000).

58. Konrad H. Jarausch, "Critical Memory and Civil Society: The Impact of the Sixties on German Debates about the Past," in Philipp Gassert and Alan Steinweis, eds., *Coping with the Nazi Past in 1960s West Germany* (Cambridge, 2006).

59. Jürgen Habermas, *Strukturwandel der Öffentlichkeit: Untersuchungen zu einer Kategorie der bürgerlichen Gesellschaft* (Neuwied, 1962), 8–9, 268 ff.

60. Ralf Dahrendorf, *Gesellschaft und Demokratie in Deutschland* (Munich, 1965), 23 ff., 480.

61. Likewise, Fritz Erler, *Demokratie in Deutschland* (Stuttgart, 1965). See Moritz Scheibe, "Auf der Suche nach der demokratischen Gesellschaft," in Ulrich Herbert, ed., *Wandlungsprozesse in Westdeutschland: Belastung, Integration, Liberalisierung 1945–1980* (Göttingen, 2002), 245–277.

62. Willy Strzelewicz, *Industrialisierung und Demokratisierung in der modernen Gesellschaft* (Hannover, 1971), 45 ff., 51 ff., 73 ff.

63. Fritz Vilmar, *Strategien der Demokratisierung*, 2 vols. (Darmstadt, 1973), 1:32–33. See also the exaggerated warning by Karl Jaspers, *Wohin treibt die Bundesrepublik? Tatsachen, Gefahren, Chancen* (Munich, 1966), 127 ff., 257 ff.

64. Bruno Heck, "Demokraten oder Demokratisierte? Eine notwendige Auseinandersetzung," *Die Politische Meinung* 128 (1969). See also Evangelischer Arbeitskreis der CDU, ed., *Unsere Demokratie zwischen gestern und morgen* (Bonn, 1969).

65. Wilhelm Hennis, *Demokratisierung: Zur Problematik eines Begriffs* (Cologne, 1970), 12–13, 32 ff., 39. See also Scheibe, "Auf der Suche nach der demokratischen Gesellschaft," 265 ff.

66. Erwin K. Scheuch, "Der Umbruch nach 1945 im Spiegel der Umfragen," in Uta Gerhardt and Ekkehard Mochmann, eds., *Gesellschaftlicher Umbruch 1945–1990: Re-Demokratisierung und Lebensverhältnisse* (Munich, 1992), 9–25, and Harold Hurwitz, *Demokratie und Antikommunismus in Berlin nach 1945*, 3 vols. (Cologne, 1983), 1:139 ff.

67. Merritt and Merritt, *Public Opinion in Occupied Germany*, 39 ff., 178–179, and Merritt and Merritt, *Public Opinion in Semisovereign Germany*, 43 ff., 61 ff.

68. Merritt and Merritt, *Public Opinion in Semisovereign Germany*, 107, 114, 118–119, 125, 135, 141, 148, 154, 158, 163, 189, 214, 219.

69. Merritt and Merritt, *Public Opinion in Semisovereign Germany*, 14, 16 ff., 138, 186 ff., 199, 223 ff., 242 ff.

70. Dirk Moses, "Das Pathos der Nüchternheit: Die Rolle der 45-er Generation im Prozess der Liberalisierung der Bundesrepublik," *FR*, 7/2/2002. See Mushaben, *From Post-War to Post-Wall Generations.*

71. Schönmeier, "Der gestorbene Idealismus," 53–54; von Bredow, *Leben in einer Zeitenwende*, 67; and Jung, *Mein Jahrhundert*, 157 f.

72. Konrad H. Jarausch, "Deutsche Einsichten und Amerikanische Einflüsse: Kulturelle Aspekte der Demokratisierung Westdeutschlands," in Arndt Bauerkämper et al., eds., *Demokratiewunder: Transatlantische Mittler und die kulturelle Öffnung Westdeutschlands 1945–1970* (Göttingen, 2005).

73. Margrit Gerste, "Der Freiheit treu: Hildegard Hamm-Brücher wird 80," *Die Zeit*, 5/18/2001. See also note 11 in this chapter.

74. Rüdiger Altmann, "Seht—welch ein Staat!" *Der Spiegel* 16 (1962), no. 46, 50; "CDU und FDP wollen in Bonn wieder gemeinsam regieren," *Die Welt*, 12/8/1962; Georg Schröder, "Kanzler für zehn Monate," *Die Welt*, 12/8/1962; and Alfred Rapp, "Keine Rückkehr nach Weimar," *FAZ*, 12/15/1962. See the press release of the annual report of 1963 of the federal government, 4/13/1964. See also Karl-Rudolf Korte, "Der Anfang vom Ende: Machtwechsel in Deutschland," in Gerhard Hirscher and Korte, eds., *Aufstieg und Fall von Regierungen: Machterwerb und Machterosionen in westlichen Demokratien* (Munich, 2001), 23–64.

75. "Wachsende Kritik am Regierungsstil," *Die Welt*, 4/9/1966; Immanuel Birnbaum, "Wechsel gehört zur Demokratie," *SZ*, 11/3/1966; Georg Schröder, "CDU sucht eine neue Politik unter einem anderen Kanzler," *Die Welt*, 11/1/1966; and "Erhard: Glücklos und verlassen," *Die Zeit*, 8/19/1966. See Klaus-Heinrich Dedring,

Adenauer, Erhard, Kiesinger: Die CDU als Regierungspartei 1961–1969 (Pfaffenweiler, 1989).

76. Theo Sommer, "Große Koalition oder nicht?" *Die Zeit*, 11/25/1966; Hans Schuster, "Das Wagnis der großen Koalition," *SZ*, 11/29/1966; "Studenten demonstrieren gegen die SPD," *Die Welt*, 11/29/1966; "Kartell der Angst," *Der Spiegel* 20 (1966), no. 50; and Golo Mann, "Was die Deutschen suchen," *Die Zeit*, 12/10/1966. Cf. Klaus Hildebrand, *Von Erhard zur Grossen Koalition, 1963–1969* (Stuttgart, 1984), and Philipp Gassert, *Kurt Georg Kiesinger, 1904–1988* (Munich, 2004).

77. "Brandt ergreift Initiative zum Regierungsbündnis," *FR*, 9/30/1969; Hans Schuster, "Das legitime Bündnis," *SZ*, 10/3/1969; Karl-Hermann Flack, "Spannende Demokratie," *FR*, 10/6/1969; and Jürgen Tern, "Der Bundeskanzler Willy Brandt" and "Brandts Stichwort: Erneuerung," *FAZ*, 10/22/1969 and 10/29/1969. See Arnulf Baring, *Machtwechsel: Die Ära Brandt-Scheel* (Stuttgart, 1982).

78. Text of the inaugural speech 10/29/1969; Brandt-Interview, "Für Bildungs- und Wissenschaftsreform," *SZ*, 10/22/1969; Brandt, "Wir wollen mehr Demokratie wagen," *FAZ*, 10/29/1969; and Rolf Zundel, "Ohne Schwüre, ohne Schnörkel," *Die Zeit*, 10/31/1969.

79. Bruno Deschamps, "Zurück zur Normalität," *FAZ*, 11/21/1972; "Bewährung im Alltag," *SZ*, 1/20/1973; Eduard Neumaier, "Noch einmal setzt die SPD auf Brandt," *Die Zeit*, 3/15/1974; "Reformansprüche zu hoch gesetzt," *FAZ*, 5/8/1974; and Wolfgang Wagner, "Kanzlerwechsel in Bonn," *DA* 29 (1974), 345 ff. See also Peter Merseburger, *Willy Brandt 1913–1992: Visionär und Realist* (Stuttgart, 2002).

80. Bruno Deschamps, "Kanzlerwechsel—Klimawechsel," *FAZ*, 5/9/1974; Hans Schuster, "Unter Helmut Schmidts Regie," *SZ*, 5/11/1974; Gerd Kübler, "Kanzler der Konzentration," *FR*, 5/13/1974; and Hans Schuster, "Nicht nur eine Schönwetter-Demokratie," *SZ*, 1/5/1974.

81. "Rücktrittserklärung von Ulbricht und erste Erklärung von Honecker," *ND*, 5/5/1971; "Ein ungewohnter Führungswechsel," *TSp*, 5/5/1971; Hans Schuster, "Ulbrichts Erbe," *SZ*, 5/5/1971; Walter Osten, "Wechsel ohne Wandel," *Die Welt*, 5/6/1971; and Dettmar Cramer, "Von Ulbricht zu Honecker," *DA*, 4 (1971), 449 f. See Kaiser, *Machtwechsel von Ulbricht zu Honecker*.

82. Report on "Innere Sicherheit," Bonn, 2/9/1967; Report on "Innere Sicherheit," Bonn, 4/2/1968. See Lutz Niethammer, *Angepaßter Faschismus: Politische Praxis der NPD* (Frankfurt, 1969).

83. "Korrekturen an der Demokratie," *TSp*, 10/8/1967; Marion Döhnhoff, "Krise der Demokratie? Resümee einer Diskussion," *Die Zeit*, 10/2/1968; and Gerhard Willke and Helmut Willke, "Die Forderung nach Demokratisierung von Staat und Gesellschaft," *APuZ* B 7 (1970), 33–62.

84. Michael Freund, "Ist der Mehrheit alles erlaubt? Über Fug und Unfug der Demokratisierung," *Die Welt*, 2/7/1970; Dieter Grosser, "Linksradikale Demokratiekritik und politische Bildung," *APuZ* B 22 (1970), 3 ff.; and Richard Löwenthal, "Demokratie und Leistung," *Berlin Stimme*, 2/26/1972.

85. "Mehr linke als rechte Radikale," *SZ*, 4/16/1971; "Die Demokratie muß verteidigt werden," *Das Parlament*, 7/24/1972; Hans Buchheim, "Zum Terror von links sind

Fragen nicht erlaubt," *FAZ*, 6/23/1972; and Peter Glotz, "Systemüberwindende Reformen?" *Berliner Stimme*, 4/14/1972.

86. "Radikalismus und Demokratie," *Das Parlament*, 7/1/1972; Hermann Rudolph, "Nach dem Radikalismus-Potential gefragt," *FAZ*, 7/18/1976; Gustav Heinemann, "Freiheitliche Gesellschaft ist Gesellschaft in Bewegung," *WdA*, 7/16/1976; and Robert Leicht, "Freiheit, die sie nicht meinen," *SZ*, 7/22/1976.

87. Fritz Ulrich Fack, "Wie jeder andere Prolli," *FAZ*, 9/1/1977; Ludolf Herrmann, "Die Republik hat sich verändert," *DZ*, 9/16/1977; Kurt Reumann, "Spiel mit den Spielregeln," *FAZ*, 9/13/1977; and Jürgen Heinrichsbauer, "So schließt sich der Kreis," *Der Arbeitgeber*, 11/10/1977.

88. Theo Sommer, "Vom Staate, den wir wollen," *Die Zeit*, 9/23/1977; Christian von Krockow, "Stabilisierung nach rückwärts?" *Die Zeit*, 9/30/1977; "Briefe zur Verteidigung der Republik," *FR*, 10/11/1977; and Walter Jens, "Der liberale Staat hat Millionen von Verteidigern," *Vorwärts*, 10/6/1977.

89. Ursula von Kardorff, "Mit rotem Punkt und schwarzen Fahnen," *SZ*, 12/31/1971; Hanno Beth, "Bürgerinitiativen," *FR*, 4/20/1972; "Heinemann ermutigt den Bürger," *SZ*, 2/12/1973; and Carl Gustav Ströhm, "Mißverständnis um den 'mündigen Bürger,'" *Die Welt*, 2/13/1973. See also Peter Cornelius Mayer-Tasch, "Bürgerprotest im demokratischen Rechtsstaat," in Hans Sarkowicz, ed., *Aufstände, Unruhen, Revolutionen: Zur Geschichte der Demokratie in Deutschland* (Frankfurt, 1998), 179–196.

90. "Polizei vertreibt die Umweltschützer von Wyhl," *FAZ*, 2/21/1975; "Reigen und Revolution," *Die Zeit*, 3/7/1975; "Ein Coup reizt zur Wut," *SZ*, 11/2/1976; and "Der Einsatz der Polizei war beeindruckend," *FR*, 12/21/1976.

91. Hans-Jochen Vogel, "Absage an die Gewalt," SPD-Pressedienst, 2/18/1977; Gerhard Schröder, "Plädoyer für einen anderen Umgang mit staatlicher Gewalt," SPD-Pressedienst, 2/25/1977; and "Erleichterung über den gewaltlosen Verlauf der Demonstrationen," *FAZ*, 2/21/1977.

92. Rainer Klose, "Die Grünen fühlen sich als Sieger von Hamburg," *SZ*, 2/25/1977; "Frage der Bundespartei droht 'die Grünen' zu spalten," *TSp*, 4/11/1978; "SPD kritisiert Parteienbürokratie," *SZ*, 1/9/1980; and Helmut Kerscher, "Der Bürger soll am Entscheidungsprozeß teilnehmen können," *SZ*, 6/12/1982. See Andrei S. Markovits and Philip S. Gorski, *Grün schlägt rot: Die deutsche Linke nach 1945* (Hamburg, 1997).

93. "Probleme und Aufgaben der Friedensbewegung," *links* (June, 1981); "Pazifismus '81: 'Selig sind die Friedfertigen,'" *Der Spiegel* 35 (1981), no. 25, 24 ff.; "Friedensbewegung: Beispiele aus diesen Tagen," *Unsere Zeit*, 8/28/1981; and Alfred Grosser, "'Diese Krise ist die schwerste,'" *Der Spiegel* 35 (1981), no. 43, 32 ff.

94. "Veranstalter der Bonner 'Friedens'-Kundgebung versichern: Wir fangen erst an," *FAZ*, 10/12/1981; "Demonstration der 250.000," pamphlet (October, 1981); "Einäugig für Frieden und Abrüstung," *NZZ*, 10/13/1981; "Der Zug der Aussteiger aus der Geschichte," *RhM*, 10/16/1981; "Das Bonner Schattenboxen und die wirkliche Politik," *links* (November, 1981); and "Die Sehnsucht nach Opposition setzt sich durch," *Morgenpost*, 10/11/1981.

95. "Koalitionsnöte in Bonn," *NZZ*, 4/4/1982; Theo Sommer, "Besser ein Ende mit

Schrecken," *Die Zeit,* 6/18/1982; and "Aus eine Parteikrise wird eine Staatskrise," *Deutsche Wochenzeitung,* 8/6/1981.

96. "Ich denke nicht an Rücktritt," *SZ,* 9/10/1982; "Ich persönlich will mich nicht länger demontieren lassen," *FR,* 9/18/1982; "Die Bonner Koalition ist zerbrochen," *FAZ,* 9/18/1982; and Peter Gillies, "Die Woche in der die Koalition zerbrach," *Die Welt,* 9/18/1982. See also Kohl, *Erinnerungen 1982–1990,* 17–25.

97. "Wenn die Parteien auseinanderstreben, ist die Politik stärker als das Grundgesetz," *FAZ,* 6/28/1982; Wilfried Hertz-Eichenrode, "Kohls Regierungsprogramm," *Die Welt,* 9/18/1982; Claus Genrich, "Ein Wechsel—zur Kontinuität," *FAZ,* 9/13/1982; and "Kohl: Bonns Politik bleibt berechenbar," *FR,* 5/10/1982. See also Andreas Rödder, *Die Bundesrepublik Deutschland 1969–1990* (Munich, 2004), 75–76.

98. Bruno Heck, "Autorität der Freiheit wegen," *RhM,* 8/26/1983; "Leben wir in einer anderen Republik?" *Der Spiegel* 39 (1985), no. 32, 30 ff.; Gunter Hofmann, "Weniger Demokratie wagen," *Die Zeit,* 3/2/1984; and Kurt H. Biedenkopf, "Der Volkssouverän überfordert den Staat," *RhM,* 5/11/1985.

99. Hans Heigert, "Erschöpfte Utopien," *SZ,* 8/4/1985; Wolfgang Bergsdorf, "Zehn Gründe für neue Zuversicht," *RhM,* 3/1/1986, versus Rudolf Wassermann, "Parteienfinanzierung und Karrieren der Politiker in der 'Zuschauer-Demokratie,'" *TSp,* 2/23/1986; and "Ein Riß geht durch das Land," *links* (January, 1982.)

100. "Dahrendorf beklagt 'gewisse Verrottung' der Politik," *SZ,* 10/9/1984, and Theo Sommer, "Kaufen und sich kaufen lassen," *Die Zeit,* 10/26/1984.

101. "Wallmann: Ich bitte um Verzeihung," *FAZ,* 12/3/1987; "Jenninger ruft zur Überwindung der 'Vertrauens- und Glaubwürdigkeitskrise' auf," *FAZ,* 1/2/1988; "Grass: Eine Republik der Skandale," *Die Welt,* 2/8/1988; and Ulrich von Alemann, "Affären und Skandale sind kein Privileg von Politik und Parteien," *FR,* 8/20/1988.

102. Hans Schuster, "Nicht nur Schönwetter-Demokratie," *SZ,* 1/5/1974, and Rörich, "Am Anfang war Adenauer," *FR,* 8/27/1983.

103. Anton Böhm, "Grundwerte und was nun?" *RhM,* 4/4/1980, and "Auf Freiheit, Gerechtigkeit und Solidarität berufen sich alle," *FR,* 2/28/1979.

104. "Hat der Bürger Anlaß zur Verdrossenheit?" and "Die politische Rolle der Bürgerinitiativen," *SZ,* 10/25/1978, and Hartmut von Hentig, "Die entmutigte Republik," *SZ,* 5/8/1980.

105. Eckhard Jesse, "Zerrbilder von einem demokratischen Land," *FAZ,* 10/7/1980, and "Die bayerische Bevölkerung ist am zufriedensten," *FAZ,* 9/4/1987.

106. "Ein Plädoyer für die Bonner Demokratie," *NZZ,* 2/15/1978; Hans Heigert, "Die Republik kommt in die Jahre," *FAZ,* 5/26/1979; and "Ein Porträt der Bundesrepublik Deutschland," *NZZ,* 5/26/1989. See also Max Kaase and Günther Schmid, eds., *Eine lernende Demokratie: 50 Jahre Bundesrepublik Deutschland* (Berlin, 1999).

107. Theodor Adorno, "Was ist deutsch?" *FAZ,* 4/2/1966, and Berghahn, *America and the Intellectual Cold Wars,* passim. See the essays in Bauerkämper et al., eds., *Demokratiewunder,* passim.

108. Claudia Fröhlich und Michael Kohlstruck, eds., *Engagierte Demokraten: Vergangenheitspolitik in kritischer Absicht* (Münster, 1999), 7–30. For an example, see Sarkowicz, *Aufstände, Unruhen, Revolutionen.*

109. Eckhard Jesse, *Die Demokratie der Bundesrepublik Deutschland*, 8th ed. (Baden-Baden, 1997), 49 ff.
110. Ralf Dahrendorf, "Wanken die Fundamente unseres Staates?" *Die Zeit*, 8/12/1977; Peter Graf Kielmansegg, "Ist streitbare Demokratie möglich?" *FAZ*, 7/2/1979; and J. Kurt Klein, "Vergangenheit darf uns nicht unfähig machen für Aufgaben der Zukunft," *Die Welt*, 4/8/1988. See Kurt Sontheimer, *Grundzüge des politischen Systems der Bundesrepublik Deutschland* (Bonn, 2000).
111. Ernst Köhler, "Einige zaghafte Einwände gegen linken Pessimismus," *Die Zeit*, 8/31/1979, and Heinz Eyrich, "Wohin führt der Weg der Bürgerinitiativen?" *DUD*, 7/27/1977. See also Grosser, "Linksradikale Demokratiekritik," 9 ff.; Hermann Rudolph, "Wissen wir wer wir sind?" *FAZ*, 6/23/1979; and Rolf Zundel, "Bonn kann nicht Weimar werden," *Die Zeit*, 12/31/1982.

CHAPTER 6

1. Eschenburg, *Letzten Endes meine ich doch*, 24.
2. Resolution of FU students of 22/23 June 1966, in Jürgen Miermeister and Jochen Staadt, eds., *Provokationen: Die Studenten- und Jugendrevolte in ihren Flugblättern 1965–1971* (Darmstadt, 1980), 45.
3. Sontheimer, *So war Deutschland nie*, 107 ff.
4. Knabe, *Die unterwanderte Republik*, and Knabe, *Der diskrete Charme der DDR: Stasi und Westmedien*, 3rd ed. (Berlin, 2001).
5. Hermann Lübbe, *Endstation Terror: Rückblick auf lange Märsche* (Stuttgart, 1978), 7–13.
6. According to Theo Pinkus, in Siegward Lönnendonker, ed., *Linksintellektueller Aufbruch zwischen "Kulturrevolution" und "kultureller Zerstörung": Der Sozialistische Deutsche Studentenbund (SDS) in der Nachkriegsgeschichte (1946–1969): Dokumentation eines Symposiums* (Opladen, 1998), 160–161, and interview with Jürgen Habermas in the *FR*, 3/11/1988.
7. Friedrich-Martin Balzer, *"Es wechseln die Zeiten . . .": Reden, Aufsätze, Vorträge, Briefe eines 68ers aus vier Jahrzehnten (1958–1998)* (Bonn, 1988), and Inga Buhmann, *Ich habe mir eine Geschichte geschrieben*, 2nd ed. (Frankfurt, 1987).
8. Claus Leggewie, "1968 ist Geschichte," *APuZ* B 22–23 (2001), 3–6.
9. Wolfgang Kraushaar, *1968 als Mythos: Chiffre und Zäsur* (Hamburg, 2000), 7 ff., 253 ff.
10. Ingrid Gilcher-Holtey, ed., *1968: Vom Ereignis zum Gegenstand der Geschichtswissenschaft* (Göttingen, 1998). See Olaf Dinné et al., eds., *68 in Bremen: Anno dunnemals* (Bremen, 1998).
11. Peifer, "1968 in German Political Culture."
12. Gilcher-Holtey, *Die 68er Bewegung*, 10, 111 ff. See also Klaus Schönhoven, "Aufbruch in die sozialliberale Ära: Zur Bedeutung der 60er Jahre in der Geschichte der Bundesrepublik," *GG* 25 (1999), 123–145.
13. Axel Schildt, "Vor der Revolte: Die sechziger Jahre," *APuZ* B 22–23 (2001), 7–13. See also Schildt et al., *Dynamische Zeiten*.
14. For a general introduction to the literature, see Philipp Gassert and Pavel A. Richter,

eds., 1968 in *West Germany: A Guide to Sources and Literature of the Extra-Parliamentarian Opposition* (Washington, 1998).

15. See Hans-Peter Schwarz, *Geschichte der Bundesrepublik Deutschland*, 5 vols. (Stuttgart, 1981), vols. 2 and 3, versus Wolfgang Kraushaar, *Die Protest-Chronik 1949–1959: Eine illustrierte Geschichte von Bewegung, Widerstand und Utopie*, 4 vols. (Hamburg, 1996).

16. "Der lange Weg," *NRZ*, 12/29/1945, and Konrad H. Jarausch, *The Unfree Professions: German Lawyers, Teachers and Engineers, 1900–1945* (New York, 1990), 202 ff. Cf. Siegrist, "Wie bürgerlich war die Bundesrepublik, wie antibürgerlich die DDR?" in Hans Günter Hockerts, ed., *Koordinaten der deutschen Geschichte in der Periode des Ost-West Konflikts* (Munich, 2003), 207–243.

17. "Richters Richtfest," *Der Spiegel* 16 (1962), no. 13, 91 ff. See Forner, "Catastrophe and Democratic Renewal."

18. "Die goldenen Sessel," *Der Spiegel* 6 (1952), no. 20, 7 ff. See Kraushaar, *Die Protest-Chronik*, 1:600 ff.

19. For an introduction to the enormous literature, see Armin Mitter and Stefan Wolle, *Untergang auf Raten: Unbekannte Kapitel der DDR-Geschichte* (Munich, 1993), 27 ff.; Kleßmann and Stöver, 1953; and Edda Ahrberg, Hans-Hermann Hertle, and Tobias Hollitzer, eds., *Die Toten des Volksaufstandes vom 17. Juni 1953* (Münster, 2004).

20. Jens Daniel, "Atomschreck Bundesrepublik?" *Der Spiegel* 11 (1957), no. 16, 8, and supporting letters to the editor, *Der Spiegel* 11 (1957), no. 19, 3–4. Numbers are from Kraushaar, *Die Protest-Chronik*, 4:2508 ff.

21. "Das Ansehen der Staatsführung steht auf dem Spiel," *Der Spiegel* 16 (1962), no. 45, 22 ff.; "Sie kamen in der Nacht," *Der Spiegel* 16 (1962), no. 45, 55 ff.; David Schoenbaum, *Die Affäre um den "Spiegel"* (Vienna, 1968); Bark and Gress, *A History of West Germany*, 1:490–509; and "'Dummheiten des Staates,'" *Der Spiegel* 56 (2002), no. 43, 62 ff.

22. "Neue Linke: Kuh und Klasse," *Der Spiegel*, 18 (1964), no. 46, 54–55. See Anson Rabinbach, *In the Shadow of Catastrophe: German Intellectuals between Apocalypse and Enlightenment* (Berkeley, 1997).

23. For the international context, ("Port Huron Statement"), see Gilcher-Holtey, *Die 68er Bewegung*, 11 ff.

24. "Blick zurück," *Der Spiegel* 18 (1964), no. 34, 28–29; "Heißer Sommer," *Der Spiegel* 19 (1965), no. 21, 76 ff. See Tilman Fichter and Siegward Lönnendonker, *Macht und Ohnmacht der Studenten: Kleine Geschichte des SDS* (Hamburg, 1998).

25. "Anstoß gesucht," *Der Spiegel* 18 (1964), no. 3, 42–43. See Dieter Kunzelmann, *Leisten Sie keinen Widerstand! Bilder aus meinem Leben* (Berlin, 1998), 25 ff. See also Buhmann, *Ich habe mir eine Geschichte geschrieben*, 24 ff., 51 ff., 85 ff.

26. Speech of Ernst Bloch, in Miermeister and Staadt, *Provokationen*, 150 ff. See also Karl A. Otto, "Thesen zur Rolle des SDS in der Antinotstandsbewegung," in Siegward Lönnendonker, ed., *Linksintellektueller Aufbruch zwischen "Kulturrevolution" und "kultureller Zerstörung": Der Sozialistische Deutsche Studentenbund (SDS) in der Nachkriegsgeschichte (1946–1969): Dokumentation eines Symposiums* (Opladen, 1998), 153 ff.

27. Michael Schneider, *Demokratie in Gefahr? Der Konflikt um die Notstandsgesetze:*

Sozialdemokratie, Gewerkschaften und intellektueller Protest (1958–1968) (Bonn, 1986).

28. Schildt et al., *Dynamische Zeiten*, 13 ff.

29. Neubert, *Geschichte der Opposition*, and Thomas Klein et al., *Visionen: Repression und Opposition in der SED (1949–1989)* (Frankfurt am Oder, 1996).

30. See the discussions from 1985, documented in Lönnendonker, *Linksintellektueller Aufbruch*, passim. See Kraushaar, *1968 als Mythos*, 254 ff.

31. Lewis S. Feuer, *The Conflict of Generations: The Character and Significance of Student Movements* (New York, 1969); Seymour Martin Lipset and Philip Altbach, *Why Students Revolt* (Boston, 1969); and Mark Roseman, ed., *Generations in Conflict: Youth Revolt and Generation Formation in Germany 1770–1968* (Cambridge, 1995).

32. Klaus R. Allerbeck, *Soziologie radikaler Studentenbewegungen: Eine vergleichende Untersuchung in der Bundesrepublik Deutschland und den Vereinigten Staaten* (Munich, 1973); Theodore Roszak, *The Making of a Counter Culture: Reflections on the Technocratic Society and its Youthful Opposition* (Garden City, 1969); and Dieter Rucht et al., eds., *Acts of Dissent: New Developments in the Study of Protest* (Berlin, 1998).

33. Kunzelmann, *Leisten Sie keinen Widerstand*, 12 ff.; Buhmann, *Ich habe mir eine Geschichte geschrieben*, 24 ff.; Gretchen Dutschke, *Rudi Dutschke: Wir hatten ein barbarisches, schönes Leben: Eine Biographie* (Cologne, 1996), 20 ff.; and Balzer, "*Es wechseln die Zeiten*," 25–26.

34. Kunzelmann, *Leisten Sie keinen Widerstand*, 15 ff.; Buhmann, *Ich habe mir eine Geschichte geschrieben*, 43–220; Dutschke, *Rudi Dutschke*, 27 ff.; and Balzer, "*Es wechseln die Zeiten*," 25 f.

35. Marion Gräfin Dönhoff, *Im Wartesaal der Geschichte: Vom Kalten Krieg zur Wiedervereinigung— Beiträge und Kommentare aus fünf Jahrzehnten* (Stuttgart, 1993), 189 ff., and Eschenburg, *Letzten Endes meine ich doch*, 242 ff.; Sontheimer, *So war Deutschland nie*, 97 ff.

36. Jörg Streese, "Das Schweigen, Die Sprache, Der Aufbruch," in Olaf Dinné et al., eds., *68 in Bremen: Anno dunnemals* (Bremen, 1998), 45 ff.; Mushaben, *From Post-War to Post-Wall Generations*; and Dirk Moses, "Conservatism and the 45er Generation of Intellectuals in West Germany," paper presented at the conference of the German Studies Association in San Diego on 10/5/2002.

37. Poiger, *Jazz, Rock and Rebels*, and Kraushaar, *Die Protest-Chronik*, 4:2504 ff.

38. Fink et al., *1968*, and Gilcher-Holtey, *Die 68er Bewegung*, 25 ff.

39. Georg Picht, *Die deutsche Bildungskatastrophe: Analyse und Dokumentation* (Olten, 1964), and "Heißer Sommer," *Der Spiegel* 19 (1965), no. 21, 76–77.

40. Cited from *Auditorium*, Peter Schneider's memorial address, leaflet on critical university, etc., in Miermeister and Staadt, *Provokationen*, 41 ff.

41. Declaration of Intellectuals on the War in Vietnam; leaflet "Erhard und die Bonner Parteien unterstützen MORD"; speech of Marcuse at the Frankfurt Vietnam Congress in Miermeister and Staadt, *Provokationen*, 73 ff.

42. Leaflet, "Studenten, Lahmärsche, Karrieremacher!" especially Kommune I, "Wann brennen die Berliner Kaufhäuser?" in Miermeister and Staadt, *Provokationen*, 25, 28.

43. "Offene Erklärung vor dem Urteil der zweiten Instanz im SPUR-Prozess," in Dieter Kunzelmann, *Leisten Sie keinen Widerstand! Bilder aus meinem Leben* (Berlin, 1998), 31; SPUR-Leaflet, in Miermeister and Staadt, *Provokationen*, 11. Cf. Dagmar Herzog, *Sex after Fascism: Memory and Morality in Twentieth-Century Germany* (Princeton, 2004).

44. Harald-Gerd Brandt, "Diese Schule ist eine Kadettenanstalt," in Olaf Dinné et al., eds., *68 in Bremen: Anno dunnemals* (Bremen, 1998), 71 ff.; "Blick zurück," *Der Spiegel* 18 (1964), no. 34, 28–29; and Flyer, "Organisieren wir den Ungehorsam," in Miermeister and Staadt, *Provokationen*, 54.

45. Anonymous poem published in *linkeck*, 2/29/1968, reprinted in Miermeister and Staadt, *Provokationen*, 37. See Streese, "Das Schweigen," 52 ff.

46. Wolfgang Kraushaar, "Denkmodelle der 68er-Bewegung," *APuZ* B 22–23 (2001), 14–27. Because many of the statements were retracted by the authors themselves, any retrospective attempt at a precise theoretical determination is likely to fail. See Lönnendonker, *Linksintellektueller Aufbruch*, 33–57.

47. Dutschke, *Rudi Dutschke*, 37 ff., 61 ff., 66 ff. See also Rudi Dutschke, *Jeder hat sein Leben ganz zu leben: Die Tagebücher 1963–1979*, edited by Gretchen Dutschke (Cologne, 2003), 39 ff., 51 ff.

48. Theodor W. Adorno, *Studien zum autoritären Charakter* (Frankfurt, 1973), and Herbert Marcuse, *Der eindimensionale Mensch: Studien zur Ideologie der fortgeschrittenen Industriegesellschaft* (Neuwied, 1967). See also Martin Jay, *The Dialectical Imagination: A History of the Frankfurt School and of the Institute for Social Research, 1928–1953* (Boston, 1973).

49. Johannes Agnoli and Peter Brückner, *Die Transformation der Demokratie* (Berlin, 1967), 13 ff.

50. Reinhard Rürup, *Probleme der Revolution in Deutschland 1918/19* (Wiesbaden, 1968); Gerhard Ritter and Susanne Miller, eds., *Die deutsche Revolution 1918–19: Dokumente* (Frankfurt, 1968); and Wilfried Gottschalch, *Parlamentarismus und Rätedemokratie* (Berlin, 1968).

51. Dutschke, *Jeder hat sein Leben*, 41; Ulrich Preuß, quoted in Lönnendonker, *Linksintellektueller Aufbruch*, 252–301.

52. Dutschke, *Jeder hat sein Leben*, 57 ff. For the search process, see Hans-Jürgen Krahl, "Angaben zur Person," in Lutz Schulenburg, ed., *Das Leben ändern, die Welt verändern! 1968: Dokumente und Berichte* (Hamburg, 1998), 351 ff., 389 ff., and Kraushaar, *Denkmodelle*, 25 ff.

53. For the international transmission of ideas, see Gilcher-Holtey, *Die 68er Bewegung*, 62 ff.

54. See the contrasting photographs in Michael Ruetz, *1968: Ein Zeitalter wird besichtigt* (Frankfurt, 1997). The Shah poster and the SS-Werner placard are in Miermeister and Staadt, *Provokationen*, 96.

55. Ruetz, *1968*, 43 ff., 69 ff., 95 ff., 102 ff., and Kunzelmann, *Leisten Sie keinen Widerstand*, 83 ff.

56. Ruetz, *1968*, 38–39, 82 ff., 122 ff., and Dutschke, *Jeder hat sein Leben*, 48 ff.

57. Heinrich Hannover, "Landgraf werde hart!" in Olaf Dinné et al., eds., *68 in Bremen:*

Anno dunnemals (Bremen, 1998), 59 ff.; Dutschke, *Rudi Dutschke,* 67 ff., 130 ff.; and Miermeister and Staadt, *Provokationen,* 177 ff.

58. BILD-Action of 6/26/1967, SDS-Program for Action, SDS-Declaration of Principles, etc., in Miermeister and Staadt, *Provokationen,* 139 ff. See Peifer, "1968 in German Political Culture," passim.

59. Ruetz, *1968,* 52–53, 98–99, versus 79 ff., 91 ff. or 308 ff., 315 ff.

60. "The mood was often so [excited], as if the revolution were about to break out," in Buhmann, *Ich habe mir eine Geschichte geschrieben,* 301; Dutschke, *Jeder hat sein Leben,* 53 ff.

61. Reinicke, "Wanderlust"; Internationale Befreiungsfront, "Mord"; and Provo Amsterdam, "Was ist das Provotariat?"—all in Lutz Schulenburg, ed., *Das Leben ändern, die Welt verändern! 1968: Dokumente und Berichte* (Hamburg, 1998), 15 ff., 20 ff., 29 ff.

62. "Von diesem Gespräch haben wir nichts zu erwarten"; "Studenten, Lahmärsche und Karrieremacher"; and "Befragung zur Person Langhans und Teufel"—all in Lutz Schulenburg, ed., *Das Leben ändern, die Welt verändern! 1968: Dokumente und Berichte* (Hamburg, 1998), 30 ff., 36 ff., 43 ff.

63. Dutschke, *Rudi Dutschke,* 87 ff., and "Empfang für Humphrey" in Miermeister and Staadt, *Provokationen,* 87 ff.

64. Christian Geissler, "Hamburg, 2. Juni 1967"; SDS-declaration, "Niederlage oder Erfolg der Protestaktion"; AUSS, "Es gibt Schüler, die machen jetzt nicht mehr mit"; and Reinicke, "Wanderlust"—all in Schulenburg, *Das Leben ändern, die Welt verändern!* 50 ff., 54 ff., 60 ff., 64 ff.

65. Hans-Peter Ernst, "Die Provos sind tot"; SDS-Hamburg, "Stürzt die Ordinarien"; Michael Buselmeier, "Rotlackierter Frühling"—all in Lutz Schulenburg, ed., *Das Leben ändern, die Welt verändern! 1968: Dokumente und Berichte* (Hamburg, 1998), 72 ff., 96 ff., 115–116.

66. Dutschke, *Rudi Dutschke,* 184 ff.. Also: SDS-Munich, "Vietnam: Das totale Kunstwerk!" and "Schlußerklärung der internationalen Vietnamkonferenz," in Lutz Schulenburg, ed., *Das Leben ändern, die Welt verändern! 1968: Dokumente und Berichte* (Hamburg, 1998), 125 ff.

67. Dutschke, *Rudi Dutschke,* 197 ff. Also: Detlev Albers, "Ostern 1968: Verlauf der Aktionen in Hamburg," and SDS-Frankfurt, "Liebe Ostermarschierer, Genossinnen und Genossen!" in Lutz Schulenburg, ed., *Das Leben ändern, die Welt verändern! 1968: Dokumente und Berichte* (Hamburg, 1998), 141 ff.; Buhmann, *Ich habe mir eine Geschichte geschrieben,* 288 ff. See also Stefan Reisner, ed., *Briefe an Rudi D.* (Frankfurt, 1968), 91–92.

68. Buhmann, *Ich habe mir eine Geschichte geschrieben,* 291 ff.

69. Gilcher-Holtey, *Die 68er Bewegung,* 91 ff.

70. Dutschke, *Jeder hat sein Leben,* 58 ff., 68, and Lönnendonker, *Linksintellektueller Aufbruch,* 302 ff.

71. Olaf Dinné, "Olafs Kryptokarriere," in Dinné et al., eds., *68 in Bremen: Anno dunnemals* (Bremen, 1998) 123 ff.; Dutschke, *Rudi Dutschke,* 190 ff.; SDS-Hamburg, "Presseerklärung," in Lutz Schulenburg, ed., *Das Leben ändern, die Welt verändern! 1968: Dokumente und Berichte* (Hamburg, 1998), 299 ff.

72. Dutschke, *Rudi Dutschke*, 230 ff.; Buhmann, *Ich habe mir eine Geschichte geschrieben*, 314 ff. Also: Zentralrat der umherschweifenden Haschrebellen, "Die APO ist tot," in Lutz Schulenburg, ed., *Das Leben ändern, die Welt verändern! 1968: Dokumente und Berichte* (Hamburg, 1998), 436.

73. Kunzelmann, *Leisten Sie keinen Widerstand*, 126 ff.

74. Willi Hoss, "Aufbruch"; Peter Schuldt, "Springerblockade und Solidarität mit Rockwell-Arbeitern"; and "Eins teilt sich in zwei"—all in Lutz Schulenburg, ed., *Das Leben ändern, die Welt verändern! 1968: Dokumente und Berichte* (Hamburg, 1998), 168–169, 191 ff., 296 ff.

75. Ronald Inglehart, *The Silent Revolution: Changing Values and Political Styles among Western Publics* (Princeton, 1977); Gerd Langguth, *Suche nach Sicherheiten: Ein Psychogramm der Deutschen* (Stuttgart, 1994), 21 ff.; and Ulrich Herbert, "Liberalisierung als Lenrprozess: Die Bundesrepublik in der deutschen Geschichte, " in Herbert, *Wandlungsprozesse in Westdeutschland. Belastung, Integration, Liberalisierung 1945–1980* (Göttingen, 2002), 35 ff.

76. "Schmeißt das gesamte Notstandsgesindel in die Außenalster"; "Wir besetzen am 27. Mai das Germanische Seminar auf unbefristete Zeit"; and Reinicke, "Wanderlust"—all in Lutz Schulenburg, ed., *Das Leben ändern, die Welt verändern! 1968: Dokumente und Berichte* (Hamburg, 1998), 176 ff., 186 ff., 219 ff.

77. Concept of Rudi Dutschke, in Dutschke, *Rudi Dutschke*, 177 ff. Also: Reinicke, "Wanderlust," in Lutz Schulenburg, ed., *Das Leben ändern, die Welt verändern! 1968: Dokumente und Berichte* (Hamburg, 1998), 218 ff.

78. Kunzelmann, *Leisten Sie keinen Widerstand*, 59 ff., and Buhmann, *Ich habe mir eine Geschichte geschrieben*, 259. See also Bernward Vesper, *Die Reise: Romanessay* (Frankfurt, 1977).

79. Frank Wendler, "Die Partei hat nicht mehr recht," in Olaf Dinné et al., eds., *68 in Bremen: Anno dunnemals* (Bremen, 1998), 97 ff., and Peter Schneider, *Lenz: Eine Erzählung* (Berlin, 1973).

80. Bommi Baumann, *Terror or Love? Bommi Baumann's Own Story of His Life as a West German Urban Guerrilla* (New York, 1978), 49 ff. See also impressive photos by Astrid Proll, *Baader Meinhof: Pictures on the Run 1966–77* (Zürich, 1998).

81. Jillian Becker, *Hitler's Children: The Story of the Baader-Meinhof Terrorist Gang* (Philadelphia, 1977), 179 ff. Cf. Hanno Balz, "Terrorismus und innere Sicherheit in der Bundesrepublik der 1970er Jahre," HSK, 10/5/2004.

82. Becker, *Hitler's Children*, 280 ff. See Anette Vowinkel, "Das Phänomen RAF," HSK, 10/26/2004, and the projects by Belinda Davis, Jonathan Wiesen, and Karrin Hanshew on German terrorism.

83. Balzer, *"Es wechseln die Zeiten,"* 63 ff., 67 ff., and Michael Filzen-Salinas, "Fünfundsechzig, sechsundsechzig, siebenundsechzig, achtundsechzig," in Olaf Dinné et al., eds., *68 in Bremen: Anno dunnemals* (Bremen, 1998), 77 ff. Cf. Klaus Schönhoven, *Wendejahre: Die Sozialdemokratie in der Zeit der großen Koalition 1966–1969* (Bonn, 2004).

84. See Kunzelmann, *Leisten Sie keinen Widerstand*, 21, 64–65, 71, 89 ff., 104–105, 127.

85. Michael Schultz, "Vanity fair auf politisch," in Olaf Dinné et al., eds., *68 in Bremen: Anno dunnemals* (Bremen, 1998), 101 ff.

86. Buhmann, *Ich habe mir eine Geschichte geschrieben*, 292 ff. Also: Hartmut Sander, "Das Schicksal einer schönen Frau" and "Rede des 'Aktionsrates zur Befreiung der Frau,'" in Lutz Schulenburg, ed., *Das Leben ändern, die Welt verändern! 1968: Dokumente und Berichte* (Hamburg, 1998), 291 ff., 339 ff.

87. Joyce Mushaben, Geoffrey Giles, and Sara Lennox, "Women, Men and Unification: Gender Politics and the Abortion Struggle Since 1989," in Konrad H. Jarausch, *After Unity: Reconfiguring German Identitie*s (Providence, 1997), 137–172.

88. Sandra Chaney, "Visions and Revisions of Nature: From the Protection of Nature to the Invention of the Environment in the Federal Republic of Germany, 1945–1975" (Ph.D. diss., Chapel Hill, 1996), and Mark Cioc, *The Rhine: An Ecobiography, 1815–2000* (Seattle, 2002).

89. Grenzen des Wachstums: Club of Rome, 1972, www.nachhaltigkeit.aachener-stiftung. de; Erhard Eppler, *Maßstäbe für eine humane Gesellschaft: Lebensstandard oder Lebensqualität?* (Stuttgart, 1974), 18–21; and Klaus Wagner, "Die Bürger wehren sich," *FAZ*, 10/27/1973.

90. Walter Mossmann, "Die Bevölkerung ist hellwach," *Kursbuch* 39 (1975), 129 ff; Christian Schütze, "Kernkraft spaltet den Rechtsstaat," *SZ*, 11/3/1976; Rolf Zundel, "Anschlag auf die Parteien oder Ventil der Verdrossenheit?" *Die Zeit*, 8/5/1977; and Cornelia Frey, "Wachsam in Holzpalästen," *Die Zeit*, 5/30/1980.

91. "Die Friedensdiskussion der Gewerkschaften," *Neue Zeit*, 7/6/1981; "Die Friedensbewegung muß gemeinsam verstärkt gegen Kriegsgefahr kämpfen," *Die Wahrheit*, 10/8/1981; Peter Meier-Bergfeld, "Der Zug der Aussteiger aus der Geschichte," *RhM*, 10/16/1981; and "Nach der Demo der 300 000 in Bonn," *Die Neue*, 10/13/1981.

92. Jeffrey Herf, *War by Other Means: Soviet Power, West German Resistance and the Battle over Euromissiles* (New York, 1991). See also Kohl, *Erinnerungen, 1982–1990*, 140–145.

93. Party platform of the "greens" in Ingrid Wilharm, ed., *Deutsche Geschichte* (Frankfurt, 1985), 2:226–230. Cf. Christian Schneider, "Den Etablierten das Grün aufzwingen," *FR*, 5/17/1978; Barbara Winkler, "Im Zeichen des Igels," *Streitgespräch* 2 (1979), 14–16; and Wilhelm Bittorf, "Die Wiederkehr der Angst," *Der Spiegel*, 6/15/1981.

94. "Wir stehen vor einem ökologischen Hiroschima," *Der Spiegel* 37 (1983), no. 7, 72–92; "Industrie-Schreck Joschka Fischer Erster Grüner Umweltminister," *Der Spiegel* 39 (1985), no. 45, 24–31; "Sie haben versagt," *Die Zeit*, 5/23/1986.

95. Hans Maier and Michael Zöller, eds., *Bund Freiheit der Wissenschaft: Der Gründungskongreß in Bad Godesberg 1970* (Cologne, 1970), 7 ff., 76 ff. See also Kohl, *Erinnerungen, 1982–1990*, 50–51.

96. For examples, see Peter Mosler, *Was wir wollten, was wir wurden: Studentenrevolte—10 Jahre danach* (Reinbek, 1977), 233 ff., and Oskar Negt, *Achtundsechzig: Politische Intellektuelle und die Macht* (Göttingen, 1995), or Heinz Bude, *Das Altern einer Generation: Die Jahrgänge 1938 bis 1948* (Frankfurt, 1995).

97. Franz-Werner Kersting, "Entzauberung des Mythos? Ausgangsbedingungen und Tendenzen einer gesellschaftsgeschichtlichen Standortbestimmung der westdeutschen '68er'-Bewegung," *Westfälische Forschungen* 48 (1998), 1–19.

98. Gilcher-Holtey, *1968*, 7 ff.

99. Ronald Fraser, *1968: A Student Generation in Revolt: An International Oral History* (New York, 1988), and Arthur Marwick, *The Sixties: Cultural Revolution in Britain, France, Italy, and the United States c. 1958–1974* (Oxford, 1998).

100. Christoph Köhler, "1968: Höhenflug und Absturz," in Olaf Dinné et al., eds., *68 in Bremen: Anno dunnemals* (Bremen, 1998), 111 ff. See Geoff Eley, *Forging Democracy: The History of the Left in Europe, 1850–2000* (Oxford, 2002), 342 ff.

101. Heinz Gollwitzer, quoted in Lönnendonker, *Linksintellektueller Aufbruch*, 205. See Peter Kuckuk, "Annäherungen an 1968: Eine persönliche Bilanz," in Olaf Dinné et al., eds., *68 in Bremen: Anno dunnemals* (Bremen, 1998), 149 ff.; and Herzog, *Sex after Fascism*, 259 ff.

102. Wolfgang Schieches, "Bruder Schieches' Weg zu Gott," in Olaf Dinné et al., eds., *68 in Bremen: Anno dunnemals* (Bremen, 1998), 143 ff.; and Konrad H. Jarausch, "1968 and 1989: Caesuras, Comparisons, and Connections," in Fink et al., *1968*, 461–477.

CONCLUSION TO PART II

1. Hans-Ulrich Wehler, *Deutsche Gesellschaftsgeschichte*, 3 vols. (Munich, 1987–2003), and Jeffrey Herf, *Reactionary Modernism: Technology, Culture, and Politics in Weimar and the Third Reich* (Cambridge, 1984).

2. Schildt and Sywottek, *Modernisierung im Wiederaufbau*.

3. Hans-Ulrich Wehler, *Modernisierungstheorie und Geschichte* (Göttingen, 1975); Jürgen Kocka, "The GDR: A Special Kind of Modern Dictatorship," in Konrad H. Jarausch, ed., *Dictatorship as Experience: Towards a Socio-Cultural History of the GDR* (New York, 1999), 17 ff.

4. Jarausch and Siegrist, *Amerikanisierung und Sowjetisierung*, and Michael Geyer, "In Pursuit of Happiness: Consumption, Mass Culture and Consumerism," in Konrad H. Jarausch and Michael Geyer, *Shattered Past: Reconstructing German Histories* (Princeton, 2003), 269 ff.

5. Detlef Pollack, "Wie modern war die DDR?" Discussion Paper 4 (2001), presented at the Frankfurt Institut for Transformative Studies. See also Dierk Hoffmann, *Die DDR unter Ulbricht: Gewaltsame Neuordnung und gescheiterte Modernisierung* (Zürich, 2003), 196 ff.

6. Merkl, *The Federal Republic of Germany at Fifty*.

7. Terminology from Konrad H. Jarausch, "Realer Sozialismus als Fürsorgediktatur: Zur begrifflichen Einordnung der DDR," *APuZ* B 20 (1998), 33–46. See also Sebastian Simsch, *Blinde Ohnmacht: Der Freie Deutsche Gewerkschaftsbund zwischen Diktatur und Gesellschaft in der DDR 1945 bis 1963* (Aachen, 2002).

8. Martin and Sylvia Greiffenhagen, *Ein schwieriges Vaterland: Zur politischen Kultur im vereinigten Deutschland* (Munich, 1993). See also Werner Faulstich, ed., *Die Kultur der 60er Jahre* (Munich, 2003), 7 ff.

9. Stefan Wolle, *Die heile Welt der Diktatur: Alltag und Herrschaft in der DDR 1971–1989* (Berlin, 1998), 82 ff.

10. As a critic of the West German development, see Erich Kuby, *Mein ärgerliches Vaterland*, (Berlin, 1990).

11. Bernd Faulenbach, "'Modernisierung' in der Bundesrepublik und in der DDR während der 60er Jahre," *Zeitgeschichte* 25 (1998), 282–294. See also Schildt, *Ankunft im Westen*.

12. Rainer Geißler, "Modernisierung," *Informationen zur politischen Bildung* No. 269 (Bonn, 2004), and Ulrich Beck et al., *Reflexive Modernisierung: Eine Kontroverse* (Frankfurt, 1996). See also Norbert Bolz, "Der Bundesphilosoph," *TSp*, 5/3/2003.

PART III

1. Konrad H. Jarausch and Volker Gransow, eds., *Uniting Germany: Documents and Debates, 1944–1993* (Providence, 1994).

2. Concept by Jürgen Kocka, *Vereinigungskrise: Zur Geschichte der Gegenwart* (Göttingen, 1995).

3. Jarausch, *The Rush to German Unity.*

4. Rainer Eckert and Bernd Faulenbach, eds., *Halbherziger Revisionismus: Zum post-kommunistischen Geschichtsbild* (Munich, 1996).

5. Ash, *In Europe's Name*, and Gale Stokes, *The Walls Came Tumbling Down: The Collapse of Communism in Eastern Europe* (New York, 1993).

6. Wolfgang Merkel, ed., *Systemwechsel: Theorien, Ansätze und Konzeptionen*, 5 vols. (Opladen, 1994–2000), 5:9–49. Cf. Winfried Thaa, *Die Wiedergeburt des Politischen: Zivilgesellschaft und Legitimitätskonflikt in den Revolutionen von 1989* (Opladen, 1996), 18 ff.

7. Friedrich Pohlmann, *Deutschland im Zeitalter des Totalitarismus: Politische Identitäten in Deutschland zwischen 1918 und 1989* (Munich, 2001).

8. Richard Bessel and Ralph Jessen, eds., *Die Grenzen der Diktatur: Staat und Gesellschaft in der DDR* (Göttingen 1996), and Thomas Lindenberger, ed., *Herrschaft und Eigen-Sinn in der Diktatur: Studien zur Gesellschaftsgeschichte der DDR* (Cologne, 1999).

9. Neubert, *Geschichte der Opposition in der DDR*, and Wolle, *Die heile Welt der Diktatur.* See also Konrad H. Jarausch, *Aufbruch der Zivilgesellschaft: Zur Einordnung der friedlichen Revolution von 1989* (Bonn, 2004).

10. Konrad H. Jarausch, "Normalisierung oder Re-Nationalisierung? Zur Umdeutung der deutschen Vergangenheit," *GG* 21 (1995), 571–584.

11. Markovits and Reich, *Das deutsche Dilemma.*

12. Dieter Gosewinkel, *Einbürgern und Ausschließen: Die Nationalisierung der Staatsangehörigkeit vom Deutschen Bund bis zur Bundesrepublik Deutschland* (Göttingen, 2001).

13. Bade, *Europa in Bewegung.*

14. Merkel, *Systemwechsel*, 5:37.

15. Klaus von Beyme, "Zivilgesellschaft: Von der vorbürgerlichen zur nachbürgerlichen Gesellschaft?" in Wolfgang Merkel, ed., *Systemwechsel: Theorien, Ansätze und Konzeptionen*, 5 vols. (Opladen, 1994–2000), 5:51–70. Cf. Nina Verheyen and Ute Hasenöhrl, "Zivilgesellschaft: Historische Forschungsperspektiven," Berlin 12/6–7/2002, HSK, 5/4/2003.

CHAPTER 7

1. Matthias Geis and Petra Bornhöft, "Jubelfeier im 'volkspolizeilichen Handlungsraum,'" *taz*, 10/9/1989. For further information, see *taz*, ed., *DDR-Journal zur Novemberrevolution* (Berlin, 1989), 41–42.

2. "Tausende demonstrierten in der Ost-Berliner Innenstadt" and "Zuversicht trotz ungewisser Zukunft," *TSp*, 10/8/1989; Karl-Heinz Baum, "Unser Forum ist der Alexanderplatz," *FR*, 10/9/1989.

3. Vojtech Mastny, *The Cold War and Soviet Insecurity: The Stalin Years* (New York, 1996).

4. "Zwei Perspektiven für 1948," *ND*, 1/1/1948, and "Gruß und Glückwunsch J. W. Stalin, dem Genius unserer Epoche," *ND*, 12/20/1949. See Sheila Fitzpatrick, *Everyday Stalinism: Ordinary Life in Extraordinary Times: Soviet Russia in the 1930s* (New York, 1999).

5. Wilhelm Pieck, "Die SU als Besatzungsmacht," *ND*, 11/7/1948, and Rudolf Herrnstadt, "Über 'die Russen' und über uns," *ND*, 11/19/1948. See Lemke, *Sowjetisierung und Eigenständigkeit*.

6. "Unsterblicher Geist des 18. März," *ND*, 3/18/1948, and Wilhelm Pieck, "30 Jahre KPD," *ND*, 11/1/1949. See Eric D. Weitz, *Creating German Communism 1890–1990: From Popular Protests to Socialist State* (Princeton, 1997).

7. Klein, *Für die Einheit und Reinheit der Partei*.

8. Klemperer, *So sitze ich denn zwischen allen Stühlen*; Mayer, *Der Turm von Babel*.

9. Ulrich Mählert, ed., *Vademekum DDR-Forschung: Ein Leitfaden zu Archiven, Forschungsinstituten, Bibliotheken, Einrichtungen der politischen Bildung, Vereinen, Museen und Gedenkstätten* (Berlin, 2002). See Corey Ross, *The East German Dictatorship: Problems and Perspectives in the Interpretation of the GDR* (London, 2002), 126 ff.

10. Eckhard Jesse, ed., *Totalitarismus im 20. Jahrhundert: Eine Bilanz der internationalen Forschung*, 2nd ed. (Baden-Baden, 1999), and Alfons Söllner et al., eds., *Totalitarismus: Eine Ideengeschichte des 20. Jahrhunderts* (Berlin, 1997).

11. Eckert and Faulenbach, *Halbherziger Revisionismus*.

12. Jarausch, *Dictatorship as Experience*, 3–14.

13. Timothy Garton Ash, *The Magic Lantern: The Revolution of '89 Witnessed in Warsaw, Budapest, Berlin and Prague* (New York, 1990), 134 ff; Helmut Fehr, "Eliten und Zivilgesellschaft in Ostmitteleuropa: Polen und die Tschechische Republik (1968–2003)," *APuZ*, B5/6, 2004; and Karsten Timmer, *Vom Aufbruch zum Umbruch: Die Bürgerbewegung in der DDR 1989* (Göttingen, 1999), 16–17, 389 ff, and 63 ff.

14. Thaa, *Die Wiedergeburt des Politischen*, 158 ff., and Arnd Bauerkämper, ed., *Die Praxis der Zivilgesellschaft: Akteure, Handeln und Strukturen im internationalen Vergleich* (Frankfurt, 2003), 7–30.

15. "Aufruf der KPD," *TR*, 6/14/1945; "Das Wollen der antifaschistischen Einheitsfront," *TR*, 8/14/1945; and Gründungsaufruf der SED, "Manifest an das deutsche Volk," *ND*, 4/23/1946. See Meuschel, *Legitimation und Parteiherrschaft*.

16. "Gibt es in der SBZ Klassenkampf?" *ND*, 10/7/1948. See Konrad H. Jarausch, "Die gescheiterte Gegengesellschaft: Überlegungen zu einer Sozialgeschichte der DDR," *AfS* 39 (1999), 1–17.

17. "Am Beginn des demokratischen Aufbaus," *ND*, 6/12/1946; "Grosser Wahlsieg der SED in der Zone," *ND*, 10/22/1946; and "Blockpolitik erneut bestätigt," *ND*, 8/6/1948. See Hermann Weber, *Die DDR 1945–1990*, 3rd ed. (Munich, 2000).

18. "Sieben Monate Wirtschaftsaufbau," *TR*, 1/4/1946; "Ergebnisse der Bodenreform in der SBZ," *TR*, 4/14/1946; "Eine demokratische Wirtschaft entsteht," *ND*, 3/18/1948; "Ein deutscher Zweijahresplan," *ND*, 6/30/1948; and "Volksbetriebe als Rückrat der Friedenswirtschaft," *ND*, 7/7/1948.

19. "Erste Gewerkschaftskonferenz für die gesamte SBZ," *TR*, 2/12/1946, and Herbert Warnke, "Sozialisten und Gewerkschaften," *ND*, 11/19/1948. See Simsch, *Blinde Ohnmacht*.

20. "Die Freie Deutsche Jugend Sachsens," *TR*, 4/11/1946, and "Deutsche Jugend für Fortschritt," *TR*, 8/15/1948. See Ulrich Mählert and Gerd-Rüdiger Stephan, *Blaue Hemden–Rote Fahnen: Die Geschichte der Freien Deutschen Jugend* (Opladen, 1996).

21. "Das hohe Ziel des Kulturbundes," *TR*, 2/19/1946, and "Kulturbund im Kontrollrat," *ND*, 2/3/1948.

22. "Demokratischer Frauenbund gegründet," *ND*, 3/7/1948. See Donna Harsch, "Approach/Avoidance: Communists and Women in East Germany, 1945–9," *Social History* 25 (2000), 156–182.

23. "SED und Christentum," *ND*, 8/30/1946; "Landespastor Schwartze an Dr. Dibelius," *ND*, 6/23/1949; and "Es bleibt dabei: Eure Rede aber sei ja, ja, nein, nein," *ND*, 6/17/1949. See Horst Dähn, ed., *Die Rolle der Kirchen in der DDR: Eine erste Bilanz* (Munich, 1993).

24. Walter Ulbricht, "Die Rolle der Partei," *ND*, 8/22/1948; Franz Dahlem, "Zur Frage der Partei neuen Typus," *ND*, 12/16/1948; and Wolfgang Hager, "Was heißt innerparteiliche Demokratie?" *ND*, 9/13/1949.

25. Wilhelm Pieck, "Die nationale Front," *ND*, 7/24/1948; Gerhard Heidenreich, "Von Brandenburg nach Leipzig," *ND*, 6/2/1949; and "Jugendparlament nimmt FDJ-Verfassung an," *ND*, 6/5/1949.

26. "Die westdeutschen Wahlen," *ND*, 8/23/1949; "Tag der nationalen Schande," *ND*, 9/7/1949; "Zustimmungserklärung der Millionen," *ND*, 5/18/1949; and "Manifest des deutschen Volksrats," *ND*, 10/8/1949.

27. "Volkskontrolle auch in der Justiz," *ND*, 9/20/1949, and "Eine Bande von Verbrechern am Volkseigentum gefaßt," *ND*, 11/23/1949.

28. Friedrich Noppert, "Mit Steuerschraube und Kautschukparagraphen," *NZ*, 8/14/1952; "Plauener Spitzen und die SED," *TSp*, 3/23/1960; "Wer den Karren aus dem Dreck zieht . . ." *Die Welt*, 6/11/1960; and Karl Pernutz, "Offensive gegen die Privatwirtschaft," *SBZArch* 11 (1960), 101–107.

29. "Die Kampfgruppe gegen Unmenschlichkeit," *TSp*, 12/10/1949; O. E. H. Becker, "Jugend im Widerstand," *SBZArch* 2 (July 1951); and Karl Wilhelm Fricke, *Opposition und Widerstand in der DDR: Ein politischer Report* (Cologne, 1984).

30. "Volksaufstand im Sowjetsektor von Berlin," *NZZ*, 6/17/1953; "Der Zusammenbruch des faschistischen Abenteuers," *ND*, 6/19/1953; and Werner Zimmermann, "Die Träger des Widerstandes," *SBZArch* 4 (1953), 306–309. See Torsten Diedrich and Hans-Hermann Hertle, eds., *Alarmstufe "Hornisse": Die geheimen Chef-Berichte der Volkspolizei über den 17. Juni 1953* (Berlin, 2003).

31. "Sowjetzonen-Arbeiter verlassen FDGB," *NZ*, 7/4/1953; "Die Gewerkschaften und der neue Kurs," *TR*, 8/19/1953; Thomas Lindenberger, *Volkspolizei: Herrschaftspraxis und öffentliche Ordnung im SED-Staat 1952–1968* (Cologne, 2003); and Burghard

Ciesla, ed., *"Freiheit wollen wir!" Der 17. Juni 1953 in Brandenburg: Eine Dokumentation* (Berlin, 2003).

32. "Die SED und die Intellektuellen," *ND*, 1/9/1949, and Jürgen Kuczynski, "Die Freiheit der Wissenschaft in der bürgerlichen und in der sozialistischen Gesellschaft," *ND*, 2/13/1949. See Ralph Jessen, *Akademische Elite und kommunistische Diktatur: Die ostdeutsche Hochschullehrerschaft in der Ulbricht-Ära* (Göttingen, 1999).

33. "Die Stellung der Intellektuellen in der Sowjetzone Deutschlands," *NZ*, 10/3/1954; "Funktionäre am Telefon," *DZ*, 6/25/1955; "SED gibt Widerstand der Intelligenz zu," *Die Welt*, 7/14/1958; and Ilko Sascha Kowalczuk, *Geist im Dienste der Macht: Hochschulpolitik in der SBZ/DDR 1945 bis 1961* (Berlin, 2003).

34. "1,8 Millionen Menschen bekamen das Junkerland," *TR*, 9/4/1949; "Dorfleben in der Sowjetischen Zone," *FAZ*, 8/9/1952; "Verzuckerte Kollektive," *NZ*, 8/13/1952; and "In der Landwirtschaft bricht sich der Sozialismus Bahn," *TR*, 2/28/1953.

35. Ernest J. Salter, "Auf dem Wege zum totalitären Dorf," *NZ*, 7/15/1954, and "Maschinendörfer für die Sowjetzone," *Die Zeit*, 2/11/1954. See Arnd Bauerkämper, *Ländliche Gesellschaft in der kommunistischen Diktatur: Zwangsmodernisierung und Tradition in Brandenburg 1945–1963* (Cologne, 2002), 493 ff.

36. Wolfgang Weinert, "So verlor der Bauer Wilhelm Niemann seinen Hof," *Die Welt*, 10/6/1959; "Bauern vor Ulbrichts Pflug," *FAZ*, 11/7/1959; "Wer auf die Partei hört, der geht den richtigen Weg," *ND*, 3/6/1960; Siegried Göllner, "Das Bauernlegen in Mitteldeutschland," *SBZArch* 11 (1960), 97–101.

37. "Razzien gegen die evangelische Jugend," *NZ*, 1/16/1953; "Atheistische Kampagne der ostdeutschen Regierung," *NZZ*, 12/29/1954; and Helmut Bunke, "Jugendweihe und Konfirmation," *Die Andere Zeitung*, 3/1/1956.

38. "SED leitet Kampagne zum Austritt aus der Kirche ein," *Die Welt*, 12/2/1957; "Scharfe Rede Grotewohls gegen die Kirchen," *FAZ*, 3/31/1959; "Stillhalte-Abkommen mit der Kirche der Zone," *FAZ*, 7/24/1958; and Ansgar Skriver, "Die Evangelische Kirche und der SED-Staat," *SBZArch* 11 (1960), 210–213.

39. Concept coined by Jürgen Kocka, "Eine durchherrschte Gesellschaft," in Hartmut Kaelble and Hartmut Zwahr, eds., *Sozialgeschichte der DDR* (Stuttgart, 1994), 547–553.

40. Christoph Kleßmann, "Relikte des Bürgertums in der DDR," in Hartmut Kaelble and Hartmut Zwahr, eds., *Sozialgeschichte der DDR* (Stuttgart, 1994), 254–270. See also Hannes Siegrist, "Wie bürgerlich war die Bundesrepublik, wie entbürgerlicht die DDR? Verbürgerlichung und Antibürgerlichkeit in historischer Perspektive," in Hans-Günther Hockerts, ed., *Koordinaten deutscher Geschichte in der Epoche des Ost-West Konflikts* (Munich, 2003), 207–243.

41. Albert Norden, "Unsere Presse: Kollektiver Organisator der sozialistischen Umgestaltung," *ND*, 4/21/1959, and "Der Sowjetstaat nach zehn Jahren," *NZZ*, 9/25/1959. See Simone Barck et al., eds., *Zwischen "Mosaik" und "Einheit": Zeitschriften in der DDR* (Berlin, 1999).

42. Klaus von Beyme, "Stalinismus und Poststalinismus im osteuropäischen Vergleich," *Potsdamer Bulletin für Zeithistorische Studien* 13 (1998), 8–23, and Juan José Linz, *Totalitäre und autoritäre Regime*, edited by Raimund Krämer (Berlin, 2000). Cf.

Gerhard Sälter, "Herrschaftswandel und Oppositionsbildung in der Ära Honecker," HSK, 8/31/2005.

43. Neubert, *Geschichte der Opposition in der DDR*; Detlef Pollack and Dieter Rink, eds., *Zwischen Verweigerung und Opposition: Politischer Protest in der DDR 1970–1989* (Frankfurt, 1997); and Christoph Kleßmann, "Opposition und Resistenz in zwei Diktaturen in Deutschland," *HZ* 262 (1996), 453–479.

44. Bessel and Jessen, *Die Grenzen der Diktatur*; Lindenberger, *Herrschaft und Eigen-Sinn*.

45. Detlef Pollack, "Die konstitutive Widersprüchlichkeit der DDR. Oder: War die DDR-Gesellschaft homogen?" *GG* 24 (1998), 110–131, as well as Pollack, *Politischer Protest: Politisch alternative Gruppen in der DDR* (Opladen, 2000). Cf. Konrad H. Jarausch, "Aufbruch der Zivilgesellschaft: Zur Einordnung der friedlichen Revolution von 1989," *Gesprächskreis Geschichte*, edited by Friedrich Ebert Stiftung, No. 55 (Bonn, 2004).

46. Karl Wilhelm Fricke and Günther Zehm, "Opposition im Ulbricht-Staat?" *SBZArch* 12 (1961), 46–47 and 144–146. See also "Zuchthausstrafen gegen Ost-Berliner," *TSp*, 8/29/1961; "Anschlag auf Güterzug in der Zone," *TSp*, 9/7/1961; and "SED fahndet nach Parteifeinden," *DZ*, 9/27/1961.

47. Hendrik Bussiek, "Die Flucht ins Private hält an," *Vorwärts*, 7/7/1977; Thomas Ammer, "Die Köpfe der Hydra wachsen immer nach," *DZ*, 2/3/1978; and Günter Gaus, *Wo Deutschland liegt: Eine Ortsbestimmung* (Hamburg, 1983).

48. "Widerstand in der Zone wächst," *DZ*, 8/30/1961; "'Polit-Information' vor dem Unterricht," *Die Welt*, 11/3/1961; "Bevölkerung fordert offene Grenzen," *Die Welt*, 2/27/1963; and "Widerstand in Dresden und Jena," *Die Welt*, 5/20/1964. See Peter Hübner, *Konsens, Konflikt und Kompromiß: Soziale Arbeiterinteressen und Sozialpolitik in der SBZ/DDR 1945–1970* (Berlin, 1995).

49. "Ulbricht soll Rechenschaft geben," *TSp*, 6/21/1961; "SED-Funktionäre in Henningsdorf ausgelacht und niedergesungen," *Die Welt*, 7/6/1961; "Offener Brief an Ulbricht," *Blätter für Politik und internationale Beziehungen*, 5/17/1962; and Alf Lüdtke and Peter Becker, eds., *Akten, Eingaben, Schaufenster: Die DDR und ihre Texte: Erkundungen zu Herrschaft und Alltag* (Berlin, 1997).

50. Wolfgang Engler, *Die zivilisatorische Lücke: Versuche über den Staatssozialismus* (Frankfurt, 1992).

51. "Gegen die dekadente Amüsierkunst," *ND*, 6/23/1949; "Musikkunst," *ND*, 6/6/1963; "Schlagerparade im neuen SED-Rhythmus," *SZ*, 8/10/1965; and Hermann Meyer, "Probleme der Beatmusik," *ND*, 6/23/1966. See Dorothee Wierling, *Geboren im Jahr Eins: Der Jahrgang 1949 in der DDR und seine historischen Erfahrungen—Versuch einer Kollektivbiographie* (Berlin, 2002), 215 ff.

52. "Musikopas in der DDR," *Berliner Stimme*, 5/27/1972; "Kraftvoll erklang das Lied des antiimperialistischen Kampfes," *ND*, 2/9/1987; "Der King vom Prenzlauer Berg kriegt die ideologische Kurve," *Die Welt*, 1/20/1979; and Poiger, *Jazz, Rock and Rebels*.

53. "Zusammenstöße mit der DDR-Polizei," *FR*, 10/10/1977; "Die Kritik der Jugend am SED-Regime wird lauter," *Die Welt*, 10/11/1977; "Brennende Uniform," *Der Spiegel* 31 (1977), no. 47, 65–66; and Lindenberger, *Volkspolizei*, 367 ff.

54. Peter Thomas Krüger, "Die Rocknacht auf der anderen Seite," *FR*, 6/9/1987; Peter Jochen Winters, "Der Ruf 'Die Mauer muß weg' wird der SED noch lange in den Ohren klingen," *FAZ*, 6/10/1987; and Robert Leicht, "Wut an der Mauer," *Die Zeit*, 6/25/1987. See Erich Loest, *Es geht seinen Gang oder Mühen in unserer Ebene: Roman* (Munich, 1998).

55. Alfred Kurella, "Wir schaffen die sozialistische Kultur für die ganze Nation," *ND*, 10/18/1982; "Lockerung der Kulturpolitik in der DDR," *NZZ*, 3/5/1964; and "Die SED hält am 'sozialistischen Realismus' fest," *FAZ*, 4/27/1964. See Angela Borgwardt, *Im Umgang mit der Macht: Herrschaft und Selbstbehauptung in einem autoritären politischen System* (Wiesbaden, 2002).

56. "Das große Reim-und-ich-freß-dich," *FAZ*, 12/22/1965; "Unbeirrbar," *ND*, 1/13/1966; "Fruchtlose Kulturpolitik Pankows," *NZZ*, 8/17/1966; and Walter Ulbricht, "Die sozialistische Nationalkultur ist unser gemeinsames Werk," *ND*, 10/9/1968. See Günter Agde, ed., *Kahlschlag: Das 11. Plenum des ZK der SED 1965: Studien und Dokumente* (Berlin, 1991).

57. "Saubere Kunst im sauberen Staat," *SZ*, 5/8/1971; "Neue Tendenzen in der Kulturpolitik der DDR," *DW Dokumentation*, 6/27/1972; "Nicht mehr so dogmatisch," *Die Zeit*, 4/20/1973; and "Wechsel in den Führungspositionen der DDR-Kulturpolitik," *NZZ*, 4/29/1973.

58. "Der sozialistische Realismus als Prinzip," *FAZ*, 5/28/1975; "Aufhebung des Toleranzedikts," *SZ*, 8/30/1977; "Honeckers Maulkorb-Edikt," *SZ*, 6/27/1979; and "Geist und Macht vereint," *FR*, 4/15/1981. Cf. Borgwardt, *Im Umgang mit der Macht*.

59. Walter Leo, "Eine neue Chance für Biermann," *Vorwärts*, 3/18/1974; Irene Böhme, "Zuckerbrot und Peitsche, *FR*, 9/18/1982; and Manfred Jäger, "Spielraum für Beherzte," *DAS*, 3/31/1989. See David Bathrick, *The Powers of Speech: The Politics of Culture in the GDR* (Lincoln, 1995).

60. Robert Havemann, "Zehn Thesen zum 30. Jahrestag der DDR," *europäische ideen* 48 (1980), 33–36. See Katja Havemann and Joachim Widmann, *Robert Havemann oder wie die DDR sich erledigte* (Munich, 2003), 35 ff., and Clemens Vollnhals, *Der Fall Havemann: Ein Lehrstück politischer Justiz* (Berlin, 1998).

61. "Havemann wünscht in der DDR Opposition und kritische Presse," *SZ*, 8/9/1976; "Weil viele noch hoffen, harrt Robert Havemann aus," *Die Welt*, 6/2/1978; "'Das ist die Tragödie der DDR,'" *Der Spiegel* 32 (1978), no. 40, 68 ff.; and "500 Personen nahmen an der Beisetzung Havemanns teil," *TSp*, 4/18/1982.

62. "Biermann bleibt in der Schußlinie," *Die Welt*, 3/16/1966; "Biermanns Rauswurf," *SZ*, 11/17/1976; "Rummel um Biermann," *ND* 11/17/1976; and Lothar Romain, "Sozialismus oder Barbarei," *Vorwärts*, 11/17/1976. See Fritz Pleitgen, ed., *Die Ausbürgerung: Anfang vom Ende der DDR* (Berlin, 2001).

63. "Offener Protest von DDR-Autoren gegen Ausbürgerung Biermanns," *TSp*, 11/19/1976; "DDR-Intellektuelle distanzieren sich in Erklärungen von Biermann," *TSp*, 11/21/1976; "Fall Biermann: Honecker im Teufelskreis," *Der Spiegel* 30 (1976), no. 48, 30 ff.; and Joachim Nawrocki, "Es knistert im Gebälk der DDR," *Die Zeit*, 11/26/1976.

64. Rudolf Bahro, *Die Alternative: Zur Kritik des real existierenden Sozialismus* (Cologne,

1977). See "'Das trifft den Parteiapparat ins Herz,'" *Der Spiegel* 31 (1977), no. 35, 30 ff.

65. "Ostdeutscher System-Kritiker Rudolf Bahro festgenommen," *SZ*, 8/25/1977; "Der Dissident, das künstliche Produkt," *FR*, 7/1/1977; "Proteste gegen die Verurteilung Bahros," *NZZ*, 7/3/1978. Bahro was released in the mid-1980s and was deported to the West where he supported the Greens.

66. "Als ihre Kritik zu laut wurde, mußten die Dissidenten in Haft," *Die Welt*, 8/29/1977; Angela Nacken "Immer mehr wagen den Kampf mit den DDR- Behörden," *FAZ*, 8/21/1976; Rainer Hildebrandt, "Menschenrechtserklärung wörtlich genommen," *TSp*, 11/7/1976; and "DDR: Die Bürger werden aufsässig," *Der Spiegel* 31 (1977), no. 43, 46 ff.

67. "'DDR' schiebt fünf prominente Kritiker in den Westen ab," *Die Welt*, 8/29/1977; "Mauer auf, Gefängnistor zu," *DZ*, 9/2/1977; and "Ein fremdes nahes Land," *RhM*, 1/12/1979.

68. "Ost-Berlin spricht der versuchten Selbstverbrennung moralische und politische Bedeutung ab," *FAZ*, 8/23/1976; "Du sollst nicht falsch' Zeugnis reden," *Universitäts-Zeitung (UZ)*, 9/1/1976 (reprinted from *ND*); and "Ich beuge mich dem System nicht," *Die Welt*, 3/31/1978.

69. Klaus Wolschner, "Jena: Vorbote eines Neuen Deutschland?" *Die Zeit*, 6/17/1983, and Marlies Menge, "Eine Art Mahnwache," *Die Zeit*, 9/9/1983. See Johann Gildemeister, "Friedenspolitische Konzepte und Praxis der Kirchen," in Horst Dähn, ed., *Die Rolle der Kirchen in der DDR: Eine erste Bilanz* (Munich, 1993), 159–173.

70. "Nackt durchs Dorf," *Der Spiegel* 37 (1983), no. 39, 44 ff.; Otto Jörg Weis, "Ein paar Graswurzeln ringen täglich mit der Erdkruste," *FR*, 2/8/1984; and ". . . wächst der Druck zu einem militärischen Präventivschlag," *FR*, 6/20/1986.

71. Founding document of the Initiative Frieden und Menschenrechte (IFM), January 1986, in Wolfgang Rüddenklau, *Störenfried: DDR-Opposition 1986–1989. Mit Texten aus den "Umweltblättern"* (Berlin, 1992), 56 ff.; "Die Reisefreiheit aller Bürger ist nötig," *Der Spiegel* 40 (1986), no. 10, 78 ff.; "Demokratie und Sozialismus," *FR*, 5/21/1986; and "Damit Vertrauen wächst," *FR*, 8/11/1986.

72. For example, see Albrecht Hinze, "Hart zugreifen, schnell loslassen," *SZ*, 10/12/1988, and "Die SED muß ihre Politik jetzt ändern," *Die Welt*, 7/30/1988. See also Havemann and Widmann, *Robert Havemann*, 71 ff.

73. Ulrich Schacht, "Bückware des Geistes aus dunklen Hinterzimmern," *Die Welt*, 9/17/1986. See Rüddenklau, *Störenfried*, 81–359, and Ilko-Sascha Kowalczuk, ed., *Freiheit und Öffentlichkeit: Politischer Samisdat in der DDR 1985–1989—Eine Dokumentation* (Berlin, 2002).

74. Helmut Lohlhöffel, "Der Stumme Kreis von Jena," *SZ*, 7/19/1983; Peter Bolm, "SED unter Druck," *Die Welt*, 12/22/1983; Sabine Katzke, "Die Haft kam prompt, als sie im Betrieb die Arbeit verweigerten," *FR*, 3/3/1984; and Peter Jochen Winters, "Jegliche 'Zusammenrottung' wird von der Polizei observiert," *FAZ*, 10/23/1986.

75. "DDR-Opposition: SED behandelt ihre Kritiker als Feinde," *TSp*, 5/19/1989; "Demokratisierung gefordert" *SZ*, 12/19/1988; and "Erneut Festnahmen in Leipzig," *TSp*, 5/10/1989. See Armin Mitter and Stefan Wolle, eds., *Ich liebe Euch doch alle! Befehle und Lageberichte des MfS, Januar–November 1989* (Berlin, 1990).

76. Dieter Dose and Hans-Rüdiger Karutz, "Symptome der Ratlosigkeit bei den ideologischen Vordenkern," *Die Welt*, 1/29/1988; "Auch das innere Feindbild schwindet," *Vorwärts*, 9/26/1987; and "DDR-Organe gehen weiter hart gegen unabhängige Gruppen vor," *FAZ*, 11/28/1987. See Gerhard Rein, *Die protestantische Revolution 1987–1990: Ein deutsches Lesebuch* (Berlin, 1990), 42–86.

77. Günter Zehm, "Das große Zittern," *Die Welt*, 2/16/1988; "Kritiker der DDR-Verhältnisse berufen sich auf Gorbatschow," *TSp*, 9/3/1988; and "Opposition in Ost-Berlin fordert von Honecker Verzicht auf Mauer," *TSp*, 1/28/1989. See Ulrike Poppe et al., eds., *Zwischen Selbstbehauptung und Anpassung: Formen des Widerstandes und der Opposition in der DDR* (Berlin, 1995), 244–272; Timmer, *Vom Aufbruch zum Umbruch*, 69 ff.; and Walter Süß, *Staatssicherheit am Ende: Warum es den Mächtigen nicht gelang, 1989 eine Revolution zu verhindern* (Berlin, 1999).

78. Bärbel Bohley, "Vierzig Jahre warten," in Bohley et al., eds., *40 Jahre DDR . . . und die Bürger melden sich zu Wort* (Frankfurt, 1989), 5–11. See Helmut Dubiel, Günter Frankenberg, and Ulrich Rödel, "'Wir sind das Volk': Die Geburt der Zivilgesellschaft in der demokratischen Revolution," *FR*, 1/2/1990, and Hartmut Zwahr, *Ende einer Selbstzerstörung: Leipzig und die Revolution in der DDR* (Göttingen, 1993).

79. "Hunderte demonstrierten in Leipzig für Ausreise aus der DDR," *TSp*, 3/14/1989; "Heute in China, morgen in der DDR?" *TSp*, 8/5/1989; "Ausreiser und Bleiber marschieren getrennt," *taz*, 9/9/ 1989; and "Sicherheitskräfte hielten sich bei Demonstrationen in Leipzig zurück," *TSp*, 9/27/1989. See Steven Pfaff, *Fight or Flight? Exit-Voice Dynamics and the Collapse of East Germany* (Durham, 2005).

80. "Festnahmen und Verletzte bei Massendemonstration in Leipzig," *TSp*, 10/4/1989; Karl-Heinz Baum, "SED wechselt die Signale auf Dialog," *FR*, 10/11/1989; and Karl-Dieter Opp and Peter Voß, *Die volkseigene Revolution* (Stuttgart, 1993).

81. "Oppositionsgruppe in der DDR gegründet," *TSp*, 9/12/1989; "Neues Forum ist staatsfeindlich," *Kieler Nachrichten*, 9/22/1989; "Wir werden immer mehr," *Der Spiegel* 43 (1989), no. 49: 25–26. See "Das Neue Forum: Selbstportrait einer Bürgerbewegung," in DGB, ed., *Materialien zur gewerkschaftlichen Bildungsarbeit* (Bonn, 1990), 4 ff.

82. Hans-Jürgen Fischbeck, Ludwig Mehlhorn, Wolfgang Ullmann, and Konrad Weiss, "Aufruf zur Einmischung," *taz*, 9/12/1989. See Ulrike Poppe, "Bürgerbewegung 'Demokratie Jetzt,'" in Hubertus Knabe, ed., *Aufbruch in eine andere DDR: Reformer und Oppositionelle zur Zukunft ihres Landes* (Reinbek, 1989), 160–162.

83. "Künstler der DDR rufen nach einer neuen Medienpolitik," *SZ*, 10/13/1989; Peter J. Winters, "Angelika Unterlauf darf unerhörte Dinge sagen," *FAZ*, 10/14/1989; and Günter Schabowski, "Mündige Bürger und mündige Journalisten brauchen einander," *ND*, 11/11/1989.

84. Hans B. Karutz, "Nachdenkliche Stimmen in den Medien der DDR," *Die Welt*, 12/10/1989; Walter Hömbert, "Klassenfeind mitten im Wohnzimmer," *RhM*, 20/10/1989; "Seit Montag guckt Schnitzler in die Röhre," *FR*, 11/1/1989; and "Immer mehr Zuschauer sehen Aktuelle Kamera," *FAZ*, 11/13/1989.

85. "Parteigründung in der DDR," *FR*, 10/9/1989; "Trügerische Hoffnungen," *Vorwärts*, 11/1/1989; and "Wir werden nach dem 6. Mai mit am Regierungstisch sitzen," *Augsburger Allgemeine*, 12/22/1989. See Konrad H. Jarausch, "'Die notwendige

Demokratisierung unseres Landes': Zur Rolle der SDP im Herbst 1989," in Bernd Faulenbach and Heinrich Potthoff, eds., *Die deutsche Sozialdemokratie und die Umwälzung 1989/90* (Essen, 2001), 52–68.

86. "In dieser Lage wird's ungeheuer spannend," *Die Welt*, 9/16/1989; "Das wird sehr bunt sein müssen," *taz*, 10/3/1989; and Christian Wernicke, "Eine neue Partei mit Bonner Bügelfalten," *Die Zeit*, 12/22/1989.

87. "Manfred Gerlach," *Stuttgarter Zeitung*, 10/7/1989; "CDU-Mitglieder in der DDR fordern zu Reformvorschlägen auf," *FAZ*, 9/18/1989; Heinrich Jämecke, "Preusse, Christ und Demokrat," *Der Stern*, 12/7/1989; and "Der Block ist zerbrochen," *ND*, 12/7/1989.

88. Gero Neugebauer, "Von der SED zur PDS 1989 bis 1990," in Andreas Herbst et al., eds., *Die SED: Geschichte, Organisation, Politik. Ein Handbuch* (Berlin, 1997), 100–116.

89. "Oppositiongruppen fordern Gespräche am Runden Tisch," *TSp*, 11/15/1989; "Alte Hasen aus dem Untergrund," *SZ*, 12/2/1989; and "Rauhe Zeiten," *Der Spiegel* 43 (1989), no. 52, 23–24. See Uwe Thaysen, *Der Runde Tisch oder Wo blieb das Volk? Der Weg der DDR in die Demokratie* (Opladen, 1990).

90. "Sturm auf Stasi-Zentrale ist die Folge der Verschleierungspolitik," *Die Welt*, 1/17/1990. See Süß, *Staatssicherheit am Ende*, 723 ff.

91. Press report of the Greens from 1/9/1990; interview with Bärbel Bohley, *Schweizer TZ*, 2/10/1990; Joachim Nawrocki, "Betäubt vom Tempo der Profis," *Die Zeit*, 2/9/1990; Klaus-Dieter Frankenberger, "Beim Stichwort Canvassing sind einige Leute ratlos," *FAZ*, 2/24/1990; and "Kinder der Demokratie," *Der Spiegel* 44 (1990), no. 7.

92. Election commentary of politicians from 3/18/1990 on channel 1 of German TV (ARD); Infas, "'Revolutionäre' rücken in den Hintergrund," *SZ*, 3/21/1990; Elisabeth Nölle-Neumann, "Ein demokratischer Wahlkampf gab den Ausschlag," *FAZ*, 3/23/1990; and Manfred Berger, Wolfgang Gibowski, and Diether Roth, "Ein Votum für die Einheit," *Die Zeit*, 3/23/1990.

93. "Gesamtdeutsche Verfassungsdebatte statt Wahlkampf," *taz*, 3/3/1990; Ulrich K. Preuss, "Auf der Suche nach der Zivilgesellschaft," *FAZ*, 4/28/1990; Gerd Roellecke, "Dritter Weg zum zweiten Fall," *FAZ*, 6/12/1990; and "Deutscher Einigungsprozeß: Nicht die Zeit für Verfassungsexperimente," CDU-press service, 6/28/1990.

94. "Wirtschafts- und Währungsunion," *taz*, 1/30/1990; "Akzeptabel ist nur eine Sozialunion," *Presse*, 4/9/1990; "Die wichtigste soziale Aufgabe für jeden ist die Stabilität der Mark," *Die Welt*, 4/30/1990; "Das gleicht Kapitulation nach verlorenem Krieg," *ND*, 5/6/1990; "Schocktherapie statt Besinnung," *taz*, 5/23/1990; and Lothar de Maizière, "Gründergeist und neuer Mut," *FAZ*, 5/28/1990.

95. Interview with Günther Krause, Deutscher Fernsehfunk, 8/25/1990; Lothar de Maizière, "Dieser Vertrag regelt den Beitritt in ausgewogener Balance," *HAZ*, 9/1/1990; "Hans-Jochen Vogels politischer Bericht vor der Fraktion," SPD-Pressedienst, 9/4/1990; and Ulrich K. Preuss, "Der Liquidationsvertrag," *taz*, 9/14/1990.

96. "Erhobenen Hauptes in die Einheit gehen," *Kölner Stadt-Anzeiger*, 8/18/1990; "DDR-Identität?" *ND*, 9/29/1990; and Thomas Bulmahn, "Zur Entwicklung der Lebensqualität im vereinigten Deutschland," *APuZ* B 40 (2000), 30–38.

97. Rainer Schedlinski, "die phase der *schönen revolution* ist vorbei," in Stefan Heym and

Werner Heiduczek, eds., *Die sanfte Revolution: Prosa, Lyrik, Protokolle, Erlebnisberichte, Reden* (Leipzig, 1990), 339–345. See Jan Wielgohs, "Auflösung und Transformation der ostdeutschen Bürgerbewegung," *DA* 26 (1993), 426–434; Detlef Pollack, "Was ist aus den Bürgerbewegungen und Oppositionsgruppen der DDR geworden?" *APuZ* B 40–41 (1995), 34–45.

98. Eckhard Priller, "Veränderungen in der politischen und sozialen Beteiligung in Ostdeutschland," in Wolfgang Zapf and Roland Habich, eds., *Wohlfahrtsentwicklung im vereinten Deutschland: Sozialstruktur, sozialer Wandel und Lebensqualität* (Berlin, 1996), 285 ff.

99. Jörn Ewaldt et al., "Zwischenbilanz der Wirtschaftsentwicklung in Ostdeutschland," *DA* 31 (1998), 371–383, and Klaus-Peter Schwitzer, "Ältere und alte Menschen in den neuen Bundesländern im zehnten Jahr nach der Wende: Eine sozialwissenschaftliche Bilanz," *APuZ* B 43–44 (1999), 32–39. See Rainer Geißler, "Nachholende Modernisierung mit Widersprüchen: Eine Vereinigungsbilanz aus modernisierungstheoretischer Perspektive," *APuZ* B 40 (2000), 22–29.

100. Karin Rohnstock, "Mentalität ist eine Haut," *FAZ*, 7/10/1999; Laurence McFalls, "Die kulturelle Vereinigung Deutschlands: Ostdeutsche politische und Alltagskultur vom real existierenden Sozialismus zur postmodernen kapitalistischen Konsumkultur," *APuZ* B 11 (2001), 23–29; and Dietrich Mühlberg, "Beobachtete Tendenzen zur Ausbildung einer ostdeutschen Teilkultur," *APuZ* B 11 (2001), 30–38. See Daniela Dahn, *Westwärts und nicht vergessen: Vom Unbehagen an der Einheit* (Berlin, 1996), as well as Hans-Jürgen Misselwitz, *Nicht mehr mit dem Gesicht nach Westen: Das neue Selbstbewußtsein der Ostdeutschen* (Bonn, 1996).

101. Peter Förster, "'Es war nicht alles falsch, was wir früher über den Kapitalismus gelernt haben': Empirische Ergebnisse einer Längsschnittstudie zum Weg junger Ostdeutscher vom DDR-Bürger zum Bundesbürger," *DA* 34 (2001), 197–218, and Detlef Pollack, "Wirtschaftlicher, sozialer und mentaler Wandel in Ostdeutschland: Eine Bilanz nach zehn Jahren," *APuZ* B 40 (2000), 13–21.

102. Karin Kortmann, "Mit mehr Verantwortung zu einer aktiveren Gesellschaft in Deutschland," *Das Parlament*, 4/16/2003. See Ansgar Klein, *Der Diskurs der Zivilgesellschaft: Politische Kontexte und demokratietheoretische Bezüge der neueren Begriffsverwendung* (Opladen, 2001).

103. Lutz Rathenow, "Mit Befürchtungen, aber ohne Angst," *Bonner Generalanzeiger*, 9/29/1990. See Bauerkämper, *Ländliche Gesellschaft*, 494.

104. "Abkehr von dem Sozialismus," *Die Zeit*, 3/19/1982, and Anette Simon, "Fremd im eigenen Land," *Die Zeit*, 6/17/1999. See also the literature cited by Corey Ross, "Grundmerkmal oder Randerscheinung: Überlegungen zu Dissens und Opposition in der DDR," *DA* 35 (2002), 747–760.

105. Wolfgang Merkel and Hans-Joachim Lauth, "Systemwechsel und Zivilgesellschaft: Welche Zivilgesellschaft braucht die Demokratie?" *APuZ* B 6–7 (1998), 3–12. Thaa, *Die Wiedergeburt des Politischen*, 357 ff., omits the East German case.

106. Thomas Ahbe, "Hohnarbeit und Kapital: Westdeutsche Bilder vom Osten," *DA* 33 (2000), 84–89; Ahbe, "Nicht demokratisierbar: Westdeutsche Bilder vom Osten (II)," *DA* 35 (2002), 112–118; and Rita Kuczynski, "Von der Wupper an die Oder," *SZ*, 3/22/2000.

107. Heiner Meulemann, "Aufholtendenzen und Systemeffekte: Eine Übersicht über Wertunterschiede zwischen Ost- und Westdeutschland," *APuZ* B 40–41 (1995), 21–33; Albrecht Göschel, "Kulturelle und politische Generationen in Ost und West: Zum Gegensatz von wesenhafter und distinktiver Identität," *BDI* 10 (1999), no. 2, 29–40; and Siegrist, "Wie bürgerlich war die Bundesrepublik."

108. Dietrich Mühlberg, "Schwierigkeiten kultureller Assimilation: Freuden und Mühen der Ostdeutschen beim Eingewöhnen in neue Standards des Alltagslebens," *APuZ* B 17 (2002), 3–11, and Joyce M. Mushaben, "Democratization as a Political-Cultural Process: *Social Capital* and Citizen Competence in the East German Länder" (manuscript, St. Louis, 1998).

109. Kocka, *Vereinigungskrise*; Thomas Ahbe, "Ostalgie als Laienpraxis: Einordnung, Bedingungen, Funktion," *BDI* 10 (1999), no. 3, 87–97; Paul Betts, "The Twilight of the Idols: East German Memory and Material Culture," *JMH* 72 (2000), 731–765.

110. Günter de Bruyn, "Deutsche Zustände," *TSp*, 8/8/1999, and Gerhard A. Ritter, *Der Umbruch von 1989/90 und die Geschichtswissenschaft* (Munich, 1995).

CHAPTER 8

1. www.Mauerspechte.de, www.ddr-im-www.de, and other websites. See Heinz J. Kuzdas, *Berliner MauerKunst* (Berlin, 1990), 77 ff., and Axel Klausmeier and Leo Schmidt, *Mauerreste—Mauerspuren* (Bad Münstereifel, 2004).

2. Müller, *Die USA in Potsdam*. See Görtemaker, *Geschichte der Bundesrepublik*.

3. "Über die Frage, wie die Deutschen die Spaltung betrieben haben," *Die Neue*, 6/28/1982, and "Bonn hält an Bemühungen um innerdeutsche Normalisierung fest," *TSp*, 7/30/1982. See also Richard Bessel and Dirk Schumann, eds., *Life after Death: Approaches to a Cultural and Social History of Europe during the 1940s and 1950s* (Cambridge, 2003), 5 ff.

4. Hans-Peter Schwarz, "Das Ende der Identitätsneurose," *RhM*, 9/7/1990; Rainer Zitelmann, *Wohin treibt unsere Republik?* 2nd ed. (Frankfurt, 1995); and Jürgen Habermas, "Wir sind wieder 'normal' geworden," *Die Zeit*, 12/18/1992. See Konrad H. Jarausch, "Normalisierung oder Re-Nationalisierung? Zur Umdeutung der deutschen Vergangenheit," *GG* 21 (1995), 571–584.

5. *Geschichte der deutschen Einheit*, 4 vols. (Stuttgart, 1998), and Alexander von Plato, *Die Vereinigung Deutschlands—ein weltpolitisches Machtspiel: Bush, Kohl, Gorbatschow und die geheimen Moskauer Protokolle* (Berlin, 2002).

6. Winkler, *Der lange Weg*, vol. 2; Kielmansegg, *Nach der Katastrophe*.

7. Mitchell Ash, "Becoming Normal, Modern, and German (Again?)," in Michael Geyer, ed., *The Power of Intellectuals in Contemporary Germany* (Chicago, 2001), 298–313, and Moshe Zuckermann, *Gedenken und Kulturindustrie: Ein Essay zur neuen deutschen Normalität* (Berlin, 1999), 21 ff. For a more alarmist view, see Stefan Berger, *The Search for Normality: National Identity and Historical Consciousness in Germany since 1800* (Providence, 1997).

8. Rudolf Augstein and Günter Grass, *Deutschland, einig Vaterland? Ein Streitgespräch* (Göttingen, 1990).

9. Schröder, *Deutschland schwierig Vaterland*.

10. Stöver, *Die Befreiung vom Kommunismus*, and Kleßmann, *Zwei Staaten, eine Nation*.

11. Egon Bahr, *Zu meiner Zeit* (Munich, 1996), 284 ff., and Strauß, *Die Erinnerungen.*

12. Wolfrum, *Geschichtspolitik in der Bundesrepublik.*

13. Hendrik Bussiek, "Visionen in Ost und West," *Vorwärts*, 8/28/1980; Jürgen Engert, "Dilemma der Halbstarken," *RhM*, 11/21/1980; and "Schmidt: Rückschläge, aber kein Ende unserer Politik der Minderung von Spannungen," *FAZ*, 4/12/1981.

14. Robert Leicht, "Turbulenz um den Begriff," *SZ*, 4/3/1981; Peter Bender, "Geisterkampf um die Nation," *Der Spiegel* 35 (1981), no. 9 , 48–49; Günter Gaus, "Politik des Friedens für Deutschland," *Berliner Liberale Zeitung*, 11/27/1981; Hermann Rudolph, "Zwischen Trennen und Verbundensein," *Die Zeit*, 4/17/1981.

15. Hans Heigert, "Die Angst vor dem Volk," *SZ*, 10/18/1980; "Die DDR schottet sich ab," *Berliner Stimme*, 11/1/1980; and "Honecker richtet Forderungskatalog an Bonn," *TSp*, 10/14/1980. See Manfred Schaller, "Das Jahrzehnt der offenen Grenze: Die DDR-Bevölkerung und Polen in den 70er Jahren" (MA thesis, Potsdam 2004), and Hans-Hermann Hertle and Konrad H. Jarausch, eds., *Risse im Bruderbund? Die Gespräche von Erich Honecker and Leonid I. Breshnew, 1974–1982* (Berlin, 2006).

16. Hendrik Bussiek, "Hoffen, dass es nicht schlechter wird," *Vorwärts*, 10/12/1981; "Treffen am Werbellinsee ist von großer Bedeutung für Frieden, Abrüstung und Zusammenarbeit der Völker," *ND*, 12/16/1981; Helmut Schmidt, "Ein aktiver Beitrag zum Dialog über Sicherheit," *ND*, 12/14/1981; and Peter Kutschke, "Bonn: Ostberlin Wieder Hoffnung für die Deutschen," *Vorwärts*, 12/17/1981.

17. "Es begann in Erfurt," *Das Parlament*, 6/6/1983; Irene Böhme, "Als wäre es das Normalste der Welt," *FR*, 12/24/1981; "Normales als Zugeständnis teuer erkauft," *BK*, 2/20/1982; and Karl-Heinz Baum, "Schielen nach dem Milch- und Honigland," *FR*, 10/2/1982.

18. Eduard Lintner, "Rechtspositionen sind kein 'Formelkram,'" *BK*, 11/13/1982; Hendrik Bussiek, "DDR-Bürger: Um Gottes willen, was habt ihr vor?" *Vorwärts*, 5/5/1983;"Kohl: Wir wollen die Teilung erträglich machen," *FAZ*, 6/24/1983; and Kohl, *Erinnerungen 1982–1990*, 83–86.

19. "Die Beziehung zur Regierung Kohl," *NZZ*, 11/19/1982, and Dettmar Cramer, "Kontinuität in der Deutschlandpolitik," *Vorwärts*, 7/7/1983. See Karl-Rudolf Korte, *Deutschlandpolitik in Helmut Kohls Kanzlerschaft: Regierungsstil und Entscheidungen 1982–1989* (Stuttgart, 1998).

20. "Jugend zur Wiedervereinigung," *Die Welt*, 8/4/1983; Eberhard Straub, "Die langwierige deutsche Frage," *FAZ*, 10/12/1981; "Burschenschaften für Einheit der Nation," *FAZ*, 5/31/1983; and "Die deutsche Frage lebendig erhalten," *Das Parlament*, 10/31/1981.

21. Dietrich Müller-Römer, *Die neue Verfassung der DDR* (Cologne, 1974), 78 ff.; Helmut Meier and Walter Schmidt, eds., *Erbe und Tradition in der DDR: Die Diskussion der Historiker* (Cologne, 1989); and Brinks, *Die DDR-Geschichtswissenschaft.*

22. Klaus Erdmann, *Der gescheiterte Nationalstaat: Die Interdependenz von Nations- und Geschichtsverständnis im politischen Bedingungsgefüge der DDR* (Frankfurt, 1996).

23. "Heftiger Disput über den Fortbestand der Nation," *Die Welt*, 3/12/1984; "Zur Deutschlandpolitik," SPD Press Service, 3/20/1984; "Bahr: Drei DDR-Forderungen zu erfüllen," *SZ*, 9/17/1984; and "Einheit der Nation heißt nicht Wiedervereinigung," *Vorwärts*, 11/20/1984.

24. "Deutsche Frage muß offenbleiben," *Die Welt*, 11/9/1984; "Wünschbares und Machbares," *BK*, 3/9/1985; "Warnung vor Kurzatmigkeit in der deutschen Frage," *Die Welt*, 11/26/1984; and "Der Weg zur Einheit über den Nationalstaat ist nicht verboten," *FAZ*, 10/16/1985.

25. "Politisches Feld mit Tretminen," *Vorwärts*, 12/22/1984; "Neue Aufregung um die deutsche Frage," *NZZ*, 5/21/1985; and "Ostpolitik nur unter dem Dach der Präambel," *Die Welt*, 2/26/1986.

26. "Von Normalität weit entfernt," *FR*, 3/16/1984; Horst Stein and Eberhard Nitschke, "Ein Arbeitsbesuch mit 16 Fahnen," *Die Welt*, 9/8/1987; and Thomas Oppermann, "Beim Klang der Hymnen hatte ich das Gefühl, das war die Besiegelung der deutschen Teilung," *Die Welt*, 9/12/1987.

27. "Das gemeinsame Kommuniqué," *TSp*, 9/9/1987; "Honecker sagt Kohl weitere Erleichterungen im innerdeutschen Reiseverkehr zu," *SZ*, 9/9/1987; Klaus Dreher, "Ein Besuch, der vieles offen läßt," *SZ*, 9/9/1984; and Hans-Herbert Gaebel, "Gemeinsam getrennt," *FR*, 9/9/1987. See also Kohl, *Erinnerungen 1982–1990*, 564–579.

28. Karl-Christian Kaiser, "Viele Wahrheiten, kein Augenzwinkern," *Die Zeit*, 9/19/1987; "Kohl spricht von Durchbruch in der Deutschlandpolitik," *TSp*, 10/16/1987; "Honecker nennt Wiedervereinigung Träumerei," *FAZ*, 9/30/1987; and "Kampagne der SED gegen innere Aufweichung," *NZZ*, 9/16/1987. See von Plato, *Die Vereinigung*, 52 ff.

29. "Reagan: Die Berliner Mauer soll fallen," *SZ*, 6/4/1987, and "'Prager Aufruf' tritt für deutsche Einheit ein," *Die Welt*, 3/13/1985. See Ash, *In Europe's Name*.

30. "Deutschlandpolitik der Regierung: Management der Teilungsfolgen," *FAZ*, 8/10/1987; Karl-Christian Kaiser, "Ein kleines Wunder für die Deutschen," *Die Zeit*, 2/1/1988; and "Ungebrochener Schrumpfkurs," *Vorwärts*, 9/24/1988.

31. Axel Schützsack, "Ein neuer Patriotismus auf der Suche nach Formen der Einheit," *Die Welt*, 8/20/1986; Kurt Sagatz, "Teilung nicht als Fluch begreifen," *TSp*, 11/24/1987; Marion Dönhoff, "Als ob endlich die Zukunft beginnt!" *Die Zeit*, 9/14/1987; "Bahr nennt CDU-Bekenntnis zur Wiedervereinigung Heuchelei," *FAZ*, 7/20/1988; and "Bräutigam: Zusammenhalt der Deutschen stärker geworden," *SZ*, 12/20/1988.

32. Eduard Schnitzler, "Kohl und die Widernatürlichkeit," *ND*, 10/27/1988; "CDU: Wiedervereinigung jetzt nicht erreichbar," *SZ*, 2/19/1989; "Im Bundestag erstmals offener Streit über das Fernziel Wiedervereinigung," *FAZ*, 12/2/1988; and Hans-Dietrich Genscher, *Erinnerungen* (Berlin, 1995).

33. "'Wir haben einen Modus vivendi,'" *Der Spiegel* 39 (1985), no. 4, 26 ff.; Carl-Christian Kaiser, "Das Geflecht wird enger," *Die Zeit*, 4/7/1989; and "Zweigleisige Politik Ostberlins gegenüber Bonn," *NZZ*, 12/25/1988.

34. "Pro und Contra: Ist die Wiedervereinigung eine dringliche Zukunftsaufgabe für Deutschland?" *Die Welt*, 5/13/1989. See Günter Gaus, "Zwei deutsche Staaten—und welcher Zukunft zugewandt?" *Die Zeit*, 1/20/1989. See Bundesministerium des Innern, ed., *Dokumente zur Deutschlandpolitik: Deutsche Einheit: Sonderedition aus den Akten des Bundeskanzleramtes 1989/90* (Munich, 1998), 276 ff.

35. D. Dose and H. Karutz, "Bundesregierung rechnet mit Honeckers Verbleiben im Amt über 1990 hinaus," *Die Welt*, 6/27/1989; "Honecker wünscht gute Beziehungen zu Bonn," *FAZ*, 9/8/1989; letter to the editor by Ingo Arend, "Statt der Lebenslüge Wieder-

vereinigung transnationale Kooperation," *FAZ*, 7/3/1989; and Gerhard Zwerenz, "Romantische Geister gibt es hüben wie drüben," *Die Welt*, 5/13/1989.

36. Rolf Hochhut, "Die deutsche Uhr zeigt Einheit an," *Die Welt*, 5/13/1989; "Mit Europa zur deutschen Wiedervereinigung," *FAZ*, 5/8/1989; "Freiheit und Einheit als Aufgabe," *Die Welt*, 5/22/1989; and "Deutsche Fragen" *TSp*, 7/3/1989. See *DzD: Deutsche Einheit*, 283–284.

37. Walter Bajohr, "Hinter den Ritualen Angst vor der deutschen Frage," *RhM*, 9/8/1989; "Ratlosigkeit in Ost und West," *Der Spiegel* 43 (1989), no. 38, 14 ff.; "Deutschlandpolitik nach der Flüchtlingswelle," *NZZ*, 24/9/1989; and "'Wir müssen Kurs halten,'" *Der Spiegel* 43 (1989), no. 39, 16 ff. See *DzD: Deutsche Einheit*, 323 ff., 393 ff., 413 ff.

38. "Wiedervereinigung ein untauglicher Begriff," *FAZ*, 9/28/1989; Karl Friedrich Fromme, "Flüchtlinge und deutsche Frage," *FAZ*, 9/26/1989; and "Kohl und Vogel über Haltung zur DDR-Führung einig," *TSp*, 10/7/1989. See also Kohl, *Erinnerungen 1982–1990*, 941 ff.

39. "Forderung Bonns nach freien Wahlen in der DDR," *NZZ*, 11/10/1989, and "Die Deutschen feiern ihr Wiedersehen: Berlins Herz beginnt wieder zu schlagen," *Die Welt*, 11/13/1989. See *DzD: Deutsche Einheit*, 425 ff., 455 ff., 504–519, and Hans-Hermann Hertle, *Der Fall der Mauer: Die unbeabsichtigte Selbtsauflösung des SED-Staates* (Opladen, 1996).

40. Gerd Prokop, "Nicht auf der Tagesordnung," *ND*, 11/14/1989; "Wider die Vereinigung," *taz*, 11/15/1989; Wolfgang Bergsdorf, "Staunen vor offenen Türen," *RhM*, 10/27/1989; and Rudolf Augstein, "Eine Löwin namens Einheit," *Der Spiegel* 43 (1989), no. 38, 15.

41. "Der Bonner Stufenplan," *FR*, 11/29/1989; *DzD: Deutsche Einheit*, 567 ff.; Horst Teltschik, *329 Tage: Innenansichten der Einigung* (Berlin, 1991), 42–86; Werner Weidenfeld, *Außenpolitik für die deutsche Einheit: Die Entscheidungsjahre 1989/90* (Stuttgart, 1998), 97 ff.; and Kohl, *Erinnerungen 1982–1990*, 988 ff.

42. "Zehn-Punkte-Plan" zur Deutschlandpolitik, *BfdiP* (January, 1990), 119 ff. See "Zehn Punkte Kohls für einen deutsch-deutschen Weg," *FAZ*, 11/29/1989, and Karl-Feldmeyer, "Kohl nutzt die Stunde," *FAZ*, 30/11/1989; and "Ein Staatenbund? Ein Bundesstaat?" *Der Spiegel* 43 (1989), no. 49, 24 ff.

43. Thomas Kielinger, "Wir haben uns die Einheit verdient," *RhM*, 12/8/1989; "SPD stimmt Plänen Kohls für deutsche Konföderation zu," *TSp*, 11/29/1989; "Die Grünen sind gegen die Wiedervereinigung," *FAZ*, 9/22/1989; "Wiedervereinigung," *taz*, 11/23/1989; and "Vereint gegen die Kohl-Plantage," *taz*, 12/11/1989.

44. Eduard Neumaier, "Der Plan, die Einheit und die Freunde," *RhM*, 12/1/1989, and "Weitgehende Übereinstimmung zwischen Mitterrand und Gorbatschow," *FAZ*, 12/8/1989. See *DzD: Deutsche Einheit*, 546 ff., 574 ff.; Philip Zelikow and Condoleezza Rice, *Germany Unified and Europe Transformed: A Study in Statecraft* (Cambridge, 1995), 102 ff.; and von Plato, *Die Vereinigung*, 125 ff.

45. "'Deutschland, einig Vaterland': Die Stimmung in Leipzig kippt," *taz*, 12/29/1989; "In der DDR wird der Ruf nach Verhandlungen über Kohls zehn Punkte lauter," *FAZ*, 12/5/1989; and "Eine Doppelseite zur Einheit Deutschlands," *FAZ*, 12/11/1989. See *DzD: Deutsche Einheit*, 590 ff., 621 ff.

46. Georg Reißmüller, "Drüben wollen viele die Einheit," *FAZ*, 12/15/1989; "Deutscher Bund ohne Waffen," *FR*, 12/16/1989; "Recht auf Einheit gefordert," *FAZ*, 12/18/1989; "Auf dem Weg zu einer Vertragsgemeinschaft," *ND*, 12/20/1989; "Brandenburger Tor wird geöffnet," *Die Welt*, 12/20/1989. See *DzD: Deutsche Einheit*, 663 ff; and Kohl, *Erinnerungen 1982–1990*, 1020 ff..

47. "Für Brandt ist die Einheit der Deutschen eine Frage der Zeit," *TSp*, 12/19/1989; editorial, *NYT*, 11/19/1989; and Peter Jochen Winters, "Deutsche Weihnachten," *FAZ*, 12/21/1989. See Harold James and Marla Stone, eds., *When the Wall Came Down: Reactions to German Unification* (New York, 1992). See *DzD: Deutsche Einheit*, 636 ff., 645 ff.

48. "Deutsche Fragen, alliierte Antworten," *taz*, 9/25/1989. See Bernhard Giesen, *Die Intellektuellen und die Nation*, 2 vols. (Frankfurt, 1993, 1999).

49. Conor Cruise O'Brien, "Beware the Reich is Reviving," *London Times*, 10/31/1989; "'Viertes Reich' mit starken Muskeln," *taz*, 2/3/1990; "Argumente gegen die Wiedervereinigung," *ND*, 12/22/1989; and "'Anderer Alltag' in der DDR: Mühsame Schwimmzüge gegen den Strom," *Vorwärts*, 2/10/1990.

50. Yonah Cohen, "The Unification of the Germanys: A World Disaster," *Ha'Zafeh*, 17/11/1989, and Günter Grass, "Don't Reunify Germany," *NYT*, 1/7/1990. See *DzD: Deutsche Einheit*, 676 ff., and Renata Fritsch-Bournazel, *Europa und die deutsche Einheit* (Stuttgart, 1990).

51. "Die Einheit liegt bei den Deutschen drüben," *FAZ*, 11/17/1989; "Aufruf 'Für unser Land' vom 26. November 1989," in Volker Gransow and Konrad H. Jarausch, eds., *Die deutsche Vereinigung: Dokumente zu Bürgerbewegung, Annäherung und Beitritt* (Cologne, 1991), 100–101; Jörg Bremer, "Dritter Weg und süße Träume," *FAZ*, 12/11/1989; and Gregor Gysi, *Wir brauchen einen dritten Weg: Selbstverständnis und Programm der PDS* (Hamburg, 1990).

52. "Modrows Entscheidung findet die Zustimmung der Bundesregierung," *FAZ*, 1/12/1990; "Geschichte entscheidet über Wiedervereinigung," *taz*, 12/13/1989; and Tilman Fichter, "Chancen für einen dritten Weg?" *taz*, 1/23/1990. See *DzD: Deutsche Einheit*, 695 ff., 707 ff., 713 ff.

53. "Genugtuung Bonns über Modrows Konzessionen," *NZZ*, 1/17/1990; "Wirtschafts- und Währungsunion vorrangig," *FAZ*, 1/24/1990; "Grüne geben Prinzip der Zweistaatlichkeit auf," *SZ*, 2/8/1990; and Jochen Dankert, "Die bessere Variante ist Rechtsgleichheit der Partner," *ND*, 3/3/1990.

54. "Vorschläge Modrows für ein 'einig Vaterland,'" *FAZ*, 2/2/1990; Peter Bender, "Ein Magnet, stärker als die Macht," *Die Zeit*, 2/9/1990; "Kohl und Modrow verabreden Schritte zur Währungsunion," *Die Welt*, 2/14/1990; and "Kohl: Chance für Einheit entschlossen wahrnehmen," *SZ*, 2/16/1990. See *DzD: Deutsche Einheit*, 722 ff., 795–813, von Plato, *Die Vereinigung*, 164 ff; and Kohl, *Erinnerungen 1982–1990*, 1062 ff.

55. Otto B. Roegele, "Beitritt und kein langes Abenteuer," *RhM*, 3/9/1990; "Koalitionsparteien und SPD bekennen sich zum Ziel der deutschen Einheit," *FAZ*, 1/13/1990; "SPD rechnet mit DDR-Beitritt," *SZ*, 2/7/1990; "Jugend in der DDR für vereintes Deutschland," *Die Welt*, 12/27/1989; and "Die 'Allianz' will die Wiedervereinigung so schnell wie möglich," *FAZ*, 3/2/1990. See *DzD: Deutsche Einheit*, 727 ff., 749 ff., 759 ff., 879 ff.

56. Interview with president George H. Bush, *NYT*, 10/25/1989; "Bush und Mitterrand für nur langsame Schritte in Richtung Wiedervereinigung," *TSp*, 12/29/1989; and "Wiedervereinigung in Polens Interesse," *FAZ*, 9/19/1989. See Konrad H. Jarausch, "American Policy towards German Reunification: Images and Interests," in David E. Barclay and Elisabeth Glaser-Schmidt, eds., *Transatlantic Images and Perceptions: Germany and America since 1776* (Cambridge, 1997), 333 ff.

57. "Deutsche Einheit nur im Rahmen einer europäischen Friedensordnung," *Die Welt*, 9/28/1989; "Bonn steht ohne Wenn und Aber zur europäischen Verantwortung," *FAZ*, 1/18/1990; and "Deutsche Einheit und europäische Integration sind kein Gegensatz," *FAZ*, 3/12/1990. See *DzD: Deutsche Einheit*, 596 ff., 771 ff., 1005 ff.

58. "Mitterrand vollzieht eine Wende," *Die Welt*, 12/21/1989; "Polen und Ungarn unterstützen deutschen Wunsch nach Einheit," *TSp*, 2/6/1990; Bernd Conrad, "Militärisch neutral?" *Die Welt*, 2/3/1990; and "Genscher erläutert in Washington Vorteile des KSZE-Prozesses für die deutsche Einigung," *FAZ*, 2/5/1990.

59. Detlev Ahlers, "Wege nach Deutschland," *Die Welt*, 3/17/1990; "DDR-Regierung will bei Vereinigung eigenständige Akzente setzen," *SZ*, 4/14/1990; and Eghard Mörbitz, "Jetzt beginnt die Arbeit," *FR*, 3/19/1990. See *DzD: Deutsche Einheit*, 961 ff., 1018 ff., and Jarausch, *Die unverhoffte Einheit*, 178 ff.

60. Hellmuth Karasek, "Mit Kanonen auf Bananen?" *Der Spiegel* 44 (1990), no. 13, 56–57; "Mit gemischten Gefühlen zur Einheit," *SZ*, 2/20/1990; and Theo Sommer, "Die Geschichte wechselt ihr Tempo," *Die Zeit*, 4/13/1990. See Konrad H. Jarausch, "The Double Disappointment: Revolution, Unification, and German Intellectuals," in Michael Geyer, ed., *The Power of Intellectuals in Contemporary Germany* (Chicago, 2001), 276–294.

61. "USA für schnelle Vereinigung," *SZ*, 3/21/1990; "'Anschluß' ist ein falscher Begriff," *Der Spiegel* 44 (1990), no. 12, 48 ff.; "Der Beitritt über Artikel 23 ist der richtige Weg zur deutschen Einheit," *Die Welt*, 3/28/1990; and *DzD: Deutsche Einheit*, 1126 ff., 1191.

62. "Genscher: Einheit trägt zur Stabilität in Europa bei," *SZ*, 2/14/1990; "Baker: Die Nachbarn werden einbezogen," *SZ*, 2/24/1990; "Die Büchse der Pandora ist weiterhin offen," *FR*, 3/27/1990; and Henryk M. Broder, "Ja zur Vereinigung," *taz*, 3/29/1990. See *DzD: Deutsche Einheit*, 860 ff., 950 ff., 1074 ff., and Zelikow and Rice, *Germany Unified*, 149 ff.

63. "Was haben wir von der Vereinigung?" *taz*, 3/19/1990; "Bonn stimmt sich vor der Zwei-Plus-Vier-Konferenz mit Washington ab," *FAZ*, 4/5/1990; and "Plädoyers und Entwürfe für die deutsche Einheit," *NZZ*, 4/8/1990. See *DzD: Deutsche Einheit*, 857 ff., 921 ff., 970 ff., and von Plato, *Die Vereinigung*, 207 ff.

64. "Erstes 2+4 Gespräch in Bonn eröffnet den Weg zur Vereinigung Deutschlands," *SZ*, 5/7/1990; "'Alle werden sehen: Es geht,'" *Der Spiegel* 44 (1990), no. 24, 18 ff.; "Genscher sieht Erfolg bei den 2+4 Verhandlungen," *SZ*, 6/25/1990; "Bekenntnis Kohls zur Einheit Europas," *NZZ*, 7/19/1990; and Richard Kiessler and Frank Elbe, *Ein runder Tisch mit scharfen Ecken: Der diplomatische Weg zur deutschen Einheit* (Baden-Baden, 1993), 106 ff.

65. "Bundestag bestätigt Garantie für Polens Westgrenze," *SZ*, 3/9/1990, and "Polen mit Grenzvertrag nach der Vereinigung einverstanden," *SZ*, 7/18/1990. In this ques-

tion Kohl was forced to make concessions through international pressure. See *DzD: Deutsche Einheit*, 937 ff., 1063 ff., 1147 ff., 1185 ff.

66. "'Zwei-Plus-Vier'-Vertrag über Deutschland vom 12. September 1990," in Volker Gransow and Konrad H. Jarausch, eds., *Die deutsche Vereinigung: Dokumente zu Bürgerbewegung, Annäherung und Beitritt* (Cologne, 1991), 224–226. See Michael Stürmer, "Entscheidung in der Mitte," *FAZ*, 6/21/1990; "Ein souveränes Deutschland in Europa," *NZZ*, 7/24/1990; Johannes Leithäuser, "Nach der Unterzeichnung nehmen die Minister die Füllfederhalter mit," *FAZ*, 9/13/1990; *DzD: Deutsche Einheit*, 1090 ff., 1249 ff., 1261 ff., 1340 ff., 1531 ff.; and von Plato, *Die Vereinigung*, 394 ff.

67. Roderich Reifenrath, "Die Deutschen haben alles—nur keine Zeit," *FR*, 2/3/1990; Günter Nonnenmacher, "Die Einheit—zu schnell?" *FAZ*, 3/10/1990; "Wirtschaft für schnelle Vereinigung," *SZ*, 3/13/1990; and "Kohl und Modrow verabreden Schritte zur Währungsunion," *Die Welt*, 2/14/1990. See *DzD: Deutsche Einheit*, 768 ff., 948 ff., 1024 ff., 1108 ff.

68. "Kohl: Chance der Einheit entschlossen wahrnehmen," *SZ*, 2/16/1990; "1:1 entzweit die Deutschen," *Der Spiegel* 44 (1990), no. 17, 100 ff.; "Entscheidender Schritt zur Einheit," *TSp*, 5/19/1990; and "Die Deutschen in der DDR vertrauen auf einen wirtschaftlichen Aufschwung," *FAZ*, 7/19/1990. See Dieter Grosser, *Das Wagnis der Währungs-, Wirtschafts- und Sozialunion: Politische Zwänge im Konflikt mit ökonomischen Regeln* (Stuttgart, 1998), 277 ff.

69. "Große Mehrheit für die Einheit," *FAZ*, 7/22/1990; "Allianz der Ängste," *FAZ*, 6/7/1990; German Bishops, "Für eine gemeinsame Zukunft," *FAZ*, 6/27/1990; and "Trend zur Einheit hat sich stabilisiert," *TSp*, 8/16/1990.

70. Ulrich Everling, "Der Weg nach Deutschland ist langwierig," *FAZ*, 3/15/1990, and resolution of 100 professors of state law, "Der Beitritt über Artikel 23 ist der richtige Weg zur deutschen Einheit," *Die Welt*, 3/28/1990. See "Ruf nach neuem Einigungsvertrag," *SZ*, 8/7/1990, and *DzD: Deutsche Einheit*, 1151 ff., 1214 ff., 1265 ff., 1324 ff., 1379 ff., 1425 ff.

71. "De Maizière will den Beitritt 'so schnell wie möglich und so geordnet wie nötig,'" *FAZ*, 7/21/1990; " 'Notanschluß unvermeidlich,'" *Der Spiegel* 44 (1990), no. 34, 16 ff.; "Nächtliche Jubelszenen in der Volkskammer," *TSp*, 8/24/1990; and Friedrich Karl Fromme, "Der 3. Oktober," *FAZ*, 8/24/1990.

72. Richard von Weizsäcker, "Einander annehmen," *Die Welt*, 7/2/1990; "Eine große Mehrheit der Deutschen in Ost und West befürwortet die Einheit," *FAZ*, 8/28/1990; and Friedrich Karl Fromme, "Spätfolge des Krieges," *FAZ*, 8/31/1990. See *DzD: Deutsche Einheit*, 1464 ff., 1490 ff., 1508 ff., and Wolfgang Jäger, *Die Überwindung der Teilung: Der innerdeutsche Prozeß der Vereinigung 1989/90* (Stuttgart, 1998), 478 ff.

73. Helmut Kohl, "Die Erfüllung eines geschichtlichen Auftrags," *FAZ*, 10/2/1990; "Vollendung der Einheit Deutschlands," *NZZ*, 10/4/1990; and "Die deutsche Einheit als Volksfest," *NZZ*, 10/5/1990. See Elke Schmitter, "Nach Toresschluß," *FAZ*, 8/12/1990, and "Nie wieder Deutschland!" *TSp*, 6/28/1990.

74. Klaus von Dohnanyi, "Deutschland: Ein normales Land?" *Die Zeit*, 8/16/1991, and Kurt Sontheimer, "Die Einheit ist kein Kuckucksei," *RhM*, 11/30/1990. For a more radical interpretation, see Rainer Zitelmann, "Das deutsche Zimmer vor dem

europäischen Haus herrichten?" *TSp*, 9/27/1990, and "Unbequeme Fragen," *Die Welt*, 10/13/1990.

75. Jürgen Habermas, "Der DM-Nationalismus," *Die Zeit*, 3/30/1990; Habermas, *Die Normalität einer Berliner Republik: Kleine politische Schriften VIII* (Frankfurt, 1995), 167 ff.; and Manfred Seiler, "Die Furcht, wieder normal zu werden," *RhM*, 12/14/1990.

76. Klaus Brill, "Die neuen Nachbarn aus der fremden Welt," *SZ*, 11/13/1990; Thomas Aders, "Keine Gefühle von gegenseitiger Fremdheit," *SZ*, 9/14/1991; and "Wie dick ist die Mauer in den Köpfen?" *FAZ*, 4/23/1994.

77. "Vom Ausweis über die Briefmarken bis zum Hausarbeitstag," *SZ*, 9/29/1990; Hans-Peter Schwarz, "Stimmungsdemokratie 91," *Die Welt*, 3/28/1991; and Karl Hondrich, "Das Recht des Erfolgreichen," versus Peter Bender, "Die Schwäche des Starken," *TSp*, 9/22/1991.

78. Friedrich Schorlemmer, "Vom Aufbruch zum Ausverkauf," *Die Zeit*, 11/9/1990; "'Plattmachen' heißt die Devise," *taz*, 10/7/1991; "Sabotage an der Einheit," *Der Spiegel* 46 (1992), no. 13, 22 ff.; and Wilhelm Bittorf, "Das Glitzern in der Wüste," *Der Spiegel* 47 (1993), no. 39, 42–43.

79. Martin and Sylvia Greiffenhagen, "Der Schock der Vereinigung," *Spiegel Dokument*, no. 2 (1994), 4–9; Kerstin Ullrich, "Demokratie als vernünftige Lebensform," *FAZ*, 9/8/1995; and Kocka, *Vereinigungskrise*.

80. "Hoffen und Bangen im anderen Deutschland," *NZZ*, 9/9/1990; Gregor Gysi, "Die ungewollten Verwandten," *Der Spiegel* 45 (1991), no. 24, 34 ff.; "Nur noch so beliebt wie die Russen," *Der Spiegel* 45 (1991), no. 30, 24 ff.; and "Fremde in der Heimat, Fremde in der neuen Zeit," *FR*, 10/2/1995.

81. Jens Reich, "Das Psychodrama um die politische Einheit," *FR*, 8/12/1994; Elisabeth Noelle-Neumann, "Aufarbeitung der Vergangenheit im Schatten der Stasi," *FAZ*, 8/6/1992; "'Distanz, Enttäuschung, Haß,'" *Der Spiegel* 46 (1992), no. 34, 30 ff.; and "'Ein schmerzhafter Prozeß,'" *Der Spiegel* 47 (1993), no. 34, 24 ff.

82. Konrad Weiß, "Verlorene Hoffnung der Einheit," *Der Spiegel* 47 (1993), no. 46, 41 ff.; "Wie erst jetzt die DDR entsteht," *Die Welt*, 1/21/1995; "Sehnsucht nach F6 und Rotkäppchen-Sekt," *FAZ*, 8/14/1995; and Dieter Schröder, "Ein Staat—zwei Nationen?" *SZ*, 9/30/1995.

83. "Einheit, von zwei Seiten betrachtet," *SZ*, 3/27/1992; Richard Schröder, "Neues Miteinander braucht das Land," *TSp*, 3/28/1993; Richard Hilmer and Rita Müller-Hilmer, "Es wächst zusammen," *Die Zeit*, 10/1/1993; and "Ost-West wächst zusammen," *Die Welt*, 1/17/1995.

84. "Deutschlands Vereinigung im Blickfeld Europas," *NZZ*, 9/30/1990; "Alle Fäden in der Hand," *Der Spiegel* 44 (1990), no. 40, 18 ff.; "Lafontaine: Nationalstaat überholt," *SZ*, 9/18/1990; and Arnulf Baring, *Deutschland, was nun? Ein Gespräch mit Dirk Rumberg und Wolf Jobst Siedler* (Berlin, 1991).

85. Peter Glotz, "Der ungerechte Krieg," *Der Spiegel* 45 (1991), no. 9, 38–39, versus Hans Magnus Enzensberger, "Hitlers Widergänger," *Der Spiegel* 45 (1991), no. 6, 26 ff.; and Wolf Biermann, "Ich bin für diesen Krieg," *Die Zeit*, 2/8/1991. See Theo Sommer, "Nur die Logik des Krieges?" versus Helmut Schmidt, "Jammern allein hilft nicht," *Die Zeit*, 2/1/1991.

86. "Germans Are Told of Gulf-War Role," *NYT*, 1/31/1991; "'Die Deutschen an die Front,'" *Der Spiegel* 45 (1991), no. 6, 18 ff.; Marion Dönhoff, "Die bittere Bilanz des Golfkrieges," *Die Zeit*, 4/19/1991; Arnulf Baring, "Schluss mit der Behaglichkeit," *Die Welt*, 10/2/1991; and Sven Papke, "Deutschland auf der Suche nach politischem Profil," *Das Parlament*, 9/27/1991.

87. Michael Schwelien, "Ein Staat zerbirst," *Die Zeit*, 8/16/1991; "Groß und arrogant," *Der Spiegel* 46 (1992), no. 2, 22; Jürgen Habermas, "Gelähmte Politik," *Der Spiegel* 47 (1993), no. 28, 50 ff. See Genscher, *Erinnerungen*, 899 ff., and Daniele Conversi, *German-Bashing and the Breakup of Yugoslavia* (Seattle, 1998).

88. Olaf Ihlau, "Nato, Bonn und Bihac," *Der Spiegel* 48 (1994), no. 49, 21, versus Rudolf Augstein, "Vater aller Dinge," *Der Spiegel* 48 (1994), no. 50, 23; "Einsatz im Machtspiel," *Der Spiegel* 55 (2001), no. 46, 34 ff.; Max Otte, *A Rising Middle Power? German Foreign Policy in Transformation, 1989–1999* (New York, 2000); and Eric Schroeder, "In the Shadow of Auschwitz: Responses to Genocide in the German Press, 1975–1999" (MA thesis, Chapel Hill, 2004).

89. Helmut Kohl, *Deutschlands Zukunft in Europa: Reden und Beiträge des Bundeskanzlers* (Herford, 1990), 163–180. See Volker Berghahn, Gregory Flynn, and Paul Michael Lützeler, "Germany and Europe: Finding an International Role," in Jarausch, *After Unity*, 173–199.

90. Adam Krzeminski, "Das neue Deutschland hat sich geändert," *TSp*, 10/3/1001, and "Planetarische Visionen," *Der Spiegel* 53 (1999), no. 45, 30 ff. Cf. Jürgen Kocka, *Consequences of Unification: German Society and Politics in a Changing International Framework* (Washington, 1995).

91. Friedrich Dieckmann, "Unsere oder eine andere Geschichte?" *TSp*, 7/31/1991; Richard Schröder, "Die Einheit macht noch wenig Freude," *Die Zeit*, 3/17/1995; and Wolf Lepenies, *Folgen einer unerhörten Begebenheit: Die Deutschen nach der Vereinigung* (Berlin, 1992). See Jan-Werner Müller, *Another Country: German Intellectuals, Unification and National Identity* (New Haven, 2000).

92. Lothar de Maizière, government program of 4/19/1990, *DA* 23 (1990), 795–809; Kurt Sontheimer, "Kein Abschied von der Bundesrepublik," *Die Welt*, 10/1/1990; Niklas Luhmann, "Dabeisein und Dagegensein," *FAZ*, 8/22/1990; and Katharina Belwe, "Innere Einheit schwieriger als erwartet," *Das Parlament*, 11/28/1991.

93. Andreas Kuhlmann, "Blick zurück im Zorn," *FR*, 1/16/1993; Friedrich Karl Fromme, "Das Selbstbewußtsein wächst langsam," *FAZ*, 10/2/1991; Monika Zimmermann, "Die Mitgift der DDR: Einheit," *TSp*, 10/2/1995; and Gerd Henghüber, "Umdenken im neuen Deutschland," *BZ*, 10/4/1994.

94. Martin Walser, "Die Banalität des Guten," *FAZ*, 12/12/1998, and Jan Holger Kirsch, "Identität durch Normalität: Der Konflikt um Martin Walsers Friedenspreisrede," *Leviathan* 27 (1999), 309–354.

95. Iggers et al., *Die DDR-Geschichtswissenschaft*; A. D. Moses, "Structure and Agency in the Holocaust: Daniel J. Goldhagen and His Critics," *History and Theory* 37 (1998), 194–219, and Konrad H. Jarausch, "A Double Burden: The Politics of the Past and German Identity," in Jörn Leonhard and Lothar Funk, eds., *Ten Years of German Unification: Transfer, Transformation, Incorporation?* (Birmingham, 2002), 98–114.

96. See texts in Heimo Schwilk and Ulrich Schacht, eds., *Die selbstbewußte Nation: "Anschwellender Bocksgesang" und weitere Beiträge zu einer deutschen Debatte* (Berlin, 1994); Zitelmann et al., *Westbindung*; Karlheinz Weißmann, *Rückruf in die Geschichte: Die deutsche Herausforderung* (Berlin, 1992); and Stefan Berger, "Der Dogmatismus des Normalen," *FR*, 4/16/1996.

97. Günter Grass, "Kleine Nestbeschmutzerrede," *taz*, 9/28/1990; Peter Glotz, "Wider den Feuilleton-Nationalismus," *Die Zeit*, 4/27/1991; Glotz, "Deutsche Gefahren," *Der Spiegel* 48 (1994), no. 17, 30–31; Hans-Ulrich Wehler, "Gurus und Irrlichter: Die neuen Träume der Intellektuellen," *FAZ*, 4/6/1994; and Jürgen Habermas, "Gelähmte Politik," *Der Spiegel* 47 (1993), no. 28, 50 ff. See Klaus Hartung "Wider das alte Denken," *Die Zeit*, 5/17/1991.

98. Christian Meier, *Die Nation, die keine sein will* (Munich, 1991), 28–29; Heinrich August Winkler, "Nationalismus, Nationalstaat und nationale Frage in Deutschland seit 1945," *APuZ* B 40 (1991), 12–24.; Richard Schröder, "Warum sollen wir eine Nation sein?" *Die Zeit*, 5/2/1997; and "Schäuble: Nationalbewußtsein stärken," *FAZ*, 4/16/1994.

99. "Biedenkopf: Die deutsche Einheit ist gelungen," *SZ*, 10/6/1995; "Träume von 'Narren, Illusionisten und Abgewickelten,'" *FR*, 11/2/1994; "Die Folgen eines 'Wunders der Geschichte,'" *BZ*, 11/10/1994; and "Fünf Jahre deutsche Einheit," *TSp*, 10/4/1995.

100. "Frau Süssmuth und Rau würdigen die Gemeinschaftleistung aller Deutschen," *FAZ*, 10/4/1995; Alfred Grosser, "Es hätte schlimmer kommen können," *TSp*, 11/9/1994; Christoph Dieckmann, "Das schweigende Land," *Die Zeit*, 6/20/1997; and Hans-Joachim Veen, "Die Einheit ist schon da," *FAZ*, 6/22/1997.

101. Günter Kunert, "Ein Sehnsuchtsziel," *Die Welt*, 10/11/1994, and Reinhard Meier, *Die Normalisierung Deutschlands: Bonner Protokolle und Reportagen aus der DDR* (Zürich, 1986), 7–30. See Joachim Perels, *Wider die 'Normalisierung' des Nationalsozialismus: Intervention gegen die Verdrängung* (Hannover, 1996); Jan W. van Deth et al., eds., *Die Republik auf dem Weg zur Normalität? Wahlverhalten und politische Einstellungen* (Opladen, 2000); and Peter Glotz, *Die falsche Normalisierung: Die unmerkliche Verwandlung der Deutschen 1989 bis 1994—Essays* (Frankfurt, 1994).

102. "Zivilgesellschaft," *info-blatt der servicestelle politische bildung*, June 2002; "Perspektiven der Zivilgesellschaft" and "Die Zivilgesellschaft in Deutschland," *Deutschland* 5 (2000; also available at www.magazine-deutschland.de).

103. "Konturen einer Zivilgesellschaft: Zur Profilierung eines Begriffs," *FJNSB* 16, no. 2 (2003). See also the Wissenschaftszentrum Berlin (WZB) working group on "Zivilgesellschaft: historisch-sozialwissenschaftliche Perspektiven." (www.wz-berlin.de).

104. "Eine deutsche Erfolgsgeschichte," *NZZ*, 9/30/1995, versus Klaus Bittermann, *Gemeinsam sind wir unausstehlich: Die Wiedervereinigung und ihre Folgen* (Berlin, 1990).

105. Martin and Sylvia Greiffenhagen, "Deutschland und die Zivilgesellschaft," *Der Bürger im Staat* 49, no. 3 (1999), 148 ff.

106. "Gemeinsame Erfahrungen auf dünnem Eis," *TSp*, 10/5/1995; Jürgen Engert, "Szenen einer schwierigen Ehe," *RhM*, 12/23/1994; and "Umgang mit der Einheit spaltet das Parlament," *FR*, 10/13/1995.

107. "Zwei Arten deutscher Gefühlshygiene," *FR*, 10/27/1993; Rudolf von Thadden, "Ein 80-Millionen-Staat ohne klare Konturen?" *TSp*, 10/3/1993; and "Ein Experiment für die Zukunft," *Der Spiegel* 53 (1999), no. 45, 40 ff.

CHAPTER 9

1. Matthias Matussek, "Jagdzeit in Sachsen," *Der Spiegel* 45 (1991), no. 40, 41 ff.; "Schwere ausländerfeindliche Ausschreitungen in Rostock," *TSp*, 8/24/1992; and "Meine Kinder die verbrennen!" *SZ*, 11/24/1992.

2. Walter Bajohr, "Die Scherben von Hoyerswerda," *RhM*, 9/27/1991; "Gemeinsame Front gegen den Fremdenhaß," *SZ*, 10/10/1991; "Lichterkette und Rockkonzert," *Die Welt*, 12/14/1992; Norbert Kostede, "Eine Erleuchtung für die Politik," *Die Zeit*, 1/29/1993; and Reinhard Mohr, "Der Casus belli," *taz*, 10/2/1991.

3. "Die dänische Minderheit will in den Bundestag," *Die Welt*, 7/18/1961. See also Eugene M. Kulischer, *Europe on the Move: War and Population Changes, 1917–47* (New York, 1948).

4. Rogers Brubaker, *Citizenship and Nationhood in France and Germany* (Cambridge, MA, 1992), and Dieter Gosewinkel, "Die Staatsangehörigkeit als Institution des Nationalstaats: Zur Entstehung des Reichs- und Staatsangehörigkeitsgesetzes von 1913," in Rolf Grawert et al., eds., *Offene Staatlichkeit: Festschrift für Ernst-Wolfgang Böckenförde zum 65. Geburtstag* (Berlin, 1995), 359–378.

5. *Grundgesetz für die Bundesrepublik Deutschland vom 23. Mai 1949*, edited by Friedrich Giese, 9th ed. (Frankfurt, 1976).

6. Bade, *Deutsche im Ausland*. See also Ulrich Herbert, *Geschichte der Ausländerpolitik in Deutschland: Saisonarbeiter, Zwangsarbeiter, Gastarbeiter, Flüchtlinge* (Munich, 2001).

7. Iring Fetscher, ed., *Rechtsradikalismus* (Frankfurt, 1967), and Peter Longerich, *Der neue alte Rechtsradikalismus*, edited by Ulrich Wank (Munich, 1993).

8. See note 4, as well as Rainer Münz et al., *Zuwanderung nach Deutschland: Strukturen, Wirkungen, Perspektiven*, 2nd ed. (Frankfurt, 1999).

9. Reinhard Mohr, "Casus belli," *taz*, 10/2/1991; Robert Leicht, "Hoyerswerda in den Köpfen," *Die Zeit*, 9/26/1991; and Beate Winkler, ed., *Zukunftsangst Einwanderung*, 3rd ed. (Munich, 1993).

10. Jürgen Kocka, "Zivilgesellschaft in historischer Perspektive," *FJNSB* 16 (2003), no. 2, 29–37, versus Roland Roth, "Die dunklen Seiten der Zivilgesellschaft," *FJNSB* 16 (2003), no. 2, 59–73.

11. Anonyma, *Eine Frau in Berlin*, 253–254. See Höhn, *GIs and Fräuleins*.

12. "Schleswig-Holsteins Flüchtlingslager sind geräumt," *DZ*, 1/4/1964.

13. Anonyma, *Eine Frau in Berlin*, 275–276. See Münz, *Zuwanderung*, 28 ff. and Klaus J. Bade, ed., *Neue Heimat im Westen: Vertriebene, Flüchtlinge, Aussiedler* (Münster, 1990).

14. Hubert Heinelt and Anne Lohmann, *Immigranten im Wohlfahrtsstaat am Beispiel der Rechtspositionen und Lebensverhältnisse von Aussiedlern* (Opladen, 1992).

15. Münz, *Zuwanderung*, 36 ff. See also the research project by Bernd Stöver on East-West migration (unpublished manuscript).

16. For two individual accounts, see Hans Herzog, "Eine bewegte Zeit," KA 6368, 107 ff.,

and Ruth Reimann-Möller, "Die Berichterstatterin von Burg: Zwischen den Schatten von Königin Luise und Hermann Matern," *KA* 6122, 286 ff.

17. "Bonn's Expulsion of Refugees Is Criticized as Too Inflexible," *NYT*, 11/10/1965. See Münz, *Zuwanderung*, 40 ff., 53 ff. See also Patrice Poutrus, "Asyl im Kalten Krieg," *Totalitarismus und Demokratie* 2 (2005), 273–288.

18. Klaus J. Bade, *Vom Auswanderungsland zum Einwanderungsland? Deutschland 1880–1980* (Berlin, 1983).

19. Herbert, *Geschichte der Ausländerpolitik*, 202 ff.

20. Ernst Müller-Meiningen, "Das Ausländergesetz in Theorie und Praxis," *SZ*, 9/16/1972; Heinz Guradze, "Etwas weniger gleich als andere," *FAZ*, 6/8/1974; and "Aufenthaltsrecht für Ausländer verbessert," *HB*, 7/12/1978. See Herbert, *Geschichte der Ausländerpolitik*, 211 f.

21. "Spanier sollen nicht zu Deutschen werden," *SZ*, 12/12/1972; "Bundesrepublik ist 'Einwanderungsland,'" *FAZ*, 6/14/1972; "Integration ja—Einwanderung nein," *FAZ*, 4/27/1973; and "Um soziale Integration der Ausländerkinder kümmern," SPD Press Service, 1/26/1978.

22. Ernst Müller-Meiningen, "Wende in der Ausländerpolitik?" *SZ*, 10/10/1972; Manfred Nitschke, "Ausländergesetz wird resoluter angewandt," *Die Welt*, 10/16/1972; and Michael Müller, "Die Disziplinierung der Ausländer," *Die Neue Gesellschaft* (May, 1973), 378 ff. See Münz, *Zuwanderung*, 48 ff.

23. "Zuzug von Ausländern wird begrenzt," *SZ*, 3/27/1975, and Winfried Didzoleit, "Das Dilemma der Ausländerpolitik," *FR*, 12/23/1976. See Herbert, *Geschichte der Ausländerpolitik*, 238 ff.

24. "Minoritäten in Ballungsräumen," *Das Parlament*, 2/22/1975; "Ausländer in deutschen Großstädten," *GK* 4 (1982); Key L. Ulrich, "Das Leben im Getto ist ihnen aufgezwungen worden," *FAZ*, 6/26/1978; and "In Frankfurt läutet die Alarmglocke," *SZ*, 6/2/1979.

25. "'Klein-Istanbul' in Berlin," *NZZ*, 1/10/1979; Stefan Klein, "Die 'Frontstrasse' von Hüttenheim," *SZ*, 11/10/1980; Hans-Joachim Hoffmann-Nowotny, "Integration und Segregation von Ausländern in der Schweiz und der BRD," *NZZ*, 10/3/1981; and "Eine geringe Bereitschaft zur Integration," *Die Welt*, 11/27/1981.

26. "Bruderkampf," *Die Zeit*, 5/5/1967; "Mit gefälschten Pässen in die Bundesrepublik," *TSp*, 3/2/1969; "Ausländische Extremisten in der BRD," *Politik und Wirtschaft*, 8/21/1974; Hans-Jörg Sottorf, "Gewaltakte nahmen zu," *HB*, 7/26/1979; and Hans-Peter Schütz, "Der Kampf um die Stammtische," *DAS*, 10/30/1988.

27. "Helmut Schmidt macht aus Türken Deutsche!" *Deutsche Nachrichten*, 9/14/1979; "NPD macht gegen Ausländer mobil," *Die Neue*, 2/21/1980; Fritz Pirkl, "Irrweg der 'Eindeutschung,'" *BK*, 11/17/1979; "Zu viele Ausländer?" *FAZ*, 12/12/1981; and Hanno Kühnert, "Rassistische Klänge," *Die Zeit*, 2/5/1982. See Herbert, *Geschichte der Ausländerpolitik*, 239 ff.

28. Renate I. Mreschar, "Von der Schule an den Rand gedrängt," *Vorwärts*, 7/14/1977; Mascha M. Fisch, "Allahs kleine Emigranten tragen Schleier und Blue Jeans," *Vorwärts*, 7/14/1977; "Zwei Drittel aller Ausländerkinder ohne Schulabschluß," *FAZ*, 1/22/1979; and Horst Heinemann, "Eingewandert, ausgeschlossen," *Vorwärts*, 5/31/1979.

29. "Kühn warnt Deutsche vor einem neuen rassischen Hochmut," *FR*, 12/17/1979; Jürgen Schmude, "Gleiche Chancen für Ausländerkinder," Bundesministerium für Bildung und Wissenschaft, *Informationen Bildung und Wissenschaft* (January 1980); "Stärkere Hilfe für Ausländer," *FR*, 3/20/1980; and Bundesministerium für Arbeit und Soziales, *Sozialpolitische Informationen*, 3/27/1980.

30. Heiner Geißler, "Eine neue Soziale Frage," *DUD*, 3/20/1980; "Kultur für die Türken?" *FAZ*, 5/28/1980; "Sich informieren und andere informieren," *FR*, 3/17/1981; and Christian Graf von Krockow, "Auf der Suche nach einer neuen Heimat," *Die Zeit*, 12/21/1979.

31. "Ausländerfeindlichkeit: Exodus erwünscht," *Der Spiegel* 36 (1982), no. 18, 37 ff.; "Sofortmaßnahmen der Bundesregierung gegen den Missbrauch des Asylrechts," *SZ*, 6/19/1980; "Bonn bremst den Ausländer-Zuzug," *FR*, 12/3/1981; and "Zuspitzung der Ausländerproblems in der BRD," *NZZ*, 4/4/1982.

32. "Das volle Boot," *FAZ*, 2/5/1982; "Einigung über Ausländer Rückkehrhilfe," *FAZ*, 6/22/1983; "Bonn zahlt für Heimkehr arbeitsloser Ausländer," *FR*, 11/11/1983; "Hunderttausend Anträge auf Rückkehrhilfe," *FAZ*, 7/5/1983; "Zimmermann betreibt stur eine Politik der Vertreibung," *FR*, 3/14/1984; and Udo Bergdoll, "Abschied von der Ausländerpolitik," *SZ*, 4/18/1984. See Herbert, *Geschichte der Ausländerpolitik*, 249 ff.

33. "Kirchen setzen sich für Ausländer ein," *SZ*, 9/25/1980; "Der offene Haß auf die Fremden," *RhM*, 9/26/1980; "Kirchen und DGB Seite an Seite," *FAZ*, 6/19/1981; "SPD-Wählerinitiative fordert mehr Rechte für Ausländer," *FR*, 16/11/1981; and "Ausländer werden gebraucht," *FR*, 5/12/1982.

34. Jutta Szostak, "Warum kommen wir mit Türken nicht klar?" *Vorwärts*, 5/16/1982; "CDU-Parolen von 'erschreckender Inhumanität,'" *FR*, 10/12/1982; "Der Preis der Multikultur," *FAZ*, 11/23/1982; "Thesen zur Ausländerpolitik," *FR*, 9/3/1983; and "Wallraffs Erlebnisse als Türke 'Ali,'" *NZZ*, 12/18/1985.

35. "Die Türken haben es am schwersten," *FAZ*, 8/16/1980; "Sie leben und leiden in einem fremden Land," *WdA*, 5/1/1980; and "Was Frau Keskin erlebte," *Die Zeit*, 3/2/1984.

36. "Wir können nicht mal sagen, was wir fühlen," *Der Spiegel* 36 (1982), no. 46, 84 ff.; "Kälte, welche die Seele krank macht," *SZ*, 8/17/1982; "Und jetzt 'Türken raus,'" SPD Press Service, 2/11/1981; and "Manche lernen Karate," *Die Zeit*, 1/16/1987.

37. Gerhard Spörl, "Die Angst vor den Fremden: Die BRD—Ein Nichteinwanderungsland mit Einwanderern," *Die Zeit*, 9/21/1984, and Hilmar Hoffmann, "Im Laboratorium fürs Überleben," *SZ*, 6/3/1989.

38. "Für Ausländerfeindlichkeit fanden Befrager keine Belege," *FR*, 12/7/1985; Dieter Strothmann, "Der alltägliche Fremdenhaß," *Die Zeit*, 8/8/1986; "Ausländerintegration nur bei Übernahme der deutschen Kultur," *FR*, 11/2/1987; and "SPD lehnt Verschärfung des Ausländerrechtes ab," *SZ*, 1/5/1988.

39. "Ausländer und Ausländerbeschäftigung in der Bundesrepublik Deutschland," *DIW Wochenbericht* 49 (1982), 455–461; Manfred Werth, "Brain Drain oder Reintegrationschance?" *AK-Journal* 4 (1977), 14–18; and "Belasten Ausländer das Sozialsystem?" *FAZ*, 10/20/1983.

40. "Strauß: Wir sind kein Einwanderungsland," *SZ*, 9/3/1984; Dankwart Guratzsch,

"Rushdie und die Multikultur," *Die Welt*, 3/20/1989, versus Gerhard Spörl, "Nirgends zu Hause: Vom Auswanderungsland zum Einwanderungsland," *Die Zeit*, 10/26/1984; and "Sorge um Weltoffenheit," *FR*, 4/25/1989.

41. "DDR wahre Heimat der Sorben," *ND*, 4/14/1961, and "Eine Minderheit, die nicht nur tanzen will," *SZ*, 8/20/1975. See Cora Granata, "Celebration and Suspicion: Sorbs and Jews in the Soviet Occupied Zone and German Democratic Republic, 1945–1989" (Ph.D. diss., Chapel Hill, 2001).

42. "Leidensweg eines Schwarzen in der DDR," *FR*, 7/18/1989. See Jan C. Behrends et al., eds., *Fremde und Fremd-Sein in der DDR: Zu historischen Ursachen der Fremdenfeindlichkeit in Ostdeutschland* (Berlin, 2003).

43. "Ausländer, die bleiben wollen," GK, 10/18/1986; "4,7 Millionen Ausländer," GK, 7/18/1988; "Mehr denn je zuvor," GK, 3/7/1989; and Münz, *Zuwanderung*, 28 ff., 53 ff.

44. "CSU: Deutschland soll kein Einwanderungsland werden," *SZ*, 11/9/1988; "'Offene Republik' kontra 'nationale Interessen,'" *taz*, 3/21/1989; and "Ausländerpolitik am Scheideweg," *SZ*, 7/11/1989.

45. "Das droht die DDR zu vernichten," *Der Spiegel* 43 (1989), no. 33, 18 ff. See also the rich material in the Press and Information Office of the Federal Government, *Deutschland 1989: Dokumentation zu der Berichterstattung über die Ereignisse in der DDR und die deutschlandpolitische Entwicklung*, vol. 4 (Bonn, 1990).

46. Hertle, *Der Fall der Mauer*, and Jarausch, *Die unverhoffte Einheit*, 100.

47. "200.000 DDR-Flüchtlinge: Wie verkraften wir das?" *BILD*, 9/3/1989; "Luftballons für die Landsleute von drüben," *SZ*, 9/12/1989; "Arbeitgeber halten Anpassungsprobleme der DDR-Bürger für überwindbar," *TSp*, 9/13/1989; and "Da brennt die Sicherung durch," *Der Spiegel* 44 (1990), no. 4, 28 ff. See further press reports in part five of the Documentation of the Federal Press Office.

48. "Dank Gorbatschow durften wir raus," *Die Welt*, 6/15/1989; "Ich bin gekommen, um in Deutschland zu sterben," *FAZ*, 7/5/1989; "Wir wären auch zu Fuß gegangen," *FR*, 7/9/1989; and "Wenn Kinder von Polen nach Herne siedeln," *FR*, 6/8/1989.

49. Astrid Hölscher, "Verwelkte Girlanden," *FR*, 5/13/1989; Arne Daniels, "Heim und reich?" *Die Zeit*, 4/14/1989; "Angst vor Aussiedlern wächst," *FR*, 6/29/1989; and "Höhere Akzeptanz für Aussiedler," *Die Welt*, 6/30/1989.

50. "Leistungen für Aus- und Übersiedler werden gekürzt," *TSp*, 6/7/1989; "Zuzug von Aussiedlern soll begrenzt werden," *FAZ*, 7/13/1989; "Lafontaine will Erwerb eines Vertriebenenstatus verhindern," *Die Welt*, 1/24/1990; and "Aussiedleraufnahme nur noch nach Verfahren im Herkunftsland," *TSp*, 3/29/1990. See also Münz, *Zuwanderung*, 32 ff.

51. "Der Rest Deutschlands soll den Deutschen vorbehalten bleiben," *FR*, 1/8/1983, and "Ausländer in Deutschland," GK, 8/10/1990. See Herbert, *Geschichte der Ausländerpolitik*, 263 ff.

52. "Deutschland nahm 1989 die meisten Ausländer auf," *SZ*, 8/14/1989, and "In diesem Jahr 800.000 Menschen in die Bundesrepublik," *FAZ*, 12/29/1989. See Münz, *Zuwanderung*, 58.

53. "Man spürt starker, dass man unerwünscht ist," *taz*, 10/2/1990. See Herbert, *Geschichte der Ausländerpolitik*, 273 ff.

54. "Von der Aufenthaltsgenehmigung zur Aufenthaltsberechtigung," *FAZ*, 9/30/1989; "Stoiber kritisiert Referentenentwurf zum Ausländerrecht," *FAZ*, 10/28/1989; "Kritik von Gewerkschaft und Kirchen unfair," *FAZ*, 11/7/1989; "Grosse Koalition gegen Ausländergesetz formiert sich," *SZ*, 3/21/1990; and "Multikulturelle Gesellschaft ade!" *taz*, 4/25/1990.

55. "Die Bonner Koalition einigt sich auf ein neues Ausländergesetz," *FAZ*, 5/12/1989; "Neues Ausländergesetz verabschiedet," *FAZ*, 4/27/1990; and "Fremde im Paragraphendschungel," *TSp*, 4/28/1990.

56. "Ein Abgrund von Fremdenhaß," *FR*, 8/22/1981; "Ventil für eigene Frustration," *BZ*, 1/8/1992; "Ausländerfeindlichkeit im vereinten Deutschland," *NZZ*, 1/19/1992; and "Jeder vierte Deutsche gehört zur 'Ausländer-raus'-Fraktion," *FR*, 9/12/1992.

57. "Überfallserie auf Ausländerheime," *taz*, 8/19/1991; "Gewalt gegen Ausländer nimmt zu," *FR*, 9/30/1991; "In der Nacht gingen sie dann 'die Neger holen,'" *FR*, 3/27/1992; "Schwere ausländerfeindliche Ausschreitungen in Rostock," *TSp*, 8/24/1992; and "Eine schleichende Vergiftung der Gesellschaft," *TSp*, 11/15/1992.

58. "Skin Heads gröhlen 'Wir sind deutsch!'" *SZ*, 5/7/1984; "Tote Hose, soweit die Füße tragen," *FR*, 8/31/1992; lyrics cited from Hans-Jochen Vogel, "Was zuerst geschehen muss," *Die Welt*, 12/4/1992, and "Die Banalität des Bösen," *taz*, 5/15/1993. See Rainer Erb, "Rechtsextremistische Jugendszene in Brandenburg," Alliance against Violence, Rightwing Extremism and Xenophobia (1999), available at: www.aktionsbuendnis.brandenburg.de.

59. Dietrich Strothmann, "Der alltägliche Fremdenhass," *Die Zeit*, 8/8/1986; "Unverstanden, benachteiligt, ausgeschlossen," *Die Zeit*, 4/5/1991; and Rainer Hank, "Ausländer sind immer die Anderen," *FAZ*, 3/20/1993.

60. Peter Jochen Winters, "Hoyerswerda: Die Anonymität und Seelenlosigkeit einer sozialistischen Stadt," *FAZ*, 9/14/1991; Heribert Prantl, "Hoyerswerda: Die letzte Rache an der DDR," *SZ*, 10/2/1991; and Otto Jörg Weis "Tote Hose, so weit die Füße tragen," *FR*, 8/31/1992.

61. Robert Leicht, "Hoyerswerda in den Köpfen," *Die Zeit*, 9/26/1991; Walter Bajohr, "Die Scherben von Hoyerswerda," *RhM*, 9/27/1991; Wolfgang Thierse, "Fremdenhaß ist kein spezifisch ostdeutsches Phänomen," *FR*, 1/13/1992; and "Erklärung der Deutschen Psychoanalytischen Vereinigung zu Fremdenhaß und Gewalt in Deutschland," *FAZ*, 11/27/1992.

62. Rüdiger Scheidges, "Die Konzepte mit der Realität in Einklang bringen," *TSp*, 4/20/1991; "Schäuble: Aussiedler werden ohne Einschränkungen aufgenommen," *FAZ*, 4/13/1991; "SPD warnt Bonn vor einer Massenabschiebung in Krisengebiete," *FR*, 6/29/1991; and "Bonn will Gewalt gegen Ausländer bremsen," *SZ*, 12/11/1991.

63. "Frau Funcke scheidet enttäuscht aus dem Amt," *FAZ*, 7/13/1991; "Bekenntnis zum Einwanderungsland," *taz*, 9/10/1991; "Deutschland längst eine multikulturelle Gesellschaft," *SZ*, 2/3/1992; and "Kein neuer Nazismus in Deutschland," *SZ*, 12/5/1991.

64. "Wir wollen mit den Ausländern leben," *SZ*, 10/11/1991; "Wer sich öffnet, erzielt mitmenschlichen Gewinn," *Die Welt*, 11/19/1991; "Deutschland profitiert von Ausländern," *FAZ*, 10/25/1991; "Handwerk ohne Ausländer nicht vorstellbar," *TSp*, 11/5/1991; and "Ausländer stützen die Sozialversicherung," *FAZ*, 12/5/1991.

65. "Wir werden die Zukunft miteinander gewinnen oder verlieren," *FR*, 7/26/1991; "Gemeinsame Front gegen Fremdenhaß," *SZ*, 10/10/1991; Eckhart Spoo, "Ohne Fremde sind wir allein," *FR*, 10/20/1991; and "Wer wagt überhaupt noch den Kopf zu schütteln," *FR*, 9/11/1992.

66. Theo Sommer, "Das Schandmal des Fremdenhasses," *Die Zeit*, 10/10/1991; "Was tun gegen den Haß?" *taz*, 10/5/1991; "Gegen Gewalt und Fremdenhaß," *taz*, 11/4/1991; and "Fremde brauchen Freunde," *FR*, 11/23/1991.

67. "Demonstrationen gegen Ausländerhaß," *FAZ*, 11//11/1991; "Aufrufe zu Massenprotesten gegen den Ausländerhaß," *SZ*, 9/30/1992; "Zehntausende demonstrieren gegen Rassismus und Fremdenhaß," *FR*, 10/5/1992; "Lichterkette und Rockkonzert," *Die Welt*, 12/14/1992; and "Kerzen über Berlin," *taz*, 1/29/1993.

68. Herbert, *Geschichte der Ausländerpolitik*, 320.

69. Richard von Weizsäcker, "Es ist hohe Zeit, sich zur Wehr zu setzen," *FR*, 11/9/1992; "Bundestag debattiert über Gewalt," *FR*, 11/26/1992; "Kohl: Terror von Rechts und Links bekämpfen," *SZ*, 12/11/1992; and "Einhellige Verurteilung von Fremdenfeindlichkeit und Gewalt," *Das Parlament*, 12/18/1992.

70. "Koalition und SPD legen Streit über Asylrecht bei," *SZ*, 1/16/1993; "Ein weltoffenes Land," *Die Welt*, 1/22/1993; "Wie weit geht die SPD?" *FR*, 1/28/1993; "Einigung über Einzelheiten des Asylrechts," *FAZ*, 2/5/1993; "Die SPD steht in der Asyldiskussion weiter unter großem Druck," *TSp*, 3/4/1993; and "Asyldebatte im deutschen Bundestag," *NZZ*, 3/6/1993.

71. "Die Deutschen investieren, die anderen parieren," *SZ*, 2/6/1993; "Es wird höchste Zeit," *BK*, 3/13/1993; "SPD geht im offenen Streit in die Abstimmung zur Asylrechtsänderung," *TSp*, 5/23/1993; and "Sozialdemokratinnen und Sozialdemokraten appellieren an die MdB," *taz*, 5/25/1993.

72. "Verabschiedung der Asylrechtsreform in Bonn," *NZZ*, 5/27/1993; Roderich Reifenrath, "Eine unheilige Allianz," *FR*, 5/27/1993; Thomas Kröter, "Der große Durchbruch in die andere Richtung," *Die Welt*, 5/27/1993; Jutta Falke, "Ende der Selbstblockade," *RhM*, 5/28/1993; and Jens Reich, "Was heisst schon 'politisch'?" *Die Zeit*, 6/3/1993.

73. Eckhard Fuhr, "Am Tag danach," *FAZ*, 5/28/1993, and Claus Leggewie, "Multi-Kulti: Schlachtfeld oder halbwegs erträgliches Leben?" *FR*, 1/29/1993.

74. "Neue fremdenfeindliche Untat in Deutschland," *NZZ*, 6/2/1993; Frank Hansen and Alexander Richter, "Fassungslosigkeit, Wut und Trauer," *TSp*, 6/1/1993; and Herbert Prantl, "Solinger Signale," *SZ*, 6/2/1993.

75. "Vorwürfe gegen Bonner Politiker," *FR*, 6/1/1993. "Türken fürchten um ihr Leben," *SZ*, 6/1/1993; Dilek Zaptcioglu-Rogge, "Jetzt weiß ich, daß ich hier keine wahren Freunde habe," *TSp*, 6/3/1993; "Dann liegt die Schuld bei uns allen," *FR*, 6/4/1993; and Thomas Kielinger, "Mitbürger brauchen Bürgerrechte," *RhM*, 6/4/1993

76. "Unfassbares Maß an sittlicher Verrohung," *FR*, 6/17/1993; "Wirtschaft sorgt sich um positives Deutschlandbild," *HB*, 9/6/1993; "Anschläge auf Ausländer kommen 'aus der Mitte der Gesellschaft,'" *FR*, 6/16/1993; and "Fremdenfeindliche Gewalt durch 'diffuse Gefühle' motiviert," *FAZ*, 5/30/1993.

77. "Die Fremden sind nicht die Ursache der Gewalt," *TSp*, 6/20/1993; "Deutschland gehört den Menschen, die hier leben und wohnen," *SZ*, 1993, no. 131; "Erst das

Grauen macht mitfühlend," *BZ*, 6/29/1993; and Renate Köcher, "Die Ausländer-feindlichkeit in Deutschland ist gering," *FAZ*, 8/18/1993.

78. "Absage Bonns an Gewalt und Extremismus," *NZZ*, 9/29/1993; "Und alles unter den Augen der Polizei," *FR*, 10/26/1993; "Die Würde des Menschen ist unantastbar," *Das Parlament*, 11/13/1993; "Ausländer und die deutsche Wirtschaft. Zehn Thesen," *Bundesministerium für Wirtschaft-Dokumentation* 339 (1994); and Ingrid Müller, "Die Deutschen von morgen werden in einer veränderten Welt leben," *TSp*, 7/23/1993.

79. "Zweieinhalb Jahre Haft für 22jährigen," *SZ*, 3/4/1993; Jasper von Altenbockum, "Die Angeklagten von Mölln erscheinen fast harmlos," *FAZ*, 8/27/1993; "Die peinigende Suche nach dem Bösen," *SZ*, 11/27/1993; "Höchststrafen für die Brandstifter von Mölln," *NZZ*, 12/10/1993; and "Angriffe auf Ausländer," *GK*, 4/25/1994.

80. "Entwicklung der Asylbewerberzahlen," *HB*, 2/4/1993; "Die Fluchtwege nach Deutsch-land," *GK*, 4/26/1993; "Wien, Budapest, Laibach, Preßburg, Prag und Warschau für klare Abmachungen," *FAZ*, 3/18/1993; and "Bonn will auf Abschiebung von bisher abgelehnten Asylbewerbern verzichten," *HB*, 3/29/1993.

81. "Asylverfahren laufen schneller," *SZ*, 1/15/1993; Sabine Sütterlin, "Nur selten hat einer noch eine Chance," *Junge Freiheit*, 8/12/1993; Martin Hagenmaier, "Die Menschlichkeit bleibt oft auf der Strecke," *Christ und Welt*, 7/1/1994; "80 Mark in zwei Raten und täglich Lebensmittelpäckchen," *FAZ*, 1/19/1994; and Kurt Teske, "Abschiebehaft," *Die Welt*, 9/13/1994.

82. Klaus-Peter Klingelschmitt, "Amnesty kritisiert deutsche Asylpolitik," *taz*, 7/9/1993; "Erste Erfahrungen mit dem neuen Asylrecht," *SZ*, 7/13/1993; and "Union und FDP werten neues Asylrecht als Erfolg," *SZ*, 1/13/1994.

83. Erwin Marschewski, "Zuzugsbegrenzung und Integration," *Das Parlament*, 11/22/1996; "Schmalz-Jacobsen fordert Konzept für Zuwanderung," *FR*, 3/4/1994; "Ein Unwort für christliche Parteien," *FAZ*, 1/11/1994; and "Härtere Gangart gegen Ausländer," *Die Welt*, 1/25/1996.

84. "Kohl droht mit Abschiebung militanter Kurden," *NZZ*, 3/25/1994; "Maßnahmen Bonns gegen Ausländerkrawalle," *NZZ*, 3/28/1996; Rainer Zitelmann, "Gewalt-Täter abschieben?" *Die Welt*, 3/14/1996; "Bundesrat billigt Visumpflicht," *FR*, 3/15/1997; and "Kanthers 'Handstreich' gegen Kinder," *SZ*, 1/14/1997.

85. "Koalition mildert Ausländerrecht," *FR*, 11/9/1995; Martina Fietz, "Wer sich hier zu Hause fühlt," *Die Welt*, 11/20/1995; Jochen Buchsteiner, "Am liebsten abschirmen," *Die Zeit*, 2/2/1996; "Koalition plant eine Einbürgerungsgarantie für Ausländer-kinder," *TSp*, 10/8/1997; and "Koalitionsgezänk in Bonn um junge Ausländer," *NZZ*, 10/29/1997.

86. "Schöne Zeiten für Schlepper," *Der Spiegel* 47 (1993), no. 27, 18 ff.; "Zahl der Asylan-träge stark gesunken," *SZ*, 3/10/1994; and "Schleuser-Büros werben fürs Paradies Deutschland," *TSp*, 10/8/1996. See Münz, *Zuwanderung*, 58.

87. Jochen Kummer, "Über 13 Millionen Menschen ziehen in diesem Jahrzehnt nach Deutschland," *Die Welt*, 9/24/1995; "Die Deutschen nahmen viermal so viele Ausländer auf wie der Schmelztiegel USA," *WaS*, 4/20/1997; and "Ausländer: Mehr als ein Viertel lebt seit 20 Jahren oder länger in Deutschland," *FAZ*, 6/20/1997.

88. Dilek Zaptcioglu-Rogge, "Leben in zwei Welten," *TSp*, 6/20/1993; "Die Welt aus türkischer Sicht," *SZ*, 5/19/1995; Wilhelm Heitmeyer, "Die Hinwendung zu einer religiös begründeten Gesellschaft," *FR*, 3/7/1997; Karin Hummel, "Die vergessen, woher sie kommen," *FAZ*, 8/2/1997; and Konrad Schuller, "Die Türken Deutschlands: Eine Minorität im Werden?" *FAZ*, 6/25/1998.

89. "Bildungsstand bei Ausländern wächst," *FAZ*, 3/3/1994; "Otto und Ali," *Der Spiegel* 47 (1993), no. 38, 117 ff.; "Die Zwitterstellung der dritten Generation," *Die Welt*, 9/10/1995; "23 Pillen und die Last zweier Herzen," *SZ*, 8/25/1994; and "Zurück in die Heimat: Nur zum Urlaubmachen," *FR*, 1/10/1995.

90. "'An kein Land binden,'" *Der Spiegel* 50 (1996), no. 29, 48 ff.; Hans-Christian Rößler, "Man kann seine Identität nicht von heute auf morgen aufgeben," *FAZ*, 7/29/1997; and Zafer Senocak, "Aber das Herz schlägt noch türkisch," *taz*, 8/22/1998.

91. Dieter Wulf, "Gute Juden—böse Israelis," *RhM*, 2/17/1985; Andreas Nechama, "Die jüdische Einwanderung besser absichern," *hagalil*, 5/9/1999; Toby Axelrod, "Deutschland für GUS-Juden attraktiver als Israel," *tacheles*, 8/8/2003; and "Ausländer in Deutschland —Deutsche Ausländerpolitik," www.schutzbund.de. See also Wladimir Kaminer, *Russendisko* (Munich, 2000).

92. "Rückkehr zur Politik," *taz*, 10/5/1998; "Kohl und Schäuble verteidigen CSU-Linie zur Ausländerpolitik," 7/10/1998; "SPD und Grüne werben für neues Ausländerrecht," *FR*, 1/11/1995; Ekkehard Wienholtz et al., "Wie die Ausländer zum Wohlstand in Deutschland beitragen," *FR*, 8/19/1998; and "Neue Ausländerpolitik gefordert," *TSp*, 11/2/1998.

93. "Bewegung in der deutschen Rechtspolitik," *NZZ*, 11/17/1998; "Mehr Zuwanderung ist nicht verkraftbar," *TSp*, 11/20/1998; "Schröder stellt sich in der Ausländerdebatte hinter Schily," *Die Welt*, 11/26/1998; and "Neues Staatsbürgerschaftsrecht noch vor der Sommerpause," *FAZ*, 1/6/1999.

94. Martina Fietz, "Deutsche zum Nulltarif," *Die Welt*, 10/17/1998; Daniel Goffart, "Legitime Kampagne mit schrillen Tönen," *HB*, 1/5/1999; "Ausländerpolitische Kampagne der CDU/CSU," *NZZ*, 1/5/1999; and "CDU hält an der Unterschriftensammlung fest," *NZZ*, 1/11/1999.

95. Giovanni di Lorenzo, "Eine ganz unsinnige Polarisierung," *TSp*, 1/10/1999; "Hitzige Kontroverse um die doppelte Staatsangehörigkeit," *HB*, 1/12/1999; "Koalition einig über neues Doppelpass-Gesetz," *Die Welt*, 1/13/1999; "Bubis verurteilt CDU-Kampagne," *FR*, 1/14/1999; and "Katholische Kirche für Doppel-Pass," *TSp*, 1/16/1999.

96. Roland Koch, "Der Wille zur Integration ist nötig," *Die Welt*, 1/15/1999; "Der Griff zur Liste," *BZ*, 1/18/1999; "Im Laufschritt zur Wurst," *Der Spiegel* 53 (1999), no. 3, 28; "Mehrheit gegen den Doppelpass," *RhM*, 1/29/1999; and "Denkzettel für die rot-grüne Koalition in Bonn," *NZZ*, 2/9/1999.

97. "SPD auf Kompromisssuche beim Bürgerrecht," *NZZ*, 2/11/1999; "Schröder will deutliche Einschränkungen beim Doppel-Pass," *TSp*, 2/10/1999; "SPD setzt beim Staatsbürgerrecht nun auf die FDP," *FR*, 2/11/1999; "Für die rasche Einbürgerung sind sie alle," *SZ*, 2/3/1999; and "CDU-Vorstand lehnt Gesetzentwurf zur Staatsangehörigkeit ab," *FAZ*, 3/16/1999.

98. "Rot-Grün lenkt bei Doppelpass ein," *BZ*, 2/25/1999; "SPD und FDP einig über deutsches Bürgerrecht," *NZZ*, 3/12/1999; "Bundestag beschließt Doppelpass," *Die*

Welt, 5/8/1999; "Fauler Kompromiss," *Die Welt*, 5/8/1999; and "Schily: Ein Zeichen für ein modernes und weltoffenes Deutschland," *FAZ*, 3/17/1999.

99. Werner Kolkhoff, "Besser die zweitbeste Lösung als gar keine," *BZ*, 3/13/1999; Eberhard Seidel-Pielen, "Mangelhaft und trotzdem gut," *taz*, 3/13/1999; Vera Gaserow, "Ein Anfang mit Schlussstrich," *FR*, 5/8/1999; and "Territorialprinzip ergänzt Abstammungsregel," *FAZ*, 3/19/1999. See Brubaker, *Citizenship*, and Gosewinkel, *Einbürgern und Ausschließen*.

100. Johannes Leithäuser, "Einbürgerung nach sechs Jahren?" *FAZ*, 10/21/1999; "Kein Ansturm auf den deutschen Pass in Bayern," *NZZ*, 1/6/2000; Elke Spanner, "Der deutsche Pass kommt in Mode," *taz*, 5/16/2000; and "Mehr Einbürgerungen in Deutschland," *FAZ*, 12/29/2000.

101. "Green Card," www.germany-info.org; "Aufholjagd um talentierte Köpfe," *Focus-online*; and "Green Card: Karriere und Gehalt locken," press release, www.wz-berlin.de, 4/9/2002.

102. "CSU und Gewerkschaften kritisieren Green Card," *Die Welt*, 3/15/2000; "Zukunft statt Rüttgers," press release, www.FIfF.de, 4/26/2000; "Schulte irrt: Green Card kein Rohrkrepierer," press release, www.gi-ev.de, 8/1/2001; and "Green Card drei Jahre alt: Verlängerung bis 2004," www.Bundesregierung.de, 7/31/2003.

103. Johannes Rau, "Ohne Angst und Träumereien: Gemeinsam in Deutschland leben," *SZ*, 5/13/2000; "Zwang zum Handeln," *FAZ*, 5/19/2000; "Streit über die Besetzung der Einwanderungskommission," *SZ*, 7/3/2000; "Das Einwanderungsgesetz kommt," *Die Welt*, 7/7/2000; and "Mit Rita Süssmuth an der Spitze," *TSp*, 7/13/2000.

104. "Schily will Gespräche zur Einwanderungspolitik," *SZ*, 5/16/2000; "Streit und Bewegung in der Asyl-Frage," *Die Welt*, 6/29/2000; Stefan Dietrich, "Fremdbestimmte Ausländerpolitik," *FAZ*, 7/6/2000; "Bonussystem für Ausländer in Deutschland?" *NZZ*, 4/19/2001; and *Zuwanderung gestalten—Integration fördern: Bericht der Unabhängigen Kommission "Zuwanderung"* (Berlin, 2001).

105. "CSU: Ausländer müssen Deutsch lernen," *SZ*, 7/9/1998; "Stoiber lehnt 'Mischmasch' ab," *SZ*, 2/18/1999; "Notfall Deutschstunde," *RhM*, 1/15/1999; "Bayern führt schriftlichen Sprachtest für Ausländer ein," *BZ*, 3/11/2000; and Dilek Güngör, "Die Augen sollen sich nicht öffnen," *FAZ*, 6/9/2000.

106. "Multikultur funktioniert nicht ohne Leitkultur," *WaS*, 11/22/2000; "Künast: Kein Abschied vom Wort 'multikulturell,'" *FAZ*, 11/2/2000; Mark Terkessidis, "Das Spiel mit der Herkunft," *taz*, 11/4/2000; and "Büffeln für die Einbürgerung," *BZ*, 12/15/2000. See Andrea Mrozek, "Heavy on the Leitkultur," *Central Europe Review* 2 (2000), no. 42; www.ce-review.org/0042/mrozek42.html.

107. "Gesetz zur Steuerung und Begrenzung der Zuwanderung und zur Reglung des Aufenthalts und der Integration von Unionsbürgern und Ausländern (Zuwanderungsgesetz)," *Bundesgesetzblatt*, 6/25/2002. "Das deutsche Ausländerrecht als Zankapfel," *NZZ*, 9/8/2001; and "Zuwanderung: Eklat im Bundesrat," *TSp*, 3/23/2002.

108. Zuwanderungsgesetz," www.aufenthaltstitel.de.zuwg; "Schwarz-rote Lösung," *TSp*, 6/18/2004; "Zuwanderung: Jetzt ist sie geregelt," *TSp*, 6/18/2004; and "Zuwanderungsgesetz kann in Kraft treten," www.bundesregierung.de, 7/9/2004.

109. "Bundespräsident nennt Umgang mit Ausländern Prüfstein für Demokratie," *TSp*, 10/4/1992; Werner Schiffbauer, "Assoziationen der Freiheit," *taz*, 12/12/1992; and

"Zivile Konfliktbewältigung ist keine deutsche Tugend," *taz*, 12/11/1991. See Wilhelm von Sternburg, ed., *Für eine zivile Republik: Ansichten über die bedrohte Demokratie in Deutschland* (Frankfurt, 1992).

110. Jochen Kummer, "Sind wir ein Einwanderungsland?" *WaS* 2 (1997); "Die Zahl der Ausländer sagt wenig über die Migrationsdynamik," *FAZ*, 11/11/2000; and Rolf Geffken, "Erst raus, dann rein?" *FR*, 3/17/2000.

111. "'Sie sind ein Utopist,'" *Der Spiegel* 52 (1998), no. 14, 48 ff.; "Generalmobilmachung gegen Ausländer," *SZ*, 2/21/1998; Klaus Weber, "Der neue Totmacher kommt aus der deutschen Normalität," *FR*, 10/15/1999; and "Familienkultur der Intoleranz und des Hasses," *taz*, 3/23/1999. See Klaus J. Bade, *Ausländer, Aussiedler, Asyl in der Bundesrepublik Deutschland*, 3rd ed (Hannover, 1994).

112. Margarita Mathiopoulos, "Europa, einig Mutterland," *ND*, 6/23/1990; Sonja Margolina, " Der Ethnizismus im multikulturellen Gewand," *taz*, 1/2/1995; "Wer zu spät kommt," *Die Zeit*, 6/10/1998; "Ein Amt zwischen den Stühlen," *taz*, 11/9/ 1999; and Daniel Bax, "Wie verkaufe ich einen Türken," *taz*, 2/1/2000.

113. "Wir brauchen Zuwanderung," *BZ*, 2/14/2000; "Das Werk des Rassismus," *SZ*, 9/25/2000; "Warnung vor Ghettos: Angst vor Vergreisung," *SZ*, 3/1/2000; and "Die Republik ist in Gefahr," *SZ*, 10/2/1992. See Klaus J. Bade and Rainer Münz, eds., *Migrationsreport 2000: Fakten, Analysen, Perspektiven* (Frankfurt, 2000).

114. Marie Luise Knott, "Fremd ist der Fremde nur in der Fremde," *TSp*, 12/16/1992; Thomas Lackmann, "Mutterheimat, Vaterland," *TSp*, 6/7/1998; and Robert Leicht, "Die List der Vernunft," *TSp*, 2/2/2001.

115. Gerd Held, "Tischsitten, Stahlbrücken, Verfassungsartikel," *FAZ*, 10/7/2001; "Was tun gegen die neuen nationalen und rassistischen Töne?" *SZ*, 4/14/1998; and "Türken bilden an vielen Orten eine ethnische Subkultur," *FR*, 12/28/1999.

116. Zafer Senocak, "Heimatwunsch in der Fremde," *TSp*, 11/3/2001; Bassam Tibi, "Hischra nach Europa," *FAZ*, 12/18/2000; "Ich bin stolz, ein Kanake zu sein," *TSp*, 11/31/2000; "Ich gehör' hier dazu," *Die Welt*, 11/11/2000; and Carsten Baumgardt,"Gegen die Wand," www.filmstarts.de. See also Matthias Konzett, "Zafer Senocak im Gespräch," *German Quarterly* 76 (2003), 131–139.

CONCLUSION TO PART III

1. Konrad H. Jarausch, "Etiketten mit Eigenleben: Wende, Zusammenbruch, friedliche Bürgerrevolution,"*Das Parlament*, 8/25/2000. See also Hans-Joachim Veen, ed., *Nach der Diktatur: Demokratische Umbrüche in Europa—Zwölf Jahre später* (Cologne, 2003).

2. Jarausch and Sabrow, *Weg in den Untergang*, versus von Plato, *Die Vereinigung*.

3. Jürgen Kocka, "Reform and Revolution: Germany 1989–90,"in Reinhard Rürup, ed., *The Problem of Revolution in Germany, 1789–1989* (Oxford, 2000), 161–179.

4. Pfaff, *Fight or Flight?* For a more sustained treatment, see Konrad H. Jarausch, "Aufbruch der Zivilgesellschaft: Zur Einordnung der friedlichen Revolution von 1989."

5. Misselwitz, *Nicht mehr mit dem Gesicht nach Westen*, and Staatskanzlei des Landes Sachsen-Anhalt, ed., *Fragen zur deutschen Einheit: Reinhard Höppner im Gespräch mit Daniela Dahn, Egon Bahr, Hans Otto Bräutigam, Erhard Eppler, Günter Gaus, Regine Hildebrandt, Günter Grass* (Halle, 1999).

6. Detlef Pollack, "Wirtschaftlicher, sozialer und mentaler Wandel in Ostdeutschland: Eine Bilanz nach zehn Jahren," *APuZ* B 40 (2000), 13–21.

7. Hermann Rudolph, "Es geht längst nicht mehr darum, ob die Bundesrepublik ein Einwanderungsland ist," *TSp*, 7/11/1996, and Ayhan Bakirdögen, "Wegbereiter für die multikulturelle Gesellschaft," *TSp*, 11/24/1996. See also "Wir öffnen die Tür einen Spalt," *TSp*, 7/3/2004.

8. Timothy Garton Ash, *The Magic Lantern: The Revolution of '89 Witnessed in Warsaw, Budapest, Berlin, and Prague* (New York, 1990), 134 ff.

9. Wilhelm Heitmann, "Feindselige Normalität," *Die Zeit*, 12/11/2003.

10. Fritz Stern, *Verspielte Größe: Essays zur deutschen Geschichte* (Munich, 1996).

11. For a Western example, see Eley, *Forging Democracy*.

12. Konrad H. Jarausch, "Die Postnationale Nation: Zum Identitätswandel der Deutschen 1945–1995," *Historicum* 14 (Spring 1995), 30–35.

13. Contributions to the issue "Der letzte Deutsche," *Der Spiegel* 58 (2004), no. 2, 38 ff. See also Bade, *Europa in Bewegung*.

CONCLUSION

1. Erich Nickel, "Der Streit um die deutsche Hauptstadt," *Berlinische Monatsschrift* 10 (2001), no. 7, 20–27. See also Udo Wengst, ed., *Historiker betrachten Deutschland: Beiträge zum Vereinigungsprozeß und zur Hauptstadtdiskussion* (Bonn, 1992).

2. Johannes Gross, *Begründung der Berliner Republik: Deutschland am Ende des 20. Jahrhunderts* (Stuttgart, 1995), 84 ff. As reply, see Habermas, *Normalität einer Berliner Republik*, 167 ff.

3. Max A. Höfer, "Die 'Berliner Republik' als Kampfbegriff?" *APuZ* B 6–7 (2001), 27–30. See also Willy-Brandt-Kreis, ed., *Zur Lage der Nation: Leitgedanken für eine Politik der Berliner Republik* (Berlin, 2001).

4. Kurt Sontheimer, "Berlin schafft keine neue Republik—und sie bewegt sich doch," *APuZ* B 1–2 (2001), 3–5. See also Roland Czada and Hellmut Wollmann, eds., *Von der Bonner zur Berliner Republik: 10 Jahre Deutsche Einheit* (Wiesbaden, 2000), 13 ff., and Dieter Dettke, ed., *The Spirit of the Berlin Republic* (New York, 2003).

5. Frank Brunssen, "Das neue Selbstverständnis der Berliner Republik," *APuZ* B 1–2 (2001), 6–14. See also James and Stone, *When the Wall Came Down*, 233–239, and Brian Ladd, *The Ghosts of Berlin: Confronting German History in the Urban Landscape* (Chicago, 1997).

6. Hans-Ulrich Wehler, ed., *Aus der Geschichte lernen: Essays* (Munich, 1988), 11–18; Peter Graf Kielmansegg, "Lernen aus der Geschichte—Lernen in der Geschichte: Deutsche Erfahrungen im 20. Jahrhundert," in Peter R. Weilemann et al., eds., *Macht und Zeitkritik: Festschrift für Hans-Peter Schwarz zum 65. Geburtstag* (Paderborn, 1999), 3–16.

7. Gerhard L. Weinberg, "Reflections on Two Unifications," *GSR* 21 (1998), 13–25. Hans-Ulrich Wehler, *Deutsche Gesellschaftsgeschichte* (Munich, 2003), 4:981 ff., remarks on this transformation without analyzing the learning processes behind it in detail. See also Horst Carl et al., eds., *Kriegsniederlagen: Erfahrungen und Erinnerungen* (Berlin, 2004).

8. *Brockhaus Enzyklopädie*, 20 vols. (Wiesbaden, 1974), 20:719–720; Johannes Weiß,

"Zivilisation," in Günter Endruweit and Gisela Trommsdorff, eds., *Wörterbuch der Soziologie*, 2nd rev. ed. (Stuttgart, 2002), 715–717; and Hans-Günther Thien, "Zivilgesellschaft," in Werner Fuchs-Heinritz et al., eds., *Lexikon zur Soziologie*, 3rd rev. ed. (Opladen, 1995), 757. See also *Kleines Politisches Wörterbuch*, 3rd rev. ed. (Berlin, 1978), 1043–1044.

9. Habermas, *Normalität einer Berliner Republik*, 167 ff. See also Winkler, *Der lange Weg*.

10. Frei, *Adenauer's Germany and the Nazi Past*. The preoccupation with the problems of memory culture has tended to exaggerate their significance compared with the more practical learning processes from the German catastrophe.

11. Jeffrey Herf, *Divided Memory: The Nazi Past in the Two Germanys* (Cambridge, MA, 1997); Annette Weinke, *Die Verfolgung von NS-Tätern im geteilten Deutschland: Vergangenheitsbewältigungen 1949–1969 oder: Eine deutsch-deutsche Beziehungsgeschichte im Kalten Krieg* (Paderborn, 2002).

12. Peter Reichel, *Politik mit der Erinnerung: Gedächtnisorte im Streit um die nationalsozialistische Vergangenheit* (Munich, 1995). Cf. Konrad H. Jarausch, "Critical Memory and Civil Society: The Impact of the Sixties on German Debates about the Past," forthcoming in Philipp Gassert and Alan Steinweis, eds., *Coping With the Nazi Past* (New York, 2006).

13. Dirk van Laak, "Der Platz des Holocaust im deutschen Geschichtsbild," in Konrad H. Jarausch and Martin Sabrow, eds., *Die historische Meistererzählung: Deutungslinien der deutschen Nationalgeschichte nach 1945* (Göttingen, 2002), 163–193, and Michael Jeismann, *Auf Wiedersehen Gestern: Die deutsche Vergangenheit und die Politik von morgen* (Stuttgart, 2001).

14. Kielmansegg, *Nach der Katastrophe*, 81. See also Wirth et al., *Das demokratische Deutschland*.

15. Edgar Wolfrum, *Die Bundesrepublik Deutschland 1949–1990* (Stuttgart, 2005), vol. 23 of *Gebhardt: Handbuch der deutschen Geschichte*, 303 ff. Kraushaar, *1968: Das Jahr*.

16. Konrad H. Jarausch, "Deutsche Einsichten und Amerikanische Einflüsse: Kulturelle Aspekte der Demokratisierung Westdeutschlands," in Arndt Bauerkämper, Konrad H. Jarausch, and Markus Payk, eds., *Transatlantische Mittler* (Göttingen, 2005).

17. Hans Misselwitz, "Die unvollendete Berliner Republik: Warum der Osten zur Sprache kommen muss," in Willy-Brandt-Kreis, ed., *Zur Lage der Nation: Leitgedanken für eine Politik der Berliner Republik* (Berlin, 2001), 32 ff.

18. See chapters 8 and 9 in this volume.

19. Hajo Funke, *Paranoia und Politik: Rechtsextremismus in der Berliner Republik* (Berlin, 2002).

20. Susanne Lütz, "Vom koordinierten zum marktorientierten Kapitalismus?" in Roland Czada and Hellmut Wollmann, eds., *Von der Bonner zur Berliner Republik: 10 Jahre Deutsche Einheit* (Wiesbaden, 2000), 651 ff.

21. Konrad H. Jarausch, "Mißverständnis Amerika: Antiamerikanismus als Projektion," in Jan C. Behrends et al., eds., *Antiamerikanismus im 20. Jahrhundert: Studien zu Ost- und Mitteleuropa* (Bonn, 2005), 34–49. See also Jürgen Maier, *Politikverdrossenheit in der Bundesrepublik Deutschland: Dimensionen, Determinanten, Konsequenzen* (Opladen, 2000).

22. Daniela Dahn, "Vereintes Land—geteilte Freude" and other texts in Willy-Brandt-

Kreis, ed., *Zur Lage der Nation: Leitgedanken für eine Politik der Berliner Republik* (Berlin, 2001), 12 ff.

23. Konrad H. Jarausch, "Normalisierung oder Re-Nationalisierung? Zur Umdeutung der deutschen Vergangenheit," *GG* 21 (1995), 571–584.

24. See chapters 1 and 2 in this volume.

25. Markovits and Gorski, *Grün schlägt rot*.

26. Günter Grass, "Mein Deutschland," in Willy-Brandt-Kreis, ed., *Zur Lage der Nation: Leitgedanken für eine Politik der Berliner Republik* (Berlin, 2001), 136 ff.; and Daniel Cohn-Bendit and Thomas Schmid, *Heimat Babylon: Das Wagnis der multikulturellen Demokratie*, 2nd ed. (Hamburg, 1993).

27. Kielmansegg, *Nach der Katastrophe*, 46 ff., 131 ff.

28. Kielmansegg, "Lernen aus der Geschichte," 8 ff.

29. Simone Barck, *Antifa-Geschichte(n): Eine literarische Spurensuche in der DDR der 1950er und 1960er Jahre* (Cologne, 2003). See also Konrad H. Jarausch, "Die gescheiterte Gegengesellschaft: Überlegungen zu einer Sozialgeschichte der DDR," *AfS* 39 (1999), 1–17.

30. "Martin Sabrow, ed., *Skandal und Diktatur: Formen öffentlicher Empörung im NS-Staat und in der* DDR (Göttingen, 2004). See also Schildt, *Ankunft im Westen*, 15 ff.

31. Herbert, *Wandlungsprozesse in Westdeutschland*, 7 ff.

32. These taboos explain the emotional reaction to Friedrich, *Der Brand*, and Anonyma, *Eine Frau in Berlin*, as well as the recent controversy over the establishment of a center against expulsion in Berlin.

33. Eric Hobsbawm, *The Age of Extremes: The Short Twentieth Century, 1914–1991* (London, 1994). See also Hans-Peter Schwarz, "Die neueste Zeitgeschichte," *VfZ* 51 (2003), 5–28.

34. Michael Staack, "Abschied vom 'Frontstaat': Deutschlands veränderte Außen- und Sicherheitspolitik," in Roland Czada and Hellmut Wollmann, eds., *Von der Bonner zur Berliner Republik: 10 Jahre Deutsche Einheit* (Wiesbaden, 2000), 159 ff. See also Hans-Ulrich Klose, "The Foreign Policy of the Berlin Republic," and Daniel Hamilton, "The Berlin Republic in a Global Age," both in Dieter Dettke, ed., *The Spirit of the Berlin Republic* (New York, 2003), 48 ff., 56 ff.

35. Till Müller, "Verfassungspatriotismus," *Mitteilungen der Humanistischen Union* 165 (1999), www.humanistische-union.de. See also Konrad H. Jarausch, "Die Postnationale Nation: Zum Identitätswandel der Deutschen 1945–1995," *Historicum* 14 (Spring 1995), 30–35.

36. Jay Julian Rosellini, *Literary Skinheads? Writing from the Right in Reunified Germany* (West Lafayette, 2000); Jürgen Habermas, *Die postnationale Konstellation: Politische Essays* (Frankfurt, 1998), versus Gerhard Schröder, "Programm für die Zukunft," speech at the SPD Congress on political change on 6/29/1998 in Berlin.

37. Edgar Grande and Burkhard Eberlein, "Der Aufstieg des Regulierungsstaates im Infrastrukturbereich," in Roland Czada and Hellmut Wollmann, eds., *Von der Bonner zur Berliner Republik: 10 Jahre Deutsche Einheit* (Wiesbaden, 2000), 651 ff.; Paul Nolte, *Generation Reform: Jenseits der blockierten Republik* (Munich, 2004), versus Oskar Negt, "Die Gewinne von heute ... sind die Arbeitslosen von morgen," in Willy-Brandt-Kreis, ed., *Zur Lage der Nation: Leitgedanken für eine Politik der Berliner Republik* (Berlin, 2001), 224 ff.

38. Friedrich Dieckmann, "*Top down* oder *bottom up*? Zum Prozess der deutschen Vereinigung," in Willy-Brandt-Kreis, ed., *Zur Lage der Nation: Leitgedanken für eine Politik der Berliner Republik* (Berlin, 2001), 79 ff.; Rolf Reißig, "Nach dem Systemschock: Transformation im Osten und Wandel der 'alten' Bundesrepublik," in Roland Czada and Hellmut Wollmann, eds., *Von der Bonner zur Berliner Republik: 10 Jahre Deutsche Einheit* (Wiesbaden, 2000), 73 ff.

39. Vladimir Handl, "Ungleiche Partner: Deutschland–aus tschechischer Sicht gesehen," in Roland Czada and Hellmut Wollmann, eds., *Von der Bonner zur Berliner Republik: 10 Jahre Deutsche Einheit* (Wiesbaden, 2000), 228 ff., and Anna Wolff-Poweska, "The Berlin Republic from a Polish Perspective," in Dieter Dettke, ed., *The Spirit of the Berlin Republic* (New York, 2003), 180 ff.

40. Friedrich Schorlemmer, "Die Forderungen der Bürger an die Demokratie—die Forderungen der Demokratie an die Bürger," in Willy-Brandt-Kreis, ed., *Zur Lage der Nation: Leitgedanken für eine Politik der Berliner Republik* (Berlin, 2001), 201 ff., and Peter Graf Kielmansegg, "Soll die Demokratie direkt sein?" *FAZ*, 4/25/2001.

41. Detlef Pollack, "Das geteilte Bewusstsein: Einstellungen zur sozialen Ungleichheit und zur Demokratie in Ost- und Westdeutschland 1990–1998," in Roland Czada and Hellmut Wollmann, eds., *Von der Bonner zur Berliner Republik: 10 Jahre Deutsche Einheit* (Wiesbaden, 2000), 281 ff. See also Hartmut Kaelble, *Wege zur Demokratie: Von der Französischen Revolution zur Europäischen Union* (Stuttgart, 2001).

42. Constanze von Bullion, "Das bewegte Dorf," *TSp*, 3/2/2003. See also "Von der APO zu ATTAC: Politischer Protest im Wandel," *vorgänge* 42 (2003), no. 4, passim.

43. "Neuregelung verschärft Kampf gegen internationalen Terrorismus," www.bundesregierung.de, 4/29/2002; "Schily: BKA erfolgreich im Kampf gegen den Terrorismus," press release, www.bmi.bund.de, 9/4/2002; and Stefan Krempl, "Schilys Geheimplan im Kampf gegen den Terrorismus," www.telepolis.de, 10/12/2001.

44. Manfred G. Schmidt, "Immer noch auf dem 'mittleren Weg'? Deutschlands politische Ökonomie am Ende des 20. Jahrhunderts," and Frank Bönker and Hellmut Wollmann, "Sozialstaatlichkeit im Übergang: Entwicklungslinien der bundesdeutschen Sozialpolitik in den Neunzigerjahren," in Roland Czada and Hellmut Wollmann, eds., *Von der Bonner zur Berliner Republik: 10 Jahre Deutsche Einheit* (Wiesbaden, 2000), 491 ff., 514 ff. Cf. Frank Thies, "The Economic and Social Fabric of the Berlin Republic," in Dieter Dettke, ed., *The Spirit of the Berlin Republic* (New York, 2003), 85 ff.

45. Konrad H. Jarausch, "A Double Burden: The Politics of the Past and German Identity," in Jörn Leonhard and Lothar Funk, eds., *Ten Years of German Unification: Transfer, Transformation, Incorporation?* (Birmingham, 2002), 98–114.

46. "Die OSTalgie-Show," www.ZdF.de, and other commercial websites; and Tobias Dürr, "On 'Westalgia': Why West German Mentalities and Habits Persist in the Berlin Republic," in Dieter Dettke, ed., *The Spirit of the Berlin Republic* (New York, 2003), 24 ff.

47. Edelbert Richter, "Aufschwung unter neoliberalem Vorzeichen: Zur wirtschaft-

lichen Lage im Osten der Nation," in Willy-Brandt-Kreis, ed. *Zur Lage der Nation: Leitgedanken für eine Politik der Berliner Republik* (Berlin, 2001), 102 ff. See also Konrad H. Jarausch, "Creative Destruction: Transforming the East German Academic System," in Jürgen Büschenfeld et al., eds., *Wissenschaftsgeschichte heute: Festschrift für Peter Lundgreen* (Bielefeld, 2001), 192–210.

48. Philippe Moreau Desfarges, "In Search of a New Balance: France, Germany and the New Europe," in Dieter Dettke, ed., *The Spirit of the Berlin Republic* (New York, 2003), 162 ff.

49. "Zuwanderung: Alle rügen die Union," *TSp*, 2/20/2004. See also Faruk Sen, "Berlin's Turkish Community," in Dieter Dettke, ed., *The Spirit of the Berlin Republic* (New York, 2003), 130 ff.

50. Herbert, *Wandlungsprozesse in Westdeutschland*, 48 f.

51. Klaus Naumann, "Die Historisierung der Bonner Republik: Zeitgeschichtsschreibung in zeitdiagnostischer Absicht," *Mittelweg* 36 (2000), no. 3, 53–66. See also Gabor Steingart, "Die Wohlstands-Illusion," *Der Spiegel* 58 (2004), no. 11, 52 ff., and Steingart, "Der deutsche Irrweg," *Der Spiegel* 58 (2004), no. 12, 52 ff.

52. Michael Gehler, "Zeitgeschichte zwischen Europäisierung und Globalisierung," *APuZ*, B 51–52 (2002), 23–35, and Gerhard Schulz, "Gegen die Vermehrung ist der Markt ein Nichts: Überlegungen zu einer Geschichte im Zeitalter der Globalisierung," *FAZ*, 7/26/2003.

53. Peter Conradi, "The Architectural Rebirth of a Capital," in Dieter Dettke, ed., *The Spirit of the Berlin Republic* (New York, 2003), 110 ff. See Anne Costabile-Heming et al., eds., *Berlin—The Symphony Continues: Orchestrating Architectural, Social, and Artistic Change in Germany's New Capital* (Berlin, 2004).

54. Sebastian Conrad, *Auf der Suche nach der verlorenen Nation: Geschichtsschreibung in Westdeutschland und Japan, 1945–1960* (Göttingen, 1999).

55. R. J. B. Bosworth, *Explaining Auschwitz and Hiroshima: History Writing and the Second World War 1945–1990* (London, 1993).

56. Gerhard Botz and Gerald Sprengnagel, eds., *Kontroversen um Österreichs Zeitgeschichte: Verdrängte Vergangenheit, Österreich-Identität, Waldheim und die Historiker* (Frankfurt, 1994).

57. Robert O. Paxton, *Vichy France: Old Guard and New Order, 1940–1944* (New York, 1972), and Henry Rousso, *Vichy: L'événement, la mémoire, l'histoire* (Paris, 2001).

58. Daniel Benjamin, "Condi's Phony History: Sorry, Dr. Rice, Postwar Germany Was Nothing Like Iraq," *Slate Magazine*, www.slate.msn.com, 8/29/2003; Robert Gerald Livingston, "Does Iraq 2004 Resemble Germany 1946?" *American Institute for Contemporary German Studies Advisor*, 1/9/ 2004.

59. Kielmansegg, *Nach der Katastrophe*, 654 ff.

60. Ute Frevert, *Eurovisionen: Ansichten guter Europäer im 19. und 20. Jahrhundert* (Frankfurt, 2003). See also Eric Frey, *Schwarzbuch US* (Frankfurt, 2004).

61. Ludger Kühnhardt, *Die Universalität der Menschenrechte*, 2nd rev. ed. (Bonn, 1991), and Jeffrey N. Wasserstrom, Lynn Hunt, and Marilyn B. Young, eds., *Human Rights and Revolution* (Lanham, 2000).

62. "Die Allgemeine Erklärung der Menschenrechte," UN-Resolution 217 A (III) of

12/10/1948, www.unhchr.ch. Further documents are available in Kühnhardt, *Die Universalität der Menschenrechte*, 314–429.

63. Kurt Schumacher, *Nach dem Zusammenbruch* (Hamburg, 1948), 10.
64. "Jahresbericht Forum Menschenrechte 2002," www.forum-menschenrechte.de., and Georg Nolte and Hans-Ludwig Schreiber, eds., *Der Mensch und seine Rechte: Grundlagen und Brennpunkte der Menschenrechte zu Beginn des 21. Jahrhunderts* (Göttingen, 2004).

INDEX

Loest, Erich, 200
Löwenthal, Richard, 112
Lübbe, Hermann, 157
Luhmann, Niklas, 234–235
Lukács, Georg, 161, 167
Lünigk, Hermann Freiherr von, 52
Luxemburg, Rosa, 161, 167

Mahler, Horst, 172–173
Maier, Charles, ix
Maier, Reinhold, 135
Maizière, Lothar de, 207, 227, 229, 234
Mangoldt, Hermann von, 114
Mann, Heinrich, 58
Mann, Thomas, 6, 10, 269
Mao Tse-tung, 167
Marcuse, Herbert, 157, 161, 165, 167
Marshall Plan, 73, 83, 89, 110, 113
Marx, Karl, 157, 167
Marxism
    K-Groups, 173, 174–175
    reform attempts, 196, 205–208
    SED orthodoxy, 67, 141, 191–196, 211–212
    student movement, 160–161, 167
Matthias, Leo L., 128
May, Karl, 122
Mayer, Hans, 109, 137, 159
McCloy, John J., 109
McNamara, Robert, 41
McNarney, Joseph T., 52
Meckel, Markus, 43, 206, 227
Meier, Christian, 236
Meinhof, Ulrike, 150, 175
Memory
    community of fate, 63
    GDR nostalgia, 213, 232
    Holocaust, 15, 157, 279
    1968, 163, 179,
    postwar, 73
    victimhood, 34, 60
    war, 33–34, 44
Merkel, Angela, 252
Merz, Friedrich, 261
Meuschel, Sigrid, 132, 147
Middle class
    dismantling of in GDR, 183, 191–196
    family tensions in, 163
    Indian Summer of, 158
    restoration of in FRG, 183
Migration from East to West Germany, 120
    mass exodus of, 1989 205, 222, 248
Militarism
    movement away from, 24, 31–32, 38, 45
    persistence of, 35, 45
    Prussian, 26

Mills, C. Wright, 161
Milosevic, Slobodan, 232
Misselwitz, Hans-Jürgen, 211
Mitterrand, François, 224, 227
Mitzenheim, Moritz, 196
Modernization, 99–101, 182–184
    catch-up, 100
    conservative, 138
Modrow, Hans, 133, 207, 223,226
Monnet, Jean, 117
Morgenthau, Henry, 6, 47, 73
Müller, Heiner, 68, 200, 201
Müller-Armack, Alfred, 83
Multiculturalism, 246, 247, 262
Münz, Rainer, 263

Nation
    cultural, 68, 216
    distancing from, 48, 68
    renationalization, 186, 215, 235
    as trauma, 69–71
Nationalism
    D-Mark, 65, 230
    negative, 63, 65, 98
    post, 63, 69
    radical, 55, 62, 63–69
    retreat from, 48, 55–63, 63–69
National Socialism
    coming to terms with, 17, 32–33, 46, 48–55, 235
    crimes of, 10–12, 45, 49, 58, 270
    judicial punishment of, 48–55, 77
NATO, 142
    creation of, 37
    dual track decision, 41–42, 151
    membership, 38, 117, 160, 183, 224, 226, 227
Naturalization, 258–261
Naumann, Klaus, 279
Neoliberalism, 80, 88, 95, 277
Neo-Nazism, 62, 137, 141,
    NPD, 149–150, 244, 252
    skinheads, 45, 252
Neues Forum, 205–206, 207, 210
Neutralism, 111
New Economic System of GDR, 91, 99
"1968," 65, 156, 162–173
    analysis of, 157, 163, 167, 173–181, 277
    as symbol, 99, 157
    as cultural revolution, 179–181
    culture of, 124, 158, 161–162, 176
    New Left, 10, 160–161, 179
New social movements, 65, 101, 178, 158, 178.
    See also environmental, peace and
    women's movements
New York Times, editorial policy of, 73, 224
Niche society, 197

376   Index

Nicholls, Anthony J., viii
Niemöller, Martin, 59, 140, 160
Niethammer, Lutz, 47
Nitschke, Karl, 202
Noelle-Neumann, Elisabeth, 63
Normalization, 215–216, 229–230, 237–238
Nuremberg Trials, 7–8, 35, 38, 54, 76–77, 270
NVA (GDR army), 40, 41, 43, 202

Occidentalism, 112
Oder-Neisse Line, 228
Ohnesorg, Benno, 157, 170, 171
Oil shocks, 92, 100, 149, 243, 274
Ollenhauer, Erich, 117
OMGUS (Office of Military Governor of US), 50, 52, 76
Opinion, freedom of, 114, 143, 158, 204
Ostpolitik, 41, 42, 67, 101, 149, 176, 215
Özdemir, Cem, 263

Padover, Saul K., 17
Palme, Olof, 204
Parliamentary Council, 36, 114, 13, 154
Pannach, Gerulf, 202
Pacifism, 42–43
Patriotism, 68
    constitutional, 66, 235
    democratic, 236, 275
PDS (Party of Democratic Socialism), 207–208, 210, 225
Peace movements
    in FRG, 41–42, 151, 160, 177–178
    in GDR, 42–43, 160, 202–203
People's Congress Movement, East German, 64, 115
Pfeiffer, Anton, 114
Picht, Georg, 164
Pieck, Wilhelm, 149, 193
Planck, Max, 40
Planned economy, 85–86, 90–94, 98, 192, 238
Plenzdorf, Ulrich, 68, 200
Plievier, Theodor, 33
Pollack, Detlef, 183
Pollock, James K., 132
Portugalow, Nikolai, 223
Potsdam Conference, 6–7, 16, 19–20, 61, 75, 111, 130 214, 239
Prague Spring, 100, 101, 164, 172, 201, 242
Press
    influence of, 134, 145
    licensing of, 54, 56–57, 134, 143
    Springer, 170
Protest culture
    FRG, 158–162
    GDR, 100, 162, 204

nonviolent, 101, 124, 151, 168–169
    student, 100, 124, 158, 168–173
    union, 159, 172
Public sphere, 134
    alternative, 170
    critical, 144, 147, 150, 154–155
Pulitzer, Joseph, 26

Rabehl, Bernd, 167
Radbruch, Gustav, x
Rau, Johannes, 260
Reagan, Ronald, 9, 221
Rearmament, 24
    in GDR, 37, 40
    opposition against, 37
    plans for, 37–38
Recivilization. *See* learning processes
Reconstruction
    effort, 80–87
    generation, 94
Red Army, 34, 37, 40, 64, 111, 116, 159, 172
Reeducation, 20, 47, 57
Reich, Jens, 206
Reich, Wilhelm, 161, 167
Reiche, Steffen, 206
Reinstatement according to article 131 GG, 139
Remigration, 108, 121,154
Reparations, 79, 142–143, 215
Resettlers, 247–249, 262
Reunification. *See* unification
Reuter, Ernst, 37, 108
Revolution
    1848, tradition of, 131, 266
    1989/90, 17, 186
Richter, Edelbert, 207
Richter, Hans Werner, 159
Riedesel, Jörn, 202
Ritter, Gerhard, 7, 63
Robertson, Sir Brian, 30
Rock music, 64, 122,
    in GDR, 125, 198–199
Rodriguez, Armando, 243
Roosevelt, Franklin D., 6, 19, 25, 47
Roosevelt, Theodore, 118
Röpke, Wilhelm, 80
Rothfels, Hans, 108
Round Table, 207, 208, 225, 265
Rovan, Joseph, 222
Rudolph, Hermann, 217
Rürup, Bert, 277
Rüttgers, Jürgen, 260

Saarland, 61, 226
Sallmann, Michael, 202
Sander, Helke, 176